Books are to be returned on
the last date

Australia: An Illustrated History

The Five Mile Press Pty Ltd
1 Centre Road, Scoresby
Victoria 3179 Australia
Email: publishing@fivemile.com.au
Website: www.fivemile.com.au

First published in 2004
Reprinted 2005
This revised, updated edition published 2008
Text © A.K. Macdougall

Designed by Geoff Hocking
Edited by Richard McGregor

Printed in China

National Library of Australia Cataloguing-in-Publication data

Macdougall, Anthony
Australia: an illustrated history.

Includes index.
ISBN 978 1 74178 958 4

1. Australia – History – Pictorial works. I. Title

994

Other books by A.K. Macdougall include:

Early Colonial Buildings of Australia, 1971
Colonial Australia, 1973
The Big Treasury of Australian Folklore, 1990
Anzacs at War, 1991
The Great Treasury of Australian Folklore, 2002
Victory: The Epic of World War II 1939–1945, 2005
Australians at War, 2002

As co-author:
Warships of Australia, 1977
Faith in Australia: Charles Ulm, 1986

As editor:
Bush Ballads of Australia, 1985
Henry Lawson: Images of Australia, 1985
Banjo Paterson: Images of Australia, 1985

As editor-in-chief:
The Australian Encyclopaedia (70th Anniversary edn), 1996

TITLE PAGE:
HMS Beagle *and her accompanying
warship off the Australian coast, 1846;
artist unknown*

Australia: An Illustrated History

From Dreamtime to the New Millennium

A.K. Macdougall

The Five Mile Press

Contents

Introduction

THIS BOOK IS AN ATTEMPT TO RELATE THE STORY OF Australia briefly and illustrate it graphically. Australians live very much in the present, seldom dwelling on the past, possibly because they see their brief history as generally a fortunate one, lacking in drama. Yet the building of a democratic nation on one of the most remote continents on earth is a story full of human drama, and I hope that this book succeeds in conveying some of its excitement. I share Mark Twain's view of Australia, written a century ago: 'Australian history is almost always picturesque. Indeed, it is so curious and strange that it is in itself the chiefest novelty the country has to offer … It does not read like history, but like the most beautiful lies … full of surprises, and adventures, and incongruities and incredibilities; but they are all true; they all happened.'

In these unsettling times it is rewarding to look back on how earlier generations responded to challenges and faced threats and overcame them. We can no longer safely predict the future but the past remains both a solid memorial and a marker post to guide us, and we ignore it at our peril.

A.K. Macdougall, 2004

Chapter 1
Island Continent

The long Dreamtime

THE LAND KNOWN AS AUSTRALIA is the world's largest inhabited island and, for most of its extent, the most desolate. The first European voyagers, sailing along its forlorn western and southern coasts, thought it to be entirely desert. With an area of 7,700,000 square kilometres, it is the smallest of continents (Antarctica is twice its size) and in geographic terms the lowest: its average height is barely 200 metres above sea level—both Africa and the Americas average 650 metres and even Antarctica averages 2000. Australia's landscape is bare of mountains, for even the rugged sandstone ranges in its north-west and the Great Dividing Range that runs the length of its eastern coastline are the remnants of high, flat-topped serrated plateaux. Lacking mountains to capture life-sustaining rainfall in all but its eastern reaches—a region of forests, chasms and waterfalls— its vast interior lies parched and dry, a seeming eternity of nothingness.

It is a continent of extremes. The heaviest rains fall in summer (the Northern Hemisphere's winter) when monsoonal rains and cyclonic storms lash its north and lakes appear in the midst of deserts, their waters later disappearing beneath the ground. In the deserts of central Australia—'the Dead Heart'—shade temperatures can reach higher than 50° Centigrade. The European notion of a climate of four contrasting seasons does not apply in Australia. For much of the year it enjoys a warm climate followed by a brief winter mild by Northern Hemisphere standards.

And above all, the skies. Most of Australia is dominated by high pressure systems and it has few clouds over its interior or grey skies in winter. The sky dominates all: by day a brilliant encompassing blue and by night a shining infinity of stars.

Life begins

Australia's land was not always semi-arid and lifeless. About 200 million years ago the climate was temperate. Forests, swamps and lakes covered the land, and plant-eating dinosaurs roamed its surface. (Their bones are still being unearthed, and the forests' rotting vegetation would later form deposits of carbonised matter—coal— and petroleum.) Life on the planet had begun long before this time—perhaps more than 2000 million years ago (Earth itself was formed 4500 million years ago) and it began in the shallow waters of the seas, where protein and organic compounds developed into single-cell 'cyanobacteria', sustained by the water's oxygen. These organisms had plants' ability to photosynthesise, and a form of oxygen emitted by them became the bluish layer of haze that rose to the stratosphere, covering almost the entire planet. This 'ozone layer' shielded organisms from the Sun's destructive ultra-violet rays and enabled life to evolve. About 400 million years ago some life forms came ashore and survived there—our vascular plants developed

OPPOSITE:
Sixteenth-century map of South-East Asia.

SCRIPTIO HYDROGRARHICA

*mmodata ad Batavorum navigatione in Javam insulam Indiæ Orien-
tis. factam ad quam postridie Calendas Aprilis anni 1595 ex Hollan-
dia solverunt et ex qua domum redierunt Idus Augusti anno 1597
Horum exitus, reditusq; via his notis demonstratur De hac navigatione extat descriptio lectu perquam admiranda*

YGENTLICHE VND AVSFVHRLICHE

*appa de Orientalissen Indien darinon auch mit punctten angezeichnet di-
vnd Wider vm Reise der Holländer nach der Insuln Java welche den andern
des Monat Aprilis im 1595 Jahr von Holland sind auß gefahren vnd den 14
Ao 1597 wider in Holland an sind komen vn di Histori hie von Meldet*

MOCORRES

India intra can
gem

INDIA extra

RE
VM

BENGALA

GOLFO DE Segrav

I. Andamaon
I. dandaman

Baixde Padua
era

e Pracçel

de Cubeis

nnaport

Corenicubor

Jaffanapatam
Capela

Chila
tala torre

Ceilam

I. de Nicubar
Gemispota

I. de Ouro

I. de Ouro
de Ouro

IALIS

S. Pe de Masca
renhas

Pomoluco

A. du
Tandu

Sumatra I.

I. de de Gracia

IENTALIS

GAN

Bengala

Pegu
Machien
Omacaca
Sumatavan

Pulo S. Bla

OEM

Pulo
Malaq

Natuna

Terra Alta

Luzon

LVCONIA I.

INSULAE

PHLIP

I. Mindanao

PINÆ

Gilolo I.

Moluc
gae I.

Ceram

I. daru

I. de Timor

Java

Baxas

JAVA

Lucach Regnum

Beach Reg.

Maletur
Reg.

Terra australis Java Minor dicitur

Petan

Java Minor Mer
catori et alys

TERRA

AUSTRALIS

ANUS

INGOGNITA

Meaco
Nagat. IA

Fungo

Tanauma

Ido Fego

Dos Reis magos
I. Fermosa

Lequio minor

9

from non-vascular algae, and from the creatures of the sea the ancestors of humankind, animal and reptile evolved. Much life died during the severe Ice Age 286 million years ago.

Gondwana

During the Triassic and Jurassic periods (between 250 and 135 million years ago), when the Earth was going through one of its periodic warm cycles, Australia formed part of a great Southern Hemisphere land mass known as Gondwana, which included Africa, South America, India, Arabia and Antarctica, and which had long separated from the super-continent, Pangaea. Australia's first reptiles appeared, including the vast family of dinosaurs, both carnivorous and herbivore. More than 100 million years ago polar dinosaurs lived in the lush forests of what is now Antarctica, and their herds migrated north along the coast of Australia-in-Gondwana when the polar winter and its two months of total darkness began. The bones, fossilised into stone, of a flying reptile known as a Pterosaur—one of the first birds—have been found at Boulia in Queensland, where it existed more than 100 million years ago.

BELOW:
Gondwana and the formation of the continents.

About 90 million years ago Gondwana began to break up and the crust of Australia (carrying with it New Guinea and Tasmania) began to drift east, separating from Africa completely and forming a new continent, Meganesia. This continental drift is continuous but fortunately gradual: Arabia is still drifting apart from Africa at the rate of two centimetres a year.

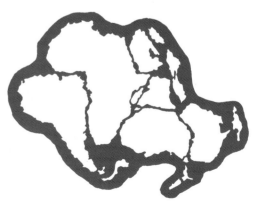

Around 65 million years ago the dinosaurs began to disappear but whether this was caused by new predators or some global

cataclysm such as a rain of meteors is still unknown. By 23 million years ago Australia had drifted further south, to its present latitudes, and the climate grew increasingly dry and harsh. Isolated from the other continents, Australia's landscape and its flora and fauna began to evolve their unique appearance. Since the 1970s archae-ologists have unearthed from a dry river-bed near Riversleigh in north-west Queensland thousands of fossils of life forms dating back 25 million years. Around 20 million years ago the 'fangaroo', a sharp-toothed relative of the kangaroo, inhabit-ed the rainforests of northern Australia.

The Earth was long subjected to periods of geo-logical upheaval (underground tunnels made from streams of lava from volcanoes are tourist attractions in southern Queensland) and tremen-dous climatic changes, which further shaped the land, ranging from howling dust storms to Ice Ages. The last Ice Age, which began about 70,000 years ago, reached its peak of severity around 20,000 years ago; between 14,000 and 12,000 years ago the world entered a long warm period. When the polar ice caps gradu-ally melted the ocean levels rose more than 100 metres, isolating Australia from its land bridges to New Guinea and Tasmania. In the same period England was sev-ered from Europe and became an island.

The Aborigines and their ancestors

But by this time Australia's first human inhabitants, the Aborigines, had already made their appearance on the continent. As recently as the 1950s it was believed that the Aboriginal people had come to Australia only about 8000 years ago, but scientific evidence accumulated since the mid-1960s (relying on the dating of bones by radio-carbon methods evolved after 1947) indicates that humankind was present in Australia as far back as 40,000 years—or even 60,000 years. Thus, at a time when Neanderthals (an ape-like relative of modern humans) were still roam-ing the valleys of the Rhine 30,000 years ago (and soon to face extinction at the hands of human wanderers), modern humans—*homo sapiens*—had already been long established on the Australian continent. The Aborigines thus form one of the world's oldest continuous surviving societies. Bones of a young Aboriginal woman of slight build found at Lake Mungo in the Willandra Lakes region of western New South Wales were discovered to be at least 26,000 years old.

Humankind's ancestors, a branch of the ape family (our closest living relative is the chimpanzee), evolved in Africa well over one million years ago (and perhaps as long as four million years); the climate there was more favourable to survival than that of the Northern Hemisphere, which was covered in glaciers. Bones of an ancestor of humans—*homo erectus*—have been found in Java and dated at one million years, but there is no evidence that Java Man crossed to Australia.

Modern humans did not appear until about 100,000 years ago and their search for food and kinder environments took him on his epic, unrecorded migrations across the globe, eventually bringing him to south-east Asia and its southernmost limits—the islands of modern-day Indonesia and New Guinea. Lying athwart the equator, where the world's two hemispheres meet, the region is prey to the monsoon, the strong—and often cyclonic—winds that bring torrential rains from the Indian Ocean to the Indian sub-continent and southern Asia from April to September. Then the winds reverse direction and this second monsoon, from April to March, deluges the northern reaches of Australia—'the Wet'. Indonesia and New Guinea are exceedingly fertile. They are heavily jungled and the volcanic soil is enriched by rotting vegetation. The island of Java alone is spanned by 100 volcanoes, some of them still active, and today supports more than 112 million people. It is one of the most densely populated places on the planet, whereas Australia has the poorest earth, much of it sand, and is one of the most sparsely populated.

ABOVE:
Aboriginal warriors of the Sydney region, from an early European engraving, 1790s.

The first Australian Aborigines were thus originally islanders, and they probably crossed to Australia at least 40,000 years ago, during a period when the waters were shallower than they are today. They came by boat or raft from the continental region of 'Sunda' (in a period when much of Indonesia was connected by land to the Philippines), or walked over the land bridge from New Guinea (which was not severed by water until about 8000 years ago), and they eventually populated every region of the great continent. Their progress was swift, for the land was easy to traverse, and there were few predators other than the crocodile, the largest of reptiles. The now extinct native peoples of Tasmania, who were negroid in appearance, were possibly the first newcomers, and were dwelling there as long as 30,000 years ago; for the mainland Aborigines are taller and of different features and skin colour. The majority of Aborigines eventually settled and flourished in the heavily wooded eastern regions of Australia. The movement of Malay people to the Indonesian islands, incidentally, did not begin until around 2500 BC.

The riddle of the megafauna

The first Aborigines experienced a climate cooler than today's and discovered forested areas and grasslands more extensive than those of the present. The plains were thick with the wild life familiar to all Australians—kangaroos, wombats, koalas, kookaburras and a variety of bird, plant and water life astonishing in its diversity. Evidence exists that about sixty species of 'megafauna'—among them giant kangaroos and wombats—existed when the first humans arrived. The largest of the megafauna was the Diprotodon, a giant wombat which stood more than 2 metres high and weighed a tonne. (The skull of a Diprotodon was found in the 1830s in a cave west of the Blue Mountains of New South Wales and a complete

RIGHT:
Re-creation of a now-
extinct Diprotodon,
once the largest
Australian marsupial.

skeleton in southern Queensland in 1847.) Other giants were a 3-metre-tall kangaroo, the Prococtodon, and the Thylacoleo, a possum the size of a lion with 60-millimetre-long teeth. There are numerous theories for the disappearance of the megafauna (which is thought to have occurred between 30,000 and 20,000 years ago). Some archaeologists maintain that the megafauna began to disappear with the coming of the first humans—who must have found them rich additions to their folklore—and who possibly hunted them to extinction; or perhaps they died out after the loss of their feeding grounds when fire claimed their grasslands. A relative newcomer, the dingo, which can sometimes be a savage predator, has often been unfairly blamed for their disappearance, but it arrived in Australia only 4000 years ago. (Neither the dingo nor the boomerang made it to Tasmania, for the seas by then had risen.)

Fire—and eucalypts

The Aborigines brought with them fire, which devastated grassland and forest. The fire-stick was as essential to them as their stone axes and wooden spears and proved a useful method of smoking out animals for food. Fatally, the fire-stick's arrival coincided with another climatic change that left the landscape parched and dry, easily ignited by lightning strikes or the hand of man. Much of Australia's vegetation was consumed by fire, as it periodically still is when the southern oscillation over the eastern Pacific draws all moisture from the western regions in which Australia lies.

'The arrival of humans had sent the land spiralling out of control. Fire storms ravaged the country,' suggests the anthropologist Dr Tim Flannery. When the rain clouds no longer came south from the monsoonal north, further climatic changes turned grassland into desert; the fast-flowing rivers dried up and so did the inland lakes, whose surfaces remain encrusted by salt. Where fire marched across the landscape only the hardiest of plants and trees regenerated vigorously; even in the temperate south-east the eucalypt dominated all. The eucalypt requires almost no water and transpires little moisture from its sparse foliage into the atmosphere. The rain clouds ceased to visit the centre of the continent.

'In an unholy alliance with fire,' suggests Tim Flannery, 'the eucalypts spread across the continent, destroying the original forests, creating the Australian landscape we know today.' In this increasingly desolate environment only the hardiest of animals adapted successfully and they did this by conserving their energy, a procedure that became an Australian characteristic. The megafauna's smaller cousins thrived, for kangaroos and wallabies—though eaters of vegetation, which produces few calories and thus little energy—bound at remarkable speed using their muscular back legs, with little strain on chest muscles, heart and lungs. In the rainforests of the north-east, some species of kangaroo have adapted so well that they can even climb trees to forage in the branches.

ABOVE:

Before the Aboriginal way of life was largely destroyed, a European artist painted this representation of an Aboriginal camp in South Australia in the 1870s.

Painting, oil on canvas, by Samuel Calvert (1828-1913).

Aboriginal society

In this unpromising environment Australia's pre-European history began and here, in a way, it stopped. The Aborigines, both in the desert interior and on the eastern and south-eastern coastal regions, did not develop from their Stone Age hunter-gatherer beginnings, for there was little impetus for progress. The only metal fired by the peoples of the north were the fragments of iron ore that they burned to obtain the rich red-orange ochre with which they painted their bodies for ceremonies.

Aboriginal society was simple and self-sufficient. The males could pursue animals by the faintest of tracks; the desert people could find fresh water and food in the form of seeds or roots in regions where nothing grew. Records tell of Aborigines at Cape

ABOVE:

The world's oldest known ground-edge axes: two axes of felspar porphyry excavated near Oenpelli in the Northern Territory and dated by radiocarbon to at least 18,000 years old (give or take 400 years).

RIGHT:
Aboriginal society was to be greatly disrupted following the arrival of Europeans, but early photographs such as these offer rare glimpses of the traditional lifestyle.

Men from south-eastern Australia, photographed in the 1870s.

York using 141 different plants as food and scientists have listed more than 100 plants that Aborigines used for medicinal purposes. They were skilled fishermen with spear and net. Though able to construct 'catamarans' they lacked the metal tools needed to build larger craft.

The land and its plants, animals, birds and fishes provided all that Aboriginal people needed. They remained nomads, moving in small groups or 'bands' ranging in size from family-size groups of a dozen in number to groups of fifty or more. To describe their communities as 'tribes' would be incorrect, for they had no kings or tribal overlords; they had elders but few chiefs; they had no common language, no agriculture and thus no villages, fixed settlements or trading centres. Necessity made them formidable warriors and skilled hunters, using boomerangs, spears and woomeras made from wood, with weapon heads from flint and bone. (In some areas the boomerang was unknown and in others rarely used—the finest hunting weapon was the spear, which some warriors could hurl a hundred metres with the aid of a woomera.) They had few possessions other than weapons, tools and a carrying bag, and saw little need for clothing other than to protect their loins.

Only the groups dwelling in cool, high regions along the east coast and in Tasmania wore clothing fashioned from animal skins. The pattern of their life was set by the seasons and they followed the food sources, knowing the times when birds migrated and eggs could be widely found, or when the Bogong moth (rich eating) arrived on the southern slopes of the Australian Alps. No form of cultivation or agriculture has been discovered, for Australia lacked the mountain ranges whose great rivers each year carried rich alluvial soils to coasts, making possible the cultivation of crops (initially grasses like wheat whose seed contained a nutritious grain) at river estuaries in Mesopotamia, Egypt, India and China. (The river waters used by these civilisations also brought with them salt, which accumulated over the cen-

ABOVE:
An Aboriginal family, New South Wales.

turies in waters—especially when they were dammed for irrigation, as happened in Mesopotamia—and eventually ruined the soil.)

For the Australian Aborigines, times of plenty were times of festivity. 'In abundant seasons many of the groups would come together and form a camp of several hundred people,' writes Geoffrey Blainey in his history, *The Triumph of the Nomads*. 'In these temporary groups most people probably were related to each other. If they were not directly related by blood or marriage they were sometimes united by the belief that they had a common totem ancestor who had pioneered the territory long ago and whose influence on the living was powerful.' Kinship is a powerful force in Aboriginal society—it is not based exclusively on blood relationship and anthropologists have long sought to understand it. Myth and ritual were merged in religion; dance was rich in symbolism.

The Aborigines' belief in their individual totem (a living creature such as an animal, bird or reptile) was their link to the land and to everything on it. For example, someone whose totem was a kangaroo would never eat the flesh of that animal, for it would be like eating part of themselves. Their mythology provided an explanation of the birth and formation of their world and their wildlife and its stories preserved tales of heroic deeds. The Australian Aborigines had more than 200 languages and a thousand dialects but no written language, so their stories—what they called the 'Dreamtime', a history without chronology—were passed down orally from one generation to the next. Some of their myths, such as that of the Rainbow Serpent which created the snaking rivers, are common throughout the country.

The native peoples felt an identity and an affinity with the land, its animals, birds and other creatures; a bond so close, and so central to their beliefs that no Europeans could understand—and few even now can interpret—it. In broadest terms, the land itself belonged to all—and to none. The European concept of individual 'property' was alien to them.

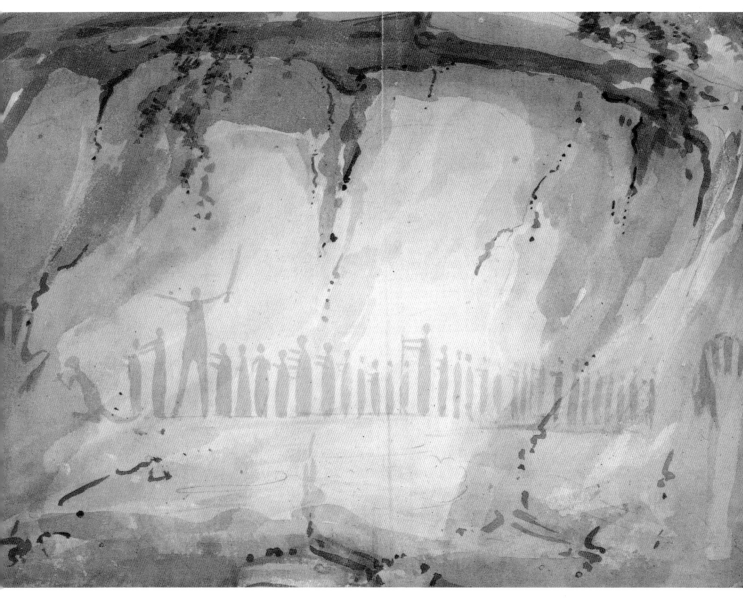

ABOVE:

The first representation by a European of Aboriginal rock painting.

Watercolour by William Westall, the artist who accompanied Flinders on his circumnavigation of Australia in 1802.

For all its simplicity, Aboriginal life could be brutal. Conflict between wandering bands was frequent and violent. Infanticide was widely practised. Young men passed from childhood to manhood through painful initiation rites, including circumcision, the details of which entered the realm of taboo, and many Aboriginal beliefs—called superstitions by the Europeans—are still barely understood. The womenfolk were treated often with brutishness. This surprised those Europeans who admired their menfolk's fearlessness and their humour, for many early European accounts mention the amused curiosity of the warriors, their sense of fun and gift of mimicry.

The number of Aborigines in Australia when the Europeans arrived will never be known. Some authorities suggest they totalled 350,000 but this figure seems far too high. (The number of American Indians in the entire continent of North America before the coming of Europeans is estimated at 900,000.) Whatever their numbers, the Australian Aborigines were among the freest peoples on the planet. They had no predators to fear and few of the tropical diseases that plagued Asia, for their climate was and remains one of the healthiest in the world. They acknowledged no kings, had no experience of slavery nor of human sacrifice. Their beliefs conditioned their art: their striking paintings on bark and rock contain no portraits, for representation of the dead is taboo.

Between the Aboriginal peoples and the future claimants to their land, the British, lay no bridge to understanding. To the English, property was the basis of wealth and its possession was the bedrock of the very Empire they ruled, and to them Australia was 'empty land'—terra nullius. Guns, diseases and—most pernicious of all—alcohol, would decimate the First Australians. But in robbing the Aborigines of the land in which they dwelled the Europeans would also rob the survivors of their soul.

First contacts

Before the coming of the Europeans, Aboriginal contact with other races, with the exception of Macassan fishermen from southern Sulawesi, was rare. Their first near neighbours, the Maori, reached New Zealand by canoes rigged with sails from the north-eastern Pacific islands around 1350 AD. A Polynesian people, the Maori made settlements strongly fortified against attack and cultivated crops, but no record exists that they navigated the storm-tossed Tasman Sea to Australia's coasts.

The great dramas of history passed Australia by. Within seventy years of the death of the prophet Mohammed (632 AD) the armies of Islam had spread from Arabia and conquered the Middle East; they reached Afghanistan in the same year that they crossed from Morocco into Spain (711) and almost reached Paris. The Arab empire was to endure more than a thousand years and the standard of its civilisation, like that of China's, was extremely high. The West learned from Arab mathematics and science and adopted Arabic numerals, but Europe was now effectively cut off from contact with the Middle East, the Near East and the lands that lay beyond, and centuries of conflict between Christianity and Islam had begun.

By 800 AD, when Baghdad was at the height of its influence and culture under the rule of Haroun-al-Rashid (the caliph of the Arabian Nights) and Charlemagne was crowned in his capital on the Rhine as ruler of an empire that embraced France, Germany and most of Italy, the Hindu rulers of Java were building the magnificent stone temples of Borobadur, and on the island of Sumatra the Hindu empire of Srivijaya was rising, with its capital at Palembang. In the twelfth and thirteenth centuries AD (the period when the Aztec and Inca empires of the Americas of Peru were at their height) the Hindu empire of the Khmers in Cambodia, which ruled most of Indochina, was constructing the great city of Angkor, whose walls stretched for sixteen kilometres and whose inhabitants numbered a million.

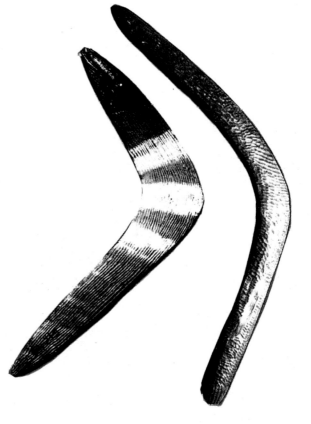

Chapter 2
Dawn of Discovery

Marco Polo and China

IN THE THIRTEENTH CENTURY A THUNDERBOLT came out of the steppes and deserts of central Asia—the Mongols. United by Genghis Khan ('Ruler of All'), Mongol hordes, in search for new lands, invaded China and conquered Persia and the Middle East. Their fleets mounted attacks on Japan and Java, and Mongol horsemen ravaged Poland and Russia and reached the borders of Germany, putting to the sword their enemies with a savagery that the world had never before witnessed. It was to the court in China of the great conqueror's more benign grandson, Kublai Khan, that three intrepid Venetian merchants ventured by the overland trade route known as the Great Silk Road. Marco Polo, who accompanied his father and uncle to the court of the Great Khan in 1275, was only one of hundreds who would make the return journey over the next century, for China—'Cathay'—was eager to trade with the West. He found employment under the Khan as a diplomat and travelled widely during his twenty years there before returning by sea to India through the waters of Malaya and Indonesia.

Marco Polo's magical book, which he dictated while languishing briefly in prison in Venice in 1295, is a blend of fact and fanciful embroidery, personal observation, hearsay, and confused sailing directions, but confirmed that fascinating realms lay beyond the known worlds of China and India, including the great island of Madagascar, which the Portuguese discovered only by accident in 1500, and which was already known to the Chinese. Indeed, a Chinese map dating from 1302 shows clearly the entire eastern coast of Africa. Marco Polo visited Sumatra on his voyage, and described Java—later known as 'the jewel of the Indies'—largely from hearsay:

> Departing from Ziamba [in south China], and steering between south and south-east, you reach an island of very great size, named Java, which, according to the reports of some well-informed navigators, is the largest in the world, being in circuit above three thousand miles. The country abounds with rich commodities. Peppers, nutmegs, spikenard, cubebs, cloves and all other valuable spices and drugs, are the produce of the island; which cause it to be visited by many ships laden with merchandise that yields to the owners considerable profit.
>
> The quality of gold collected there exceeds all capacity and belief. That the Great Khan has not brought the island under subjection to him, must be attributed to the length of the voyage and the dangers of navigation.

OPPOSITE:
A Dutch map of the 'East Indies', but including Africa and 'New Holland' (Australia), published by van Keulen and dating from around 1690.

BELOW:
China's fabulous admiral, Zheng Hi, whose voyages in northern Australian and Indonesian waters pre-dated Columbus's discovery of the Americas by sixty years.

Beyond Java—which since the twelfth century had supplanted Sumatra as the power in the archipelago—lay another great land, Australia, which Marco Polo heard was termed Locach or 'The Golden Realm of Beach'. In some old maps it was shown as part of Java—'Java la Grande'—and extended to Antarctica.

Marco Polo's record was not the first written by travellers to China but it was the best, and it stimulated interest in Asia and the East to an extraordinary degree, as it still does. Prince Henry of Portugal treasured his manuscript copy, constantly referring to it, and after it was set in type and printed as a book in 1483 (becoming one of Europe's first best-sellers) Columbus carried a copy with him on all his voyages.

The Chinese voyages

The Mongol dynasty lasted little more than a century and the new Ming rulers of China sent a mighty fleet into the Indian Ocean on seven great voyages between 1405 and 1433 under the command of an astonishing admiral, a eunuch named Zheng Hi. He sailed to India through the Indonesian archipelago, exacting tribute from local rulers, and then crossed to the shores of Arabia and Africa. Hundreds of his giant junks laden with goods to trade and with soldiers carried as many as 400 men and were armed with primitive cannon, for the Chinese had invented gunpowder. 'It is at least possible, but not proved, that some of the Chinese ships touched the northern coasts of Australia. One object found near Darwin many years ago suggests that they did so. They certainly visited Timor, the nearest island of Indonesia,' writes the historian C.P. Fitzgerald. The tiny, fertile island of Timor, endowed with forests of sandalwood and fine harbours, was destined to be a pawn for centuries in the game for dominance played by the European powers.

ABOVE:
Chinese wood engraving of a warship of the type used by their fleets in the time of Zheng Hi.

'Thus, sixty-four years before the Portuguese discovered the Indian Ocean—with all the consequences this had for Europe, Asia and later Australia—the Chinese had made themselves masters of the Indian Ocean and could easily have established lasting and strong bases on its coasts,' writes Fitzgerald. 'The whole course of Asian history could have been different, and the "colonial era" in south and south-east Asia might never have come about.' Yet the great fleets of China—a recent chronicler suggests that they may have even reached the Americas—soon curtailed their forays, possibly because the cost outweighed the return in terms of trade, and were left to rot.

Possibly as early as the 1400s boats from Macassar began sailing annually to the shores of Arnhem Land—as many Indonesian fishermen still do. They came for sea-slug (bêche-de-mer or trepang), a delicacy when smoked and cured, and they came

ABOVE:
Fifteenth-century maps imagined Australia as part of a super continent that included a polar region (Antarctica had not yet been discovered).

in the summers when the monsoonal winds carried their sailing boats easily on the 1000-mile voyage to Australia's coasts. They returned to their island home when the winds reversed direction in March. Rock carvings record their presence. A few Indonesians intermarried with the Aborigines—the first of thousands of intermarriages between Aborigines and Indonesians, Chinese, Japanese and Europeans—and some trading took place, though Australia's inhabitants had little to trade.

The same monsoonal winds would soon bring sailing ships across the Indian Ocean from the tip of south Africa to the riches of India, Arabia and south-east Asia, carrying with them to Australia's waters the first Europeans: Portuguese and Spanish, Dutch and English, and Australia would be awoken from its deep sleep.

The search for the South Land

Terra Australis

Long before Europeans ventured into the Southern Hemisphere, geographers had fantasised about the existence of a southern continent at the uttermost end of the earth. The Greeks, whose ships sailed the coasts of Arabia, the Persian Gulf and north-western India, knew of the existence of the northern Polar region, and their successors the Romans were sure that great lands lay to the south beyond their known world. The Latin name *australis terra* (south land) or *terra australis incognita* was later applied to this imagined region. Much classical learning and speculation was lost during the Barbarian invasions (Greek maps of 200 AD for example showed the entire outline of Africa, which later had to be rediscovered) and for close to a thousand years Europe showed no interest in the wider world. Early initiatives were killed by the epidemic of bubonic plague—'the Black Death'—which came from Asia and was carried by ships from the Crimea to Europe's ports in 1348, killing in two years 25 million people, a third of Europe's population. The Muslim world now separated Europe from contact with the East and it would be nearly two centuries before other European venturers could confirm the truth of Marco Polo's writings.

In the time of Marco Polo the great island of Java was the furthest
land south known to navigators.

The Portuguese voyages

The Portuguese were the first to try to solve the riddle of the East, and their searches were prompted by the lure of gold. Since the times of the Greeks and Romans this metal had never lost its allure, and fables told of kingdoms in Africa built on its riches. It has remarkable properties, being not only lustrous and heavy but also malleable and resistant to corrosion, making it ideal for jewellery and coinage. The discovery of gold in Australia in the 1850s was to transform our history, and today gold's chemical inertness makes it a perfect conductor in electronics. Other commodities would also prove valuable and stimulate a search for new markets: Europeans had developed a taste for spices brought overland from the East and then carried by the ships of the great maritime power, Venice, to the ports of Europe. Spices made palatable the Europeans' stodgy diet of meat and bread—spices such as pepper were also used as preservatives for meat, and many herbs and spices had prized medicinal uses. Slaves formed another developing market. African kings freely traded their own people and Europe's overseas empires would be based on slavery.

In 1411 the Portuguese had driven the last Moors from Portugal, and four years later they launched their own conquests, capturing the Moorish stronghold of Ceuta on the North African coast. Soon followed a series of bold maritime excursions planned and dispatched by Prince Henry, younger brother of the King of Portugal, to explore the west coast of Africa and gather riches on the way. The enterprise would also be another blow in the war against Islam, whose galleys dominated the southern Mediterranean and whose armies under the Ottoman Turks had for a century been established in the Balkans.

The Turks' capture of Constantinople (1453), three years before the death of Prince Henry, merely administered the coup de grâce to a moribund Byzantine Empire, but to historians it provides an event from which to date the remarkable rebirth of European culture then under way, the golden age of learning, art, architecture, science and maritime discovery celebrated as the Renaissance. And it was the early voyages of the Europeans to Africa and India that opened the way to the discovery and exploration of Australia.

By the 1450s the Portuguese had already ventured down Africa's jungled coast as far south as the Gulf of Guinea, the richest region for obtaining slaves. Over the next four centuries European ships would carry 13 million Africans across the Atlantic to work as slaves in the plantations of North and South America and the West Indies, and Portugal's ships carried 4.65 million of them. The trade grew in importance and profits with every year that passed, as did the human misery.

The European seafarers

The voyages of the early navigators are well recorded, for the age of discovery coincided with the birth of printing in Europe, and soon ships sailed with printed charts, a product of the new age, though it was a century (1570) before enterprising publishers bound the maps into volumes known as 'atlases'.

Advances in science—particularly in astronomy and the making of glass lenses for telescopes—and ordinary human inventiveness were making navigation easier. European seamen were venturing further from their own coastlines and the shores of the Mediterranean lake, where, because of indifferent winds, oar-driven galleys

ABOVE:
A nineteenth-century depiction of da Gama meeting the ruler of Calicut.

were the fastest and most reliable of vessels. Humans knew that the sun rose in the east and set in the west; even primitive compasses showed the magnetic north. They had long learned to set a course by the stars, whose position in the heavens changed imperceptibly each night as the Earth rotated. The historian Samuel Eliot Morison writes that 'rough estimates of latitude could be made from the height of the North Star above the horizon and its relation to the two outer stars (the Guards)' and by a 'meridial altitude of the sun, corrected by the sun's declination, for which tables had long been provided'. Wooden sextants and quadrants (later made of metal) helped in fixing a ship's degree of latitude (which were imaginary lines running across the world from north to south), but were no use if the sea was not dead calm. Some voyagers such as Columbus relied on their knowledge of the winds and currents and on 'dead reckoning'—plotting a course and position (like our early aviators) on a chart from the three elements of direction, time and speed. ('Longitude', or position running east to west, was largely guesswork until the English invented the maritime chronometer in the mid-eighteenth century.) Speed could be calculated by observing the rate ('knot') at which a piece of knotted rope drifted past a vessel but the only widely used time-pieces, apart from sun dials, were sand clocks; when these emptied every half hour and were reversed by a ship's boy, a mark was made on a slate and a bell rung. Eight bells marked a four-hour 'watch'. It was crude but it worked.

Ship design was undergoing a revolution of its own, and the Portuguese led the world. Ships were getting larger, and sails of tough flax or canvas was replacing wool, with hemp from the Baltic providing strong ropes and rigging. The Portuguese sailed swift 20-metre-long caravels, with three masts often rigged with lateen (triangular) sails—ships strong enough to brave the unknown seas; and they armed them with small cannon, a weapon that had been fairly ineffective in land battles because of its short range but which proved ideal for close bombardment when fired by ships. The Portuguese invented a runner that absorbed the recoil of cannons firing, for ships firing broadsides had often capsized. The 500-tonne square-rigged galleon, designed specifically as a warship and armed with rows of cannon, came later, after the 1570s, when the need grew for escorts for merchantmen. With its giant square-rigged sails, it was less responsive than a caravel, had little space for cargo, and was slow and ponderous—as English seamen in smaller and faster craft discovered early in sea fights.

Fired also with Catholic determination to convert the heathen, this remarkable kingdom of Portugal and its two million people (their enemy Spain had a population of eight million and France nearly double that) would soon dominate one-third of the oceans of the globe.

Spain and the Americas

In 1488 Bartholomeu Dias sailed as far as Africa's southern tip—the Cape of Good Hope, returning to Lisbon with word that a great sea lay beyond Africa: the Indian Ocean. The age of European Renaissance discovery had begun and some of the most outstanding of its figures were Italians. Cristofo Colombo (Christopher Columbus), a Genoan seaman who had fought the Turkish galleys (shipwrecked once, he reached the coast of Portugal on a plank), tried to interest the Portuguese court in financing a voyage to India by sailing west, across the Atlantic. In an age when many people believed the world was flat and that navigators who ventured too far beyond Europe would fall off its edges, the wise knew it to be a sphere, while Columbus himself thought it was pear-shaped. The English were obsessed with the idea of sailing to Cathay and India by following the icy coasts of northern Russia by way of the elusive 'North-East Passage', and the Asian face of every captured Eskimo confirmed their belief that China lay just beyond the northern horizons.

His expedition financed by the Spanish court, Columbus left in command of three ships in August 1492. Avoiding a course due west which would lead him into the stormy north Atlantic seas, he made a south-westerly course before turning sharply north (a trick known as latitude sailing) and after only seven weeks at sea sighted an island (on 12 October), one of the Bahamas, which lie off Florida. Here he made landfall, gave thanks to God and raised the flag of Spain. Believing he had found India, he called its inhabitants 'Indians', and explored the coasts of Cuba and Hispaniola. On later voyages Columbus charted the islands of the Caribbean (soon known as the Spanish Main) and the northern coast of South America in a futile search for a passage to India. It was another Italian in the Spanish service, Amerigo Vespucci, who first sailed the entire length of the Atlantic coast of South America (possibly in 1499) and his name, not Columbus's, would be bestowed on the new continent: America. The Americas would give Europe the potato, the tomato, the peanut, the pineapple, rubber and tobacco—and within twenty years Spanish conquistadors would plunder richer prizes: the gold and silver of Mexico and Peru, deflecting their kingdom's attentions for two generations from the search for India.

1498: Vasco da Gama and India

Where the Spanish sailed west, the Portuguese sailed south. They were obsessed with the notion of a gold-rich Christian kingdom in eastern Africa, Ethiopia, which would provide treasure and serve as an ally in the war against the Muslims, but they delayed further attempts to search for India until a truce was signed with Spain; in 1494 the Pope divided the New World between the two Catholic powers, granting Spain most of the Americas, and Portugal everything east of 'the Pope's Line'. (Thus Brazil, which jutted east into the Atlantic, soon became a Portuguese domain.)

In July 1498 four ships commanded by Vasco da Gama sailed from Portugal for the Cape of Good Hope. The Portuguese had established a presence in Angola as early as 1491; their sailors kept to the African coast to avoid getting lost, despite the dangers of currents, rocks and headwinds, but da Gama sailed south through the Atlantic Ocean itself, navigating by the stars, and rounded the Cape in

November after a voyage of four and a half months. Expecting to find the Indian Ocean an expanse of blue sparkling waters, the Europeans met with storms and strong currents. They made landfall several times on their progress up Africa's eastern coast, pretending to be Turks in their dealings with the Muslims, and when attempting to enter Mombasa had to fight off attacks with cannon and bombard. Most worrying of all, they found no trace of Christian allies. At Malindi, however, da Gama, whose men were now restless, obtained the services of an Arab sea captain, for the inhabitants were now fearful of the Europeans' guns. With the aid of their pilot and his charts, the Portuguese reached the coast of India near Calicut on 18 May 1498, after what has been called 'the longest sea voyage in history'. They were astonished by the opulence of Calicut, at that stage the richest port in India, where the wealthy were borne on palanquins, their progress preceded by musicians blowing trumpets of gold.

On entering the ruler's palace the Europeans saw a statue of a beautiful woman and fell to their knees, offering prayers to the Blessed Virgin Mary, but then saw paintings of females with six arms and animal-like tusks, and realised that they were among Hindus. The ruler (the Zamorin) received them, reclining on a divan beneath a silken canopy, naked to the waist, and chewing betel nuts, for the heat was oppressive. He wore bracelets of diamonds, emeralds and pearls. When da Gama presented a letter from his king and explained that he wished only to replenish his ships, buy spices and depart, the ruler offered to trade 'cinnamon, cloves, pepper and precious stones' for gold, silver and cloth. The Portuguese gifts of trinkets, hats and jars of honey were rudely rejected and the newcomers were thrown into captivity. Strident negotiating combined with threats by the Portuguese aboard ship saw them freed several days later and they sailed away pursued by a fleet of forty ships, which da Gama destroyed ruthlessly in a night attack. East had met West in an atmosphere of mutual distrust that would never abate. Battling against contrary winds, with two ships abandoned and two-thirds of his men dead, da Gama rounded the Cape in March 1489 and returned to Lisbon to be acclaimed a hero and recount to his king tales of fabulous realms and trade for the taking. The route to India was now opened and early in March 1500 a great fleet of thirteen ships under Cabral set sail from Portugal, reaching India in just six months. Only six vessels returned to Portugal a year later but their holds were bursting with spices, paid for in gold. Later navigators would learn that the secret of an easy crossing of the Indian Ocean was to catch the winds of the summer monsoon (which blew from the south-east from April to September, and carried them to India) and return to the shores of Arabia and Africa's great trading centres of Zanzibar and Sofala (the port of Great Zimbabwe) when the winds changed direction to north-easterlies in November–March (the period when the monsoonal rains also strike Australia).

The Indian Ocean

Portugal established her power in the Indian Ocean in a blaze of fire. Her seafarers discovered Madagascar and in 1505 established posts in Mozambique. In 1508 Almeida destroyed off Diu a combined fleet sent by the Indian rulers and the Muslim suzerains of Egypt; in the close combat, fought without quarter, the Portuguese killed 4000 Muslims for the cost of 300 casualties. But it was the genius of Afonso de Albuquerque that established Portugal's domination of the East. He destroyed Muscat by bombardment, seized Goa on India's west coast in 1510 (boasting in his report to his king that his men slaughtered 6000 of its Muslim inhabitants to make the colony safe for Christians and Hindus) and went on to plant his nation's flag in the islands of the 'East Indies', as the Malay Archipelago (Malaya and Indonesia) became known.

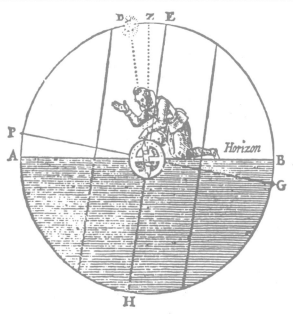

He captured Malacca on the coast of Malaya from its Muslim rulers in 1511, giving Portugal domination of the trade route, and on his return voyage along the coasts of Arabia pondered the chances of sacking Mecca and ransoming the bones of the Prophet Mohammed, for there was no limit to his boldness nor to his blasphemy. Thinking better of this, Albuquerque stormed and secured Hormuz on the Persian Gulf, thus presenting the crown of Portugal with the three well-distanced ports of call her ships needed on voyages to the East: Hormuz, Goa and Malacca. In 1512 Serrao discovered the Moluccas—known thereafter as the Spice Islands—and other mariners explored trade in the Gulf of Bengal and invaded Ceylon. Only China and Japan (Xipangi) remained untouched, but in 1517 the Portuguese sailed from Malacca to anchor at Canton, where they obtained trading privileges, and in 1557 established a permanent colony on a small island at Macao, where the flag of Portugal flew until 1999. One of their captains, de Menes, is credited with being the first European to sight the north coast of New Guinea (1525) and another explorer, de Retes, gave the island its name nineteen years later, for its fuzzy-haired Melanesian tribesmen reminded him of the natives of Guinea.

1512: Portugal in Timor

Cinnamon from Ceylon, cloves from the Moluccas (they grew nowhere else), pepper from India, nutmeg from the Banda Islands, camphor from Borneo, oils from Macassar, sandalwood from Timor—these were southern Asia's gifts to Europe. They were profitable cargoes but the Portuguese had to fight for them and possessed too few ships and men to defeat the strongest of the local rulers, the sultan of Acheh. Acheh on the northern tip of Sumatra was 'enterprising in business, warlike and fanatically Moslem' (in the words of the historian J.H. Parry) and it remained semi-autonomous, even under centuries of Dutch rule. The island of Ambon, however, which was visited by St Francis Xavier in 1543, became a Christian stronghold and would provide the Dutch with their most loyal Indonesian soldiers, long after the Portuguese had vanished, their endeavours crippled by lack of capital and the decimation of their manpower.

ABOVE:
Magellan's ship *Victoria*.

In 1512 the Portuguese first visited the island of Timor and in 1561 a Dominican friar arrived at Ocussi on its north coast to convert the pagan tribes. Thus the Portuguese, who valued eastern Timor's fine harbour at Dili and its stands of sandalwood, were established on an island lying only 350 miles (600 kilometres) from Australia's northern coast, and to many historians it seems inconceivable that they failed to explore the continent's reaches, if only out of curiosity. Perhaps they did, but kept their discoveries secret, for French map-makers at Dieppe produced a chart known as the Dauphin Map, circa 1547, that has been described by recent authorities as 'one of the most puzzling' of the Dieppe map-makers' works. It was apparently copied from a Portuguese chart and when errors in longitude are allowed for, it shows clearly the Queensland coastline from Cape York as far south as Cooktown. 'It seems likely that the map is of the eastern Australian coastline, and, if so, that Portuguese mariners under Christoval de Mendonca charted that coastline some years before 1536, most likely between 1521 and 1523,' states *The Australian Encyclopaedia*. Two cannons were found near the entrance to Broome Bay, Western Australia, in 1916, and both bore the rose and crown of Portugal. Tales of shipwrecked galleons on the coast of Victoria are part of our folklore.

But by the 1570s Portugal's ebbing strength would be challenged by the Spanish, and in 1580, with the end of her royal line, the Kingdom of Portugal was absorbed by Spain. The strains of empire had proved beyond her resources and population. Recovering her independence and possessions in 1640, she then faced a new and stronger challenge—the Dutch—and what was left of her ocean empire became, like Portugal itself, a backwater.

1550s: The spread of Islam

If Portugal's short-lived supremacy in the Indies was complete by the 1550s, so also was the eastward progress of another powerful force—militant Islam. The Islamic empire would endure and grow.

By the late sixteenth century most of the peoples of Indonesia had adopted Islam; the religion had been spread over the previous three centuries, not by conquering armies but by Arab missionaries and traders, and Muslim power under the Moghuls had supplanted Hindu rule in India, strengthening Islam's domination by the conquest of Bengal after 1555. The Moghul conqueror's son Akbar the Great would prove one of the most enlightened of rulers, tolerant of Christianity and welcoming Western envoys and traders to his vast dominions.

It is not hard to understand why Islam was quickly accepted in the Indonesian islands and why so many Hindus quickly converted to its faith (an exception being Bali), enabling it to become the common religion of peoples reaching from the Straits of Gibraltar to islands in the Philippines. Based on the holy book, the Koran (Qur'an), it is devoid of ritualistic ostentation and states that all men are equal, whereas Hinduism and its many deities is based on a rigid system of classes and castes. Split mainly into two antagonistic sects—the Sunnis (who comprise 80 per cent of Muslims) and the Shias (who are concentrated in the Arab lands), it is in some ways more tolerant than Christianity: Jews and Christians in Islamic lands were generally left unmolested and free to practise their religion (though forbidden to bear arms), for they shared Islam's belief in a single almighty God. Muslims shared with Christians, however, an intolerance of unbelievers, consigning them to slavery or death without compunction.

Religion and territorial rivalry would bring the Christian West and the Islamic East to centuries of almost continuous conflict: crescent and cross, scimitar and sword.

1519: The Pacific Ocean—Magellan

In 1504 the Spanish conquistador Balboa had gazed from Panama on the waters of the Pacific Ocean, beyond which, men thought, lay the fabled realms of India and China. In 1519 Ferdinand Magellan, a Portuguese who had fought in the East Indies before offering his services to the Spanish, sailed from Spain with five ships, having been commissioned by King Philip to find an eastward passage to the Indies, which were thought to lie only 300 miles east of Panama. Unable to find a channel through the American continent, he sailed towards its southern tip, wintering there for five months. When summer came, he navigated a tortuous passage through the island group at Tierra del Fuego, and after thirty-eight days entered the Pacific. (It would be almost another century before another navigator, a Dutchman, would brave the storms of the southern oceans and round Cape Horn itself.) Making for a more northern latitude, Magellan then sailed due west across the ocean's enormous expanse—it was three times wider than the Atlantic— whose waters were so tranquil that he called it the 'Pacific Ocean' and so empty that in two months he sighted only two islands, his men marvelling at the new constellation known as the Southern Cross which dominated the sky, outshining all others. Magellan sailed for more than three months before he reached Samar in the island group that he named the Philippines in honour of his king (April 1521). Unwisely involving himself in a war as ally to a local ruler he fell in battle on an island near Cebu only three weeks later. So died needlessly the only navigator whose achievements rivalled those of Columbus. Only one ship survived Magellan's expedition, but Spain now had claim to the Pacific. Unfortunately, for nearly fifty years it proved an empty acquisition: vessels found it almost impossible to sail east across its waters, for the winds between the two tropics constantly blew from the direction of South America and seldom the other way. When seamen learned to sail in a great arc through the Pacific's northern waters, galleons laden with the riches of the East would make regular voyages from Manila to the ports of Peru.

But what lay in the Pacific's southern latitudes? In 1567 Mendana sailed from the coast of Peru with orders from the viceroy to try and locate the legendary Unknown Southern Continent believed to lie in the ocean west of South America. He discovered the Solomon Islands, which lay north-east of Australia and proclaimed them the South Land, but their position on the map was then lost and they were rediscovered 200 years later by James Cook.

ABOVE:
Ferdinand Magellan (1480–1521), the Portuguese who sailed in the service of Spain.

1577: The English challenge—Francis Drake

The English now appear in the Southern Seas. Only ten years after Mendana sailed, three ships left England for the Pacific under the command of Francis Drake. English maritime activities had previously been concentrated in the north Atlantic and the Americas. It was King Henry VIII, in rejecting the omnipotence of the Pope, who founded two institutions to defend his Protestant kingdom: the Church of England and the Royal Navy, though the latter consisted for fifty years of barely two dozen sizeable warships. It was his daughter Elizabeth who, while establishing peace in her own realm and protesting friendship with Spain, made no attempt to limit the initiative of her seamen; when war came with Spain (an almost inevitable result of her support of the Dutch Protestant struggle and the depredations of English privateers), England was strong enough to triumph.

When Francis Drake, a Devon man who had raided Spanish treasure ships with success, sailed from Plymouth with five ships in the autumn of 1577 with the avowed intention of circumnavigating the world, his merchant backers believed he was seeking to discover Australia, the Unknown South Land and its possibilities for trade, his crew thought they were signing on for the Mediterranean, and only Queen Elizabeth (a shareholder in the voyage) and her ministers knew the true purpose—to return with Spain's treasure and establish English influence in the East and the Pacific, 'the Spanish Lake'.

Drake sailed via the Atlantic, navigated the Straits of Magellan, and then encountered a ferocious storm that lasted fifty-two days, separating his fleet, and forcing his ship south, where he sighted Cape Horn through the gale before being driven north again, back to the islands of Tierra del Fuego and the Straits of Magellan. As the mountainous seas threatened to crush them, the Englishmen prayed to God for salvation and one wrote:

BELOW:
Sir Francis Drake (c. 1540-96), the first English navigator to venture into the Pacific Ocean and the waters to Australia's north; from an old engraving.

The winds were such as if the bowels of the Earth had set all at liberty, or as if all the clouds under Heaven had been called together to lay their force upon that one place. The seas, which by nature and themselves, are of a weighty substance, were rolled up from the depths, even from the roots of the rocks ... [until] God—whom not the winds and seas alone, but even the devils themselves and powers of hell obey—did so wonderfully free us, and make our way open before us, as if it were his holy angels still guiding and conducting us ...

Anchoring in calm waters once more, Drake was now sure that the coastline he had sighted formed the southern-most tip of the Americas, and was not connected to the Unknown South Land. One of the many accounts of the voyage stated: 'It hath been a dream through many ages, that these islands have been a main [land], and that it hath been Terra Australis, wherein many strange monsters live ...'

Drake, whose command was now reduced to one ship, his own vessel the *Golden Hind*, then sailed up the coast of Chile and Peru, capturing Spanish merchant ships as he went, sailing almost the entire extent of the west coast of the Americas before careening his ship in San Francisco bay and heading west. He landed in the Moluccas, where he signed a treaty with the sultan of Ternate and crammed his overladen ship with a cargo of cloves, careened his damaged ship on the south coast of Java, and returned to England in triumph in 1580, having circumnavigated the world, the first Englishman to do so. He had made no attempt to explore the Pacific's southern waters. The inevitable clash between England and Spain came in 1588, and the defeat of the Spanish Armada in that year extinguished Spain's slackening hegemony in the East.

ABOVE:
The extraordinary role played by Dutch navigators in the discovery of Australia was later commemorated in postage stamps.

1606: Quiros and Torres

Some last Spanish voyages had a bearing on the history of Australia and its surrounds. In 1595 Mendana, now an old and querulous man, sailed for the Solomon Islands from Peru with a fleet of prospective colonists, who happened to be the most undesirable individuals who could be coaxed aboard at short notice by a sceptical viceroy. Mendana made landfall on an island far to the east of the Solomons—Santa Cruz, a palm-fringed malarial flyspeck that centuries later would be immortalised in the musical South Pacific and whose waters in 1942–43 saw massive air and sea battles between the fleets of Japan and the United States. Here Mendana's men shot natives for sport, slaughtering hundreds before being in turn decimated by arrows and disease. Mendana died but his resolute Portuguese pilot, Pedro de Quiros, took command and led the survivors back to Spain. In 1605 de Quiros, seemingly consumed by Catholic zeal to convert the heathen, set sail from Peru for the elusive Solomons in Spain's last great voyage of exploration. He discovered instead the New Hebrides islands, which he also thought were the Unknown South Land, and named them, confusingly, 'Australia del Espiritu Santo'.

BELOW:
Navigators' accounts of their voyages were quickly translated into English and published widely.

Quiros's second-in-command, Torres, was sceptical of his commander's claim that the New Hebrides (Vanuatu) were the long-sought continent, and after Quiros, faced with a mutinous crew abruptly departed for Peru, it was Torres who decided to return to Spain by sailing west. He sighted the tip of New Caledonia and then the easternmost cape of New Guinea before sailing along the island's southern coast through the strait that today bears his name, and became possibly the first European to see Cape York. Spain kept secret the discovery that New Guinea and Australia were separated by water, and copies of Torres' charts were not discovered until 1762 when an English fleet captured Manila.

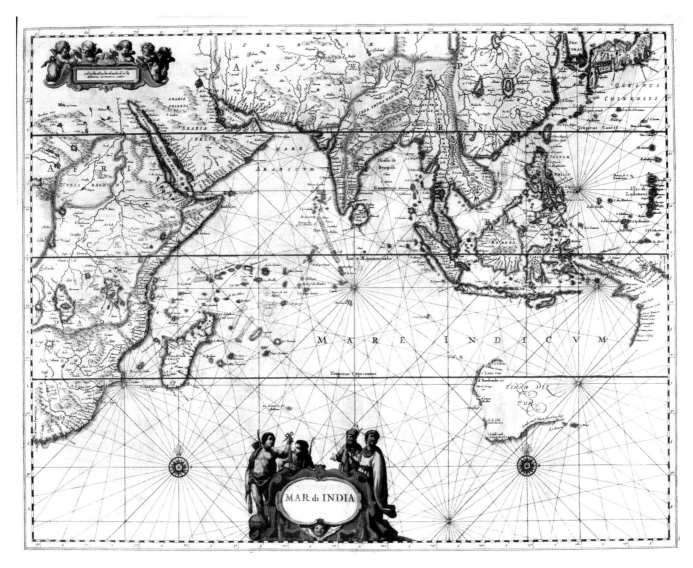

ABOVE:

Chart of the Indian Ocean by J. Jansson, Amsterdam, 1650. Eight years earlier Tasman had discovered the coast of Tasmania but his finds were apparently not yet incorporated on charts.

1606: The Dutch

In the same year, 1606, as Quiros's attempt to settle the savage Solomons, a Dutch vessel, the *Duyfken* (Dove), under the command of Willem Janz, sailing from Bantam in Java, entered Torres Strait from the west and sighted Cape York peninsula— the first recorded sighting of the Australian mainland, which he named Cape Keerweer—but turned back before exploring the full extent of the strait. Exploring several inlets to its south, he then sailed north, where some of his men landing in a boat were attacked by the inhabitants. The captain's report of the reefs of Torres Strait and the reception given him by the natives was sufficient to deter further Dutch exploration.

On the last day of 1600 the ageing Queen Elizabeth issued a charter to the 'Honourable East India Company', set up by leading English merchants and bankers, to exploit the trade of the East Indies. An unexpected new rival, the Dutch, followed suit, creating their own East Indies Company in 1602. The Dutch provinces, having driven the Spanish armies from their Lowland home, achieved a truce with Spain in 1609. In the same year the Dutch founded the Bank of Amsterdam to fund their ventures and a Dutch ship crossed the Atlantic and reached the Hudson River (prelude to the founding of a settlement on Manhattan Island fifteen years later, the birth of New York). Dutch ships went in search of trade with boldness and vigour, rapidly filling the vacuum left by the decline of the Portuguese and Spanish seaborne endeavours, and the wealth from trade that flowed to Amsterdam and its richest province, Holland, would give birth to a Dutch Golden Age, a cultural and artistic renaissance.

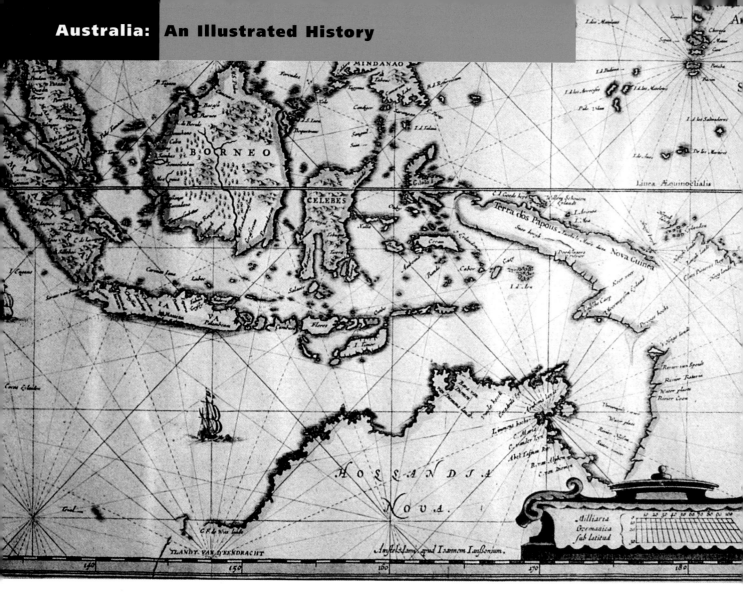

ABOVE:

Australia slowly takes
shape: Further Dutch
discoveries in the early
seventeenth century
provided an accurate
chart of Australia's northern waters, but the east
of the continent remained
a mystery.

Unlike the Spanish and Portuguese, whose trading was generally a royal monopoly, undercapitalised, often inefficient and prey to corruption, the Dutch
approached overseas trade as a business proposition and reaped the benefits.
The Dutch—and later the English—developed a commercial sense before they
took to the seas.

The Dutch were the first seafarers to sail round the stormy tip of South America—Cape Horn was rounded and named by Schouten in 1616—and in 1619 they
established their base in the East Indies at the harbour near Java's western tip,
which they named Batavia (it later grew into the great city of Jakarta), and which
seven years later became their principal port, supplanting Bantam. In 1622 the
Dutch captured Malacca, which soon dwindled in importance. They even contested Portuguese control of Timor, establishing a trading post at Koepang on the
island's south-western tip. In 1652 they founded a settlement at the Cape of Good
Hope, where European ships had often watered and bartered with the natives on
their way to and from India. Their ships later blockaded the Portuguese in Goa
seven years in succession, when the monsoonal winds kept at bay any chance of
a fleet sailing to the outpost's rescue. The seventeenth century would belong to
the Dutch, the eighteenth to the English.

The Dutch and 'New Holland'

'Credit for the discovery and early exploration of Australia should go entirely to the
Dutch, who not only found the new continent but put definite limits to it as well,'
wrote Boise Penrose, the American maritime historian. 'This indeed is the outstanding contribution of the Netherlands to the cause of discovery, a contribution
recognised in the early name of the land—New Holland.' This remarkable nation

ABOVE:
Dutch ship from a chart
dating from 1622.

of barely 1.25 million people would redraw the maps of the world and establish an empire that would endure for nearly three centuries.

Beating across the Indian Ocean to Java, Dutch skippers noticed that stronger winds prevailed south of the tropics, and after 1613 they began sailing due east across the Indian Ocean in 40 degrees latitude ('the Roaring Forties') before making north when they struck the trade winds. Inevitably, some Dutch vessels were destined to sight the western coast of Australia and others to collide with it.

The first Dutch reports of the continent were not encouraging. Late in August 1616, the *Eendracht*, commanded by Dirck Hartog, left Table Bay at the Cape of Good Hope, and sailed due east. Her captain became the first European to sight the Western Australian coast, and on 21 October he made landfall on the island that bears his name and left there an inscribed pewter plate nailed to a tree to mark the occasion. Hartog then sailed north up the coast for 300 miles (500 kilometres) and completed his voyage in Java.

Other Dutch vessels charted sections of our coast. In May 1616 the *Zeewolf* sighted the coast and in July the *Mauritius* landed a party near Exmouth Gulf before departing. In July 1619 two ships under the command of Frederik de Houtman explored to the south of the west coast, anchoring near Bunbury and then landing at Rottnest Island near Perth; on his voyage north to the Indies Houtman also sighted midway up the Western Australia coast the islets and coral reefs 50 miles (80 kilometres in land terms) off the coast of present-day Geraldton, and named them the Abrolhos Group from the Portuguese words for 'Look out!'— 'Abro holes'.

ABOVE:
Dirk Hartog's plate: the pewter plate that the navigator nailed to a tree on an island in Shark Bay, Western Australia, to mark his landfall there in his ship *Eendracht* in October 1616.

The region was long known as Eendracht Land.

But the first ship to be wrecked off the Western Australian coast was an English one. On 25 May 1622 the East India Company ship *Tryal*, bound from Plymouth to Bantam, and carrying 143 souls, ran aground on a reef off the Montebello Islands, and began to sink. Captain Brookes recounted: 'I strucke down my sails and got out my skiffe and by their sounding about ye shippe they found sharp sudden rocks half a cable length astern …' The gallant captain set out for Java with nine others in the skiff, followed by thirty-six others in the longboat; these two boatloads were the only survivors.

Few English ships ventured in these waters, for in the following year the Dutch turned on English merchants on Ambon and massacred them, effectively curtailing England's incursions into the East Indies.

1622: The 'most barren region'

In 1622 the Dutch ship *Leeuwin* sighted the cape that bears her name: Australia's south-western tip. In 1623 the *Pera* and the *Arnhem* were dispatched by the Dutch East India Company to explore Torres Strait; after a skirmish with the natives on the New Guinea coast they sighted Cape York and followed its western shore to the south, into the Gulf of Carpentaria, where they were attacked by natives. The small yacht *Arnhem* then sailed west to explore the coast further—Arnhem Land—while Captain Carstenz on the *Pera* investigated Cape York Peninsula. Of the inhabitants of its desert coast, Captain Cartensz wrote:

> These blacks showed no fear and were so bold as to touch the muskets of our men and to try to take (them) off their shoulders. They are coal-black, with lean bodies and stark naked, having twisted baskets or nets about their heads; in hair and figure they are like the blacks of the Coramandel coast, but they seem to be less cunning, bold and evil-natured than the blacks at the western end of Nova Guinea ...

> 'During all the time we have searched and examined this part of the coast,' he continued, 'we have seen not one fruit-bearing tree; there are no mountains or even hills, so that it may be safely concluded that the land contains no metals, nor yields any precious woods. In our judgement this is the most arid and barren region that could be found anywhere on the earth ...'

ABOVE:
More gaps in the coastline are filled in: By 1665, when this map in French was published, Tasmania had appeared and New Guinea was represented as separate from the Australian mainland.

ABOVE:
The shipwreck of the Dutch ship *Batavia* on a reef in the Abrolhos Islands off the Western Australian coast in 1626 became one of the horror stories of the sea, a tale of mutiny and murder.

In 1627 the *Gulden Zeepard* was blown off course and the captain decided to follow the coastline along the south-western coast beyond Cape Leuwin. This was the first voyage into the Great Australian Bight and the ship sailed for 1000 miles (1600 kilometres), as far as Nuyt's Archipelago (midway along South Australia's coast), before turning back. No detailed record exists of this astonishing voyage but it enabled the map of Australia's coastline to be extended. The outline of almost the entire western half of the continent known as New Holland was now charted.

The shipwreck coast

Despite their fine charts of the west coast, Dutch vessels making for Java often came to grief on its shores: the *Batavia* failed to look out and ran aground on the Abrolhos reefs in June 1629, sinking four days later. Her survivors marooned there with little to eat but seabirds endured a horror story of rapine and murder at the hands of drunken crewmen while her captain was sailing to Batavia in a small boat. He returned to rescue survivors and exact harsh justice on the mutineers. The same shoals claimed the great 600-tonne *Vergulde Drueck* (Gilt Dragon) in 1656 (only eight survived from the 194 souls aboard), and the *Zeewyck* in 1727 (when 120 died), only fifteen years after Holland's biggest ship, the *Zuytdorp*, had disappeared completely off the Australian coast, giving birth to one of the great mysteries of the sea. No trace of the ship or her 286 passengers and crew was

found until 1927 when a stockman riding along the coast 240 kilometres north of Geraldton saw wreckage on a beach, which proved to be from the *Zuytdorp*. The bleak shores of Western Australia became a coast of ghosts, dreaded and forbidding.

1642: Tasman's first voyage

What lay to the east remained a mystery. Whether New Holland extended almost to South America, forming with Antarctica a land mass larger than Asia, was a question that tempted the curiosity of Antonio van Diemen, Governor-General of the Dutch East Indies in Batavia, who in one historian's words 'broke the back of Portuguese sea power in the Indian Ocean between 1636 and 1645'. Indeed, when the United Provinces of the Free Netherlands achieved total independence in 1648, their fleet of vessels that could serve as warships numbered 14,000; Portugal could muster only thirteen warships.

Van Diemen was eager to find a southerly route to the west coast of South America and in 1642 he dispatched his most resourceful officer, Abel Tasman, and the ships *Heemskirk* and *Zeehan*, to determine the extent of New Holland by sailing around its eastern and northern coasts.

Tasman left Batavia in August 1642, putting in to Mauritius before leaving the island on 8 October to sail south-east and then due east, into the waters below the Great Australian Bight. He kept well away from the southern coast, which he did not sight, and on 24 November he sighted land—the west coast of Tasmania, which he named Anthony van Diemenslandt (Van Diemen's Land). After making landfall in Sorell Bay, Tasman followed the coast to the east, the Dutchmen anchoring a week later in a harbour (Cape Frederick Henry Bay), where they went ashore but found little of interest, for the inhabitants hid from them. The seafarers saw smoke from campfires, and notches high in the trunks of the towering trees that led them to believe they were in a land of giants. Nevertheless, Tasman claimed the land for his nation.

Resuming his voyage east, to latitude 42° 10'S, Tasman again sighted land—the coast of one of the two islands he named Nieuw Zeeland, and whose western coasts he mapped. He remarked on the savagery there of the Maori, who killed several of his crew, and he charted incompletely the coastlines before sailing north for the Solomons and thence via the northern coasts of New Guinea to Batavia, which he reached in July 1643.

But Tasman's ten-month voyage had produced no riches and his reports (later published in book form) gave little hope of any important trade, though he speculated that New Holland might be rich in gold. He had also made an error in assuming that New Zealand was part of Australia and formed its eastern extremities and he had failed to discover whether Australia was connected to New Guinea and Van Diemen's Land.

ABOVE:
Title page of Captain Pelsaert's account of the *Batavia* horror.

ABOVE:
A portrait of the Dutch navigator Abel Tasman and his wife, c. 1637.

Painting by J.G. Cuyp.

1644: Tasman's second voyage

In 1644 Tasman was again despatched to Australian waters, this time commanding three vessels, but he contented himself with exploring the northern coasts and he failed even to sail the length of Torres Strait or to confirm whether Arnhem Land was an island, but he charted much of the coastline of the Gulf of Carpentaria and Groote Eylandt. From this point on the Dutch, who were soon to be distracted by commercial wars with England, appear to have lost interest in what Tasman called 'New Holland', and by the late 1690s the Netherlands itself was in decline and subject to the growing power of France.

1697: The last Dutch visitors

The Dutchman Vlamingck explored and named the Swan River—on whose banks would rise the future city of Perth—in 1697. He reported on the beauty of the black swans on its waters and of the verdant nature of the land, but found nothing at *Swaenerevier* to barter or trade. On his voyage he saw Hartog's plate and removed it, leaving his own inscribed pewter plate nailed to a tree to record his landfall. The Hartog plate is now in the Rijksmuseum on display with the master-pieces of Rembrandt and Vermeer but the Vlamingck plate was taken back to France by a later navigator, Freycinet, in 1818 and lost until 1940 when it was found in a cupboard in a Paris museum. It now stands on display in its natural home, Perth.

1688: The English reappear— Dampier's first voyage

England's East India Company followed Dutch activities closely and saw no possibilities in opening trade with Australia. Thus the landing on our northern coasts of an English adventurer, William Dampier, was almost accidental. Dampier, who had gone to sea as a boy, had served on warships in the Second Dutch War, and spent several years managing a plantation in the West Indies, before joining in 1683 a group of privateers (little better than buccaneers or pirates in that they preyed on native vessels and passing Spanish shipping). Two years later he sailed with them on the *Cygnet*, commanded by Captain Swan, for the Mariana Islands, before heading for the Philippines. These waters were thick with native seaborne trade, which European ships raided with impunity. Under a new captain, Read, the *Cygnet* put in at Timor and then made course for the north-western coast of Australia. The Englishmen sighted land at a point near the present-day Buccaneer Archipelago on 4 January 1688, and anchored in a bay next day. Seeing figures ashore, the *Cygnet* sent a small boat to shore, but the inhabitants waved spears at the newcomers, who fired a gun to scare them. While the ship was careened and its hull scraped at low tide, Dampier explored the shore and came across a group of Aborigines. The women ran away with their children, crying, but the men remained unmoved, and refused both Dampier's offer of clothing or his orders to carry water to the ship's boats. Dampier recorded his impressions of the place, obviously sharing Dutch pessimism about the country:

> The 4th of January, 1688, we fell in with the land of New Holland, having made our course due south. New Holland is a very large tract of land. It is not yet determined whether it is an island or a main continent; but I am certain that it joins neither to Asia, Africa nor America. This part of it that we saw is all low even land, with sandy banks against the sea; only the points are rocky, and so are some of the islands in this bay. The land is of a dry, sandy soil, destitute of water, except you make wells; yet producing divers sorts of trees; but the woods are not thick; nor the trees very big …

Dampier saw gum oozing from the bare eucalypts. 'There was pretty long grass growing under the trees, but it was very thin. We saw no trees that bore fruit or berries. We saw no sort of animal, nor any track of beast but once, and that seemed to be the tread of a beast as big as a great mastiff dog [possibly a kangaroo]. Here are a few small land birds … Neither is the sea very plentifully supplied with fish, unless you reckon the manatee or turtle as such …'

> The inhabitants of this country are the miserablest people in this world …
> They are tall, strait-bodied and thin. They have great heads, round forheads,

and great brows. Their eyelids are always half-closed, to keep the flies out of
their eyes, they being so troublesome here, that no fanning will keep them [off]
... The colour of their skins ... is coal black, like those of the natives of Guinea
... They have no houses, but lye in the open air, without any covering; the earth
being their bed and the heavens their canopy.

Dampier then speculated as an anthropologist:

Whether they cohabit one man to one woman, or promiscuously, I know not;
but they do live in companies. Twenty or thirty men, women and children live
together. Their only food is a small sort of fish, which they get by making wears
[dams] of stone across little coves ... In other places at low water they seek for
mussels, cockles and periwinkles ... I did not perceive that they worshipped
anything.

The *Cygnet* sailed from Australia on 12 March. At the Nicobar Islands Dampier,
having determined to leave the ship, took to a canoe with seven others and made
for the Sumatra coast from where, after numerous side-voyages (one of them to
Indochina aboard an English vessel), he returned to England in 1691, bringing with
him a Filipino whom he passed off as a 'prince' and whom he intended to place
on show.

1699: Dampier's second voyage

BELOW:
Dampier's chart of
Shark Bay, Western
Australia, 1699.

Tasman's journal of his 1642 voyages was published in England in 1694 and
Dampier, who read it with fascination, began to wonder if his judgement of
Australia was too harsh. After the publication in 1698 of his famous book, *A New
Voyage Round the World* (which was read and enjoyed
by thousands, including the Irish cleric who would write
the novel *Gulliver's Travels*), Dampier began to lobby
the Admiralty and the Royal Society to sponsor another
voyage to New Holland. He was commissioned by the
Admiralty to investigate the eastern coasts of New Holland and New Guinea, this time as captain of HMS *Roebuck*. Dampier was now a lion of London society and in
August 1698 the diarist John Evelyn dined with his ageing friend and fellow diarist Samuel Pepys, the former
naval administrator and president of the Royal Society:

Shark's Bay

I dined with Mr Pepys, where was Captain Dampier,
who had been a famous Buccaneer, [and] had brought
hither the painted Prince Job, and printed a relation
of his very strange adventure, and his observations.
He was now going abroad again by the King's encouragement, who furnished a ship of 290 tons. He seemed
a more modest man than one would imagine by the
relation of the crew he had assorted with. He brought
a map ...

Dampier sailed in January 1699 in the *Roebuck*, which
he quickly realised was barely seaworthy, by way of Brazil, arresting and abandon-
ing his first lieutenant there after an argument. He rounded the Cape of Good
Hope in early June and twenty-five days later sighted the Western Australian coast,

which he followed north, landing at Shark Bay in August 1699 to further explore the land, but apart from sighting small kangaroos found only a monotony of desolation. After only two days he raised anchor, sailed north, putting into the Dampier Archipelago to obtain water. There he saw dingos ('like hungry wolves') and was attacked by Aborigines and had to shoot one to drive them away, an act that sorrowed him. He then headed for Timor and in January 1700 sighted the southern coast of New Guinea. He sailed around the island's western and northern coast, discovering a large island he named New Britain and then the strait that separates it from New Guinea (Dampier Strait). But by now his ship was leaking, his crew stricken with scurvy and his spirit almost broken. He made for Batavia and the Cape of Good Hope but the *Roebuck* foundered off Ascension Island (February 1701). Dampier was rescued by a passing English ship. He reached London, his only achievement being the sighting of New Britain, to face a court-martial, which found him unfit to command a ship of the Royal Navy. He had sold his Filipino prince, and wrote an account of the experiences, *A Voyage to New Holland*. Undeterred by official doubts of his competence, he set sail two years later (1703) in command of a privateer, the *St George*, but again met with failure; his second ship sailed off, and he had to abandon his own vessel as unseaworthy and was placed under detention by the Dutch when he reached the East Indies as a passenger. When he returned to England in 1707, his reputation was tarnished but in the following year he took ship as a pilot for Captain Woods Rogers, a successful privateer, to plunder Spanish shipping in the Pacific—a profitable venture at last. They returned with booty valued at £180,000—and an additional crew member, Alexander Selkirk, who had been marooned on a Pacific island in 1704 by one of Dampier's captains. Selkirk's story inspired Dampier's contemporary Daniel Defoe to write *Robinson Crusoe*, a rival in high adventure to the circumnavigator's own books.

An opportunist and poor leader of men but fearless and with brilliant skills as a writer, Dampier has been called an attractive character but hardly a hero. He was, however, fairly summarised by a later historian, Captain Burney: 'It is not easy to name another voyager or traveler who has given more useful information to the world.'

European arrival had been premature. For the next century, European exploration of the South Seas languished.

The first decade of the eighteenth century saw England (united to Scotland in 1707) at war with France, beginning fifty years of conflict from which she would emerge with the strongest navy and the greatest empire the world had known.

The Antipodes: 'Topsie-turvey fellows'

For the best part of the eighteenth century, Australia—'the Antipodes' (meaning, though not literally, the opposite ends of the earth)—was a realm of fable, fantasy and mockery. As early as 1638 a play opened in London called *The Antipodes*, about a country where everything was upside down, including the people, and especially their society, for parrots talked and the women ruled the men. In the Restoration dramatist Congreve's play *The Way of the World* a hearty character confides: 'Your Antipodes are a good rascally sort of topsie-turvey fellows—if I had a bumper I'd stand upon my head and drink a health to 'em.' In the satire

By the mid-eighteenth century England's shipyards and ports hummed with activity.

Painting by John Clevely.

Gulliver's Travels, published in 1726, Jonathan Swift shipwrecked his hero in the kingdom of Lilliput in present-day South Australia: 'We were driven by a violent storm to the north-west of Van Dieman's [sic] Land,' Gulliver recounts. When he came to, he felt something on his chest and saw a 'human creature not six inches high, with a bow and arrow in his hands and a quiver on his back'.

While sections of the coasts of Australia and New Zealand were now appearing on maps, they were still thought to be part of one immense southern continent, and it was in search of Terra Australis Incognita (which was thought to be far larger than Australia alone) that a Dutchman, Jacob Roggeven, sailed from Holland in 1721. He found nothing of note and European interest in the region subsided.

The world we came from: Georgian England

When the cannons boomed their salutes from London's Tower Hill to proclaim the accession of the young King George III in 1760, Englishmen counted themselves the luckiest race on earth, the most favoured, the most powerful. Only a year earlier—in the *annus mirabilus*, 1759—the bells of London had pealed in celebration of a succession of victories: General Wolfe's capture of Quebec and Admiral Hawke's destruction of the French fleet and invasion force at Quiberon Bay. They came only two years after Robert Clive's victory at Plassey that delivered Bengal to British rule. Now Canada had fallen with India into England's lap, along with rich plums in the West Indies, the fruits of the genius of William Pitt (later Lord Chatham). France's long hegemony in Europe was in decline.

England's new king, only twenty-two years old, was the first Hanoverian to speak without a thick German accent, for he had been English-born. He was to prove a conscientious and popular (but meddlesome) monarch, and a devoted husband. Attending the coronation, Benjamin Franklin, agent for the colony of Pennsylvania, felt proud to be a Briton and wrote afterwards that England had 'the best Constitution and the best King a nation was ever blessed with'. George III's long reign from 1760 to 1820 encompassed both the Age of Reason and the Age of Revolution.

Only two years later (1762) British fleets took Havana and Manila and the world lay open to English ships, English enterprise; by decade's end the voyages of Wallis, Carteret and James Cook would reveal the extent of the new world of the Pacific. 'Yet in the half century before George III's accession,' wrote historian Sir Keith Feiling, 'the national advance was slow and uneven. This limited progress was much due to the fact that the whole mechanism of life was antiquated.'

ABOVE:
English-made seafarers' compass, 1750.

The rise of English power

The sudden growth of England's strength and influence by 1760 had been phenomenal. Through the course of the seventeenth century England had been a negligible power: the Dutch ruled the seas and the French ruled not only the battlefields but taste and culture as well. The last of the Tudors, the great Elizabeth, had asserted English power but her Stuart successors had squandered it. Threatened with the reintroduction of the Catholic religion imposed by a monarch who treated Parliament with contempt, the English had fought a civil war, beheaded their king, experimented with a Republic, restored the monarchy, and in 1688 invited the displaced king's daughter Mary to share the crown of England with her husband, the Dutch Stadtholder William of Orange—under strict conditions, among them being their acceptance of a Bill of Rights that deprived the Crown of arbitrary power while investing its subjects with freedoms unknown in other lands. Unlawful arrest was abolished (habeas corpus), torture was outlawed, the primacy of the Protestant religion and Parliament permanently established.

In 1685 the Bank of England was created, modelled on the Dutch banks. It was the initiative of a Scot, William Paterson (Australia's national poet 'Banjo' Paterson claimed him as a kinsman) and with it came the consolidation of the national debt. The debt could never be paid off, but the bank became the bedrock of England's new financial stability. The first banknotes were issued and England's debased coinage was called in and replaced with coins of real gold and silver. The soundness of sterling was established. For more than two centuries inflation was unknown and despite a mounting national debt England became the banker of Europe, able to finance her allies in forming coalitions against whichever European power threatened her own standing. Financial speculation was rife, sound investments few, but institutions of some integrity date from this time—the shipping insurers Lloyds of London being one of them. The navy was reformed and English troops under a general of genius, John Churchill, Duke of Marlborough, served with distinction in the Low Countries and Germany against the armies of France. Inviting the Elector of Hanover to assume the crown in 1714 to ensure a Protestant succession, England found herself, when peace came, possessing Gibraltar and Minorca, and with her North American colonies and West Indian islands intact.

France and Spain no longer dominated Europe's destinies. Austria–Hungary, Russia and Prussia were now pre-eminent powers on the continent. Modern Europe was being shaped.

ABOVE:
His Britannic Majesty George the Third, By the Grace of God, King of Great Britain and Ireland, 1760.

Yet the first decades of the eighteenth century gave little promise of the transformation to come, a revolution so profound that historians describe the Britain of half a century later as the birthplace of the modern state. In 1700 half of England's exports were cloth, and other industries was stagnant. It was the age of three of Europe's greatest geniuses—the architect Sir Christopher Wren, the philosopher John Locke and the scientist Sir Isaac Newton, who had discovered the principles of gravity, the calculus and light and its spectrum before the age of twenty-five—but public taste was primitive, Parliament was corrupt and life cruel.

An Empire built on trade

England's most valuable prize from the Treaty of Utrecht in 1713 was obtaining the asento— the monopoly in supplying slaves to Spanish America. In an early foray into privatisation the Crown sold the rights to the South Sea Company, whose shares by 1720 were trading at £1000 each; in one of the West's most sudden and spectacular corporate collapses, profits proved illusory, directors were found to be playing free with shareholders' money—and shares fell 80 per cent in value, ruining speculators, among them Sir Isaac Newton, who lost £20,000.

'The sole purpose of government is the Preservation of Property,' John Locke had written. No slavers were more feared than the English, for the Englishman saw slaves not as souls worthy of redemption but as property to be sold at a profit. 'We have been sitting this fortnight on the African Company,' wrote the fastidious and humane Horace Walpole (son of the former prime minister) in 1750, when the slave company's abuses were under investigation by the House of Commons. 'We, the British Senate, that temple of liberty, and bulwark of Protestant Christianity, have this fortnight been pondering methods to make more effectual the horrid traffic in the selling of negroes. It has appeared to us that six-and-forty thousand of these wretches are sold every year to our plantations alone!—it chills one's blood.'

Slaving was lucrative. In an age where soldiers were paid a shilling a day (the rate of pay remained unchanged until 1918), slaves fetched up to £35 each and some £100 or more. The English were not too troubled by religious strictures or conscience, and they were extraordinarily efficient. English slave ships were to carry nearly 3,000,000 slaves to the Americas before national revulsion found parliamentary support and led to slavery's abolition.

Where European nations contemplated war with horror, the British seized it as an opportunity. Constant clashes with the Spanish over trade saw England involved in war against them in the 1740s—when Commodore Anson completed his famous circumnavigation of the world (1740-44), bombarding Manila on the way. He returned with only one of the six ships he had sailed with but her hold was bursting with plunder.

'United Kingdom'

Near bankrupt, Scotland had joined England in a 'United Kingdom' in 1707, but the union was unpopular and in 1715, only a year after a Hanoverian ruler assumed the throne to ensure a Protestant succession, the Highland clans (strongly Catholic) rose in rebellion against 'German George', as they were to rise against his son in 1745. Scots were soon to march with Englishmen into a wider world, providing the Crown with regiments of Highland soldiers, and a body of highly educated men out of all proportion to Scotland's small population (1.5 million). The Lowland Scots of Edinburgh and Glasgow were renowned for their humourless ambition but they would provide the Empire with merchants, administrators, generals, engineers, writers and tough pioneers.

Ireland remained ungovernable and a constant threat. Its Catholic population was growing at an alarming rate (it soon had four million people, half the size of England's) but they were forbidden to practise their religion and remained in dark poverty and surly bondage.

England's own freedoms were unique, and even her critics and occasional enemies—including Voltaire and Montesquieu, who fled to England to escape arrest in their own country, as thousands have done for centuries—found stimulation in her atmosphere free of religious dogmatism where political discussion, literature, science and the arts flourished. The London journals mocked king and ministers with impunity, theatre flourished and the crudity, energy—and bawdy humour—of the age lives in the novels of Defoe, Smollett and Swift.

Parliament and patronage

The first Hanoverian king, George I (who reigned 1714-27), ceased attending and presiding over meetings of his key ministers because of petulance, laziness or language difficulties and deputed the Chancellor of the Exchequer, Robert Walpole, to be his First (Prime) Minister and duly report proceedings to him, thus initiating cabinet government.

England's much vaunted Parliament was an archaic mockery of representative rule. Patronage and power were cultivated by the ambitious. Parliament was an oligarchy, often corrupted by vested interests, but at least it existed; France was ruled by a royal bureaucracy, its society a feudal one, and its parliament (the Estates-General) had not met since 1614. England's portly 20-stone (120 kilo) Prime Minister, Sir Robert Walpole seemed immovable, and became the dominant if corrupt leader of thirty years of Whig rule, presiding over a long period of peace and seeming prosperity. 'In truth,' wrote the historian Sir Keith Feiling, 'matter was being heaped up for explosion. An industrial revolution was proceeding, the realm was weakened by social injustice.'

ABOVE:
Portsmouth Point, by
the English satirical artist
Thomas Rowlandson,
1790.

The Industrial Revolution

Historians would date the Industrial Revolution from the 1760s, when England, benefiting from social and political stability, began to apply her natural resources and accumulated scientific knowledge to manufacturing on a scale never before seen. In 1769 James Watt, a Scot, patented an effective steam-powered engine (it was not the first steam engine, but Watt invented the condenser that made it function). Its widespread adoption marked the introduction of mechanisation. In 1740 a Yorkshireman had discovered how to blend iron with carbon to make steel by the crucible method. Coal, in which England was rich, also fired all manner of steam engines. In 1769 Arkwright invented a powered spinning machine and by 1790 power was driving weaving machines, soon making Lancashire the centre of the cotton cloth industry.

England gave birth to an equally significant agricultural revolution. In 1760 a House of Commons dominated by the gentry began passing the first of 4000 Enclosure Acts over the next twenty years (during the previous sixty years only 280 were passed), which were framed to increase the size of agricultural holdings to allow more economic farming. Allied to improvements in agriculture, they destroyed England's yeoman peasantry by driving them from the smallholdings they had tilled and farmed for centuries. The rural dispossessed would drift in time to the cities where factory work was plentiful but living conditions abysmal. The products of the iron foundries of Birmingham and Sheffield, the mills of Manchester and Leeds, the potteries of Staffordshire, would be transported by remarkable systems of improved roads and new inland canals to the ports of London, Liverpool and Bristol, whence they would be carried on English ships to all corners of the known world.

Maritime supremacy

A series of Navigation Acts conferred on English shipping a monopoly of trade within her Empire; American ships were barred from trading with Europe and high taxes and tariffs were imposed on the American colonies after 1765 by the government in London to offset Britain's high cost of defending them. The Yankees, despite their respect for the monarchy, early showed a spirit of independence by simply refusing to pay the taxes or duties. The Americans and the Irish rankled under the English laws that prohibited them from establishing industries of any kind. King George unwisely exercised his royal prerogative to appoint his ministers and invariably appointed the worst. In desperation both peoples would later resort to armed rebellion.

Meanwhile, riches flowed to the ports of England: 'The splendour of this monarchy is supported by commerce', declared a prosperous London merchant, 'and commerce by naval power.' The English had solved the riddle of finding longitude with John Harrison's invention in the 1750s of a reliable maritime chronometer: navigators could now calculate their exact position by comparing local time to that at the Royal Observatory at Greenwich, where the zero meridian of longitude began. The Royal Navy was the nation's pride, controlled not by the king but by the Board of Admiralty. Unlike the army (in which commissions in regiments were bought and sold by their colonels like shares in a company), the navy was an essentially professional service demanding high qualities of leadership and seamanship among its officers. The King's young son Prince William went to sea in a man-o'-war as a 13-year-old midshipman; the Royal Navy's greatest navigator, Captain James Cook, was the son of a penniless farmer.

No Englishman was conscripted to serve in the king's armies or navy. The ranks were recruited from among the poor, officered by the gentry and reinforced in war by foreign levies. Yet Britain, unprepared for a long war, emerged after initial disasters in the war against France (1756–63) with a Royal Navy of 400 ships, having raised an army of 250,000 men, and with a new Empire in Canada and India. By 1788 more than 9000 ships flew the British flag (though the majority of them were under 200 tonnes).

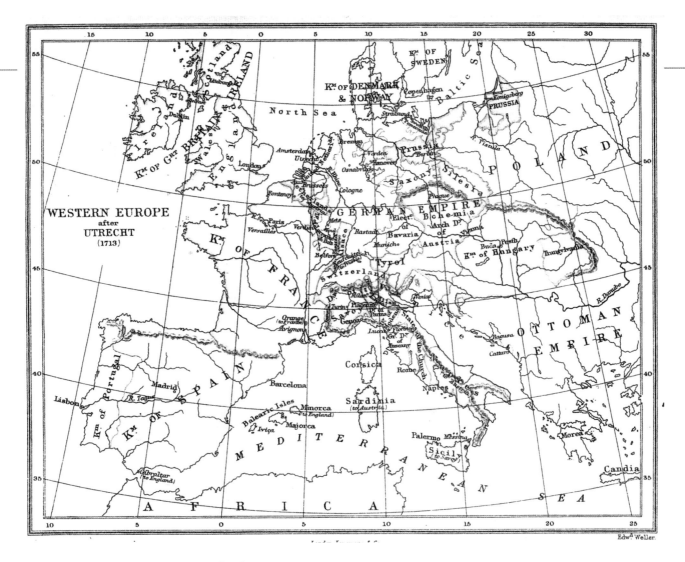

ABOVE:
Map of Westen Europe at
the time of the Treaty of
Utrecht, 1713.

English society

Englishmen were developing a mighty self-conceit. 'Though a stern, true-born Englishman, and fully prejudiced against all other nations,' wrote the Scot James Boswell of his idol, Dr Samuel Johnson, 'he had candour enough to censure the cold reserve too common among Englishmen towards strangers.' The French in turn still regarded the English with some distaste—as *nouveaux riches,* lacking true culture. 'Culturally, the eighteenth century was an Anglo-French condominium, and under that sign America was born,' writes the historian Albert Guerard. The English had mastered the arts of combining grace with simplicity in architecture and furniture design, painting, ceramics and fashion, for this was the age of Gainsborough and Romney; of Wedgwood, Copeland and Chippendale. But J.H. Plumb reminds us: 'Yet somehow there was no development, no increase of stature, no burgeoning of a culture, literary, scientific or artistic, which could compare with France.' England excelled in mass production.

The wonders of the age were many. In 1728 an Englishman named Chambers had been the first to compile and publish an 'encyclopaedia' (in two volumes) incorporating the knowledge of the burgeoning Age of Learning, and this inspired the French intellectuals to prepare their own *Encyclopaédie*—in thirty-five volumes. Learned Scots in Edinburgh published the first edition of *The Encyclopaedia Britannica* in 1768, again in two volumes. The great French venture began appearing in 1751 but its articles questioning orthodox belief on subjects from religion to philosophy and reflecting the humanism of the Enlightenment, so angered the French Church and State that its printers and authors lived in fear of arrest; the last of its majestic volumes of plates did not appear until 1780.) Adam Smith, another Scot, would found a new school of learning, economic theory, and in his great work *The Wealth of Nations* (1776) provide British commerce with a philosophy. In one historian's words he propounded the theory that 'economic production and exchange would automatically find their most efficient form if human nature, inspired by rational self-interest, was allowed full scope'. No government laws were imposed on slavers and factory owners; indeed, some Royal Navy captains had found occasional slave-trading a profitable sideline.

ABOVE:
An eighteenth-century intellectual whose books are still read widely: Adam Smith (1723–90).

English law

English law was impartial but harsh and it fell with equal savagery on rich and poor alike. It was a curious law. 'Common law' was not a result of statutes but had evolved since the Norman Conquest as a commonsense solution to disputes. Lawyers could draw on precedents to influence a magistrate's or judge's ruling; the common people provided juries to decide the rights and wrongs of cases while a judge decided the punishment. In the 1760s the jurist Sir William Blackstone began setting out English legal structure and principles in his *Commentaries on the Laws of England*, a work of enormous influence. Oddly, students at the great university of Oxford studied Roman law, not common law, and this had irked Blackstone.

In 1760 a peer of the realm was sentenced to death for murder and hanged in public, but so also were two teenage children, sentenced to death for stealing. England's poor lived in conditions not far removed from slavery. Dukes and marquesses could be hauled before a magistrate like commoners for failing to pay their tradesmen's bills, but children under the age of ten worked in the factories and the darkness of coalmines. Crimes against property such as stealing and embezzlement were regarded as offences against the fabric of society and were punished with a severity not found in other European countries: by 1765 a total of 165 offences carried the death penalty. Men, women and children alike suffered hanging for stealing trifling amounts. Others suffered 'Transportation' to the American colonies to toil there as 'indentured servants' (the term convicts was not used). The plight of the poor and the increase in petty crime in the cities would reach bursting point in the 1780s.

Poverty amid riches

'Fabulous riches mingled with dire poverty,' writes J.H. Plumb, 'and the wonders of the age belonged to a few.' England was a paradox. Life for the poor was brutish. No crowd was louder and coarser than the London Mob. Elections and public executions alike were rowdy and festive affairs where bear-bating, among other amusements, competed for the crowd's attention. Henry Fielding, the blind magistrate at Bow Street who wrote the rollicking novel *Tom Jones*, wondered why the practice of 'jesting at misery' was peculiarly English. Soldiers and sailors were seldom executed for minor offences: instead they were flogged until their backbones were bared, a punishment widely deplored on the Continent. 'The violence, the rioting, the gambling and cruelty were all facets of the Englishman's turbulent nature,' writes Plumb.

'This House,' Lord Chatham's precocious son William Pitt the Younger would cry, 'is not representative of the will of the people.' The House of Commons was the catspaw of vested interests: the growing city of Birmingham, soon to be the centre of the industrial Midlands region, had no Member of Parliament, yet the deserted Parish of Old Sarum—a 'rotten borough'—was represented in the Commons.

No representative of the North American colonies sat in the Commons, nor any from Ireland or the West Indies. They had their own legislatures, but these were powerless, mere debating societies. The slave trade continued, but only the Quakers denounced slavery for the crime that it was and their efforts to alleviate its miseries were widely mocked until the 1780s, when the new Prime Minister, William Pitt, introduced legislation to alleviate its horrors.

Englishmen would ascribe their wealth, power and influence to the vigour of their Protestant faith, one that excused commercial enterprise and its sins by insisting that Man could reach the new Jerusalem most surely not by piety but by his endeavours on this earth. In a society so little regulated, so open to new ideas, liberalism would in time evolve and from it would spring reform and acts that redeemed the worst abuses of the past.

For all the iniquities, England's society and its achievement were remarkable. 'As Italy had led the Renaissance, as Germany had guided the reformation, as France had dominated the Age of the Great Renewal, so England kindled the Enlightenment,' wrote an American scholar, and American historian Roy Porter has recently gone further, stating that in the eighteenth century England was evolving into 'the creator of the modern world'.

The voyages of the 1760s

With the end of the Seven Years War (1756–63), England initiated a new series of voyages to the Pacific, the first of note since Anson's in the 1740s. In 1764 Commodore the Hon. John Byron (grandfather of the poet), who had been a midshipman with Lord Anson, left England in command of HMS *Dolphin* on a voyage 'to

ABOVE:
Engraving of Captain Wallis, discoverer of Otaheite (Tahiti), meeting the island's queen.

advance the honour of this nation as a maritime power' and, after surviving near disaster off Chile, sailed across the Pacific, returning after completing a two-year circumnavigation of the world. Within a month of *Dolphin*'s return she sailed again for the Pacific (1766) under a new captain, Samuel Wallis, accompanied by the *Swallow*, commanded by Philip Carteret. Their voyage also added little to knowledge of the Pacific Ocean but Wallis discovered Tahiti—apart from Hawaii the loveliest of Pacific island groups—and his second lieutenant, Tobias Furneaux, raised the Union Jack there, formally annexing it to the Crown. On the voyage home via the Straits of Magellan Carteret, who had become separated from Wallis, in January 1769 hailed a passing ship, which turned out to be a French vessel under the command of the Chevalier de Bougainville, himself returning from a voyage to the Pacific. As both nations were at peace, they proceeded peacefully on their separate ways.

France was once again challenging England at sea. By the 1760s England was showing increased interest in the Bay of Bengal, where India's trade with China (particularly in the importing of Chinese tea, silks and porcelain) was often contested by the French. English ships in the Indian Ocean had long fought under a disadvantage, for they lacked a safe port on the eastern coast apart from Madras and when the monsoonal hurricanes blew from the north-east in October–November, they had to break off action and seek refuge on the west coast at Bombay, reappearing on the east coast no earlier than April. The need for a naval base to defend India's Coromandel Coast and secure control of the Indian Ocean was to prompt the East India Company to look for ports in southern Burma and in Malaya.

1768: Bougainville and the French

Only France matched England in maintaining interest in the Pacific. In 1756 Charles de Brosses's *Histoire des Navigations aux Terres Australes* appeared, a stimulation to navigators and to geographers. In 1767 the Bourbon King of France, Louis XVI, dispatched a remarkable officer, Captain Louis Antoine de Bougainville, to the Pacific with the specific intention of investigating the extent of the Unknown South Land and circumnavigating the world.

Bougainville was a child of the Enlightenment. A prodigy, he had already written a treatise on mathematics and had served in the French embassy in London, where he was elected a Fellow of the Royal Society. He had joined the army and like his great contemporary James Cook served in Canada during the battle for Quebec in 1759. The Marquis de Montcalm's trusted aide-de-camp and second-in-command of troops in the campaign, Bougainville transferred to the French navy in 1763, and

LEFT:
Bougainville being received in state by the people of Tahiti, 1768.

colonised the Falkland Islands (they were later transferred to Spain and later still seized by England) and in 1766 sailed in command of the first French voyage around the world. Steering west from Tahiti in 1768, Bougainville sighted a curious phenomenon: a line of breakers crashing over coral. He had reached the Great Barrier Reef off the Queensland coast.

'The sea broke with great violence on these shoals,' wrote Bougainville, 'and some summits of rocks appeared above the water to it.' All his efforts to navigate a passage through the reef proved fruitless and on the following day he gave up and steered north, making a course for home via the Solomons and the Louisades, little suspecting that an entire Australian continent lay just beyond the reef. The largest of the Solomon islands, Bougainville, bears his name, as does the genus *Bougainvillaea*. The navigator, who returned to France via the East Indies in 1769, supervised the publication of his magnificent work *Voyage Autour du Monde*, fought again in the navy in the wars against England, was honoured by Napoleon and lived until 1811.

A reef of coral lay between Australia and possession by the flag of France. More French voyages followed. They resulted in no important discoveries, nor in fine illustrated volumes describing their adventures, and they are now almost forgotten. In October 1771, only two years after Bougainville's return, two ships left Mauritius, originally bound for Tahiti. They were under the command of Marion du Fresne. Deviating from his original course du Fresne sighted Van Diemen's Land on 3 March 1772, where he skirmished with Aborigines, before setting sail for New Zealand. There he and twenty-six of his men were killed by Maori in the Bay of Islands.

In the year of du Fresne's death another two French ships left Mauritius; one of them discovered Kerguelen Island (which was named after her captain); the other ship, separated by a storm, reached the Western Australian coast at Shark Bay, where her captain, St Allouarn, took possession in the name of the King of France before proceeding to Timor. Would a French settlement have survived seizure by the British in the wars that followed? Probably not. There is an air of inevitability about English colonisation of Australia.

The voyages of James Cook, RN

The full dimensions of the Pacific Ocean and the Unknown South Land could still only be guessed at. The historian of voyages, Alexander Dalrymple, whose volume *Discoveries in the South Pacific* (it summarised voyages prior to 1764) did much to stimulate scholarly interest in further exploration, suggested that

BELOW:
The Queen Anne (Union Jack) Flag flown by Cook. It was changed after Ireland became part of the United Kingdom in 1801.

LEFT:
Captain James Cook, Royal Navy, the foremost
explorer and navigator of his day.

*From the posthumous portrait by Webber
painted in 1782.*

the southern continent matched Europe and Asia in size and stretched from the Pole as far as the coast of Chile.

In 1767 the Royal Society and the Admiralty decided to send a scientific expedition under naval command to Otaheite (Tahiti) in the Pacific Ocean to time the transit of Venus across the face of the sun and thus calculate the distance of the earth from the sun. It was an event that would not be witnessed again for a century, and one that excited scientists in numerous countries. On the return voyage the expedition was authorised to try to establish the dimensions of New Holland.

Dalrymple lobbied for appointment as the expedition's commander, but Admiral Lord Hawke selected instead an experienced seaman, James Cook, who was hastily made a commissioned officer with the rank and single gold epaulette of Lieutenant, and appointed captain of His Majesty's Bark *Endeavour*, a 368-tonne former Whitby collier undergoing conversion to a warship, with ample space for scientists and botanists. It was a rare compliment to a sailor of such low rank, but Cook was no ordinary man.

James Cook's life would encompass the Age of Enlightenment and the Age of Revolution and he looked the part of a hero. More than six feet tall—immensely tall for a man of that time—and quiet of speech, he possessed all the dour nature and commonsense of the Yorkshireman. Born in 1738 and brought up there on the farm of his Scottish-born father, he had left the village school at the age of twelve (his education had been paid for by his father's employer) and worked in a store in the town of Whitby, where he went to sea as an apprentice on the colliers, and gained experience in the rough waters of the North Sea. He studied diligently and became mate on a Whitby bark before resigning in 1755 to enter the Royal Navy, where he thought greater opportunities lay. He joined as a humble Able Seaman,

BELOW:
Construction drawings
of the bark *Endeavour*.
The ship was barely 35
metres long and less than
30 metres in breadth.

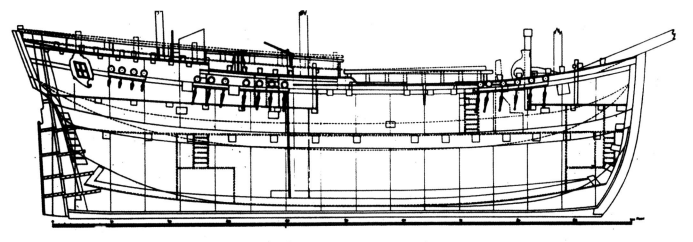

but soon advanced to the post of master of a ship, HMS *Pembroke*, and served in Canada, where his soundings and charts of the St Lawrence River were of assistance to General Wolfe before he captured Quebec in 1759.

Cook married Elizabeth Batts in 1762 and fathered six children, but he was to see little of his family. His meticulous charts of Newfoundland also impressed the Admiralty, as did some observations he wrote on the eclipse of the Sun in 1766. His fellow officers would remember Cook as a tall, taciturn man (he would often dine with them without saying a word), hot-tempered but kind to his crew; he was never heard to swear and was morally righteous. If allied to character and genius, a humble background was no bar to advancement in the Royal Navy of the day.

Among the Royal Society's scientists aboard were Joseph Banks, a well-born and wealthy 25-year-old who had been a passionate collector of plants since his schooldays at Eton, and Daniel Solander, a Scandinavian botanist. Their writings and drawings, and Cook's journals, would record the greatest voyage of discovery in the history of mankind. Oddly, Cook did not carry one of Harrison's new chronometers (designed to calculate exact longitude) on this voyage, which makes his achievement as a navigator all the more remarkable.

1768: Cook's first voyage

Endeavour left Plymouth in August 1768 for Cape Horn and reached Tahiti without mishap in April 1769. Here the friendliness of the natives made the landfall a pleasant one, the observation of their pagan customs fascinating and fruitful. When the astronomers' work was completed, Cook opened the Admiralty's orders that contained the secondary reason for his voyage:

> Whereas the making of discoveries of countries hitherto unknown, and the acquiring of knowledge of distant parts will redound greatly to the Honour of this Nation as a Maritime Power, as well as to the Dignity of the Crown of Great Britain ... and whereas there is reason to imagine that a Continent or Land of Great Extent may be found to the Southward of the Track lately made by Captain Wallis, you are to proceed to the Southward in order to make discovery of the Continent abovementioned ...

After exploring the extent of the continent and preparing charts of its coast, bays and harbours, its land, soil, and vegetation—showing towards its natives 'every kind of civility and regard'—Cook was to take possession of the land 'with the Consent of the Natives'. If failing to locate New Holland, Cook was to sail to New Zealand and explore its coasts, providing that the health of the crew and his provisions was adequate to the task.

1770: Australia's eastern coast sighted

Endeavour sailed from Tahiti on August 1769, having lost none of her crew to scurvy (Cook's crew ate pickled cabbage and drank lime juice to balance their unhealthy diet of salt meat, cereal and rum.) Discovering the Society Islands en route, Cook reached the latitude of 40 degrees south, and having still found no sign of land, with gales mounting, set a course for New Zealand, sighting the North Island in October 1769. Here *Endeavour* spent six months charting the coast and investigating the land and its impressive inhabitants, a Polynesian folk called the Maori, whose ancestors had killed many of Tasman's crew. 'The natives

SUPPLEMENT PRESENTED GRATIS, WITH CHRISTMAS NUMBER OF THE TOWN & COUNTRY JOURNAL, DEC. 21st 1872.

CAPTAIN COOK'S LANDING AT BOTANY, A.D. 1770.

ABOVE:
Captain Cook's landing
at Botany Bay, 1770.

of this country are a strong, raw-boned, well-made native people, rather above than under the common size, especially the men,' Cook wrote. He was fascinated by their clothing, which reminded him of mats and was woven from plants and often decorated with feathers. He noted that they had a reputation for cannibalism.

On 31 March 1770 Endeavour set sail, her captain resolved to discover the eastern-most dimensions of New Holland by heading for Van Diemen's Land and then sailing up its eastern coast; on the morning of 19 April land was sighted. Continuing north Cook saw a headland that he named Point Hicks after his First Lieutenant and late next day saw another point he named Cape Howe. These were the first recorded European sightings of the Australian mainland's eastern coast. On the following day (sailing past the coast south of Wollongong) Cook was able to see figures ashore who seemed very dark in colour. On 28 April Cook tried to land in a small boat and make contact with 'the Indians' but the surf was too heavy.

1770: 'Botany Bay'

Sailing further north, Cook reached, early on 29 April 1770, the entrance of 'a bay which seemed to be well sheltered from all the winds' (Botany Bay) and entered it, anchoring off its southern shore (Kurnell). He saw on land 'a small village consisting of about six or eight houses', two Aborigines in canoes spearing fish and an old woman and half a dozen children gathering wood to make a fire. None of the

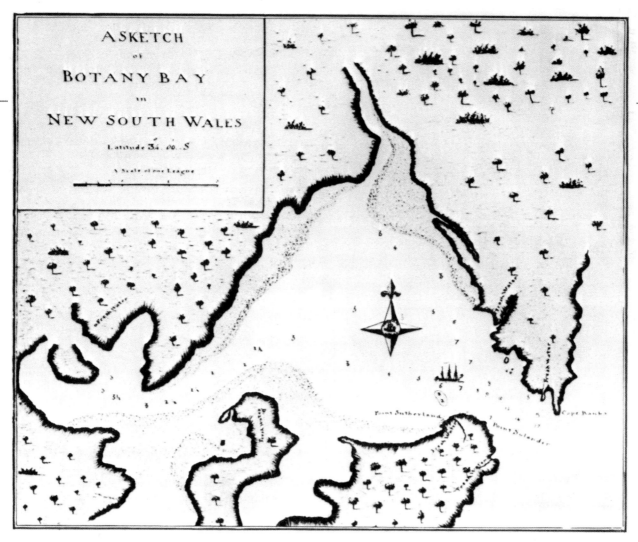

ABOVE:
Cook's precise chart of
Botany Bay, his first landfall on the eastern coast
of Australia, 1770.

Aborigines paid any attention to the ship. When Cook hoisted out a boat to go ashore, two men on the beach brandished spears, apparently, in Cook's words, 'resolved to defend their coast to the uttermost, though they were but two and we were forty'. The warriors were joined by others and shook their spears. Neither Cook nor Tupia, his Tahitian friend, could understand their language, and Cook threw them trinkets. When an Aborigine retaliated by throwing a stone at the boat Cook tried to frighten them off by firing a musket. One of them then threw a spear, and Cook ordered another musket fired, the shot slightly wounding one warrior in the leg.

Landing next day with Banks, Solander and seven others, Cook set out to explore the sandy shores of Botany Bay (so named because of its abundance of plants). The shores have changed little since the first Europeans strolled along them. Cook found open land covered in tufted grasses and the trees were 'tall, straight and without under wood,' standing well apart. 'The whole country, or at least a great part of it, might be cultivated without one's being forced to cut down a single tree,' he wrote, noting also the prevalence of shellfish. The newcomers left trinkets at the numerous native huts, but saw only one 'Indian'. Cook wrote:

> The natives do not appear to be numerous, neither do they seem to live in large bodies, but dispersed in small parties along by the water-side. Those I saw were about as tall as Europeans, of a very dark-brown colour, but not black, nor had they woolly, frizzled hair, but black and lank like ours. No sort of clothing or ornaments were ever seen by any of us upon any one of them, or in or about any of their huts; from which I conclude that they never wear any. Some that we saw had their faces and bodies painted with a sort of white paint or pigment.

ABOVE:
HMS *Endeavour* narrowly
avoided shipwreck on the
Great Barrier Reef off the
Queensland coast.
This drawing by Sydney
Parkinson of *Endeavour*
being careened during
repairs is thought to be
the first European artistic
impression of the Aus-
tralian landscape.

Banks was impressed by the country, which he described as possessing soil rich enough 'to support a very large number' of people. The bird life and the wildflowers—all of them so strange to English eyes—fascinated him, and he collected hundreds of botanical specimens. Oddly, the newcomers saw no kangaroos.

Unable to make any contact with the inhabitants, Cook charted the bay and ordered anchors raised on 6 May 1770, and *Endeavour* sailed north, passing two headlands several miles up the coast that led into a large harbour which Cook neglected to enter but which he named Port Jackson—the site of the future harbour city of Sydney.

The Queensland coast

Progressing north, Cook passed 'a wide, open bay which I called Moreton's Bay' (site of present-day Brisbane) and soon observed palm trees, and on 23 May went ashore, finding deserted native campfires. His men shot a bustard—'the best bird we had eaten since we left England'—and ate abundant fish and oysters. Proceeding up the tranquil waters between the coast and the Great Barrier Reef, which stretches 2000 kilometres along the coast of Queensland, Cook on 4 June sighted 'Whitsunday Passage' and was passing Trinity Bay (sighted on Trinity Sunday) when disaster struck. 'Hitherto we had safely navigated this dangerous coast, where the sea in all parts conceals shoals that suddenly project from the shore, and rocks that rise abruptly like a pyramid from the bottom,' Cook wrote, 'but here we became acquainted with misfortune.' On 11 June, when *Endeavour* had navigated the coast past the present site of Cairns and was off that of Cooktown, the ship suddenly struck coral, and started taking in water. Ordering all hands to the pumps, Cook beached her at the estuary of the Endeavour River, where kangaroos abounded on the fringes of the tropical jungle. There, for seven weeks, Cook's men repaired the ship's hull, astonished by the abundance of food—edible plants, turtles, fish, mussels so large that one made a meal for two men, and kangaroos, which the sailors found good eating. For a month, the 'Indians' kept their distance, though some of them accepted gifts from Cook while refusing an invitation to dine with him. Cook wrote that:

> They were wholly naked, their skins the colour of wood soot. Their hair was black, lank, and cropped short and neither woolly nor frizzled ... Some parts of their bodies had been painted with red, and one of them had his upper lip and breast painted with streaks of white, which he called carbanda. Their features were far from being disagreeable, their voices were soft and tunable, and they could easily repeat any word after us ...

1770: Cook claims 'New South Wales'

After a month, the Aborigines began burning grasses around the camp to drive the newcomers away—'in an instant the whole place was in flames'. Cook, with his customary patience and humanity, tolerated this behaviour for three weeks, before setting sail north again, taking *Endeavour* outside the Barrier Reef to avoid the coral, but on 17 August the Pacific easterly wind struck the ship, pushing it towards the breakers, and only a last-minute shift in wind or current saved the vessel. Finding a break in the reefs, Cook re-entered the channel and, keeping a sharp eye to port for the entrance to Torres Strait, made landfall on an island off the northernmost point of Queensland, Cape York. On 22 August 1770 he raised the Union Jack, taking possession of the entire east coast of New Holland 'from the latitude 38 degrees South, to Possession Island in the north' for the crown of England and naming it (possibly in honour of the young Prince of Wales) 'New South Wales'. Cook then took his ship through Torres Strait, confirming that the strait indeed separated Australia from New Guinea.

BELOW:
The young Joseph Banks shared Cook's rosy view of Australia.

Thanks to Cook's discoveries the extent and dimensions of the entire continent of Australia and New Zealand were now known, but where New Holland (the western part) exactly ended and New South Wales began remained somewhat in doubt—and entire sections of its serrated coastline remained uncharted, a task that was completed by Matthew Flinders and a later generation of Royal Navy captains. The land had been claimed *without* 'the consent of the natives', and England thereafter regarded their new acquisition as *terra nullius*—empty land.

Owing to the diet of vegetables and lime juice consumed with salted meat and imposed on the crew by the captain, not a single man on *Endeavour* had succumbed to scurvy, but on leaving Australia's healthy clime for the 'unwholesome air' of Batavia to refit, thirty men contracted fever and died in just three

AUSTRALIA 90c

NEW HOLLAND · COOK'S VOYAGE

months. Dr Solander and Joseph Banks were also stricken, but survived. *Endeavour* left Batavia on Boxing Day 1770, a passing East Indiaman saluting her with three cheers and a 14-gun salute, and reached England in June 1771, after a voyage of three years. There she was greeted with an acclaim that surprised her captain and ship's company.

In his journal—later edited by other hands into a widely read volume—Cook wrote in glowing terms of Australia's eastern coast: 'The Coast of this Country … abounds with a great number of Fine Bays and Harbours, which are sheltered from all winds.' He informed the Admiralty that the country produced nothing in the way of trade: 'However, this eastern side is not that Barren and Miserable Country that Dampier and others have described the Western Side to be,' he wrote. It was in a 'pure state of Nature' where 'most sorts of grain, fruits, roots etc. of every kind would flourish'.

'From what I have seen of the Natives of New Holland they may appear to some to be the most wretched people upon the earth,' Cook wrote, 'but in reality they are far more happier than we Europeans … They live in a Tranquillity which is not disturbed by the Inequality of Condition; the Earth and Sea of their own accord furnishes them with all the things necessary for life …'

RIGHT:
Sir Joseph Banks (right) in later years, with his colleague Dr Solander and Omai in London.

1772: Cook's second voyage

Cook was given command of a second expedition, 'to complete the discovery of the Southern Hemisphere'. This time the expedition consisted of two warships, HMS *Resolution* and HMS *Adventure*. On this voyage Cook took with him Hadley's chronometer to facilitate calculating longitude.

Leaving Plymouth in July 1772, Cook in *Resolution* sailed by the Cape of Good Hope and then south, crossing the Antarctic Circle in January 1773 and sailing further into the cheerless realm of ice than any men had been before. The two ships passed icebergs that towered above them, while whales played in the seas; the livestock on deck froze to death, and at night the sky was lit with the eerie waving lights of the *aurora australis*. In February Cook lost contact with HMS *Adventure*, whose captain, Tobias Furneaux, took the opportunity to chart the southern and eastern coasts of Van Diemen's Land, before meeting up again with *Resolution* at Queen Charlotte Sound in New Zealand.

Facing contrary winds, Cook had given up his intention to investigate Van Diemen's Land and had set course for New Zealand; when he arrived there he had sailed 11,000 miles (19,000 kilometres) without sighting land. In New Zealand a group of Furneaux's crew came under attack by Maori, who killed ten of them, and *Adventure* soon again lost contact with Cook's ship and returned to Spithead, where she arrived in July 1774.

Cook in the aptly named *Resolution* sailed south once more into the world of icebergs, then on to Easter Island, the Marquesas and to Tahiti. Leaving Matavai bay in Tahiti in May 1774 Cook again set course for the Antarctic, discovering en route the New Hebrides (the Spanish had not investigated the entire sprawling island group) and New Caledonia, where he landed and found fine trees perfect for ships'

BELOW:
Norfolk Island.

masts. A week after raising anchor Cook sighted a small island that he named Norfolk Island, after England's premier Duke. Landing by boat, he found it uninhabited, but possessing fresh water, numerous plants and 'a sort of spruce pine, which grows in abundance'. This remote and forlorn island was to play an important part in Australia's history.

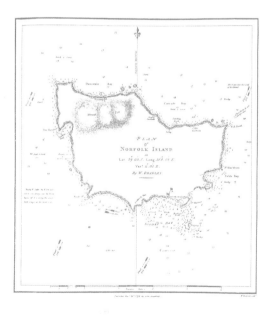

A week later Cook sighted Mount Egmont, which was covered in snow, and spent three weeks in New Zealand waters repairing his sails and reprovisioning before making a course for England via the south Atlantic. Rounding Cape Horn, Cook sighted and named the bleak mountainous island of Georgia (later New Georgia), which he was astonished to see was covered in snow, even though it was summer. HMS *Resolution* anchored at Spithead early in June 1775 and Cook was acclaimed the greatest of navigators, promoted to Captain and appointed a Fellow of the Royal Society.

1776: Cook's third voyage

Only a year later, in July 1776, Cook left on his last voyage of Pacific exploration, commanding the ships *Resolution* and *Discovery*, with orders to seek in the waters of the Arctic Circle 'a northern passage by sea from the Pacific to the Atlantic Ocean'. Sailing by way of the Cape of Good Hope, Cook anchored briefly

ABOVE:
Painting by Clevely of Cook's ships at anchor in the Society Islands during his third—and last—voyage to the Pacific.

at Adventure Bay on the coast of Van Diemen's Land (Tasmania) in January 1777, where a group of Aborigines visited his camp. Cook wrote that:

> They approached us from the woods without betraying any marks of fear, or rather with the greatest confidence imaginable; for none of them had any weapons, except one, who held in his hand a stick almost two feet long, and pointed at one end. They were quite naked, and wore no ornaments. They were of the common stature, but rather slender. Their skin was black, and also their hair, which was as woolly as that of any native of Guinea … their features were far from being disagreeable … Most of them had their hair and beards smeared with a red ointment, and some had their faces also painted …

They rejected Cook's gifts with disdain, but accepted two pigs with glee and grabbed them by the ears. Cook rescued the animals but left them behind when he sailed. He never returned to the Australian mainland, and departed under the impression that Tasmania was the southernmost point of the continent.

Crossing to New Zealand waters, Cook reprovisioned there and then sailed by way of the Friendly Isles to his familiar anchorage, the even friendlier waters of Tahiti. In December 1777 he took his ships north, discovering en route Christmas Island and then the Hawaiian Islands, which he named the Sandwich Islands, before making for the cold waters of Nootka Sound in mid-1778, where ice blocked any attempt to push further through the Behring Strait.

Cook's voyage, rich in discoveries, ended in tragedy. He returned to the Hawaiian Islands in January 1779, and when a cutter was stolen he went ashore to confront the chiefs. Word reached the islanders that an English sailor had fired on a canoe and killed a chieftain. As Cook was returning to his ship, he was felled and killed on the beach by the blows of native knives and clubs, as were four of his marines. 'So fell our great and excellent commander!' an officer wrote.

Cook's two ships returned to England in October 1780. The world heard of his death with grief. No man had added more to humankind's knowledge of the geography of the earth, its oceans and peoples.

Chapter 3
Farewell to Old England Forever

'IT WAS THE BEST OF TIMES, IT WAS THE WORST OF TIMES, it was the age of wisdom, it was the age of foolishness, it was the epoch of belief, it was the epoch of incredulity, it was the season of light, it was the season of darkness, it was the spring of hope, it was the winter of despair …' Charles Dickens' famous description of England in the 'dear old year', 1775, was an eulogy for a age on the edge of revolution. The pride, stability and graceful symmetry of the England of the 1760s was now shaken and darkened by the smoke of revolution, war and social upheaval.

1776: Age of revolution

In July 1776, when Cook left on his last voyage, the rebellious colonists of America declared their independence from the Crown. Seemingly stable Georgian England entered a period of defeat and decline, accompanied by economic and social woes that seemed about to tear the nation's fabric apart. Economically and politically disadvantaged for decades by British policies, the Thirteen Colonies of America were also at risk of defeat until 1778, when France pledged aid to them, gathering European allies on the way. Against the combined fleets of France, Spain and Holland, the Royal Navy lost command of the Atlantic sea lanes, dooming General Cornwallis's army on the peninsula at Yorktown. The policies of King George and his Prime Minister Lord North lay in ruins. At a meeting convened by King George in January 1781, the Earl of Sandwich (an old patron of Cook) stated bluntly that if Russia joined in the war against Britain, 'we shall then, literally speaking, be in actual war with the whole world'. With the surrender of Cornwallis's army at Yorktown in 1781, all knew that the war was lost and England by the coming of peace in 1783 faced not only the humiliating loss of America but internal turmoil.

In the summer of 1780 London was aflame with rumours that Roman Catholicism was returning. To ensure the loyalty of French Canada, Britain had allowed the establishment there of the Catholic Church in 1777, and the London mobs went on a rampage throughout the City and Southwark, burning churches, looting and killing. Order was restored only by troops firing on the crowds—285 people died in the violence. While his ministers panicked, King George remained calm; his monarchy, he knew, was too solidly established to be brought down by a mob.

France's was not, and revolution was to overturn the regime of Louis XVI in 1789. Thomas Jefferson, arriving in Paris in 1785 to take up the post of the United States ambassador to France as successor to Benjamin Franklin, nevertheless described the French people as amiable, polite, hospitable and good, while in a private letter to Abigail Adams (and using some hyperbole to amuse her) he reminded her that the English were 'rich, proud, hectoring, swearing, squibbling carnivorous animals', and that England was their new nation's greatest enemy. But France's

OPPOSITE:
By the 1780s Portsmouth's busy harbour was crowded with prison hulks; from a painting by an unknown artist.

THE LONDON CONVICT MAID.

But sin my youthful heart betrayed,
And now I am a Convict Maid.

To wed my lover I did try,
To take my master's property,
So all my guilt was soon displayed,
And I became a Convict Maid.

Then I was soon to prison sent,
To wait in fear my punishment,
When at the bar I stood dismayed,
Since doomed to be a Convict Maid.

At length the Judge did me address,
Which filled with pain my aching breast
To Botany Bay you will be conveyed,
For seven years a Convict Maid.

For seven years oh, how I sighed,
While my poor mother loudly cried,
My lover wept, and thus he said,
May God be with my Convict Maid.

Charlotte W——, the subject of this narrative, is a native of London, born of honest parents, she was early taught the value and importance of honesty and virtue; but unhapily ere her attaining the age of maturity, her youthful affections were placed on a young Tradesman, and to raise money to marry her lover, she yielded to the temptation to rob her

20 million people lived in poverty so extreme that Jefferson wrote that at least 19 million of them were 'more wretched, more accursed in every circumstance of human existence' than the lowliest American Negro. On visiting England, Jefferson wrote: 'I could write volumes on the improvements which I find made and making here in the arts.' He observed agricultural methods and steam-powered innovations, but was saddened by the conditions of the workers: 'The less dexterous individuals … the class of paupers … furnish materials for armies and navies to defend the domination and vicious happiness of the aristocracy … Such is the happiness of scientific England.'

ABOVE:
Scene in a London prison, late eighteenth century. The figure on the right is thought to be Francis Greenway, later Australia's first notable architect.

Crime and punishment

During the 1780s the gulf between Britain's rich and poor grew steadily wider. The pressure on society increased, for the nation's population of eight million, after centuries of stagnation, was growing 5 per cent annually and poverty and its accompaniment, crime, grew every year more widespread. This was seen most disturbingly in England, home of six million Britons. The Poor Laws of the Elizabethan era, framed to provide work for all and punish vagrancy, had become an instrument of forced labour for the poverty-stricken of all ages, for children as young as five were forced into 'apprenticeships' for a period of seven years, while their parents faced the prospect of ending their lives in the misery of the Poor House. In 1788 an act was passed forbidding children under the age of eight to be employed as chimney sweeps, but it was not enforced, and subsequent bills to relieve the misery of the working class that were passed by the Commons were thrown out by the House of Lords.

Parliament sought to deter crime by making the punishment of criminals ever more horrific. For comparatively minor crimes, from sheep stealing and picking pockets, the convicted faced death by hanging, irrespective of age or sex. The total of 165 crimes punishable by death in the 1760s had, by the 1780s, grown to nearly 200. 'So dreadful a list, instead of diminishing, increases the number of offenders,' wrote the wise jurist, Blackstone. Men were hanged for counterfeiting banknotes, for stealing to feed their starving families, or for poaching rabbit or deer from rural estates; women and children were hanged for stealing food, clothes, silver spoons or silk handkerchiefs—or indeed any property worth more than five shillings.

England, in giving birth to the Industrial Revolution, was now the first country to face the phenomenon of an urban crime wave: it began in 1783 with the end of the war in America and the discharge of thousands of soldiers and sailors into England's overcrowded cities; and it reached a peak in 1786.

By 1785, when no fewer than ninety-five criminals were publicly hanged in London (a dramatic rise from the average of twenty hangings a year), the City's streets were so infested by gangs of thieves that it was no longer safe to walk them at night. King George himself was once relieved of his gold watch in Kensington Palace garden by a footpad who had climbed its walls. When an alderman of the City announced that at least 600 persons in London 'lived by crime alone', the Solicitor-General claimed that the situation was far worse and that 'between two and three thousand lads, from the ages of 10 to 15, were employed in thieving every night of their lives'. (By day these Artful Dodgers slept under bridges, or in alleys and the hollow trees in Hyde Park).

Transporting felons

Even in this heartless age, judges and juries often exercised mercy, condemning the convicted, particularly first offenders, to the lesser punishment of gaol or 'transportation' overseas. Since 1717 'transportation' to America had long been England's remedy for overcrowded gaols. 'All told, between 1717 and 1776, approximately thirty thousand convicts from England and Scotland, and ten thousand from Ireland, were transported to the colonies in America,' the historian Manning Clark relates. But after 1783 the former American colonies, while still accepting black slaves, refused to admit more English felons.

A new Empire rising

But during these grim years when Britain's American colonies had slipped away, the foundations of a new British Empire were already being established in India and the Pacific, and one of its enduring creations would be Australia. In 1785 Warren Hastings, who had been appointed India's first Governor-General in 1772, returned to England to face impeachment before the House of Commons on charges that he had misused his near-absolute power. Yet during his rule modern 'British India' had been created, unchallenged by any foreign power (for French influence in India had been extinguished), and 'ruling through Indian means and Indian law, and doing justice to the tillers of the soil ... He almost alone saved the British Empire and character during the ignominy of Lord North,' wrote the historian Keith Feiling. Hastings would be acquitted of all charges after a trial lasting twelve years, but his impeachment was evidence of another force for change— the growing power of Parliament.

In 1786 the East India Company, now capitalising on the decline of Dutch power in the East Indies and the opportunities afforded by trade with China, established a presence at Penang, an island off the western coast of Malaya. This was the result of the persistence and enterprise of a former naval officer named Francis Light, who gained the concession by promising the Company's military aid to the local sultan in his wars with his rivals. The promise was never fulfilled, but British infiltration of the Malay Archipelago had begun. Light's son by a Malay mother would be Colonel William Light, one of the founders of Adelaide.

ABOVE:
Among the convicts sent to Botany Bay were a number of children.

1779: Banks and Botany Bay

Early in 1784 the House of Commons began to debate the question of where to send transportees, in order to improve the appalling conditions in gaols now filled to bursting with 100,000 prisoners. To relieve congestion the first of some 10,000 prisoners had been transferred in 1776 to old ships—'prison hulks'—moored in the Thames or in harbours, but here death rates from disease were high and conditions a disgrace; their 'tween-decks were cesspools of vice. In 1779 a House of Commons committee exploring the fanciful idea of founding a colony of felons 'in a distant part of the Globe' called Sir Joseph Banks to give his opinion of the scheme. Some had recommended Africa as the ideal site for a settlement but Banks suggested 'Botany Bay'.

Joseph Banks was no longer the slim young companion so affectionately described by Cook in his journals; he was now a portly figure of power and great renown. One year earlier he had been elected President of the Royal Society and he was to hold the post for forty-one years. From his house in Soho Square crammed with books and specimens of insects, plants and minerals, he invited learned men for breakfasts where deep discussion sometimes lasted until lunch. He had become 'the great Panjandrum of British Science'.

Banks told the committee that Botany Bay's climate was moderate, possessed adequate fresh water and that there was nothing to fear from the natives; while the good soil was small in comparison to the barren, he had no doubts that it would support a large number of people and that crops and animals could be raised there—if colonists were given a year's supply of seeds, victuals and adequate tools and implements. (Shortly after the First Fleet reached Australia in 1788 the tireless Banks was plunging into fresh fields for colonisation, founding the African Association, a learned society for the exploration of Africa for the benefit of England. He would dispatch his first explorers to the Dark Continent only five months later.)

In 1784, James Matra, who had also sailed with Cook (and aroused his displeasure), was emboldened to suggest New South Wales as a perfect site for a convict colony and in 1785 Sir George Yonge, an eminent naval officer, also pointed out the benefits of New Holland. When it was announced in Parliament that Gambia, on the coast of Africa, had been chosen for a convict colony, the persuasive Irish orator Edmund Burke demolished the plan, describing the place, quite correctly, as a graveyard for Europeans.

In March 1786 convicts mutinied on board a prison hulk in Plymouth. The revolt was crushed for the cost of nearly fifty killed and wounded, and William Pitt, the 27-year-old Prime Minister, had to calm a noisy House of Commons with assurances that the problem of penal overcrowding was being closely considered. Action came in April 1786, when Lord Sydney, the Secretary of State for War and the Colonies (England's government considered the two as indivisible) wrote to the Lords of the Treasury:

The several gaols and places of confinement of felons in this Kingdom being in so crowded a state that the greatest danger is to be apprehended ... His Majesty has thought it advisable to fix upon Botany Bay, situated on the coast of New South Wales, which, according to accounts given by the late Captain Cook, is looked upon as a place likely (to support a settlement).

I am therefore commanded to signify to your Lordships His Majesty's pleasure that you do forthwith take such measures ... for providing a proper number of vessels for the conveyance of 750 convicts to Botany Bay, together with such provisions, necessaries, and implements for agriculture as may be necessary for their use after arrival.

Three companies of His Majesty's Corps of Marines would accompany the convicts; enough provisions to last two years would also be provided. The command of the settlement would be entrusted to the care of a 'discreet naval officer'.

1786:
Captain Arthur Phillip, RN

Chosen as Captain-General and Governor-in-Chief of the new settlement of New South Wales was an obscure naval officer, Captain Arthur Phillip. The son of a German father with Jewish blood and an English mother, he was on half-pay, farming in Kent after service in the Royal Navy and in Portugal's navy. He was living alone—his marriage had broken up after only three years—when news of his commission reached him. Admiral Lord Hawke, the fiery Cornishman then serving as First Sea Lord, had recommended Captain John Hunter, a Scot, as Governor-designate, and Phillip possibly owed his appointment to his mother's connections with people of influence. Either man would have been a fine selection—but Phillip proved to be outstanding.

The notion of founding a colony of convicts appealed to the English sense of humour, and still does. Street ballads and broadsides greeted the idea with mockery or delight—even a comic opera *Botany Bay* was staged in London in 1787. But the dour Scottish navigator and publicist, Dalrymple, regarded 'this Mad Scheme' as absurd and one hardly calculated to discourage crime. He wrote:

> The plan the ministry proposes must be considered as encouraging rather than deterring felons, for what is the punishment intended to be inflicted? Not to make the felons undergo servitude for the benefit of others, as was the case in America, but to place them, as their owner masters, in a temperate climate, where they will have every object of comfort and ambition before them ...

Those convicts sentenced to fourteen years' transportation would view Botany Bay as a death sentence; in later decades when punishments increased and men were sentenced to chain gangs, their life was one long hell. As Robert Hughes has written in *The Fatal Shore*, the colony was intended to form a giant prison to which social outcasts would be consigned and then be duly forgotten.

There was a certain strategic value in having a Pacific Ocean settlement—the Spanish suspected this to be England's prime reason for founding the colony—and

Cook's reports of the fine quality of Norfolk Island timber and New Zealand flax (ideal for the masts and sail cloth needed by the Royal Navy) were inducements to colonise Botany Bay, but they were minor in importance.

Because of the small number of female convicts being transported, Lord Sydney hoped that the prisoners would intermarry and interbreed with native women, 'as without a sufficient proportion of that sex it is well known that it would be impossible to preserve the settlement from gross irregularities and disorders'. Phillip had his own simple remedy for homosexuality among the felons: he would maroon its practitioners along with murderers on the New Zealand islands and let the cannibals eat them.

Arthur Phillip, the Governor-designate, was no ordinary naval officer. Elevation from obscurity to a governorship and the challenge of creating a colony was both a compliment to him and a challenge. In his meticulous letters to Lord Sydney's patient Under Secretary, Evan Nepean, the Governor-designate respectfully submitted that the government's allowances were insufficient: he would need twenty scythes, not the six provided; he required two saddles, for he intended to explore the new land on horseback; one of the vessels should serve as a hospital ship; the bread allowance for the convicts must be increased. 'The women in general,' Phillip wrote in words typical of the age, 'I suppose possess neither virtue nor honesty,' but he proposed that the petty thieves among the female convicts might still possess 'some degree of virtue' and these would be segregated from the worst so that they be 'not abused or insulted by the ships' company.' And he was determined to introduce English laws into the colony, writing boldly and firmly: 'There can be no slavery in a free land and consequently no slaves.'

The convicts

The 741 convicts—565 men, 165 women, six boys and five girls—had by early 1787 been transferred to Portsmouth, where at anchor lay the transports *Alexander*, *Charlotte*, *Scarborough*, *Friendship*, *Prince of Wales*, *Lady Penrhyn*, three store ships and the warships HMS *Sirius* (540 tonnes) and HMS *Supply*. The sailors, a handful of officials and the force of 206 Marines, who were accompanied by 27 of their wives and 19 of their children, brought Phillip's charges to a total of 1400 souls.

Before transportation ceased in 1868 nearly 162,000 convicts would be sent to Australia. They would even be romanticised by some writers as victims of society, martyrs to a cruel system and basically law-abiding, but records show that only 3600 of them were political prisoners (and of this number 2500 were Irish rebels). The majority of them were indeed petty criminals and they were to commit an average of six further offences after their arrival in Australia—minor and trivial crimes in modern-day terms, but crimes nonetheless. They were the unlikely pioneers of a new nation.

On Sunday 13 May 1787 the eleven ships raised anchor in Portsmouth and sailed into the Channel for the voyage to Botany Bay. They were embarking on the longest voyage of colonists ever undertaken both in terms of distance—14,000 miles or nearly 19,000 kilometres—and in time, for it would take more than seven long months.

Those among them who returned to England would find themselves in a world hardly recognizable from the one they had left. In July 1789 the Paris mob tore down the Bastille. Within three weeks France's feudal system would be swept away in one day and her king would be a prisoner of his people. France would be wracked by revolution and by 1793 be at war with England, a conflict that would last, except for two brief periods, until the final fall of Napoleon in 1815. In 1797 England's fleets at the Nore and Spithead would hoist the red flag of mutiny and in 1798 the Irish—Protestant and Catholic alike—would rise up in bloody rebellion. The Age of Revolution had arrived.

The voyage of the First Fleet

At landfall in Tenerife, the Reverend Richard Johnson, the Chaplain-designate, witnessed a Catholic procession carrying the image of the Virgin Mary and wrote, as a good Anglican: 'Alas, alas, what superstition and idolatry is all this—God make us thankful.' The 'First Fleet' reached Rio de Janeiro in August and Cape Town in October, where two of Phillip's officers witnessed a native being broken on the wheel before execution by the Dutch and thanked God that English justice had outlawed these horrors. Deciding to sail ahead of his slow ships and reconnoitre the landfall, Phillip transferred from *Sirius* to *Supply*, handing over command of the convoy to John Hunter, captain of *Sirius*.

Bligh and La Pérouse

While Phillip's fleet was making its leisurely progress to Australia, three other vessels were beating their way to the South Pacific and by an extraordinary coincidence they too would anchor in Australian waters in 1788. Commanding HM brig *Bounty*, a small ship of 215 tonnes, was Lieutenant William Bligh, who had sailed under Cook. *Bounty* was making course for Tahiti to collect seedlings of the breadfruit plants, described by Cook, that the authorities decided would be suitable food for England's slaves in the West Indies. Her commander had been chosen on the personal recommendation of Sir Joseph Banks.

William Bligh's voyage and life would be stormy, dramatic and contradictory. After anchoring in Van Diemen's Land in August 1788, he sailed direct for Tahiti and there abused his officers and men so cruelly that on the return voyage they mutinied, casting him adrift in a ship's boat with a handful of loyal crew members, and tossing overboard the hundred breadfruit plants as they sailed away. Bligh would steer this tiny craft in an epic of navigation more than 3600 miles (6000 km) to Timor, survive the humiliation of court martial in England and sail again for Tahiti to pick up breadfruit as captain of HMS *Providence* (1791-93), charting the coast of south-east Tasmania on the way. He would reappear in Australian history again as Governor of New South Wales in 1806, where he would again be the cause—and victim—of mutiny.

ABOVE:
Evidence of France's reviving interest in the Pacific Ocean: the Comte de la Pérouse receiving his last instructions from King Louis XVI before sailing in 1785.

The Comte de la Pérouse, commanding two vessels, had been sent by King Louis XVI of France in 1785 on a long voyage of discovery in the Pacific. After exploring the coasts of north-west America and north-east Asia, he was to land at Botany Bay only a week after Phillip's arrival there, take on fresh water and then disappear into the expanse of the Pacific, his fate a mystery for decades.

1788: The colony is founded

On 18 January 1788, HMS *Supply* entered Botany Bay and three days later the entire fleet lay at anchor there, after a voyage that ranks as testimony to the skills of command and seamanship of Phillip and his captains. 'I cannot say, from the appearance of the shore, that I will like it,' wrote Ralph Clark, a Lieutenant of Marines. 'Upon first sight, one would be induced to think this a most fertile spot,' wrote Captain John Hunter, but on going ashore he found the grass dry and coarse, the timber unsuitable for building and the soil 'nothing but black sand'. They had arrived in the middle of the Australian summer, when all is parched. Phillip, exploring the sandy shore of the huge, open bay in search of fresh water, was puzzled by the aridity of the place. Cook had seen the ground in April, when the autumn brings with it rain and the vegetation is thick. The few Aborigines they met displayed no fear of the Europeans. Phillip attempted to give trinkets to one of the men, who seemed astonished by the newcomers. 'I think it is very easy to conceive the ridiculous figure we must appear to these poor creatures, who were perfectly naked,' wrote Lieutenant Philip Gidley King, one of Phillip's closest friends and a man of some humour. Both Hunter and King were later to serve as governors of the colony.

On 21 January, Phillip and Hunter took several of the longboats manned by seamen and marines and rowed up the coast nine miles to investigate the harbour that Cook had called 'Port Jackson'. The tiny boats passed between the two giant sandstone headlands to enter a harbour whose size and myriad coves and reaches delighted Phillip. Fortune had smiled. Phillip clambered from his boat onto a beach, just inside North Head, where a group of natives brandished spears, appearing quite unintimidated by the whites. 'Their confidence and manly behaviour made me give the name Manly Cove to the place,' he recorded. Further up the harbour, Phillip found a wooded cove with a stream of fresh water; this, he decided, would be the perfect site for the settlement. He named it 'Sydney Cove'.

'The party returned this evening', wrote Surgeon White on 23 January, 'full of praise for the extent and excellence of the harbour, as well as the superiority of the ground, water and situation, to that of Botany Bay.' On the morning of 26 January Captain Hunter was astonished to see two strange ships enter Botany Bay and drop anchor. They were the Comte de la Pérouse's vessels. The English and French officers exchanged pleasantries in a state of mutual puzzlement and suspicion that existed until the two French ships sailed on 10 March.

BELOW:
First contact: Europeans landing on the shores of Sydney Cove, Port Jackson (Sydney Harbour).

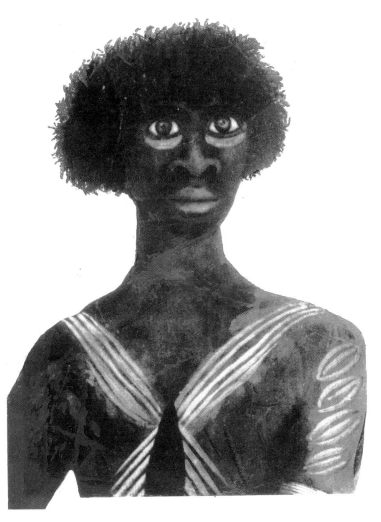

ABOVE:
A warrior of the Sydney region, painted in 1790.

1788: Sydney founded

On 26 January, when the Fleet was at anchor in Sydney Harbour, Surgeon White wrote: 'Port Jackson, I believe to be, without exception, the finest and most extensive harbour in the universe, and at the same time, the most secure.' At dusk the Governor and his officers assembled around a crude flagstaff on the shore, and while the Marine detachment fired volleys from their muskets, Phillip formally took possession of the country and toasted 'His Majesty and the Royal Family and success to the new Colony'. Thus was Australia founded.

'I am much charmed with the place,' Lieutenant Clark wrote. 'The tents look pretty among the trees; I hope to be on shore tomorrow.' Over the next few days the cove echoed to the smack of axes as a hundred convicts from the *Scarborough* cleared timber on the shores of the cove and its two headlands. The days were hot, the air humid, the work delayed by Sydney's midsummer rainstorms. 'Remarkably hot,' Clark to his beloved wife on 31 January, after sleeping the night under canvas: 'In all the course of my life I never slept worse, my dear wife, than I did last night. What with the hard ground, spiders, ants and every vermin you could think of was crawling over me. I was glad when the morning came …'

We know nothing of what the convicts thought of their new home (all of the males were landed amid great uproar in the first week), or of what the other mute players in the drama, the Aborigines, thought of this intrusion by white men. But some of Phillip's officers kept journals and diaries. 'The Governor gave strict orders that the natives should not be offended, or molested on any account,' wrote Surgeon Wogan, 'and advised that, whenever they are met with, they were to be treated with every mark of friendship.'

The women were landed on 6 February, drenched to the skin by a thunderstorm; predictably, the night was one of nakedness and debauchery, for not even the marine sentries could prevent the men from sneaking through the bush into the female tents. None was shot, though many were bleary from drinking when the Governor lectured them next day on the follies of their conduct.

'One of the sailors was caught in the women's tents and drummed out of the camp with his hands fastened behind him, and the Fife and Drums marching before him playing "The Rogues' March"' wrote Surgeon Wogan two days later. On the same day, 9 February, a Marine was sentenced to 200 lashes for striking a woman, Elizabeth Needham, 'a most infamous hussy' when she refused to go into the woods with him.

'The anarchy and confusion which prevail throughout the camps and the audacity of the Convicts, both men and women, is not to be equalled by any set of villains upon the Globe,' Clark opined. 'The men seize upon any sailors on shore who are walking near the women's camp (and) beat them unmercifully …' The convicts pilfered ill-guarded stores with ease and traded food and rum for favours. In February, a court martial sentenced a seaman to 100 lashes for trying to trade a possum for a gallon of stolen rum; Phillip reduced the punishment to fifty lashes of the cat-o-nine tails. To augment their daily ration of a pound (approx. half a kilo) of salted meat and a pound of bread or flour, three convicts stole a quantity of 'butter, pease and pork'. All were sentenced to death and marched 'to the place of execution', a tree midway between the male and female camps. Here, two were reprieved and the third was hanged before the assembled convicts and Marines. He was just seventeen years old. Executions were to increase as the plight of the colony worsened.

Winter came in June. In Australia all realities were reversed. 'The climate is fine and temperate,' a Marine officer later wrote to Sir Joseph Banks. 'We have had a great deal of rain in the months of June, July and August, which seems to constitute the rainy season here.' It was winter but the skies remained clear and blue between storms. There had been an earthquake in July; it lasted only three seconds but it sounded like the ships' cannon were firing. The new moon, the officer added, always coincided with thunder, and lightning had killed many of the sheep they had landed. It was a strange new land indeed. 'The birds are not so numerous as you would expect in a wild country, but are very beautiful, especially those of the parrot kind,' he wrote. Kangaroos abounded, and their 'flesh is not bad eating, something like coarse mutton'.

ABOVE:
A newcomer: Watkin Tench, Captain of Marines, and author of a valuable and entertaining account of the early years of settlement at Sydney Cove.

'The climate is certainly a very fine one, but the nights are very cold,' Major Ross wrote to Under-Secretary Evan Nepean on 10 July 1788. 'This country will never answer to settle in …' Corn might grow, Ross opined, but nothing else. 'It would be cheaper,' he wrote, 'to feed the convicts on turtle and venison at the London Tavern than send them here.' This cheerless Scot refused to permit his officers to sit on tribunals to show his contempt for the convicts and for the Governor.

Governor Phillip's belief in the success of the colony never wavered. 'The sending out of settlers', he wrote to Lord Sydney in July, 'appears to be absolutely essential' and confirmed that his Lordship's instructions to treat the natives with civility had been followed: 'The natives have been treated with the greatest humanity and attention.' The inhabitants, who were of the Eora people, showed little interest in the Europeans and within months many of the Aborigines began to sicken, manifesting signs of smallpox. Even the briefest contact with European maladies was sufficient to kill off half the Aborigines on the harbour's shores in the first year of settlement.

1788: Norfolk Island settled

On 15 February Phillip had despatched HMS *Supply* under Lieutenant King's command to found a settlement with twenty-three people (half of them convicts) on
Norfolk Island, the lonely Pacific island nearly 800 miles (1400 km) east of the Australian mainland and lying midway between New Caledonia and New Zealand. It
possessed the splendid pine trees that had caught Cook's eye (and which were
later used to build Matthew Flinders' ship *Norfolk*), and quantities of flax. Unfortunately the island possessed no harbour; everything reaching and leaving it had
to be transhipped in small boats across a treacherous sand bar. Both the timber and
the flax had intrigued the Admiralty, for during the war with America, the Royal
Navy's Baltic source of flax and timbers had been closed to British shipping. Thus
the Colonial Office selected the tiny island as Australia's second European settlement, but its only real use, a generation later, would be as a prison, one of the cru-
ellest in our history.

Early difficulties

By September 1788, when the first crops failed, stealing was still prevalent, the
convicts morose, the Marines mutinous. Major Robert Ross, Phillip's difficult Scottish second-in-command, wrote to Nepean: 'I do not scruple to pronounce that in
the whole world there is not a worse country than this. All is so very barren and
forbidding that it may in truth be said that nature is reversed; if not so, she is nearly worn out, for nearly all the seed we have put into the ground has rotted …' His
missive was one of the last letters to leave the colony for nearly two years, as in
October 1788 the remaining transport ship left Sydney Cove—'this vile country'
as one of the merchant captains described it—for India and the return voyage to
England. A terrible sense of loneliness settled over the colony.

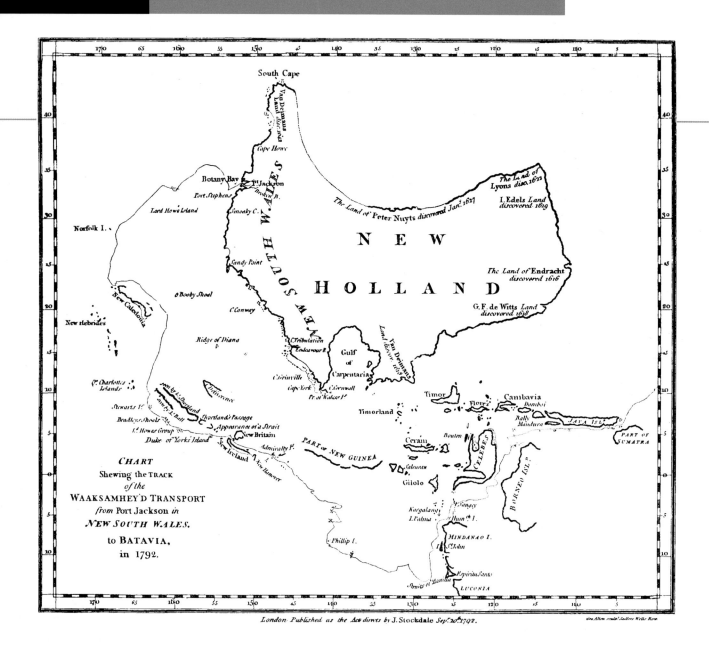

London Published as the Act directs by J. Stockdale Sep.r 20.t 1792.

ABOVE:

Upside-down, down-under: an odd view of the course taken by a Dutch transport sailing from 'Botany bay' to Batavia in the Dutch East Indies during Hunter's governorship.

So ended 1788. In November King George had gone mad and was not restored to sanity for four months; his bouts of insanity were to persist for the rest of his long life.

In March 1789 some of the Marines were caught stealing food from government stores. All six, 'the flower of our Batallion [sic]' as Captain Watkin Tench recorded sadly, 'were hanged in public in this awful and terrible example of justice'.

In his explorations by small boat and on foot, Phillip had discovered fine farmland. A major western reach of the harbour was in effect the estuary of a broad river, and by following its course he found, twelve miles upstream, perfect pasture with good soil. Here at Parramatta, early in 1790 he granted the convict James Ruse an acre of land (0.4 hectares) to till. North of Sydney, another broad river flowed into Broken Bay: the Hawkesbury. Its river flats—often subjected to flooding—proved the richest of all. The crops and animals farmed in these two areas would, in time, support the colony.

In November 1789 Governor Phillip kidnapped two male Aborigines, Bennelong and Colebee, in an attempt to learn their ways. Although he treated them with kindness, both later escaped. But when Phillip was speared by Aborigines while exploring Manly Cove near the entrance of the harbour, Bennelong returned to Sydney Cove, apparently concerned about the Governor's wounding. An unusual

ABOVE:
His Britannic Majesty
George the Third, By the
Grace of God, King of
Great Britain and Ireland.

*From the portrait by Sir
William Beechey, 1800.*

friendship between the two men began, and Bennelong moved into a house constructed for him on the point later named in his honour. Today Bennelong Point is the site of the Sydney Opera House.

In March 1790 food supplies were dwindling so rapidly that Phillip sent half the marines and convicts to Norfolk Island in order to conserve rations at Sydney Cove and ordered HMS *Sirius* to then sail on to China to purchase provisions. Her wreck on the bar at Norfolk Island plunged the Governor into deep gloom. Rations were reduced by half and HMS *Supply*, now the only vessel remaining at Sydney Cove, was ordered to sail to Batavia to seek help from the Dutch. 'In the name of heaven, what has the Ministry been about,' wrote Surgeon White. 'Surely they have quite forgotten us ...'

A Second Fleet had in fact left England in July 1789, but its voyage proved to be one of the longest and most disastrous in our history. The *Guardian* was sunk just out of Cape Town and the eleven-month voyage of the remaining transports, all of them crammed with convicts subjected to intolerable suffering, saw the prisoners die in their hundreds. Their bodies were thrown overboard.

In the early evening of 3 June 1790, the eve of the King's birthday that few felt in a mood to celebrate, a flag was seen hoisted on South Head—signal of an incoming ship. Beating up harbour was a vessel 'with English colours flying'. Rowing out to greet her with shouts of 'Pull away, my lads!' and cries of 'She's from old England!' Phillip's officers clambered aboard, beseeching the masters and crew for news from home. She was the *Lady Juliana*, a transport laden with provisions. The colony would survive.

1790: The New South Wales Corps

On 26 June the *Scarborough* entered harbour, followed two days later by the *Surprize* and the *Neptune*. All were carrying convicts and detachments of a regiment raised to replace the unruly Marines—the New South Wales Corps. Of the 1026 male and female convicts who had left England, 267 had died on the voyage and most of the survivors were so ill and half-starved that scores more died soon after they were carried ashore.

One officer of the Corps, Captain Hill, was sufficiently enraged by the dreadful sufferings of the convicts to write a letter that in time reached both William Wilberforce, the Christian reformer, and the Admiralty:

> Humanity shudders to think that of 900 male convicts in this fleet, 370 are already dead, and 450 are landed sick and so emaciated and helpless that very few, if any of them, can be saved by care or medicine ... The irons used on these poor wretches were barbarous. The contractors had been in the Guinea trade ... The slave trade is merciful compared to what I have seen in this fleet.

He begged his recipient to urge the appointment of naval officers to exercise control over 'these low-lifed, barbarous' civilian ships' masters.

He noted brightly: 'It would be impossible for me to convey to your mind a just idea of this beautiful heavenly clime,' but he added that everything except the climate seemed unpromising. He was critical of Phillip's failure to explore the hinterland; the soil was poor and attempts to farm it pathetic. 'All here, the officer, soldier, sailor and convict have the same ration allowed by the Governor … Here I am, living in a miserable thatched hut, after six months at sea, obliged to live on a scanty pittance of salt provision, without a vegetable …'

John Macarthur

Among the newly arrived officials was an Irish surgeon, D'Arcy Wentworth, a well-connected man who for some reason (there were rumours of charges of highway robbery) had chosen self-exile in New South Wales. Posted to Norfolk Island, he fathered numerous children by a convict lass, Catherine Crowley: his eldest son would be the stormy petrel of the early colony, William Charles Wentworth, 'Australia's greatest son'.

BELOW:
In 1793 a Spanish expedition under Malaspina put in at Sydney Cove. One of the Spanish artists drew an officer of the New South Wales Corps and his wife—the couple are believed by many to be Captain John Macarthur and his wife Elizabeth.

The officers of the New South Wales Corps included one in particular who stood out from his fellows. Lieutenant John Macarthur, English-born but the son of a Scottish Highlander, was a handsome, headstrong 22-year-old of violent temper, who was accompanied by his wife, Elizabeth, of sweeter nature but with a character to match his own. Their lives would encompass the dramas of Australia's first thirty years.

The character and composition of His Majesty's New South Wales Corps were little different from any other regiment in the army. Its officers were men of some means, for even the purchase of a lieutenant's commission required considerable outlay (though it was also an investment, for it could be sold to a younger officer if needs arose). The rank and file, recruited by beat of drum and promise of enlistment bounty among the poor of England's cities, had signed up for seven years' service in the colony (enlistment in the army was normally for life). It was hoped that all would remain in the colony as settlers.

In July 1790 Lord Grenville, Sydney's successor as Secretary of State, authorised Phillip to give conditional pardons to those convicts whose conduct made them worthy of it, and as an enticement to them to remain there as settlers. Few took up the offer. In 1791 the Third Fleet arrived—a total of ten transports, which had left England with 1800 convicts, 200 of whom had died on the voyage.

By 1792 Phillip was disillusioned by the convicts' surly attitude and was also tired and broken in health. He left the colony in December 1792, handing over power to his Lieutenant-Governor, Lt-Colonel Grose of the New South Wales Corps, taking with him his black friends Bennelong and Yemmerrawannie, who became objects of fascination

to London society. (Only Bennelong survived the trauma to return to his tribe and die in 1813 in a tribal fight, sodden by drink.)

Phillip's achievement had been great. In his five years of rule the colony had not only survived but had reached self-sufficiency. The farms at Parramatta and the Hawkesbury were flourishing. In 1792 the first ships of the East India Company began putting in to Sydney Town, followed by the American trader *Philadelphia*. Soon the waters of the southern coast of New South Wales would be thick with sealers and whaling ships.

1792: Rule by the Rum Corps

From the departure of Phillip in 1792 until the arrival of a new Governor, John Hunter, in 1795, the colony was ruled by the officers of the New South Wales Corps. Their commanding officer, Grose, was a far from commanding figure. Ailing, paunchy, trusting and easy-going he was soon reporting to London: 'I have alotted such officers as have asked, one hundred acres which with great spirit they, at their own expense are clearing.' Given free convict labour, the task of clearing the land was not an arduous one for the new landowners, whose military duties were few.

ABOVE, TOP:
Gouache drawing of an Aborigine of 1790, by the 'Port Jackson Painter'.

ABOVE:
A fish, from *The Zoology of New Holland* by George Shaw, London, 1794.

One of the major beneficiaries of Grose's largesse was Captain Macarthur, Paymaster of the Corps, who was appointed Superintendent of Public Works and granted 250 acres at Parramatta, a land holding he named Elizabeth Farm in honour of his wife. Here the Macarthurs began experiments in sheep breeding by importing four merino ewes and two rams from the Cape of Good Hope in 1796. The merino, originally a Spanish breed and one inured to extremes of heat and cold, had thrived at the Cape, where the climate and grasslands resembled Australia's.

'I find that the late Lieutenant-Governor made it a rule to grant every private soldier under his command 25 acres of land where ever he chose to have it', Governor John Hunter would write with concern after his arrival in September 1795. Untrained in farming, the men had invariably sold the land to officers. Officers of the Corps soon progressed to trading in all commodities. There was no currency, so rum was freely used for barter or payment for services and rum shipments were purchased by the Corps' officers and resold at vast profit. The first free settlers arriving in 1793 found a military oligarchy established, one that was to dominate the colony for the next seventeen years.

From 1793 on, England's links with the colony would be tenuous ones. The demands of a new war, barely ten years after the American rebellion had ended, relegated the far-distant penal colony to the lowest of imperial priorities. Grose

From a Sketch by Governor King   *Blake Sculpt.*

sailed for home in December 1794, handing over control to Major William Paterson, a Scottish officer who was happiest sharing a bottle with his officers or out on exploring expeditions. Paterson was one of the first Europeans to attempt to find a way across the Blue Mountains, the blue smudge on the western horizon that formed an impenetrable barrier to the inland, but he kept entering valleys that ended in walls of cliff. (In 1793 another Scot, Alexander Mackenzie, tracked the river that bears his name to Canada's Arctic Circle and then crossed the Rockies; the colony of New South Wales lacked, it seemed, enterprising men.)

The Reverend Samuel Marsden, who arrived in 1794, was to provide the colony with faith, fire, enterprise and energy. Obsessive, pugnacious, a Protestant zealot, Marsden was soon appointed to the magistrate's bench and granted nearly 2000 acres for farming. His hatred of the Irish was pathological. History would remember him both as a sadist—the 'Flogging Parson'—and as a missionary and visionary who later took the gospel to the Maori and merino wool to England.

The first shipload of Irish convicts had embarked for New South Wales in 1791 and they introduced a new fractious element into the colony's society. Two years later the four 'Scottish martyrs' were sentenced in Edinburgh to transportation for daring to preach dangerous Jacobin notions of the brotherhood of man. Unlike the Irish prisoners, criminal and political, the Scots, men of education, would be treat-

ABOVE:
'A family of New South Wales'; engraving after a drawing by Governor King who was, like his predecessor, Governor Hunter, a talented artist.

LEFT:
Lieutenant Philip Gidley King, who succeeded John Hunter as Governor. King was the first of the Governors to leave progeny in the colony and his descendants are many.

LEFT:
Lieutenant Philip Gidley King, who succeeded John Hunter as Governor. King was the first of the Governors to leave progeny in the colony and his descendants are many.

ed with leniency and allowed almost full liberty in the colony. One of them, Thomas Muir, considered this a mockery of freedom and in 1796 stole aboard an American vessel and escaped, to end his days in Paris a hero of the French.

There was little growth during Hunter's rule, but considerable exploration. One hundred miles north of Sydney, at the mouth of the Hunter River, coal deposits were found in 1797. Worked by convicts, the penal settlement there would become the town (and future great city and port) of Newcastle. In 1795 Surgeon Bass and Lieutenant Matthew Flinders began to explore the coast south of Sydney and in 1798, with Hunter's blessing, ventured to Van Diemen's Land in the cutter *Norfolk,* returning with the astounding news that a great strait separated the island from the mainland.

1800: Governor King

The 1798 rebellion in Ireland broke out, resulting in what all colonists dreaded: an influx of Irish rebel prisoners, the 'croppies'. They were Catholic and thus in Protestant eyes belonged to a religion tinged with superstition and hypocrisy; they also spoke in Gaelic, a language none but the Highland Scots could understand. Hunter, normally a warm and humane man, regarded them as 'diabolical' and 'turbulent'. His successor, Governor King, who assumed rule when the first shiploads of rebels reached Sydney Town in 1800, viewed them as a danger in a settlement that numbered barely 5000 Protestant souls. 'They are extremely superstitious, artful and treacherous,' their tormentor, the Reverend Marsden, wrote. 'They have no concern whatever for any religion nor fear of the Supreme Being, but are fond of riot, drunkeness [sic] and cabal ...'

In 1798 Robert Campbell, a Calcutta merchant, arrived in Sydney Town to seek permission to open trade between the two centres; his fellow Scot, Hunter, refused his request but King soon obliged him. Campbell remained in Sydney to become one of the colony's most respected merchants, a pillar of integrity, and to build in

ABOVE:
Captain John Hunter, RN, who succeeded Phillip as Governor in 1792. A Scot, Hunter was a talented artist.

From a portrait by an unknown artist.

1804 the colony's first sailing vessel.

Few could recognise the bright and engaging young First Fleet officer of 1788 in the corpulent and choleric naval captain who now sat in Government House, but Philip Gidley King was energetic and unintimidated by the power of the Corps. He attempted to regularise the trade in rum and when Macarthur wounded his commanding officer, Paterson, in a duel in September 1801, King ordered MacArthur from the colony, sending him to London to face a court martial. Realising that he

had probably over-reached himself, Macarthur was to resign his commission on arriving in London and devote himself to lobbying for favours—Sir Joseph Banks treated him with cold disdain—in an attempt to create a fortune for himself by raising sheep to provide wool for England's mills.

1802: Matthew Flinders, explorer

The immense extent of New Holland and New South Wales and the fact that its coasts remained largely uncharted, obsessed Matthew Flinders after his return to England from the colony. References to his work as a navigator were glowing (he had sailed with Bligh on the captain's second breadfruit voyage), his energy apparent. In July 1801 HMS *Investigator* left Spithead under Flinders' command, charged by the Admiralty with charting the entire coastline of the continent of New Holland. Reaching the continent's south-western tip near King George Sound, which Captain Vancouver had found and named in 1771, Flinders sailed east along the Great Australian Bight to be the first European to explore Flinders Gulf and Spencer Gulf, encountering there, to his astonishment, two French vessels. Their commander, Nicolas Baudin, had been dispatched by the First Consul of France, Napoleon Bonaparte, to combine scientific exploration of Australia with a little spying.

Sailing further east Flinders entered and charted Port Phillip Bay and rounded Wilson's Promontory to reach Sydney early in May 1802, having filled in all the gaps on the southern outline of Australian maps. His voyage was also a tribute to the pre-eminence the Royal Navy had achieved in the care of seamen's health and well-being: he had lost not a single man to scurvy while in Baudin's vessels, which

Australia's exotic flora and fauna fascinated naturalists and provided subjects for talented artists in the 1790s.

ABOVE LEFT:
A banksia depicted in an engraving commissioned by Sir Joseph Banks.

ABOVE RIGHT:
A rosella painted by the anonymous 'Port Jackson Painter'.

BELOW:
Matthew Flinders, from a miniature.

BELOW:
Title page of Flinders' celebrated
account of his voyages of
1801–03, and the title of his chart
of 'Terra Australis', the land he
suggested be called 'Australia'

A

VOYAGE

TO

TERRA AUSTRALIS;

UNDERTAKEN FOR THE PURPOSE OF COMPLETING THE DISCOVERY OF THAT
VAST COUNTRY,

AND PROSECUTED IN THE YEARS

1801, 1802, AND 1803,

IN

HIS MAJESTY'S SHIP THE INVESTIGATOR,

AND SUBSEQUENTLY IN THE ARMED VESSEL PORPOISE AND
CUMBERLAND SCHOONER.

WITH AN ACCOUNT OF THE

SHIPWRECK OF THE PORPOISE,

ARRIVAL OF THE CUMBERLAND AT MAURITIUS, AND IMPRISONMENT OF THE
COMMANDER DURING SIX YEARS AND A HALF IN THAT ISLAND.

BY MATTHEW FLINDERS,

COMMANDER OF THE INVESTIGATOR.

IN TWO VOLUMES, WITH AN ATLAS.

VOL. I.

LONDON:

PRINTED BY W. BULMER AND CO. CLEVELAND-ROW,
AND PUBLISHED BY G. AND W. NICOL, BOOKSELLERS TO HIS MAJESTY,
PALL-MALL.

1814.

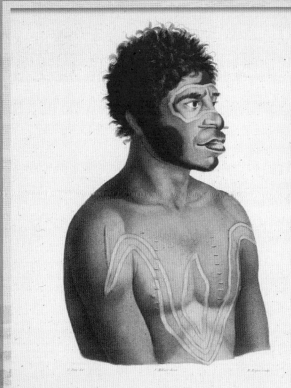

NOUVELLE-HOLLANDE.

Y-ERRAN-GOU-LA-GA

ABOVE:
Investigator careened on the shore.

LEFT:
Drawing of an Aboriginal man at Port Jackson.

reached Sydney two months later, only 12 of the 170 seamen were fit for duty. France and England were enjoying a brief period of peace—a treaty had been signed in 1802—and the French were treated with consideration, courtesy, and the usual suspicion.

Proceeding up the Queensland coast to round Cape York, Flinders charted the coastline of the Gulf of Carpentaria where, to his alarm, the *Investigator*'s timbers began falling apart and his crew began to sicken. The navigator put into Timor and then returned to Sydney, finally departing for England in September 1803 in the *Cumberland*. Unaware that war had once more broken out with France, he was detained on Mauritius and spent seven years there as a prisoner, using his energies despite failing health to complete the journal of his explorations.

Broken in health, Flinders returned to London, living in time to see his epic *A Voyage to Terra Australis* published on the day before his death in 1814. It is to Flinders that we owe the popularisation of the name 'Australia' for the continent that all still referred to as New Holland.

ABOVE:
A British man-o'-war at anchor in Sydney Cove, c. 1800; artist unknown. This view looks towards Bennelong Point, the site of today's Opera House, with the west side of Sydney Cove in the distance.

1803: Van Diemen's Land

Perturbed by the presence of the French, whose designs on Australia were still unknown, Governor King in May 1803 ordered Lieutenant John Bowen to establish a settlement of convicts and soldiers in Van Diemen's Land, the future Tasmania, on the banks of the Derwent close to the present site of Hobart.

The British Government was equally disturbed by French activities and dispatched Lieutenant David Collins, a former First Fleet Marine officer, from England in April 1803 in HMS *Calcutta* with 299 convicts and 19 settlers (accompanied by their wives and children) to found a settlement at Port Phillip Bay. This proved to be the first of many failed and half-hearted attempts to create a colony on unsuitable shores. The soil on the eastern coast of the bay was sandy; nothing grew, and in November Collins received permission from King to transfer the settlement to the Derwent. On arriving there in February 1804, Collins immediately decided to move Bowen's small colony from Risdon Cove to the opposite shore and there, beneath the towering slopes of Mount Wellington, snow-capped in winter, Hobart Town was founded. On 3 May a large group of Aborigines approached the Risdon Cove camp and for some reason the troops opened fire on them, killing several. Within seventy years Van Diemen's Land's small Aboriginal population were dead.

With the establishment of a settlement on the island's north coast at Port Dalrymple in November 1804, Bass Strait was now effectively guarded against any foreign designs.

BELOW:

Map of Australia and the Pacific Ocean showing 'the New Discoveries'. Tasmania is now shown as an island, following its circumnavigation by Bass and Flinders in 1798.

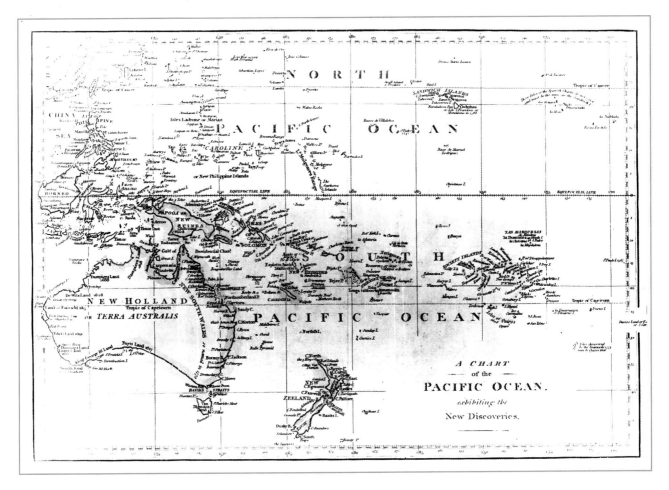

Major Johnston with Quarter: Master Laycock One Serjeant and Twenty five Privates of ye New S Wales Corps ——— defeats Two Hundred & Sixty six Armed Rebels 5 March 1804.

1804: The Irish Revolt

As early as 1803 Governor King had requested that he be relieved of duty. He was almost crippled by gout; the colony seemed ungovernable, and persistent rumours were current that the Irish were hiding pikes and planning a revolt. The Reverend Marsden attempted to beat information out of several of the Irish 'croppies' in his charge at Parramatta: a convict named Fitzgerald and a 20-year-old named Paddy Galvin each got 300 lashes, but both remained silent as their flesh left their bones. 'I am sure (Galvin) will die before he reveals anything,' Marsden wrote to King.

On 4 March 1804 the Irish convicts near Castle Hill, north-west of Sydney Town, broke out and marched on neighbouring homesteads searching for weapons and vengeance for the treatment they had suffered. Shouts of 'The croppies are coming!' were heard in Parramatta and the Reverend Marsden promptly packed himself and his family, accompanied by Elizabeth Macarthur, onto a river boat bound for Sydney, for some of the rebels had sworn to flog him first of all.

The revolt was quickly and bloodily crushed. Martial law was proclaimed, and a detachment of fifty soldiers of the New South Wales Corps were marched overnight to Parramatta with Major Johnston riding at their head. They caught up with the convicts next day in the Hawkesbury hills. Opening fire, the troops killed twelve of the rebels and wounded six others. Another twenty-six were taken prisoner. They suffered summary justice. Nine of the prisoners were hanged at Parramatta without trial, nine were flogged, and a total of fifty others later sentenced to servitude at Coal River.

ABOVE:

A contemporary impression of the Castle Hill Rebellion of 1804.

The Irish rebels can be seen fleeing from volleys fired by the New South Wales Corps while Major Johnston and Quarter-Master Laycock point their pistols at the ring-leaders.

1805: Macarthur builds his power

John Macarthur returned to Sydney in June 1805, bringing with him a consignment of merino rams and an order to the Governor from Lord Camden, the Secretary of State for the Colonies, to grant him 10,000 acres of land in the rich pasture land south-west of Sydney, the Cow Pastures. It is said that when Governor King saw him he burst into tears of rage.

Macarthur's grant was equal to the entire area under crop in the colony. King was also ordered to provide Macarthur with a labouring force of thirty convicts on 'assignment'. The landholding—and its fine merino stud—would be the making of the Macarthur dynasty.

Other dynasties were in process of formation. In 1806 Gregory Blaxland, a gentleman farmer from Kent, arrived in Sydney with his family; his brother John arrived the following year. Both would benefit from land grants and the colony's growing opportunities. They would become, with the Macarthurs, founding members of the 'Pure Merinos', the 'Exclusives', in a society soon to be split asunder.

1806: Governor Bligh arrives

In August 1806, King's replacement as Governor of New South Wales, Captain William Bligh, RN, arrived in Sydney. Bligh's reputation was formidable. He had survived mutiny on the *Bounty* and a voyage of survival and the humiliation of a protracted court martial to command HMS *Glatton* under Nelson's approving eye at Copenhagen. He had been recommended to the government by Sir Joseph Banks as a man who would brook no nonsense. This was an understatement. Bligh was victim of a hot temper, and prone to express his frustrations in foul language.

One of Bligh's first actions was to forbid the 'exchange of spirits as payment for grain, food, labour, wearing apparel; or any other commodity whatever', ordering that all transactions be expressed in sterling. His predecessor King had licensed the first brewery in Sydney Town two years earlier to reduce the populace's addiction to the demon rum, but cheap beer had only increased the general drunkenness.

Bligh's measure won the Governor the support of the smaller settlers but aroused the anger of the wealthy. He alienated the Blaxlands by refusing them a land grant and earned Macarthur's enmity by threatening to cancel his 10,000-acre grant. He antagonised the New South Wales Corps by requesting its removal lock, stock and barrel, and its replacement by a Regiment of the Line. Accustomed to naval discipline, he was appalled by the slackness and insolence of the Corps officers and men, some of whom he abused to their faces as 'buggers and wretches'.

By late 1807 Macarthur could write with satisfaction that 'the Corps is galloping into a state of open warfare with the Governor'. Matters came to a head when Bligh determined to enforce the law to the letter, but the spark that led to his downfall was a relatively trivial affair. When Macarthur in December 1807 was served with a summons to pay a forfeited bond (one of his convicts had absconded) he drove the constable from his doorway with dire threats to end Bligh's 'horrid tyranny'.

All appeared peaceful on New Year's Day 1808 when Governor Bligh was presented with a loyal address bearing the signatures of more than 900 citizens—a rare affirmation of their support for his policies. Missing were the signatures of the Macarthurs, the Blaxlands, the wealthy merchant Simeon Lord—and of all officers of the New South Wales Corps.

Above:
Captain William Bligh, RN, survivor of the 'mutiny on the *Bounty*', who arrived as Governor of New South Wales in 1806. Within two years he was the victim of another mutiny against his authority—in the form of military rebellion.

1808: The Rum Rebellion

On 25 January 1808 John Macarthur appeared before a court of six officers who sat in full dress uniform; the president of the court was the Judge-Advocate, Richard Atkins, a notorious drunk. In the first minutes Macarthur angrily challenged the competence of Atkins to sit as president. When Atkins threatened to charge Macarthur with contempt of court, one of the officers, Anthony Fenn Kemp, shouted to Atkins 'We will try you!' Atkins stormed from the court to report to Bligh. Rejecting the court's 'treasonable' demand for Atkins to be replaced, Bligh ordered his Provost, William Gore—an even worse drunk that Atkins—to arrest Macarthur.

Major George Johnston, the commanding officer of the Corps, was now dragged unwillingly into the drama. Informed by Surgeon Harris that 'an insurrection' was threatened, Johnston went to the Barracks, called the troops to arms and proclaimed Martial Law, announcing that, as senior military officer and Lieutenant-Governor, he was assuming the administration; he also ordered Macarthur's release. Fortified by a letter signed by some of Sydney's leading citizens imploring him 'instantly to arrest Governor Bligh', Johnston led the regiment uphill to Government House to the strains of 'The British Grenadiers'. 'Liquor was liberally and indeed profusely served to the soldiers,' one witness recalled. 'Bonfires blazed in all parts of town, and scenes of riot, tumult and insubordination ensued ...'

The hot and humid evening was, by coincidence, the twentieth anniversary of the colony's founding and the crowd of onlookers were naturally good-humoured. The guard at Government House gates melted away and the only defence offered was that by Bligh's young widowed daughter, Mary Putland, who broke an umbrella over the head of a soldier entering the doorway. Bligh was discovered

ABOVE:
The Baudin expedition to Australia left this drawing by Leseur of ships in Sydney Cove in 1802. Matthew Flinders' ship *Investigator* is shown, fully rigged, alongside the *Supply*.

upstairs attempting to hide his papers under a bed and was arrested; for the next year he was confined to Government House.

In July 1808 Lt-Colonel Foveaux arrived in Sydney en route to Norfolk Island, but he chose not to reinstate Bligh; Lt-Colonel Paterson, returning from Tasmania, unwillingly assumed the Governorship and in March 1809 authorised Bligh to leave for England on the *Porpoise*. Bligh immediately sailed for Van Diemen's Land and moved into Government House in Hobart. There he remained for almost nine months.

For a year London did nothing. John Macarthur, who had left for England with Johnston to explain to the authorities the extent of Bligh's 'tyranny of oppression', correctly surmised that the affairs of 'our insignificant Colony' would create little excitement. George Johnston's court martial for mutiny in 1811 resulted in his being cashiered from the army, but he was allowed to return to the colony as a free citizen.

Macarthur was warned that he could face charges if he returned to Sydney Town. He remained an exile in London until 1817, years of great loneliness that contributed to his later mental deterioration, and which were made bearable only by the presence of his sons Edward, John, James and William. In London he met young William Charles Wentworth—'a pleasing lad'—who was hopeful of marrying Macarthur's daughter Elizabeth and thus creating a colonial dynasty. The Macarthur family's rejection of Wentworth deeply wounded him, as he considered himself every inch as noble as a freeborn Englishman.

John Macarthur was also sustained by his wife's letters and her unswerving devotion, and by her careful management of the farms; but in 1815 he was chiding her for neglecting small details: 'Your letter contained no return of the Stock, no

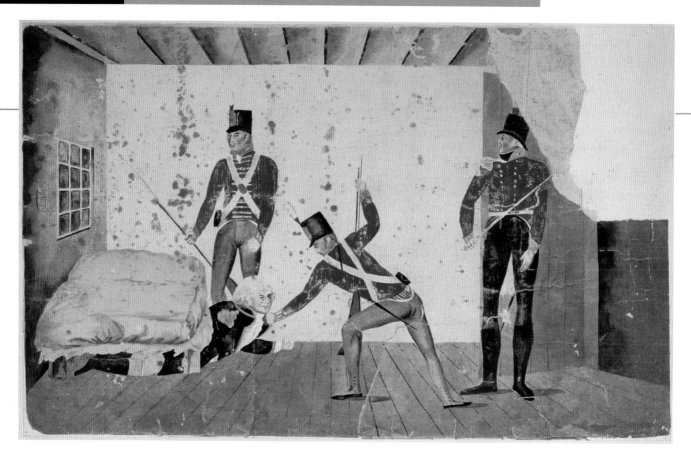

mention of the current Prices, nothing of the sale of Rams,' he wrote. 'Indeed, my dearest Elizabeth, I feel as ignorant of the state of my affairs as any Stranger, and when I am interrogated upon the subject I can only stammer and look foolish ...'

1809: Macquarie arrives

Rule of the difficult colony could no longer be entrusted to naval officers. The Governors would henceforward be military officers, men with their feet firmly on the ground.

'We are shortly to be Transported', the commanding officer of the 73rd Regiment, Lt-Colonel Lachlan Macquarie, wrote with amusement to a friend early in 1809. 'We have been expecting every day to receive orders to embark for the Land of Exiles ... I am appointed Lieutenant Governor of New South Wales (alias Botany Bay!) ... so I shall probably have all the trouble, plague, responsibility and odium of new modelling the Government duty.' The 73rd Regiment of Foot (previously a kilted Scottish regiment, but now uniformed in red coats and gaiters) had been chosen by the Commander-in-Chief to accompany the new Governor, Major-General Miles Nightingall, but two days later, owing to Nightingall's sudden resignation on grounds of illness, the regiment's Commanding Officer, Macquarie, found himself appointed Governor-in-Chief in his place, and was promised a pension if he remained in the colony for at least eight years.

Duty was no stranger to Lachlan Macquarie. He was forty-eight years old and had eaten the King's salt as a loyal soldier for thirty-two years in Canada, India and Egypt. He was a Scot from Ulva in the Inner Hebrides and had spent his boyhood

ABOVE:

A cartoon of the arrest of Governor Bligh by soldiers of the New South Wales Corps, 1808. The artist shows the Governor attempting to hide under the bed—an assertion denied by Bligh, who maintained that he was trying to secrete important papers.

BELOW:

Commanding Officer of the New South Wales Corps—but absent in Tasmania when the rebellion took place: Colonel William Paterson played an ambivalent role in the affair. A Scot, he was a venturesome explorer with an interest in natural history, but was lax in his duties and a heavy drinker. He had first arrived in the colony in 1790, was invalided back to England in 1796 but had returned to the colony in 1799.

ABOVE:
Colonel Lachlan Macquarie, from the portrait by Richard Read, Snr. Macquarie was a stopgap Governor who proved to be the most far-sighted and benevolent the colony had known.

in the Highlands that produced Scotland's hardiest soldiers. Born into a proud but poor clan, he had strength of character and sympathy for the less fortunate in life; he was deeply Christian in an age that mocked Christ's teachings. Tall and handsome, he possessed the Scottish characteristic of ambition leavened by intelligence. Hostile to 'the infernal and destructive principles of Democracy' (he had written these words in 1795), he was nevertheless humane, liberal and just.

Macquarie, who had been ordered to restore Bligh to power for the token period of one day before assuming rule, arrived in Sydney in December 1809. On New Year's Day 1810 he stood before a crowd of colonists and the assembled ranks of the New South Wales Corps and the 73rd Regiment and called for an end to 'dissensions and jealousies' and the birth of a 'spirit of conciliation and harmony between all classes'.

The disgraced New South Wales Corps was shipped back to England, renamed the 102nd Regiment, and later fought (unkindly nicknamed 'The Botany Bay Rangers') in the Americas, where its men proved to be good soldiers after all.

The new Governor appealed to the citizens to observe their religious duties, to treat the natives with kindness, promising that 'the honest, sober and industrious inhabitants, whether free settler or convict, would ever find him a friend and protector'. Bligh, whom Macquarie found 'a most disagreeable person', soon departed for England to attend the court martial of George Johnston; to his horror the New South Wales Corps accompanied him.

With Scottish thoroughness, Macquarie established the pattern his rule would follow. He would deal with applications for land grants on Mondays; on Tuesdays he would receive citizens. The Sabbath would be observed as a day of rest and piety: to enforce sobriety he reduced the number of inns from seventy-five to twenty.

1810: Macquarie the builder

In order to provide the money to build Sydney's first hospital, Macquarie signed a contract in December 1810 with three Sydney businessmen—one of them D'Arcy Wentworth—allowing them to import 45,000 gallons of rum. The Rum Hospital, later the state Parliament, still stands in Macquarie Street. It was the first of a number of Georgian public buildings and churches of rare distinction and

RIGHT:
Curiosities of Botany Bay, as shown in London broadsheets and booklets.
The 'giant' proved to be Australia's first tall story.

RIGHT:
Curiosities of Botany Bay, as shown in London broadsheets and booklets.
The 'giant' proved to be Australia's first tall story.

grace, many of them designed by the convict architect Francis Greenway, whose genius the Governor quickly recognised.

In November 1810 the Governor set off to inspect his domain. Escorted by a mounted bodyguard and taking with him his Bengal tents, he travelled by coach to the site of Liverpool, writing, 'I determined to erect a township' (naming it not after the port but after the prime minister of the day). In 1811 Macquarie voyaged to Van Diemen's Land, his other fief; the island's new Lieutenant-Governor, Tom Davey, impressed Macquarie as a dishonest buffoon.

By 1812 the Secretary of State was writing that he was 'very angry' about the colony's threefold increase in expenditure; Macquarie replied that he had found 'no public buildings and works of any description' when he arrived, and was merely initiating long-overdue improvements. 'I found the colony barely emerging from infant imbecility, and suffering from various privations', Macquarie was to write in his defence when he relinquished the governorship in 1821. 'I left it reaping incalculable advantages from my important and extensive discoveries in all directions …'

A thriving township on the harbour's edge: The west side of Sydney Cove (site of the Rocks and the southern pylons of today's Harbour Bridge) in 1803; from a painting by John Eyre.

Sydney and its harbour in
1823, from a painting by
Major Taylor of the 48th
Regiment. Part of a
panorama, it provides
a rare view of everyday
life at the close of
Macquarie's rule: the
windmills that ground
the colony's grain, newly
constructed government
buildings, cottages, along
with military officers and
convicts at work.

The river flats along the
broad Hawkesbury River
to the north of Sydney
and Parramatta proved
to be some of the most
fertile in the early colony,
and communication was
easy by water transport.
An 1809 view of the
township of Windsor, then
known as Green Hills.

VIEWS IN AUSTRALIA
OR NEW SOUTH WALES, & VAN DIEMEN'S LAND
DELINEATED,
In Fifty Views, with descriptive Letter Press.
Dedicated by Permission, to
The Right Honble Earl Bathurst &c &c.
BY J. LYCETT,
Artist to Major General Macquarie, late Governor of those Colonies.

1813: Crossing the Blue Mountains

In 1812 Macquarie ordered George Evans, the Surveyor, to explore the land south of Sydney—the rich Illawarra and in 1813 encouraged the first attempts to cross the Blue Mountains. In May 1813 Gregory Blaxland, D'Arcy Wentworth's son William (an imp of fortune whom the Governor looked upon with affection and indulgence) and Lieutenant William Lawson, formerly of the New South Wales Corps, set out with four convict servants, four horses and two dogs to find a route across the mountains. By following the ridge line instead of the valley floors they reached its western edge to see below them rich plains rolling as far as the horizon. They had unlocked the key to Australia's interior.

In 1815 Macquarie was among the first to travel up Cox's mountain road to the Bathurst Plains, where he selected and named the site of Bathurst, nearly 200 kilometres from Sydney on the banks of the river that Evans had discovered and named the Macquarie. (In the same year the Governor laid out no fewer than five towns on the banks of the Hawkesbury.)

In January 1818, in the sweltering heat of summer, the first ten settlers to cross the Blue Mountains left the Nepean to drive their drays up Cox's road to Bathurst. From the government stores they had been given a cow for milk and wheat for sowing. Five months later John Oxley set out to trace the Macquarie River to its source. He was to find only impassable marshes that blocked his progress, but striking north he discovered the rich Liverpool Plains above the Hunter Valley, before crossing overland to the coast and returning to Sydney to recount his discoveries.

ABOVE:
Transported for forgery and pardoned in 1821, Joseph Lycett was a talented convict favoured by Macquarie. Lycett published a series of views of New South Wales and Tasmania between 1823 and 1825. He, too, helped popularise the term 'Australia' for the continent still referred to as New Holland or New South Wales.

Circumnavigating Australia:

Filling in the gaps

In 1817 Governor King's son, Lieutenant Phillip Parker King, sailed from England under Admiralty order to chart Australia's northern coastline and thus fill in the gaps on Flinders' map of the continent. The young officer had been born in Australia and had settled on a naval career like his father. In five epic voyages by 1822, King carefully carried out his instructions. He retired from the Royal Navy in 1032 to live in New South Wales, dying in 1856 a rear-admiral, his great achievements remaining until recently a footnote in the history books.

Emancipists and Exclusives

By 1813 Macquarie was complaining that the conduct of his former regiment was disgraceful and recommended that no garrison regiment be posted to the colony for more than three-year periods. Its replacement, the 46th Foot, which arrived in 1814, was no better. Its officers refused to sit at the same table as former convicts (Emancipists)—'men so much our inferior in rank and station'—and the Governor requested its 'speedy removal'. The new garrison regiment, the 48th (Northamptonshire), which disembarked in 1817, was exemplary, and among its officers were a number who rendered good service as commandants, engineers and magistrates: Erskine, Macalister, Druitt, Mitchell, Close, Cimitière, Cuthbertson and Bell among them.

Calling together fourteen of Sydney's leading merchants in 1817, Macquarie encouraged them to form the Bank of New South Wales to regulate the issuing of currency and to fund development. This aroused the ire of the Bank of England, but soon banknotes replaced the old collection of Spanish dollars that had, with rum, served as legal tender.

In 1815 Macquarie closed down Norfolk Island prison. He reduced the severity of punishments meted out to convicts and sought above all to bring former convicts—'Emancipists'—into the ranks of society as citizens with full rights, and to heal the widening breach between them and the freeborn 'Exclusives'.

When John Macarthur returned to Sydney with his boys in 1817, their mother wrote that 'they are delighted to return to their native land and breathe not a regret for the gay scenes of the English metropolis'. Macarthur, his sons and his nephew Hannibal, would rise to leadership of the 'Exclusives'.

'The colony is, I believe, the only one of the British possessions inhabited by Englishmen in which there is not at least the shadow of free government', young William Wentworth, a great favourite of Macquarie's, would write in the book on New South Wales which he published in London in 1819. Smarting from the embarrassment of being not only the first 'Australian' the graduates had met, but also the son of a man said to have been 'Transported to Botany Bay', William Wentworth would be an impassioned patriot—probably our first. He, too, would later become a conservative.

ABOVE:
The young William Charles Wentworth. Like Lang, he would be a turbulent figure in Sydney society and politics.

1819: The Bigge Report

Macquarie's style of government, if humane, was certainly autocratic: he spent grandly, stood much on ceremony and dispensed justice like a Roman emperor. Between 1813 and 1816 he was constantly at loggerheads with his Judge-Advocate, Ellis Bent and with the latter's brother, Judge Jeffrey Hart Bent, an ally of Marsden. Constant complaints to Lord Bathurst by critics of Macquarie's liberalism saw John Thomas Bigge appointed by London to report on the administration of New South Wales in 1819.

The Bigge Report was highly critical of Macquarie's policies and his leniency. Macquarie called it 'vile and insidious'; William Wentworth would label it 'dirt and filth and scandal'. Bigge was a meticulous note-taker and listened perhaps too much to John Macarthur, who after his return in 1817 became an outspoken enemy of what he called Macquarie's 'absurd and mischievous policy'.

The Governor's program of buildings and public works was especially criticised for its extravagant cost and nature but Macquarie was past caring. He had already tendered his resignation to 'the great folks' in Downing Street. Defending his lenient treatment of Emancipists, Macquarie wrote to the Colonial Office: 'It is true, indeed, that you send us from the Mother Country men, who are stained by "vice and crime" of every description, but happily for them and us, many who come out vicious, do not remain so … and some few would be an honour and a credit to any country.'

Macquarie regretted that the colony generated no income, for its costs to the government exceeded the profits from its exports, but reminded London that a

ABOVE:

'Macquarie the Builder' was responsible for the rebuilding in 1815–16 of the Government House at Parramatta that remained in use until the 1850s. Like many of his buildings, it still stands.

By the 1820s a definite Australian style was emerging in the design of public and private buildings: a fusion of Georgian and Regency symmetry with local innovations such as broad verandahs to reduce the effects of the summer heat. The Officers Quarters at Victoria Barracks, Sydney, was completed in the 1840s, before the onset of Victorian Gothic and Italianate styles.

growing population necessitated 'an increase in all the accommodations of civilised life'. Macquarie believed in an equable society but Macarthur, in a letter to Bigge, dreamed of a future in which 'a body of really respectable settlers   men of real capital' could form with their 'fine woolled sheep' a 'wealthy and powerful aristocracy' to keep 'the democratic multitude' at bay. It was a crazy idea, but Macarthur was already showing signs of the intransigence and irrationality that would leave him insane.

1822: Farewell to the 'Old Viceroy'

Against civil servants as painstaking as Bigge and enemies as artful as Marsden and Macarthur, the 'Old Viceroy' had no hope. A new governor, Major-General Sir Thomas Makdougall Brisbane, arrived in Sydney in November 1821 and Macquarie made a farewell journey through the colony before leaving for England in February 1822. Promoted to the rank of major-general and grudgingly given a small pension late in 1823, he died in London in June 1824. If the Bigge Report was critical of Macquarie's record, it at least shared his vision of Australia as a home for the free—it recommended a program of immigration—and detailed the expansion of the colony under Macquarie's benevolent rule: it had grown from 12,000 people in 1810 to nearly 40,000 in 1821; the number of sheep had increased tenfold, from 26,000 to nearly 290,000.

Macquarie's last victory had been to obtain from London an undertaking to restore the rights of free men to all Emancipists. He is buried on Ulva, in a granite tomb inscribed 'The Father of Australia'.

Macquarie was a Prince of Men,
Australia's pride and joy,
We ne'er shall see his like again,
Here's to the Old Viceroy!

The words of the old patriotic song, and the grief with which news of his death was received are testimony to the love that he inspired. In the dark decades that followed, Macquarie's rule would be looked back on as a brief golden age.

BELOW:
Cross-belt buckle of the 48th (Northamptonshire) Regiment, one of the best British regiments to serve in Australia. Its discipline was high, and many of its officers proved to be outstanding administrators.

BELOW, RIGHT:
Merino ewes. By the end of the century Australian Merino sheep were yeilding nearly 2 kilos of wool per year, and by the the 1990s were each yielding up to 4.5 kilograms of fine wool.

Currency and Sterling

Derided as 'Currency' by the proudly 'Sterling' free settlers of English birth, the white 'Native Australians' (as the children of the early convicts were known by the genteel) had by the 1820s developed into a distinct breed, speaking with a pleasant drawl with faint Cockney undertones that became a recognisable Australian accent.

Their tallness was often remarked upon. They were bigger and healthier than their parents, for they had grown up in sunshine (a natural source of vitamin D) and on nutritious food rich in vitamin C. Their nature was friendly and open, their language blunt and frequently coarse: they used the word 'bloody' freely, because their history had been bloody. They teased emigrants as 'New Chums'—the words became a humorous form of abuse—but lacked spite in any form. 'The inhabitants born in the colony are generally tall in person, and slender in limbs,' reported Commissioner Bigge in 1821. 'They are capable of undergoing more fatigue, and are less exhausted by labour than the English … In their temper they are quick and irascible, but not vindictive …' They had little reverence for the law that had sentenced their parents to years of suffering and showed an abiding sympathy for the underdog. Currency lads in the pubs of The Rocks area often fought with off-duty redcoats (known as 'the Lobsters' by their brick-red jackets and heavy packs) and chased them back to their barracks for a lark. Convicts absconding into the bush could rely on 'the Currency' to feed and shelter them, and few were ever betrayed. A national type had been born.

In 1824 the newly arrived English official George Boyes wrote from Sydney to his wife in England:

> The Native born—I mean the children of Convicts or Settlers—are a different race from the old stock—they have nothing of the strength and solidity of form of their fathers. They have generally light hair, blue eyes, and shoot up as fast as mushrooms to a very considerable stature—very few of the women are pretty …

BELOW:
A family of Sydney Town; from an old broadside.

Several years later, however, he was writing from his new post in Hobart Town:

> You cannot imagine such a beautiful race as the rising generation in the colony … as they grow up they think nothing of England and cannot bear the idea of going there. It is extraordinary the passionate love they have for the country of their birth … there is a degree of liberty here which you can hardly imagine …

The 1820s and 1830s would also witness a degree of suffering by the colony's convict population that dwarfed previous horrors. Van Diemen's Land, created as a separate colony in 1825, would become a metaphor for brutality.

1822: Governor Brisbane

It was General Sir Thomas Brisbane's fate to rule a colony that was beginning to enjoy belated growth at a time when England itself was undergoing renewed social turmoil and France was again emerging from defeat as a major European power.

Like Macquarie, Brisbane was a Scot and a soldier (he had commanded brigades with distinction under Wellington in the Peninsular War). Intellectually gifted, he was a respected astronomer and liberal in his views. John Dunmore Lang found the Governor 'disinclined to business and deficient in energy' and the ever-critical Marsden viewed Brisbane's tolerant attitude to Catholics with misgiving. Brisbane delegated much of his authority but worked harmoniously with his lieutenants in Van Diemen's Land, Sorrell (who had succeeded the incompetent 'Mad Tom' Davey) and his successor, Arthur.

Brisbane's short rule was benevolent and his achievements considerable. In 1823 the first step towards giving the colonists some say in their affairs came with the appointment of a Legislative Council of six members to advise the Governor and with the institution of a Supreme Court; in 1824 the Chief Justice, Sir Francis Forbes, introduced trial by jury to replace military courts in civil cases. Brisbane also introduced freedom of the press, in keeping with English political tradition.

BELOW:
The Reverend John Dunmore Lang, a Presbyterian cleric who became a fiery politician.

John Dunmore Lang

Scots were few in the first decades of Australian history—only three of Phillip's First Fleet convicts had been Scottish—but in 1823 arrived the first of a flood of Lowlanders and Highlanders. John Dunmore Lang led them. Born in Greenock and educated at the University of Glasgow, Lang was a Presbyterian cleric who had taken it upon himself to establish the Kirk in the godless colony. He loved the climate but deplored the character of the inhabitants ('Oh, nest of vipers!') and energetically set about the building of the first Scots church. From its pulpit Lang thundered against those who renounced the Son of God, calling them bastards. Alarmed by the growing number of Irish Catholics, he returned to his birthplace in 1825 to bring out more Scots.

William Charles Wentworth

Australia's patriot son, William Wentworth, returned to Sydney in July 1824. Like John Dunmore Lang, Wentworth was a physically huge man with a gift for language that could inspire or damn men in equal parts. Seven years spent practising law in London had served only to make him yearn more for his homeland—indeed while

studying briefly at Cambridge in 1823 he had written a poem which had failed to win a prize but was much recited by his fellow countrymen, especially its closing stanza:

> And, oh, Britannia! Should thou cease to ride
> Despotic Empress of the Ocean's tide—
> May this, thy last-born infant then arise
> To glad thy heart, and greet thy parent's eyes
> And Australia float, with flag unfurled,
> A New Britannia in another world!

Wentworth was determined to introduce to his new Britannia all the rights enjoyed by Englishmen—namely a free press, a 'free constitution', an elected parliament and the blessings of self-government. His book on the colony published in London in 1819 contained passages critical of John Macarthur, whom Wentworth now described in conversation as 'the yellow snake'. In October 1824 Wentworth formed a partnership with Robert Wardell to publish a newspaper, the *Australian*, which became the bane of Brisbane's successor, Darling, and a platform for the Emancipist cause. The death in 1827 of his beloved father, D'Arcy Wentworth, left William Charles a wealthy man, squire of Vaucluse on the harbour's edge, a rival to Government House as the centre of what little brilliance existed in Sydney society.

ABOVE:
John Blaxland, a prominent member of a family close to the heart of the 'Exclusives'—the 'Pure Merinos' who prized power.

'Pure Merinos'

The 'Pure Merinos'—the Exclusives, who boasted no convict blood or connections—increased in influence during the 1820s. Land grants had always been offered to military and naval officers in the colony; grants of 2000 acres were now offered to the growing number of officers in Great Britain who had been placed on half-pay after the Napoleonic Wars. Posting of a regiment to Australia usually resulted in a flurry of exchanges into home-based regiments by officers who dreaded three years' exile in a penal colony and a further three years in India (the graveyard of English soldiers). Those who accompanied their battalions to Australia sold their commissions in increasing numbers to settle on the land. 'It really is a delightful country and ought to make a respectable settlement,' Captain Francis Allman of the 48th Regiment, Commandant at Port Macquarie, wrote in 1824 to his friend Captain John Piper. 'I would have no objection, from what I have seen, to put off the red coat and remain.' Like his brother officers Robert Close, Lachlan Macalister and Surgeon Mitchell (father of the founder of the famous library that bears his name), Allman sold his commission and remained in Australia, taking up a land grant in 1824 and becoming a pioneer of the rich Hunter Valley region.

Word of John Macarthur's success in growing fine wool encouraged English farmers to emigrate with their families: in 1821 James Henty, a Surrey sheep farmer who had secured merino rams as early as 1796, saw his neighbour, John Street, depart for the Antipodes. Street wrote glowingly of the opportunities in the new land, and he founded a dynasty that has produced four generations of farmers, soldiers and jurists. Henty and his brothers Charles, William, Stephen, John and Francis and their sister Jane began emigrating in 1829. The freeborn landholders were soon to form a colonial 'aristocracy' or landed gentry, natural allies of the Pure Merinos.

ABOVE:

In 1835, when Sigismund Himely painted this view of 'Vooloo-Moloo', the future congested inner city suburb of Wool-loomooloo was an idyllic harbour-side pasture.

RIGHT:

Sydney Harbour from Vaucluse, painted in the 1850s.

1824: The Australian Agricultural Company

In 1824 the largest monopoly of all was granted to the 370 shareholders (who included some of the most prominent members of London society and banking) of the new Australian Agricultural Company: a million acres in the Hunter Valley region, the colony's richest region in pasture and in coal. The AAC was a colony within a colony. It was the creation of Macarthur's son John, a solicitor in London and to Wentworth its creation was proof that the 'yellow snakes' dominated both the colony and the Colonial Office in London; he greeted its early growth pains with glee. In 1825 John Macarthur took a seat on the Legislative Council, where he was soon joined by his son-in-law, Dr John Bowman. The Pure Merinos were supreme. The AAC has survived to this day.

Hobart Town was a thriving settlement by
the late 1820s.

The growth of settlements

1824: Hume and Hovell

In 1823 John Ovens discovered the Monaro region
near the present site of Canberra; and in 1824
Hamilton Hume, a pioneer of the Yass district, and
William Hovell, an Englishman, sighted the Australian Alps and reached the Murrumbidgee River.
The two men fought almost all the way, and Hume
was the first to cross the river, taunting his hesitant
companion to join him. They rode further south
and discovered an even broader, fast-flowing river –
the Murray River – which Hume named after himself. They then rode on to the shores of Corio Bay.
On their return they reported that the country – the
future Port Phillip region (Victoria) – was well-
watered and verdant.

1824: Brisbane founded

In 1824 Governor Brisbane was ordered to send
a group of convicts and a detachment of soldiers
under Captain Miller to Moreton Bay, a region
previously explored and described in glowing
terms by Oxley. Within months the settlement was moved to the banks of
the broad Brisbane River, where grew the future city of Brisbane. Captain Patrick
Logan, an officer of the 57th Regiment then garrisoning Sydney, arrived

ABOVE:
The first outstanding Australian-
born explorer, Hamilton Hume
in old age.

ABOVE:
Captain Joseph Logan, explorer and administrator of the settlement that became Brisbane. He was hated by his convict charges and many rejoiced when he was speared to death by Aborigines.

there as Commandant in 1826. He was a martinet who worked his convicts until they dropped; Governor Brisbane's successor, Darling, increased Logan's power to include summary punishment of free settlers and other excesses by Logan elicited no rebuke from Darling. Few wept when Logan was speared to death by Aborigines in 1830.

Forlorn settlements

Persistent fears of French designs on the unclaimed area of New Holland were balanced by a reluctance on the part of the Colonial Office to add any more financial burdens to the Crown. The value to England of a trading post in the far north had been pointed out by Captain Phillip Parker King after his charting of the northern coasts in 1817, and the establishment in 1824 of a small military post on Melville Island (which with Bathurst Island forms the Tiwi Islands) was seen as a step towards establishing a trading port that might rival Batavia as a port of call for the Indies trade. But the enervating heat—and competition from the new port of Singapore (founded by Stamford Raffles in 1819)—left the forlorn trading post to languish. It was transferred to the mainland, to Port Essington, but the only lasting result of this westerly expansion was Britain's claim to a further slice of the continent, by moving the border of New South Wales west from 129 degrees to 135 degrees.

Again, fear of the French claiming possession of the western extremities of the continent prompted Governor Darling in October 1826 to send a motley detachment of soldiers and convicts to King George Sound to claim the area for Great Britain in July 1827. In that same year, Captain James Stirling sailed from Sydney to investigate the Swan River region. Stirling reported on his return that the area was fertile and capable of supporting a settlement, and began lobbying in London for the establishment there of a colony.

In April 1829 Captain Charles Fremantle of the warship HMS *Challenger*, which had been dispatched on Admiralty command from the Cape of Good Hope, raised the Union Jack at the Swan River to formally claim Western Australia for the British Crown. The entire Australian continent now lay under the British flag.

The repressive 1820s

The 1820s was a bleak decade of English history; a period of economic and social distress. The coming of peace in Europe in 1815 coincided with the introduction of the Corn Laws, which imposed a high price on grain to safeguard the fortunes of the rural gentry but resulted in the poor being unable to afford even bread.

107

England's iniquitous Poor Laws, which placed the care of the indigent on parishes, led to the workhouse and to degradation, the break up of families and children being put to work in conditions of squalor. By 1818 the Royal Navy's 700 warships had been reduced to a strength of only 120 and discharged sailors and soldiers had no work and little hope of finding any. Habeas corpus (freedom from arbitrary unrest) was suspended for the first time in a period of peace and artisans attempting to form unions and workers assembling in groups faced arrest. Those who smashed the mills and machines of the Industrial Revolution faced death by hanging.

In 1819 a peaceful crowd gathering to hear the radical 'Orator' Hunt at Manchester were dispersed with bloodshed. In the same year the 'Cato Street Conspiracy' was uncovered: its leaders had planned to assassinate the entire Cabinet at Downing Street; its plotters went to the block unrepentant. The old King George III was dying and mad; the Prince Regent who succeeded to the throne in 1820 as George IV, was hated as the symbol of an overfed, effete ruling class. In Ireland Protestants and Catholic 'Whiteboys' raided, burned and killed and in Glasgow a mob of striking mill workers clutching pikes was dispersed by the troops in 1820 and three of its leaders faced the fearful fate of convicted traitors—hanging and the headsman's block. Even the English soldiers guarding the executioner were seen sobbing at the beheadings. (Accomplices of the Cato Street Conspiracy and the Glasgow radicals and the Irish Whiteboys were all sentenced to transportation to New South Wales.)

1825: Governor Darling arrives

'Come with us if we should go to "Bottomless Bay", which is still our favourite scheme if it can be accomplished.' So wrote Lady Darling, the wife of the new Governor-designate of New South Wales, to her brother late in 1823. It would be a year before the Darlings sailed for their new appointment, and both would later regret their decision. 'Australia has proved a curse to me, and I wish it had been sent to the bottom of the sea before I had any connexion with it,' Darling wrote many years later, when his colonial investments had been lost in the crash of 1847. Darling's term of office would be as stormy as Bligh's and Australia would ruin not only his fortune but also his reputation.

Sir Ralph Darling and his wife and entourage arrived in Sydney in December 1825. Sydney society found Darling a cold, austere man and his wife, who was many years his

ABOVE:
In Britain the recession following the end of the Napoleonic wars in 1815 coincided with growing industrialisation and social distress. Militia charged a crowd of workers in Manchester in 1819 and the loss of life added to the mounting anger of workers.

BELOW:
An officer of a British regiment, 1830s. After the leather bell-shaped shako (cap) was introduced in the 1830s, the British soldiers' red-coated uniforms barely changed until the 1850s.

BELOW:
Soldiers embarking at Sheerness on a transport as guard for convicts
on the long voyage to Australia; from a painting by an unknown artist.

ABOVE:
The new Governor of
New South Wales with
a reputation as a harsh
administrator:
Sir Ralph Darling.

junior, flighty in nature. She was a Dumaresq and she and her three brothers formed Sir Ralph's only close friends. Gossips said that the Governor was not highborn (his father had been a sergeant), that he had not commanded men in battle (he had indeed been a staff officer) and that he was a protégé of the Duke of York—in other words, a High Tory.

Before Darling left for the colony, Lord Bathurst at the Colonial Office had advised him to 'initiate a measure to control the press', perhaps by imposing a licence or stamp duty, measures that were proving effective in controlling England's press in an age of repression.

The rigour of Darling's rule was soon evident. The British government decided in 1825 to re-open Norfolk Island as a prison for the most dangerous criminal and political prisoners. It would be 'a place of the extremist Punishment, short of Death', Darling ordered; no women would be allowed there, in case their softer natures be scarred by witnessing the punishments. Under Captain Morrissett, who in London had lobbied the Colonial Office for the command of the prison, citing his success on the mainland as a magistrate in dealing with unruly convicts, Norfolk Island would become a living hell.

To Ralph Darling, New South Wales was a penal settlement, not a colony. 'It seems absurd to talk of the interests and imprescribable rights of Englishmen,' he wrote to Whitehall in February 1827. 'These rights have been forfeited by the Emancipists and Prison Population here …'

1825: Van Diemen's Land: island prison

In 1825 Van Dieman's Land was removed from the control of the Governor in Sydney and made a separate colony under the rule of a colonel who had previously been administrator of the slave colony of Honduras: George Arthur. Van Diemen's Land's fate had been decided: the remote island was a natural prison and would remain one. The new Lieutenant-Governor was to rule Van Diemen's Land like an autocrat from 1824 to 1836.

Macquarie Harbour, the bleak prison on Van Diemen's Land's west coast backed by a range of impassable mountains, was equal to Norfolk Island in loneliness and horror. Many convicts killed themselves rather than endure the punishment and the despair.

Macarthur supreme

In 1825 John Macarthur wrote to his sons: 'Five newspapers are being published, all in the convict interest, and the editors all are dangerous radicals. Our Chief Justice is their idol.' Macarthur had little cause to worry about his position, for it was unassailable. The census of 1828—the first undertaken in the colony's history—revealed that the Macarthurs were among the greatest landholders in New South Wales, their sheep numbering 20,000 and their holdings widespread. 'King John' Macarthur yearned only for heirs to his dynasty. His son John, a lawyer in London, died young and childless; Edward was embarked on a military career; William and his nephew Hannibal helped him in his business affairs, as did James in London, but none of his sons had fathered children. To his father, James wrote in 1830

ABOVE:
British soldiers suffered the same dreadful punishments as convicts: a flogging being observed by officers (including the surgeon).

'I shall sit down peaceably amongst our sheep folds and under the shade of our own fig tree.' The authorities in London, he added, 'have too many troubles of their own to think of the complaints of poor Australians…' He returned to Australia with a bride, Emily Stone; their daughter Elizabeth would marry Lieutenant Onslow, RN, and continue the line. It was James Macarthur who would ally himself with William Wentworth to fight to keep Australia free of the taint of democracy—he was truly his father's son.

Sydney Town in the 1820s

When Roger Therry, an Irish lawyer, arrived in Sydney in 1829, he noted that 'nothing met the stranger's eye to convey the notion that he was in the capital of a penal colony … The streets were wide, well laid-out, and clean. The houses were for the most part built in the English style, the shops well stocked, and the people one met with in the streets presented the comfortable appearance of a prosperous community.' George Street was brilliant with jewellers' shops, and 'commodious verandahed cottages around which English roses clustered, with large gardens, were scattered through the town.' The presence of two regiments of redcoats, the 39th and 57th, the numerous officers to be seen and the regimental bands playing at dusk 'imparted quite a military aspect to the place,' especially on summer evenings.

Harsh justice

At daybreak, however, the delusion was dispelled.

'Early in the morning the gates of the convict prison were thrown open, and several hundred convicts were marched out in regimental file, and distributed amongst the several public works in and about the town. As they passed along—the chains clanking at their heels—the patchwork dress of coarse grey and yellow cloth marked with the Government brand in which they were paraded—the downcast countenances and the whole appearance of the men, exhibited a truly painful picture. Nor was it much improved throughout the day, as one met bands of them in detachments of twenty yoked to wagons laden with gravel and stone, which they wheeled through the streets; in this and in other respects they performed all the functions of labour usually discharged by beasts of burden at home.'

In an enclosed yard of the (Hyde Park) Barracks, shut out from the public road by a very high brick wall, flogging was administered. A band of from ten to twenty were daily at one period marched into this yard to be flogged. As I passed along the road about 11 o'clock in the morning there issued out of the prisoners' barracks a party consisting of four men, who bore on their shoulders a miserable convict, writhing in the agony of pain—his voice piercing the air with terrific screams ...

As a good lawyer, Therry (who would be a Judge of the Supreme Court between 1846 and 1859) was angered that magistrates, many of them corrupt, could order the same 'rough and ready justice' as naval or military officers—twenty-five or even fifty lashes a day to any convict they found 'insubordinate'.

ABOVE:
Convicts dreaded being sentenced to a chain gang, for conditions were barbarous and the men often incorrigible.

Chain gangs under military guard built roads and bridges throughout the colonies.

DESCRIPTION

OF THE

MANNER OF PUNISHMENT,

With the Instruments of Torture

INFLICTED ON THE PERSONS OF

JAMES SUDDS AND PATRICK THOMPSON,

SOLDIERS IN THE 57TH REGIMENT,

BY ORDER OF

GOVERNOR DARLING,

AT SYDNEY, NEW SOUTH WALES.

(Vide Parliamentary Papers, No. 56, July 1, 1830, and July 26, 1832.)

* The irons were made of round bolt iron formed into A COLLAR FOR THE NECK, with two projections extending from a foot to eighteen inches from the collar, and weighing about fourteen or fifteen pounds each."—Minute of the Executive Council of Sydney, May 28th, 1829.

London:

PUBLISHED BY BENJAMIN FRANKLIN,

No. 378, STRAND.

1833.

ABOVE:

The punishment of two soldiers of the 57th Regiment was seen by liberals as an example of Governor Darling's inhuman rule.

1826: The Sudds and Thompson case

British military punishments often exceeded those meted out to convicts. Even the humane Captain Charles Sturt of the 39th admitted that 100 lashes was the norm for insubordinate soldiers. In 1826 two privates of the 57th Regiment, Joseph Sudds and Patrick Thompson, decided that a convict life was preferable to their own and robbed a Sydney shopkeeper with the sole intention of being discharged and sent to gaol. Darling was incensed by their sentence of seven years in prison and changed it to seven years on a chain gang, ordering the felons to be drummed out of the regiment in neck irons and leg-chains. Sudds, who was already ailing, died ten days later.

Wentworth, whom Darling thought 'a vulgar, ill-bred fellow' and Edward Smith Hall, who had founded the *Monitor* in 1816, seized upon Darling's brutal sentencing of the two soldiers to attack the Governor's 'tyranny'. Hall was charged with the first of seven offences of criminal libel and was finally sent to gaol in 1829 (he continued to write his editorials from his cell).

But Darling's attempt to impose a stamp duty was challenged by Wardell and Wentworth in the pages of the *Australian*, and Chief Justice Forbes supported their stance. Freedom of the press was confirmed.

1828: The Bushrangers

In the same month that three young burglars, a highway robber and a murderer were hanged together in Sydney, three men holding pistols emerged from the bush on the Windsor Road and bailed up a dray, relieving the driver of his valuables before disappearing into the scrub.

Without horses, the three were caught in March 1828, clapped in irons and sent to Sydney Town for trial and execution. They were Irishmen, escaped convicts named Donahoe—a fair-haired, blue-eyed Dubliner—Kilroy and Smith. On the way to the condemned cells Donahoe broke free, clambered over a wall and escaped—into legend.

'Bold Jack Donahoe' was Australia's first 'Wild Colonial Boy', the earliest hero of a convict population that in the 1820s outnumbered the free by four to one. He was born in 1806 and sentenced to transportation for life in 1823. He arrived in Sydney in 1825, the same year as Governor Darling, and escaped from assignment on a farm two years later.

For two years after his escape from gaol, Donahoe led a group of fugitive convicts on a spree of highway robbery—bushranging—on roads from Bathurst to the

McCabe   Matthew Brady   Patrick Bryant

Illawarra, his gang sheltered by more than thirty sympathisers on farms in the area. He was tracked down and shot at Bringelly in 1830, the year that Darling introduced the Bushranging Act to defeat the new wave of crime. Donahoe would live on in the rousing last lines of the folksong:

> Together we will conquer,
> Together we will die!
> 'For we scorn to live in slavery
> Bound down by iron chains!'

The Bushranging Act meant summary justice for any escaped convict who carried arms. The guilty would be executed 'within a day or two' of sentence; anyone harbouring or 'aiding and abetting' bushrangers or even 'stealing from a dwelling' also faced the death penalty.

Darling's first ten victims were walked to the gallows outside Bathurst Prison on 2 November 1830. Their leader, an English convict named Ralph Entwhistle, had been sentenced to transportation for life in Lancaster in 1827 for stealing clothes. A likeable young man, and certainly no rogue, he had worked as an assigned convict for a settler near Bathurst who treated him well and who trusted him sufficiently to take a drayload of wool down to Sydney. Entwhistle and his mate were bathing in the Macquarie River one sweltering afternoon in November, 1829 when Darling's entourage passed by. The local magistrate, a former officer named Evenden, ordered both convicts punished by fifty lashes.

ABOVE:
British soldiers apprehending bushrangers; a fanciful illustration from a German book of the period.

ABOVE, TOP:
The 'bushranger' Matthew Brady and two of his confederates in court.

LEFT:
High rewards were promised for the apprehension of
convict absconders and bushrangers

COLONIAL SECRETARY'S OFFICE,
SYDNEY, 12TH NOVEMBER, 1833.

SEVENTY
POUNDS REWARD.

WHEREAS it has been represented to the Government, that on the 5th Instant, SIX PRISONERS OF
THE CROWN, assigned to Messrs. MUDIE and LARNACH, of Hunter's River, together with another
individual at present unknown, after ROBBING Mr. MUDIE's House, and committing various OUTRAGES
on his Farm, took to the Bush, and, it is supposed, intended making for Sydney, conceiving that they would
escape detection by being dressed in the Clothes taken from Mr. MUDIE, and having with them Provisions, and
the following PROPERTY; viz.

Three Horses ; one a Bay Horse, with short tail, and another, a Jet-black Mare, about 4 years old, short
tail, star in face and branded L on off shoulder;

A Quantity of Wearing Apparel ; consisting of black and blue cloth coats and trowsers, white shirts, and
white trowsers, and coloured waistcoats ;

A Quantity of Plate ; consisting of table and tea spoons, and forks, some of which are crested with an Arm
in Armour, grasping a Scimetar ;

One double-barrelled gun; one single Hill; one pistol ditto, and masked I .I ; one ditto fowling piece ditto;
one new musket ; one old musket ;

Two large pistols and a tomahawk constructed with a knife and saw ;

NOTICE IS HEREBY GIVEN, THAT A REWARD OF
TEN POUNDS

will be paid for each of the said Offenders who may be apprehended and lodged in any of His MAJESTY's Jails.

NAMES, DESCRIPTION, &c. OF THE MEN.

ANTHONY HITCHCOCK, *alias* HATIL, *Lord Mobile,* 41 years of age, a native of Essex, a fisherman and bricklayer, 5 feet 6½ inches in height, ruddy fair complexion, light brown hair, grey eyes; slight scar on left cheek, large scar back of right leg, and was dressed when last seen in a blue cloth coat, with long tails, white duck trowsers, white shirt, when waistcoat, and straw hat.

JOHN POOLE, *Claudine,* 25, Dublin, joiner, 5 feet 3½ inches, ruddy freckled complexion, dark brown hair, blue eyes, fish on left arm, crucifix mark and sun on back of hand; small scar under left eyebrow, J P upper part of right arm; worn white duck trowsers, and has been lately punished.

JAMES REILLY, *Boswell Merchant,* 23, Dublin, carter and laborer, 5 feet 3½ inches, ruddy fair freckled complexion, brown hair, grey eyes, and wore a white shirt, dark trowsers, white jacket, and straw hat.

DAVID JONES, *Guildford,* 24, Drogheda, butcher, 5 feet 4 inches, ruddy freckled complexion, brown hair, light brown eyes, large scar between eyes, scar on left eyebrow, large scar outside upper part of left arm, and was dressed in white shirt, white trowsers, dark frock, and straw hat.

JOHN PERRY, *Asia (5),* 24, Essex, farm labourer, 5 feet 5½ inches, ruddy complexion, light brown hair, light brown eyes, and had on a white shirt, dark trowsers, dark jacket, and straw hat.

JAMES RYAN, *Eliza (6),* 17, County Tipperary, shoemaker's apprentice, 5 feet 1 inch, fair freckled complexion, brown hair, grey eyes, wart on back of right thumb, and another on back of left hand.

The INDIVIDUAL not known, is a fresh good-looking man, stands about 5 feet 5 inches high, and was dressed in a blue cloth jacket, yellow buttons, and fustian trowsers

BY HIS EXCELLENCY'S COMMAND.
Alex^{r.} McLeay.

ABOVE:
Captain Charles Sturt of the 39th Regiment. Humane but
ambitious, he became an outstanding explorer of the inland
and the first European to follow the Murray River to its mouth
in South Australia.

His 'heart boiling with hatred and revenge', Entwhistle talked a body of assigned convicts into joining him and raided the magistrate's homestead; in the
confrontation an overseer was shot and killed.
The group quickly decamped into the bush, calling on
other assigned convicts to join them. Estimates of the
gang's number ranged from 20 to 184; retreating into
the Abercrombie Ranges, the rebels drove off three
attacks mounted by police and troops sent from
Bathurst, Sydney and Goulburn (several of whom
were killed by the rebels). The ten survivors, half-
starved and out of ammunition, were finally captured
in October 1830 and were executed in Bathurst less
than a month later.

It was the largest rising since Castle Hill. Half the
convicted were Irish, the balance English and Scots,
and Entwhistle had led his men wearing a hat festooned with green ribbons, emblem of an Irish rebel.
This doomed insurrection by men driven to despair is
forgotten even in folklore; in the colony of the time it
increased the irrational fear of the Irish.

1828: Charles Sturt, explorer

Ralph Darling was a master of paperwork. He
reformed the civil service, which had grown overweight under Brisbane, organised an effective Customs Service and in 1829 formed a force of Mounted
Police from men in the garrison regiments. He
encouraged the plans of his aide-de-camp Captain
Charles Sturt (who had arrived in 1827 with the 39th
Regiment) to explore the Macquarie River beyond
the marshes Oxley had found. Given the extreme
drought, Sturt thought the marshes may have dried
up, facilitating their crossing.

Sturt's expedition leaving Bathurst in November
1828 included Hamilton Hume—already a renowned
bushman—as second-in-command, two soldiers and
eight convicts. Following the Macquarie, the party
reached the marshes to find them still thick and
impassable. The party trekked west, reaching a point
70 kilometres from Bourke and finally came upon 'a
noble river', which Sturt named the Darling. Parched
by thirst, the men dashed eagerly for its water only to
discover it was salt (caused by brine springs within
the river itself). They came across an Aboriginal camp
of seventy huts whose inhabitants were all dying of
disease, possibly smallpox.

Returning to base camp in February 1829, Sturt wrote out a report for the Governor and set out after two weeks' rest in an easterly direction, there to discover that the Macquarie River emerges from its marshes to join the Castlereagh about 15 kilometres from its junction with the Darling.

Though eager to discover the extent of the Darling River, Sturt was instead sent to discover the course of the Murrumbidgee. In November 1829 his expedition, proceeding along the river's northern bank, discovered that the Murrumbidgee, too, appeared to end in marshes. Undeterred, Sturt and his men felled trees and in seven days they built two boats, launched them and found a way past the reeds. Nearly 30 kilometres down the Murrumbidgee, they passed the entrance of the Lachlan, and three days later the river again contracted into reeds, which they rowed through to find the waters growing turbulent. On 14 January 1830 the explorers noticed that the river suddenly swung south and the boats were swept with increasing speed towards a river junction. In minutes they were carried into 'a broad and noble river'—the Murray, the westerly course of which Sturt was to follow past its junction with the Darling, on its long voyage to the sea.

Aboriginal tribesmen on both banks appeared to threaten them; and 600 of them one night surrounded Sturt's camp, but they proved friendly and inquisitive. In the course of the long river journey the tribesmen on the banks offered no violence to the Europeans. Following the Murray when it swung south, Sturt's expedition found themselves entering (on 7 February 1830) a huge lake—Lake Alexandrina—which was separated only by a sand bar from Encounter Bay.

The return journey, rowing against the current, was an even greater ordeal. Exhausted, Sturt's party reached Yass three months later and its leader rode into Sydney on 25 May 1830 to report to Darling that the Murray flowed from its modest stream in the Alps westward to South Australia itself.

The extent of the colony seemed infinite. By 1829 so many settlers were pasturing their flocks of sheep in areas still unmapped that Darling issued an order limiting settlement strictly to the nineteen counties around Sydney. His edict was ignored. Where the sheep wandered, settlers followed. The Squatting Age was about to begin.

1831: 'He's Off!'—Governor Darling recalled

In August 1831 the Government Notices in Sydney announced and explained a radical new decision by the Colonial Office: no land was to be disposed of by the Governor by grant—all crown lands would in future be sold by auction and the proceeds used to bring out free settlers. Two months later Ralph Darling received a letter from the Colonial Office recalling him to England. To celebrate the event Wentworth held a memorable gala ball at Vaucluse House where bands played and oxen were roasted for the delight of his friends and Darling's enemies. On the day of the Governor's departure the *Monitor* proclaimed 'He's Off—The Reign of Terror is Ended!'

Darling returned to the humiliation of having to defend his name in court: the echoes of the Sudds–Thompson case were still sounding when he died in 1864, reviled, unjustly, as a tyrant.

OPPOSITE:
Disturbing the tranquil growth of the colonies was increasing friction with the Aborigines.

In 1816 Governor Davey of Van Diemen's Land issued this broadside for the native peoples to remind them that Aborigines and Europeans would suffer the same harsh punishment for disturbing the peace. It had little effect.

Chapter 4
The Struggle for Freedom

From the 1830s to 1851

1830s: The colony becomes a problem

THE UNEXPECTED GROWTH OF THE AUSTRALIAN settlements during the 1820s left the British government with increased costs and a growing quandary. The colonies had been planned as convict settlements, they were developing far beyond expectations and free settlers were demanding a say in their future. Yet free settlers were few. The bulk of the population were convicts, and there were practically no women.

The 1828 census, the accuracy of which Governor Darling was rightly proud, had revealed the alarming imbalance between the sexes. Well into the late 1830s there were 333 males for every 100 females in New South Wales, and moralists were describing the colony as a 'Sink of Iniquity and Depravity'. Several shiploads of English females had been brought out, but they proved to be unruly at best, drunken viragos at worst. Many were veterans of English gaols, where conditions contributed little to their manners. The Irish girls were more subdued and better behaved but few young Protestant males favoured a Catholic marriage, despite Catholic Emancipation in 1829 (when all restrictions on Catholics practising their religion and holding official office were removed).

Australia had not been won by military conquest but had simply been claimed. According to Crown Law officers, the king and his ministers had no right to levy taxes from the colonists, nor had the governor. 'New South Wales cannot be administered with reference to the ordinary and established maxim of good government,' the respected civil servant James Stephen informed the Secretary of State in July 1830. 'To combine the discipline required of a gaol with the freedom of action essential to a remote and increasing Colony is a problem which the founders of New South Wales left to be resolved by their successors …'

He added, in postscript, that 'a Perfect Solution being evidently impossible, recourse must be had to Compromise and Anomalies.' Australia would grow from the English genius for compromise.

OPPOSITE:
Thomas Peel was seen by satirists as plucking clean the Swan River migrants.

BELOW:
Most convicts gained a ticket of leave that made them workers under contract to landowners or wealthy families, with some freedom of movement.

The birth of Western Australia

The first free colony: Swan River

The Swan River colony, founded in 1829, was the first to be made by free settlers and encouraged by a government cognisant of the fact that convict colonies were fraught with abnormalities. Captain James Stirling, who had investigated the Swan River region in 1827 and rhapsodised over its beauty and suitability for settlement, met with nothing but frustration in his attempts to convince the British government that the French might well annex western Australia unless a decision was made. In the summer of 1828 Stirling wrote to his brother from London: 'About three weeks ago I persuaded the Colonial Office people about the necessity of immediately occupying that Territory and I left town convinced that they would set about it immediately. I returned there last week but found them trembling at the thought of increased expenditure, and nothing as yet done...' On visiting Downing Street again in October 1828 he was frustrated to discover that the officials had left for their autumn holidays.

James Stirling

James Stirling was another of the determined Scots who shaped Australian history by qualities of sheer persistence. He was also well connected by marriage to powerful members of parliament. As a young naval captain on half-pay he had married Ellen, the daughter of John Mangles, MP, a wealthy farmer from Surrey: He had fallen in love at first sight of her. She was a girl of uncommon beauty and spirit. On a visit to Mangles' farm, he saw Ellen trying to ride two donkeys at the same time. She was fourteen at the time and he proposed to her on her fifteenth birthday.'She prefers riding on horseback, swinging, driving the donkey-chaise and rowing the boat to dancing and communing sentimentally with the Beaux,' Mrs Mangles wrote in announcing her daughter's engagement.'Indeed it was but yesterday she said she did not like any gentleman much, but doubtless in that respect her taste will alter!' But she had a good deal of character and Captain Stirling was 'unimpeachable for honour and integrity, intelligent mind, handsome face and figure'. James and Ellen Stirling would be the makers of Western Australia.

ABOVE:
Captain James Stirling, RN, later one of the founding fathers of the Colony of Western Australia.

Five months after Stirling's latter complaint of government inactivity, the Colonial Office was instructed to claim New Holland for the British Crown and establish a colony at Swan River; Stirling would be its Lieutenant-Governor. In April 1829 the warship HMS *Challenger* was ordered to sail forthwith from the Cape of Good Hope and establish British sovereignty at the Swan River before French ships reached the area. If a French settlement was found, it was to be politely evicted. According to legend a French diplomat called at the Colonial Office shortly afterwards to enquire about which parts of Australia were under the British flag; he received the smug answer 'All of it.'

ABOVE:
A view of Perth on the Swan River in 1842.

In June 1829 HMS *Sulphur*, carrying a detachment of soldiers and the transport *Parmelia* carrying the Governor and a group of emigrants, reached the Swan to find *Challenger* at anchor.

1829: Surviving at Swan River

The first brave attempt to settle Western Australia almost ended in failure. The *Parmelia* ran onto rocks, and was only with difficulty floated off. One of the colony's founders and Chairman of the Swan River Company was Thomas Peel (cousin of Sir Robert Peel), who had proposed that he settle 400 pioneers at Swan River in return for a grant of 250,000 acres (100,000 hectares). For every £3 contributed by settlers, they would receive 40 acres. The British government would face no financial outlay, and would provide only administrators.

Eighteen shiploads of English settlers landed at the Swan River during 1829. One of the emigrants, James Henty, wrote:

> The Governor has behaved very civilly to me, although in consequence of the first establishment being founded at Garden Island (which is nothing but sand) and subsequently removed to a place called Perth about 13 miles up the river, nothing whatever was prepared for our arrival and we had nothing to place our property, stock, or ourselves in; everybody lives in tents ... including the Governor.

The Stirlings set an example to all, though the Lieutenant-Governor occasionally walked around barefoot. One settler called Ellen Stirling 'a paragon of perfection'. In the historian Marnie Bassett's words: 'Aged 23, a brunette, she was a happy mixture of sense and simplicity, sweetness and vivacity; moreover she was ready to rough it with the rest.'

By 1830 more than 4000 emigrants were clearing the bush. Disappointment and financial ruin were their only rewards. The soil proved poor, crops failed, vegetation was insufficient to feed their sheep and cattle. Axes broke on the hard Karri

ABOVE:
The era of immigration began in the 1830s: a vessel from England arriving in Sydney Harbour. In the background is the new Government House, completed in 1845.

and Jarrah timber. 'The Land here is very unpromising and the capabilities of the Colony have been vastly overrated,' Henty wrote before deciding to leave and try his luck in Van Diemen's Land. With English commonsense he informed his family: 'My plan is not to lay out a shilling unless I can do so to sell again with advantage …' He would attempt to exchange his grant for one in Van Diemen's Land, establish a sheep farm and trade in imported goods.

By 1832 only 1500 hardy pioneers remained, the majority having left for New South Wales or Van Diemen's Land. Among the many who returned to England was Thomas Peel, who had lost his £50,000 capital and died bankrupt.

The dispossessed Aborigines had begun to dispute European settlement. In 1834, following attacks on settlers south of Perth Governor Stirling led a detachment of soldiers and colonists to 'punish the natives'. They tracked down two fleeing groups of Aborigines and killed up to fifty of them. One soldier was killed in an action known later as the 'Pinjarra massacre'.

The Stirlings stubbornly stayed on until 1839 (apart from a two-year absence in England to report to the authorities) to manifest their faith in the settlement. They won nothing but praise from the settlers. But even before the end of the first decade the colony had been admitted a failure and settlers soon petitioned the British government to provide them with convict labour to ensure the settlement's survival. London was happy to provide them, for the eastern colonies were threatening revolt unless transportation to their shores ceased. The convict age in Western Australia was mercifully brief, from 1850 to 1868, but the west would remain the cinderella of Australian colonies until the golden glow of the 1890s.

The birth of South Australia

If Western Australia's birth was unusual, South Australia's would be even more so. It would be not only free of the convict taint, but a New Utopia, a social experiment without precedent.

Kangaroo Island, at the mouth of the St Vincent's Gulf, was considered an ideal place for settlement, close to the sea lanes and, from all reports, possessing abundant fresh water. In 1819 a sea captain named Sutherland had spent seven months there during a sealing voyage. 'There were no natives on the island,' he wrote, but there were numerous whites—a motley tribe of escaped convicts and seamen who lived there with black women. 'They are complete savages,' Sutherland wrote, 'living in bark huts like the natives, not cultivating anything, and living entirely on kangaroos, emus and small porcupines, and getting spirits and tobacco in return for skins. They dress in kangaroo skins, without linen', he added in disapproval, 'and smell like foxes.'

Edward Gibbon Wakefield: flawed visionary

Edward Gibbon Wakefield was living in uncivilised surroundings in Newgate Gaol, and also lacking adequate linen, when he began scribbling his theories on colonisation. He too had lived with women, and for abducting his second wife, a young heiress, was now behind bars. The circumstances were bizarre even in an age when ambitious men would go to extraordinary lengths to marry money.

Like James Stirling, Wakefield had determined to make a 15-year-old girl his wife. She was also named Ellen. Miss Turner, the object of his affections, had been enticed from her home on the ruse that her mother was ill. By the magic of his charm Wakefield had convinced her during the long coach ride to the Scottish border that they should marry, and this they did, at Gretna Green. The happy couple had then left for France and were living in domestic bliss when the girl's father charged Wakefield with abduction. To prove that he was an English gentleman, the offender returned to London to face the charge and in a sensational trial in 1827 was found guilty and sentenced to three years in gaol.

Prison transformed Wakefield into a social reformer. From his cell in Newgate Wakefield published in 1829 a collection of writings called *A Letter from Sydney*, which purported to be a description of the glowing opportunities awaiting emigrants in Australia. It aroused great interest; for everything Wakefield wrote—unlike everything he did—was based on common sense.

Wakefield's imaginative *Letter* described the attempts of a young emigrant to create a home in a land of beauty and opportunity in which he was thwarted by an

ABOVE:
Edward Gibbon Wakefield, dreamer and publicist extraordinaire.

indolent convict population who practised upon each other unnatural vice. This was particularly shocking to English readers for the 1828 census had confirmed that the population of New South Wales was not only predominantly criminal but also three-quarters male. The convict experiment was, to all intelligent sensibilities, a disgrace and a failure, a blot on England's name.

What Wakefield propounded in his writings was nothing less than a complete rethinking of colonial policy; in time the gaolbird would be ranked with Lord Durham, the champion of colonial self-government, as one of the makers of the modern British Empire—one based not on coercion but on English freedoms. Wakefield proposed a 'systematic colonisation' of the Antipodes for England's surplus population, by the establishment of settlements in which people of sound character, the sexes neatly balanced to promote a normal society, would create new lives and enjoy all the democratic rights of people of moderate wealth in the Old Country.

ABOVE:
The Third Earl Grey, the long-suffering Colonial Secretary and son of Prime Minister Lord Grey.

1830: Age of reform

Wakefield's theories were revolutionary, but the 1830s was a decade of revolutionary reform. In 1830, while Europe was wracked by revolution, the men of Kent marched from village to village smashing mills and machinery. The 'Swing Riots' were suppressed brutally: nine workers were hanged and 415 men sentenced to transportation to Australia. (Five years later Governor Arthur would grant pardons to 250 of these unfortunate men in Van Diemen's Land.) England itself was approaching a political watershed. In November 1830 the Whigs were swept into power under Lord Grey to begin a half-century of Liberal reform broken only briefly by short-lived Tory governments. In that year rebellions had broken out in Paris, Vienna, Brussels, toppling rulers and autocracy. Upheaval was in the air and the English averted revolution by rapid reforms.

England's population, now 14 million, had doubled since 1800; pressure everywhere was for reform. In 1832 the Great Reform Bill was passed, enlarging England's minuscule electorate from 500,000 to 750,000 but sweeping away the system of rotten and pocket boroughs that had made Parliament a mockery. In 1833 Goderich, the future Earl of Ripon, fumblingly introduced a Bill to abolish slavery within the British Empire; it was enacted into law the following year. In 1837 when both British and French Canada broke into revolt, Prime Minister Grey's son-in-law, Lord Durham, would be despatched to Quebec and Ottawa to report on affairs; he took with him Wakefield to draft the document that granted Canada self-government,

There was obviously more to Wakefield than met the eye. He was, it transpired, a devout Quaker—of all sects the most respected—a cousin of Elizabeth Fry, the prison reformer, and a descendant of the great historian Edward Gibbon, with whom he shared a wonderful way with words. He had abducted the young girl and whisked her to Gretna Green, he explained, because a rich wife's dowry would enable him to enter the House of Commons and devote his life to social reform.

1831 The Wakefield Scheme

In 1831 Wakefield formed the first of his Colonisation Committees with his follower Robert Gouger and was gratified when some of Lord Grey's most trusted colleagues and friends joined it: Grey's own son, Viscount Howick; Goderich; the philosopher John Stuart Mill; George Grote the historian; and William Molesworth, later chairman of the committee that in 1838 would recommend the cessation of transportation. The age of the colonial reformers had begun.

Wakefield regarded the ill-organised attempt to colonise the Swan River as an example of ineptitude. He saw the orderly sale of land as the key to any colony's success. If it were too cheap, anybody could buy it; if it were too expensive few could afford it. He recommended a 'sufficient price'—in excess of £1 an acre—as being within the reach of most emigrants who had the energy to work to pay for it and the financial resources to employ labour. This land must be surveyed in advance of the arrival of emigrants. Proceeds from the sale of land would be used to sponsor the emigration of family groups and honest tradesmen—decent, law-abiding folk who could be entrusted to develop political institutions that would reflect credit on Great Britain.

In 1831 British colonial policy underwent a radical change. Ripon's Land Act ended the system of grants and introduced the sale of land. The new scheme, so perfect in theory, also worked perfectly in practice: 'The extent of revenue raised from the sale of unsettled crown lands in New South Wales exceeds the most sanguine expectations,' the Permanent Under Secretary, James Stephen, wrote in 1837, 'and there is reason to believe that the amount arising from this source during the present year will not fall short of £100,000 ...' Even the Lords of the Treasury were happy, for the colonies were finally returning money.

The stimulus to the Ripon reforms was Ripon's Under Secretary of State, Howick, who, on succeeding his father as the 3rd Earl Grey, would play a dominant role in formulating British policy towards the Australian colonies during his period as Colonial Secretary from 1846 to 1852.

Grey, like his father the Prime Minister, was firmly committed to a program of gradual reform. 'I conceive that, by acquisition of its Colonial Dominions, this nation has incurred a responsibility of the highest kind,' he would write in the 1840s, and among these responsibilities he numbered 'diffusing among millions of the human race, the blessings of Christianity and civilisation'. He was obstinate, haughty but intensely intelligent. The gossip Grenville wrote of him: 'Those who know him are aware that a man more high-minded, more honourable and conscientous [sic] does not exist, but he ... cannot be relied on ... The House of Commons swarms with his enemies.'

BELOW:
Early pamphlets encouraging migration often painted too rosy a picture of conditions in Australia.

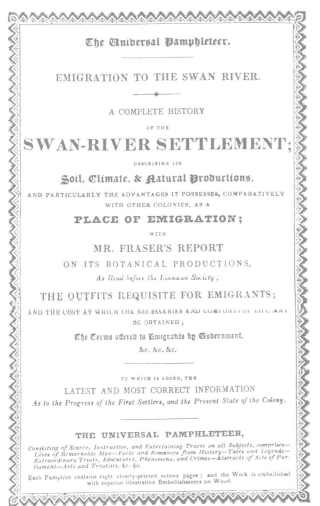

Grey never ceased to give credit to Wakefield for producing the theories that he put into practice. 'A clever scoundrel,' was the nobleman's view of the bustling Quaker, and their uneasy relationship came to a sudden end in 1846 with an unseemly shouting match in Grey's office. Two days later Wakefield had a stroke from which he never completely recovered. 'Yet Wakefield was indispensable,' writes the historian of Empire Charles Carrington. 'He boasted that thirty-six Members of Parliament called one weekend at his little house in Riegate to consult him about colonial questions. He drafted the constitution of New Zealand sitting with [C.B.] Adderley one afternoon in the garden of the latter's house. Provided he remained in the background all went well.'

Wakefield later emigrated to New Zealand, as two of his brothers had done before him (one of them to be killed by Maori) and lived to see the Canterbury Pilgrims and the Scots at Dunedin create the settlements he had dreamed of in his cell in Newgate.

ABOVE:
The scene that greeted migrants to Adelaide in the 1840s.

South Australia—the new Utopia

In 1832 Wakefield and his associate Gouger formed a joint stock company with the object of founding a settlement in South Australia and in 1834 Parliament passed an Act setting up this Utopia—the Province of South Australia.

The province would be revolutionary in other aspects: the governor would be nominated by the board of the South Australian Company, not appointed by the British government. When the number of males of voting age and qualifications exceeded 10,000, there would be an elected Legislative Assembly: a democracy. There would be complete freedom of worship. All Christian denominations would be welcome and all would be supported financially in proportion to the number of their members. This last freedom attracted many German Lutherans, who were just the type of sober, industrious folk the board saw as ideal emigrants.

There would be no settlement before the land was surveyed. Land would be sold for £1 an acre. Wakefield felt this was far too cheap, and quickly lost interest in the colonial child he had fathered. The Colonisation Commissioners stipulated that every 80 acres of rural land purchased would include a bonus of one acre of city land. There seemed to be no problem of settlement for which a solution had not been already provided. When insufficient land was sold, a wealthy Baptist, George Fife Angas, purchased it in order to provide the colony with funds; he also funded the passages of 200 Prussian Lutherans and followed them out to the colony in 1851.

In 1835 the board offered the governorship to Colonel Charles Napier, the dashing soldier who had commanded the 102nd Regiment—the Botany Bay Rangers—

in the West Indies and who had won fame in the Peninsular Wars. Napier doubted that the colony could be self-supporting, as the board claimed. 'I have no ambition to be the head of such a milk and water colonial government,' he informed them. Five years later he wrote: 'I was mad not to go out as Governor. I could have founded a kingdom.'

Colonel Francis Light

A duller alternative to Napier was found: Captain John Hindmarsh, RN, a choleric man who stood on ceremony and alienated all by his manner. A better choice would have been Colonel Francis Light, who was appointed Surveyor-General and sent on ahead of the main body of emigrants in order to explore the region and establish a site for the settlement.

Light was half Malayan—his mother was said to have been a Malay princess—a brave officer and a talented artist, highly regarded and well liked by his brother officers. He had in turn sent his deputy on ahead, George S. Kingston, an Irishman, whom some credit with having chosen the site of the colony's future capital of Adelaide. Light arrived in Spencer Gulf on the Rapid in August 1836, and quickly rejected Kangaroo Island as an unsuitable birthplace for a settlement. But to its north, on a broad river that flowed into the Gulf lay flat country whose backdrop of hills seemed a perfect setting for a city. Its only drawback was the intense heat of its summer.

1836: Adelaide founded

Light and Kingston laid out the future city of Adelaide in grand style, providing boulevardes of immense width and a town centre lapped by hectares of parkland. Like much in South Australia, its planning reflected thinking ahead of its time. Already weakened by tuberculosis and soon broken completely in health by his exertions, Light wrote to Wakefield in May 1838 in answer to criticisms of the slowness of his surveying: 'The Commissioners know not the manner I was compelled to work myself, trudging along the banks of this river carrying my own theodolite on my shoulders with often only two other men to help me … and be obliged also to travel the same ground over and over again placing my flags—this in the very hottest month of the year—and then to get nothing but abuse from my masters at home.'

By 1838 nearly sixty ships carrying 6000 colonists had left Europe for South Australia. Among them was Colonel Gawler, who arrived to succeed Hindmarsh and found chaos. Few emigrants had settled on the land and most were living despondently in Adelaide. Under Gawler, 7000 acres were soon under cultivation and 5000 emigrants were arriving annually, but the expenses of good administration were so high that the commissioners were refusing to honour the bills Gawler was drawing. South Australia was producing an abundance of wheat and sheep but was effectively bankrupt.

To the colonists' humiliation the Province of South Australia was declared a Crown Colony in 1842 and Captain George Grey of the Royal Engineers appointed Governor. Only twenty-seven years old but already famous for his exploration of the Western Australian coast, Grey ruthlessly cut government expenditure. As if in token of better times, the settler Francis Dutton discovered copper at Kapunda; more deposits were found at Burra Burra. In the beautiful Barossa Valley the settlers found that vine cuttings brought from Germany grew vigorously. In 1843 John Ridley, a miller and lay preacher, invented a reaping and threshing machine for the colony's high-standing wheat and by the late 1840s South Australia was the only colony exporting the grain.

The province had, in less than seven years, proved to be the model of economic growth and social harmony its founders had planned. It was the only colony untarnished by convict pain and native bloodshed. It would remain a model of progress for a century.

In 1863 South Australia was given the huge uninhabited segment of northern Australia later known as the Northern Territory and by 1869 the government in Adelaide had founded a capital for the region at Port Darwin and was laying plans to connect it by an overland telegraph line.

1831: Governor Bourke — liberal rule

When Major-General Sir Richard Bourke, formerly acting Governor of Cape Colony, was offered the governorship of New South Wales in 1831 he wrote to a friend: 'I seem to alternate between the land of Hottentots and the land of Pickpockets.' He had been hoping for the offer of Canada or Bermuda (a non-slave Crown Colony)—two of the plums on the vice-regal tree—for his reputation as an enlightened administrator stood high.

The salary of £5000 a year was a princely inducement to a distinguished soldier living

BELOW:
An enlightened and popular Governor: the Protestant Irishman Sir Richard Bourke.

ABOVE:
News from Home:
Impression by the English
artist Baxter of Australian
settlers receiving letters.

on half-pay in Ireland with a young family to support, as was a colleague's opinion that 'the Australian colonies are the most thriving colonies of the present day, and every day increase in importance'.

Bourke and his family arrived in Sydney in December 1831 to one of the warmest receptions ever given to a new Governor. His reputation as a liberal had preceded him. Every inch the soldier, Bourke was of the Protestant Anglo-Irish Ascendancy yet sympathetic to the Catholic Irish who had suffered in his home-land under what he called an 'abominable system of government'. A former Grenadier Guards officer, he had also attended Oxford University. 'This place has astonished me,' Bourke wrote soon after arriving. 'With a little care it will become a very valuable colony'.

'I cannot tell you how delighted I am with this superb country … the climate, the soil and the unknown resources it contains,' wrote another new arrival, Potter Macqueen.

The Squatters

Bourke's arrival coincided with the belated introduction of land sales and the arrival of government-sponsored free emigrants. But again the peculiar conditions in New South Wales made a mockery of the law's good intent: settlers were already running their flocks and herds and building shepherd's huts and homesteads on land beyond the Nineteen Counties—land for which they had not paid.

'Squatting' was impossible to prevent or police. 'Not all the armies in England, not a hundred thousand soldiers scattered through the bush', Governor Bourke wrote to London in the mid-1830s, 'could drive back those herds within the

Nineteen Counties.' How to deal fairly with this new breed—enterprising pioneers to some, greedy land-takers to others—would consume the efforts of administrators for the next forty years.

Bourke the reformer

Bourke's administration came like a summer breeze to a discontented colony. In the year of Bourke's arrival convicts or former convicts comprised 43 per cent of the population but the arrival of free-born emigrants would see the convict component fall to 23 per cent a decade later, and the free majority were soon demanding wider freedoms and greater rights.

During Bourke's period in office the Governor consulted the Legislative Council 233 times; Darling had summoned it on only 85 occasions. Juries of military officers for criminal cases remained until the end of his period in office but in 1833 Bourke used his casting vote to confirm trial by jury for all civil cases. He confirmed Catholic emancipation in the colony in 1835, appointing Bishop Polding Vicar-General to his Catholic flock; in 1836 a Church Act extended this equality.

The Governor's attempt to introduce 'national schools' (non-denominational) foundered on the bitter opposition mounted by Bishop Broughton, the Church of England primate and conservative voice in the six-man council. Chief Justice Forbes, a liberal, commiserated with the Governor: 'I do not think the Aristocracy of New South Wales are sufficiently advanced with the times to understand that poor people have any right to education at all—it is considered a very democratic and dangerous thing'. Bourke advocated the abolition of transportation, abolished the death penalty for forgery and sheep-stealing and was delighted when Chief Justice Forbes restored full civil rights to Emancipists.

In 1836 the Governor forwarded to the Colonial Office a petition requesting a democratically elected Assembly signed by 6000 names. (A petition requesting no change in the status quo bore only 329 names, the Macarthurs being among them.) Bourke suggested the enlargement of the Legislative Council, with two-thirds of its members being elected. 'If you tax free men in a convict colony, you must in common honesty, let them have some voice in the spending of their money,' his ally Forbes warned the Colonial Office.

There was little alleviation of the sufferings of the convicted. During the 1830s when transportation was reaching a peak (4000 felons a year were arriving by 1835) no fewer than 330,000 strokes of the lash were ordered and given in New South Wales alone. Three regiments, scattered in detachments across Australia, were required to act as guards for convicts—a role the soldiers hated. Macquarie's vision of a land where all would be equal and past sins expunged had become a nightmare of cruelty.

ABOVE:

The rule of law: Judge
Roger Therry, a friend
of Bourke's and one of
the first Irish Catholics
to hold high office in
New South Wales.

'A sturdy manliness'

The free migrant Alexander Harris, whose reminiscences of life in the 1830s are the brightest and best of the colonial portraits, described former convicts as good men all, law abiding and honest. 'Like most of those who had risen from the ranks of the prison population by their own efforts,' Harris wrote of one Emancipist farmer, 'there was a sort of sturdy manliness about his character which was very agreeable'. Judge Therry who, as noted earlier, had seen a convict sentenced to fifty lashes for failing to raise his hat to a magistrate, agreed that even hardened criminals—London pickpockets and thieves from other English cities who had grown up in ignorance, 'knowing nothing on their arrival, beyond criminal practices'—became useful and hardworking citizens when they earned their freedom.

Harris was also sickened by the punishments he saw meted out in Sydney—prisoners lashed to the triangle to endure floggings without uttering a cry, a groan or a prayer for mercy. Those property owners who treated their convicts with humanity, he stated, were rewarded with loyalty and a 'willing obedience', while cruel masters drove their servants into surly rebelliousness.

Bourke did away with summary sentences by tyrannic magistrates and with the corrupt methods used to 'assign' convict labourers, replacing these practices with a committee to regulate this valued and much abused source of free labour. The Governor was meticulous in his attention to convicts' applications for probation, or tickets of leave. 'I should indeed be an unworthy representative of His Majesty if I refused to receive a petition from a man in bonds,' he wrote to Therry.

1834: Mutiny on Norfolk Island

In 1834, 200 of the convicts on Norfolk Island, shouting 'Liberty or death!' had attacked their guards and taken up crude weapons in an attempt to seize Morrisett and his equally hated lieutenant, Captain Fyans. Fifteen of them were shot down by the garrison and fifty wounded before order was restored. Judge Burton, sailing to the island to conduct their trial, was horrified by the punishments meted out to the prisoners. 'This abomination on earth,' Therry called the prison, where 'the lash, the dungeon, and the scaffold were the only instruments used to reform and reclaim fallen man'. No guards had been killed but thirty of the prisoners were sentenced to death. Burton begged Bourke to spare the lives of sixteen of the condemned, and Bourke did this. But fourteen others were hanged on Norfolk Island, dressed in white, on the scaffold overlooking the ocean.

In 1834 the rule of the autocratic visionary, George Arthur, was coming to an end. His was a difficult fief to rule. While the proportion of convicts in New South Wales was falling, in Van Diemen's Land it was rising. In 1830 Arthur began building the enormous prison at Port Arthur and decided to end black–white conflict by

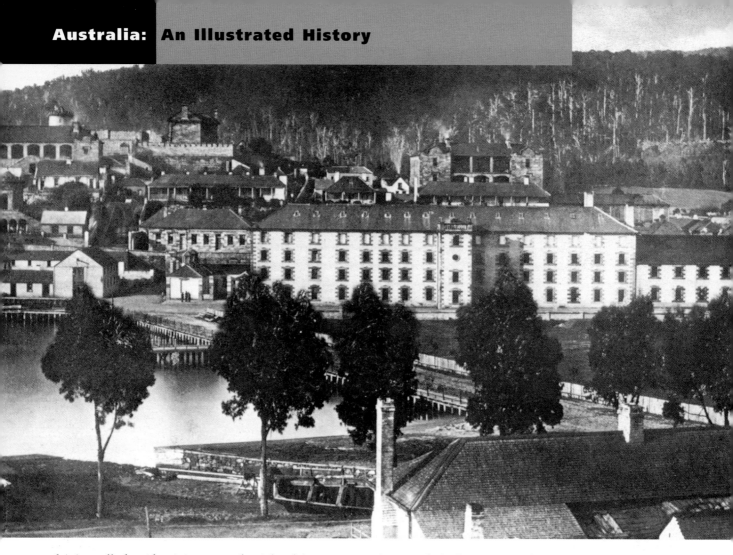

ABOVE:
Port Arthur prison.

OPPOSITE:
Relics of the convict days.

driving all the Aborigines on the island into one region, with ludicrous results. Organised with military precision, a line of soldiers and settlers was formed into a human chain that moved across the island; it ended with the capture only of an old man and a boy. The expensive operation was much criticised. Arthur's 'Protector' of Aborigines, George Robinson, succeeded where soldiers had failed, convincing the remaining tribes to follow him to a new land where they would be safe from the white man's gun. The Aborigines of Van Diemen's Land were removed to reserves on the islands of Bass Strait, where they seemed to lose the will to live. Truganini, who died in 1876, was the last full-blood Tasmanian Aborigine. A century later, the part-Aboriginal descendants of Tasmania's original inhabitants would be among the leaders of the movement that achieved recognition of Aboriginal rights in Australia.

1833: Port Arthur

In 1833 Governor Arthur opened the Port Arthur prison that became his pride and joy. It was one in which convicts would work their way to redemption, where harsh regulations would change their natures. The public buildings and bridges that grace Tasmania and Port Arthur's crumbling ruins are all memorials to George Arthur's single-minded desire to create a form of civilisation from nothingness. Arthur's sentencing of a convict found attending the races to 100 lashes and a swift hanging saddened his few remaining supporters. At a mass meeting in Hobart in July 1834 the lawyer J.T. Gellibrand proposed to acclamation 'That we consider trial by Jury the indispensable Right of all citizens of the Crown'.

Reforming 'The System'

Arthur was recalled to London in 1836 and his replacement, the naval hero and Arctic explorer Sir John Franklin, arrived in the following year to govern a colony

that on one hand demanded democratic institutions yet on the other depended for its growth on convict labour. Franklin was both brave and humane; icebergs had failed to terrify him but he had trembled with grief in witnessing his first naval flogging. His loving wife Jane sustained his spirit and his private secretary, Captain Alexander Maconochie, became a spokesman for reform.

Maconochie, a former naval officer who had been captured by the French and knew the soul-destroying nature of prison, became, in the words of Robert Hughes, 'the one and only inspired penal reformer to work in Australia throughout the whole history of Transportation'. The Captain's report on the failure of 'The System' and the suffering it inflicted reached Secretary of State for the Colonies Grey and his Prime Minister, Lord John Russell, in 1838; it was just the ammunition Russell needed to swing parliamentary attitudes towards reform.

The end at Norfolk Island

In 1837 a House of Commons committee had met to decide whether transportation should be discontinued. The evidence it collected disturbed the gentlemen who interviewed witnesses of the horrors of convict life in the Australian colonies. The Reverend Naylor, chaplain at Norfolk Island, stated: 'I saw very young boys seized up and lost; I saw decent and respectable men, nay gentlemen, thrown among the vilest villains, to be tormented by their bestialities.' Bourke's successor, Governor Gipps, confirmed that homosexuality was indeed rife among the English convicts, though hardly known among the Irish Catholics. Life was just as bestial

ABOVE, LEFT:
Captain John Franklin, naval officer and explorer, who was Governor of Van Diemen's Land from 1836 to 1843.

ABOVE:
Jane, Lady Franklin, devoted wife and inveterate traveller. She conducted classes for young girls during her time in Van Diemen's Land.

on the chain gangs. Norfolk Island itself was such a cesspool of brutality and vice that 'many preferred death to being in that penal settlement'.

Maconochie was appointed Commandant of Norfolk Island in 1840 to put into practice his theory that kindness and humanity could improve all but the most hardened. On his first day he proclaimed a public holiday and opened the prison gates, permitting the prisoners to go anywhere on the island providing they returned at bugle call. The new Commandant requested musical instruments in order to form an orchestra, enough books to form a library, and instituted a points system with the promise of a ticket of leave for prisoners of good behaviour. (Of the 920 second-offenders who earned their ticket and were returned to the mainland only twenty were subsequently arrested for a crime.) He and his wife and children walked among the prisoners without protection and without harm befalling them. News reached Governor Gipps that the convicts were eating at tables at mealtime instead of squatting in the dirt, and performing in amateur theatricals. The reforms created great criticism. Even Gipps, normally a fair and far-sighted man, thought that Maconochie was going too far.

To counter the rising crime wave in the England and Ireland of the 1840s, a new experiment in punishment was being adopted: isolation of felons in tomb-like prisons. Maconochie was recalled in 1843 (as was Governor Franklin, who was also a victim of intrigue by his enemies) and replaced by a harsh bully, Major Childs. Floggings were resumed with gusto but unnatural vice flourished and discipline deteriorated. 'The curse of Almighty God', the Anglican chaplain on the island wrote in horror to Earl Grey, 'must sooner or later fall upon a nation which can tolerate the continuance of a state of things so demoniacal and unnatural.' His cry from the heart failed to move Whitehall.

In 1846 a set of hardened convicts—'the Ring'—led another revolt, killing four soldiers. Twelve convicts were hanged for their murder. The new Commandant, John Price, was a cold-eyed sadist who instituted a reign of terror and was forced to resign in 1850 when his cruelties were exposed.

Norfolk Island itself was closed down in 1855. The staff departed and the prisoners were transferred to Port Arthur, the chilling 'model' prison. Norfolk Island had witnessed the six ages of punishment: execution, banishment, brutality, reform, probation and isolation.

'Transportation is slavery'

'Transportation, though chiefly dreaded as exile, undoubtedly is much more than exile,' a House of Commons committee stated, 'it is slavery as well.'

While admitting that many, possibly most, of the convicts may have experienced reasonable treatment as assigned servants or under tickets of leave, the committee recognised that the cruelty suffered by others was ineffective in deterring crime. Instead it hardened the sufferers. The committee in 1838 recommended the cessation of transportation. It was the first clear, rational judgement to come from the Commons in fifty years.

Yet it would be a mistake to think that moral outrage was the main reason for the announcement of the ending of transportation in 1840. The British government ceased transportation when it suited it to do so, Professor John Ward has reminded us, and just as promptly reintroduced it when conditions changed.

The Birth of Victoria

ABOVE:
'Australia the Pleasing':
a view of the rich
countryside of the future
Colony of Victoria.

The Port Phillip District

'This colony is like a healthy Child outgrowing its Clothes,' Governor Bourke informed Whitehall in October 1836. 'We have to let out a tuck every month ...' He had just dispatched Captain Lonsdale of the 4th Regiment to the new settlement at the head of Port Phillip Bay where colonists were arriving daily. The future colony of Victoria would be the first to be founded by Australians.

Hamilton Hume had discovered the rich hinterland at the head of the bay in company with Hovell in 1824, but had thought he was on the shores of the great bay of Westernport (which, confusingly, lies to its east). His report of the rich countryside excited the curiosity of land seekers.

In 1834, the Henty family, disappointed at both the Swan River settlement and Van Diemen's Land, crossed Bass Strait and settled on the mainland coast at Portland. In the same year other settlers from Van Diemen's Land—the 'Overstraiters'—began landing on the mainland's shores, where land lay for the taking.

John Batman

One of them was a 'loose-limbed Sydney native', a bounty hunter and farmer and the son of convict parents, John Batman (or Bateman). He had been farming near Launceston, married to a Currency Lass, Eliza Callaghan, by whom he had a brood of children. It was Batman who in 1826 had captured the bushranger Matt Brady, the Wild Colonial Boy of Van Diemen's Land. Batman was a man with big appetites—he was mad when drunk and voracious in his love of women—and yearned for status and riches.

In June 1835 Batman formed the Port Phillip Association with Swanston, Simpson, Wedge and Gellibrand. He crossed Bass Strait in the *Rebecca* with three servants and seven Aborigines, whom he hoped would serve as interpreters; and laden with trunks of blankets, mirrors and cheap trinkets to use as currency.

On the banks of the Yarra Batman explained to the chiefs of the Dutigallar tribe that he was coming to live among them and wished to purchase much land. For the cost of twenty pairs of scissors, fifty pounds of flour, twelve red shirts and other items, Batman signed with the seven chiefs (three of whom all answered to the name Jaga Jaga), a treaty granting him 600,000 acres of the richest land in the world. He agreed to pay an annual rent of blankets, tomahawks, scissors, clothes and flour.

Batman's treaty was declared null and void by Governor Bourke, who declared the settlers to be trespassers. Wedge arrived in August 1835 to find another group of interlopers: Batman's rival John Pascoe Fawkner, an inn-keeper and printer of the *Launceston Advertiser*, had sent them ahead of his own band of colonists.

Australia Felix

In March 1836 the Surveyor-General in Sydney, Major Mitchell, set out from Orange to explore the extent of the Darling River. His party numbered twenty-five men in all, equipped with bullock teams and herds of sheep, organised like an army. Mitchell was often prone to setting courses in conflict with his instructions and in June, having reached the Murray, he decided to follow its course west and 'explore

BELOW:
The founding of Melbourne: John Pascoe Fawkner treating with Aborigines.

From a drawing by William Strutt

the unknown regions beyond it'. Reaching the future site of Swan Hill he then progressed south-west into promising country, reaching the rugged Grampian ranges, which rise through winter mist like giant rocks. Crossing a river known to the Aborigines as the Wimmera, Mitchell and his party found to the south country that grew more verdant with every mile, and over which they 'moved merrily over hill and dale'.

Ten weeks after crossing the Murray, Mitchell reached the coast and a week later sighted a brig at anchor. He had reached Portland Bay and the Henty homestead. Returning overland to Sydney—he had been puzzled to sight through his telescope what appeared to be tents on the northern shores of Port Phillip Bay—Mitchell retraced his steps over 'flowering plains and green hills, fanned by the breezes of early spring', and reached Sydney to inform Governor Bourke that he had discovered another Eden. He named the future colony of Victoria 'Australia Felix'—Australia the Pleasant.

1837: Melbourne founded

The Port Phillip settlement was undergoing a lawless birth. The tribesmen speared sheep and an occasional stockman; Fawkner grew wealthy dispensing grog to Vandemonians whose thirst seemed unquenchable.

In September 1836 Bourke, in answer to the settlers' pleas for some 'established authority', dispatched Captain Lonsdale and a party of surveyors and soldiers to create a colony on the English model. Lord Glenelg at the Colonial Office had agreed that the circumstances were indeed 'novel and peculiar'.

In March 1837 Bourke and his vice-regal party arrived to proclaim the founding of Melbourne. In the full dress uniform of a Lieutenant-General, Bourke stood with Captain Hobson RN, Lonsdale, Surveyor Hoddle and the Vandemonians—John Batman, Fawkner and their confederates. 'At a respectable distance viewing the scene with a mixture of curiosity and fear were grouped about 200 aborigines, mostly men,' a witness wrote. 'Sir Richard looked remarkably well, with his usual soldierly bearing.'

ABOVE:
Charles La Trobe, first Lieutenant-Governor of the Port Phillip District.

TOP:
An early view of the infant township of Melbourne.

ABOVE:

The capable William Hobson (1793–1843), commander of HMS *Rattlesnake*.

Irish-born, he explored reaches of Port Phillip (his name was given to Hobson's Bay) and was entrusted with negotiating the Treaty of Waitangi in 1840.

'Melbourne is a beautiful site for a town,' Bourke informed Whitehall after naming the capital after the Prime Minister. 'I have had the satisfaction of affixing Whig names to the Bush.' The vice-regal party later dined sumptuously on a feast of kangaroo.

Victorians would adopt the comforting fiction that their colony grew to prosperity without great bloodshed, but the facts speak otherwise. Killings of the Aborigines became common. In 1840 a group of 300 Aborigines from around Melbourne under a leader called Jacky Jacky stole nearly 1500 sheep from stations on the Upper Yarra and were rounded up by troopers and dispersed. Attempts by Protector Robinson, the paragon of Van Diemen's Land, to form a 'native reserve' at Narre Warren—a small area surrounded by an ocean of squatters—resulted only in the Aborigines melting away into the bush: village life was not for them. The Gippsland pioneers were particularly ruthless in exacting vengeance on tribes if whites or sheep were speared.

Aboriginal customs and practices appalled the settlers. In intertribal battles the dead were often fallen upon and eaten raw by warriors—the internal organs, particularly the kidney fat, were highly prized. Constant killings of shepherds and stealing from the flocks—for the Aborigines found sheep ('jumbucks') delicious—were answered by punitive action that reduced the Aboriginal population of 10,000 by perhaps three-quarters in just five years.

'When our people find it necessary to defend themselves, a number of blacks, I am sorry to say, were shot', confessed W.J.T. Clarke, a squatter whose holdings covered 184,000 acres.

1840: New Zealand claimed

'Here's a pretty go!' wrote a young officer of the 80th Regiment in Sydney in his journal in March 1840. 'Who would ever have thought that I should have been ordered to New Zealand to have my head tattooed and baked after the savages have eaten me?' In that year New Zealand was proclaimed part of New South Wales and Bourke's invaluable naval captain Hobson sailed from Sydney with a detachment of the 80th Regiment to assert British sovereignty.

As early as the 1790s the remote, beautiful islands charted by Tasman and Cook were visited by traders and sealers (the first sealing ship from Sydney had put into

RIGHT:
A French artist's depiction of a Maori warrior. French interest in
New Zealand stimulated the British decision to claim the islands.

the Bay of Islands on the North Island in 1792). Samuel Marsden was active there and in 1815 brought Maori chieftains to Sydney to meet Macquarie. Europeans introduced Christianity, potatoes, pigs and guns to the Maori and took timber, shrunken heads and women in return. The lively trade forced the Colonial Office to remind Macquarie in 1817 that New Zealand 'is not part of His Majesty's dominions'.

Persistent reports of lawless behaviour by the whites, murders and tribal warfare caused Darling to request that the home government establish some form of British presence there. Rumours were also current that the French were planning to annex New Zealand.

In 1833 James Busby arrived as Resident Officer and in 1837 the first 2000 British settlers, followed in 1839 by a shipload of pioneers led by Edward Gibbon Wakefield's brother. In 1840 the British government was forced to act: New Zealand was annexed (it ceased to be part of Australia in 1841) and Hobson signed a treaty with the Maori chieftains at Waitangi confirming their land rights. The Treaty of Waitangi, however, failed to safeguard their rights and in 1845 the North Island broke out into open warfare between Maori and settlers. British regiments were sent across the Tasman from Sydney and in a spirited series of actions the troops, and the enlightened policy of the new Governor, Captain George Grey, restored peace. By 1854 New Zealand had its own extremely democratic constitution—and embarked on its own path to nationhood.

1836: Charles Darwin in Australia

When HMS *Beagle* arrived in Sydney in 1836, one of her passengers, the naturalist Charles Darwin, was impressed by its astounding growth. 'In the evening I walked through the town and returned full of admiration for the whole scene. It is a most magnificent testimony to the power of the English nation'. The *Beagle* had spent much time in Spanish America where poverty and slavery showed in every face, and Darwin wrote with some conceit: 'My first feeling was to congratulate myself that I was born an Englishman.'

Darwin's views of Australia were ambivalent. He found the society 'rancorously' divided, with 'much jealousy between the children of the rich emancipists and the free settlers'. He was depressed by the 'uniformity of vegetation' but thought the countryside and inns quite reminiscent of England. 'The iron gangs, or parties of convicts who have committed here some offence, appeared the least like England they were working in chains, under the charge of sentries with loaded arms.' He left Australia's shores, however, 'without sorrow or regret', disturbed by its strange evolution.

BELOW:
Charles Darwin.

The Squatters

The mainland colony was growing at the pace it takes sheep to move over grassland. In 1836, just before his term expired, Governor Bourke sought to regulate the movement inland by proclaiming areas 'Squatting Districts'. The settlers—the 'squatters'—were allowed to take out leases for payment of a nominal £10 a year for each property, irrespective of its size. Two years later Border Police were organised to collect the tax of a halfpenny per head of sheep and protect the shepherds and stockmen from attack by Aborigines.

'Wool is our wealth,' Bourke explained to a Colonial Office perplexed about his lenient attitude towards the squatters. In 1831 nearly 25 million pounds' (approx. 12.3 million kilos) weight of wool was exported from the Australian colonies, the majority of it from Van Diemen's Land; by 1837 the quantity had risen to more than 70 million pounds, 47 million pounds of which was produced by the graziers and squatters of New South Wales.

Even the Chief Justice was, until 1836, an illegal trespasser on crown land. 'I am a squatter!' Forbes told Bourke. (Chief Justice Forbes, recipient of the largest land grant ever made to a civil servant—10,000 acres (4050 ha)—had flocks on his station in the Hunter Valley and depastured them occasionally on the Liverpool Plains.)

The squatters, and their overseers, herdsmen and shepherds (squatters were mostly men of substance, with the means to employ others) probably did more to open Australia to settlement than any other set of individuals, but they had few champions and earned the enmity of the growing number of poorer free immigrants. But even the squatter's foe, Governor Gipps, would admit: 'The persons who form these stations may be said to be in Australia, the pioneers of civilisation.'

In 1836 Edward Henty was writing to Major Mitchell hoping to locate the fine pastures in Australia Felix that the Surveyor-General had described. Henty received no reply but he rode north 70 kilometres from Portland Bay and simply staked out a sheep run there.

In 1840 John Robertson, who had made a fortune in Van Diemen's Land, took up land next to the Hentys. 'They pointed out their land and I took possession of the land adjoining', he explained. But another hopeful, James Ritchie, who set out on foot to find land, was met with less kindness by the Hentys—'little tyrants' and 'cold-hearted misers' he called them. He soon staked out his own property, calling it Blackwood.

By 1839 the three Manifold brothers, originally from Cheshire in England, were squatters in rich country near Purrumbete. W.J.T. Clarke, a butcher who had left England in 1829 for Van Diemen's Land, was to build a dynasty at Sunbury; 'Big Clarke' soon had holdings that made him Victoria's largest landowner. The Scot Niel Black at Glenormiston and Samuel Winter at Murndall were another two of nearly eighty squatters who by the early 1840s had sequestered the best land in the Port Phillip District.

It was men's country—there were very few women. In 1836 Charles Darwin spent a night in the Bathurst Plains homestead of two newly arrived settlers. They were the Archer brothers from Scotland. 'The total want of almost every comfort was not attractive but future and certain prosperity was before their eyes,' Darwin wrote, 'and that not far distant'. The Archer brothers would later pioneer Queensland in epic cattle drives.

The overlanders

The 1830s gave birth to another breed of Australian folk hero. Men began to drive their sheep and cattle overland to new settlements to sell them for a profit or discover unclaimed land on the way. In 1836 Joseph Hawdon, a Durham man, drove a mob of sheep from Sydney to Port Phillip and two years later, accompanied by Charles Bonney, took sheep and cattle from near Albury to Adelaide in the first of the epics of overlanding.

The new settlers put up simple dwellings close to springs or creeks, of wattle-and-daub or slab timber, the interiors of which were as unfinished as the exteriors. Pots, pans and muskets hung over a stone fireplace. A slaughtered sheep or kangaroo (a favoured dish when stewed as 'steamer') provided ample meat. Flour mixed with water and baked in the ashes—'damper'—formed their bread. Old bouillon tins made a perfect kettle or 'billy' and tea was drunk black with plenty of sugar. The fastidious grew vegetables or planted fruit trees. Horses, the settlers' most valuable possessions, were tethered outside, saddles removed.

Apart from attacks by Aborigines, the settlers' only fear was loneliness. Strangers were welcomed. Because ex-convicts were ashamed of their past, men were taken at face value, seldom asked questions, and seldom asked to pay for a night's food and shelter. It became an Australian tradition.

The wealthier, married squatters built stone homesteads of simple Georgian design with high-pitched roofs and wide verandahs similar to the bungalows of India; servants' quarters lay beyond the main building and stables. In the genteel age of the late Victorian era, mansions would rise in their place.

ABOVE:
Droving cattle overland.

BELOW:
Hawdon's great feat was celebrated with a public dinner.

PUBLIC
DINNER
TO
MR HAWDON

A number of persons having expressed a desire to testify their sense of the spirited and enterprizing conduct of Mr. HAWDON in bringing CATTLE overland from *New South Wales* to *Adelaide*, it is proposed

THAT A

PUBLIC DINNER

Shall be given to that gentleman, and that a

PIECE OF PLATE

Shall be presented to him in commemoration of the event, and as a Testimony of the feeling of the Colonists.

Persons desirous of evincing their sentiments are invited to record their Names in a paper left for this purpose at the POST OFFICE.

N.B. An early day will be fixed for the DINNER, of which due notice will be given.

Adelaide, 4th May, 1838.

Printed at the office of the *Southern Australian.*

'The typical squatter of the period would probably be Scottish,' writes the historian Michael Cannon. The Scots were clannish, physically tough and very ambitious. Patrick Leslie, one of the six sons of a Scots laird, arrived in Sydney Town in 1835 with two of his brothers. Resolving to acquire land of his own he set off in 1840 into the future colony of Queensland, riding with a single companion, a convict named Murphy, to explore the Darling Downs inland from Moreton Bay, and find there some of the richest pasture land in Australia. Joined by a brother and the latter's flocks, Leslie—hailed by his admirers as 'the Prince of Bushmen'—married James Macarthur's daughter Kate in 1842, was almost ruined in the depression (he briefly cursed 'this felonious land') but soon re-established himself as one of the leading squatters and stud-breeders on the Downs.

Few squatters rivalled the Dangar family in influence. Henry Dangar founded the family's fortunes in the 1820s with land grants and purchases. In 1839 his brother took up land nearby at Scone; a third brother, Richard, opened the first in Muswellbrook; the fourth, Thomas, ran the inn at Scone.

In 1839 Robert Delhunty, a ship's surgeon, married a daughter of Major Gibbes, the Collector of Customs, and within a few years was leasing 80,000 acres at Mudgee—for £10 a year.

BELOW
Aboriginal corroboree.

The 'squattocracy'

The squattocracy's daughters provided acceptable brides for the sons of their friends. In 1843 Terence Aubrey Murray, an immense man, a Catholic Irish-Scot, married another Gibbes daughter; she would be chatelaine of his large estate at Yarralumla, not far from Robert Campbell's Duntroon property at Canberra. (The Murray mansion is now the home of Australia's Governor-General, Duntroon homestead part of the Royal Military College.)

Angus McMillan and Lachlan Macalister jointly claimed the honour of settling Gippsland in 1839. McMillan named the rich hill country and rugged mountains Caledonia in honour of his homeland. The Scots, in fortitude and Calvinistic faith so reminiscent of the intransigent Boers of South Africa, were more cruel than the English in their treatment of the Aborigines. McMillan boasted of the number of Aborigines he had to shoot; when Macalister's son was speared to death by Aborigines in 1845, Old Lachlan's men killed 150 of them in revenge.

ABOVE:
Scottish explorer and landowner Angus McMillan, pioneer of Gippsland, seen in this photograph wearing traditional highland bonnet and tweed just before his death in 1865.

'The squatters were much discussed by the townspeople, and particularly by the ladies,' one squatter, Edward Curr, wrote. They were 'pictured as living in remote loneliness, much given to emu and kangaroo hunting and constant encounters with hordes of blacks … and at night, sleeping anywhere, with their saddle for a pillow.'

If many of the squatters were gentlemen, few looked it: 'They were distinguished by their hirsute appearance, whiskers, beards and mustaches being decidedly in the ascendant among them,' Curr wrote. 'Many of them, I noticed, indulged in blue serge shirts in lieu of coats, cabbage tree hats, belts supporting leather pouches and, in a few cases, a pistol which, with breeches, boots and spurs, completed the costume.'

Most rode horses, and set out with drays laden with some of the comforts of home—furniture, tools, books and, in some cases, wives. In the Monaro one traveller hardly saw a woman and called the region 'entirely masculine'. The unknown land had decreed that the pioneers, like the convicts, would be predominantly unmarried men, reinforcing the male ethos of the Bush. They needed to be tough. In the summer of 1838–39 the colony endured its worst drought since settlement, and within two years came its first economic depression.

'The results of Bourke's land legislation were incredible,' writes Michael Cannon. 'In less than seven years, almost the entire fertile area outside the established counties, ranging from Brisbane in the north to Melbourne in the south, had been opened up'. The squatters' wool brought Australia the first wealth the colonies had known and established the industry that carried the country—on the sheep's back—through good times and bad for the next century.

1837: Governor Gipps

When Sir Richard Bourke sailed for home in 1837 grateful citizens raised a statue by public subscription to commemorate his benevolent rule. No statue has been raised to his successor, Gipps, but few Governors deserved one more than he. Colonel George Gipps of the Royal Engineers was unlucky enough to administer a colony during the first economic depression in Australia's history and at a time when his policies pleased neither the Haves nor the Have Nots.

BELOW:
Governor George Gipps.

In fifty years of settlement no colonist had paid the full penalty of the law for killing Aborigines (several had been sentenced to death, but the sentences had been commuted). In April 1838 Gipps warned the colony that the killing of Aborigines must cease:

As human beings ... as the original possessors of the soil from which the wealth of this country has been principally derived, and as subjects of the Queen ... the natives of the Territory have an acknowledged right to the Protection of the government, and the sympathy and kindness or every separate individual. In disputes between Aborigines and whites, both parties are equally entitled to demand the protection and assistance of the laws of England ...

The year 1837 saw the onset of a drought that would last until 1842 and in its first harsh year the Aborigines of the Liverpool Plains were particularly bad, according to reports, killing shepherds, stealing sheep and pilfering from homesteads.

1838: The Myall Creek massacre

In June 1838 the magistrate at Muswellbrook in the Hunter Valley reported to Sydney that a stockman, an Irishman, had confessed to taking part in killing Aborigines at Dangar's station at Myall Creek on the plains. An overseer had discovered the charred remains of twenty-eight Aboriginal men, women and children and called on the remorse-stricken Irishman to confess his part in the crime.

On the orders of Gipps' Attorney-General, John Hubert Plunkett, a high-minded Protestant Irishman, a party of mounted police was sent up from Sydney to arrest the murderer's accomplices; fifty-three days later their commandant reported that he had arrested eleven men for complicity in the murders, all of them former convicts.

They were ready enough to tell their story. Constant stealing by Aborigines and the killing of a European drove them one day to make an example of the local tribe. They had driven the twenty-eight victims into the stockyard and slaughtered them all.

At their trial on 15 November 1838 all were acquitted of murder after the jury had deliberated only twenty minutes. It was a popular verdict. 'I look upon the blacks as a set of monkeys, and I think the earlier they are exterminated, the better,' one juryman was later heard to say.

ABOVE:
Watercolour by Augustus Earle, (1793–1838), of 'Desmond' a New South Wales chief painted for a corroboree.

Gipps and Plunkett saw the case for what it was: the first real test in the colony of the justice of English law. They immediately ordered a retrial. Law, or its pretence to fairness and justice to all, was the bedrock of British civilisation. It protected all men, white or black. Justice must not only be done, but must also be seen to be done. Offering four of the accused immunity if they turned Queen's Evidence, Plunkett charged the remaining seven with the murder of Aborigines not named in the first indictment. At the trial on 29 November 1838 all were found guilty and sentenced to death. Gipps and the Executive Council rejected all pleas for mercy and the seven men were hanged in public in Sydney on 18 December.

Spasmodic killing of Aborigines continued, but men no longer boasted about it. Poisoned flour would be part of the new recipe for genocide. But the consequences of the Myall Creek massacre and trials were widespread and lasting. 'If you touch me, the Gubbner will hang you,' an Aborigine at Portland warned a bullock master who was about to strike him. The trial was a turning point. Australia was saved from becoming another South Africa, its racism legally condoned.

The Explorers

George Grey

In July 1837, only two weeks after Princess Victoria has ascended the throne of England, Her Majesty's Ship *Beagle* left Plymouth on a six-year commission to chart Australia's north-western coastline and the waters of Torres and Bass Straits. Already notable as the ship that had carried Charles Darwin round the world, she numbered among her passengers a young captain of the 83rd Regiment named George Grey and a party of soldiers, whose task it was to explore the north-western coast by land.

'Our soldiers are very well and happy—and make themselves quite at home,' Captain Wickham wrote to the Admiralty as the ship beat its way towards Cape Town. Captain Grey's nature melted the reserve of even such hardened sea dogs as Wickham and his formidable second-in-command, John Lort Stokes. Born in 1812, the son of a soldier who had fallen in Wellington's army in the storming of Badajoz, Grey had entered the army and served in Ireland. There British policy towards the Irish had so disturbed him that he had decided to give up military life for one in the colonies, where the founding of new settlements might relieve the terrible distress suffered by the poor. Lord Glenelg had given Grey his official backing, the Royal Geographical Society had sponsored the young man's expedition, and the navy had provided the ship to carry him there.

Scrambling ashore at the estuary of the Prince Regent River in December 1837, Grey led his party, later equipped with Timor ponies, south through the suffocating humidity of the northern Australian summer, surviving an attack by Aborigines and the removal of three spears from his body. In March he reached the Glenelg River and pushed inland to explore its majestic plateaux where, lost in amazement, he saw and sketched the eerie and inexplicable cave paintings—unlike any other Aboriginal art—called the Wandjina.

ABOVE:

The young Captain George Grey, army officer, administrator and explorer.

George Grey was the first European to discover and draw the eerie Aboriginal rock paintings known as the Wandjina.

Terminating his expedition shortly afterwards, Grey re-equipped at Cape Town and landed near Shark Bay early in 1839, before exploring on foot the entire bleak coastline to its south. He led his party into Perth two months later.

The expedition brought to Grey great fame and launched him on one of the most romantic careers in Imperial history. In 1842 he was appointed Governor of South Australia and in 1845 Governor of New Zealand (he served there again in the 1860s, during the Second Maori War). In 1891 Grey would pledge support to Billy Hughes in the new Labour Party's call for 'One Man, One Vote'. He was one of the most remarkable Englishmen of his time.

1841: Eyre crosses the Nullarbor

Grey's expedition over impossible country ushered in a decade of epic feats of overland exploration. In November 1840 Edward John Eyre and a small party set out from Streaky Bay to walk from South Australia to Perth across the unknown wastes of the Nullarbor Plain. Eyre had arrived in Sydney as a 17-year-old in 1833, and had already won fame for overlanding a thousand sheep from Sydney to Adelaide and for forays into the deserts of South Australia. Alternately harassed by Aborigines (who killed his companion Baxter) and weakened by hunger and thirst, Eyre and his Aboriginal guide Wylie reached Albany in July 1841, having crossed 1800 kilometres of scrub and desert. Eyre was appointed Lieutenant-Governor to Grey in New Zealand in 1846 but quarrelled with his superior; he ended his colonial career in disgrace as a bloody-handed Governor of Jamaica in the 1860s.

Mount Kosciuszko

Across the continent a small party of explorers was leaving the Yass Plains in January 1840. Their leader was a Polish count, a self-taught geologist named Paul Strzelecki, who had arrived in the colony nine months earlier after a life of wandering and discovery in the Americas. One of the group was James Macarthur. They reached the site of today's Gundagai and proceeded south-east into the Australian Alps first seen by Hume and Hovell. On 15 February Strzelecki climbed to the sum-

ABOVE:
The explorer and navigator John Lort Stokes, speared in the lungs while investigating the Victoria River in northern Australia, 1839; from the oil painting by Richard Beechey. The intrepid naval officer survived the encounter.

mit if its highest peak and, picking some Alpine flowers to press for the woman he loved, named the mountain Mount Kosciuszko, in honour of the Polish national hero. Even in summer, patches of snow lay on its slopes: he was standing on the highest point in Australia. He returned to his companions overcome by emotion, moved by the Alps' majestic beauty. The party pushed on through the mountains into Gippsland, which Strzelecki named in honour of the Governor, and reached the coast at Westernport without mishap.

The riddle of the interior

In the 1830s the map of Australia appearing in atlases and on emigration-office walls showed a coastline and little else. What lay in the continent's interior? Was there some inland sea, or even jungles similar to those of central Africa? Perhaps some great inland river system like America's mighty Amazon or Mississippi reached into the unknown heart of the continent. Or did the desert seen on the fringes of New South Wales by Sturt and Mitchell stretch as far as the forlorn coast of Western Australia?

Australia would prove to be a continent like no other. Its rivers seemed to end in waterholes. Its mountain ranges were not peaks but monolithic rocks or disfigured plateaux. Its northern deserts were drier than the Sahara, yet whipped by storms and soaked by monsoonal floods during the months of the Wet.

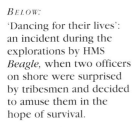

BELOW:
'Dancing for their lives': an incident during the explorations by HMS *Beagle,* when two officers on shore were surprised by tribesmen and decided to amuse them in the hope of survival.

Ludwig Leichhardt

In February 1842 a ship entered Sydney Harbour. Among its passengers was a 29-year-old German naturalist named Friedrich Wilhelm Ludwig Leichhardt. Precociously talented and by nature romantic, he had become fascinated by Australia's flora and determined to explore the continent's interior.

The continent's unique natural wonders were attracting scholars from all over the world—the Poles Lhotsky and Strzelecki, the English ornithologist John Gould, who had arrived in 1838 (his masterpiece, *The Birds of Australia*, would be published in London a decade later in seven handsome folio volumes now regarded as the loveliest of Australian books). The botanist and explorer Ferdinand von Mueller would arrive in 1847 and six years later be appointed Government Botanist of Victoria, devoting his life to collecting and naming Australia's indigenous plants.

Leichhardt bore letters of introduction to Sydney society but he was surprised by the bitterness of its divisions and decided to avoid much contact with it. 'Those who came free regard themselves as a superior class,' he wrote to a friend. 'The effect of this has been to unite the emancipists, so there are two parties, two social circles, in continuous confrontation.' There was talk that Sir Thomas Mitchell was planning a major expedition into the interior and Leichhardt was offered a position on it, but the delay annoyed him and he instead spent two years 'botanising' on a series of forays in the coastal regions from Sydney to Moreton Bay. With financial support from Sydney squatters and businessmen Leichhardt set out in September 1844 with a party of five men and teams of horses and bullocks to explore the land from Moreton Bay to Port Essington on the northern shores of Arnhem Land. Of all Australian epics of exploration this was to be the most brilliant.

'The mornings and evenings are very beautiful, and are surpassed by no climate that I have ever lived in,' Leichhardt wrote in his journal as his party approached the Gulf of Carpentaria. The party reached the Gulf in July 1845. 'We had discovered a line of communication by land between the eastern coast of Australia and the Gulf of Carpentaria; we had traveled along never failing and for the greater part, running waters; and over excellent country available, almost in its whole extent, for pastoral purposes,' Leichhardt wrote. As the days grew hotter and the humidity intensified their bullocks began collapsing; they were slaughtered for food. Weary and starving, the explorers sighted a group of houses on the coast in December 1845. They had reached Port Essington. Leichhardt returned to Sydney in triumph in March 1846.

ABOVE:
Ludwig Leichhardt, the mysterious German naturalist and explorer whose life and disappearance have prompted legends.

OPPOSITE:
The explorer Thomas Mitchell, seen here in his uniform as Surveyor-General of New South Wales, was also a talented map-maker and artist.

Mitchell and Sturt: last forays

In the meantime Mitchell's long-delayed expedition to the interior had left Orange in December 1845, consisting of thirty men, eleven carts and drays, with 112 bullocks as beasts of burden and 250 sheep to provide food on the hoof. Leaving most of his men behind at a depot under the command of Edmund Kennedy, Mitchell set out north with a small party but heard several days later that Leichhardt had beaten him to the Gulf. Mitchell nevertheless pushed on with ten others and in June reached the river named the Maranoa, marching further north to cross the tropic of Capricorn in August. In September he reached the present site of Blackall, having followed a river he was sure flowed north-west into the Gulf of Carpentaria. He named it the Victoria in honour of his Queen; it is known today as the Barcoo. Threatened by hostile Aborigines and short of provisions, Mitchell returned to his depot before leading the expedition back to Sydney, which he reached in December 1846. It was Mitchell's last great expedition into the interior.

Mitchell's great rival Charles Sturt had left Adelaide in August 1844, also intending to reach the interior and solve the riddle of the inland sea. He led an expedition of fourteen men, including a nuggetty Scots surveyor, John McDouall Stuart, and carried on drays two boats in which to sail the waters of the fabled sea.

Sturt found only desert. By October he and his party had reached the Barrier Ranges, near the site of present-day Broken Hill; proceeding north another 300 kilometres they made camp to sit out the worst of the summer. Here the expedition was marooned from January to July 1845, in heat so intense that the mercury in their barometers burst and the ink dried on their pens before they had time to record their discomfort. When the rains came, Sturt pushed on, discovering a river he named Coopers Creek, before encountering a 'gloomy, stone-clad plain'.

He crossed the expanse (now known as Sturt's Stony Desert), only to discover even more desert—sand dunes and ridges reaching to the horizon. The terrain proved impassable. He turned back, broken in health and half-blinded, to reach Adelaide in January 1846. This journey was Sturt's last.

LIEUTENANT-COLONEL SIR T. L. MITCHELL, D.C.L., SURVEYOR-GENERAL OF NEW SOUTH WALES

1848: Kennedy of Cape York

Edmund Kennedy, Mitchell's second-in-command in the 1845 expedition, was determined to discover whether the Barcoo flowed into the Gulf of Carpentaria. He led an expedition from Sydney in March 1847, reaching the Barcoo in October and soon discovered that if flowed into Coopers Creek, thus solving the riddle of Australia's inland drainage system.

Two months after returning to Sydney, Kennedy and a small party sailed from there in April 1848 with the intention of proceeding overland from Rockingham Bay on Queensland's coast to Cape York. Kennedy's progress up the coast was hampered by swamps, river estuaries, thick rainforest and mountain ranges. By early November the expedition was so weakened that the leader decided to leave nine men at a camp and push on with his guide, an Aborigine called Jacky Jacky, and three others. In December Kennedy, who judged the Aborigines to be friendly, was speared to death in a sudden attack and only Jacky Jacky escaped to reach the coast and the ship that was waiting for them. Of the other twelve Europeans, only two were later found alive by rescuers.

Tragedy also awaited Leichhardt. Fascinated by the possibility of crossing the continent from east to west, he set out in April 1848 from the Darling Downs, heading for the Barcoo from where he intended to march west and eventually reach Perth. When a shepherd asked them their destination, Leichhardt replied: 'To the setting sun.' The expedition was never seen again. Leichhardt and his six companions vanished from the face of the earth as if they had never existed. Legends persist that all were killed by Aborigines; others that some of the party reached the Gulf, but no possessions or human remains have been discovered. This abiding mystery brought to an end the last of the great explorations of the 1840s.

ABOVE:
Kennedy speared by Aborigines, 1848.

TOP:
Smith O'Brien.

ABOVE:
John Mitchel.

The hungry forties

The Irish

Between 1830 and 1850 more than 100,000 emigrants braved the horrors of the sea voyage to Australia. Nearly half of the total (48 per cent) were Irish.

The 1840s was another period in the cycle of severe economic distress in the United Kingdom. No empire was greater than Britain's and no poverty so deep. Walking the back streets of Liverpool, the American consul Nathaniel Hawthorne saw 'every two or three steps a gin shop … men haggard, drunken, care-worn … hopeless but with a kind of patience, as if all this were a rule of life'. By 1841, a census year, the population of England and Wales had risen to 16.5 million, Scotland's to 2.7 million.

Ireland's population had reached nearly 8 million and the Irish lived in degradation that went beyond poverty. William Ewart Gladstone was to call England's centuries-long attempt to crush the Irish 'the one deep and terrible stain upon our history'. Driven from their land and deprived of all rights for refusing to renounce their Catholic faith, yet taxed heavily by absentee landlords, the Irish lived and died like animals. Of the Irish peasants a shocked English observer wrote in 1836: 'Their habitations are wretched hovels, several of a family sleep together upon straw or upon the bare ground … their food commonly consists of dry potatoes, and with these they are obliged to stint themselves to one spare meal a day …'

In 1846 the Irish potato crop was stricken with a strange blight that reduced the tubers to a noxious, oozing pulp. Famine and its followers, cholera and typhus, brought about the death of one million Irish men, women and children in just one year and forced the emigration of another 1.5 million. (Ireland's population growth, once the highest in Europe, has never recovered. Where the English population has now risen to 55 million, Ireland's has fallen to under 6 million in the 150 years since the Famine.)

1848: The Irish exiles

Ireland finally rose in protest in 1848. It was the fifty-fourth recorded insurrection against English rule. In March 1848, as word came of revolution in the capitals of Europe, the leaders of the Young Ireland league called for freedom. The garrison in Ireland was reinforced, until thirty-six regiments were based in the island—a force greater than that in India. In April the Chartists marched on London and the House of Lords rushed through a Treason and Felony Act; in July habeas corpus was suspended. The revolt was quickly crushed, with the loss of only one life, for the mass of the Irish were too weak to take up arms. Charles Gavan Duffy, editor

of the *Nation*, was charged with treason; he faced five packed juries, challenged their right to try him and was acquitted at his fifth trial. Four other Irish leaders, all of them men of education and some standing—William Smith O'Brien, Terence McManus, Patrick O'Donohoe and Thomas Meagher—were sentenced to death for treason.

The medieval penalty meted out to traitors horrified all those sympathetic to Ireland's plight. 'England is guilty towards Ireland and reaps in full measure the fruit of fifteen generations of wrong doing', protested the Scottish historian Carlyle. All the condemned were respectable men: Smith O'Brien was not only a Protestant, educated at Harrow and Cambridge University, but had also been a popular and respected member of the House of Commons. The sentences were commuted to transportation to Australia. John Mitchel, another patriot, had already been condemned to transportation; the four convicted men, accompanied by two other Irish leaders, John Martin and Kevin O'Doherty, became with Mitchel the 'Seven Irish Exiles' of Van Diemen's Land.

As political prisoners in Australia they were treated with relative leniency by the Governor, Denison. Only Smith O'Brien rejected the offer of parole, and suffered for his obstinacy a month in solitary confinement, which left his spirit undimmed. When three of the exiles, given the freedom to roam the island, met up in the wilds of Van Diemen's Land at Lake Sorrell they burst out laughing at the implausibility of the whole affair and sat on the stumps of gum trees to eat damper and plan an escape. They were treated with kindness by settlers, particularly the Irish and Scots. The Vandemonians, Mitchel wrote, 'grow up frequently tall, straight and handsome, with mild expressions of countenance, and manners always affable, gentle and kindly. On the whole, our species grows to splendid perfection here.' McManus was the first to bolt, stealing aboard a ship bound for America in 1851; Meagher and O'Donohoe were smuggled onto ships heading for America in the following year. Mitchel's escape was arranged by Irish Vandemonians and two English sympathisers whom he described with affection as 'bold horsemen, indefatigable bushmen, (who) seem to have come into our present enterprise for the sake of the excitement as well as from a sincere regard for Irish rebels'.

Gavan Duffy, now a member of the House of Commons, sought repeatedly for pardons for Smith O'Brien and the remaining exiles. Pardons were granted in March 1854. Of these colourful men, O'Doherty settled in Queensland, Duffy later became Premier of Victoria. O'Brien returned to Ireland, and Meagher led the Irish Brigade of the Union Army, carrying the Stars and Stripes and the flag of Erin in the famous six charges at the battle of Fredericksburg in 1862 that caused an admiring Confederate general to shout through the battle smoke: 'There are those damned green flags again!'

Irish and Scots

In Scotland the 1840s saw the last of the major Highland Clearances, when the lairds drove their own clansmen from the mountains and islands where they had dwelled for centuries. The landowners then introduced sheep, which returned them a good profit. This heartless program depopulated Scotland's north. The clearances continued into the 1850s.

In 1848 the untiring John Dunmore Lang arrived in England to sing the praises of his beloved adopted land Australia. For two years he wrote a weekly letter in a journal replying to emigrants' enquiries for two years and published *The Golden Lands of Australia* in 1850; he travelled to the Orkneys and the Shetlands to encourage them to emigrate and chartered the ships to carry them. His experience of Scotland's misery and his growing regard for the United States (where he had been received with courtesy by a President who lived in surroundings of greater simplicity than most colonial Governors) made Lang an ardent republican.

The Highland Scots and the Catholic Irish came ashore in Australia like bewildered sheep, speaking their harsh Gaelic that made the English laugh. The Celts were physically strong. Scots were valued for their patience and hardiness as stockmen and overlanders; the Irish were suspected of rebelliousness and truculence; their women and children were beguiling but often went barefoot. Yet the Scots and the Irish—the outsiders—would in time intermarry as they had in Glasgow and Belfast, breeding offspring who combined all the charm of the Irish and the canniness of the Scots. Separately or together the Scots and Irish would produce Australian politicians, soldiers, writers and priests in numbers far exceeding their proportion of the colony's population—barely 35 per cent. Denied power in the land of their birth, they sought it with ferocity in their new homeland.

The wealthy Irish Protestant lawyer William Stawell emigrated to Australia in style in 1843 with twenty-three family members and servants. But conditions on board most migrant ships were appalling. During the 1840s nearly 17,000 emigrants to the Americas and Australia died at sea. Overcrowding led to the rapid spread of contagious diseases; in the *Layton* sailing from Bristol in 1837, seventy two children died from measles. Nearly 2000 emigrants were to lose their lives in shipwrecks during the course of emigration to Australia and New Zealand—369 men, women and children drowned in a single disaster when the *Cataraqui* hit rocks in Bass Strait on a dark, stormy night in 1845.

Caroline Chisholm

The preponderance of males—by the 1850s there were still two men for every woman in the colonies—had prompted the disinterested and the opportunists to sponsor the emigration of unmar-

BELOW:

When economic depression struck the Australian colonies in the 1840s Caroline Chisholm (1808-70) provided assistance for penniless females and began a personal crusade that forced the authorities to support the establishment of hostels for new arrivals.

ABOVE:
Sydney picnic party en
route to Botany Bay;
the name already was a
reminder of a past the
colony wished to forget.

ried women in the 1830s. The fortunate and pretty were quickly snapped up by the wealthy in Sydney and Hobart Town as servants and housekeepers; the unfortunate slept in the streets or in strange beds.

In 1838 an English officer, Captain Archibald Chisholm and his wife Caroline and their children arrived in New South Wales, where they established their home at Windsor. Caroline Chisholm had become a Catholic convert and was appalled by the plight of unemployed and homeless women she saw in the streets of Sydney. She pestered Governor Gipps about the issue until he provided the old Immigrant Barracks as a 'half-way' home for the women in 1841. Chisholm then accompanied groups of young women to country towns, ensuring that they received employment, and successfully established sixteen other half-way houses. Within six years she had cared for 11,000 people.

She sailed for London in 1846 to lecture on the plight of her waifs, raise money for their welfare, and encourage the poor to leave England for the Promised Land. In the following years two shiploads of children from workhouses sailed for a better life in Australia, and in 1850 the Family Colonisation Society, which she had helped to found, dispatched to Australia a chartered ship carrying 250 entire families; it was the first of many. Charles Dickens mocked her earnestness; but one London newspaper praised her as 'a Moses, with bonnet and shawl'. Her fame spread far. Michelet the French historian wrote 'Australia has a saint, and she is an English woman …' Caroline Chisholm returned to England in 1866 and died eleven years later, shortly after her husband's death. She left six children of her own. In a dark age of callousness, she shines like a star. No other individual in Australian history has won more praise for raising the dignity of women.

Transportation: beginning of the end

On 20 October 1840 Governor Gipps announced in Sydney the British government's decision to cease transportation of convicts throughout the British Empire. Two islands alone would continue to receive England's unwanted felons: Van Diemen's Land and Norfolk Island, and the next decade would witness renewed horrors there. 'The System' was not yet dead.

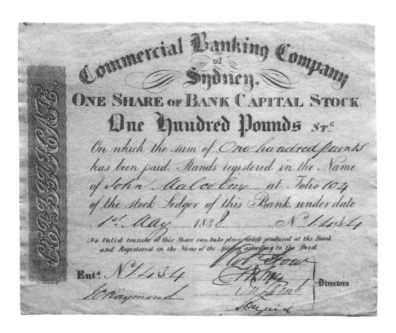

Tough times

'In this country, money is the great idol, and for it they will do anything or undergo any hardship,' a Scots emigrant wrote of the Australian colonists in 1839. Louisa Meredith, who arrived in the colony with her husband in the same year, was distressed to hear the men talk of nothing but money and sheep. But the boom was about to end.

Emigrants arriving in Sydney Town in the early 1840s found work non-existent and conditions hard. The first cold winds of recession were blowing. The previous decade—one of untrammelled growth—had seen squatters and land speculators borrow heavily to build up herds and homes, and wool prices in England were falling. Bankruptcies were soon an epidemic.

A Warwickshire emigrant and a staunch Chartist, Henry Parkes, arrived in 1840 to find homes being rented at six times the amount charged in England, and cursed his decision to leave his homeland. The future 'Father of Federation' spent his first year in the colony in poverty, working as a labourer on the Jamison estate at Penrith, and sleeping with wife and babe on a bed made of a sheet of bark and an old door.

An elected Legislative Council

In 1842 the British government acknowledged Australia's maturity: the New South Wales Legislative Council would be enlarged to thirty-six members, twenty-four of them elected. Municipal and local councils would be created. (Sydney officially became a city with its own Lord Mayor in 1842.)

Of these twenty-four elected members eighteen were elected from country areas with nearly 66,000 people. The towns, with 47,000 people elected only six members: the City of Sydney would have two members, Melbourne only one. This gerrymander left power securely in the hands of a conservative squattocracy. The radicals quite properly called the Act 'a mockery of self-government' and they were soon joined by unexpected allies, for a companion Act had stipulated that 'waste land' would in future be sold for a minimum of 20 shillings an acre. 'Bourgeois, gentry, squatter and working man, Tory, whig, liberal radical and chartist, the Protestant and the Catholic', wrote Manning Clark, 'joined hands to demand self-government for New South Wales.' As the economy sputtered into depression, the demand for self-rule rose to a crescendo.

1842: The first depression

In 1842 the Bank of Australia collapsed and emigration was suspended. But in the same year a steamship entered Sydney Harbour carrying the man many predicted would be the colony's saviour. Ben Boyd was a giant of a man, a London-born Scot with a silver tongue and charm to match his grand ideas. As with most transparent frauds, few could see through him.

Before leaving London Boyd had founded a bank to finance a steamship service to the colonies—his steamers were already plying between Sydney and Melbourne—and received from Lord John Russell a promise that the colonial government would provide him with all assistance in establishing ports and facilities for his services.

Ben Boyd, our first entrepreneur, blazed across Australia's sky like a comet. With his shareholders' money he took out enormous leases, stocked them with sheep and then built his own town on Twofold Bay to export the wool from his flocks on the Monaro; Boyd Town included a factory for his whaling fleet.

ABOVE:
Benjamin Boyd, entrepreneur.

Boyd's sheep runs extended as far as the Port Phillip District (the region soon elected him as their representative on the Legislative Council), and not even the depths of the depression—the first months of 1843— appeared to dent his wealth. To the dismay of Sydney society Boyd imported the first Pacific Islanders into the colony to work as shepherds, but these unfortunate men, paid a pittance, soon wandered back into Sydney and demanded to be taken back to their island homes.

As the price of wool fell and squatters faced sudden ruin, 'Black Harry' O'Brien, pioneer of Yass, began slaughtering his flocks and boiling them down for tallow. Other squatters followed his lead. It was a drastic move but it saved many of them from bankruptcy, for tallow for candles was a difficult item to import from England (it melted on its passage through the tropics) and was always in short supply. In 1843 Thomas Sutcliffe Mort, a 27-year-old Lancashire man whose employers had gone bankrupt, began holding Sydney's first regular weekly wool auctions.

Auctioneers never lost money. This was the foundation of the company that later merged with Mort's rival, Thomas Goldsborough, to form the giant stock and station firm of Goldsborough Mort.

Mort possessed the keenest business mind in the colony; he would become in succession Australia's pioneer in cheese-making, profit-sharing with employees, and the refrigeration of meat for export; an advocate of assisted immigration, railway construction and steam navigation (he built Sydney's first graving dock at Balmain); a man of vision in a world of opportunists.

In 1843 William Wentworth, newly elected Member for Sydney, pushed an extraordinary emergency Bill through the council that allowed squatters to mortgage their sheep. Some wondered if the squatters would next try to mortgage their convicts. The young patriot had not just drifted into the arms of the oligarchy but had become its leader.

As rumours began circulating that his investments were going sour, Boyd took up a new role: the Patriot. At a dinner in October 1844 to celebrate his election to the council, Boyd declared to his guests: 'We are all squatters to a man—I glory in the name!' and called for the granting of self-government.

Relations between the squatters and the Governor were soon at breaking point. On 2 April 1844 Gipps announced a new law for the squatters. Instead of one £10 licence to cover all their holdings, they would henceforth pay £10 for each of their sheep runs; for licensing purposes no single station was to cover more than 20 square miles, and each licence would cover no more than 4000 sheep or 500 head of cattle.

'The monster squatters', as Gipps called them, reacted angrily. Seven days later William Wentworth addressed a crowd of some 350 gentlemen at the Royal Hotel, with his ally, Dr William Bland (who had been transported for killing a man in a

BELOW:
Whaling off Boyd Town on the southern coast of New South Wales in the 1840s.

The coming of steam: Her Majesty's Steam Ship *Driver* entering Sydney Harbour in 1846.

Propellers or paddlewheels driven by steam engines provided additional power to the sail-rigged vessels of the time.

duel) in the chair. Wentworth cursed 'Gipps the oppressor' and, declaring the Governor's edict unconstitutional, cried: 'These wilds belong to us, not to the British Government.' He then called for the immediate granting of self-government. Ben Boyd called Gipps an agent of 'grinding oppression'. The result of the meeting was the formation of the Pastoral Association of New South Wales to defend the interests of the propertied class.

1847: Introduction of the 14-year leases

In 1846 the Colonial Office promulgated a compromise: from 1847 the squatters' licences would be extended, but giving them rights of occupancy for only another fourteen years. In June 1847 Robert Lowe, the educated Englishman who had emigrated to Australia for his health (he was an albino, sickly of appearance but a thunderous champion of democratic rights) declared in the Legislative Council that the interests of the public had been sacrificed for the benefit of one class. When Wentworth reminded Lowe that 'the squatters were the colony', Lowe called the squattocracy 'highwaymen with money'. But the argument about who should control the land was effectively postponed until 1861, when the leases would expire.

The squatters of Port Phillip now voiced their demands for separation from New South Wales. To show their disgust

BELOW:
Satirical view of drunken squatters.

ABOVE:

A prosperous and progressive city: view of Sydney in the 1840s.

with their lords and masters in Sydney, the gentlemen of Port Phillip in 1848 elected Earl Grey, the Colonial Secretary, as their member; others put the Duke of Wellington's name on the ballot paper to prove its absurdity.

Ben Boyd: eaten by cannibals?

By 1848 Ben Boyd's bank had collapsed with debts, his sheep runs were deserted and his name dishonoured. He was left with nothing but his elegant yacht, the *Wanderer*, in which he sailed out of Sydney Harbour to try to mend his fortunes in California. Unsuccessful there, he left San Francisco in a hurry in 1850 to try his luck in the Pacific, perhaps in recruiting or kidnapping islander labour. He moored his yacht at Ta'na, went ashore and was never seen again. Legend has it that the burly Scot suffered the fate of many failed entrepreneurs: his intended victims ate him.

1846 Governor FitzRoy

Governor Gipps, nearly prostrate with asthma, returned to England in 1845. His successor, the genial soldier Sir Charles FitzRoy, who was related to the royal family, arrived in June 1846, to rule for the next nine years. The depression was over but a new storm was strengthening: a vehement demand by the colonists for self-government. Shortly after FitzRoy's appointment, the Tories fell in London and were once more succeeded by the Whigs, two of whose well-meaning liberal-minded ministers showed how ignorant they were of Australia's changing attitudes.

Having ceased transportation of convicts and admitted its iniquity, the British government attempted to reintroduce it. Faced by overcrowded gaols whose population was being increased by 40,000 new criminals every year, Secretary Gladstone, after gazing at the maps of Australia's blank areas, ordered FitzRoy to establish a new penal colony on the coast of northern Queensland, to be called North Australia. Its citizens would be convicts working off their sentences—'Exiles' as the government called them. It was a failure. Northern Queensland's tropical coastal regions were as enervating as the West Indies. The first group of convicts arrived there in July 1847 and were transferred to Sydney the following April. The scheme's only lasting memorial was the founding of the small town of Gladstone.

1848: Transportation resumed

Sounding out the NSW authorities on the possibility of renewing transportation, Gladstone's successor, the ubiquitous Earl Grey, received the pleasing news in October 1847 that the Legislative Council favoured the proposal. The squatters depended on convict labour and those on the Darling Downs were demanding convicts. In September 1848 Grey informed FitzRoy that by Order-in-Council the British government had decided to renew transportation to New South Wales.

The historian John Ward has called this decision a 'disastrous error of judgement' and its consequence 'the only serious storm in Britain's relationship with Australia'. The colonies had outgrown the convict age. They wished only to bury it.

1849: 'No more convicts!'

When the convict transport *Hashemy* dropped anchor in Sydney on 11 June 1849 a crowd of 5000 protestors stood in the rain at Circular Quay to stop the felons landing. 'Australia wants them not,' shouted Robert Campbell (nephew of the merchant). 'The men of Australia have wives and children and are not content to subvert the land' and 'absorb British criminals and British misery'.

'The threat of degradation has been fulfilled. Our city, the beautiful waters of our harbour are this day again polluted with the presence of this floating hell—a convict ship,' cried Robert Lowe. He called upon those assembled to make 'a declaration that they will not be slaves—that they would be free!' The time was coming, cried Lowe, when the free colonies would assert this freedom 'not by words alone … As in America, oppression was the parent of independence—so would it be in the colony,' he said. Just as a plant grows into a tree 'so will injustice and tyranny ripen into rebellion, and rebellion into independence!' He was cheered to the skies.

Henry Parkes, now finding his feet as a champion of popular causes, mspoke for the 'emigrant working man' who demanded to be protected from the 'degradation

ABOVE:
Sir Charles FitzRoy, Australia's first 'Governor-General'.

FitzRoy gave his blessing to the establishment of Australia's first university, in Sydney, in 1850.

THE SHIP 'NILE'

WITH

MORE CONVICTS

IS IN THE HARBOUR.

Remember the *LEAGUE.*

REMEMBER the Lieutenant-Governor's **DESPATCH** of the 20th August, 1847:

" AS HER MAJESTY'S GOVERNMENT *have decided that* TRANSPORTATION IS TO CEASE, and as that decision has been PUBLICLY " MADE KNOWN in the Colony, I do not consider that it would be *possible* or *desirable* to attempt to carry out the suggestions contained in my " Despatch No. 88. The feelings of a large portion of the Community are so fully enlisted in the Opposition which has been raised to the " Convict System here, that ANY attempt now to revive the System in ANY form would be looked upon by them as a BREACH OF FAITH."

GOD Save the QUEEN !

Hobart Town, 3rd October, 1850.

ABOVE:
Growing public anger with the continuation of transportation of convicts led to the formation in the 1840s of groups dedicated to its abolition.

of working with convicts'. A deputation of these spokesmen of the middle class— none of them was Australian-born—walked uphill in the drizzle to Government House to deliver their resolution to FitzRoy and found the gates barred and defended by troops. But next day they were permitted to present their resolution: 'We protest against the landing again of British convicts on these shores ... because it is incompatible with our existence as a free colony desiring self-government, to be the receptacle of another country's felons ...'

One week later another protest rally was held. Lowe called for the dismissal of Lord Grey—'remove that Nobleman from Her Majesty's counsels!'—and a quick end to rule by a 'remote, ill-informed and irresponsible Colonial Office'. He called for the right of self-government and asked his audience to 'brave death' itself to achieve it.

Two months later, in August 1849, the convict ship *Randolph* moored at Port Melbourne and mobs of colonists again gathered to block the wharves. In the next week Queen's Theatre was packed with colonists who resolved to reject any convicts sent to them and to go to 'any extremity' rather than submit to the new indignity. They would declare independence from Britain, with a government of their own—'and an army of our own!' one voice cried. 'The die is cast,' said the chairman in attempting to restore order, ' Victoria will be free!'

Convictism and the colonists' own interests had resulted in nothing less than a demand for independence. But the squatter-dominated NSW Legislative Council reaffirmed the need for convict labour, Lowe within months was to return to England, and the shiploads of 'exiles' were later quietly landed and sent up country on tickets of leave.

In April 1850 the convict ship *Neptune* anchored in Hobart with 282 convicts on board. They rapidly found employment and cheekily named their own price. To the horror of all, a shipload of Irish convicts had arrived six months earlier bearing some of the rebels of the 1848 uprising. It seemed that Van Diemen's Land was

163

to be not only a dumping ground for common felons but for dangerous traitors as well. The whole idea and business of convictism—free men starved while convicts worked for wages—was becoming repugnant. The Reverend John West called for an end to 'this servile bondage' and sailed for the mainland to organise Anti-Transportation Leagues. 'The efforts of the Tasmanian people to cast off the convict yoke have excited unbounded admiration,' West wrote. 'It is from among the people—trampled underfoot, insulted, taunted, and threatened—that an irresistible confederation has sprung up!'

In mid-1850 the reverend gentleman, John Dunmore Lang, returned from his two years in Britain to form the Australian League and began lecturing on the need for an Australian republic; with his usual droll wit he thanked Lord Grey for paving the way for a United States of Australia. Lang went further. In September 1850 he told his audience that they must struggle for 'independence' and if Britain remained obdurate they must haul down the Union Jack and hoist the flag of the Southern Cross.

LIST OF THE

Traitors,—Trimmers,—Rose-water Liberals,—and Political Tidewaiters, who voted for MR. WENTWORTH'S ARTFUL DODGE, the adjournment of the Question of NO TRANSPORTATION!!! in the Legislative Council of New South Wales, August 30th, 1850.

W. C. WENTWORTH
J. B. DARVALL
S. A. DONALDSON
COL. SNODGRASS
THE COLONIAL TREASURER
THE AUDITOR GENERAL
THE COLLECTOR OF CUSTOMS
MR. EBDEN
MR. ICELY
MR. MARTIN
MR. JAMES MACARTHUR
MR. WILLIAM MACARTHUR
MR. NICHOLS
C. NICHOLSON, Speaker.

ABOVE:
Reformers branded the oligarchy as traitors for supporting the continuation of transportation of convicts.

The rise of a radical: Henry Parkes

Lang found a natural ally in Henry Parkes, who was running a shop in Sydney and had begun publishing the *Empire* in 1850. A newly arrived Scottish emigrant, the Chartist David Blair, has given us a vivid picture of these two patriot sons:

> I was walking along Hunter Street in company with Doctor Lang. He stopped suddenly before a little shop, the window of which was filled with children's toys.

> He said, 'Come in here, I want to introduce you to somebody.'

> Stepping into the shop, we found a young man about thirty. He was of striking and remarkable appearance. His coat was off and he was engaged in unpacking a case of toys. Introductions were exchanged and at once the doctor and the remarkable shopkeeper fell to talking politics. I had not listened for many minutes before I felt that here were two statesmen of nature's own making.

With Parkes' support, Lang stood successfully for a seat in the Legislative Council; his victory celebrated by 400 'Friends of Progress' who sang 'Auld Lang's Side' until the wee hours.

1850: New colonies, new freedoms

On 1 October 1850 the Legislative Council pushed through a resolution calling on Great Britain to end Transportation forever. The conservatives—'the dreadful oligarchy' as Hawkesley's *People's Advocate* called them—had been outvoted. Wentworth left the chamber without uttering a word, to mourn the end of rule by aristocrats. Two days later, to the astonishment of the colonists, Governor FitzRoy announced that he had received a significant communication from London. The British Parliament had passed an 'Act for the Better Government of the Australian Colonies'.

The Australian colonies had become the bane of Lord Grey's life. Early in 1849 he had requested the sharp legal minds of the Privy Council to draw up a Bill granting wider powers to the colonists. Their suggestions were extensive and unexpectedly liberal; indeed they redrew the map of Australia. The Act ordained that the Port Phillip District would be separated from New South Wales and form a new colony, Victoria; all colonies would enjoy self-government with the establishment of Legislative Councils in which two-thirds of the members would be elected (by a franchise safely limited to the wealthy). The 'northern region' of New South Wales would, in time, also form a separate colony, Queensland.

The transportation question was left unresolved. Van Diemen's Land—soon to be renamed Tasmania—would continue to receive convicts (though only until 1853). Western Australia alone was considered too small to be granted self-government. (Indeed transportation to Perth began in 1850 in response to the settlers' pleas for convict labour. By 1868, when it ceased, 10,000 convicts had been sent there.)

The Act was Lord Grey's last attempt to provide the framework for a federation—a united Australia. The Governor of the senior colony, New South Wales, would become 'Governor-General', the other colonial viceroys would bear the title of lieutenant-governor. But the Act fell short of granting 'full self-government', which is what the colonies wanted. To many it was merely an extension of the 1842 liberalisation. It gave the colonies no control over their revenues, nor did it solve the problem of land ownership, nor of convicts.

1851: Victoria: 'Separation at last!'

Australia was now poised on the edge of the most dramatic decade of its history. The remote, struggling, quarrelsome colonies were about to enter a Golden Age. On 1 July 1851 Victoria celebrated her emergence as a colony with bonfires and fireworks. 'Separation at Last!' proclaimed the papers. Thirteen days later a fossicker named James Esmond slammed his pick into rocks at Clunes in the hill country north of Melbourne and struck gold. Two weeks later a seam of gold was discovered only thirty kilometres north of Melbourne.

The Gold Rushes had begun. Friedrich Engels predicted that they would change the world. In little more than two years freedoms vainly sought in the 1840s fell like stars on the Australian colonies, transforming them by decade's end into the world's youngest, wealthiest and lustiest democracies.

ABOVE:
While Melbourne began overtaking Sydney in prosperity and size, Sydney's shipbuilders continued to dominate the industry: a rare photograph of ships (including a paddlewheel steamer) undergoing repair or construction in a reach of the harbour near Balmain, 1850.

OPPOSITE:
Separation at last! The new Colony of Victoria celebrates its birth, freed from what its people regarded as the odious influence of New South Wales.

V R

**THE MELBOURNE
MORNING HERALD
EXTRAORDINARY.**

Vol. XI.   MELBOURNE, MONDAY EVENING, NOVEMBER 11, 1850.   No. 1508.

GLORIOUS NEWS!
SEPARATION
AT LAST!!

We lose not a moment in communicating to the PUBLIC the Soul-stirring Intelligence that

SEPARATION HAS COME AT LAST!!
The Australian Colonies' Bill,
WITH THE AMENDMENTS MADE IN THE LORDS, ON THE 5th JULY,

WAS AGREED TO IN THE COMMONS ON THE 1ST AUG.,
AND ONLY AWAITS THE QUEEN'S SIGNATURE TO BECOME

THE LAW OF THE LAND.

The long OPPRESSED, long BUFFETED Port Phillip, is at length an

INDEPENDENT COLONY,
Gifted with the Royal name of VICTORIA, and endowed with a flourishing revenue and almost inexhaustible resources.
Let all classes of Colonists then lose not a moment in their hour of triumph in celebrating the Important Epoch in a suitable manner, and observing one

GENERAL JUBILEE.

The " Public Rejoicings " Committee lately nominated by the Citizens of Melbourne will assemble without delay; let one and all co-operate with them heart and hand in giving due effect to the enthusiastic ovations of our

New-born Colony!

167

Chapter 5
The Golden Years

From 1851 to 1860

1851: Gold discovered

IT WAS EDWARD HARGRAVES, an English emigrant, who first realised that Australia was a huge gold-field. Like 'Big' Clarke the squatter, he was physically huge, with ambitions and energy to match. Digging in California in the 1849 rush, he was struck by the similarity of the landscape there to the country around Bathurst—quartz country, with myriad gullies and creeks. On returning luckless to Sydney in mid-1851 he hurried to Bathurst and, with a companion, began panning in the creeks there, searching for alluvial gold.

He found gold specks gleaming. 'There it is!' he cried. 'I shall be a baronet, you will be knighted and my old horse will be stuffed and put into a glass case and sent to the British Museum!' In March Hargraves rode to Sydney to inform the authorities and claim a reward. He found the Colonial Secretary, Deas Thomson, cool and non-committal. More than ten years earlier the Reverend William Clarke had shown samples of gold to the Governor and Gipps had cried 'Put them away, Mr Clarke, or we shall all have our throats cut!' An influx of lawless gold diggers was the last thing the government wanted.

Returning to Bathurst, Hargraves went down on 6 May to the Lewis Ponds Creek site with his partners, two locals named Lister and Tom, and found more gold, which he proudly displayed in town two days later. Hargraves named the site 'Ophir' after the city of gold in the Bible. On 15 May 1851 the *Sydney Morning Herald* announced that another goldfield had been discovered at Wellington. In Manning Clark's words, 'A great madness was about to begin'.

The gold rush begins

'From the oldest to the youngest every one was talking of it,' wrote one aspiring digger. 'The spruce officials, the absorbed merchants, the busy tradesmen, the labour-featured artizans, the whip-cracking drivers, the active servants, the bachelors, the newly-married husbands, the matrimonial veterans, the strong, the healthy, the sick, the maimed, the lame, and the lazy saw visions of gold ...'

In the first days of news reaching Sydney, hundreds of hopefuls set out for the new El Dorado in the west, most of them by coach or on horseback, others on foot,

ABOVE:
Edward Hammond Hargraves, the burly English migrant who is celebrated as the discoverer of gold in Australia.

OPPOSITE:
Gold miners panning for gold in Victoria.
From a painting by S.T. Gill.

V. R.

NOTICE!!

Recent events at the Mines at
Ballaarat render it necessary for
all true subjects of the Queen, and
all strangers who have received
hospitality and protection under
Her flag, to assist in preserving

ABOVE:
Heading for the gold-
fields was often a festive
affair; the well-to-do rode,
the poor trudged on the
long journey.
*From a drawing by
William Strutt.*

carrying picks and shovels, blankets and pans. 'Carts and drays were piled with stores, implements, cradles, tents and bedding.' It was the same in Melbourne:

> Bullock drays, in long line, are moving northward, surrounded with companies of men and lads. Occasionally a female is seen among them. Whips are cracking, the drivers shouting, all are talking or busy aiding the departure. All kinds of vehicles, from the horse cart to the wheelbarrow, are pressing on. Yonder goes a team of four bull-dogs yoked to a nondescript carriage ... two thousand men are leaving Melbourne this morning, hurra!

Within ten days more than a thousand men were digging and panning at Ophir. Governor FitzRoy informed Lord Grey of 'the excitement which prevails in the community' (one of his aides had asked for leave and ridden off to the diggings) and proclaimed that no miner could disturb the soil without payment of 30 shillings a month. The following month, in June 1851, gold was reported on the Turon River, north-west of Bathurst. By the end of July gold valued at nearly £30,000 sterling had been unearthed in New South Wales. 'In gold', proclaimed a radical journal, 'lie the elements of all our future greatness—yes, we shall be a NATION, not a dependency of a far-off country!'

1851: The Victorian gold rush

The Victorian finds were even richer. By the end of 1852 more than 100,000 people had poured into the colony and crew members of incoming ships were joining the armies of prospective miners trudging to the northern goldfields. Ships were soon unloading six tons of gold in London every other day. The gold rush enriched and transformed the British economy: the Bank of England held so much of the precious metal in its vaults that golden sovereigns became commonplace in the coinage.

Diggers had struck gold in the ground at Sandhurst (Bendigo) and Ballarat and by the end of 1851 both areas were miniature cities of tents, shanties, weatherboard pubs. Among the immigrants, former convicts, and native-born staking out claims were lawyers, merchants, doctors and even clergymen.

Tent cities clustered on the banks of the Yarra as emigrants poured from ships that arrived daily in Port Phillip Bay. The tents on the goldfields were scenes of much violence, dissipation and debauchery, but observers were impressed by the self-imposed discipline of the diggers during the long hot days as they sweated below their mullock heaps. Picks and shovels could be left unattended; possessions were seldom stolen. There was an unwritten law that few were silly enough to break, for digger justice was quick.

BELOW:
Off to the diggings;
drawing by S.T. Gill.

'Tens of thousands of Englishmen were off to the diggings as fast as sailing ships and steam vessels can carry them to the Golden Fields of Australia, the Great South Land,' wrote the novelist Charles Dickens after going down to the Port of London in 1851. 'What a sight there was upon the jetty. I would have fancied the whole export trade of this country had gone stark staring mad with the gold fever … On the convict hulks "Warrior" and "Woolwich" the prisoners seized weapons and hurling dire threats demanded to be swiftly conveyed to "the diggings"!'

Off to Australia

Even Dickens' Mr Micawber and his family set sail for Australia. As early as 1850, before the gold rush, the colonies were seen as a land of hope for those strong enough to survive the sea voyage on overcrowded ships.

'It was such a strange scene to me,' related David Copperfield when he farewelled the Micawbers on board the vessel at Gravesend, and so confused and dark that, at first, I could make out hardly anything; but by degrees, it cleared, and as my eyes became more accustomed to the gloom.

> Among the great beams, bulks and ringbolts of the ship, and the emigrant berths, and chests, and bundles, and barrels, and heaps of miscellaneous baggage—lighted up, here and there, by dangling lanterns; and elsewhere by the yellow daylight straying down a windrail or a hatchway—were crowded groups of people, making new friendships, taking leave of one another, talking, laughing, crying, eating and drinking; some already settled down into the possession of their few feet of space …

Two of Charles Dickens' sons would emigrate to Australia, as would a son of his rival Anthony Trollope, the brother of Henry Kingsley, and the son of Dr Arnold of Rugby School. In 1853 Adam Lindsay Gordon emigrated. Poet, horseman, trooper, Gordon would be Australia's first popular balladist.

ABOVE:
A young emigrant leaves his family in England for a new life in Australia.

The long voyage to Australia was long and fraught with danger and discomfort.

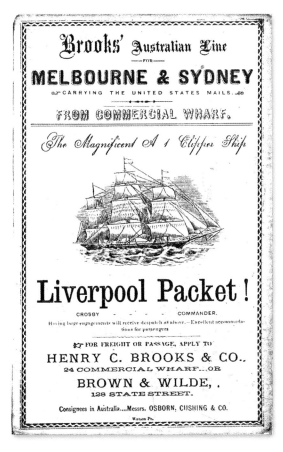

The Scots

'A continuous run of bad luck in the mother country has induced me to emigrate and see if fortune will smile more propitiously in the Antipodes,' a Scottish schoolteacher named George Morrison wrote pedantically to his brother Alexander before sailing out to join him in Melbourne in 1858. Three years after arriving George established Geelong College; Alexander rose to be headmaster of Scotch College. From Scotland came a future prime minister, George Reid, in 1852; the Scottish ancestors of three other conservative prime ministers—Malcolm Fraser, Robert Gordon Menzies and Stanley Bruce—emigrated to Victoria in the 1850s. One group of newly arrived Scots marched to the diggings in the kilt behind their pipers, with their wives and bairns following on drays. By the end of the 1850s one-quarter of Victoria's population was Scottish, and they gave the colony a Calvinistic stamp.

1855: Charles Gavan Duffy

Charles Gavan Duffy, the Irish patriot whose attempts to liberalise Victoria's constitution during its passage through the Westminster Parliament had made him a hero to the Irish and to the Protestant democrats in Australia, emigrated to Victoria with his family in 1855. 'I have laboured till my health broke down. I have neglected my family and lived only for the Irish cause,' he wrote to Smith O'Brien. 'After twelve years of fruitless struggle my heart is weary and longs for tranquillity.' A London paper crowed: 'Mr Duffy is going as a volunteer to Australia, once our Siberia, but now one of the most flourishing, independent, and comfortable communities within the British dominions.' Duffy arrived in Melbourne to be greeted by a Address of Welcome signed by ninety-five of the city's leading radicals (including the Syme brothers, owners of the *Age* newspaper, and the dedicated reformer and editor of the *Argus*, the towering Englishman Edward Wilson). 'Let me not be misunderstood,' Duffy told his admirers at the banquet of welcome, 'I am not here to repudiate or apologise for any part of my past life. I am still an Irish rebel to the backbone!'

Duffy was astonished by Melbourne, this enormous city, still half-timber, half-brick and whose streets were full of wild, drunken men 'who galloped furiously through the town'. The last celebrity the colonists had seen was Lola Montez (who was also Irish) and they took Duffy to their hearts. 'The accession of talent like his is more important that the discovery of a goldmine!' announced the rising politician John O'Shanassy. Travelling to Sydney, Duffy was

BELOW:
Irish rebel and premier of Victoria: Charles Gavan Duffy.

acclaimed by Henry Parkes and John Dunmore Lang as a future political leader, and they urged him to stand for Parliament. The Victorians raised the bulk of the £5000 Duffy needed to qualify as a man of property; this enabled him to buy a home and stand for election. Charles Gavan Duffy took his seat in Victoria's first Parliament on its opening by General Edward Macarthur in November 1856. 'If a man can find a second home on this earth, I have found it here,' Duffy wrote to his brothers in Ireland.

'Hell or Melbourne!'

Less prosperous emigrants enjoyed none of the luxuries of cabin class and little warmth of welcome when they arrived. The voyage to Australia for the poor and the assisted-passage emigrant families coming steerage was hell on high water, a three-month ordeal of suffering and terror. In 1852, when 368,000 Britons emigrated (225,000 of them Irish) to the Americas or the Antipodes, no fewer than 100,000 emigrants reached Australia. But thousands died on the voyage, victims of disease or malnutrition, the result of overcrowding by dishonest or venal ship's masters. 'Hell or Melbourne in Sixty Days,' Captain 'Bully' Forbes vowed, and to break all records he sailed the Great Circle Route following the earth's curvature, one that took his ship 700 miles south of Cape Town into the icy fringes of the Antarctic. (He made it in sixty-eight days.)

'The impulse given by the Gold Discovery and Assisted Immigration has been very great, no less than 42 ships carrying in all 15,744 souls have anchored in our waters,' a Victorian health officer reported in 1852. 'I regret to state that the number of deaths amounted to 849 …' On one ship, the *Ticonderoga*, carrying 811 Scottish emigrants, 96 died during the voyage. (Some of the English said it was the Scots' own fault, for the Highlanders seemed strangers to soap.) Laws introduced in 1853 forbade overcrowding of vessels and eventually reduced the death rate from 5 per cent to 0.5 per cent.

The Great Circle Route cut a third from the ninety days ships normally took but exposed suffering passengers to great danger—icebergs in their hundreds—and intense cold. One vessel carrying 546 souls disappeared in 1855: according to legend she ran onto an iceberg and was unable to float free. For many migrants the first land they saw after leaving England was Cape Otway near the entrance of Port Phillip, and even the overcrowded, jerry-built town of Melbourne at the onset of the gold rush looked like Paradise.

Most migrants never made it to the diggings, working instead in the towns, where wages were good and jobs plentiful. 'Rank and title have no charms in the Antipodes,' new arrivals were warned in one of the many handbooks published by enthusiastic migrants, but golden opportunities awaited the hardworking and enterprising. One female migrant advised a friend in London who was considering emigration that if she had good health and was willing to work hard 'the only risk she would run is getting married and being treated with twenty times the regard she would receive in England'; for women were few and far between in the colonies, and a good wife was prized.

ABOVE:
Madame Lola Montez, The 'Darling of the Diggers'.

OPPOSITE, TOP:
Gold Escort arriving at the Melbourne Treasury.
From a drawing by William Strutt.

OPPOSITE, BOTTOM:
'Native Police' bring in a law-breaker.
From a drawing by William Strutt.

arrival of the Gold Escort in Melbourne. conveying the chests into the Treasury, Spring Street. From sketch taken from nature in 1851. by William Strutt.

Black Troopers escorting a prisoner, from Ballarat to Melbourne 1851

The Ballarat–Bendigo goldfields began to peter out by 1854; machines took over the quartz crushing and it seemed that 'the digger', a new folk hero, was about to disappear. But new finds at Beechworth (where one show-off rode a horse with gold horseshoes) and at Walhalla on the banks of the Snowy River deep in Gippsland, gave a second life to the rush. By then Melbourne was solidly established.

'In 1845 Bourke-street contained but a few scattered cottages, and sheep were grazed on the thick grass then growing in the street,' wrote Judge Roger Therry:

> In 1856 this same Bourke-street was as crowded with fine buildings, and as thronged and alive with the hurrying to and fro of busy people, as Cheapside at the present day … In the principal street, Collins-street, here was but one jeweller in 1845 … In 1856, there might be seen in the same street jewellers' shops as numerous and brilliant as those that glitter in Regent-street. The harbour of Hobson's Bay (in 1846) contained two large ships, three brigs, and a few small colonial craft. In 1856 the same harbour was filled with about 200 large London and Liverpool A1 ships, and countless other vessels from America, New Zealand, and various foreign parts …

'Marvellous Melbourne' was the wonder of the world.

1852: The reward: self-government

Self-government came out of the blue. In December 1852 the Colonial Secretary in Lord John Russell's new government informed the Governor of New South Wales and the Lieutenants-Governor of South Australia, Victoria and Tasmania that 'the extraordinary discoveries of Gold' had created 'new and unforseen features to the political and social conditions'. The British government had decided that the new prosperity of the colonies had made it urgent 'to place full powers of self-government in the hands of a people so advanced in wealth and prosperity'.

The colonies were asked to urgently attend to the drawing up of Constitutions for their parliaments, so that the colonies could frame their own laws (as long as these laws were 'not repugnant to the Laws of England'). In May 1853 Wentworth was selected to head a committee to draft a constitution for New South Wales.

It was Wentworth's last dramatic appearance on the stage of Australian history. The constitution he had fought for would soon be a reality but the erstwhile young Patriot Son was now an embittered conservative who dreaded democracy's face and form, hating the vulgar mob—the 'Cabbage Tree Boys'—who bayed for power. He would recommend the

ABOVE:
The British Empire's growing boy: cartoon of British prime minister, Lord John Russell measuring the strapping figure of Australia for self-government.

BELOW:
The fiery radical who became a conservative: William Charles Wentworth in old age.

William Strutt's sketchbooks contain these striking images of the 1850s.

RIGHT:
An Aboriginal Christian convert.

BELOW:
Women left behind after their men had gone to the goldfields.

creation of an Australian aristocracy, a nobility drawn from the squatter kings who could control the upper house—the Legislative Council—and thus moderate or thwart the dangerous bills emanating from the Legislative Assembly. The committee members 'have no wish to sow the seeds of a future democracy,' Wentworth announced, and he denied that the middle classes—the merchants and city businessmen—had any role in law-making.

BELOW:
The British prime minister, Lord John Russell.

It was these absurd attempts to deny power to the middle classes and professional classes that brought down upon Wentworth's leonine head a torrent of

ridicule. In August 1853 a meeting was held in Sydney to protest against Wentworth's plans for a gerrymandered parliament ruled by a squatter aristocracy. Henry Parkes, Charles Cowper, the Chartist Hawkesley, the merchant Thomas Sutcliffe Mort and the Catholic Archbishop McEnroe all spoke, but the star turn was Dan Deniehy, lawyer son of Irish convict parents and one of the liveliest wits in the colony. A tiny man—'a perfect little dandy, fairly overflowing with wit, learning and vivacity' as one admirer described him —Deniehy called Wentworth's nobility a lot of 'harlequin aristocrats', a 'bunyip aristocracy' and the whole idea 'claptrap'; the colony rocked with laughter.

Charles Harpur, a friend of Parkes, and Australia's first poet of note, wrote his 'revolutionist' battle cry:

We'll plant a Tree of Liberty
In the centre of the land,
And round it ranged as guardians we,
A vowed and trusty band ...

V. R.

NOTICE!!

Recent events at the Mines at Ballaarat render it necessary for all true subjects of the Queen, and all strangers who have received hospitality and protection under Her flag, to assist in preserving

Social Order

AND

Maintaining the Supremacy of the Law.

The question now agitated by the disaffected is not whether an enactment can be amended or ought to be repealed, but whether the Law is, or is not, to be administered in the name of HER MAJESTY. Anarchy and confusion must ensue unless those who cling to the Institutions and the soil of their adopted Country step prominently forward.

His Excellency relies upon the loyalty and sound feeling of the Colonists.

All faithful subjects, and all strangers who have had equal rights extended to them, are therefore called upon to

ENROL THEMSELVES

and be prepared to assemble at such places as may be appointed by the Civic Authorities in Melbourne and Geelong, and by the Magistrates in the several Towns of the Colony.

CHAS. HOTHAM.

BY AUTHORITY: JOHN FERRES GOVERNMENT PRINTER, MELBOURNE

ABOVE:
Governor Hotham of Victoria.

ABOVE LEFT:
Trouble on the goldfields, alarm in Melbourne, 1854

He vowed 'woe' unto the traitor who would 'break one branch away'.

Yet the constitution's provisions for a bicameral parliament—the lower house elected by voters of moderate wealth—were acceptable even to Parkes (who was elected to Parliament in 1854), and Wentworth, assuring James Macarthur that the draft constitution was one of 'sufficiently conservative character,' left for London with Deas Thomson to shepherd the document through the Westminster Parliament.

Ahead lay two years of revision and discussion, a period described by one Sydney newspaper as an 'isthmus' leading from a quagmire to a verdant future. Australians' wild nationalism was dampened by the news of Great Britain's war with Russia in 1853, and men outdid each other in protesting loyalty to the Crown. Fearful of Russian attack, New South Wales raised volunteer regiments, built a warship and converted Pinchgut, the small island in the harbour where once convicts hanged in gibbets as a warning to others, into a Martello fort armed with cannon and named Fort Denison after the martinet governor who succeeded Fitzroy in 1855. (In 1899 and again in 1914 the voice of a quietly strengthening Australian nationalism—men and women who loved Australia more than they loved England—would also be drowned out by the drumbeats of Empire patriotism.)

Progressive British members of the House of Commons attacked the 'property qualifications' that restricted candidates for election to 'Men of Property'. 'These "diggers" created the wealth, and paid the taxes and, to a great extent, constituted the strength of the colony—to shut them out from political action in the government is madness,' declared Charles Gavan Duffy in Westminster. Whitehall struck out some of the worst 'property qualifications'—but not all, for the British government had no wish for the colonies to pass into the hands of the mob—and simply deleted all reference to a colonial nobility.

LEFT:
Peter Lalor, leader of the Eureka rebels.

Wentworth didn't return to Australia to live or even witness the opening of the New South Wales Parliament in 1856. Apart from one brief visit he lived out his days in England, where he died in 1872; but his body was brought home to the country that, for all his faults, he had honoured, and was buried at Vaucluse House amid the panoply of the colony's first state funeral.

1854: *In the goldfields*

Victoria's draft constitution was on a fast steamer heading for London when the goldfields exploded into insurrection. It was a constitution, like Wentworth's, that placed the control of the Legislative Council securely in the hands of the wealthy landowners—the 'Money Bags'—and contained no provision for extending the vote to the diggers so heavily taxed by the gold licence system. 'No Taxation without Representation' had been the rallying cry of the American colonists seventy-five years before; Governor Hotham, who succeeded the amiable Charles La Trobe in June 1854, had failed to learn the lessons of history.

Hotham was a naval officer accustomed to having his orders obeyed without question. He inherited a government deficit exceeding £1 million, which he was determined to reduce. As most of Victoria's police force had thrown off their uniforms and headed for the diggings, police strength was augmented by recruiting men of dubious character; the mounted troopers whose duty it was to collect the monthly £10 licence fees included ex-convicts—'Vandemonians'—who were as violent as the diggers who fought them. As the gold grew more scarce diggers were arrested as criminals for evading payment of a fee that all regarded as a harsh injustice: £10 was close to an average town worker's monthly earnings.

There was another element that possibly made conflict inevitable: the Irish. There were more Irishmen on the diggings than any other race and they had an innate inability to bend the knee to English authority and the arrogant 'Traps' who marched off their mates as criminals. One of the Irish was Peter Lalor (or Lawlor), brother of Fintan Lalor, intellectual leader of the short and

BELOW:
The cost of the hated licence was reduced later from £10 to £1.

RIGHT:
Rewards were offered to anyone knowing the whereabouts
of the rebels Peter Lalor (Lawlor) and Black.

near-bloodless Irish revolt of 1848. 'Eureka merits
closer attention, for it entered not only Irish but general Australian democratic mythology as a prime genera-
tor of Australian liberties,' writes the historian Patrick
O'Farrell; he reminds us also that when the Irish took
command of the rebellious miners most of the English
and Scots, foreseeing a bloody outcome, deserted the
cause.

The spark that detonated rebellion came in October
1854 with the murder of a digger. The culprit, his mates
had good reason to think, was the publican of the Eureka Hotel at Ballarat and a known crony of the goldfields
police. A mob of 5000 angry diggers burned the pub
down. Three diggers who were marginally involved in
the bonfire and riot were arrested: yet another injustice. When a deputation of diggers—Humffray, Black
and Kennedy—went to Melbourne to petition for their
mates' release, Governor Hotham promised to look into
the affair but then ordered police and companies from
two regiments, the 12th (East Suffolk) and the 40th
(Somerset) to march to Ballarat, a decision that broke
any trust the diggers had in him.

On 29 November 1854 thousands of diggers gathered
in the sunshine on Bakery Hill, beneath a flag of their
own devising, the Southern Cross. The German
Friedrich Vern called upon them to burn their licences
rather than submit to the government. Peter Lalor
spoke next, reminding the men that here was tyranny
as bad as that in old Ireland. The Italian Raffaello
Carboni, who had come to Australia to find happiness,
wine and song, called on them to fight tyranny. Not for
the last time in dramatic episodes in Australian history,
the grog had been freely passed around, and when a
couple of diggers burned their licences hundreds more
threw theirs into a great bonfire.

Next day, when Commissioner Rede and his force
attempted to inspect licences he was greeted with
jeers, oaths and laughter. 'We've burned them!' the diggers shouted and marched in a mob through the heat
to Bakery Hill. Here, in the late afternoon, Lalor again
hoisted the Southern Cross and called upon all those
among the 2000 assembled who were willing to fight,
to stand together. Kneeling in the dust, he led them in
an oath: 'We swear by the Southern Cross to stand truly
by each other, and fight to defend our rights and liberties.' It was stirring, but it was treason. Others shouted
for the vote, for short parliaments, for democracy.

1854: Eureka Stockade

Over the next two days the diggers built a fortress from timber slabs on Bakery Hill—Eureka Stockade—and fashioned crude pikes from staves and knives. Lalor organised them into 'divisions' like an army, under the command of his confederates, Ross (a Canadian) and Thonen, a German. Few of the rebels had guns. By Saturday night only 150 diggers were still with Lalor, the rest having melted away.

In the early hours of Sunday 2 December 1854 companies of the 40th and 12th regiments and a detachment of Mounted Troopers moved silently towards the stockade, intending to overcome the defenders by surprise. The diggers fired the first shots. The battle was all over in fifteen minutes. Raffaello Carboni's graphic description is livelier than any official report of the brief action:

> The shots whizzed by my tent. I jumped out of the stretcher and rushed to my chimney facing the stockade. The forces within could not muster above 150 diggers.
>
> The shepherds' holes inside the lower part of the stockade had been turned into rifle-pits, and were now occupied by Californians of the I.C. Rangers' Brigade, some twenty or thirty in all, who had kept watch at the 'outposts' during the night.
>
> Ross and his division northward, Thonen and his division southward, and both in front of the gully, under cover of the slabs, answered with such a smart fire … that the command 'Forward' from Sergeant Harris was put a stop to. Here a lad was really courageous with his bugle. He took up boldly his stand to the left of the gully and in front: the red-coats 'fell in' in their ranks to the right of this lad. The wounded on the ground behind must have numbered a dozen.

181

Another scene was going on east of the stockade. Vern floundered across the stockade eastward, and I lost sight of him. Curtain whilst making coolly for the holes, appeared to me to give directions to shoot at Vern; but a rush was instantly made in the same direction [Vern's] and a whole pack cut [bolted] for Warrenheip. There was, however, a brave American officer, who had the command of the rifle-pit men; he fought like a tiger; was shot in his thigh at the very onset, and yet, though hopping all the while, stuck to Captain Ross like a man.

The dragoons from south, the troopers from north, were trotting in full speed towards the stockade.

Peter Lalor, was now on the top of the first logged-up hole within the stockade, and by his decided gestures pointed to the men to retire among the holes.

He was shot down in his left shoulder at this identical moment: it was a chance shot, I recollect it well.

A full discharge of musketry from the military now mowed down all who had their heads above the barricade. Ross was shot in the groin. Another shot struck Thonen exactly in the mouth, and felled him on the spot.

Those who suffered the most were the score of pikemen, who stood their ground from the time the whole division had been posted at the top, facing the Melbourne road from Ballarat, in double file under the slabs, to stick the cavalry with their pikes.

The old command 'Charge!' was distinctly heard, and the red-coats rushed with fixed bayonets to storm the stockade. A few cuts, kicks and pulling down, and the job was done too quickly for their wonted ardour, for they actually thrust their bayonets into the body of the dead and wounded strewed about on the ground. A wild 'Hurrah!' burst out and 'the Southern Cross' was torn down, I should say, among their laughter, such as if it had been a prize from a May-pole.

Of the armed diggers, some made off the best way they could, others surrendered themselves prisoners, and were collected in groups and marched down the gully. The Indian dragoons, sword in hand, rifle-pistols cocked, took charge of them all, and brought them in chains to the lock-up.

Seventeen soldiers and one trooper were killed or wounded, twenty-four diggers lay dead; another twenty or more wounded (including Lalor, who was hidden by a priest and later lost his arm to a surgeon.) The 114 prisoners were thrown into gaol to await trial.

ABOVE:
The miners' flag and symbol of rebellion—the 'Southern Cross'.

BELOW:
Edward Wilson, the crusading editor of the *Argus* of Melbourne continues to joust with the British lion for wider franchise, greater democracy.

ABOVE:
Victoria's Chief Justice, William a'Beckett (in wig), is shown next to the wealthy squatter W.J.T Clarke ('Big Clarke') and other 'notable personages' in this drawing by William Strutt on the occasion of the opening of the colony's parliament in 1856.

The bourgeois shuddered at word of Eureka. Even Henry Parkes called the revolt an 'un-British error', probably caused by foreigners. He was correct: of the fourteen diggers killed on the day, eight were Irish and two German. One was an Englishman and only one was Australian-born. Hotham made one last error: he ordered that thirteen of the ringleaders be charged with high treason, the only penalty for which was death. The trial became a farce and the sentences were lenient. David Syme's Age pronounced the general feeling: It was the government that was rotten, not the people. When Governor Hotham caught a chill and died in early 1855 much of the bitterness of Eureka was buried with him.

Eureka would live on in folklore as the day of the Good Fight. 'Stand up my young Australian, in the brave light of the sun, and hear how Freedom's battle was in the old days lost—and won,' Victor Daley (another Irish nationalist) would write in ballad. 'Ere the year was over, Freedom rolled in like a flood / They gave us all we asked for—when we asked for it in blood.'

1850s: *The coming of democracy*

In Victoria, Eureka resulted not only in the abolition of oppressively expensive gold licences but also sweeping revisions to the electoral boundaries and suffrage: eight goldfields members were admitted to the Legislative Council in 1855. Property qualifications were changed so that 'men without property' could stand for election to the Assembly. Not only that: all voting would be by secret ballot, though in 1858—the 'Diggers' Election'—only one man in eight bothered to vote.

South Australia extended the vote to nearly all adult males in 1856; Victoria followed suit in 1857, New South Wales in 1858, Queensland in 1859. On Federation Australia became, after New Zealand, the first nation in the world to give the vote to women.

'By the year 1859 the colonies holding more than 90 per cent of the colonies' people were governed by politicians for whom nearly every man could cast his

183

vote,' writes Geoffrey Blainey. In less than ten years Australia was transformed from a convict reformatory into one of the world's most advanced parliamentary democracies.

The 'secret ballot'—and more

The secret vote—the 'Victorian ballot'—became the envy of reformers in England and Europe where voters were notorious for declaring their loyalties by wearing coloured ribbons and offering their vote to whoever would pay them best. Wealthy electors had the right to vote for more than one seat, and as late as 1918 only 60 per cent of adult males in Britain had the vote. Hugh Childers attempted to introduce the secret vote in England after returning there from Victoria, but it was not adopted by law in Britain until 1872. Australia had left the Mother Country behind.

In 1892 Queensland introduced another innovation—'preferential voting', in which electors could indicate a second or third (or fourth or more) preference among candidates, and this system was later adopted by the federal government. In 1894 Premier Kingston's South Australia introduced votes for women—the first colony after New Zealand in the British Empire to do so. In 1915 Queensland made failure to vote an offence, and the other states and the Commonwealth (in 1924) followed suit. (In both the United States and Great Britain up to half the electors never bother to exercise their right to vote.) In 1978 New South Wales was to introduce 'optional preference' voting for both Houses.

Australia had the honour of leading the world in electoral reform and in the rigorous application of democracy.

Progress and profits

The results of the Gold Rush were almost all beneficial. Improvements in transport were the most dramatic. An American, Freeman Cobb, answered the need for a coach service to the goldfields by forming a company running coaches from Melbourne to Bendigo in 1853; Cobb and Co was to eventually cover the eastern part of the continent, maintaining the world's largest coach service. Steam-powered locomotives arrived and the first railway opened in Sydney in 1854. It reached Parramatta in 1855 but Melbourne quickly took the lead in most things, including railway construction. The first steam-powered riverboat appeared on the Murray in 1856, initiating a colourful era of steamers that rivalled the Mississippi's. By the 1870s more than a hundred river boats were steaming on the Murray–Darling system carrying wool and wheat; only the extension of railways in the 1880s brought the growth in river transport to a sudden end.

Australia's first university was founded in Sydney in 1850; W.C. Wentworth is celebrated as one of its founders. In 1853 the University of Melbourne opened. Intercolonial cricket matches began in 1856 and to keep cricketers fit during the winter months the wild form of football

ARRIVAL OF THE FIRST RAILWAY TRAIN AT PARRAMATTA, FROM SYDNEY.

185

NEW SOUTH WALES.

ANNO DECIMO QUARTO

VICTORIÆ REGINÆ.

By His Excellency SIR CHARLES AUGUSTUS FITZ ROY, *Knight Companion of the Royal Hanoverian Guelphic Order, Captain-General and Governor-in-Chief of the Territory of New South Wales and its Dependencies, and Vice-Admiral of the same, with the advice and consent of the Legislative Council.*

No. XXXI.

An Act to Incorporate and Endow the University of Sydney. [Assented to, 1st October, 1850.]

WHEREAS it is deemed expedient for the better advancement of religion and morality, and the promotion of useful knowledge, to hold forth to all classes and denominations of Her Majesty's subjects resident in the Colony of New South Wales, without any distinction whatsoever, an encouragement for pursuing a regular and liberal course of education: Be it therefore enacted by His Excellency the Governor of New South Wales, with the advice and consent of the Legislative Council thereof, That for the purpose of ascertaining, by means of examination, the persons who shall acquire proficiency in literature, science, and art, and of rewarding them by academical degrees as evidence of their respective attainments, and by marks of honor proportioned thereto, a Senate consisting of the number of persons hereinafter mentioned, shall within three months after the passing of this Act be nominated and appointed by the said Governor, with the advice of the Executive Council of the said Colony, by Proclamation, to be duly published in the *New South Wales Government Gazette*, which Senate shall be and is hereby constituted from the date of such nomination and appointment a Body Politic and Corporate, by the name of "The University of Sydney," by which name such Body Politic shall have perpetual succession, and shall have a common seal, and shall by the same name sue and be sued, implead and be impleaded, and answer and be answered unto in all Courts of the said Colony, and shall be able and capable in law to take, purchase, and hold to them and their successors, all goods, chattels, and personal property whatsoever, and shall also be able and capable in law to take, purchase, and hold to them and their successors, not only such lands, buildings, hereditaments, and possessions

Preamble

A body politic and corporate, to be named "The University of Sydney," constituted with certain powers.

THE FIRST APPEARANCE OF MISS CATHERINE HAYES AT THE VICTORIA THEATRE, SYDNEY, ON TUESDAY, SEPTEMBER 26TH, 1854.

later known as 'Australian Rules' was invented in Victoria in 1858. Three years later, in 1861, the first Melbourne Cup race meeting was held, for the free money of the 1850s had stimulated gambling until it became almost a national obsession. By 1856 Melbourne had thirty-five flourishing breweries (most would be combined fifty years later in the giant Carlton and United company).

Artists from overseas—S.T. Gill, William Strutt, Eugène von Guérard, Nicholas Chevalier—found Australia a rich subject for painting during the 1850s. The English music hall performer Charles Thatcher, a gifted rhymster and a popular turn with goldfields crowds, wrote dozens of popular songs about the digger's life, creating a body of work that joined the Irish rebel ballads to form the basis of a national folksong. Another Englishman, George Robertson, a bookseller, opened for business in Melbourne in 1852, publishing his first book—a sermon—three years later. The first novel by an Australian-born writer, John Lang's *The Wetherbys*, appeared in London in 1853; Henry Kingsley's *Geoffry Hamlyn*, the first Australian best seller, in 1859. The influx of a literate population saw the founding of quality newspapers and the growth of numerous illustrated weeklies: in 1853 the *Sydney Morning Herald* was purchased by the Fairfax family, who installed Australia's first steam press; the Melbourne *Age* was founded by two Scottish brothers, the Symes, in 1854, and the Hobart *Mercury* in the same year; the *Adelaide Advertiser* dates from 1858. In 1855 a citizen who had grown rich during the gold rush

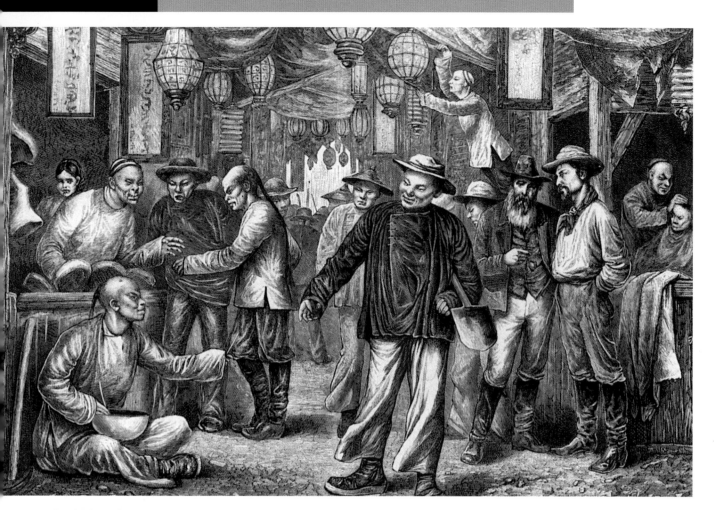

built the Theatre Royal in Melbourne for an outlay of nearly £100,000, and George Coppin, catering to the public demand for musicals and drama, imported and constructed a prefabricated iron theatre for Melbourne, naming it the Olympic.

The Chinese

The gold rush had seen nearly 20,000 Chinese enter Victoria in the 1850s. There had been Chinese in Australia since the 1830s, when hundreds came as 'indentured labourers' working for £15 a year plus rations; by living communally most managed to remit the bulk of their earnings to their families in China. The Chinese population was almost totally male; they smoked opium and rumours spread that they were given to other 'appalling practices'. They were also intensely hard workers. For all these reasons they aroused the hatred of the Europeans and clashes between the two races were common.

The Chinese became so numerous on the goldfields that in 1854 Hotham levied a tax of £10 on each arrival, but the newcomers simply landed in South Australia to escape paying it and walked overland to the diggings. In 1855 the importation of Chinese was forbidden and Hotham attempted to establish Chinese villages on the goldfields, well apart from the Europeans. In 1858, when news spread of new gold finds in south-western New South Wales, 12,000 Chinese landed in Sydney to make their way there. The result was a wild series of riots at Lambing Flat in July 1860 when the miners drove the Chinese from their diggings and burned down their shanties. When the Chinese returned, the

ABOVE:
Most of the Chinese who had reached Australia during the gold rushes later returned to their own country. But thousands remained, and Chinese have made a significant contribution to Australian society since that time.

BELOW:
The Lambing Flat flag.

LEFT:
Here the prominent Adelaide couple Charles and Alice Todd pose for one of the early daguerreotypes taken in Australia, 1855. By the late 1850s photography was widespread. Charles Todd became famous as the engineer who supervised the building of the 'Overland Telegraph Line' linking Darwin to Adelaide in 1872.

diggers attacked them. Some Chinese were killed, but no record exists of their numbers. From Sydney the government despatched a regiment of red coats by rail, naval bluejackets and a field gun to reimpose law and order, and Lambing Flat was renamed Young in honour of the Governor of the day.

Chinese continued to arrive in Australia until the 1880s, more than 20,000 of them joining the Palmer River gold rush of 1877, but Australian xenophobia was growing. Most Chinese were happy to return to their homeland when the gold ran out and only 30,000 of the great influx chose to settle in Australia when all colonies adopted a ban on Asian immigration during the 1890s, prior to Federation.

1856: The first unions

In April 1856 stonemasons downed tools in Melbourne and demanded a reduction of the working day to eight hours; as craftsmen were few, their demand was met, but other industries whose workers could be quickly replaced would continue the fight for decades for shorter hours and better conditions.

BELOW:
In the 1850s Australians pioneered the eight-hour working day—but most workers had to wait another fifty years before achieving it.

LEFT:

For Australia's original inhabitants there would be no gold rush, no rise in living standards: painting by Robert Dowling of 'King Tom' of the Mount Elephant tribe at Meningoort station, painted around 1855–56.

By the end of the 1850s Australia was supplying 50 per cent of the wool needed by England's mills and mining 40 per cent of the world's gold. Gold to the value of £124 million had been dug and assayed, dwarfing the £4 million earned by the colonies' wool exports.

Rabbits abounding

A blight on the decade arrived in 1859 in the shape of twenty-four fine rabbits, a gift from England to the Austin family who had a large property on the Barwon, near the shore of Port Phillip. The rabbits were released into the wild to provide sport for Austin and his neighbours but they quickly ran wild, multiplying at a rate that threatened to eat him out of house and home. Within ten years the rabbits had spread through Victoria's Western District, where the pickings were rich, and they reduced pasture lands to dead paddocks, eating not only the blades of grass but the roots too. No natural predators existed to cull their numbers for the European had

BELOW:

The Australian middle-class responded enthusiastically to appeals to their patriotism: a meeting in Sydney in aid of the Patriotic Fund after the outbreak of the Crimean War (1853–56).

shot the native birds of prey for sport. The rabbit armies crossed the Murray into New South Wales in 1872 and reached Queensland in 1882; more of these intrepid pioneers hopped across the Nullarbor to reach Western Australia in 1894. They had conquered the continent and would continue to devastate the land for a century.

Lastly, the colony of Victoria announced in 1859 its intention to organise an expedition to cross the continent from south to north and back again. There seemed to be no end to the triumphs and challenges of the Golden 1850s.

PUBLIC MEETING AT THE VICTORIA THEATRE, SYDNEY, IN AID OF THE PATRIOTIC FUND.

Emigrants continued to face unseen dangers on the voyage from England. The fast clipper *Dunbar* struck the rocks near South Head at the entrance of Sydney Harbour on a stormy winter night in 1857; of the 121 souls aboard only one survived.

Bushfires scourged Victoria and southern New South Wales in the early 1850s: a William Strutt watercolour of cattle racing from the flames. Often a year later floods swept away entire townships. It was a land of extremes.

Chapter 6
Conquering a Continent

From 1860 to 1901

O N NEW YEAR'S DAY 1860 two white men stood in the shimmering heat on the edge of the dry expanse of Lake Eyre in the northern deserts of South Australia. They struck picks into the rocks, hoping to find gold, but found none. The bones of fish lay caked in the dried salt: a lake without water and rocks without gold—the desert of Australia.

One of the men was a small Scot, John McDouall Stuart, his companion an Englishman, William Kekwich. They turned back from the desert, deciding to wait until the worst of the summer heat had abated before going any further. On 2 March 1860, accompanied by an 18-year-old station hand, they set out to ride from South Australia to the north coast of the continent.

Hampered by rain, and then by expanses of rounded rocks—the gibber plains— Stuart and his companions pushed north for six weeks into the wilderness, until they sighted a reddish smudge in the horizon: the MacDonnell Ranges. They had reached the centre of Australia.

On 22 April 1860 Stuart and his men climbed a nearby hill, which Stuart named Central Mount Sturt in honour of his old chief, and planted the Union Jack, symbol of 'civil and religious liberty'.

Weakened by scurvy and half-blinded by ophthalmia and the sun's glare, Stuart pushed further on, plodding 150 kilometres over country devoid of water. Attacked by nearly a hundred tribesmen, the trio retreated under a hail of spears and next day made the heart-breaking decision to head back to Adelaide. Stuart and his men reached there in September to be feted as heroes. The Scot decided to make another attempt to reach the northern coast, this time with a larger expedition, possibly a dozen men.

1860: Burke and Wills

While Stuart's party was struggling back to Adelaide, a great cavalcade of explorers was parading through the streets of Melbourne. They were en route to the Gulf of Carpentaria. The Colony of Victoria was sparing no expense. The amazing expedition consisted

OPPOSITE:
After the bodies of Burke and Wills were brought back to Melbourne for a public funeral, a memorial was raised to their memory.

BELOW:
Robert O'Hara Burke.

E. GILKS. LITH?. FROM A PHOTOGRAPH BY HILL

R. O'Hara Burke
Leader
ROBERT O'HARA BURKE,
Leader of the Victorian Exploration expedition
DIED, JUNE 28TH 1861, AT COOPERS CREEK

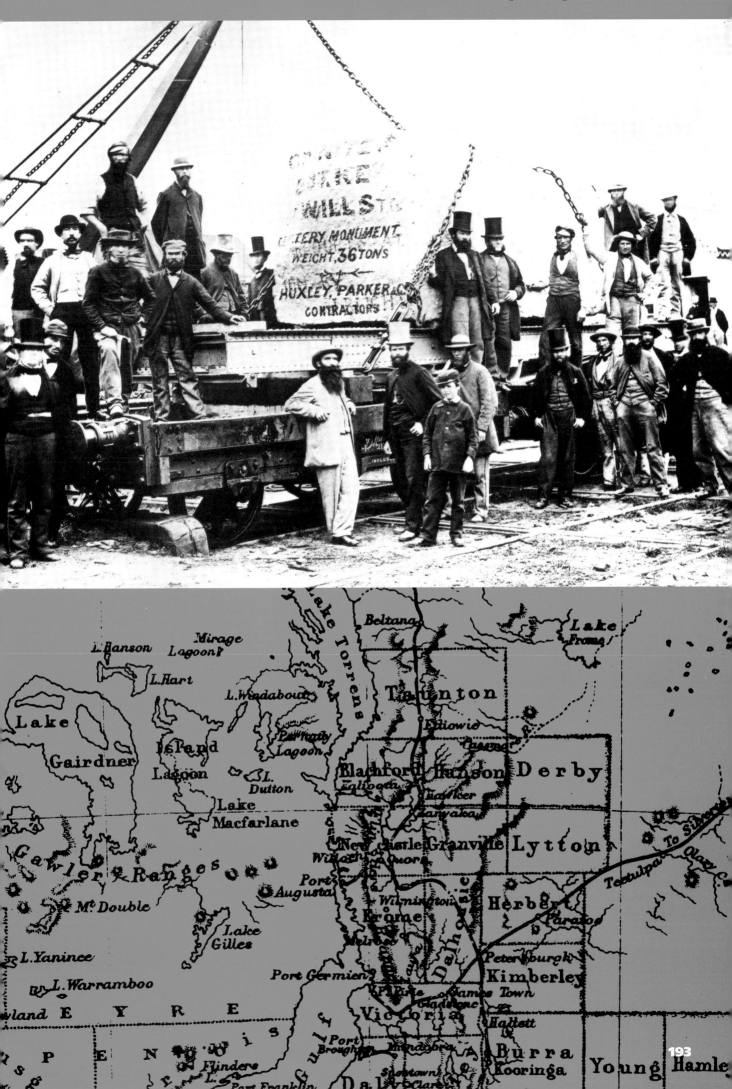

ABOVE:
The Burke and Wills expedition ride their camels out of Melbourne, 1860.
From a watercolour by William Strutt.

of fifteen men, twenty-seven camels and twenty-three horses. Led by Robert O'Hara Burke, a 39-year-old Irishman and former police superintendent at Beechworth, they departed from Melbourne's Royal Park on 21 August 1860, cheered by crowds of well-wishers.

'I have just heard', Victoria's Chief Justice Stawell wrote to Burke, 'of Stuart's expedition ... As he is now to start with an increased number—12 in all and 36 horses—it will be to a certain extent a race between you and him (but) you are much better equipped ...' The race for the north had begun.

Burke's expedition moved at a snail's pace across Victoria to Balranald on the Murrumbidgee, where he left the wagons and dumped the stores that were delaying his progress. Several tonnes lighter, the party set out next day for Menindee—the last inhabited settlement they would see. Here Burke quarrelled with his subordinates and appointed an English surveyor, William Wills, as second-in-command.

Burke and Wills left Menindee accompanied by six other men, including the foreman, Brahe, and reached Coopers Creek (first discovered by Sturt) in November 1860, establishing a base camp on the banks of a stream near the present site of Innaminka. Instead of sitting out the worst of the summer heat, Burke decided to push on to the Gulf with Wills, King and Gray and six camels and a horse. He instructed Brahe and the others to wait three months for their return. Burke was determined to beat Stuart in the race.

They headed north from Coopers Creek on 16 December and reached the impassable Gulf swamps on 11 January 1861. Now the tragedy began. The full fury of the northern wet season struck as the party struggled south through thunderstorms and mud and an enervating humidity that sapped their already exhausted health. Gray died on 17 April. The survivors were so weakened that it took them a whole day to scrape and dig his shallow grave. The three men reached Coopers Creek to find that Brahe's party had left only hours before.

I hope we shall be done justice. We fulfilled our task but we were atuad not followed up as I expected and the Depot party abandoned their post.—R.O'H Burke

Burke and his companions found rations buried for them; they rested for three weeks and then set out for Mount Hopeless, where a police post was established. The going was terrible. The camels were almost dead and unable to traverse the boggy ground. The three men decided to return to Coopers Creek. In their absence Brahe had returned to the base there, but finding no sign of Burke's party, had again left. Close to death, the three explorers awaited rescue, or death. Burke was the first to die; Wills next. King, kept alive by Aborigines, was the only survivor.

Burke's failure to return to Coopers Creek in April led to months of anxiety—and to a series of rescue expeditions that, ironically, discovered more of Australia's secrets than any previous attempts. In July 1861 the first of three relief expeditions set out. It was led by Edward Howitt, a 30-year-old Englishman who had some knowledge of the desert. He and seven others left Melbourne on 4 July and on 13 September reached the Coopers Creek depot. They found the bodies of Burke and Wills on the banks of Coopers Creek and, returning with the one survivor, King, took them back to Melbourne for burial.

In August 1861 Will Landsborough, a Scot who had discovered the Thomson River with Nat Buchanan, left Queensland for the Gulf of Carpentaria; he felt that Burke's party might have reached the Gulf and were perhaps stranded there. In an epic journey, Landsborough's party worked their way south from the Gulf of Carpentaria (from the site of Burketown), proceeding along the Gregory River to the Flinders River, discovering en route the Barkly Tablelands of Queensland; they then travelled via the Darling River to Melbourne. Of Landsborough a companion wrote: 'He was the very model of a pioneer. He could starve with greater cheerfulness than any man I ever saw.'

1861: McKinlay

John McKinlay, another Scot, led South Australia's attempt to rescue Burke, heading north from Adelaide in August 1861 in charge of an expedition of nine men, with camels and horses. In October they reached the Coopers Creek area, where Aborigines showed them the remains of dead Europeans. 'All Burke's party killed and eaten,' McKinlay informed the authorities with little regard for the truth, adding he was intending to push on to the Gulf of Carpentaria himself. Astonished to discover huge lakes, McKinlay's party was then caught by floodwaters. They reached the Gulf and

then marched east, to struggle into a settlement near Bowen in Queensland on 2 August. (McKinlay led an expedition to the Darwin area three years later. Trapped by floods, he and his party ate their horses and made boats from the skins in which they floated downriver to Palmerston.)

1862: McDouall Stuart's last journeys

John McDouall Stuart's second attempt to reach the northern coast was delayed by his illness and by lamed horses; it started in January 1862 and progressed via Newcastle Waters to the Roper and Adelaide rivers. On 26 July Stuart's party sighted the Indian Ocean. They returned to South Australia the way they had come. Close to death on several occasions, Stuart was nursed by his companions and his party returned in triumph to Adelaide in December 1862. This astonishing feat was Stuart's last contribution to the exploration of Australia. 'The 'King of Explorers', as one of his companions called him, died in poverty in London four years later. Stuart's path, a line from south to north, would be that followed by the builders of the Overland Telegraph nearly ten years later.

1870: The Overland Telegraph Line

In 1870 the South Australian Postmaster-General, Charles Todd, began the herculean task of linking Adelaide by telegraph to Darwin, capital of the colony's vast Northern Territory, a distance of nearly 3000 kilometres. He divided the construction teams into three: the northern would construct poles from Darwin to Tennant Creek; the southern would work north from Port Augusta for 800 kilometres and lay poles across the treeless wastes of the gibber deserts. The central party, under John Ross and Alfred Giles, was to find a gap through the MacDonnell Ranges in central Australia. Exploring the region on horseback in 1871, the two men discovered a beautiful natural spring, ideal for a base camp: they named it Alice Springs after Todd's wife.

By February 1871 the northern team, battling monsoonal rains and floods, their men stricken by scurvy, had carried the line barely 400 kilometres and the luckless contractor was sacked. An army of 500 workers under a new engineer was shipped north and the men offered a bonus for overtime. On 22 August 1872 the Overland Telegraph lines were ready to be connected at Frew's Creek. The engineer in charge walked forward to link the two ends. By some miscalculation the wires did not meet. He grabbed a short length of thin wire, twisted it round the two ends and made the connection, jumping back with shock as the currents met. Australia was now connected by electric impulse to London. The continent had been conquered.

ABOVE:
John McKinlay.

BELOW:
The man who succeeded where Burke failed: the Scot John McDouall Stuart, 'King of Australian Explorers'.

ABOVE:
Stuart and his party planting the flag on the shores of the Indian Ocean, 1862.

BELOW:
Ernest Giles.

Gosse and Giles: The 'Dead Heart'

The Overland Telegraph Line—the 'OT'—became a famous landmark and departure point for a new series of expeditions into Australia's centre. In 1873 the South Australian surveyor William Gosse set out from it and discovered the huge monolith the tribes called 'Uluru'; Gosse named it Ayer's Rock after his colony's Premier. In the same year Ernest Giles pushed into the wastes of the Gibson Desert (named after his companion, who perished there). In 1874 one of the last unexplored segments of the mighty continent, the Kimberley region, was crossed by John Forrest, who set out from Perth and discovered beyond its forbidding sandstone plateaux areas of land perfect for cattle raising. In the following year, 1875, Ernest Giles—the last great explorer—set out from Beltana, crossed the desert to Perth and then traversed the Gibson Desert to Peake telegraph station before finishing his epic journey in Adelaide.

Giles called the centre the 'Dead Heart'. Other Australians called this alien world of parched desert, red mountain ranges and what they perceived as savage tribesmen the Never Never.

Law and order

Australia in the 1860s was still a frontier society making the painful transition to order and law. When Henry Parkes, the Colonial Secretary in Sydney, set out by coach for Melbourne in 1866 he rode in a two-horse buggy, escorted by mounted troopers, and carried two pistols and a rifle for protection. They would be

ABOVE:
An expedition to search for Ludwig Leichhardt departs in 1865.
Painting by Nicholas Chevalier

LEFT:
Burke and Wills remain enshrined in Australian folklore, but Augustus Gregory's explorations of northern Australia during the mid-1850s are largely forgotten. His accompanying artist, Thomas Baines, painted these memorable scenes of the difficulties Gregory encountered in the Victoria River region of Northern Australia.

LEFT:
The search parties mounted to search for lost explorers discovered much of Australia for the settlers.

ABOVE:
The classic painting by
Tom Roberts, The Bail Up,
depicts the robbery of the
Forbes gold coach at
Eugowra Rocks in central-
west New South Wales in
1862 by bushrangers
including Frank Gardiner,
John Gilbert and Ben Hall.

riding through bushranger country. 'The arms of our party will enable us to fire 54 shots without loading. Our journey will lie right through the country infested by the bushrangers Clarke and his companions,' Parkes wrote to his wife. 'This will give you some idea of the pleasures of travelling nowadays through the bush of Australia!'

At Albury Parkes was met twelve kilometres out of town by a group of armed and mounted settlers and escorted to a reception in which he was treated royally. (Nine months later the Clarkes would kill four troopers in cold blood at the latters' bush campsite. The murderers were eventually caught by police aided by an Aboriginal tracker and hanged in 1867.)

1860s: *The bushranger epidemic*

The rash of bushranging reached its peak in the mid-1860s and then quickly declined as police became more numerous and aggressive, and public sympathy waned for the last of the Wild Colonial Boys. Few of them were violent men, but they raided country properties and stole horses without conscience, showing little concern for those they robbed with such obvious enjoyment.

The hold-up of the gold escort at Eugowra by Frank Gardiner's gang in 1862 and their escape with £14,000 is part of our folklore, but Gardiner thought it expedient to leave the colony and the gang soon split up.

In 1863 police gunned down Fred Lowry, whose last words also live in legend: 'Tell 'em I died game.' The only real psychopath among them, 'Mad Dog' Morgan, was surrounded in 1865 on a property near Benalla that he had been terrorising, and was shot dead. In the same year, 1865, Gardiner's old confederate, Ben Hall, was gunned down near Forbes and by December of that year 'Flash Johnny' Gilbert was killed by troopers at Binalong, near Yass. The last gang member, Dunn, was wounded and captured; he was later hanged, for the murder of a constable at Braidwood. 'Captain Thunderbolt'—Fred Ward—was pursued and shot by a Mounted Police trooper in 1870.

BELOW:
Daniel Morgan (1830–65) terrorised the Riverina and earned
the name 'Mad Morgan'. He was shot down and killed in 1865.

ABOVE
Ben Hall remains the most romanticised
of Australian bushrangers.

BELOW:
Hall, Gilbert and Dunn sticking up the mail at Black Springs, 1865.

With the bushranger menace defeated, bush settlements now held few terrors apart from loneliness. The 1860s was a decade of steady, uninterrupted growth. These were also years of exploration, but most of the country would be discovered by stockmen—overlanders—driving cattle across country into which surveyors had never ventured.

Land replaced gold as Australians' obsession. Luckless diggers crossed the Tasman in 1862 in their thousands to fight the Maori, on the promise of land grants after the fighting was done. Australia itself remained a land for the taking, and the settlers took it all.

Ned Kelly: The last bushranger

The bushranger Ned Kelly and his gang appeared a decade after the end of the wild bushranger period of the 1860s. Everything about him was original.

BELOW:

As Australia settled into middle-class prosperity, the 'last bushranger' appeared: Ned Kelly.

When he faced trial in Melbourne in 1880 for shooting policemen and was hanged, the Colony of Victoria breathed a sigh of relief, yet soon tales of his derring-do, wild humour and occasional acts of chivalry saw him transformed into a hero of sorts.

Edward Kelly, born at Wallan, Victoria, in 1855, the son of a former Irish convict, grew up with a hatred of the police, who he claimed victimised his family. By 1878 he was hiding out in the Wombat Ranges near Benalla with his brother Dan, Steve Hart and Joe Byrne. After Kelly ambushed and shot three police troopers (October 1878) he and his gang were declared outlaws. The gang eluded capture. After raiding Euroa, they crossed the border into New South Wales and held up the bank at Jerilderie. From here Ned dictated an extraordinary letter explaining his anti-social behaviour, blaming everything on the police—'big, ugly, fat-necked, wombat-headed, fat-bellied, magpie-legged, narrow-hipped, splay-footed sons of Irish bailiffs or English landlords'. He complained of the cruelty meted out to the Irish by the English, and praised those who died 'true to the Shamrock and a credit to Paddy's land'. When the gang raided Glenrowan in June 1880 and holed up in the pub they were soon surrounded by police. Ned, wearing his hand-made armour as he emerged from the burning pub, guns blazing, was the only one of the gang to survive the siege, and he was hanged for murder in Melbourne Gaol on 11 November 1880, bringing to an end a colourful but over-romanticised chapter of colonial history. His last words were 'Such is life'.

His courage and gift of the blarney made him a folk hero and the phrase 'game as Ned Kelly' is still widely bestowed as a compliment.

Colonial politics

Free trade or protection?

The post-1850s era was an age of turbulent politics, but there were no political parties. Factions ruled and strong personalities dominated. Conservatives and progressives (or radicals) jousted or jockeyed for power. With democracy achieved, the breaking of the squatters' hold on the land consumed energies well into the 1870s.

ABOVE:
Unsung pioneers of the outback: surveyors at work.
From a drawing by S.T. Gill.

Thereafter, fiscal policies overrode all other priorities, and these were reduced to two conflicting philosophies—free trade and protection. New South Wales, like the United Kingdom, was ferociously in favour of free trade; Victoria passionately protectionist.

'The political instability was extraordinary,' writes American historian Hartley Grattan, who describes the rise and fall of governments as 'almost South American'. From the mid-1850s until the 1890s, Victoria had twenty-eight ministries, New South Wales twenty-nine, South Australia thirty-seven, Tasmania twenty-two, and Queensland twenty-one. It was an age of political mediocrity not untinged by ruthless self-interest and corruption, one in which progressives could claim only one victory: the breaking of the squatters' power.

Squatters and Selectors

In 1860, when John Robertson, Minister for Lands in the Cowper government in New South Wales, rose in the Assembly to introduce a Bill devised to break the squatters' holdings, fewer than 3000 landholders controlled 7,000,000 acres (about 3,000,000 hectares) of the richest land in New South Wales. It was an affront to justice.

The squatters paid annually an average of a farthing an acre—just one-thousandth of the amount outlaid by farmers purchasing land at the standard price of one pound an acre, and who were saddled with interest. The 14-year leases obtained by the major landowners in 1847 would expire at the end of 1861, and the cries 'Unlock the land' and 'Free selection for all!' could no longer be ignored.

The Cowper government, of which Jack Robertson was Lands Minister, fell soon afterwards; but on taking office again Robertson reintroduced his Bill and forced it through, becoming a folk hero. 'The agitation on the land question has driven the people wild,' Governor Young informed London late in 1860. He wondered why the poor imagined land to be the way to riches and predicted that there would be little change to the status quo whatever the legislation.

The Robertson Land Acts permitted new settlers to 'select' 320-acre blocks of crown land in squatters' regions and purchase them on a small down payment. Robertson was a landowner himself but he was also a democrat—and a politician, like Parkes, with a keen sense of the popular will. He too was English-born. All listeners were amused by 'Hen-ery' Parkes' odd pronunciation; John Robertson had a cleft palate, which left his orations puzzling in delivery yet unmistakeable in meaning; his range of adjectives was alarming. His other liability was an adherence to high principles. Both Robertson and Parkes were men of the people, larger than life. Originally rivals, they would later share the premiership of New South Wales during the 1870s in a form of uneasy coalition—like the Spartan kings, who ruled on alternate days.

In Victoria the Nicholson Land Acts had changed nothing. In 1862 Gavan Duffy, the former Irish rebel, introduced a Bill in the Assembly that would make available, after survey, 10 million acres for selectors with enough capital to buy 640-acre lots for one pound an acre. The survey clause saw it defeated.

In 1865 a new Victorian Minister for Lands, James McPherson Grant, warned the squatters, in a blaze of fire and brimstone, that he 'had a guillotine in his heart' and would 'cut off the heads of the squatters rather than they should hold the land'.

Neither the Robertson Acts nor the Grant Acts achieved their purpose of completely breaking the squatters' hold. Land auctions became a farce when squatters financed 'dummies' to purchase land for them. Some squatters overborrowed and went bankrupt but the majority retained their properties, or shed the least valuable areas. They maintained their grip on land along river frontages or adjacent railway lines, leaving the scrub for the new buyers. It was not until the mid-1870s that the squattocracy lost its domination of colonial parliaments and submitted to increasingly severe land acts that opened up the bush for all.

Most selectors lacked the capital to buy large holdings or to purchase stock or herds, tools or implements, and many barely scratched a living from the soil before selling out. Like the 'soldier settlers' of a later century, they were the 'battlers' who formed a national ideal but went broke in the process.

The Colony of Queensland

Queensland began as a frontier society and remained one. On the separation of the region from New South Wales in 1859, the newly arrived Governor Bowen found only seven-pence-halfpenny in the Treasury, and it was stolen the next day. To add to his financial problems, New South Wales presented Queensland with a bill for £20,000 for expenditure it had incurred there before separation.

During the 1860s Queensland's settled area almost tripled in size. In 1859 Nat Buchanan and Will Landsborough struck inland and set up Bowen Downs station; in 1853 Charles and William Archer discovered the rich Fitzroy River region, north of the Darling Downs: 'Upon topping the ranges a most astonishing

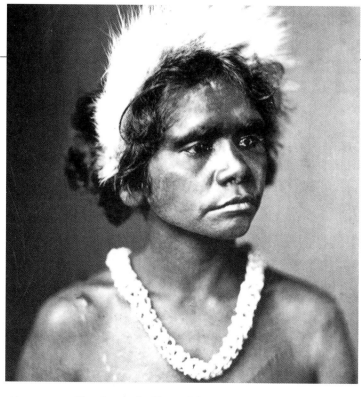

view lay beneath us. Through a large and apparently open valley bounded by table-topped and pyramidal domite mountains with here and there fantastic sandstone peaks, a large river wound its way towards the sea,' they wrote. In the following year Charles and Colin Archer (six brothers in this remarkable Scottish-Norwegian family came to Australia) opened up the land at Peak Downs, inland from Rock-hampton. In 1864 Buchanan overlanded stock to the Gulf, took up land at Burke-town and in 1878 established the first cattle station in the Northern Territory.

Tempted by the government's offer of 100 square miles of land on 14-year leases, if stocked within a year to quarter-capacity, the Duracks and Costellos drove a mob of 400 cattle up from Goulburn to the Channel Country in 1867 to carve out

ABOVE
By the 1890s, when this photograph of a young Aboriginal woman in Queensland was taken, the indigenous peoples had been decimated.

BELOW:
Into the semi-tropical jungles of Queensland; drawing from a German account of travels in the colony.

BELOW
In 1859 the revered reigning monarch lent her title to the new colony of Queensland.

cattle empires totalling 10 million acres. The Channel Country, the Barkly Tablelands, the Atherton Tablelands and the stations of the central west would be Australia's land of legend.

The Queensland squatters

Queensland squatters were a breed apart, and none were more arrogant or typical of their species than those of the Darling Downs. 'These gentlemen live in patriarchal style among their immense flocks and herds, amusing themselves with hunting, shooting and fishing,' Governor Bowen reported to the Colonial Office. They reminded him of the Virginian planters in Thackeray's novels. 'You would not send a governor here who cannot ride and shoot,' he advised. On one station at Warwick, 17,000 animals, nearly all kangaroos, were shot in six weeks. Soon afterwards squatters held a koala hunt that yielded 25,000 skins. At race meetings the squatters 'hold themselves aloof from the ordinary race of colonials' and 'after the races drink themselves blind drunk in their own exclusive booth'.

'The normal squatter hates the "free selector" almost as thoroughly as the English country gentleman hates the poacher,' wrote Anthony Trollope when he visited his son in Queensland. He was astonished to hear that six of the colony's seven cabinet ministers were squatters. 'I don't know that there can be a much happier life than that of a squatter,' he wrote. Those on the Downs lived 'a plentiful, easy life, full of material comfort, informal, abundant, careless, and most unlike life in England'. Another Englishman, William Astley (better known as the writer 'Price

205

Warung') recorded the bitterness that existed between squatter and selector on the flat, dry plains of the Riverina and saw them 'spending their energies' in cutting one another's throats, instead of combining 'in the eminently useful work of cutting the throats of the legislators'.

The Selectors

The underdogs, the selectors, would live on in the affectionate memory—the folklore—of Australia as true pioneers. One of them, a Welshman named Thomas Davis, set out for his Darling Downs selection in 1875 to put up a hut on his 160 acres at Emu Creek ahead of his wife and eight children.

He had been transported to Sydney in 1849 for stealing clothes and as an 'exile' headed for Queensland as a ticket-of-leave man, there to marry an Irish lass, Mary Green, three years later. By hard work he saved sufficient to pay the deposit of 3s 9d per acre. His wife and children followed on drays laden with furniture, pots and pans. They found their home was a hut of slab timber with an earth floor. The family cleared four acres of timber to plant corn. Their only horse, an old mare, died in foal. The ground was too hard for a spade. When the waterhole dried up, the boys walked seven kilometres there and back to a spring. One of Davis's sons wrote:

> No mistake, it was a real wilderness—nothing but trees, 'goannas', dead timber and bears; and the nearest house—Dwyer's—was three miles away. I often wonder how the women stood it in the first few years; and I can remember Mother, when she was alone, used to sit on a log, where the lane is now, and cry for hours. Lonely! It was lonely …

ABOVE:
For settlers in the bush life was primitive: a bush hut in rural New South Wales.

The photograph dates from 1900 but is a valuable record of the slab huts built by the pioneers a generation earlier.

TOP:
Travellers in Queensland, from a photograph by Richard Daintree.

ABOVE:
Blackbirders: Europeans with armed escort coerced thousands of Pacific Islanders into working in Queensland and often resorted to outright kidnapping.

But they survived; and twenty years later the writer of the above, Arthur, would publish a collection of stories drawing on his life there. Published in the *Bulletin* and later in book form in 1895 as *On Our Selection*, the stories would give immortality to Dad, Dave, Mabel and all the characters Arthur Davis ('Steele Rudd') had known as a child.

Fighting the Aborigines

'While Governor Bowen hailed "the triumph of peaceful progress",' writes historian Ross Fitzgerald, 'Queensland's history was being written in blood.' It was the only colony where the Aboriginal people—the Myalls—strongly resisted white incursion, and Aborigines were killed on a scale that amounts to genocide.

By 1865 a southern visitor was protesting against the 'wholesale, indiscriminate, cold blooded cruelty on the part of whites'. After the massacre of nineteen white settlers at Cullen-lo-Ringo in 1861, whites and native police went on an 'Abo Hunt', killing up to 500 people from one tribe alone. 'When savages are pitted against civilisation, they must go to the wall ... Much as we deplore the necessity for such a state of things, it is absolutely necessary in order that the onward march of civilisation may not be arrested,' stated the *Cooktown Herald* in January 1874 with no trace of remorse.

1863: The Blackbirders

The Queensland colonists' attitude to non-whites remained a puzzle to the moralistic southern colonies. In May 1863 the Sydney shipowner Robert Towns commissioned a Pacific trader, Ross Llewin, to recruit fifty South Sea Islanders—'Blackbirds'—to work on his plantations, where he was experimenting in growing cotton. The islanders would work in Queensland for a year, for pay of 10 shillings a month. When missionaries criticised his use and misuse of islanders, Towns told them that working on his plantation 'will do more towards civilizing the natives in one year than you can do in ten'.

The cotton crops failed, but in 1862 Captain Louis Hope discovered that sugar cane grew luxuriantly on Queensland's tropical coast. By 1864 he was employing fifty-four 'Kanakas' on his estates. The 'recruiting' process was little short of kidnapping and slavery. The Royal Navy in the South Pacific constantly arrested vessels carrying Blackbirds but local courts failed to achieve prosecutions against the owners. The Colonial Office in London was disturbed, for in 1808 England had been the first European nation to prohibit the slave trade. Lord Granville warned Governor Blackall that 'Queensland will be severed from her sister colonies … the impact of slaves, under the name of free labour, may make her a second South Carolina'.

'I would venture to offer your Lordship my own opinion', replied Blackall, 'that there is no reason to [suspect] any unfair treatment of these islanders.'

Bland assurances like these were contradicted by reports to the Admiralty from Royal Navy captains that the Islanders were being taken by force and transported to Queensland in hideous conditions. In 1872 the British government passed laws over the head of the colony ordering that all vessels engaged in Blackbirding must be licensed and established a flotilla of six patrol vessels on the Queensland coast. This removed the worst rogues but abuses continued.

By 1883, when the sugar boom was under way, 11,000 Kanakas were employed in the colony's plantations and the new liberal Premier, Samuel Griffith, who had pledged to end the trade, had to reverse his policy: sugar was too important a part of Queensland's economy to replace and repatriate its coloured cane-cutters.

More than 50,000 Kanakas worked in the colony's plantations before most of them were repatriated by 1908. They left the bodies of 10,000 of their kin on Australian soil, most of them dead from diseases to which they had no immunity.

FACT AND FICTION.

"AND RUN ALOFT ST. GEORGE'S CROSS, ALL WANTON LET IT WAVE, IN TOKEN PROUD THAT UNDER IT THERE NEVER TREADS A SLAVE."
—*Patriotic Song.*

ABOVE:
In this engraving the British government is represented as conniving in the enslavement of Pacific Islanders; in truth, the Royal Navy in Australian waters fought a losing battle to arrest vessels carrying captive islanders.

ABOVE:
Sir Henry Parkes and his wife Julia. Even in old age Parkes was a formidable and dominating figure.

New Zealand: the 1860s wars

Even in stable, progressive New Zealand violence had flared into open war between Maori and settlers. In 1860 fighting broke out in the Taranaki and spread to the Waikato. In 1861 George Grey was reappointed Governor and brokered a truce but the war erupted again in 1863. Australians, promised land by the New Zealand government, volunteered for a militia that saw some service, but most of the fighting fell to the British regiments and Royal Navy warships rushed across the Tasman. A form of guerrilla war was to last for ten years but in 1867 the Maori people were given four seats in Parliament—this was a rare step in any British colony. In that year the English historian James Anthony Froude visited the Antipodes—'Greater Britain', as he called it—and described New Zealand as aristocratic and Australia as democratic. He may have equated democracy with roughness of manners. 'The young Australians ride as well, shoot as well, swim as well, as the New Zealanders; are as little given to book-learning; but there is more shrewd intelligence, more wit and quickness, in the sons of the larger continent.' Froude spoke of 'the eager burning democracy' that was unique to Australia—and Australians' 'high capacity for personal enjoyment' that marked them out from Americans and British.

The age of progress

In 1861 Henry Parkes proposed in Cabinet that officials be sent to England to set about encouraging emigration to Australia. It came as no surprise when he offered himself for the duty.

Parkes was sobered and saddened by the misery and unemployment he saw. Lancashire seemed to him a 'wilderness' of silent factories, its streets full of 'crowds of men with hunger as plain as winter daylight' on their faces. When he extolled the joys of life in Australia and informed a meeting in his birthplace, Birmingham, that the colonial parliament was elected by manhood suffrage and secret ballot, 'not a single cheer' was heard. Parkes wondered what had happened to the English radical tradition, when men marched, risking the gallows, for better conditions.

The age of revolution had ended. The age of docility had begun. Parkes returned in 1862 to the country where everyone shouted noisily, and where the horizons were limitless.

1866: Parkes the reformer

In 1864 Parkes stood for the seat of Kiama and won, despite noisy Irish opposition, and became Colonial Secretary in 1866. In his first year in office he set up the Sydney Infirmary and invited Florence Nightingale to send trained nurses out to the colony. When they arrived two years later he was the first to bound up the

gangway to greet them, for he was never known to pass up an opportunity to meet pretty women.

In September 1866 Parkes introduced a Public Schools Bill to reform education and replace the two boards—Catholic and Protestant—that ineptly ran 'the multiplicity of small inefficient schools … The clergy of the various churches, in this as well as in the Mother Country, are the most powerful enemies that popular education ever had,' Parkes said. Henceforward a single Council of Education would administer and fund all schools and would train their teachers. The common tenets of Christianity would be taught and a clergyman might visit schools for one hour a week to teach dogma. The Catholic bishops were understandably opposed; but Parkes' system was still, in essence, in operation a century afterwards.

1867: The Queen's son shot

The visit to Australia in 1867 of Queen Victoria's younger son, Prince Alfred, Duke of Edinburgh, nearly ended in tragedy. Between Government House banquets, which left him bored, the Prince attended a corroboree in South Australia and the horse races in Melbourne, where the suburb of Coburg was named after the royal family (Saxe-Coburg-Gotha) and sailed up the Hunter River by steamer while colonists on its banks fired their rifles in the air in ragged salutes and children on its bank sang:

> Welcome, welcome, Royal Alfred,
> Son of our beloved Queen!
> Welcome to our rustic valley
> Welcome to our autumn scene!

ABOVE:
On the first royal visit to Australia Alfred, Duke of Edinburgh, was wounded by a lunatic at a picnic in Sydney in 1868. Alfred survived the attack.

OPPOSITE:
With the Royal Navy's 'Australia Squadron' reduced to a few obsolete warships and a batch of gunboats, the arrival of the British 'Flying Squadron' on a brief visit on a voyage round the world cheered the colonists. Here Victoria's own flagship, the antique HMCS *Nelson* (built in 1815) proudly leads the squadron down Port Philip Bay in 1870.

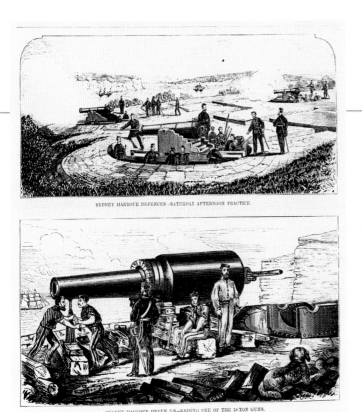

SYDNEY HARBOUR DEFENCES—SATURDAY AFTERNOON PRACTICE.

SYDNEY HARBOUR DEFENCES—RAISING ONE OF THE 18-TON GUNS.

LEFT:
With the departure of the last British regiments in 1870 the Australian colonies were forced to attend to their own defence. The first permanent military forces in New South Wales were artillery to man the guns at the entrance to Sydney Harbour.

At a picnic at Clontarf on Sydney Harbour an Irishman shot him, causing only a superficial wounding, for the bullet had bounced off the royal braces. The assailant was thought to be an Irish terrorist—one of the Fenian Brotherhood—but was only insane; nevertheless he was Irish and was hanged, and Australia spun in a new storm of anti-Catholic feeling. The Duke lived on to distinguished old age, dying in 1900, one year before his mother, the Queen.

1870: The Redcoats depart

In 1870 the last of the British regiments were withdrawn from Australia, New Zealand and Canada by Gladstone's government, leaving only the warships of the Royal Navy's Australia Station as evidence of Britain's imperial might. Queen Victoria was upset, chiding Gladstone's minister: 'The Queen could never forgive herself if she found she had inadvertently given her assent to anything that could risk the safety of her colonial possessions.'

Fear of the Americans, fear of the French, fear of the Russians and soon fear of Germans and Japanese, stimulated the Australian colonies into periodic war scares. Victoria led the way, forming her own navy in the 1860s—a motley fleet that included an old battleship from Nelson's days, a steam yacht and an armour-plated

LEFT:
A century after rabbits were let loose they had turned much of Australia into baren land. This photograph dates from the1950s.

BELOW:
Australia's stormy coast: the lighthouse at Seal Rocks, New South Wales, photographed in 1876.

monitor, the *Cerberus*. Australia's militia units date from the last decades of the nineteenth century: Queensland volunteers formed Highland regiments who sweltered in red coats and woollen kilts; graziers served as officers in units of lancers and light horse. Sir William Clarke, Australia's first baronet (and a son of Big Clarke) maintained a horse-drawn Nordenfeldt gun battery on his property at Sunbury as a contribution to his colony's defence.

ABOVE:
Hobart in 1870. More than one visitor described the city, nestling beneath the snow-capped peak of Mount Wellington, as the most attractive of Australian capitals.

Parkes and Duffy

In 1870 Parkes, anti-Catholic when it suited him, was declared bankrupt for the second time in twenty years, but two years later became Premier. By now snow-bearded, for his financial woes had aged him, but still striking in appearance, Parkes would continue to dominate NSW politics for the next twenty years. Five times Premier, thrice married—a distinction he shared with Robertson and Duffy —and the father of 12 children, Parkes was to survive another bankruptcy to become a figure of such renown that the President of the United States and the Emperor of Germany were flattered to meet him; the flawed giant in time became the prophet of federation.

BELOW:
Two lively NSW premiers: Sir Henry Parkes (right) and Sir George Dibbs.

In Victoria a form of stability came in 1863 and the election of the McCulloch government which lasted until 1871, when Gavan Duffy—despite howls of 'No Popery!'—briefly became Premier. A champion of federation, Gavan Duffy endured the faction-fighting of colonial politics until 1880 when he decided to return to Europe, writing to Parkes of his weariness

ABOVE:
Melbourne's fine Government House was first occupied in 1876. Previously the Governor had resided in Toorak. Both residences still stand.

with parliamentary life, 'so petty and so rancorous, so dead and driftless'. To his old friend he wrote: 'Where are the dreams of a noble, generous free state in which the wise can rule, and the fool and the knave are absent?' (Of Duffy's children, one son became Attorney-General of Victoria, another helped to draft the federal Constitution, a third became President of the Irish High Court and a daughter took part in the Irish Uprising of 1916.)

Inching towards federation

'For the first time in the history of these Australian colonies, they have all, including New Zealand, met with nothing but the desire to effect a common end, to suit the views of all. The time has come when these colonies should be united by some federal bond of connexion.' Henry Parkes' speech at the gathering of colonial authorities in Melbourne in 1867 was the first of his public calls for union. The circumstances were possibly inappropriate for the eastern colonies had met to decide on ways of improving the speed of the postal service from Australian ports to Suez (from where fast steamers sped letters to Britain).

'I am confident that a majority of fellow colonists are looking to me now for important services,' Parkes wrote to his second wife. 'The position I was allowed to take has compelled the respect even of my enemies ...'

Gavan Duffy of Victoria—by now the leading colony in wealth and population—was the next formidable figure to promote union. In 1870 he called for a royal commission to report on federation. His call fell on deaf ears. The Act of 1850 had been drawn up by the British government as a framework for a united Australia, one in which goods and produce could pass as freely between the colonies as freight did between the counties of England, but colonial rivalries had erected tariff barriers that were as effective as guarded frontiers in protecting their own interests. All colonies feared domination by Victoria, the dynamo of growth.

In 1881 Parkes, pleading for the institution of common tariffs, suggested the creation of a Federal Council of Australasia and in 1883 Victoria's Premier James Service delivered a speech at Albury during the connection of the Melbourne–Sydney rail link that gave supporters of federation their battle cry: 'We have long been separated, and rivalries and jealousies of each other have sprung up in consequence. But now we are looped together with bands of iron … Gentlemen, we want federation and we want it now!'

Ironically, the railways of his metaphor served only to perpetuate disunity. The colonies had rail gauges of differing widths: New South Wales had adopted the English gauge—4 feet 8.5 inches; Victoria and South Australia chose the Irish gauge—5 feet 3 inches—because the former colony had already ordered rolling stock to fit these rails; Queensland and Western Australia used gauges 3 feet 6 inches wide, because of the cost saving. Long after federation the differing rail gauges plagued the efficiency of the nation's railways.

At an Intercolonial Conference also held later in 1883, Premier Griffith of Queensland proposed forming a Federal Council made up of two members from each colony, with the power to legislate on matters of universal concern, one of these being a common front against French and German activities in the Pacific. Oddly, New South Wales and New Zealand both voted against participating.

1884: New Guinea and Papua

The Australian colonies' sense of isolation and fear of external threats became the most powerful impulse towards federation. The great island of New Guinea lay across Australia's north, but no European power had yet claimed it. (The Dutch had claimed the western half in 1829, but the east remained the preserve of tribesmen, of little interest even to explorers and anthropologists. The Russian scientist Nicholai Miklouho spent time among the tribes at Madang on the north coast in the 1870s, and the Italian explorer Luigi d'Albertis ventured several hundred kilometres up the mighty, fast-flowing Fly River in 1876, accompanied by an adventurous young Englishman, Lawrence Hargrave, who would later be Australia's pioneer of flight. Everything about New Guinea was forbidding—its mist-shrouded mountains, its suffocating humidity, its diseases, its tribal warriors, its sheer size.

MURDEROUS ATTACK BY NATIVES AT SANTA CRUZ ON COMMODORE GOODENOUGH AND BOAT'S CREW.

RIGHT:
In the latter quarter of the nineteenth century Britain began extending its domain in the South Pacific in response to French and German moves and increasing bloodshed between Europeans and Islanders. When Commodore Goodenough sailed from Sydney to negotiate with the chiefs in the Santa Cruz Islands he fell victim to a poisoned arrow. In 1874 Fiji became a British dependency.

A new commodore, Sir George Erskine, raises the British flag in Port Moresby in 1884 behind a guard of British sailors and Marines, claiming Papua for the Crown. Steaming in his flagship HMS *Nelson*, Erskine then planted the Union Jack on headlands around Papua's southern coastline.

Workers lived simply, in tenements that duplicated the workers' dwellings of the industrial cities of England. Terraces in Darlinghurst in 1870. Sydney's inner-city slums were few but became notorious for rowdiness, drunkenness and vice.

Queensland had claimed the Torres Strait Islands in 1878 and went so far as to despatch a magistrate to claim eastern New Guinea for the Crown in 1883, but the Imperial Government repudiated the act. 'If the Australian people desire an extension beyond their present limits, the most practical step that they could take … would be the confederation of those colonies in one united whole,' Lord Derby announced.

German warships steaming to annex the north-eastern coast of New Guinea and the islands of New Ireland and New Britain (which they named the Bismarck Archipelago) in 1884 forced Britain to act: the Commodore of the Australia Station was ordered to take possession of the remaining part of New Guinea—Papua—and this he did, steaming from Sydney in his flagship HMS *Nelson*, and raising the flag at Port Moresby in November 1884.

The war scare of 1884 after Russian incursions into Afghanistan, during which the colonies purchased gunboats to protect their shipping from the Russian Pacific squadron, and the French seizure of the New Hebrides in 1886 (Britain later occupied the islands jointly with France), intensified concerns about Australia's defences.

ABOVE:
St Andrew's Cathedral and the new Sydney Town Hall, photographed by Charles Bayliss in 1879.

ABOVE:
Henry Lawson in the
1890s.

TOP:
By the 1880s Australia's
Aboriginal people were
so reduced in numbers
that it was thought they
would soon disappear
completely.

An Aboriginal couple and
their child in New South
Wales.

New Zealand opts out

The Federal Council—'a rickety body', Parkes called it—continued to meet between 1886 and 1899, achieving little. New Zealand attended out of politeness and curiosity. Her Premier Richard Seddon—'King Dick'—a mammoth Yorkshireman who had prospected for gold in Australia in the 1860s, saw New Zealand's destiny as a colonial power in Polynesia, not as an adjunct to Australia. 'Am returning to God's Own Country,' he cabled midway through one abortive conference, after boarding a steamer for Wellington, and he never came back.

1888: The Centenary

As the end of the first century of British civilisation in Australia approached, her three million people congratulated themselves on their wealth and progress. Public buildings in Italianate grandeur—like ornate birthday cakes—were built in suburbs and country towns to celebrate the great Queen's reign. Australians had duplicated England, laying the pattern of borough, shire and municipality on a harsh and unwelcoming land.

Premier Parkes tried to mark the centenary by changing the name of New South Wales to Australia; the Bill failed, despite the support of Sir John Robertson, who wrote: 'We introduced civilized man. If this colony is not Australia, I should like to know what colony is.'

'Leaving out the rum, the cat and the gallows, there is little cause for exuberance,' stated the radical Sydney weekly the *Bulletin*, which had begun publication in 1880. 'The spirit of Labour and Lang is the spirit that we look for in our public men,' it said—an Australia of 'pioneers, diggers and Democrats'. In the *Bulletin*'s view the present Australia was one of 'toadies, grovellers and lick-spittles' of whom 'Sir Henery' was the worst. Louisa Lawson published the first issue of her progressive journal *Dawn* as a similar act of protest against middle-class smugness and her son Henry, a gangling boy teased by his fellows for his deafness, was also infatuated with republicanism and wrote in verse of the grief he had seen in the faces of the poor. 'Faces in the Street' was published in the *Bulletin* in July 1888. It was the beginning of his troubled writing life.

At a banquet on Foundation Day 1888 Sir Henry Parkes toasted 'Australia, her trials and triumphs, her union and progress in the future'. Well-attended anniversary celebrations followed and numerous lavish volumes recorded the success of all the Australian colonies. The future looked bright.

THE BULLETIN

SYDNEY, SATURDAY, JANUARY 31, 1880. Pric

The Bulletin.

SATURDAY, JANUARY 31, 1880.

MATTER OF PUBLIC CONCERN.

DAY we send broadcast throughout the colonies first number of THE BULLETIN. That it to an appreciative public we have no doubt. ellence is the passport to success in colonial and THE BULLETIN bids to win. The aim of

THE PRESS SNUBBED.

As it is hardly likely that the Sheriff would on his own responsibility have excluded reporters from the gaol on the occasion of the execution of the Wantabadgery bushrangers, it may fairly be assumed that the action alluded to was solely a result of instructions received from the Colonial Secretary. SIR HENRY PARKES, now a professional politician, was once a pressman himself, and not only a pressman, but a newspaper proprietor. In the good old days, when there was as yet "no such a person" as "SIR HENRY," the present Premier was editor of the EMPIRE.

AN UNTIMELY CRAZE.

JUST as Mr. BUCHANAN begins to agitate for Protection the news of the successful voyage of the Strathleven comes to render Protection forever impossible, in this colony at least. For we want to send our beef and mutton to the English market, and the proof that we can do so will send the price of every bullock up to £15 or so in the course of a very few months. But if we are to send shiploads of meat for English mouths we must, if freight is to be cheap and prices high,

friends. He knew that something more was study, earnest study, and patient, and practice. He determined to place his daugh Conservatoire de Musique of Paris, and, desp insurmountable obstacles, succeeded after a p struggle of nine months; Camilla was admit age of seventy-six. She was the first girl and paved the way for several others on whom was subsequently bestowed. De Beriot, dire Conservatoire at Brussels, visited Paris and child; he was so delighted that he offered to Brussels and give her a complete musical but the plan was frustrated by the pover realising a considerable sum; and she then her studies. Each year she gained more honour at the examinations, and at the end bationary period of three years she went to with her diplomas, under engagement to a

The Australians

In 1877 the Melbourne journalist Marcus Clarke, author of the first great Australian novel, *His Natural Life*, had discerned a definite 'national type' and had predicted that the Australian a century hence would be a 'tall, coarse, strong-jawed, greedy, pushing, talented man, excelling in swimming and horsemanship,' his national politics 'a democracy tempered by the rate of exchange'. James Hogan in 1880 described the Australian's main characteristics as 'an inordinate love of field sports and a great dislike of mental effort'.

Richard Twopenny's *Town Life in Australia*, published in 1883, provides an entertaining and perceptive portrait of the Australian of the day. 'The general feeling in Australia is democratic,' he wrote. The typical Australian youth he described thus: 'His impudence verges on impertinence, and his want of respect for everybody and everything passes all European understanding' (Twopenny was Englishborn) but he is 'able to ride almost as soon as he can walk, he is fond of all athletic sports ... Generally intelligent and observant, he is here, there and everywhere; nothing escapes him, nothing is sacred to him.' He observed that while English boys dutifully played cricket at school, most of them gave up the game on leaving; in Australia boys and men

ABOVE:

First issue of the *Bulletin* in 1880; the weekly has survived to this day as a news magazine.

BELOW:

As sportsmen Australians were achieving renown in cricket: a scene from the famous test match at Kennington Oval in 1882 as England's W.G. Grace faces 'demon bowling' from Australia.

LEFT:
The weekly journals such as the *Bulletin* attracted
numerous artists whose work reflected a uniquely
relaxed way of life.

played it with an almost religious dedication. (In 1882 the Australian team had rewritten the history of the game, trouncing England, who needed only 85 runs in the last innings to win, by a demonic display of bowling by Freddie Spofforth. A supporter of the beaten English team had put an obituary notice in the paper announcing the death of English cricket, notifying readers that its 'ashes' would be taken to Australia.)

Sport became a powerful shaper of Australian national pride and the male character. 'For Catholic and Protestant boys alike, sport was probably the main teacher of morality,' writes historian Geoffrey Bolton. 'To play by the rules and obey the umpire, within reason, meant more in the here and now of Australians than any amount of Sunday preaching.' Rugby and its Irish offshoot, 'Aussie Rules', produced generations of Australians who were taught to take hard knocks for the sake of the team and to never whinge. On Gallipoli the Australians charged into battle, an English observer later wrote, 'like a football team'.

Australian males, compared with Englishmen, seemed to have 'greater independence of manner and thought, more tolerant views, less reserve, more kindliness of heart.' Twopenny wrote. 'In Australia a man feels himself a unit in a community, a somebody; in England he is one amongst 27 million, a nobody.'

One the whole, 'colonial girls' were good-looking but true 'beauties' were rare, for 'the sun plays the devil' with fair complexions. The Englishman found the Australian girl refreshing: 'Her frankness and good-fellowship are captivating and all her faults come from her head, and not from her heart. She is rarely affected, and is singularly free from "notions".' In choosing a husband, Australian girls married for love, not money.

'In no country in the world is the legal freedom of worship more firmly established than in Australia. All churches and sects are absolutely equal,' Twopenny recorded. 'Generally speaking, food in Australia is more plentiful than in England but poorer in quality.' Meat appeared to be the staple of the colonial diet and the only two beverages consumed seemed to be tea—and champagne.

The American writer Mark Twain visited Australia in 1893 in the course of a world tour, and found Australians refreshingly like Americans—easy and cordial in their manners, as friendly as the English 'but with the English shyness and self-consciousness left out'. On the train journey to Maryborough a trainee clergyman warned the American that the pub there was 'a hell of a hotel'

BELOW:
The engineers who carried out the monumental task of linking Adelaide to the telegraph cable from Europe that had reached Australia's northern coast at Darwin. South Australia's postmaster-general, Sir Charles Todd, stands second from the right.

with no beds—'just sandbags'—and the cupboard consisted of 'two nails on a wall'. The visitor enjoyed the laconic humour.

George Morrison, the son of Dr Morrison of Scotch College, was a man Twopenny and Twain might have been tempted to hold up as a typical Australian of his time. Finding himself in Normanton on the Gulf of Carpentaria in December 1882, he decided to walk home to Melbourne. He set off alone, just as the Wet was about to break, and, like Burke and Wills, had to wade through flood for much of the way. He strolled into Melbourne in April after crossing the continent, a journey of 3200 kilometres in 123 days. The London *Times* called the feat 'one of the most remarkable of pedestrian achievements', and later appointed Morrison correspondent in Peking, where he survived the siege of Peking by the Boxers and became an adviser to the Chinese republican government.

Without sufficient great men in their short history, Australians would idealise certain male qualities they felt were common to all. Mateship was pre-eminent. The shearer, the stockman and the overlander, the miner and the prospector, the bushranger, the selector, and later the sundowner and swaggie 'waltzing his matilda' down the wallaby track, would become folk heroes, and bit players in the comedy of Australian life. They were later joined by the soldier—the Digger; even the larrikin, the street kid, would be idealised, because mateship and irreverence towards authority were common to all Australians, whether they were 'Micks' or 'C of E.' Henry Lawson would write:

They tramp in mateship side by side,
The Protestant and Roman,
They call no biped lord or 'Sir',
And touch their hats to no man!

Australians spoke their own idiosyncratic language, a humorous one that city folk took up. Selectors were 'cockies' because they scratched out a living. The summer was drier than a dog's bone, some coves were lower than a snake's belly, a shearer who couldn't get through a hundred wethers in a day was a learner, hard workers were 'flat out like a lizard drinking'. Lacking a known history, Australia evolved a folklore instead and mythologised tragedies.

Other Australians, like Walt Whitman in the USA, found poetry in the place names of the land itself: Goondiwindi, Cunnamulla, Toowoomba, Chinchilla; the Barcoo, Bulloo, Paroo, Diamantina, Maranoa, Warrego; Gundagai, Cootamundra, Mareeba, Meekathara, Wangaratta, Oodnadatta; and cocky names like Donnybrook, Springsure, Longreach.

The slow march to federation

In 1887 the Colonial Conference had requested that a senior British officer be sent to Australia to report on the colonies' defences. Major-General Edwards, who arrived in 1889, reported briskly that Australia could not defend her shores without some form of unified central command, which could only come through federation. This widely discussed report caused Parkes to call, in a speech soon afterwards at Tenterfield, for a 'Federal Parliament' to coordinate Australia's defence.

A Federal Conference was called to sit at Melbourne in February 1890. In a speech there Parkes toasted a 'United Australasia' and said: 'The crimson thread of kinship runs through us all … Even the native-born Australians are Britons, as much as the men born within the cities of London and Glasgow …'

The rising Victorian politician Alfred Deakin wrote of Parkes: 'His huge figure, slow step, deliberate glance and carefully brushed-out aureole of white hair combined to present the spectator with a picturesque whole. His voice … was pleasant and capable of reaching and controlling a large audience'. It was an impressive performance by the Grand Old Man.

BELOW
Now a prophet of Federation, Sir Henry Parkes is shown fancifully presenting his plan for a 'Commonwealth of Australia' to Queen Victoria.

The Queen, with memories of Cromwell's Commonwealth, is not amused.

The extension of railways from the 1860s onwards, made possible by British banks, opened up the inland and spelt doom for the horse-drawn coaches.

ABOVE:
As in all periods of boom, profits were there to be made. A suburb is planned in Sutherland, to the south of Sydney.

Within a week, Griffith of Queensland, the keenest of legal brains, was chosen to head a committee to draft a federal constitution for the country which, on Parkes suggestion, would be called 'The Commonwealth of Australia.' Legend has it that Griffith wrote most of the Constitution himself, on his government's yacht.

The age of expansion: 1870–1890

The period from 1860 to 1890 was one of unparalleled growth. Between 1875 and 1891 railway lines grew sixfold from 1600 miles to 10,000 miles, linking wheat fields to townships. The railways—probably the greatest achievement of the period—were built with loans raised in Britain.

During the 1880s the Australian colonies went on a spending spree, borrowing nearly two hundred million pounds from British banks. The results were to be calamitous. The 1880s also saw the transformation of the cities in a building binge that was hastened by speculation and fired by borrowed capital. Mark Twain was astonished that Australian towns spent thousands of pounds on town halls, municipal offices and banks where Americans spent only hundreds, and he wondered where the money came from to erect such monuments to progress.

The pinnacle of Sydney's construction boom of the 1880s and probably one of the greatest buildings of its time: the new General Post Office on its completion in 1887.

The building served as the GPO for more than a century. The newly renovated building still dominates Martin Place.

The second rush

Continuing gold strikes and unexpected mineral finds fuelled progress and hopes. None approached the size of the 1850s finds, but discovery of gold at Gympie in 1867 saved Queensland from the devastating consequences of a rural slump, and bankruptcy; next year gold was found at Ravenswood. In 1870 copper was discovered at Cobar and more gold in 1872 at Charters Towers. When diggers were thinking the Turon–Tambaroora fields were nearing exhaustion two Germans, Holtermann and his partner Beyers, found a massive nugget at Hill End in 1872, sparking a rush that turned the place into a miniature city. In the previous year the world's largest tin deposit had been found at Mount Bischof in Tasmania.

1883: Silver at Broken Hill

In 1883 another German, Charles Rasp, who was working as a boundary rider on the McCulloch property near the Barrier Ranges in the far south-west of New South Wales, decided to investigate a curious, broken-backed hill that he thought must contain some minerals of value. Silver had recently been found nearby at Silverton and Rasp had bought himself a mineral recognition handbook. He took some rock samples from the hill and, positive that they contained minerals, rode to a trooper's homestead to write out a claim. Staking out a small area Rasp then informed his employer who, to his surprise, said 'There's only one thing to do, that's peg out the lot!'

Five other investors each contributed £7 as capital. The syndicate of seven was astonished by the geologist's report: the rocks contained silver-lead ore in high quantities. The Broken Hill Proprietary Company—BHP—was floated on the market in the same year. It would become the nation's largest mining and steel-making combine.

Laying the international telegraph cable linking
Australia to New Zealand at Botany Bay in 1876.

The birth of the Broken Hill mines:
McCulloch's shaft, June 1887.

LEFT:
The 1880s boom begins: businessmen
and investors gather for the latest stock prices.

The prolonged drought from 1877 to 1891 prompted the Victorian government to consider methods of conserving water in the parched north-west of the colony. In California desert had been turned into productive orchards by irrigation. On Alfred Deakin's initiative the Chaffey brothers of California were invited to Victoria in 1886 to repeat the miracle at Mildura, and at Renmark in South Australia.

A definable Australian culture

The 1880s saw the birth of both a recognisable Australian culture and an Australian nationalism, a complex of aggressive pride in the country and irreverence for many things British.

The parent of Australian literature was the *Bulletin*, a weekly journal founded in 1880 by a Scot named Traill, who three years later sold shares to John Haynes and J.F. Archibald. Haynes had little money but had great self-confidence and wide social contacts. 'I knew everybody who was anybody in Sydney,' he boasted. Archibald was an editor of genius, an Irish-Scottish Australian and a francophile (he changed his Christian names to Jules François as token of his love for French civilisation). From the start the journal was democratic but racist to a degree that tarnishes its larrikin charm; it spoke for the common man—particularly the bushman—and mocked the pretensions of the bourgeoisie. Archibald had conceived a hatred of the English ruling classes,

BELOW:
Shearing the Rams,
c. 1890, by Tom Roberts
(classic painting from
National Gallery of
Victoria).

particularly the aristocratic sprigs who occupied Government House: they were ripe subjects for satire at the hands of his writers and cartoonists (the English artist Phil May and the American Livingston Hopkins in particular). Archibald welcomed contributions from his readers and published ballads, verse and fiction in every issue.

In A.G. Stephens, who joined Archibald in 1894 and three years later founded the literary page—the 'Red Page' of the back cover—Australian literature found another champion. In printing verse, ballads or stories by Henry Lawson, Andrew Barton ('Banjo') Paterson, Will Ogilvie, Harry Morant, Victor Daley, E.J. Brady, Edward Dyson, Barcroft Boake and a host of others Archibald and Stephens turned the *Bulletin* into the 'Bushman's Bible'. Archibald encouraged the English journalist William Astley ('Price Warung') to expose the cruelties of the convict days in a famous series of articles later published in book form. Australians were already adopting a comforting national amnesia about those terrible years but Archibald reminded them: 'We did not make our history. We only tell it. We only flay the carcase of the hybrid and moribund monstrosity ...'

Stephens, a beefy, flamboyant man, was also given to damning anything British ('I have nothing against Oxford men. Some of our best shearers' cooks are Oxford men') and overpraising anything Australian. Like Archibald, he had a weakness for the Celts—artists and writers such as Norman Lindsay, Hugh McCrae, Mary Gilmore, Miles Franklin, Joseph Furphy, A.H. Davis ('Steele Rudd'), Bernard O'Dowd and John Shaw Neilson received, and returned, his admiration. He was to compile twenty books out of his contributors' writings and rival George Robertson as a founding father of a national literature.

ABOVE:
Andrew Barton ('Banjo') Paterson in 1900.

Archibald inspired great love; even his letters to contributors rejecting their verse were treasured by the recipients. 'His resentments—against cruelty, oppression, wealth, jingoism, established religion, and conformism—explain many of the extreme *Bulletin* policies,' writes one historian of Archibald's editorship. This mercurial man had a nervous breakdown in 1907 while attempting to found a purely literary journal, the *Lone Hand* (Stephens took over the editing) and was committed to a mental home by his business partner, McLeod. ('Why did you chuck me in Callan Park?' he protested.) Archibald retired from the journal in 1914 and died five years later; Stephens continued under full sail until his death in 1933.

The city or the bush?

The city or the bush? The debate became a favourite of those attempting to delineate the Australian character, but Australians had already decided the issue. They were a nation of city dwellers, the world's first urban nation. In 1892 two of the public's favourite balladists decided to debate the relative virtues of bush and town life in the pages of the *Bulletin*.

Henry Lawson led off, and ended his first poem bleakly:

Bush! Where there is no horizon!
Where the buried bushman sees
Nothing but the sameness of the ragged, stunted trees.

Banjo Paterson replied in mock indignation:

You found the bush was dismal and a land of no delight,
Did you chance to hear a chorus in the shearers hut at night?

and suggested to his sparring partner:

You had better stick to Sydney and make merry with the Push
For the bush will never suit you, and you'll never suit the bush …

Paterson first achieved fame in the *Bulletin*; his ballads spoke of life in the saddle and the wonder and majesty of the great land:

the vision splendid of the sunlit plains extended
And at night the wondrous glory of the everlasting stars

Paterson was a lawyer who had grown up on his father's properties—his first years were spent in the hill country at Binalong, near Yass, and his love of bush life and horsemanship was sincere.

It is doubtful whether Henry Lawson ever felt happy on a horse. A gawky youth, son of a Norwegian farmer and a formidable mother who herself wrote voluminously, he was separated by deafness from his fellows, whom he regarded with a wise and sardonic eye.

OPPOSITE, TOP:
In 1893 much of Brisbane lay under water: violent floods turned the city into an antipodean Venice. When the waters of the Brisbane River receded the colony's two gunboats were found stranded among the palm trees in the Botanic Gardens.

BOTTOM:
Map of Australia on the eve of Federation: South Australia, by administering the Northern Territory, had become the second largest Australian colony.

His sympathy and admiration for the poor of the city and for the bush people was deep, yet he feared the bush. His early republicanism drifted into a proud nationalism on a sea of drink. Alcohol first made him a buffoon and then destroyed him.

A century after the verse of Paterson and Lawson was first published they remain the best loved of all Australian writers. They were published by a firm that has also survived (though its imprint now appears only on Australian titles published by its owner HarperCollins): Angus & Robertson. Its founders were two Scots who set up in bookselling in Sydney in 1882; Angus soon sold out to his partner and George Robertson began publishing books in 1886. Angus & Robertson was soon synonymous with Australian writing, specialising in the bush ballads and humorous verses that Australians loved.

A new Australian school of painters held their first exhibition in Melbourne in 1889. Their names were Arthur Streeton, Tom Roberts, Frederick McCubbin and Charles Conder. They had discovered the drowsy, hazy beauty of the Australian bush when camping at Box Hill and at Heidelberg on the Yarra and they rendered the landscape in the manner of the impressionists whose work some of them had seen in Europe. Critics were unkind: 'At an exhibition of paintings you would naturally look for pictures, instead of which the impressionist presents you with a varied assortment of palettes,' wrote the *Argus* critic. He described nearly all of the small paintings as 'a pain to the eye'.

The radical tradition

Australians were not yet political, but a radical tradition was being born, one that combined Irish and Scottish nationalism, English trade unionism, a good dose of Methodism, and the Australian bush values of mateship.

In 1884 a new Catholic prelate arrived in Sydney: Patrick, Cardinal Moran, the great builder of souls and churches. He trained a generation of priests 'who learned a passionate patriotism the hard way, by training under Irishmen'. In Australia the Catholics became more Irish and the Irish became more Catholic, one Celtic historian has remarked. Irish Catholicism was a hard and cheerless church (totally different in spirit to Italian Catholicism) and rigidly conservative; but it produced uncompromising men and women of profound faith and troubled social conscience, dreamers, writers and Labour prime ministers.

In the same year a London-born Welshman, William Morris Hughes, emigrated to Australia. Two more future prime ministers, Andrew Fisher and Joseph Cook (a conservative) arrived in Australia in 1885. In 1886 John Christian Watson, reputed to have been born in Chile and educated in New Zealand, emigrated to Australia. He too would become, in 1904, a Labour prime minister, the first leader of a socialist government in the world.

BELOW:
A formidable spokesman for Roman Catholics and champion of his faith: Patrick, Cardinal Moran, head of the Catholic Church in Australia on the eve of Federation.

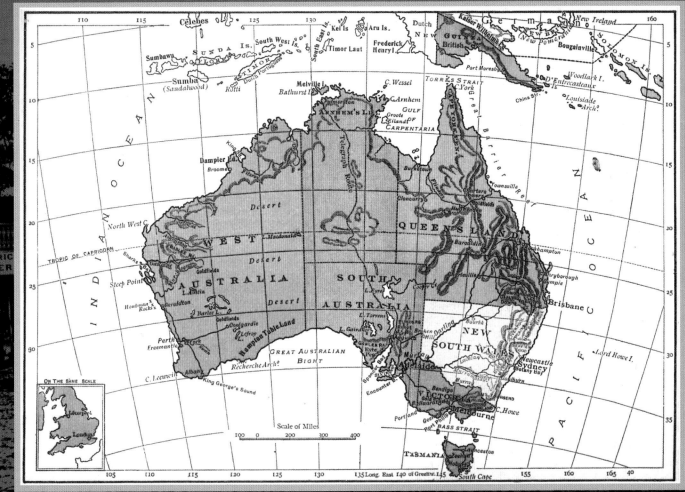

The 1890s: The grim decade

Wealth from the land —and unions

'Unionism came to the Australian bushman as a religion,' wrote William Guthrie Spence. 'It had in it that feeling of mateship which he understood already.' Spence had arrived in Geelong with his Scots parents in 1852, aged six, and had worked as a shepherd and a butcher's boy before becoming involved in union activities in Melbourne. He formed the Australian Miners Union and by the late 1880s had so effectively spread the unionist cause that 2600 of the 3000 shearing sheds in eastern Australia were unionised, their members pledged to united action to protect their interests.

Conflict began when wool fell in price in the mid-1880s to 7d a pound. In 1886 Victorian pastoralists and graziers ('squatter' was now a dirty word) tried to reduce shearers' pay from 20shillings a hundred sheep to 17shilling. The shearers went for advice to W.G. Spence, who formed them into the Australian Shearers' Union. Within a year 16,000 shearers had joined it. (In 1894 it would merge with the largest union of all—the Australian Workers' Union).

The 1880s was a revolutionary decade on the land. The extension of railways spelled doom for the river boats but connected cities to country towns. Water reached the inland: the first artesian bore was drilled at Barcaldine in 1884; two years later George Chaffey from California began the country's first major irrigation scheme at Mildura, channelling the waters of the Murray into dry paddocks.

It was the founding of Australia's citrus and dried fruit industry—Sunraysia country.

In 1884 a 19-year-old Victorian, Hugh Victor McKay, built with his brother's help a strange machine, dragged by a team of horses, that could strip, thresh and clean wheat grains in one operation; five years later he set up a factory at Ballarat to manufacture his invention. He called the machines 'Sunshine Harvesters.'

In 1886 William Farrer, an Englishman, the son of a Westmoreland farmer, resigned from the public service to work a property on the Murrumbidgee and experiment in crossbreeding wheat to produce a strong hybrid immune to 'rust' and other blights. Three years later he made his first successful cross-breeding. Farrer's most famed hybrid came in 1901; he named it 'Federation' in honour of the new Commonwealth.

Methods were changing in the sheds. In 1886 an Irish immigrant, Frederick Wolseley (a brother of Field Marshal Wolseley, the Empire's pride), demonstrated his steam-powered 'machine shears' at McCaughey's Dunlop station west of the Darling River. Machine shears took off more wool than blades but were originally no faster: in 1892 Jack Howe, already a legend on the Barcoo, shore 321 sheep in 7 hours 40 minutes using blades—'glorified scissors'—at Alice Downs station in Queensland, establishing a record that stood for fifty-eight years.

When Queensland graziers announced pay cuts in 1884 the shearers there went on strike, picketing the stations and dumping 'blackleg' (non-union) shearers in the water tanks. For most of the next decade Queensland would be the scene of Australia's first bitter confrontation between capital and labour.

By the 1880s wool, Australia's main export, was mainly being stored and auctioned in Australian cities; only 40 per cent was being shipped to London for auction there. The era saw the rise of the great wool companies—Elder Smith of Adelaide, Dalgety & Co (incorporated in 1884), Goldsborough Mort (formed in 1888). Their great mausoleum-like warehouses still tower over docks and wharves.

The worldwide recession of the 1880s coincided with a major Australian drought lasting from 1880 until 1888 (it broke even later in some parts of the country). It mainly affected the wheat belt but nine million sheep and three million head of cattle died. Sidney Kidman of Adelaide—the 'Cattle King'—built his fortunes in the 1880s by buying up cattle stations that soon stretched the length of the continent. He began modestly in 1880 by purchasing Owen Downs in the MacDonnell Ranges near Alice Springs, the first of 100 properties totalling 270,000 square kilometres in the Northern Territory, Queensland and New South Wales. This chain of properties enabled Kidman to drive his herds south during drought to wherever feed was available. A man notorious for the low wages he paid his drovers and station hands, Kidman became a millionaire, a knight and a benefactor.

ABOVE:
At the time of Federation Australia lay in the grip of drought, but William Farrer's rust-resistant strain of wheat, which he named 'Federation wheat', would yield bumper crops by decade's end. Farrer, who died in 1906, was later honoured on a postage stamp.

FEDERATED MINING EMPLOYEES' ASSOCIATION OF AUSTRALIA

NEW SOUTH WALES BRANCH.

ABOVE:
Union banners were the rallying point of workers and became an art form in themselves.

The 1890s strikes

Trouble was brewing on the waterfront. When pastoralists announced further pay cuts in 1890 the Seamen's Union rallied to the shearers' cause and threatened strike action. Their battle would be caught up in one of the great sagas of Australian political history and folklore—the shearers' strike.

In May 1890 the owners of Jondaryan station in Queensland brought in non-union shearers and the Shearers Union called on dock workers to refuse to handle wool from the property. Settlement was reached. In July 1890 the station owners formed their own union—the Pastoralists' Union—and decided to break strikes by employing non-unionists, whatever the consequences.

The British Seamen's Union and the London dockers pledged solidarity with their fellow unionists in Australia. In August 1890 Australian ships' officers walked off their ships in Melbourne to demand better pay, improved conditions. Ten days later, on 26 August, miners' demands for better pay and conditions resulted in a lockout by mine owners throughout south-eastern Australia. The battle was on.

ABOVE:

During the 1890s the railway line was extended from Melbourne south-east into Gippsland, a region rich in coal: a photograph of the first load of coal dug from Korumburra, October 1892.

'In this fight we are going to prove that the old narrow trade unionism is gone in Australia,' the radical, William Lane, declared in his new paper, the *Worker*: 'The bushman, the townsman and the waterside workers are united'.

In September 1890 the miners at Broken Hill went on strike. In Sydney and Melbourne angry crowds gathered to prevent 'black' wool from leaving the wharves—'Fire low and lay them out!' was Colonel Tom Price's order to his militia troops in Melbourne, but the confrontation ended without bloodshed.

When the Australian Shearers' Union was called out on strike many members did not comply, and non-unionists were quickly recruited. In the words of one historian 'the graziers and other employers resolved to beat the unions to their knees'. After three months of unemployment—for thousands of strikers the grimmest winter of their lives—the strikes began to collapse, one by one, over September and October 1890.

In Queensland the shearers stood their ground. When blacklegs from the south came up to work, hundreds of striking shearers gathered in a camp at Barcaldine and armed themselves as the Eureka diggers had done. By March 1891 more than 500 militia and 'special constables' had been deployed there and the situation was explosive. On 1 May 1891 the shearers marched in the first 'May Day' parade seen in Barcaldine.

ABOVE:

As the recession deepened into a depression during the 1890s, unions grew in strength. A Labour Day procession in Melbourne.

1891: Birth of the labour movement

Barcaldine is celebrated by some historians as the true birthplace of the labour movement and the Australian Labor Party (the odd spelling was not made official until 1916). Others trace the ALP's birth to a meeting of unionists in Balmain in the same month, convened to select the first socialist candidate for parliament.

To escort the 'black' wool to Brisbane a total of 1400 police and troops armed with Gatling guns and field artillery were called up. Stray shots were fired by the shearers but, as in Melbourne, no one was killed.

The Queensland government, declaring a State of Emergency, now brought down the mailed fist. After a disturbance, police arrested twelve of the Barcaldine ringleaders and sentenced them to three years in gaol, under an archaic English law of 1825 relating to conspiracy. 'Justice here is a farce, patriotism a mockery,' wrote William Lane of the trials and decided that Australia was no place for a radical. In 1893 he sailed for Paraguay to found a utopian settlement—'New Australia'. His flock objected to his authoritarian ways and all but a handful soon returned.

The repressive laws in Queensland eased after 1894, when the shearers admitted defeat. But the Labour Party was now an active force. In 1899 the first socialist government in the world took power in Queensland. It lasted only a week, but it predated Britain's first Labour government by twenty-four years.

'*Marvellous Melbourne*'

'Look out Sydney, Melbourne is streaking ahead', a newspaper warned New South Wales readers in the 1870s as the younger colony catapulted past the older in population and wealth. 'Victoria the Golden' its citizens called it. 'Although Sydney is the older town, Melbourne is justly entitled to be considered the Metropolis of the South Hemisphere,' Richard Twopenny recorded in 1883. Sir John Robertson and his constituents called the upstart colony the 'cabbage patch'—a small green area 'only good for growing vegetables'. But in Victoria everything people touched turned to gold.

Victoria, which founded Australia's first public art gallery (in 1861), led the older colonies in social legislation too. State schools were instituted there in 1872 but Parkes' great dream of free education was not fully realised in New South Wales until 1880. The first trade unions were also founded in Victoria in 1872. In the mid-1880s Victoria, with 1.5 million acres under cultivation for wheat in the Wimmera and the Mallee, was overtaking South Australia as Australia's bread basket.

Unions could exist, but they were not strictly legal. Their existence was legalised first by New South Wales 1881—ten years after Britain had legalised them—and in 1886 by Victoria and Queensland.

Social harmony reigned. The Scots dominated politics in Victoria as the Irish did in New South Wales. With wealth came shameless cronyism, and all factions were guilty of it. In the words of the upright banker George Turner, Graham Berry's accession to power in 1875 'marked the commencement of an era of political intrigue, Parliamentary degradation and shameless self-seeking'.

ABOVE:
Work continued on the completion of Victoria's Parliament House in Spring Street, Melbourne, a grandiose project that elicited much speculation and derision.

Begun in 1856, it received its imposing facade (pictured) only in 1892. The dome originally envisaged has never been added to the building. It served as Australia's Federal Parliament House from 1901 to 1927.

The newly built South Melbourne Town Hall, 1880s.

ABOVE:

The Exhibition Building in Melbourne was built for the great Exposition of 1880.

The wooden structure still stands and became the scene for the official celebration of the Commonwealth of Australia's first centenary in 2001.

In 2004 an international body named it as a 'World Heritage' building.

After the boom

In 1888, the last golden year, a total of 270 new companies were registered in Melbourne; almost as many went bankrupt within a year. In 1889 Melbourne's building boom and the speculation in real estate ended when finance began drying up. By 1890 the Australian colonies, whose borrowings from British banks amounted to nearly £200 million found difficulty in obtaining further loans. British investments in Argentina had gone sour; Barings Bank crashed in 1891 and the City of London panicked.

First to go broke were the swindlers and speculators. The Melbourne property millionaire Benjamin Fink went bankrupt and fled to London owing £1.5 million to banks and investors. (He died leaving an estate valued at £250,000.) Premier Munro, founder of the Federal Bank which declared losses of £2 million, introduced legislation permitting bankrupts to effect a 'compact' with their creditors, and then left quickly for London to weather the storm there as Victoria's Agent-General. One of the largest property-owners, Henry Heyter, went broke and paid his creditors, by compact,

threepence in the pound; the other 237 pence in every pound he borrowed were never recovered.

Visitors to Australia were astounded by the number and size of banks. Their head offices in Melbourne's Collins Street were larger, their ground floors grander and more ornate than even those of London or New York. Most country towns had three or four competing banks.

1893: The banks crash

In August 1891 the long-established Bank of Van Diemen's Land closed its doors. A run on deposits had revealed an embarrassing lack of reserves and the fact that its customers' savings had been lent out under dubious circumstances.

In January 1893 the Federal Bank in Melbourne closed its doors. In April the Bank of South Australia closed. On 5 April there was a run on the Commercial Bank of Australia. On 15 April the English, Scottish and Australian—'the Scotty'—closed its doors to customers. On 17 April the National Bank of Australasia paid out 45 per cent of its gold before closing its doors in panic.

By year's end nineteen of the twenty-eight commercial banks in Australia had closed (some of them temporarily, as an act of self-preservation). 'Nothing in the history of English banking could match our disaster of 1893,' Geoffrey Blainey has written.

ABOVE:

'The Queen's Navee': officers and men of HMS *Miranda* pose for the photographer on a visit to Norfolk Island in 1884.

The Royal Navy was popular in Australia, with its ships regularly visiting Australian ports as they patrolled her coasts and New Zealand's, and it remained in Australian waters until 1913, when the Royal Australian Navy was born.

Coaching party
photographed outside
Government House,
Sydney, in 1877.
The Gothic sandstone
residence was
completed in 1845

Much of the panic could have been averted. People were obsessed by gold, seeing it as the only possession of true value. By law, banknotes could be exchanged —on demand—for gold. The banks had indeed lent money for speculative purposes but most were forced to close their doors because they could not immediately pay out gold to their customers. Early in 1892, when the venerable Bank of New South Wales had to close its doors, Premier Dibbs stood at its entrance and assured customers that the government would back their savings. In the next year he allowed banks to issue banknotes as legal tender.

The experience of the 1890s embittered a generation. The little people suffered most. Families lost their savings, selectors lost their farms in foreclosures. The photographs of the period show sombre faces: family groups in their Sunday best, gloomy as undertakers; school children without a trace of laughter in their eyes. Australia was the only British dominion with a strong republican sentiment and this republicanism was channelled into nationalism or into socialism, now seen as the great hope of humankind in the world dominated by greedy capitalists and fossilised monarchies that extolled the dubious virtues of imperialism. When the Australian Labour Party announced its platform after Parkes called an election in 1891, the *Bulletin* endorsed and summarised its aims: 'Co-operation in place of Capitalism, national insurance instead of relief works and benevolent asylums, and a universal 8-hour system'.

Rise of the Labour Party

In the 1891 elections thirty-six of Labour's forty-five candidates won seats in the NSW Parliament; they would have won more but for the 'plural voting' system. It was a stunning success for party only a few months old. 'One Man, One Vote' became the Labour battle cry. From New Zealand, Sir George Grey, delighted by the political demise of Parkes (whom he detested), cabled his congratulations to the Labour Party, saying: 'If you continue to move so wisely, the four millions of Australians will establish a Federation which will be a glory to generous England, and a blessing to all mankind'. Of the first thirty-six Labour members only twelve were Australian-born.

The trade unions were Labour's solid financial base, but the party attracted individuals from all walks of life. An American (some said he was Canadian) who reminded Australians of a cross between a hot gospeller and a snake-oil salesman, King O'Malley, entered the South Australian Parliament in 1896; he graduated to Federal Parliament in 1901 and would become one of the most innovative of Labour ministers. Another whose origins are shrouded in mystery later became the world's first Labour prime minister: John Christian Watson, born in Chile of an English mother. 'Chris' Wilson was educated in New Zealand and emigrated to Australia in 1886. William Morris Hughes, the Welsh schoolteacher (though born in London) who had emigrated to Australia with a mate in 1884, to knock around Queensland for a few years, left his bookshop at Balmain in the care of his wife in 1892 and rode on horseback from Bathurst to Forbes and to outlying country towns enrolling hundreds of members for the Labour League. 'The unionist was a

pariah,' Hughes recalled. 'Every man's hand was against him; his organization was tabooed, his efforts at redress ruthlessly crushed. He was both despised and detested.' He entered Parliament in the elections of 1894, when only twenty-seven Labour candidates won seats. In the following year the party adopted the 'pledge'—members vowed to support policy framed by Caucus, to provide the party with unbroken solidarity.

The most significant reform of the decade came from South Australia, where the Kingston Liberal government introduced a Court of Conciliation in 1890 and votes for women in 1894 (New Zealand under King Dick Seddon had pioneered female suffrage in the previous year). Western Australia introduced votes for women in 1899.

Elsewhere small and growing groups of dedicated women led the battle for reform of the conditions for women and children. In 1891 Rose Scott became secretary of the Women's Suffrage League while fighting to improve working conditions for children; among her achievements was the raising of the age of consent in 1910 from fourteen to sixteen. (The visiting American feminist Jessie Ackermann felt that sixteen was still too young for girls to be considered women.)

In 1899 Daisy O'Dwyer Bates, who had come to Australia in 1884 from her native Ireland, made a disastrous marriage and returned to Britain, was commissioned by the London *Times* to report on stories of ill-treatment of Western Australia's Aborigines. She chose to live among them for the rest of her life, recording their ways while predicting their passing. She lives in the legend of two cultures as 'Kabbarli'—the grandmother.

1897: Diamond Jubilee

In the summer of 1897 the streets and malls of London were festooned with flags and bunting and lined with Guards as the biggest precession ever seen in the city left Buckingham Palace. The Diamond Jubilee was celebrating Queen Victoria's sixty years on the throne. Jingling behind the sailors, Guards, Dragoons, Hussars, Lancers, Highlanders, Light Infantry and red-coated Regiments of the Line came the contingents from the Empire and Dominions—Indians, Africans, Canadians and 'Australasians': mounted men from the Australian colonies and New Zealand in broad-brimmed hats. The New South Wales Lancers were the first Australians the English had seen and many onlookers were astonished to see they were white men. In Australian cities loyal citizens raised bronze statues to their beloved Queen and outdid each other in protestations of loyalty to the Crown.

Where the Protestants built statues of the great, the Catholic Irish raised tombs to their martyrs. In the following year an enormous procession moved through the streets of Sydney towards Waverley Cemetery. Protestant Australians were astonished by the number of people and priests—for it was larger even than the Jubilee marches of 1887 and 1897. Nor would the towering memorial at Waverley, bearing numerous Irish names and the simple legend 'Remember '98' have meant much to them. The memorial to the Irish Rebellion of 1798 was a Catholic protest against Protestant dominion. For the next half-century Australia would be a battleground of Protestant imperialism and Irish nationalism.

ABOVE:
Queen Victoria, whose reign was to last from 1837 to 1901.

The Golden West

In 1890 Western Australia achieved self-government and John Forrest, better known as an explorer, became the colony's first Premier. Gold had been found at Halls Creek in the north in 1885 and in the rugged Kimberleys one year later; then in the Pilbarra and on the Murchison. Few suspected it, but the colony was rich also in iron ore.

In September 1892 two prospectors at Coolgardie, 600 kilometres east of Perth, struck gold in large quantities, and news of their find sparked off a rush that attracted thousands in an Australia wracked by depression. In June 1893 two diggers, Paddy Hannan and Tom Flanagan, seeing that the alluvial gold was nearly exhausted at Coolgardie, walked further east for three days. At Mount Charlotte they began digging and panning. There they discovered the biggest seam of gold in Australia—

Kalgoorlie's 'Golden Mile'. By the time Hannan got back from claiming the reward, hundreds of miners were there. Thousands more came, many of them from Victoria. A century later they are still unearthing gold in Kalgoorlie.

Western Australia's population was only 50,000 in 1891; it rose to 135,000 by 1896 and the newcomers—the 'Other Siders'—brought with them not only their eastern accents but also strident demands for the vote.

Inching towards federation

The end of Sir Henry Parkes's career in 1891 (he died in 1896) robbed the federation movement of its figurehead. Labour's priorities were social improvement. Edmund Barton, Parkes's protégé and Alfred Deakin, who had turned his back on Victorian politics in shame at the disgraceful corruption of the 1890s, became articulate advocates of federation.

It was the people who led the way. In 1893 various citizens groups—most notably the friendly society founded in 1871, the Australian Natives' Association—sponsored a conference at Cowra where delegates suggested that a convention, one whose members were elected by the people, draw up a constitution for submission to the electorate in each colony. In 1894 the *Bulletin*, always stridently opposed to a union of colonies under a British crown, finally gave up the cause of a republic, announcing: 'The fact has slowly dawned on us that nine-tenths of the population takes no real interest in the future Australian nation … or in any of the abstract glories of a United Australia. The *Bulletin* is now willing to accept Federation on the plan of the Convention.'

TARIFF DUTIES OF THE AUSTRALIAN COLONIES

Also **New Zealand** *duties on goods not specified in table, and N. Z., C. O. decisions since last edition.*

(When no duty is mentioned the article is free, except in the case of N.S.W., see Note at end.)

Articles.	Q'land.	S. Aus.*	Tas.	Victoria.	W. Aus.	N. Zea.	N.S.W.
ABDOMINAL Belts	15 p.c.	10 p.c.	12½ p.c.	...	...	...	10 p.c.
Acid—Acetic	3d. lb.	3d lb.orpt.	12½ p.c.	3d.p.orlb†	12½ p.c.	1½d.per lb.	2/6 p. gal.
Acid—Sulphuric	2/6 p. cwt.	5/- cwt.	...	5/- cwt.	12½ p.c.	...	2/6 p. cwt.
„ Muriatic	15 p.c.	5/- cwt.	...	5/- cwt.	12½ p.c.		
„ Nitric	15 p.c.	5/- cwt.	12½ p.c.	5/- cwt.	12½ p.c.		
„ Tartaric	...	...	4d. per lb.	...	...	1d. per lb.	....
Advertising matter	...	...	...	...	...	...	15/ p. cwt.
Adzes	...	...	12½ p.c.	...	12½ p.c.	20p.c *ad.v.*	....
Aer. and Min. Waters	15 p.c.	20 p.c.	12½ p.c.	10 p.c.	20 p.c.	20 p.c.	6d. dz. pts.
Aerated Limejuice	15 p.c.	1/- gal.	12½ p.c.	10 p.c.	20 p.c.	...	6d. „
Agricultural Impl.	...	15 p.c.(not enum.	...	20 p.c.	5 p.c.		
Air Beds	15 p.c.	25 p.c.	12½ p.c.	...	12½ p.c.		
Air Bellows	15 p.c.	25 p.c.	12½ p.c.	25 p.c.	5 p.c.		
Air Bricks—Iron	3/- p. cwt.	25 p.c.	12½ p.c.	35 p.c.	12½ p.c.	20 p.c.	
„ Clay or Erthwr.	15 p.c.	25 p.c.	12½ p.c.	...	12½ p.c.		
„ Galvanized	3/- p.c.	25 p.c.	12½ p.c.	35 p.c.	12½ p.c.		
Air Mattresses	15 p.c.	25 p.c.	12½ p.c.	...	12½ p.c.		
Albuminized Paper	15 p.c.	...	12½ p.c.	2d.lb.if ct.	12½ p.c.		
Albums—Confession	15 p.c.	25 p.c.	12½ p.c.	20 p.c.	12½ p.c.		
„ Not enum.	15 p.c.	25 p.c.	12½ p.c.	20 p.c.	12½ p.c.	25 p.c.	
„ Autographic or Stamp	15 p.c.	25 p.c.	12½ p.c.	20 p.c.	12½ p.c.		
Ale—In Bulk	9d. p. gal.	1/- p. gal.	9d. p. gal.	9d. p. gal.	1/- p. gal.	...	6d. p. gal.
„ In 6 reputed qts. or 12 reputed pt. bts.	1s. p. gal.	1/- p. gal.	1/3 p. gal.	9d. p. gal.	1/- p. gal.	1/6 p. gal.	9d. p. gal.
Alkali	15 p.c.	...	12½ p.c.	Crystals, 40/- ton	12½ p.c.		
Almonds	15 p.c.	3d. per lb.	2d. per lb.	2d.p.or lb.	12½ p.c.	3d. p. lb.	1d. per lb.
Aloes	15 p.c.	...	12½ p.c.	...	...	...	....
Alum	15 p.c.	10 p.c.	...	...	12½ p.c.	...	....
American Leather—(not Oil Baize)	...	...	...	...	5 p.c.		
Ammonia	...	10 p.c.	10 p.c.	Car.& Liq. 2d. p. lb.			
Ammunition (including Caps)	15 p.c.	10 p.c.	Cps.12½p c	Pwdr. 3d. lb.cps.fre.	12½ p.c.	...	3d. per lb.
Anchors	15 p.c.	Over 3 cwt. free	...	...	5 p.c.	...	....
Animals, Living—Horses, Horned Cattle, Sheep, Pigs, Poultry, Unen.	...	‡ ...	(*See* Live Stock)	(*See* Live Stock)	(*See* Live Stock)	...	....
Anti-fouling Composition	15 p.c.	...	10 p.c.	...	12½ p.c.		
Antimony (in Ingot)	...	...	...	...	12½ p.c.	...	....
Anvils	...	...	...	...	5 p.c.	...	....
Apparel and Slops	15 p.c.	25 p.c. excpt. moleskin15p.c.	10 p.c.	25 and 35 p.c.	12½ p.c.	25 p.c.	
Apples—Dried	2d. per lb.	3d. per lb.	2d. per lb.	2d. per lb.	3d. per lb.	...	1d. per lb.
„ Fresh	...	1/- p. bsh.	1/- p. bsh.	1/6 p. bsh.	12½ p.c.	½d.lb. (fr.)	1/- p. bsh.
Archery Material	15 p.c.	25 p.c.	12½ p.c.	25 p.c.	12½ p.c.		
Architraves	15 p.c.	1/6 100f.lnl	20 p.c.	7/- p.100ft. lineal ovr. 3 in	20 p.c.		
Arms—Military	15 p.c.	10 p.c.					
Arms—Firearms, Sport.	15 p.c.	10 p.c.	12½ p.c.	...	12½ p.c.		
Arrowroot	1d. per lb.	...	2d. per lb.	2d.lb.or pt	12½ p.c.	...	1d. per lb.
Arrows—Surveyors'	15 p.c.	25 p.c.	12½ p.c.	35/- p.c.	1d. per lb.		
Arrow Links (Iron)	25 p.c.	25 p.c.	12½ p.c.	...	12½ p.c.		
Arsenic	15 p.c.	10 p.c.	...	...	12½ p.c.		
Artists' Brushes	15 p.c.	25 p.c.	12½ p.c.	...	12½ p.c.	...	....
„ Colours	15 p.c.	...	...	...	12½ p.c.		
Asbestos, Unmanufac.	15 p.c.	10 p.c.	...	...	12½ p.c.	...	pckg. f.
Ash Timber (in plank)	15 p.c.	...	...	...	...	...	15 p.c.rgh. free
Aspirators	15 p.c.	...	12½ p.c.	...	12½ p.c.		
Asphalt	15 p.c.	...	12½ p.c.	...	12½ p.c.		

Articles.	Q'land.	S. Aus.*	Tas.	Victoria.	W. Aus.	N. Zea.	N.S.W.
Atlases	...	...	...	Mntd.20pc	...		for school use free
Augers—Screw & Shell	...	...	...	...	12½ p.c.	...	....
Axes	...	...	...	...	12½ p.c.	...	....
Axe Handles	15 p.c.	25 p.c.	10 p.c.	25 p.c.	12½ p.c.	...	....
Axles, Arms and Boxes	15 p.c.	25 p.c.	Axles,5 pc	3/- to 10/- p. arm;common dray 25 p.c.	12½ p.c.		
BACK Chains	15 p.c.	...	12½ p.c.	...	12½ p.c.		
Backs, Wooden (for Brushes)	15 p.c.	...	12½ p.c.	25 p.c.	12½ p.c.		
Bacon	3d. per lb.	4d. per lb.	2d. per lb.	2d. per lb.	3d. per lb.	2d. per lb.	2d.lb. grn. or partly cured
Bagging	15 p.c.	...	12½ p.c.	Jute free	12½ p.c.	...	....
Bags & Sacks (new), viz.:—				Under 3 bsh. 6d. doz. (except gns. and sugar-mat) hnd. fcy. or travelling 25 p.c.	...	...	....
„ Bran	15 p.c.	...	½d. each		6d. p. doz.	...	....
„ Corn & Flour	15 p.c.	...	...		6d. p. doz.	20 p.c.	....
„ Gunny	15 p.c.	...	...		6d. p. doz.	...	....
„ Ore	15 p.c.	...	...		3d. p. doz.	...	....
„ Other	15 p.c.	...	12½ p.c.		6d. p. doz.		15 p.c. fancy & trav.
„ Unenu.	15 p.c.	printed 25 p.c.not pr. 10 p.c.	12½ p.c.			15 p.c.	
„ Woolpacks	15 p.c.	...	4d. each	3/- p. doz.	4d. each	...	....
Bags, Canvas (Water)	15 p.c.	25 p.c.	12½ p.c.	...	12½ p.c.		
„ Paper (not prntd.)	5/- p. cwt.	10/- cwt.	...	...	...	...	7/6 p. cwt.
„ „ (printed)	7/6 p. cwt.	15/- cwt.	...	...	...	...	15/-p.cwt.
Baize—In the piece (ex. Oil Baize)	15 p.c.	15 p.c.	12½ p.c.	...	12½ p.c.		
Baize—Oil	15 p.c.	...	12½ p.c.	...	12½ p.c.		
Baking Powder	15 p.c.	10 p.c.	12½ p.c.	20 p.c.	12½ p.c.	15 p.c.	1d. per lb.
Balks	15 p.c.	...	12½ p.c.	...	12½ p.c.		
Bark (for tanning)	15 p.c.	10 p.c.	12½ p.c.	...	12½ p.c.	...	....
Barley (*See* also Pearl)	9d. p. bsh.	1/6 p. bsh.	½d. per lb.	3/- p. cntl.	4d. p. bsh. 50 lb.	...	10d.100 lb.
Barometers	15 p.c.	...	12½ p.c.	...	12½ p.c.		
Baskets	15 p.c.	25 p.c.	12½ p.c.	25 p.c.	12½ p.c.	20 p.c.	
„ Carpenters' tool	15 p.c.	2[illegible] p.c.	12½ p.c.	...	12½ p.c.		
„ Painters' brush	15 p.c.	25 p.c.	12½ p.c.	...	12½ p.c.		
Bass, for brushmaking	15 p.c.	...	...	...	12½ p.c.		
Battens	15 p.c.	2/6 per 40 cubic ft.	If under 3 in. 2/6 100 sup.feet; over exempt.	...	12½ p.c.		
Bay Rum	12/- p. gal.	25 p.c.	15/- p. gal.	24/- p. gal.	15/- p. gal.	...	20/- p. gal
Beans and peas (other than split)	1/- p. bsh.	2/- 100 lbs.	...	2/11 cental	12½ p.c.	...	10d.100 lb. incld.split
Bedford Cord (cloth)	15 p.c.	15 p.c.	12½ p.c.	20 p.c.	12½ p.c.		
Bed Keys	15 p.c.	25 p.c.	12½ p.c.	...	12½ p.c.		
Bedsteads	15 p.c.	25 p.c.	12½ p.c.	35 p.c.	12½ p.c.		
Beef or mutton	15 p.c.	...	1/6 100 lbs.	...	1d. lb. in pkle. presrvd., 12½ p.c.		
Beer of all kinds (draught)	9d. p. gal.	1/- p. gal.	In btls.1/3 wood, 9d.	9d. p. gal. lager,qts. 3/- pts. 1/6 p. doz.	1/- p. gal.	...	6d. p. gal. wood or jar

* The Tariff of the *Northern Territory* is the same as South Australia; viz.—Engines under 60 H.P., Pumps over 3-inch Bore, Boilers, Chaff Cutters, Corn Crushers, Grain Sowers, Horse-powers, Mowing Machines, Reaping Machines, Scarifiers, Horse Rakes, Ploughs (triple, double, single), Harrow, Moulding Boards, Ploughshares, and all parts of above, 5 per cent., others free.
† In *Victoria*—Acid (Acetic), containing not more than 50 per cent. acidity, 3d. per pint or lb.; for every extra 10 per cent. or part thereof, 1d. per pint or lb.
‡ Horses and Horned Cattle, 5/-; Pigs, 2/-; Sheep, 6d.

ABOVE:
By the eve of Federation the number and variety of tariffs imposed by the Australian colonies on each other had become a powerful argument for Federation, if only as a way of rationalising the problem by adopting a single system, common to all.

The Cowra Convention

The Cowra Convention plan, broadly, was the idea adopted by the colonies. In 1895 New South Wales passed an Act providing for the election of four delegates to a Federal Convention; Victoria, South Australia and Tasmania soon followed her example. The delegates who assembled in Adelaide in March 1897 found little of substance to alter in the constitution framed a decade earlier by Samuel Griffith, but Labour (only one member of the party had been elected) challenged the clause that provided for each state to have an equal number of senators.

'We are not Federationists at any price,' announced William Holman, the normally progressive Labour leader of New South Wales. At an intermediate meeting in Sydney in September 1897, Victoria's Alfred Deakin called for an end to delay and procrastination: 'I trust that all of us recognize that upon this Convention rests a responsibility for framing a Constitution for all time', he said, 'that upon this Convention, and upon this Constitution alone, rests the whole burden of federation.'

The Constitution soon adopted with minor changes has withstood over a century of stress. The founding fathers drew inspiration from both American and English political models: the upper house—the Senate—would consist of six senators from each state and would form the house of review. The House of Representatives—'the People's House'—would consist of seventy-five members elected by proportional voting. A High Court of three learned judges would be the safeguard of the Constitution. The monarch would be represented by a Governor-General.

The federal government would assume responsibility for all matters of truly national importance—defence, immigration, foreign trade, diplomacy and some forms of taxation, returning to the colonies three-quarters of the revenue raised from taxes.

In his own vivid reminiscences Deakin would write of the colonial premiers who gathered there—Braddon of Tasmania, as dapper as a French diplomat; Forrest of Western Australia, 'a Henry VIII figure'; 'the portly Sir George Reid' of New South Wales who would prove obstructive enough to wreck the federationists' hopes by neither endorsing nor supporting the cause.

BELOW:
Pillars of the Protestant Establishment: the Governor of New South Wales, the rear-admiral commanding the Royal Navy's Australia Station, and a senior military officer, 1880s.

The draft Constitution was ready to be submitted to the people. In the first referendum of March 1898 the affirmative vote fell just short of the 80,000 votes needed to bring the senior colony into the Federation: 77,965 Yes votes were recorded. Calling a Premiers' Conference, 'Yes-No Reid' (as he was by now known) suggested more amendments (one of them a sop to his voters: the federal capital would be located within New South Wales). He ordered another referendum.

The outbreak of the South African War in 1899 and the dispatch to the scene of fighting of volunteer units from all colonies was a powerful influence in fostering national sentiment and this time the electors—including Queensland's—voted overwhelmingly for federation. Only Western Australia remained outside the new nation-to-be.

1899: Boer War

For a decade Australians had made their way to the Boer Republic of the Transvaal where gold and diamonds had been discovered. The Boers, who had left Cape Colony to escape British rule in the 1830s and had founded their own republics across the Orange River and the Vaal, resented the influx of English-speakers, for the native peoples, whom they treated appallingly, provided adequate labour in the mines. Britain's Colonial Secretary Joseph Chamberlain supported moves by the millionaire Cecil Rhodes to destabilise the Boer administration, and the possibility of war between the British and the Boers loomed closer.

LEFT:
High society: a function in Melbourne at the turn of the century.

Two Nellies:

BELOW, LEFT:
She sang like a bird and swore like a trooper: young Nellie Mitchell of Melbourne began her career as a soprano in the opera houses of Europe, calling herself 'Madame Melba' in honour of her birthplace.

BELOW, RIGHT:
English-born beauty Nellie Stewart became the darling of the Sydney stage.

ABOVE:
Convention delegates
meet in Victoria's parliamentary chamber to
debate the projected
federal constitution.
Seated at the table on
the left is Edmund Barton
of New South Wales,
destined to be Australia's
first prime minister;
opposite him is the large
figure of Sir George Reid.
Western Australia's beard-
ed Sir John Forrest can
be seen seated behind
Barton.

RIGHT:
Alfred Deakin,
eloquent spokesman
for Federation.

In October 1899 the Boers struck first. Their horsemen quickly surrounded Lady-smith in Natal and the towns of Kimberley and Mafeking on their western border, and defeated the British columns sent against them.

The Australian colonies were the first to offer troops to Britain, and their offers were gratefully received. As early as 1885 a small contingent of volunteers had sailed from New South Wales to assist the British in the Sudan, but they saw no action, and the British evacuated the region. It was not until 1898 that British forces under General Kitchener returned to the Sudan and reconquered it. Britain decided that she would not face a similar humiliation at the hands of the Boers of South Africa, but the succession of defeats in 1899—'Black Week'—was further humiliation.

'Banjo' Paterson sailed from Sydney as a war cor-respondent with the first New South Wales volun-teers in October 1899, and covered the early stage of the conflict in vivid prose. By February 1900 Australian horsemen were scouting ahead of the great army (a role they seemed by nature to enjoy) that marched north to relieve Kimberley, com-manded by Field Marshal Lord Roberts VC ('Lord Bobs') and Lord Kitchener, and they were among the first to gallop into the Boer cities of Bloem-fontein, Pretoria and Johannesburg.

Britain's early reverses had provided mischie-vous pleasure to Queen Victoria's grandson, the young Emperor of Germany, Wilhelm II, who had

249

ABOVE:

As the nineteenth century ended the Australian colonies looked back on a century of peace and progress, but the twentieth century began in war. Volunteers had sailed to aid the British in South Africa in 1899, intending quickly to crush the Boers. The Australians, who had no military tradition, were to prove outstanding if undisciplined soldiers in the two-year conflict. An officer of the New South Wales Lancers prior to sailing for war, 1900.

ABOVE:
Harry 'Breaker' Morant.

succeeded to the throne in 1888. In February 1900 he wrote to his uncle, the future King Edward VII, that England should take her setbacks like good sports, the way they accepted their defeats in cricket at the hands of the Australians. Edward replied testily: 'I am unable to share your opinion … in which you liken our conflict with the Boers to our Cricket Matches with the Australians, in which the latter were victorious and we accepted our defeat. The British Empire is now fighting for its very existence, as you know full well, and for our superiority in S. Africa. We must therefore use every effort in our power to prove victorious in the end!' Germany's rising economic and naval power and the impudent incursions of the Kaiser into the realm of foreign policy were to lead to growing anxiety in Britain, which emerged from the war in 1902 victorious in South Africa but isolated among the Great Powers.

The defeat of the Boer field armies in June 1900 did not end the war. It degenerated into a cruel guerrilla war that lasted until 1902, and it would take an Imperial army of more than 400,000 men to finally defeat Boer forces that seldom numbered more than 30,000 horsemen. More than 16,000 Australians saw service against the Boers, losing 251 killed in action but winning a remarkable reputation for initiative, insubordination and bravery. Nearly all had been mounted troops, men from the bush, capable of fighting Boer 'commandos' on their own terms. Yet the war had been divisive. Many Australians felt sympathy for the Boers and anger that two of their men—one of them the balladist Harry Morant—had been shot by British firing squads for killing enemy prisoners. The 'Colonials' from Australia, New Zealand and Canada had not responded well to the harsh discipline of the British army and had harsh things to say about the competence of British generals. Equally embarrassing was the information that an Australian from a prominent Irish Catholic Melbourne family, Arthur Lynch, whose father had fought at Peter Lalor's side at Eureka, had led an Irish brigade against British forces in South Africa. When he was elected to Parliament in Westminster for the Irish seat of Galway, the British threatened to hang him as a traitor. They later relented and Lynch became, like the defeated Boer generals Botha and Smuts, an enthusiastic Anglophile and supporter of the British Empire.

1900: Boxer Rebellion in China

While shiploads of Australian volunteers were sailing for South Africa, other Australian ships were steaming for China, where the European legations in Peking were besieged by Chinese forces pledged to banish Europeans from the country. When the Manchu court protested that it was unable to control the actions of the armed and violent bands of the 'League of Harmonious Fists' (known to Europeans as 'Boxers') who had massacred Christian missionaries and converts late in 1899, a column of European troops set out from the coast for Peking and finally raised the 55-day siege. The Colony of South Australia dispatched to China its gunboat *Protector* and New South Wales sent a naval brigade of volunteers, but both arrived too late to play any part in the fighting. China had to pay a crippling indemnity, and the Manchu monarchy itself fell in 1911.

The Australians' prompt despatch of forces to China and South Africa showed plainly that when the British Empire was threatened Australians would be the first to sail to its defence.

1900: Federation—the last act

Premier Forrest of Western Australia was now under pressure from Joseph Chamberlain, the Colonial Secretary in London, to step into line. The miners of Coolgardie and Kalgoorlie—nearly all of them easterners—were demanding the vote and threatening to declare the goldfields independent of the rule of Forrest and the 'Six Families' who clung to his coat-tails. In a referendum in July 1900 Western Australia's electors endorsed federation with one proviso: the federal government would pay the cost of completing the transcontinental railway linking Perth to the eastern states. Forrest fell from power soon after, moving on to Federal Parliament and the Ministry of Defence. (In 1918 the old explorer became the first Australian to be made a peer of the realm, as Baron Forrest of Bunbury. 'I would have made him a Duke to get rid of him,' Prime Minister Hughes later said.)

The delegates who carried the new Constitution to London for approval received high praise for their handiwork. Joseph Chamberlain again used his remarkable powers of persuasion: predicting that British commercial interests in Australia might receive short shrift in judgments from the High Court, he suggested that the colonies accept a clause permitting rights of appeal to the Privy Council in London, over the head of the High Court. With this amendment, the Bill for the federation of the Australian colonies passed the British Parliament and the Act received Queen Victoria's assent on 2 July 1900. The date chosen for the transformation of the six colonies into states of a single Commonwealth of Australia was 1 January 1901.

In December 1900 A.G. Stephens of the *Bulletin* reminded his readers of their new responsibilities:

> It is the duty of every father and mother and teacher of Australian children to intensify their natural love for Australia and to point out in how many ways Australia is eminently worthy to be loved—both the actual land and the actual ideals. Good and evil are mingled everywhere; but there is no land with more beautiful aspects than Australia, no ideal with greater potentialities for human achievement and human happiness.

OPPOSITE:
At the turn of the century this group of schoolchildren was photographed at Tilba Tilba, on the south coast of New South Wales in 1899.

RIGHT:

The venturous English explorer Lawrence Hargrave, who had explored the Fly River in New Guinea, became a pioneer of flight.

He is shown with his box kites on the coastal cliff at Stanwell Park, south of Sydney, in 1894.

Hargrave understood that if motive power was applied to a glider, it would be possible to direct the 'aircraft', but his steam engines were too heavy for his frail airframes.

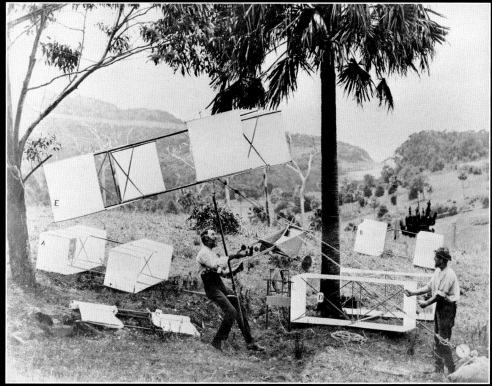

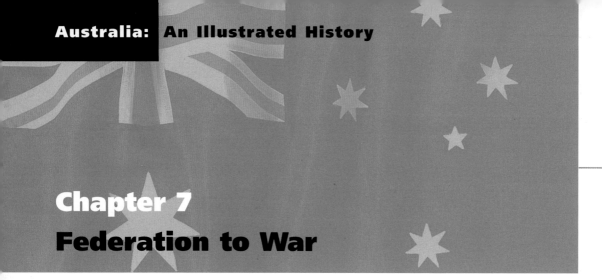

Chapter 7
Federation to War

From 1901 to 1919

THE COMMONWEALTH OF AUSTRALIA, born on the first day of the twentieth century, was one of its most optimistic creations. The celebration of nationhood began in Sydney where 100,000 people gathered in Centennial Park on 1 January 1901 to see the Governor-General, Lord Hopetoun, sworn in beneath a plaster-of-Paris cupola crowded with dignitaries. The Catholics arrived separately: Cardinal Moran, piqued that the Church of England primate had been given precedence in the ceremony, had formed his own procession on the steps of St Mary's Cathedral and led it to Centennial Park.

The new nation had no parliament house, and no flag (the Union Jack with Southern Cross was adopted in 1903)—and almost no government, for Hopetoun had chosen as Prime Minister in mid-December Sir William Lyne, Premier of New South Wales, a notorious opponent of federation, and all ministers refused to serve under him. Edmund Barton had been appointed in his stead only one day before the ceremony.

The celebrations continued across the continent to the sound of brass bands and military salutes. A week later the first of the troops returning from South Africa paraded through Sydney. A month earlier Victoria's first contingent had returned to a wild reception in Melbourne, but on the following day many were still so drunk that they staggered and fell over during the official march, repaying kisses from women with lewd gestures.

BELOW:
Sister Mary McKillop (1842–1909), born in Melbourne of Scottish Catholic stock, founded the Congregation of the Sisters of Saint Joseph of the Sacred Heart to care for and educate poor children and orphans in the South Australian bush. Her death in 1909 passed unnoticed but in 1995 she was beatified, the first step to her canonisation as Australia's first saint.

The drought: a dry beginning

Australia lay dried and desiccated. The worst drought on record had seen 14 million sheep die and in 1902, before it broke, Nellie Melba returned to her homeland to honour the new federation with a series of public appearances. Travelling south by train from Queensland, she recalled that 'all along the line from Brisbane to Melbourne I had noticed out of my window the carcases of sheep and cattle lying dead and rotting under the gum trees whither they had crawled to eat the leaves. And when they could reach no more they had dropped dead. Everything was desolate with the desolation of the desert. Not a blade of grass.' She was touched to hear that country people had driven for days 'just to hear me sing' and brought the house down in Melbourne by following the mad scene from *Lucia di Lammermoor* by a rendition of 'Home Sweet Home'. She was appalled, however, when her plans to hold a Sunday dinner

Scene in Queen's Square, Sydney, on Federation Day, 1 January 1901.
Crowds wore their 'Sunday best' to celebrate the birth of the
world's newest nation. On the right can be seen St James Church,
dating from the Macquarie era, and on the left, Hyde Park. The tower
of the Town Hall and the dome of the Queen Victoria Building are
seen on the skyline.

party at her home in Toorak were dashed when the cook walked out: nobody in Australia worked on Sundays.

Those dedicated English Fabian socialists Sydney and Beatrice Webb, visiting Australia for the first time, were disappointed by Sydney and its inhabitants—'a crude chaotic place' where 'money making and racing seem their only concern'—and found Queenslanders even worse: 'bad manners, sullen insolence, and grasping-ness'. They were enchanted by Hobart—'the neatest little town that the sun shines on'—and impressed by Melbournians: 'These men are certainly a better type than the rich men we met in Sydney, superior in intellectual culture and vastly so in public spirit.'

ABOVE:
The British army had left the Australian colonies in 1870, but a contingent of British officers, seen here in their full dress uniforms with a handful of Australian officers, added a touch of splendour to the Federation celebrations.

The first years of Federation

In May 1901 King Edward's eldest son the Duke of York (for the Queen had died on 21 January, after a reign of sixty-three years) proclaimed the opening of Australia's first Federal Parliament in Melbourne, where both Houses would sit until Canberra's Parliament House was built in 1927.

Alfred Deakin found it convenient: as Prime Minister in 1903 he would often walk to his office through the Botanic Gardens from South Yarra or simply catch a tram. Other ministers would accept a lift from a friend driving one of the new-fangled automobiles. A century later Australian prime ministers still sit in the front seat of their limousines next to the driver. It's an Australian tradition.

The first years of Parliament were conducted by gentlemanly English-Australians with a personal courtesy and decorum now vanished. There were no established political parties as such, only factions—Free Traders and Protectionists. Only sixteen of the seventy-five members of the House were Labour but the party itself was divided on the tariff question.

ABOVE:
King Edward's son the Duke of York (the future King George V) opened Australia's first federal parliament in Melbourne's Exhibition Building in May 1901.

Prime Minister Barton, standing before his cabinet ministers, reads the royal guests a speech of welcome.

From this sketch Tom Roberts made his formal panting of the event.

RIGHT:
Edmund Barton (1849–1920), the successful Sydney barrister who became Australia's first Prime Minister.

On one matter all members of Parliament were in agreement: Australia would stay European. 'The Commonwealth of Australia shall remain a White Australia,' Deakin announced on introducing the Immigration Bill in 1901. The nation, he explained, shall be founded 'on the firm foundation of unity of race', one whose people shared common ideas, ideals, character, traditions and loyalties. One dissenting member described the Bill as 'racial prejudice' and reminded the House of Deakin's own admission that Australians feared the Japanese because of the latter's known industriousness and intelligence. Immigration of Asians would be controlled not by armed borders but by a dictation test: all 'coloured' applicants for residency would be subjected to a literacy test in any European language. It proved effective in keeping out individuals whose politics might prove disturbing to a government: as late as 1934 an anti-Nazi Czech journalist was refused entry when he failed a test in Gaelic and a New Zealand communist had to sit for a test in Dutch.

When Edmund Barton retired (he had collapsed in his rooms in Parliament) to become a judge on the High Court in 1903, Deakin succeeded to the prime Ministership and he dominated parliament until the coming of Labor in 1908. He was a brilliant and impressive speaker—eloquent if loquacious—and a tall, poised and elegant figure. A progressive conservative, he contributed much to the making of what William Morris Hughes was to call 'one of the most socially advanced and democratic nations of the time'.

1902: Australia—powerhouse of reform

In 1902 the vote was extended to women in federal elections; this Act forced those states that had not yet enacted female suffrage in state elections to follow suit. In 1903 the High Court was established, its bench of three judges soon expanded because of pressure of work.

Deakin was a Protectionist, and protectionism triumphed. Leading a minority party, he remained in power by the good grace of Labor, whose members supported—and often initiated—his program of social reform. The various colonial tariffs were phased out gradually and replaced by federal ones.

In 1904 Australia created a Court of Conciliation and Arbitration, the first in the world, but disagreement about its application brought about the fall of Deakin.

Labor took power under 'Chris' Watson in April 1904 but lost office in August when deserted by its coalition partners: it was the world's first Labor government. Sir George Reid—with whom Deakin refused to serve—took over as Prime Minister until June 1905, heading a government of 'fiscal misfits whose common attitude was a hostility to Labor'.

ABOVE:
Ernest Wunderlich's building-materials factory in the inner-Sydney suburb of Redfern, established in 890, was part of Australia's growing light manufacturing industry early in the century.

BELOW:
A future Prime Minister, Andrew Fisher was elected to the Federal Parliament in 1901.

With seven parliaments for a population of just over four million people (the United Kingdom's 40 million got by with one parliament), Australians derived continual amusement from the antics of politicians, here parodied by the artist Norman Lindsay (1879-1969).

Lindsay was already famous for his koala cartoons in the *Bulletin.*

Pledged support by Watson, Deakin was asked to form a new government by the Governor-General: the introduction of old age pensions in 1907 and the initiation of a strong, independent defence policy were two of its lasting achievements. In 1908 Deakin cheekily invited the American Great White Fleet to visit Australian ports without informing London, to demonstrate to Australians the value of a strong navy; the visit was a sensational success, and the beginning of a decades-long love affair with America.

1907: *The basic wage*

An attempt to introduce a tariff on certain goods to provide the finance to reward local manufacturers adopting enlightened wage policies was unsuccessful: the High Court found Deakin's innovative 'New Protection' unconstitutional. But the legislation had one important result. Hugh McKay, who had moved his Sunshine Harvesters factory to the outskirts of Melbourne in 1907, asked for exemption from the new excise clause, but the High Court in 1908 found that the company was paying uneven wages, and introduced for all Australian workers a 'basic wage'. Mr Justice Higgins of the Arbitration Court decided that the minimum 'fair and reasonable' wage for the average worker—a man with a wife and three children to support—was a healthy £2 2s 0d a week. The basic wage, reviewed annually, was an Australian innovation and remained part of law for almost a century.

BELOW: Australian women obtained the franchise in 1902. In this banner an Australian woman pleads with Britannia to grant the vote to the women of Britain. It was carried in suffragette processions in Britain in 1908 and 1911.

The devastating drought ended in 1903 and recovery was rapid. The following year a statistician produced figures showing that Australians had higher disposable incomes than Americans, Britons and Canadians. With the worst of the 1890s depression just a bad memory, the government began a successful immigration campaign in 1905 that enticed nearly 400,000 British migrants to Australia (and the first sizeable number of Italians); this boosted the Commonwealth's population by 1914 to nearly five million.

Industrial growth was slow. Australia's iron industry dates from the building of BHP's blast furnaces at Newcastle, near the Hunter Valley black coal deposits; the plant—the creation of BHP's Guillaume Delprat—opened in 1915 but was a prewar initiative. Soon Newcastle's furnaces and foundries, factories and shipyards, and Wollongong's smelting works would make New South Wales once more the economic heart of Australia.

When Labor withdrew support over the New Protection legislation Deakin resigned and Andrew Fisher (Watson's successor) headed the second, equally short-lived Labor government from November 1908 to April 1909. Deakin's decision to irrevocably dump Labor and merge—

LEFT:
In 1904 J.C. ('Chris') Watson became Australia's first Labor Prime Minister. He is shown in this poster from *The Worker* with his cabinet; it included two future prime ministers, the Welshman William Morris Hughes (top portrait) and the Scot, Andrew Fisher (bottom right portrait).

BELOW:
By 1904 the drought had ended and the country began a boom period. A farmer is seen here inspecting the fleece of his prize Merinos, western New South Wales, c. 1910.

or 'fuse'—with Lyne's Liberals attracted abuse, insult and charges of 'ratting' from Labor members so unremitting that the Speaker collapsed and died from a heart attack, murmuring 'Dreadful, dreadful'. Hughes, in Celtic fury, compared Deakin to Judas, and Deakin, though he continued to serve in Parliament until 1913, never really forgave him.

In the election of 1910 the Liberal-Fusion Party was soundly beaten by Andrew Fisher's Labor Party. The new Prime Minister was a Scot, 'a tall handsome man, a slow thinker,' wrote Deakin, 'a man of integrity'. Fisher's deputy and Attorney-General was neither handsome nor a slow thinker: 'Billy' Hughes was, in the words of one journalist, 'endowed with nervous, physical strength beyond belief. He is as tough as a whipcord, has the endurance of a camel and the pluck of a prize-fighter. Some men fear him, many admire him, a very few hate him.' But no man worth his salt, the writer agreed, lacks enemies.

The drift to war

The century of European peace—the Pax Europa—was drawing to a close. The elaborate 'balance of powers' on the Continent had been displaced by the extraordinary economic growth of a united Germany; since its defeat of France in 1870 the new German Empire had outstripped France's population of 40 million by 20 million and its coal and steel production by a similar ratio. Germany's young Kaiser Wilhelm developed an obsessive Anglophobia and began embarking on a strenuous naval building program to challenge Britain's naval power. Britain, remote for a century from European squabbles, was drawn into a 'naval race', launching in 1906 HMS *Dreadnought*, an armoured capital ship mounting heavy guns; Germany countered this move by intensifying the construction of a High Seas Fleet. France and her ally Russia faced an alliance between Germany and Austria. Europe had become two large armed camps.

It was Labor that created a navy for Australia but Deakin had prepared its keel. The Admiralty had objected strongly to the idea of an Australian navy until the beginning of the naval race after 1906. Britain's naval supremacy was clear but the gap was closing: in 1909 both Australia and New Zealand had offered to pay for dreadnoughts for the Royal Navy and Deakin's government placed an order for three destroyers with British shipyards. In 1911 the Fisher–Hughes government created the Royal Australian Navy; its nucleus was the colonial flotilla taken over by the Commonwealth but its strength lay in the battle cruiser HMAS *Australia,* and the three cruisers and the destroyers that steamed into Sydney Harbour in October 1913.

The war clouds in Europe were gathering. In 1909 a form of military conscription for Australian youngsters was instituted and in 1910 Lord Kitchener was invited to Australia to advise the nation on how best to improve its military preparedness. In 1911 a military college was opened at Duntroon, a direct result of his report; a naval college followed in 1913 to train as future officers the first intake of 13-year-old Australian midshipmen.

The first decade of the new century had been a revolutionary one. As early as 1905 motor cars—the first automobile had been built in Australia in 1900—were reaching speeds of 70 km/h and pedestrians were demanding that their drivers be licensed or in some way controlled. In 1907 Sydney and Melbourne were linked by telephone. In 1912 William Hart, holder of Australia's first pilot's licence, won the air race from Botany to Parramatta (there was only one other competitor) and two years later a Frenchman, landing

ABOVE:

As early as 1901 Australians were becoming concerned at Germany's belligerent attitude, and foresaw a time when conflict would eventuate.

BELOW:

Australians were proud to buy 'Austral' suits and trousers made from 'Marrickville' tweed as evidence of national pride. The firm of Gowings still trades in George Street, Sydney.

ABOVE: The commercial heart of Melbourne: Bourke Street in the early 1900s. At the top of the street stands Parliament House.
BELOW: Australian cities reflected an inevitable sameness: George Street, Sydney, in 1907.

in paddocks to refuel, made the first flight between Melbourne and Sydney.

If the British thought of Australians at all it was as sportsmen, the one field in which they excelled. In the first decade of the new century the Australian cricket team won fourteen Test matches to England's nine; seven were drawn. In the 1902 tour of England the Sydney batsman Victor Trumper scored 2570 runs, including eleven centuries. In 1906 another prodigy from Sydney, Annette Kellermann, who had taken up swimming after being nearly crippled by infantile paralysis, won the 40-kilometre race down the Danube in just over thirteen hours, and then tried to swim the English Channel. (In the same year the first Life-savers began patrolling Sydney beaches.) In 1907 Australia and New Zealand, playing together as 'Australasia', won the Davis Cup; the star, Norman Brookes, also won the Wimbledon singles and defended it successfully three years running.

Apart from sports, Australia had made little impact on the world and seemed to have little to offer. Australians spoke English, but with a nasal drawl, and the language and slang appeared comic to 'New Chums' and their unhurried approach to life hardly characteristic of such a businesslike Empire as the British.

ABOVE:
Bounding down the crease in his usual style, Victor Trumper (1877–1915) was the first Test cricketer to make a century between the start of play and lunch. One of Australia's first national heroes, he died of kidney disease.

264

LEFT:
Pianist and composer Percy Grainger (1882–1961) of Melbourne was already acclaimed in Europe when he returned to Australia to give concerts in 1903 and 1908. An eccentric genius, he left to live permanently in the United States in 1914.

BELOW:
The young Stella Miles Franklin (1879–1954), novelist, who grew up on Brindabella station near the future capital of Canberra.

ABOVE:
Annette Kellermann (1886–1975) of Sydney, a state swimming champion, found fame and fortune overseas after 1907 as a swimmer, dancer and Hollywood film star. Seen here in *A Daughter of the Gods*, 1916.

Pride among Australians was muted. In 1905 Dorothea Mackellar wrote the poem *My Country*, the words of which, later to be chanted by generations of school children, joined Peter Dodds McCormick's 'Advance Australia Fair' as unofficial national anthems. The same year saw the publication of Jeannie Gunn's *We of the Never Never*, and the first novel by Henry Handel Richardson, *Maurice Guest*. (Its author was a young woman, Ethel Richardson.)

In Australia's masculine world, another woman writer of genius also chose to write under a male pseudonym: Stella Maria Miles Franklin wrote *My Brilliant Career* when she was sixteen; it was published six years later, in 1901, with a preface by Henry Lawson, and astonished readers by its precocity. It was a romantic novel in which the strong-willed heroine, Sybylla, rejects marriage in order to pursue an independent career. The author faced her family's anger and then sudden fame, which was equally traumatic.

'Miles Franklin' wrote a sequel to it in 1903, titling it whimsically *My Career Goes Bung* (though she chose not to publish it for another forty-three years) and left for the United States to involve herself in the feminist cause. Joseph Furphy protested her decision: 'Stay among the eucalypts, Miles … Mind you, I love the Americans, but Australia cannot spare you.' Rose Scott, who had acclaimed the novel, complained: 'And so you are really going to America … Why this long journey? Why, Why, Why?' In her unpublished sequel, Miles Franklin explained why: 'I loved to learn things—anything, everything …' She refused to accept a future working as a governess, or a cook or a housemaid or a 'despised lady doctor … I rebelled against every one of these fates.' She left for the United States with letters of introduction from Rose Scott and Vida Goldstein to Alice Henry, one of the leaders of America's women's

MANLY, SYDNEY HARBOUR, N.S.W.

THE LONE HAND—February 1, 1913

"Into the thick of the dance Dad and Mother trundled furiously."

reform movement. There she chose to write a series of novels with Australian settings under a pseudonym, 'Brent of Bin-Bin', and ended her self-imposed exile only in 1933.

Joseph Furphy wrote his great but difficult novel *Such is Life* (published in 1903) under the name 'Tom Collins'—the Irish-Australian nickname for a tale-spinner. The famous opening line of his masterpiece struck readers as typically Australian: 'Unemployed at last!' When in 1908 the *Bulletin* asked readers to contribute lines for a new national anthem the humorous Irish-Australian journalist C.J. Dennis sent in one that began:

> Fellers of Australia,
> Blokes and coves and coots,
> Shift yer b——carcases
> Move yer b——boots ...

It became instantly popular, showing only that Australians had a rich, idiosyncratic sense of humour and alone among the Dominions hardly took themselves seriously

Furphy's book reflected his nationalism ('temper democratic, bias offensively Australian') and extolled the mateship found among his heroes, the bushmen—the 'men without property'. But few bought it; the book took ten years to sell one thousand copies. Educated Australians spoke like the English and read English books, English magazines.

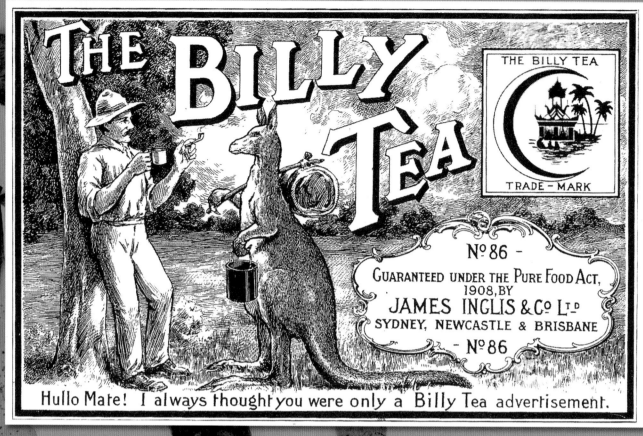

ABOVE: Billy Tea, already popular, was 'guaranteed under the pure Food Act of 1908.

ABOVE:

A slow-growing patriotism: Melbourne-born singer and actress Dorothy Brunton (1890–1977) sang this 1910 composition with fervour during the coming war and became known as 'The Diggers' Delight'.

LEFT:

A century later they remain household names: Arnott's biscuit factory opened in 1904.

ABOVE:
While most entertainers loved Australia some left it to pursue opportunities overseas. This piece dates from 1908.

TOP:
The visit of America's 'Great White Fleet' to Australian ports in 1908 created public enthusiasm and stimulated an appetite for an Australian navy. The world cruise indicated that the United States was now a world power.

'Australia presents a paradox,' wrote a perceptive British journalist, Foster Fraser, who travelled through the Commonwealth in 1909.

There is a breezy, buoyant Imperial spirit. But the national spirit, as it is understood elsewhere, is practically non-existent—though one sees the green leaf sprouting.

There is a warm and generous love for the Motherland. When the Australian uses the word 'home' he does not mean his home. He means England.

But you drop from Imperialism to something like parochialism in Australia, with little of the real nation's spirit intervening—though it exists and must increase. There is a warm pride in forming part of the Empire. There is more evidence of loyalty in Australia than I have ever met with in any other part of the King's dominions. But it is loyalty to the Empire, not to Great Britain. Not out of State patriotism, but out of Imperialism a healthy nationalism will grow.

In the same year, an English-Australian of sensitivity revealed where his heart truly lay:

There is a certain pure old cross of St George which the smallest grey gunboat carries about the world ... It stands for generosity in sport, for a pure regard for women, a chivalrous marriage tie ... for every British principle of cleanliness in body and mind, of kindness to animals, of fun and fair play, for the British Sunday, for clean streets and a decent drainage ... and a thousand and one ideas wrung out by British men and women from the toil and sweat of nine hundred years, that make the Anglo-Saxon life worth living ...

The writer was a Sydney journalist of higher than average intelligence, Charles Edwin Woodrow Bean, and his words—from the concluding pages of a book on the Royal Navy in Australia—were described by one Sydney reviewer as 'flamboyant flapdoodle'. Bean's editor on the *Sydney Morning Herald* soon sent the young reporter into the west of New South Wales to write about flood and drought, shearers and roustabouts. Here Bean found a new set of heroes. As Australia's

'Official War Correspondent' on Gallipoli he
would discover among the Anzacs even greater
heroes. He would lose his admiration for the
ways of the British Empire and curse England's
society as 'a relic of the Middle Ages'.

Even before the Imperial gift of Gallipoli as a
seedbed of national pride, there were other
indications that Australians were developing a
quiet pleasure in asserting their individuality
and forging a society in their own image. In
1910 the Labor government introduced—
despite the disapproval of the Bank of England—Australian banknotes and coins to
replace the mixture of British sterling currency
and local notes. The following year it set up a
'people's bank', one owned by the taxpayers—
the Commonwealth Bank—which in 1913
began competing against the private trading
banks. The bank was the creation of King
O'Malley, the American of whom Hughes
would say: 'We never knew what he was going
to do next.'

1913: Canberra founded

As Minister for Home Affairs, O'Malley was the
driving force also behind the building of a
national capital. Andrew Fisher had been the
first Prime Minister to demand a Commonwealth car and driver; the search for the perfect site for a national capital became the first
'junket' as scores of politicians were transported at some expense around south-east New

A COMPARISON
The Melbourne Girl   The Sydney Girl

South Wales. Canberra was chosen over Tumut in the House of Representatives by
nineteen votes to seventeen. Hundreds of fanciful and grandiose architectural
plans were submitted for the capitol but the design adopted was that by an American, Walter Burley Griffin, and his wife, who planned a garden city of circular
boulevards and modest buildings. King O'Malley drove the first builder's peg into
the hard ground at Canberra in 1913. Not since the building of Washington had a
nation created a capital city from scratch.

Geographically, the nation was growing. British New Guinea—Papua—was presented to Australia in 1907; in the following year Hubert Murray (one of the sons
of the squatter king and laird of Yarralumla, Terence Aubrey Murray), was appointed Lieutenant-Governor. He would rule Papua until 1940, protecting Papuans
against any repetition of the Blackbirding era in a remarkably enlightened if paternalistic administration. In 1908 Douglas Mawson and Edgeworth David sailed with

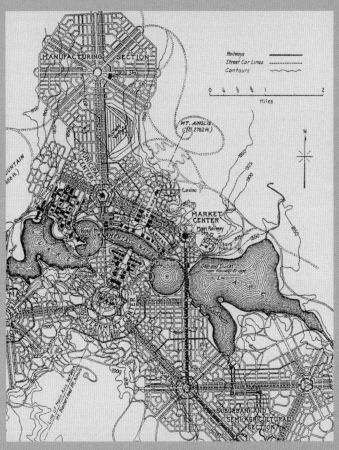

ABOVE:
The American Walter Burley Griffin's original design for Canberra.

LEFT:
Publication of the period before the First World War.

BELOW:
Corner store in the suburbs of south-western Sydney around 1910.

Shackleton's expedition to the Antarctic; in the following year they became the first men to stand on the lip of the snow-covered volcano, Mount Erebus, and several months later, the first to fix the site of the magnetic South Pole.

In 1911, when the Commonwealth took over the Northern Territory, hauling down the South Australian flag at a ceremony in Darwin (the population of which totalled 400), Douglas Mawson left again for Antarctica to (in his own words) 'hoist the Australian flag in land which geographically should belong to Australia ... and to uphold the prestige of the British race in the Australian Antarctic'. Australia's great polar hero was English-born, a maker of empires, and the government expedition to Antarctica explored and claimed for the Commonwealth an entire, empty new world. Mawson was knighted in 1914, one year after his return.

In 1913 the first truly Australian postage stamp appeared, breaking with tradition by bearing the image not of the king, but of a puzzled kangaroo. In January 1914 the cover of the literary magazine the *Lone Hand* carried what soon became another national icon, metaphor for a nation of innocents—Bib and Bub, May Gibbs' cherubic gumnut twins, small plump English babies wearing little gumnuts for hats, clinging to a gumleaf, as if they were about to fall off.

1914: The outbreak of war

The early months of 1914 were the hottest and driest for more than a decade, onset of the worst drought to devastate the land since the '1902'. When General Hamilton, Inspector General of British overseas forces, visited Australia in March 1914, he saw Australia's militia go through their paces at Lilydale on a sweltering day on which bushfires burned furiously on the surrounding hills. He was impressed by the enthusiasm displayed by the troops and by several of the officers he met, notably Colonel Monash, who had handled his brigade with great dexterity; but Hamilton would later write privately that the Australians had been less orderly than the New Zealanders and that it would take three colonial soldiers to equal one British regular.

In the election of June 1913 the Labor government unexpectedly lost power to the Liberals under Deakin's successor, Joseph Cook, who took office with a major-

ABOVE:
Australians at the South Magnetic Pole: Edgeworth David (1858–1934) (centre), Douglas Mawson (1882–1958) and Mackay, 16 January 1909.

ABOVE:
English-born William Holman (1871–1934) won the state seat of Cootamundra for Labor in 1906. He is pictured visiting his electorate after he became NSW Premier in 1913.

RIGHT:
The monoplane in which French aviator Maurice Guillaux made the first flight from Melbourne to Sydney in 1914, dropping off 'airmail' on the way. Early 'aeroplanes' were so simple in construction that many aviators made their own.

ity of one seat; after a year of frustration the Prime Minister asked the Governor-General for a double dissolution, and the calling of a new election. Parliament was dissolved on 30 July 1914. Five days later Australia was at war.

Europe was also basking in an unusually warm and glorious summer. The British Fleet was paying a courtesy visit to German ports, the French President was visiting the Tsar of Russia, and Asquith's Liberal government had just enacted the Home Rule Bill giving Ireland self-government when, on 28 June 1914, the heir to the Austro-Hungarian throne was assassinated by Serbian fanatics in the Bosnian town of Sarajevo. But during the next four weeks people in Europe breathed a sigh of relief, for it seemed that diplomacy had again averted another Balkan war. But on 28 July Austria declared war on Serbia. Three days later Russia, having mobilised her army, received Germany's declaration of war. While Winston Churchill, the First Lord of the Admiralty, ordered the Grand Fleet to war stations and cabled the Dominions that a European war seemed likely, on 3 August Germany declared war on Russia's ally, France. On 4 August German armies entered neutral Belgium in an act the German Chancellor admitted was contrary to international treaty, but militarily necessary. It was in fact part of the long-prepared plan to take the French from the rear and encircle Paris.

'This simplifies matters, so we sent the Germans an ultimatum to expire at midnight,' Prime Minister Asquith wrote in London. 'Winston, who has got on all his war paint, is longing for a sea fight … The whole thing fills me with sadness.' No reply to Britain's demand for an evacuation of Belgium was received from Berlin. At midnight on 4 August Great Britain declared war on Germany.

The Herald

EXTRAORDINA EDITION

No. 12,087. | MELBOURNE, SUNDAY EVENING, AUGUST 2, 1914. | (4 PAGES) PRICE ONE 1ª

CONTINENT OF EUROPE THREATENS TO BECOME A HUGE BATTLEFIE

KAISER DECLARES WAR

POWERS FEVERISHLY ARMING,
EXPECTING INSTANT WARFARE

AMBASSADORS LEAVE CAPITALS

KING GEORGE SEES PRIME MINISTER AT 2 A.M

BRITISH EXPEDITIONARY FORCE
READY TO GIVE AID TO FRANCE

GREAT BRITAIN PREPARES FOR STRUGGLE

PREMIER SEES KING AT TWO O'CLOCK IN THE MORNING

TROOPS MOVE FROM ALDERSHOT

(Published in "The Times" This Morning).

LONDON. Mr. Asquith, the Prime Minister, interviewed the King at 2 o'clock on Saturday morning, and Ministers subsequently conferred together.

His Majesty the King sent an urgent message to the Czar as a final effort to avert calamity.

There has been a general exodus of troops from Aldershot.

Sixteen thousand officers and men moved to Frensham, in Surrey, miles away.

It is understood that an expeditionary force of 115,000 men is ready to cross the Channel at the shortest notice.

It is believed that the Government will take over all his strategic rail-

however, is feeling the persistent pressure of the minority.

Australia's response has greatly heartened Great Britain.

People are only commencing to realise the gravity of the situation.

The main streets of London are crowded with people wishing to buy special editions, and places of amusement are suffering loss, the houses being only half full.

CANADA TO ASSIST

OFFER OF TROOPS EXPECTED

MEAT SUPPLIES WANTED

BRITAIN MAY KEEP STOCKS

LONDON. Beef and pork in the London markets has advanced, and Continental buyers are arriving.

Several large buyers arrived in London, but did not operate.

It is possible existing supplies will be reserved Great Britain and France. Germany withdrawing her restrictions importation of

WHEAT PIT MAD

DEALERS SCRAMBLE FOR GRAIN AND MANY ARE RUINED

(United Service, Special Cable.)

NEW YORK The maddest excitement ever seen prevails in the wheat pit at Chicago. The price of grain is bounding upward phenomenally.

Men are struggling on the floor, con-

PARIS GETS I

TENTS VEGETARIAN

(United Service Special

Paris is not in any danger having reserved a stock amounting to 75,000 tons.

During the mobilisation troops railway tracks are able for live stock, but the rounded by a belt of mark The Parisians are practising vegetarian diet.

M. Messimy, the French for War, went to the Cen in Paris to obtain a person of the spirits of the t found them singing patriot whistling military marches for the fray.

SMALLER PO

MANY DECLARE NEUTR BUT SEVERAL

(United Service Special

The First World War, 1914–18

Australia at war

When the British Empire went to war in 1914 for England, Home and Glory it did so to the command of Scots. From Canada Prime Minister Robert Borden, a Nova Scotian, had pledged to Britain on the eve of war an army of 20,000 men; from New Zealand Prime Minister William Fergusson-Massey offered a force of 6000 men. In Sydney the Governor-General, Sir Ronald Munro-Ferguson, a former Scottish Liberal who had taken up his post earlier in the year, suggested to the Prime Minister that Australia indicate what support the Commonwealth could offer the British government. In Colac the Scot Andrew Fisher, who would succeed Joseph Cook as Prime Minister on 5 September, promised the crowd in his soft Ayrshire burr that if war came Australia 'would rally to the Mother Country and defend her to our last man and our last shilling'.

Australia as part of the British Empire was thus at war with Germany, but her involvement in the conflict was seen as minor, for all military experts were predicting that the European war would be over by Christmas. Few factions could find fault with Britain's decision to declare war. The Irish both in Australia and in their homeland pledged loyalty to the Crown; a Lutheran bishop whose voice was taken as representative of Australia's 100,000 citizens of German birth or parentage also pledged his flock's loyalty to Australia and 'to our beloved King'. The government called for volunteers for an army to assist Great Britain.

The Australian Imperial Force (AIF)

The recruiting of an Australian expeditionary force began on 10 August 1914. The officer nominated to command the planned army of 20,000 volunteers was Scots-born, but a descendant of the Throsbys of Bowral, Major-General William T. Bridges. The three infantry brigades of Bridges' '1st Australian Division' were entrusted to the command of two lawyers who had reached militia rank as colonels—McLaurin and M'Cay—and to a British regular, Sinclair-MacLagan. A Light Horse brigade was raised under the command of the Queens-lander Colonel Harry Chauvel and the Artillery was placed under the command of Colonel Talbot Hobbs, an English-born architect from Perth.

ABOVE:
The experience of the First World War left an enduring impression on the nation. The bravery of the Anzacs was extolled as an example to the young; the slouch hat and the 'rising sun' cap badge of the 1st AIF are still worn by the Australian Army.

So many volunteers were accepted that a 4th Infantry Brigade was formed under the command of Colonel John Monash, a former dux of Scotch College who had been attracted to the militia because of its 'gorgeous uniforms' and had become Melbourne's leading structural engineer. He was the son of German-Jewish parents. Four years later he would be regarded as the only general capable of leading the British Empire's armies in France to victory.

Bridges decided that this new army would be called the 'Australian Imperial Force'. The name is significant. Men came from banks, from shearing sheds, from railway yards, from schools and farms, motivated by both pride in Empire—sheer patriotism—and by an urge for adventure, though many afterwards would find it difficult to articulate their reasons for joining up. 'All my mates were going, so I went too,' one Australian would later say. 'The last thing I thought of was King and Empire.'

In the middle of the Western Australian desert a bunch of gangers working on the Transcontinental Railway line heard that war had broken out; they were not sure who the enemy was but they dropped their tools and hopped a freight car into Fremantle, where they enlisted. On sighting a red-tabbed staff officer one of them burst out laughing, shouting 'Cripes, a galah!' which made his mates laugh, and after dumping their swags several of them told the sergeant that they were going down to the pub for a few hours; they were quickly shown to their barracks. They were the nucleus of the 11th Battalion, destined to be among the first to land on Gallipoli.

By late September an Australian naval and military force had seized German settlements in New Guinea and at Rabaul in an almost bloodless conquest, and troops gathering in hastily erected training camps thought the war would be over before they reached it. Only Lord Kitchener said it would be a long war—'possibly three years'. H.G. Wells predicted that the war would destroy civilisation.

A Welsh-born music hall star scribbled the official marching song of the AIF and troopships of Australian volunteers echoed to its throaty chorus as they pulled away from wharves crowded with proud and tearful loved ones:

ABOVE:
The sinking of the
Emden, from the painting
in the Australian War
Memorial, Canberra.

Rally round the banner of your country
Take the field with brother o'er the foam
On land and sea, where ever you may be
Keep your eye on Germany!

But England Home and Beauty have no cause to fear,
Should auld acquaintance be forgot?
No! No! No! No! No!
Australia will be there!
Australia will be there!

The convoy of thirty-eight transports, ten of them carrying two brigades of the Fernleafs—New Zealand Expeditionary Force—left the spacious waters of King George Sound on the south-west tip of Western Australia on 1 November 1914, setting a course for Egypt from where officers and men alike hoped to go on to the battlefields of Belgium and France. The only excitement came seven days later when the convoy was passing the Cocos Islands in the Indian Ocean. From the wireless operator at Cocos came a message that a strange warship was offshore: this could only be the German raider *Emden.* The escorting cruiser HMAS *Sydney* steamed west, smoke belching from her funnels as the stokers laid on coal, and opened fire at five miles range from *Emden*, suffering fifteen hits from the under-gunned enemy cruiser before the latter, in flames, ran herself onto the reef. News of Australia's first naval victory thrilled the nation. The convoy arrived in Egypt to hear that a new enemy had joined Germany and Austria—Turkey.

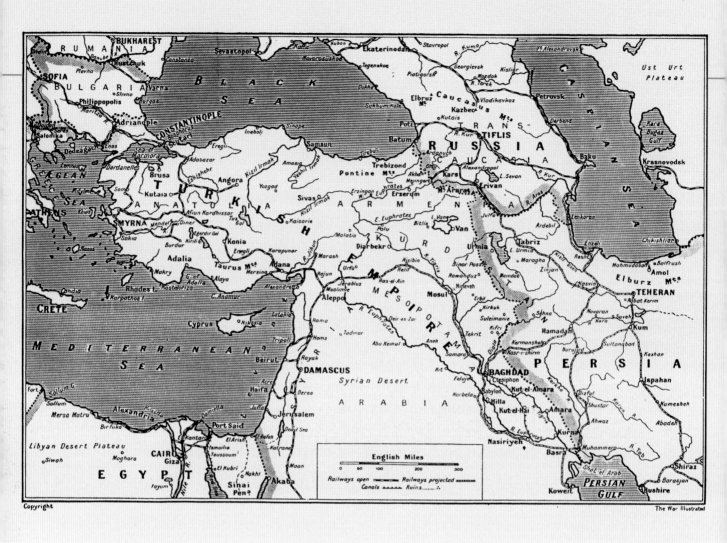

Copyright

The War Illustrated

Gallipoli: The Dardanelles plan

In Egypt a great Imperial army was gathering for one of the most extraordinary campaigns in history. Turkey had entered the war on Germany's side in November 1914 and the known weakness of the ramshackle Ottoman Empire prompted the British War Cabinet in January 1915 to decide on a bold plan to re-open the sea link to embattled Russia. They would seize the Dardanelles, the narrow strait that led from the Black Sea to the Aegean and Mediterranean, and capture Constantinople. The idea was Winston Churchill's. The 40-year-old First Lord of the Admiralty proposed that a fleet of old pre-dreadnought British battleships (they were due for scrapping anyway) be used to destroy the forts, force the minefields of the Narrows and thus open the way to Constantinople, the heart of Turkey's empire.

On 18 March 1915 a mighty fleet of British and French battleships steamed into the Dardanelles, bombarding the forts on the Gallipoli peninsula with devastating results; but it ran into minefields; within hours three battleships were sunk and three damaged.

On 22 March the admiral confessed that seaborne attack alone could not force the narrow channel. An army would be required to capture and neutralise the Gallipoli peninsula. Churchill was appalled to see his naval venture become a military campaign cobbled together in a hurry. The First Sea Lord, Admiral Fisher, was even angrier, later writing to Churchill: 'You are simply eaten up with the Dardanelles. Damn the Dardanelles! They will be our grave!'

ABOVE:

It was decided in late 1914 that Australian troops would train in Egypt before moving to the battlefields of France.

The Middle East was destined to be a battlefield for Australians in two World Wars — and in Iraq as late as 2004.

ABOVE:
Australians in Egypt: Almost the entire 11th (West Australian) Battalion poses on a pyramid on teh eve of Gallipoli invasion. The 11th was among the first units to land on Gallipoli.

1914: The Australians in Egypt

'I can only form the guess that for the time being the Australian troops will be left to garrison Egypt and may quite possibly be left there until the end of the war,' Colonel John Monash of Melbourne wrote as his troopship approached Aden in December 1914. The first convoy of Australians and New Zealanders were sent into camps at Mena and at Zeitan respectively, for camps in England were full to bursting point of volunteers for the divisions Kitchener was raising—Britain's 'New Armies'.

The Australians' conduct in Egypt soon caused complaints to flow back to Australia about their lack of discipline and insubordination towards officers, most particularly British officers of all ranks. 'They seem a slack lot,' the New Zealand Colonel Malone wrote, and advised his men to have nothing to do with the Australians. The troops were appalled by the unsanitary conditions in the cities and became bored and restless; on leave in Cairo they tended to drink too much and seemed to take out their frustrations on the Egyptians. There was no point of contact between the Australians and the English garrison troops—the latter were quickly dubbed 'Chooms'—for the Australians were puzzled by the British soldiers' calm acceptance of harsh discipline and their comical Lancashire accents. The New Zealanders were not innocent of disorderly behaviour but the Australians were generally regarded as a disorderly mob whose value as fighting troops was questionable.

ANZAC is born

In December 1914 a new general arrived to command the 'Australian and New Zealand Army Corps' (or ANZAC), which was by now a force of 30,000 men consisting of the 1st Australian Division and the 'NZ and A Division'. He was Lieutenant-General William Birdwood, who had had ample experience commanding Indian Army regiments, and was one of Kitchener's favourites. 'A fine, dapper little chap,' Monash described him. 'Birdie' was to command the AIF until the war's end.

On 5 March 1915 Kitchener ordered the first of two British divisions to sail for Egypt to form part of the Constantinople Expeditionary Force and seven days later appointed General Sir Ian Hamilton as its commander. The bulk of the invasion army would however consist of the 'Anzacs' who, for all their ill-discipline at least looked like soldiers.

'They walked the earth with daredevil self confidence,' wrote another Englishman, the war correspondent Henry Nevinson. 'Gifted with the intelligence that comes from freedom and healthy physique, they could be counted upon to face death but hardly to salute an officer.' Many English observers found it impossible not to compare the Anzacs to Greek gods; the novelist Compton Mackenzie, who served as an officer at Gallipoli, saw them as the engravings in Flaxman's *Homer* come to life, Ajaxes and Hercules in khaki.

The Australians exert an almost physical presence in all accounts of the Great War; no other soldiers left such enduring and affectionate images among those who knew them. Their character was completely guileless, their nature frank, open and generous. 'A strange mixture of toughness and sentimentality,' a British general would write.

The landings on Gallipoli would begin on Sunday 25 April 1915. To distract the Turks, a French force would land on the Asian shore, on the plain of Troy. The British regulars—the 29th Division—would land on the southernmost tip of the peninsula, at Cape Helles, and then strike north. The Royal Naval Division comprised a mixture of marines, naval reservists and young Oxford dilettantes; the officers included Asquith's son, the Australian composer 'Cleg' Kelly, the poet Rupert Brooke and a giant New Zealander called Bernard Freyberg (who was certainly no dilettante). They were to cruise off the neck of the peninsula to mislead the enemy.

The Anzacs were given what was considered an easy task: to land north of the British zone, on a broad beach north of Gaba Tepe headland, from where they could advance easily across the plain towards the Dardanelles and thus cut off the Turkish retreat. The British high command was hopeful of clearing the Gallipoli peninsula and reaching Constantinople in a few weeks. The Turks were known to be poor soldiers. Only 5000 Allied casualties were expected.

The Gallipoli campaign would last not two weeks but eight months and cause nearly half a million casualties, 200,000 of them Allied; and of these 40,000 would be Anzacs.

1915: Landing on Gallipoli

The first Australians landed on Gallipoli at 4.29 am, 25 April, scrambling from small boats on a narrow beach below sloping cliffs. They had been landed at the wrong headland, on a small promontory called Ari Burnu, nearly two kilometres north of Gaba Tepe. After several minutes of confusion in the darkness—for Turks on the

ABOVE:
Australians charge into battle on Gallipoli. The 'Colonials' charged like footballers, according to one British officer. Gallipoli veterans later wore a bronze 'A' on their colour patches to mark them as original 'Anzacs'.

cliff top were firing into incoming boats—the Australians calmly began to climb the slopes, clawing at tussocks of grass to steady their ascent, and plunged inland into a terrible terrain of ridges, gullies and ravines.

The battle raged all day. Turkish counterattacks mounted in intensity in the mid-afternoon, driving the Australians back from the crest of the dominating 700-foot-high hill ('Baby 700') to a narrow neck—'The Nek'—which lay beneath it, and pushed the main force back to the seaward edge of '400 Plateau'. The bridgehead by nightfall was barely one kilometre deep and snaked along a broken crest line for four kilometres. Far to the south, at Cape Helles, the British 29th Division—the 'Tommies', nearly all of them English and Irish regulars—had been decimated on the beaches by machine-gun fire but were digging in on a similarly tiny bridge-head.

For the next eight months 'Anzac Cove' would be the Australians' and New Zealanders' battleground, every day of it shattered by the rattle of rifle and machine-gun fire, the groans of men, the crash of shellfire. General Hamilton ordered the Anzacs: 'Dig, dig, dig, until you are safe.'

The campaign had got off to a bad start, and things didn't improve. There was no fresh water, so water was carried up in cans and drums from the jetties on the beach. A few 18-pounders were hauled up the slopes but the troops would have to rely on the guns of the Fleet for artillery support and live under a continuous hail of Turkish shrapnel. Officers were astonished at how quickly the Australians adjusted to their strange conditions—'the most extraordinary position in which an army has ever found itself,' according to an English correspondent.

281

OPPOSITE, TOP:
The trenches of Gallipoli:
Two of the soldiers are
using periscopes to keep
an eye on the Turks.

After the first days the troops looked upon their plight with a laconic humour. 'Throughout the fighting there has never been a word of complaint,' Monash would write in May. 'They are always cheerful, always cracking jokes, always laughing and joking and singing.' On the night before his 14th Battalion went up to the front trenches he heard them laughing, chiacking and pulling each other's legs in the rowdy verbal horseplay that was Australians' special form of humour. They were coming through it well.

The Australians were also proving to be formidable soldiers, heedless of danger, very steady under fire. On 10 May an Australian brigade had advanced on Krithia, on the Helles front, marching for nearly half a kilometre through shrapnel and point-blank machine-gun fire, some of the men holding their spades to deflect bullets from their bodies, while Tommies sheltering in the trench tried to pull them back or cheered their valour. After Krithia the British called them the White Gurkhas, for only Gurkhas had been known to follow their British officers without wavering.

In a massive Turkish attempt to drive the Anzacs into the sea on 18 May, nearly 10,000 Turks were killed or wounded by the defenders for the loss of only 628 Australian and New Zealand dead. These enemy losses seem incredible, perhaps overstated. But six days later a truce was arranged and the Anzacs helped the Turks bury nearly 3500 corpses, for the stench of putrefaction was making the men ill. Closely observing his fellow countrymen, Captain Charles Bean, the official war correspondent, decided that Australia, though it produced wild men, also produced superb soldiers.

News of Gallipoli reached Australian newspapers on 30 April 1915 and Australians were surprised, and proud, to read that their men had been acclaimed as heroes. By 25 June the papers had listed a total of 10,000 killed and wounded men; in July, when the government called for every man to do his duty for King and Empire, 37,000 Australians joined the colours.

1915: The August offensives

BOTTOM:
Australian Light Horse
served as infantry on
Gallipoli and suffered
crippling losses. Their
charge at the Nek formed
the climax of the film
Gallipoli.

*From the painting by
G.W. Lambert in the
Australian War
Memorial, Canberra.*

With summer came heat and flies, thirst and dysentery, a collapse of supply lines and widespread erosion of morale; troops recuperating on Lemnos looked to one newly arrived officer like a 'beaten army'. In August 1915 General Hamilton landed a new British army in the north, at Suvla Bay, and launched the Anzacs in a series of bloody offensives, mainly to absorb the Turks' attention and reserves. Australian losses at Lone Pine, the Nek and Hill 60 were terrible and their survivors related alarming stories that the British New Armies had let the side down at Suvla, barely advancing off the beaches. When Keith Murdoch visited Anzac Cove in late August 1915 he found the Australians and New Zealanders despairing of the British, in low morale but determined to do their duty for the sake of their countries. Murdoch, astonished by the bland assurances from the British staff that all was jogging along nicely, broke his pledge of secrecy and wrote a report damning the campaign, sending it to Prime Minister Fisher, who circulated it among members of the British Cabinet. Its criticisms soon became public knowledge.

'The latest English papers talk of the whole undertaking as a strategic blunder, and say that the whole future effort should be concentrated in Flanders, which means that the sacrifice of 15,000 magnificent Dominion troops has been useless and to no purpose,' Monash wrote bitterly.

ABOVE:
The home front: mean-
while the women of
Australia waited. Raising
money for the war effort.

On 11 October 1915 the Cabinet in London recommended evacuation of Gallipoli. The evacuation was carried out without loss in December, as the first winter snows were falling on the trenches and as gales were lashing the beaches, sweeping away jetties. Buried in crude graves in the hard earth were the bodies of 7500 Australians and 2500 New Zealanders; another 30,000 Anzacs were incapacitated by wounds or disease. Newspapers described the campaign as 'the most splendid failure in history,' a humiliating military defeat but a triumph of spirit of the soldiers on both sides who had endured its horrors.

The Australian government considered it expedient to celebrate Gallipoli as the occasion of the birth of Australian national pride and the anniversary of the landing, 25 April, was henceforward observed as a day of remembrance. Gallipoli was romanticised and mythologised by men who had never experienced the terror, stench and putrefaction of war as a symbol of Australia's true character, one brave, loyal and indomitable. No official inquiry was made into the mismanagement of the campaign. School children would be taught that the Australians and New Zealanders stormed the beaches and cliffs of Gallipoli with a bayonet charge; but there were no Turks on the beach and few cliffs, only a handful of enemy soldiers on the crest of an easy slope, and no New Zealanders had landed until noon. Criticisms of the British High Command and the Suvla disaster were softened lest they offend Great Britain. The truth was best left buried with the dead. All that Australians knew was that their men had performed heroically, better than most, and for the first time in their history they felt proud.

Of the Australians and New Zealanders on Gallipoli a later British historian would write:

Nobody had seen such soldiers before. They were truly like men from a new world, or survivors from an older one. Tall, lean, powerful, cocky, their beauty was not merely physical, but sprang from their air of easy freedom. Their discipline was lax by British standards; they made terrible fun of the British officers, and regarded the British other ranks with a mixture of pity and affectionate condescension; but they brought to Hamilton's army a loose-limbed authority all their own, as though they were not the subject of events, but their sardonic masters.

ABOVE:
German detainee being
photographed by police,
1917.

France, 1916

The Gallipoli veterans returned to camps in Egypt and the misery of the Khamsin—the sand storms that rage from March to June. The men found that an even greater army was gathered there, for a total of 60,000 Australians were by March 1916 regrouping or training in Egypt, their destination unknown. In France a massive German offensive had fallen on the French lines at Verdun; it was a battle intended to bleed France white and was destined to claim 500,000 French and German casualties. On 13 March 1916 the first of the two 'Anzac Corps' in which the four Australian divisions and New Zealanders were grouped, began to embark for France, where the position was critical.

The British and French High Command had decided to launch a joint offensive against the German line near the Somme: this would be the first major battle fought by massed British armies on the Western Front since the beginning of the war, the long-awaited 'Big Push' that would break the German front.

The Irish rebellion

On the late morning of 25 April 1916 columns of Australian and New Zealand troops marched through the streets of London to an Anzac Day commemoration at Westminister Abbey, where the service was attended by the King and Queen and Lord Kitchener. Here 'the brave young sons of the Empire' were extolled as examples of valour and self-sacrifice. Prime Minister Hughes of Australia was also present; he had succeeded Fisher in October 1915 and had come to England to discuss the conduct of the war with the British Cabinet and to determine what increased part Australia could play in defeating Germany.

At the reception held after the service Hughes acclaimed the Australians as heroes; they had 'put on the toga of manhood'. Those Australians strolling into the streets afterwards would have seen evening papers whose headlines reported an uprising in Dublin, for on 24 April, Easter Monday 1916, several hundred Sinn Fein Irish Nationalists had seized public buildings in gun fights with British troops. The rebels had despaired of Britain's ability to honour its commitment to Irish independence in a war that seemed to have no end.

The revolt was quickly crushed and British and Irish moderates agreed that it had been foolish and disloyal. But in May the British military in Dublin, after summary courts martial, began executing by firing squad the first of fifteen rebel leaders.

The executions horrified Ireland and the world and made the continuation of British rule in Ireland, in any form, impossible. The Easter Rebellion also served to widen the religious division in Australia between Protestants and Catholics into a schism that remained unbridgeable for half a century. In Sydney the poet Christopher Brennan wrote a bitter poem, 'Irish to English':

I am not of your blood;
I never loved your ways;
If ever your deed was good
I yet was slow to praise

and proclaimed himself 'Irish and rebel both—and both unto the end'.

ABOVE:
The 'Little Digger',
Prime Minister W.M. 'Billy'
Hughes, being cheered
by Australian troops at
war's end, 1919.

Billy Hughes in London

In London Hughes had become spokesman of the Empire, addressing crowds throughout England and Wales on the necessity of harnessing all the resources of the Empire to achieve victory over German brutality. Not for the last time in Australian history, an Australian prime minister had been charmed by the English. The emigrant who had left London penniless in 1884 was now dining with the royal family at Buckingham Palace and being acclaimed by his fellow Welshman, Lloyd George, for his 'ability to instruct, persuade and move the multitudes'.

Billy Hughes, Sydney's *Labor Call* announced, is having a 'royal time in London … Ye Gods, a Laborite dining with monarchs.' The paper promised to keep its readers informed of 'Billy's progress from jingoism to imperialism'.

1916: The Somme—Pozières

'France is a picnic compared with Gallipoli,' an Australian wrote in May 1916, when the Anzacs were established in a quiet sector of the Front well north of the Somme. For many of them the picnic was to end at Fromelles, where on 19 July 1916, the 4th Division was sent into the attack in the first major Australian action on the Western Front. In one night 5533 Australians were lost in action, a figure higher than the nation's 4000 casualties incurred by the ten-year war in Vietnam.

Worse was to come. On 1 July 60,000 British troops had fallen on the first day of the Somme offensive and in three weeks the British line had barely advanced three kilometres. On 23 July 1916 the Australians were sent in to seize Pozières, the small village on a low ridge that blocked the road to the great objective, Bapaume. They took the village, which had resisted no fewer than four British assaults, in less than six hours. Within a day a German bombardment, heavier than any seen on the Western Front apart from Verdun, fell on the Australians digging in amid the rubble and sweltering heat on Pozières ridge. The bombardment continued, as did ceaseless German infantry attacks, for the next seven weeks. The British front, its advance everywhere halted, held its collective breath to see if the Australians could hold their ground. They not only held their ground but pushed forward a narrow salient towards the German defences at Thiepval, fighting to clear the enemy from the defence system at Mouquet Farm that blocked their way. By 3 September when the Canadian Corps was called down to relieve the four AIF divisions, more than 23,000 Australians had been killed or wounded pushing their line forward little more than a kilometre.

'They looked like men who had been in hell,' an officer wrote of the first Australians to stumble out of Pozières, 'so dazed that they seemed to be walking in a dream'. Officers noted that their men had lost their bright spirits and were 'strangely quiet, far different from the Australian soldier of tradition'. At Pozières, the horrors of bombardment and machine guns and constant attacks (the Australians mounted nineteen offensives, nearly all of them at night) had decimated the proud battalions and destroyed what few romantic notions they still had about the war.

BELOW:
The battles of the Somme added to the growing reputation of the Australian troops as fine soldiers, but frontline photographs of them in 1916 are rare.

By late 1917 official photographers such as Frank Hurley were accompanying the troops: This glass-plate shot shows Australians resting between attacks near Ypres, 29 September 1917, when the 'Diggers' had become the shock troops of the British army.

The Light Horse in the Middle East

The British High Command's claims that the German front was crumbling were not borne out by close study of the newspaper maps, which showed barely any advance being made. But from Egypt came heartening news: on 4 August 1916 the Turks had been stopped at Romani and 10,000 of the enemy were killed, wounded or captured. Anzac mounted troops—the Australian Light Horse and the New Zealand Mounted Rifles—had proved outstanding desert fighters, and bore the bulk of the 1100 British casualties. There was talk that General Royston had worn out fourteen horses galloping amid the bullets. 'We have fought and won a great battle', the Anzac horsemen's commander, Major-General Harry Chauvel, wrote to his wife, 'and my men put up a performance which is beyond all precedent, although worn out with harassing an enemy day and night for almost a fortnight. The fighting in the early morning of the 4th was the weirdest thing I ever took on. It was over rolling sand dunes and the enemy, who were in thousands, on foot, could see our horses before we could see them. Our losses have been heavy of course …' But the Turkish hold on Egypt was broken and in December the Anzac Mounted Division led the advance into Palestine, where another year of hard fighting lay ahead before they broke the Gaza line blocking the road to Jerusalem.

ABOVE:
An entire Australian Light Horse brigade on the march in Egypt. By early 1917 these skilled horsemen were leading the advance into Palestine.

1916:
The first conscription battle

In late August 1916, only a week after arriving back in Australia, Hughes received a cable from the Army Council in London requesting more men. Recruitment figures were falling. The possibility of conscription being introduced was almost the sole topic of conversation in Australia, for Britain in January 1916 had introduced compulsory military service for the first time in its history. At mass meetings Hughes addressed crowds on the importance of increasing Australia's contribution to the Empire's cause, but hesitated to mention conscription, for his own party was overwhelmingly opposed to it. Though nearly 300,000 Australians had volunteered for overseas service, another 200,000 men aged between eighteen and thirty-five had not come forward. At a public meeting in Sydney Premier Holman turned to Hughes and said: 'Tell us what Australia has to do! The democracy of Australia will rally round its leader, and will not flinch until the task before it is completed!' Hughes still hesitated.

Finally announcing to Caucus his decision to introduce conscription, Hughes met with bitter opposition.

ABOVE:
The government appealed to Australian men's tradition of volunteering to keep the Australian forces up to strength.

He agreed to compromise: he would call on the 'shirkers' to register for military service but offered to let the people vote on whether the troops should be sent overseas. A referendum would be held on 28 October 1916.

Opposition to conscription was led by Melbourne's Catholic Archbishop, the Irish-born Dr Daniel Mannix and by the Labor Premier of Queensland, Tom Ryan, the son of an illiterate Irish immigrant, who had emerged as one of the strongest

289

BELOW:
Australian government plans to enforce conscription found a ferocious opponent in Daniel Mannix (1864–1963), Catholic Archbishop of Melbourne, seen here in Sydney after the war.

figures of Australian Labor. Members had already walked out of the party and when the trade unions proclaimed a national strike in protest against Labor's imperialist policy, Hughes declared strikes illegal. (Among the 9000 men who refused to register for the army was a Victorian Labour official, John Joseph Ambrose Curtin, who was arrested in Melbourne and spent three nights in gaol.) Hughes issued government leaflets stressing the need for Australia to pull its weight in the great battle for civilisation: 'Women of Australia, mothers, wives, sisters of free men, what is your answer to the boys at the front? Will you be the proud mothers of a nation of heroes, or stand dishonoured as the mothers of a race of degenerates?'

BELOW:
Australian government plans to enforce conscription found a ferocious opponent in Daniel Mannix (1864–1963), Catholic Archbishop of Melbourne, seen here in Sydney after the war.

The inflammatory nature of the first conscription campaign was further intensified when twelve members of the radical International Workers of the World (IWW) were charged with planning sabotage. Hughes now added the IWW to the Catholics and the Sinn Fein as enemies of the nation and the Empire. The referendum rejected conscription.

1916: Hughes splits Labor

On 14 November 1916 the Labor Party passed a motion of no confidence in the Prime Minister. After listening to a bitter attack on himself in the party room, Hughes gathered his papers and said: 'Enough of this. Those who are prepared to stand by the British Empire and to see the war through to the end, please come with me.' He stood up and walked out of the room. Only twenty-three members followed him, but they included George Pearce, the Defence Minister, Spence and Holman. All were expelled from the Labor Party, as was Hughes. Labor had 'blown out its brains'; those who remained, led by Frank Tudor, renamed the party the 'Australian Labor Party'.

The Native Premier and the Imported Prime Minister.

ABOVE:
Premier Tom Ryan of Queensland was a vocal opponent of Prime Minister Hughes' conscription plans and war measures.

Hughes formed a coalition with Cook's Liberals to form the Nationalist Party, and won the May 1917 elections handsomely. The ALP lay in ruins. John Curtin, Prime Minister in a future war, left for Western Australia to become editor of the Perth Labor paper. 'In Jack Curtin, the Labor movement of Victoria loses one of its most brilliant expositors', ran the announcement. 'As a speaker he has few equals and being still a young man will go far.'

1917: The Western Front

The British Armies could count few victories during the course of 1917. In April, one week after the French had launched their first major offensive of the year, the British armies mounted a new push along the front near Arras that promised in the first week to be a stunning success. On the first day the Australians were ordered to attack in their south, to break the Hindenburg Line at Bullecourt. The Australians attacked the German defences without tanks or a preliminary bombardment and, in one of the most remarkable actions of the war, broke into the German trench system. One Australian officer signalled back that they could hang on till the cows came home if only they got artillery support; but it never came and a German counterattack forced them out. As at Pozières, many were seen strolling back across no-man's-land amid shell bursts in the famous slow, steady stride that became the hallmark of Australian infantry in two world wars. Birdwood inspected the survivors and wept. Of the 3000 men in the 4th Brigade only 641 survived.

News of the Australians' feat spread the length of the Western Front but could not save them from another 7000 casualties in continuous attacks to wrest Bullecourt from the Germans late in May.

1917: Flanders—to Passchendaele

In June 1917 the 2nd Anzac Corps lost 12,000 men in five days but were instrumental in storming Messines Ridge, through hails of gas shells, in one of the few clear-cut victories of the year. In July, General Haig resolved to exploit the Messines victory by launching a major offensive just to its north, from Ypres.

Again the Anzacs, who had achieved like the Canadians, a remarkable reputation for always gaining their objectives, seized Menin Road Ridge, and Polygon Wood one week later. Eight days after this all five Australian divisions and the NZ Division formed the centre of the attack on Broodseinde Ridge, which also fell in one day.

On the evening of 4 October 1917, the day the Australians took Broodseinde, the rains began to fall, turning the fine Flanders soil into a morass, and the victors were

stranded waist deep in the mud under the heaviest bombardment of poison gas shells they had ever endured. 'Mates I have played with last night and joked with are now lying cold. My God it was terrible. Just slaughter. The 5th Div. were almost annihilated,' wrote an Australian sapper after Polygon Wood. 'We certainly gained our objectives but what a cost …'

On 6 October the Australians and New Zealanders began the last one-kilometre advance on Passchendaele but the Front was now liquid beneath their feet and the floundering infantry were decimated by fire from German blockhouses. Another 5000 Anzacs fell. The Canadians, well rested, were brought up to Ypres and took Passchendaele on 6 November, a week before the murderous offensive was closed down. It had cost more than 250,000 British and Dominion casualties. A total of 38,000 Australians had been killed or wounded since Messines.

'It is bad to cultivate the habit of criticism of higher authority, and I do so with some hesitation … Our men are being put into the hottest fighting and are being sacrificed in harebrained ventures, like Bullecourt and Passchendaele, and there is no one in the War Cabinet to lift a voice in protest,' wrote Major-General Monash of the 3rd Division in October 1917.

Of this grim year of slaughter, the English journalist C.E. Montague wrote: 'French soldiers sneered at British now, and British at French. Canadians and Australians had almost ceased to take the pains to break it to us gently that they were the 'storm troops', the men who had to be sent in to do the tough jobs.' He had seen at Messines and Ypres the advancing British divisions falter and lose their cohesion 'while the Dominion troops still marched steadily on, their ranks closing …'

ABOVE:
'The Diggers': spirited exuberance even as their losses mounted.

ABOVE:
Outstanding soldiers in
the deserts of Egypt and
Syria: Australian Light
Horse at the charge at
Beersheba, October 1917.

In the Sinai desert the Light Horse had ridden in the last great cavalry charge in history, galloping headlong through shellfire to take Beersheba, the key to Gaza, the last fortress blocking the road to Jerusalem. The Holy City fell in December 1917—the only victory of a terrible year.

The 'Diggers'—as all the Anzacs in France called themselves—were formed into their own army, the Australian Corps, on the first day of 1918. This was a great compliment from the British.

The Home Front

While the Anzacs were pushing rail lines over mud to trundle forward howitzer shells at Ypres in October 1917, gangers in the heat of the Western Australian desert were hammering in the last spikes of the Transcontinental Railway, linking west to east in 'a band of iron'. In September 1917 the government broke a two-month strike by 100,000 workers that had paralysed the country. 'The recent strike, the most serious in the history of Australia,' said Prime Minister Hughes, 'was the fruit of a deliberate conspiracy ... on the part of the IWW, Sinn Fein and every disloyal section in Australia.' It had begun when railway workers struck for higher pay—prices had risen 60 per cent since the coming of war—and for discontinuation of a new card timing system, but Hughes saw in it the seeds of conspiracy. It was, however, two eggs thrown at him in Warwick in November that created the most impact. Carrying his new conscription campaign to the heartland of Tom Ryan's Queensland, the Prime Minister was pelted with these harmless missiles by two Irishmen. A couple of policemen in the hall, Kenny and Duffey, refused to arrest the assailants. The Irish were everywhere. Two weeks later, on 12 December 1918, Hughes ordered the creation of a Commonwealth Police Force to protect prime ministers. (Its powers were to grow.)

BELOW:
On top of the conscrip-
tion battle, in 1917 Prime
Minister Hughes was
faced with nationwide
strikes by unions that had
once been his strong
supporters.

SOLIDARITY

A PERPETUAL TRIBUTE
TO THE SELF-SACRIFICING
HEROES WHO TOOK
PART IN THE 1917
STRIKE AGAINST
INDUSTRIAL
TYRANNY

Irish enlistment in the AIF had plummeted. It seemed that the Protestant Australians in France were carrying the weight of the war and suffering the losses. 'I have been called disloyal,' Archbishop Mannix explained to anti-conscription crowds. 'If I put Australia and Ireland before the Empire, it is not that I love the Empire less, but because I love Australia and Ireland more.' In the December 1917 referendum the electors again voted No to conscription, this time by a margin of 94,000 votes. Two weeks later the Prime Minister resigned; again the Governor-General appointed Hughes to lead the government, for the Nationalists still held a majority. 'The people won the conscription referendum,' writes Manning Clark. 'The comfortable classes won the struggle for political power.'

The Australian Imperial Force in France would continue to fight its battles as an all-volunteer army, the only one on the Western Front—its reinforcements barely making up its losses.

George Morrison returned to Australia for the first time in fifteen years just before the referendum. 'I am much depressed by the outlook,' he wrote in his diary in Brisbane. 'What a shocking condition is Australia. Disloyalty. Governed by the unfit. Drunkenness. Prostitution. Much drunkenness among soldiers in uniform.' He had been appalled in Townsville by the sight of 'large bodies of vigorous young men who ought to be serving their country, loafing around the pub bars'. He wondered at the sanity of Hughes' policy. 'The wonder is not that conscription failed,' he wrote, 'but that so many voted in its favour … But most to blame are wholly misleading optimistic reports from England … Daily we were duped with stories of Germany's disintegration.'

ABOVE:

Before the war ended Russia had dissolved into civil war between Reds (Communists) and Whites (royalists). The Australian destroyer *Swan* found herself in the Black Sea on a mission to aid the local White general, who poses with the Australian officers and men.

1918: The German offensives

Far from disintegrating, Germany was about to launch the heaviest offensive yet seen on the Western Front. Her Eastern Front now secure with the collapse of a Russia rent by the Bolshevik revolution, the German High Command dispatched to France no fewer than thirty-five divisions. The offensive—'The Kaiserbattle'—was Germany's last attempt to break the Allied armies before the Americans, three-million strong but still under training, could reach France.

The offensive began at dawn on 21 March 1918, the first day of the European spring, when forty-three German divisions, following a barrage from 6000 guns, attacked through the mist the nineteen weakened divisions of the British 5th Army and plunged them into retreat. The German tide flowed on towards Amiens.

On 25 March Field Marshal Haig called upon his last reserve, the Australian Corps. Like Winston Churchill in a later war, Haig disliked Australians intensely, admiring their prowess as soldiers but regarding them as uncouth and ill-disciplined. More Australians, proportionally, were in military prisons than any Empire troops (nine per thousand AIF compared to one per thousand British soldiers) and he ordered that Australians be kept apart from Tommies because the colonials 'put such revolutionary ideas' into his men's heads. Haig had constantly pressed Birdwood to introduce the death penalty, especially for men absenting themselves from their units (desertion), but Hughes' government was outraged at the thought.

BELOW:
Heavy guns of
2nd Australian Siege
Battery in action.
Passchendale,
September 1917.

ABOVE:
Faces of exhaustion:
Germans captured
by Australians in the
Third Battle of Ypres,
September 1917.

1918 would be—in the official historian's words—the 'Year of the Digger'. As the Australians began moving south to the Somme and Amiens, Birdwood asked his 'Boys' to 'take the strain' for the sake of their country and everything they held dear. One of their brigadiers promised them they were facing 'the fight of their lives'. They left Flanders, division by division, with bands playing as the troops crowded onto trains and their gun teams filled the roads. The sudden appearance of the columns of Australians astonished refugees and beaten troops. 'You're going the wrong way Digger!' one retreating Tommy shouted. 'It makes one feel proud to be an Australian to see our boys after all this, pass through a village singing,' a 3rd Division officer wrote home. 'They are magnificent.'

On 26 March Major-General Monash of the 3rd Division drove through the night past thousands of retreating British troops to locate the local Corps headquarters. He found a deserted chateau at Montigny, and in one of the rooms two British generals hunched over a table covered with maps, lit by a flickering candle. 'Thank Heaven, the Australians at last,' one said. Monash's orders were to hold the ground

between the Somme and the Ancre. Sinclair-MacLagan of the 4th Division soon arrived; he was to deploy his 4th Division near Dernancourt.

The Australians did all that was asked of them—and more. In the following week the Germans encountered the first strong resistance since the offensive had started. The Australians at Hébuterne, assisted by their old comrades the New Zealand Division, stopped the enemy in his tracks and at Villers-Bretonneux, a village only two hours' march from Amiens they counterattacked. Charles Bean wondered if Australians and New Zealanders at home would ever be told that their men were now holding half of the collapsed front.

1918: Villers-Bretonneux

On 24 April, after the Australians had handed over Villers-Bretonneux to young English troops, the Germans attacked and drove them out. Instead of waiting for days to bring up tanks and artillery, Elliott and Glasgow sent their brigades into a counterattack after nightfall, without a bombardment. By dawn of Anzac Day 1918 'Villers-Bret' was retaken. 'A magnificent performance,' Monash called it.

Only one week later John Monash was promoted to Lieutenant-General and to the command of Australian Corps. This meticulous man with a capacity to plan his battles with care to minimise loss of life launched a sudden attack on Hamel on 4 July in which his infantry were accompanied by tanks and supplied by aircraft. 'A très bon stunt,' one Digger called it, for Hamel fell in one day for losses considered light (1400 casualties) and Haig ordered Monash's battle plans copied and circulated to every British division as an example to other generals of how to fight a battle. A week later Haig asked Monash to look into the possibility of launching an offensive from the Villers-Bretonneux sector where the German salient, its line so extended, presented the best opportunity to break the front. Monash asked his Army Commander, Rawlinson of 4th Army, for tanks and aircraft and a reliable Corps to guard his flank. He was given everything he asked for—500 tanks, 800 aircraft, 2000 field and siege guns and the redoubtable Canadian Corps.

1918 The Battle of Amiens

On 8 August 1918 the Australian Corps and the Canadian Corps launched their sudden offensive east of Amiens and by midday had advanced nine kilometres. The British tanks, whose crews almost suffocated in the heat, had been magnificent. (By next day only 145 tanks were fit for service.) 'The Canadians have done splendidly and the Aussies even better—I am full of admiration for these two Corps,' Rawlinson wrote in his diary. There was no German counter-blow. 'August the 8th was the Black day of the German Army in the war,' General Ludendorff later wrote, and informed the Kaiser that the war must be ended. Amiens was the battle that marked the beginning of the end.

On 21 August the British 3rd Army opened their offensive before Bapaume (the New Zealanders entered the town eight days later). On 31 August the Australians stormed up the slopes of Mont St Quentin, the key to Péronne on the Somme bend, in a feat that rivalled 'Villers-Bret' in audacity. The enemy was now withdrawing to the Hindenburg Line, which ran from St Quentin in the south to east of Arras in the north.

On 24 September 1918 the French and Americans in the Argonne launched the first of the four massive Allied blows on the German front; on 27 September the British attacked at Arras-Cambrai; on 28 September the British and Belgians attacked in Flanders; and on 29 September the 4th Army, spearheaded by the Australian Corps, mounted the vital thrust in the St Quentin Canal sector. Only two Australian divisions were still strong enough to enter battle, so the first assault was entrusted to two eager but untested American divisions. The American attack fell to pieces on the first day, and the Australians had to fight the battle on their own through the ten-kilometre-deep defence line of barbed wire and machine-gun posts.

It was the last great triumph of a remarkable body of men, for on 5 October, when the last German position fell, Australian Corps was withdrawn for rest. Their losses since March totalled 22,000 but they had led the offensives in their sector from the beginning. Barely 10 per cent of Haig's armies, the Australians had taken 23 per cent of all German prisoners and guns. The Australians' fame was immense, their reputation second to none.

Barely one month later Germany, torn asunder by workers' and soldiers' revolts, signed the Armistice; at 11 am on 11 November 1918 the guns fell silent and the great bloodbath ended. The warring powers had suffered 8 million dead. British Empire dead alone totalled one million— 750,000 men from the United Kingdom and 250,000 from the Empire. Australia and Canada had each lost 60,000 killed; New Zealand, with a population of just one million, had lost 60,000 killed and wounded.

BELOW:
Lieutenant-General Sir John Monash (1865–1931); and his staff.

Born of German-Jewish stock and a wealthy Melbourne civil engineer before the war, he was an unlikely figure to be acclaimed as one of the most brilliant generals of the war. 'I hate war,' he wrote in a letter home.

1919: Versailles—the peace that could not last

When the self-governing Dominions' leaders gathered in Paris in June 1919 they signed the Treaty of Versailles as separate nations alongside France and Britain, and were parties to all the discussions that preceded the treaty.

The treaty inflicted on Germany was one of punishment: forced to accept 'guilt' for beginning the war (the true guilt lay with Austria–Hungary, but the Hapsburg Empire lay in ruins), Germany agreed to pay reparations to the victims and victors. These helped to cripple its economy and instil among her people a despair that later became a palpable desire for revenge.

At Versailles Hughes demanded and obtained a League of Nations 'mandate' over the German territories of north-east New Guinea and the islands of the Bismarck Archipelago adjacent to the Solomons to serve as a 'chain of defence' against the southward progress of any new enemy (namely, the Japanese). Hughes was preoccupied by the growth of Japan's empire at little cost to herself.

Australia's government and people would raise their soldiers to demi-god status as an example of valour and self-sacrifice, creating in the Anzac and the Digger powerful icons for the generation growing up in their shadow. They had earned respect for Australia, for the first time in the nation's history, and were thus revered.

The Great War had destroyed a generation of men and split Australian society asunder, producing only a sense of national pride. The troops themselves had

been organised on a national basis, with Victorians serving alongside Queenslanders, Tasmanians with Westralians, and though the city boys acknowledged the bush men as the born leaders, all Diggers looked upon themselves with some pride at war's end simply as 'Australians'.

Australia's domestic turmoil only underlined the extraordinary strength of the national effort. Canada, 'the Great Dominion' of seven million people, had produced an army of four divisions, strengthened in 1917 by conscription (which produced a political catfight that divided Canada between the Anglo-Scottish Protestant majority and the Catholic minority as bitterly as the conscription issue had divided Australia). Australia, with barely five million people, fielded an army of five divisions in France and the equivalent of 1.5 divisions of mounted troops in the Middle East, an air force (the AFC) and a navy, all of them manned by volunteers. For 315,000 Australians who served overseas, 221,000 battle deaths and wounds were recorded—a casualty rate of 65 per cent, the highest of any nation involved in the war. The terrible superlatives accumulate: 11.2 per cent of the male population were fighting troops, compared to 6.8 in Canada and 5 per cent in Great Britain. For Australia the Great War was a holocaust.

Australia's role in the war consolidated her nationhood. In mid-1921 when the prime ministers of Australia, New Zealand, Canada and South Africa met in an Imperial conference in London, Prime Minister Lloyd George greeted them as 'equal partners' with the United Kingdom in the new British Empire, a step forward incorporated in the Balfour Declaration of 1926, which described the Empire as a 'Commonwealth of Nations'.

"The Australian and New Zealand troops have indeed proved themselves worthy sons of the Empire."
GEORGE R.I.

Chapter 8

Between Two Wars

From 1919 to 1939

THE GREAT WAR HAD BOTH UNITED AND DIVIDED AUSTRALIA. By the middle of 1919 more than 200,000 soldiers had sailed home from Europe to an Australia wracked by strikes and demonstrations. They brought also a virus that was devastating Europe. Puzzled doctors called it a virulent form of influenza, which turned quickly into pneumonia. It claimed up to 40 million lives before running its course late in 1919; 11,000 of them were Australian men, women and children. (One of the fatalities was Premier Tom Ryan of Queensland, the only figure capable of rebuilding Labor, who died, weakened from the effects of 'flu in 1921.) It seemed that the world was blighted with war, disease and pestilence—and another 'virus', Bolshevism, which advocated a violent overthrow of the capitalist system.

In March 1919 trade unionists protesting against the continuation of the War Security Acts in Brisbane were attacked by returned soldiers; nineteen men, most of them described as Bolsheviks or 'Reds', were wounded. The returned soldiers' association (the future RSL) was militantly anti-communist. Most returning Diggers never joined it—they were apolitical men, regarding all politicians and pressure groups as rat-bags—but it became a right-wing grouping of great strength. British reprisals against Sinn Fein supporters in Ireland during 1920 further aggravated Protestant–Catholic antagonisms. Even the Australia–England Test matches, which resumed late in 1920, were marred by a new nationalist rowdiness—violent barracking and abuse of players had never before been known in cricket. The Commu-

OPPOSITE:
The Melbourne artist Percy Leason (1889–1959) captured the comic aspects of Australian country and suburban life in the era between the wars.

The Sydney Mail, February 5, 1919.

GALLANT SOLDIERS AND SAILORS BACK FROM THE WAR

AN ANZAC WELCOMED BY HIS MASKED RELATIVES.

nist Party of Australia was formed in 1920, but it was never to attract sufficient votes to put a single member into Federal Parliament (and only one into a state House). Australians remained rigidly conservative, for even Labor proclaimed loyalty to the institutions of the British Empire.

'The British flag has never flown over a more powerful and united Empire,' Lord Curzon had said after the victory in 1918. In September 1919 Prime Minister Hughes addressed the House before asking members to ratify the Treaty of Versailles. He spoke movingly of the great battles and sacrifices of the Australian army in the 'titanic struggle' between 'autocracy and democracy' that had left Germany

ABOVE:
The epidemic of influenza that struck the armies in France in 1918 reached Australia at the end of the year. The flu strain was easily spread and was deadly for it could turn overnight into pneumonia, for which no cure existed.

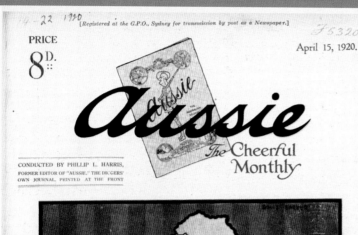

To the People of New South Wales

A danger greater than war faces the State of New South Wales and threatens the lives of all. Each day the progress of the battle is published in the Press. Watch out for it. Follow the advice given and the fight can be won.

Already the efforts made by the Government have had the effect of keeping the New South Wales figures down. But everybody is not yet working, so from to-morrow on the Government insists that the many shall not be placed in danger for the few and that

EVERYONE SHALL WEAR A MASK

Those who are not doing so are not showing their independence—they are only showing their indifference for the lives of others—for the lives of the women and the helpless little children who cannot help themselves.

CABINET DECISIONS:

At a special meeting of the Cabinet, held yesterday, the following recommendations of the Consultative Council (Medical Section) were adopted:—

1. Long-Distance Trains.—No need to restrict railway travel in New South Wales as yet, although it may be necessary to do so at any moment.
2. Hotel Bars, Restaurants, Tea Houses.—Not to be closed at the present time, but the 250 cubic feet regulation to apply to them.
3. Retail Shops.—Space regulation to apply; also prohibition of Bargain and Clearing sales, and a recommendation that orders be telephoned.
4. Church Services.—Prohibition of both indoor and outdoor services.
5. Auction Rooms.—Prohibition of all sales in rooms.
6. Libraries.—Reading rooms to be closed down.
7. Billiard Rooms.—To be closed.
8. Race Meetings.—Prohibited.
9. Theatres, Music Halls, Indoor Public Entertainments.—Prohibited.
10. Beaches.—No restrictions to be placed upon the free uses of the beaches on the ground that the risk of infection is likely to be more than counterbalanced by the benefits that will ensue.
11. Open Air Meetings in the Domain and Other Places.—Prohibited.
12. Churches and Schools Outside the County of Cumberland.—Not to be closed. Local authorities not to act on own initiative, but to be asked to refer to Public Health Department in every instance.

GENERAL RECOMMENDATION.

That, as far as possible, the people be encouraged during the course of the epidemic to take all possible advantage of fresh air as a means of increasing the natural resistance to infection, and of lessening the risk of infection, and also to avoid crowds.

W. A. HOLMAN, Premier.

ABOVE:

After the horrors of war, a sense of humour soon returned: Aussie had been a popular magazine with the troops but it did not long survive.

BELOW:

By 1930, when this photograph of tribesmen was taken by the Williams expedition, Australians were slowly venturing into the interior of New Guinea.

ABOVE:

The government of New South Wales declares a state of emergency, 1919. By the last quarter of the year the flu had disappeared after claiming up to 40 million lives worldwide.

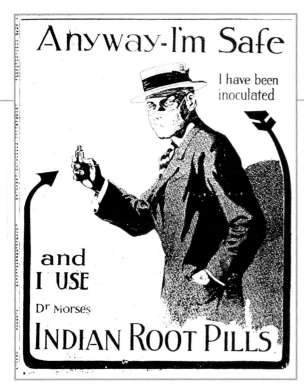

Anyway-I'm Safe

I have been inoculated

and
I USE

Dr Morse's

INDIAN ROOT PILLS

broken, 'for this generation, at all events'. Australia had joined the new League of Nations, which would ensure the preservation of peace; Germany had been asked to pay Australia what the war had cost her—£350 million. (Germany was to pay barely £6 million before reparations ceased in 1932.)

Hughes called on Australians to put aside their differences now that the years of 'trial, tribulation and turmoil' were past. Months later he moved to expel from the House the member for Kalgoorlie, who had called the British troops in Ireland 'thugs and murderers'. Hughes shouted: 'He forgets the millions or more who died for the Empire, who, by their deaths brought us liberty and safety … In the name of Heaven, how can he help Ireland by bitterly insulting and humiliating the people of this country by calling the Empire "bloody and accursed" …'

Some Australians continued to put themselves at risk even though the war was over. A small number signed on for service against the Bolsheviks in north Russia (two were awarded VCs).

Aviation: *the trail blazers*

In January 1919 an Australian pilot in England, Captain Andrew Lang, wearing five pairs of socks and similarly thick clothing, flew an open-cockpit biplane up to the highest altitude humans had ever reached—nearly six miles (30,500 feet) or ten kilometres above earth, before his engine died from lack of oxygen. In true Australian tradition he had neglected to obtain permission for this 'unauthorised flight' and after gliding to earth was placed (briefly) under arrest by his British CO. In May 1919, after the London *Daily Mail* had offered of £10,000 to the first per-

BELOW:
Keith and Ross Smith with photographer Frank Hurley, 1919.

son to fly the Atlantic, Harry Hawker, a 32-year-old Australian airman who had achieved fame in his flights around England, took off with a co-pilot in a single-engine Sopwith with a dinghy strapped to the fuselage; they had to ditch in the sea and were picked up by a passing freighter. Several airmen decided to fly home. When Billy Hughes offered a £10,000 prize in June to the first airmen to fly from England to Australia, the ace pilot Captain Ross Smith, who had fought with the Australian Flying Corps' crack 1 Squadron against the Turks, accompanied by his brother Keith and two AIF aircrew, took off from near London in a

giant, open-cockpit Vickers-Vimy bomber. They flew through sandstorm and blizzards to touch down at Darwin in December 1919 after a flight of twenty-eight days and became Australia's first postwar heroes. (Both Harry Hawker and Ross Smith were later killed in air crashes.)

The 1920s

People craved a return to the pleasures of peace. By 1922 the wartime boom was ending and unemployment rising. Peace came to Ireland in 1922 when the British granted independence to the southern counties, thus defusing Irish Catholic militancy. On the urging of Australia and New Zealand plans were made to create a great naval base at Singapore for a British Pacific Fleet to act as a deterrent to Japanese expansion southward.

The prospect of another invasion of the Dardanelles was also averted in 1922 when Kemal Atatürk's armies expelled the Allies from Turkey and Lloyd George, after appealing vainly to the Dominions for military assistance, accepted the fait accompli. By the end of 1922 Lloyd George had been forced to resign the prime ministership, Winston Churchill had lost his parliamentary seat; and Billy Hughes followed them out of power in the New Year.

By 1923, when the recession was growing and BHP had to close down its blast furnaces temporarily because of lack of orders, Hughes' unpopularity was extreme. Victory had produced only further distress. The Soldier Settlement Scheme was already failing: of 40,000 ex-soldiers provided with cheap blocks of land, many had already given up trying to make a living there. The mallee scrub and the distress showing on the faces of their wives and children were tougher to bear than war. Within ten years, six out of ten soldier settlers had drifted back to the towns; ten years later barely two in ten were left. A scheme to settle British immigrants in Western Australia's south-west similarly failed. The timber there was even harder to clear than in the east; the settlers, many from English cities, had few rural skills; and commodity prices were falling.

1923: The fall of Billy Hughes

The growth of a new political party, the Country Party, was a direct result of the growing distress and dissatisfaction among rural people, rich and poor alike. In the elections of December 1922, Hughes' Nationalists lost nine seats, emerging with twenty-eight members in the House against thirty Labor. Dr Earle Page's Country Party—'the hayseeds', as Hughes mocked them—won fourteen seats and held the balance of power. It offered to join the Nationalists in a coalition on one condition: Hughes must go. John Latham, one of two surviving Liberal members, and Herbert Brookes, the Melbourne power broker who had married one of Alfred Deakin's daughters, made the overtures to Page that forged a new coalition.

Faced with a party revolt, Hughes resigned as Prime Minister in January 1923 in favour of his Treasurer, Stanley Melbourne Bruce, who immediately effected a coalition with Page. The Country Party had polled 12.5 per cent of the vote, yet obtained five of the twelve Cabinet posts. The 'Little Digger' with the heart of a lion was tired, anyway, by eight years of attack and counterattack, abuse and

acclaim. 'I am a Celt, and so intensely superstitious,' Hughes would write. 'I have never been able to shake myself wholly from the idea that all is predestined, that we all have a mission in life, and if that work be worthwhile, we are given the opportunity to do it.' He continued to sit in Parliament until his death, constantly warning Australia of the threat it faced from Japan, and became a minister again. But his remaining years were haunted by the ghosts of the war dead, 'the gallant boys who had not died in vain'.

Return to conservatism

Stanley Bruce was as conservative as his appearance. Patrician and handsome, seemingly devoid of political ambition, he gave promise of dignity and stability. A product of the Melbourne Establishment and a scion of the old Scottish-

ABOVE:
Disarmament begins: Following the Washington Naval Treaty of 1922 limiting the size of the world's navies, Britain ordered the scuttling of most of her older battleships and battle cruisers. As a result, the RAN flagship *Australia*—already obsolete—was stripped of her fittings and sunk outside Sydney Heads in 1924.

Australian merchant house of Paterson, Laing and Bruce, the new Prime Minister had been educated at Melbourne Grammar and served in a British regiment in the war. 'Mrs. B is among Toorak's most tastefully-dressed matrons. Her mother was a Manifold,' reported the *Bulletin*. 'There are no little Bruces, but a well-manicured fox terrier does his best to keep the pair from feeling lonely.' Bruce had a valet and wore spats, reminding Australians of an English lord.

The 1923 meeting in London of Empire prime ministers resulted in affirmations of unity of 'The Great Imperial Firm of Wealth, Progress and Opportunities Unlimited' just as economic conditions were deteriorating. Australia and New Zealand were particularly insistent that Britain act on the recommendations of Admiral Jellicoe's report that Singapore be developed as a naval base for a British Far Eastern Fleet to balance the growing naval power of Japan. The British Treasury pleaded shortage of funds.

'Men, Markets, Money' was Bruce's recipe for growth after his return from the London conference. There would be little social reform in the country that only ten years earlier had been the powerhouse of social improvement. The basic wage was raised to

ABOVE:

The twenties saw the beginning of high immigration from Italy. The worst aspects of Mussolini's Fascist rule there were not yet evident, and most immigrants came for economic reasons: work was plentiful in the cane fields of Queensland. Italians such as these staff members of Mario's Restaurant transformed Melbourne's nightlife with the founding of fine eateries and wine bars.

OPPOSITE:

Two sober conservatives from the Melbourne establishment: Prime Minister Stanley Melbourne Bruce (1883–1967) (left), the image of an English gentleman, and his Attorney-General, John Latham. (1877–1964).

ABOVE: By 1924 George Coles had been joined in business by three brothers, Edgar, Kenneth and Norman, and had opened a giant store in Bourke Street, Melbourne. The Myer Emporium was opened nearby. Half a century later the two large chains merged and Coles-Myer now dominates Australian retailing.

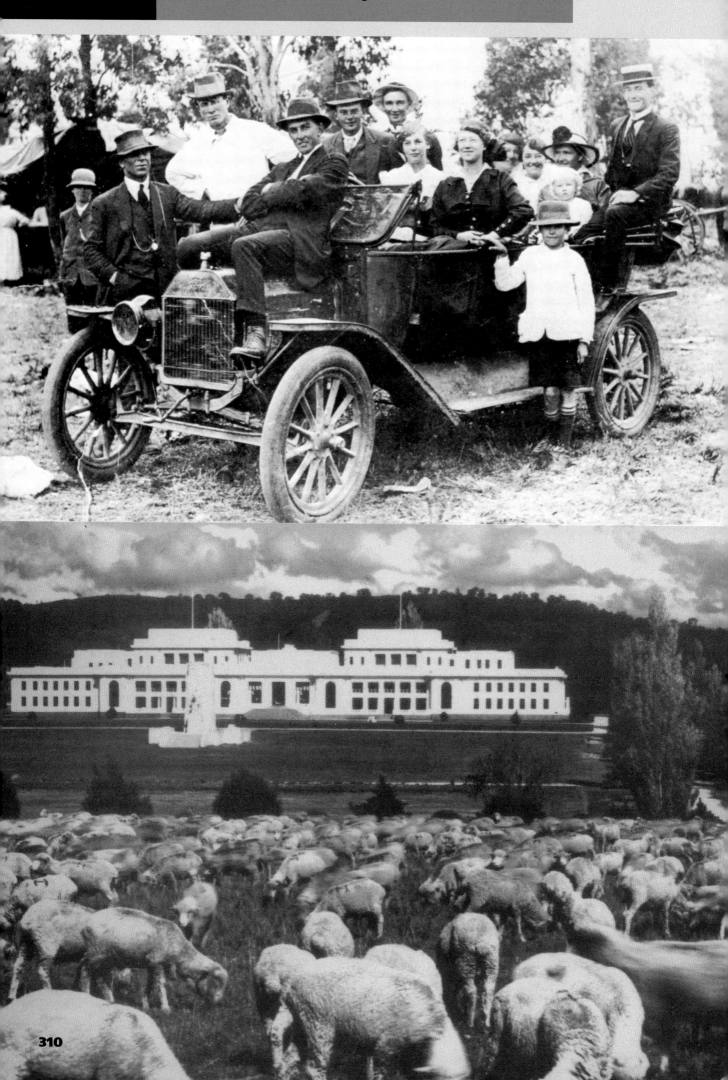

LEFT:
The Australian bestseller *The Sentimental Bloke* was make into a film in 1919, complete with C.J. Dennis's verse as subtitles.

ME PAL 'E TROTS 'ER UP AN' DOES THE TOFF
'E ALLUS WUS A BLOKE FER SHOWIN' OFF.
"THIS 'ERE'S DOREEN," 'E SEZ. — "THIS 'ERE'S THE KID."
— I DIPS ME LID —

£5 16s 0d in the mid-1920s, but there would be little else done to improve living conditions. Under the Bruce–Page government the Commonwealth-owned businesses were sold off—the Commonwealth Line of freighters that Hughes had purchased during the war years, the Commonwealth Woollen Mills and other examples of 'socialistic' enterprise.

The late 1920s were a period of confrontation between government and unions. The new Attorney-General, John Latham, who was appointed in 1925, was extremely antagonistic to union demands. A bitter seamen's strike came in 1925, the formation of the Australian Council of Trade Unions (ACTU) in 1927.

In 1927, when the Duke of York came out to open the new Parliament House in Canberra, more than 400,000 new cars were sold in Australia. The motoring craze and the high sales of wirelesses and other electrical goods were financed by a new innovation: hire purchase (a contradiction in terms, but an arrangement that enabled one to acquire goods before paying them off). Parents and religious leaders

ABOVE:
Cinemas–'picture theatres'–of the 1920s were built like Hollywood palaces.

OPPOSITE, TOP:
The Hides family of Batlow in New South Wales head for a picnic in the town's first hire car.

OPPOSITE, BOTTOM:
Sheep graze on the lawns opposite the new Parliament House, Canberra in the 1920s.

despaired at the sight of the young enjoying themselves for the first time in Australia's history. Young women wore scandalously short skirts, some ('even convent girls') smoked cigarettes in public and surfed alongside their boyfriends on weekends. In 1928 'talkies'—films with sound—arrived to further subvert morals.

Australians in the air: Qantas and the RAAF

The 1920s would be the decade of barnstorming and epic flights when it looked as if Australians were taking over the future of air travel. Australians, already the first to attempt to fly the Atlantic, became the first to fly the Pacific and, later, the Indian Ocean; and the first to fly airmail between England and Australia. In 1920 Hudson Fysh, , the wartime pilot 'Paddy' McGinness and the businessman Fergus McMaster formed an air service at Longreach—QANTAS (Queensland and Northern Territory Air Service) and two years later began flying airmail between Charleville and Cloncurry. Fysh's partners were skilled pilots, and Fysh was an astute businessman who guided QANTAS's growth for the next forty years.

Aware of the promise that aircraft held, Billy Hughes formed the Royal Australian Air Force in 1921, appointing to its command Group Captain Richard Williams, who had led 1 Squadron AFC in the Middle East. In 1924 two RAAF pilots flew the first 'Around Australia' flight. Development of the RAAF would languish, for the

OPPOSITE, TOP:
Larger and powerful aircraft
were needed for long dis-
tance flights to prove the
feasibility of transoceanic
passenger routes, and in the
1920s the Dutch genius
Anton Fokker produced
a solution: in the hands of
a master pilot, Charles
Kingsford Smith, the tri-motor
'Southern Cross' proved
capable of crossing the
Pacific and flying around the
world. Here the aircraft lands
at Melbourne in 1928.

OPPOSITE, BOTTOM:
The 1920s were trail-blazing
years in aviation and in sheer
audacity Australians led the
world. Queenslander Bert
Hinkler, a wartime pilot, was
the first man to fly solo from
England to Australia in 1928.
He was killed in an air crash
in 1933.

BELOW:
Following their epic flight
across the Pacific Ocean in
June 1928 the Australians
Charles Kingsford-Smith
(1897–1935) (right) and his
'co-commander Charles Ulm
(1898–34) (second from
right) decided to attempt the
first aerial crossing from Australia to New Zealand. They
flew the stormy Tasman in a
14-hour flight in September
1928 and are seen on arrival
in New Zealand with their
crew members Harold Litch-
field (left) and T.H.
McWilliams.

1920s were a period of disarmament, when Britain gave up her lead in aircraft design and production with near calamitous results as the 1930s progressed.

In 1921 Norm Brearley, a former AFC pilot, founded West Australian Airways to fly mail between Derby and Geraldton. Two of his pilots were Charles Kingsford Smith, a Queenslander who had flown in the RFC and Keith Anderson, ex-AFC, both of whom were flying in Sydney in 1927, where they met Charles Ulm, anoth-er AIF veteran (he had served on Gallipoli as a 16-year-old before being shipped home as under age).

'Southern Cross' flies the Pacific

In 1927 'Smithy' and Ulm decided to fly the Pacific. To get publicity and to show that aircraft, though primitive, were safe, they flew around Australia in a war sur-plus two-seater Bristol Fighter, topping up the fuel tank in the air from cans, and arrived back in Sydney in June 1927 to find a crowd of 50,000 cheering them as national heroes. They sailed for America three weeks later to purchase an aircraft powerful enough to fly the Pacific.

The Americans thought the two Australians were mad. The Atlantic had been flown in 1919, but the Pacific was three times as wide—close to 4500 nautical miles (nearly 7000 kilometres) of empty ocean. In August 1927, seven aviators had crashed into the sea in attempting to fly from San Francisco to Hawaii. Charles Ulm did not even have a pilot's licence: he had taught himself to fly. The whole thing appeared to be madness.

Undeterred, Smithy and Ulm found their aircraft: a three-engine Dutch Fokker that Captain Hubert Wilkins, another AIF man, had used to fly over the North Pole. An American millionaire took a shine to the Australians and advanced them a loan; Kingsford Smith and Ulm bought the Fokker, rebuilt it, fitted it with new Wright engines and began making flights to train themselves to keep awake for forty hours or more.

They left nothing to chance. They fitted wireless and sophisticated navigation equipment and appointed two Americans as wireless operator and navigator. Aviation was like every venture in life: 90 per cent preparation— and the rest perspiration.

On 21 May 1928 the 'Southern Cross', as she had been dubbed, took off from San Francisco. Seven hours later she touched down in Honolulu to cheering crowds. On 3 June she took off for the most dangerous leg of the flight—3000 miles of ocean—to Fiji. Flying through storms that forced Smithy to take the aircraft down to sea level and then up to 10,000 feet (3000 metres) to get above the clouds, 'Southern Cross' landed in Fiji after thirty-six

hours in the air, the four aviators too deafened by the engines to hear the cheering of the crowd. 'Southern Cross' flew on to Brisbane through the worst weather of all, touching down there after another twenty deafening hours in the air.

At a civic reception in Sydney for Kingsford Smith and Ulm, a speaker hailed them for possessing 'the Anzac spirit'. They then made the first Trans-Tasman flight, risking worse weather conditions than those encountered in the Pacific, to be similarly acclaimed.

By the end of the fabulous year, 1928, Bert Hinkler had flown solo from England to Brisbane, the Reverend John Flynn—'Flynn of the Inland'—had created the Flying Doctor Service, the Australian Hubert Wilkins and C.B. Eilson flew a Lockheed Vega in the first crossing of the Polar basin, and Kingsford Smith and Ulm had formed an airline company—the first ANA—to link Brisbane, Sydney and Melbourne. There seemed no limit to Australian aviation enterprise.

Early in 1929 'Southern Cross' took off from Sydney to fly to England, despite adverse weather reports from northern Australia. Over the northern coast of Western Australia, the aircraft struck the heavy rainstorms of the Wet and, flying blind, was forced down on the mud

When 'Smithy' and Ulm disappeared on their flight to Britain in 1929, their friend Keith Anderson (left) and his mate Bob Hitchcock (right) set off to find them. Their ill-equipped two-seater 'Kookaburra' landed for repairs in the Tanami Desert and the stranded fliers died there of thirst.

flats of the Glenelg river. News that 'Southern Cross was' missing devastated Australia. The starving airmen were found twelve days later, but only after a nationally coordinated air search that had claimed the lives of Keith Anderson and his co-pilot Bobby Hitchcock, who had been forced down in the Tanami Desert, where they perished.

Kingsford Smith and Ulm never recovered from slanders that the forced landing had been a publicity stunt, but they went on to pioneer the England–Australia air route and survived the collapse of ANA in 1931. Australians had a habit of celebrating heroes and then questioning their motives, thinking the worst of them. In the 1930s Australians, having pioneered air routes, would be among the first to break speed records, but today there are few reminders of their achievements. 'Southern Cross' itself survives, preserved at Brisbane airport as a memorial to the brief and turbulent years when Australian aviators led the world.

ABOVE:

The public was angered by the federal government's slowness in organising a search for *Southern Cross*, and Prime Minister Bruce was held responsible for failing to order the RAAF to control operations. The aviator Les Holden later spotted the stranded aircraft on the Glenelg River flats near Wyndham.

Drifting into depression

By the mid-1920s, as the economy improved (a heartening discovery was Mount Isa's wealth in 1923), Bruce became increasingly worried about the high borrowings by the states for expenditure on public works. American and British capital

Smithy and Ulm's airline ANA was one of the first modern airlines in the world. Another wartime flier, Les Holden, began carrying passengers in his aircraft *Canberra*.
All three pioneer aviators had been killed in air crashes by the end of 1935.

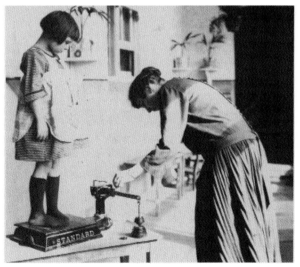

ABOVE:

A schoolteacher's responsibilities were many: in an age of poor diet and undernourished children, teachers often had to check the weight of their pupils. By the 1950s governments were supplying free milk for schoolchildren.

LEFT:

The enterprising Sydney publisher Sydney Ure Smith (1887–1949) published the nation's first 'glossy' magazine *The Home* in 1920 and it captured the elegance and optimism of the twenties, using the talents of leading artists. It too became a victim of the Depression, and was sold in 1934.

flowed into Australia at an alarmingly high rate, stimulating booms in real estate and speculation on the stock market.

By late 1927, however, there were growing signs that the brief boom was ending. In December of that year Bruce and Latham brought in amendments to the Arbitration Act that included stiff penalties for industrial law breakers. 'As capitalism develops and class clashes become sharper,' the *Worker* stated, 'the parasite class is compelled to tighten its chains on the worker class'. The new Labor leader, James Scullin, attempted to mediate in the wharf strikes of September 1928, referring to government-paid strike-breakers as elements of a new 'martial law'. In November police opened fire on striking unionists, wounding four of them. The Bruce–Page government, the symbol of law and order in an era of industrial anarchy, was returned to power in the November 1928 elections with forty-two seats to Labor's thirty-one.

In January 1929, as the economy worsened, timber workers went on strike when their hours were increased from forty-four to forty-eight a week. In May coal miners in the Hunter Valley were locked out until they accepted pay cuts. Three months later Prime Minister Bruce moved to repeal the Conciliation and Arbitration Act—in other words, to leave industrial disputes to the states to solve. Labor was in uproar. Hughes now sought and took his chance to bring down Bruce, the man who 'betrayed' him in 1923: 'The honourable gentleman has on two occasions been wafted into power on the battle cry of the maintenance of industrial peace. This cry cannot serve him again'. The Hughes faction withdrew support from Bruce who, faced with an impasse, asked the Governor-General for a double dissolution.

ABOVE:
By the mid-1920s the economy had begun to pick up. In 1927 BHP had a record year for steel output and the company had launched a fleet of five freighters. *Iron Warrior* is seen here at Newcastle wharf. Less than three years later came the Great Depression.

1929: Scullin leads Labor to victory

The election on 12 October 1929 was a landslide victory for Scullin's Labor Party, which won forty-six seats in the House; only fourteen Nationalist and ten Country Party members survived. Bruce and Latham both lost their seats. Seventeen days later the stock market crashed in New York. In one day, 29 October 1929, $40 billion was wiped off the value of shares, turning paper millionaires into paupers. It was the spark that fired the Great Depression.

James Scullin was the antithesis of Bruce. He was the first of the Irish Catholic prime ministers and Labor leaders who would joust for power with Scottish-Australian conservatives for nearly forty years— a true clash of Celts. A physically diminutive man, Scullin possessed a magnificent voice and a powerful eloquence—there were few finer speakers in Parliament. Yet he proved incapable of leading Australia out of the economic catastrophe that fell on her or of raising her spirit. No leader could. Only a massive infusion of loans could have revived the West's economies, but the United States, after Britain and France had failed to repay their war debts, had turned its back on the world's woes, and was soon to face its own slump.

A miner, killed by police bullets when a mob of strikers threatened police at Rothbury in the Hunter Valley in December 1929, was the only official fatality of the Depression, but millions in a land of plenty knew hunger, malnutrition and soul-destroying despair.

BANK OF ENGLAND

AUSTRALIA

1930: The Depression

The first years of the Depression were the worst. There had been slumps before—in the 1840s and 1890s—but nothing to equal this worldwide collapse of trade and economic confidence. Between late 1929 and late 1931, Australian export prices fell by 50 per cent, income fell 30 per cent and unemployment reached as high as 33 per cent in New South Wales. Unemployment grew in the first months of 1930. There were mass demonstrations in February of unemployed in Sydney and Melbourne. 'The banks are full of money, and all the big shops filled with goods, money is being spent at racecourses and picture shows,' a Labor member said to a crowd in Melbourne, 'while hundreds of people in Victoria are starving and sleeping in parks at night—hunger, want, misery and destitution stalk the land.' After a fall in wool prices, Prime Minister Scullin urged farmers to grow more wheat.

Politicians and economists differed on how best to fight a recession that was deepening into depression. Scullin's Treasurer, E.G. Theodore, favoured 'inflation' by increasing borrowings to fund public works and maintain a money flow. (Theodore, son of a Rumanian father and an Irish mother, and a successor to Tom Ryan as Queensland Premier, was a charismatic man, one of the most formidable of Scullin's cabinet ministers. But he was soon tainted by allegations of corruption during his years as Queensland Premier—the Mungana scandal—and he resigned to clear his name.)

The bankers recommended tough measures—'deflation' by reducing spending and workers' wages. Britain was growing increasingly concerned about returns on its £500 million of investments in Australia. In August 1930 Sir Otto Niemeyer of the Bank of England visited Australia to confer with the premiers. He suggested that Australia

ABOVE:
As the Depression began to bite deeply, the fire-brand Irish-Catholic Labor Premier of New South Wales, Jack Lang (1876–1975) took radical measures. His criticisms of British financiers caused concern in political and financial circles and his tactics led to his dismissal by the Governor.

BELOW:
Hero of the 1930s and an Australian hero for ever-more: cricketer Don Bradman in action.

'tighten its belt' and reduce its inordinately high standard of living. His closing words were: 'I assume that everybody is in agreement that costs must come down.'

The resultant 'Premiers Plan' revealed their intention to balance budgets over 1930–31 in order to repay or convert loans maturing in the next few years. Spending on public works would be cut.

Jack Lang

In October 1930 Jack Lang and Labor were returned to power in New South Wales. Lang was another spellbinding Labor leader—a huge man, a doctrinaire socialist, and a brother-in-law of Henry Lawson (they had each married a Bredt sister). His enemies were many; they said he could afford to be a socialist because he was wealthy (he had made his money in real estate in Auburn). In his two governments in the 1920s Lang had introduced child endowment and a 40-hour week. His solution to the economic hardship was simple: to suspend interest payments to Britain and to reduce interest rates on loans. He denounced the Bank of England as one of a number of 'sinister financial interests' that were ruthlessly 'dragging this country down'.

In January 1931 matters came to a head. The currency was devalued to make export prices more competitive. Now £125 Australian was needed to buy £100 sterling (this exchange rate remained until 1967) and the Arbitration Court ordered a 10 per cent cut in wages. When Theodore was returned to the ministry—before being cleared of corruption charges—Joseph Lyons, former

Labor Premier of Tasmania, resigned in anger from the Cabinet. Lyons' conscience was in turmoil, he was 'at his wits' end to know where to turn and what course to follow'.

'Honest Joe' Lyons, the Irish Catholic family man, had been the best-liked of all Labor ministers; he was a warm, human, widely respected figure; he and his wife Enid were to have twelve children. Distraught at the predicament of Australia, and of Labor, he responded quickly to overtures from the conservative parties, and to their flattery.

It was a period when swift and extreme action was seen as the only alternative to chaos. In February 1931 former AIF officers formed the New Guard to fight Bolshevism and 'Langism'; their motto was 'All for the British Empire', but their opponents pointed out that their military uniforms and salutes were similar to those of the Italian Fascists and German Nazis.

In March 1931, Lang defaulted on an overseas debt repayment. 'It was simply a question of whether the unemployed would be left to starve or whether the bond holders were repaid,' he explained. Faced with a run on the banks, Lang ordered the State Savings Bank to close its doors. As Lyons left Canberra station to catch the train to Melbourne for a meeting with the Nationalists, a Labor man shouted 'Don't do it, Joe!' But Lyons had made his decision.

ABOVE:
The 1931 federal election was one of the first to be reported by wireless. As votes were tallied an announcer relayed the latest results. The result was defeat for Labor.

TOP:
The arches of the new Sydney Harbour Bridge, which began construction in 1923, were joined in 1930 and the bridge opened for traffic in 1932.

THE SUN NEWS-PICTORIAL, MONDAY, DECEMBER 21, 1931   3

Nation's Crushing Verdict Against Scullin Rule

LIKELY CHOICE AS MINISTRY

Strong Team Available For Mr. Lyons

MR. BRUCE RETURNING

ON his arrival from Tasmania this week Mr. Lyons probably will have a preliminary conference with Mr. Latham on the personnel of the new Ministry.

The main consideration in picking the Cabinet will be that it is imperative the Ministry comprises the best brains and experience among the anti-Labor forces. Personal claims will be disregarded.

It is almost certain Mr. Bruce will be included, and places may be found for the Leader and Deputy-Leader of the Country Party.

Mr. Bruce, who is returning from England on the Oronsay, will reach Fremantle on January 5.

The following is the probable personnel of the new Government:

Mr. Lyons, Prime Minister and External Affairs.

Mr. Bruce, Treasurer.

Mr. Latham, Attorney-General.

Mr. Gullett, Minister for Trade and Customs.

Dr. Page, Postmaster-General and Minister for Works.

Mr. Paterson, Minister for Markets.

Mr. Marr, Minister for Home Affairs.

Mr. Hawker, Minister for Health

MR. LYONS EXPECTED TO HAVE MAJORITY
OF 27 AT LEAST IN NEW HOUSE

Six Ministers Likely To Lose Seats In Heaviest Turnover In Australia's Political History

THRILLING FIGHTS IN BATMAN AND BOURKE

THE Scullin Government suffered a crushing reverse at Saturday's general election in the biggest electoral turnover in Federal history. Mr. Lyons, the United Australia Party, was returned to office with a majority of at least 27 seats.

SIX Ministers seem likely to lose their seats, including the Treasurer (Mr. Theodore), who came third on the list in Dalley. The other Ministers were: The Attorney-General (Mr. Brennan), who provided the biggest surprise in Victoria by falling behind in Batman; the Minister for Markets (Mr. Parker Moloney), the Minister for Health (Mr. McNeill), the Minister for Defence (Mr. Chifley), who is not likely to hold Macquarie, and the Assistant Minister (Mr. Cunningham).

VICTORIA provided the biggest sweep, and may have only three Labor members in the new Parliament—the Prime Minister (Mr. Scullin), Dr. Maloney in Melbourne, and Mr. Holloway in Melbourne Ports. Mr. Anstey is in grave danger in Bourke.

THE Lang group gained several seats in the Sydney metropolitan area, but the issues are in doubt there because of the uncertainty of the allotment of second preferences.

MR. SCULLIN will consult his colleagues today about the resignation of the Government, and decide when he will return to Canberra.

MR. LYONS is in Tasmania, but will return to the mainland in a day or so. He promised yesterday that the new Government would penalise no section of the community in the measures it proposed to adopt for rehabilitation.

A DEFINITE reaction against Labor was expected by most political observers, but the electors of Australia responded to Mr. Lyons's call in a manner

Probable Changes In House				
	Old.	New.	Gains.	Losses.
U.A.P.	23	36	13	—
Labor	35	13	—	22
Lang Labor	5	10 (4 doubtful)	5	—
C.P.	11	14	3	—

The Speaker (Mr. Makin) was hard pressed for a time in Hindmarsh by Mr. Evans (Ind. Emergency Committee), but will retain the seat. The Lang candidate (Mr.

ANALYSIS OF VOTING

Anti-Labor Majority of 625,273

LANG v. LABOR

WHEN counting ceased last night 2,709,617 votes in the House of Representatives had been counted, out of a total of 3,654,110 persons entitled to vote.

Anti-Labor votes were in a majority of 625,273, the totals being:—Anti-Labor, 1,667,445; Labor 1,042,172.

The feature of the voting in New South Wales was that the Lang Labor

1931: Lyons heads the UAP

The Nationalist leader, the upright but coldly intellectual John Latham, inspired little popular support and he was intelligent enough to realise this. He offered to stand aside if Lyons chose to lead a party of renewal. In May 1931 Lyons agreed to lead a new movement—United Australia—to attract Nationalists and disenchanted Laborites. In the December 1931 federal elections Labor was swept from office, retaining only nineteen seats (five of which were 'Lang Labor') in a House dominated by Lyons' new conservative creation, the United Australia Party, which won forty-seven seats. The UAP was to retain power for the next ten years.

ABOVE
As unemployment increased the federal government seemed unable to cope with the disaster. The Scullin Labor government was voted out of office after just two years.

BELOW:
Melba, the first Australia to achieve world-wide fame, died in 1931.

Lang dismissed

Only Lang remained as a symbol of radical socialism. At the official opening of the Sydney Harbour Bridge (built with British capital) in March 1932, an officer of the New Guard charged forward on a horse with sword upraised and cut the ribbon before the Premier could complete the ceremony. The officer, who was hustled away by police, protested 'You can't arrest me! I'm a Commonwealth officer.' 'So am I,' a policeman said.

More farcical scenes followed. When the federal government confiscated New South Wales income tax to meet the state's debt payments, Lang sent police to block federal officials' access to the Treasury building in Martin Place. The trade unions began forming a 'Red Army' of militants to guard the Premier, but the Governor of New South Wales, Sir Philip Game, brought an end to the drama by sacking Lang on 13 May. In the resulting June election Lang's Labor was swept from office.

All the giants were disappearing. Both Melba and General Monash had died in 1931; they were the only two figures apart

from Hughes whom Australians from all walks of life regarded as truly great (at least in newspaper polls which, like the new craze, crosswords, were products of the Depression). Now Lang, the idol of the poor, 'the Big Fella' who had been corrupted by power, was gone too.

1930s: Dark clouds gathering

By 1933 Australia was emerging from the worst of the Depression's dramas, just as the world was sinking into a new dark age. In January 1933 Adolf Hitler was summoned to lead a coalition government in Germany. It was a dangerous appointment, for Hitler's Nazi Party, though a minority in the Reichstag, was committed to tearing up the Treaty of Versailles and to rearm; it was violently anti-Semitic, blaming the Jews (along with the Communists) for Germany's collapse in 1918 and its current domestic ills. By 1934 Germany was effectively a dictatorship. Europe's only consolation was the fact that Mussolini's Italy had no sympathy for the idea of German hegemony.

Florey, Burnet, Oliphant

While Germany was closing its borders and echoing to the march of armies, numerous Australians were travelling freely and some were achieving a reputation in the wider world. Two future Nobel Prize-winners were studying in the quiet reaches of the great universities of England. In 1935 Howard Florey of Adelaide, a Rhodes Scholar, became Professor of Pathology at the University of Oxford, a post he was to occupy until 1962. Working with a German scientist, Ernst Chain, who had fled Nazi Germany in 1933, Howard Florey began to develop penicillin, the first antibiotic (the remarkable bacteria had been discovered growing by the Scot Alexander Fleming in 1928). By 1944, thanks to Florey's tireless efforts, American laboratories were producing the drug in massive quantities (much of it was

LEFT:
Unsung hero of the 1930s: Howard Florey (1898–1968) of Adelaide studied in England and developed penicillin in time for the antibiotic 'wonder drug' to be used by the Allies in the coming war. He later shared the Nobel Prize for medicine, was ennobled as Lord Florey and commemorated on an Australian banknote.

BELOW:
Joseph Lyons' decision to quit Labor caused bitterness in the ALP but the majority of Australians liked and trusted him. Cartoonists often portrayed him as a lovable koala. He is shown here with the nation's billiards champion Walter Lindrum.

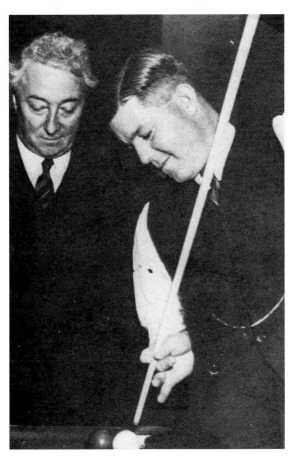

cultured in warehouses of rotting fruit in southern states of the USA). Penicillin arrived in time to be used to treat hundreds of thousands of wounded soldiers in the last year of the war and Florey, Chain and Fleming shared the Nobel Prize for medicine and physiology in 1945.

Frank Macfarlane Burnet, who graduated from the University of Melbourne in 1922, became a research fellow at London's Lister Institute in 1926 before returning to Melbourne's Walter and Eliza Hall Institute in 1928. He was fascinated by bacterial viruses. With Jean Macnamara of Queensland he discovered that the deaths of a dozen children had resulted from the diphtheria inoculations being infected by staphylococcus; and found that there was more than one poliomyelitis virus. In London in 1932–33 Burnet began research into the influenza virus, which he succeeded in isolating. Returning to the Hall Institute (where he was to remain until his retirement in 1965), Burnet pioneered the manufacture of influenza vaccine by growing non-infective strains in fertile hen's eggs. He shifted his (and the institute's) emphasis from virology to 'immunology'—the study of the body's natural defence system, where his discoveries saw him later awarded a Nobel Prize.

In 1927 young Adelaide scientist Mark Oliphant won a scholarship to the University of Cambridge and worked in the Cavendish Laboratory on the structural disintegration of atomic particles. By 1935 he was assistant research director and two years later Professor of Physics at the University of Birmingham. Oliphant was to direct astonishing developments in microwave radar and be a member of Britain's Atomic Energy Technical Committee during the coming war, though he was later to campaign strongly against the atomic bomb as a weapon in war.

In Paris in 1933 Louise Hanson-Dyer (sister of a Lord Mayor of Melbourne) began publishing under the Lyrebird imprint—the famed *Éditions de l'Oiseau-Lyre*—the forgotten music of the sixteenth to the eighteenth centuries; while in the same year a young Tasmanian named Errol Flynn, who had left Australia hurriedly for the United States determined to be a film star, appeared in the Hollywood film *In the Wake of the Bounty*. Handsome and completely amoral, he never returned to Australia and never lost his larrikin ways.

In 1933 also the former Prime Minister, Stanley Bruce, who enjoyed being near the centre of events in London, became Australia's representative there—High Commissioner—and represented his country in that year at the World Economic Conference and on the League of Nations Council.

BELOW:
By 1934 the worst of the Depression was past and Australia
was pictured as steaming ahead into a bright future.

Sport, films—and radio

Australians lined up at suburban theatres every week to see Hollywood
films ('the flicks')—and danced to
American tunes, but generally showed
as little interest in the outside world as
the world showed in them. The 10 per
cent wage cut was removed in 1934 but
unemployment would be a fact of life
for the rest of the decade (it still stood
at 10 per cent as late as 1939).

BELOW:
By 1934 the worst of the Depression was past and Australia
was pictured as steaming ahead into a bright future.

Sport replaced politics as the people's
obsession. Australians were stimulated
into argument by the death in the United States of the great racehorse Phar
Lap in 1932 and by the 'bodyline' con-
troversy of the 1932–33 cricket season,
when English bowlers under their captain Douglas Jardine
persisted in hurling the ball at the Australian batsmen instead
of at the wickets. It led to a minor crisis in Anglo-Australian
relations. At the third Test in Adelaide in January 1933, the
Australian captain, Bill Woodfull, was struck over the heart by
a ball from Harold Larwood, and another ball hit wicket-keep-
er Bert Oldfield on the head. The crowd of 50,000 roared
their disapproval. 'There are two teams here,' a spectator said
with typical Australian understatement, 'but one of them isn't
playing cricket.' England went home with the 'Ashes' but
some Australians began to wonder about the Englishmen's
reputation as gentlemen.

Australian Rules football first became a passion to Melbur-
nians during the Depression, for the entrance fee was cheaper than the pictures and it was a relief from the drudgery of
the other six days of the week.

The ABC (Australian Broadcasting Commission), based on
the British (BBC) model, was created by the federal government in 1932. Unlike the BBC—and the NZBC—which
enjoyed a monopoly of the airwaves (commercial radio was

ABOVE:
Radio arrives: By 1932,
when wireless sets were
common in many homes,
the Australian Broadcast-
ing Commission began
regular broadcasting.
Two of the first directors,
Stuart Doyle (left) and
Frank Albert, appear
before the microphone
on the first night.

banned in both countries), Australia's national broadcaster had to compete from
its birth with commercial stations, and its growth would be a triumph. It began
broadcasting programs of classical music, news bulletins and discussions for those
tired of commercial stations' diet of popular songs, serials and corny advertise-
ments. Radio broke the severe isolation endured by country people and gave all
Australians a sense of identity—a shared past, common language, concerns and
pleasures—in a way that nothing else had done. Only a minority listened to it, but
they were among the 'changers of society'—informed individuals. Not least, the
ABC was impartial. Prior to general elections politicians from all major parties
were allowed to use radio to announce their programs without payment.

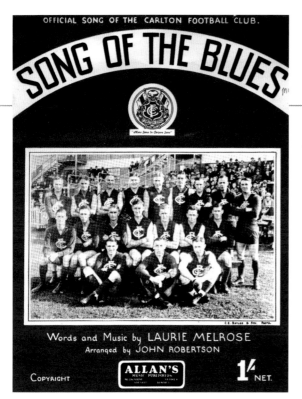

OFFICIAL SONG OF THE CARLTON FOOTBALL CLUB.

SONG OF THE BLUES

Words and Music by LAURIE MELROSE
Arranged by JOHN ROBERTSON

COPYRIGHT   ALLAN'S
MUSIC PUBLISHERS
1⁄4 NET.

LEFT:
The 1930s saw sport become an obsession. Improved public transport, increased leisure time and widespread broadcasting contributed to the popularity of cricket and football. In Victoria the Carlton Football Club ('The Mighty Blues') even had a song written in tribute to their prowess in 1935.

BELOW:
Charles Meere's *Australian Beach Pattern*, painted in 1938–40, has become an Australian icon.

An Australian identity?

For all Australians' resilience and the apparent soundness of their institutions, the people themselves struck visitors as parochial and lacking independence of thought. One of the best-known observers, a musician, Dr Thomas Wood of Oxford University, spent two years travelling the Commonwealth between 1930 and 1932—at the height of the Depression—and became almost a household name for his broadcasts over the new medium of ABC wireless, and for the book he wrote, affectionately entitled *Cobbers*.

Wood found Australians—'98 per cent British'—to be 'as pro-British as they are pro-Australian' but the intensely nationalistic feeling of the 1890s had all but disappeared. He was amused to hear them 'interminably discussing matters that the rest of the world had settled and forgotten' and felt that this parochialism could be traced to isolation—not so much from other people, as from other people's ideas. Australians were great readers of newspapers, but not of books, and those they read were British books, not Australian ones. He was puzzled by Australians' 'easy going casualness' and utter indifference

to precision; but thought them likeable, generous, practical and warm hearted, with positive qualities of youthful self-confidence and easy optimism. (Others called it the 'Give it a go' attitude to life). 'If I were in a tight corner,' Wood wrote, 'the Australian is the best man in the whole world to get me out of it. And he would succeed, if resource, good humour, and sheer unmatchable bravery would do the job.'

Others bemoaned the fact that in 150 years Australia had produced no great literature nor any form of identifiable culture. Australia remained a cultural backwater ruled by wowsers. Until 1938 fedcral Customs banned Boccaccio's fourteenth-century classic *The Decameron*, as it was deemed injurious to morality (despite the fact that Shakespeare had borrowed freely from the bawdy stories for plots for his plays). Also on the proscribed list were novels by Ernest Hemingway, John O'Hara and James Joyce, all of which were freely read in Britain and the United States.

Australia's national genius, Norman Lindsay, whose celebration of the female form so shocked the straitlaced, was vilified as a pervert and his novel *Redheap*, published successfully in England by Faber (publishers of T.S. Eliot and James Joyce), was banned as indecent in 1930, as was a special issue of *Art in Australia* devoted to his work. Lindsay attacked his detractors in the pages of the irreverent paper, *Smith's Weekly*: 'Do they really think they can keep this country as an ignominious little mental slum, isolated from the world of serious intellectual values?'

RIGHT:
In a period of economic austerity the Labor Party portrayed the Lyons government's policies as a form of slavery. The then weekly basic wage of 51 shillings and sixpence (equivalent to about $5) was in world terms reasonably high.

He left for New York embittered, sending a telegram from the ship as it went through the Heads: 'Goodbye to the best country in the world, if it was not for the Wowsers.'

In 1934 G.H. Cowling, an English professor of literature at the University of Melbourne, announced that Australia had no literature and little chance of creating one. 'There are no ancient churches, castles, ruins—the memorials of grandeur departed,' he wrote. 'From the point of view of literature this means that we can never hope to have a Scott, a Balzac, a Dumas—nor a poetry that reflects past glories.'

Whether Cowling was lamenting the vacuity of life or merely 'stirring the possum' hardly matters; but several Australians responded with energy. P.R. Stephensen, who had founded the Endeavour Press with Norman Lindsay's support in order to publish Australian writers, wrote: 'The culture of a country is the essence of its nationality. A nation is nothing but an extension of the individuals comprising it, generation after generation of them.' But he agreed that 'until we have a culture, a quiet strength of intellectual achievement, we have nothing but our soldiers to be proud of'.

BELOW:
An Irish-Australian Catholic family: The Labor politician who became a conservative Prime Minister, Joseph Lyons and his family at the Lodge in Canberra, 1938. Lyons' widow Enid Lyons, mother of twelve children, became one of the first two women elected to the House of Representatives in the 1943 elections and lived until 1981.

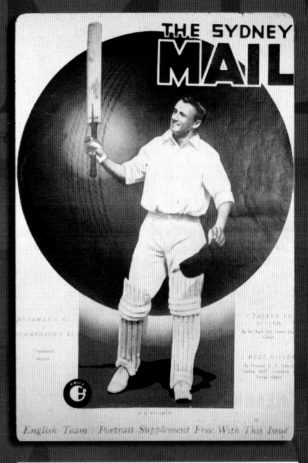

Images of the 20s and 30s.

LEFT & BELOW LEFT:
Australians went to the films—'the flicks'—but theatre was also popular; the comedian George Wallace starred in Brisbane vaudeville shows and also appeared in the popular musical of 1932, *Collitt's Inn*, alongside Gladys Moncrieff.

BELOW:
Steele Rudd's bush yarns about Dad, Mum and Dave were still providing Australian film-makers with fare the public liked.

*The Foundations of
Culture in Australia*

An Essay towards National Self Respect
by
P. R. Stephensen

AUSTRALIA: PUBLISHED BY W. J. MILES
4 ROSEDALE ROAD, GORDON, N.S.W.

ABOVE:
Katherine Susannah
Prichard, widow of the
war hero Hugo Throssell
VC, joined the Communist
Party of Australia and
channelled her political
convictions into novels
exposing hypocrisy and
racial injustice.

LEFT:
The Rhodes Scholar P. R. Stephensen urged Australia to develop
an all-Australian culture but with only limited success.
During World War II he was he was considered a dangerous
fascist and imprisoned.

The Jindyworobaks

A young poet, Rex Ingamells, challenged Cowling's assertion that Australia was devoid of a past rich in great traditions. 'But we have other traditions worth having, such as no other country possesses, and these are the things that are valuable to us culturally,' he wrote in 1938. 'The history of Australia abounds in a wealth of dramatic material, ready to be shaped by the careful artist … Our history goes back to the early navigators … and the country of native legends; of the tjuringa, the boomerang and the spear. Life has been lived fully and the human heart has experienced intensely …' He would be a founder of the Jindyworobaks, who drew their inspiration chiefly from Australia's unique Aboriginal symbols, spurning Englishness.

One Australian whose heart had experienced intensely never ceased to write. Katherine Susannah Prichard had joined the Perth branch of the Communist Party on its foundation in 1920, the year after she had married Captain 'Jim' Throssell VC, a hero of Gallipoli. Prichard would remain a communist, fighting racial intolerance; a passionate activist and prolific novelist. Despite their political differences they were inseparable (Prichard confessed that their arguments were followed by love-making). Depressed by financial problems and the pain of his war wounds, Throssell shot himself in 1933, leaving a note praising his wife as the best mate a man ever had.

'I love every inch of Australia,' Katherine Prichard wrote in 1936. 'The rugged coasts from Gabo and Otway to the Leeuwin, our western shores with all their jade green bays and little towns …' But there was much that she hated also: the poverty of her people and the poverty of their culture, 'a culture built on cheap foreign patterns,' imitations of the antique. 'We have submitted to a censorship of literature that neither the English nor the American people would tolerate.'

Australians were uninterested bystanders in the dramas unfolding in Europe. The Westminster Statute of 1931, an extension of Lord Balfour's Declaration of 1926, had confirmed that Australia and the other self-governing Dominions were independent nations, bound to Britain only by ties of blood and loyalty to the monarch. For more than a decade neither Australia nor New Zealand bothered to ratify and thus legalise the statute, for the Dominions' dependence on Britain in defence and the economy was absolute. The emotional bond was strong, though Australia often felt like an unloved child, the rowdy boy who was sure to embarrass the family. The statute empowered Australia to initiate an independent foreign policy and establish her own diplomatic relations with the great powers, if she so desired. But no diplomats were appointed or embassies opened until 1940 when Sir John Latham was sent to Tokyo to open a legation.

A generation later Manning Clark was to end his multi-volume history of Australia at 1935. It was a watershed year, though few at the time knew it. Henry Lawson had written that Australia's destiny lay in either the 'old dead tree' of the British Empire—or the 'young tree green' of their own growing. Australians had opted for the former, and the Empire was soon to need their help. In 1935 'collective security' began to break down in Europe as Nazi Germany announced a rearmament program, and Britain followed suit.

In the elections of September 1934 Lyons' new conservative creation, the United Australia Party–Country Party government was confirmed in office. It won a total of forty-two seats, the 'Liberal' faction five seats, Labor only twenty-seven. Among the new Labor members in the House was John Curtin, born in country Victoria and now representing the voters of Fremantle. Lyons' new Attorney-General was Robert Gordon Menzies, who had come from Victorian politics, and his new assistant Treasurer was another Victorian, Bruce's protégé, Captain Richard Gardiner Casey, MC.

The rise of R.G. Menzies

Robert Menzies had carved out a brilliant career in Victorian politics. Like General Monash he was the son of a storekeeper in a Victorian country town and like Monash he was a prodigy. Born in the small Wimmera town of Jeparit in 1894, third of the four sons of a father of Scottish Presbyterian origin, he had been educated at Wesley College in Melbourne and progressed to the University of Melbourne, where he graduated in law in 1916. His two elder brothers were serving overseas in the AIF. Menzies wrote patriotic verse for the university paper but did not volunteer for military service, a decision that his future opponents would label as typical of the man, a failing of character. Menzies was called to the Victorian Bar in 1918 and stood successfully for a Legislative Council seat as a Nationalist (conservative) ten years later. Appalled by the corruption and cronyism in Parliament, he formed the 'Young Nats', stood successfully for a seat in the Lower House and emerged from the 1932 victory as Victoria's Attorney-General. In the 1934 elections he stood for the seat of Kooyong, and entered Federal Parliament.

Two months later Menzies forbade entry to an anti-Nazi Czech journalist named Egon Kisch, whom he classified as an 'undesirable visitor'. Kisch had come to tell Australians that evil things were happening in Europe. When his lawyers appealed

ABOVE, LEFT:
Thirties elegance: Pioneer film-maker Ken Hall and his wife arrive at a Sydney premiere.

ABOVE:
Performers and news readers broadcasting on ABC radio were required to dress as if attending a society function.

LEFT:
Robert Gordon Menzies in the early 1930s,
just before he entered federal parliament.

against the ban, Mr Justice Evatt lifted the prohibition. Chagrined, Menzies left for London by liner to attend King George V's 25th Jubilee celebrations.

Menzies had always loved England, now he loved it even more. He loved the winding lanes, 'the green and flowering things—a beauty no new country town in Victoria could ever possess,' as he wrote in his diary. It was a world so different from the bare plains of the Wimmera where he had grown up. Here was the world 'of civilised beauty', of Shakespeare, Wordsworth, Housman and Rupert Brooke, whose works he loved. He was thrilled to be treated as a 'person of consequence,' instead of being the butt of jokes by the 'yahoos' and 'squirts' of Australian politics. 'Although Australian born,' recorded the London *Sunday Times*, 'Mr Menzies speaks precisely in the manner of a cultivated Englishman.' *The Australian Worker* retorted: 'We want our representatives to speak not like cultivated Englishmen but like cultivated Australians. We want them to look at the world through Australian eyes … We are creating a new nation, not duplicating an old one.' Menzies would mostly look at the world, and at Australia, with English eyes.

Menzies returned to Australia in September 1935 to be mocked by the Labor Opposition. 'Chuck it, Bob!' one of them said after listening to one of his reports. A week later, when Sir Isaac Isaacs retired as Governor-General, Lyons appointed a retiring state Governor, the Scottish soldier and future General Lord Gowrie VC, in his place. The bonds with Britain were strengthening. (Three years later Canada's Prime Minister Mackenzie King, looking for another sound Scot, appointed as viceroy the novelist John Buchan, who was enobled as Lord Tweedsmuir.)

On 1 October 1935 John Curtin was elected leader of the Australian Labor Party by a majority of one, for James Scullin was dying. Curtin swore to his colleagues that he would keep off alcohol, and he kept the pledge. The international situation, Curtin warned Australians, was one in which 'the portents of evil are grave and ominous,' for Germany was building an air force—the *Luftwaffe*—and enlarging its army. Only days later Mussolini's Italy invaded Ethiopia and the League of Nations proved powerless, as did British–French sanctions against the aggressor.

Only in New Zealand was the ideal of a better world being made reality: in 1935 the Australian-born Michael Joseph Savage was swept into office in the Labour landslide. Before his death in 1940, 'Mick' Savage created in his adopted home the first welfare state outside Scandinavia.

BELOW:
Following his success with the comic novel *Here's Luck*, Sydney humorist Lenny Lower published a collection of his pieces *Here's Another* in 1932.

Aviation: the last of the trail blazers

In 1934 Victoria celebrated its centenary, marked by a royal visit by the King's son the Duke of Gloucester and his wife and a much publicised England–Australia Air Race. On 20 October two English pilots flying a fast two-seater De Havilland Comet touched down in Melbourne, after a flight of just three days. On the same day a Douglas airliner flown by KLM touched down, winning first place in the handicap section after a flight of three days, eighteen hours. On the next day Sir Charles Kingsford-Smith, who had been unable to participate in the Centenary Air Race, made the first west-to-east flight across the Pacific in a two-seater Lockheed Altair named 'Lady Southern Cross' with P.G. Taylor as co-pilot.

The incentives to the establishment of regular international air services were mail contracts, not passengers (but if fee-paying passengers could be carried with sacks of airmail, profits could be considerable). Charles Ulm, Smithy's former colleague, was determined to establish regular services across the Pacific but his plane and its four occupants, flying from California, disappeared in the ocean near Hawaii in December 1934, and a year later Sir Charles Kingsford-Smith and his navigator, flying 'Lady Southern Cross' from London to Australia, crashed into the sea off the Burma coast. With the deaths of these two outstanding Australian airmen and their crews so also died initiatives to open fast, regular airline and mail services across the Pacific.

In December 1934 Qantas Empire Airways (its new name betraying its large British shareholding) initiated the Australia–England airmail service, flying from Brisbane to Darwin and landing in eight Queensland towns on the way. At Darwin the mails were handed over to an Imperial Airways aircraft and flown to London. In February Qantas made its first international flight, flying mail and passengers from Darwin to Singapore. In 1938 Qantas adopted Empire flying boats for the new England–Australia route. For passengers it was a leisurely but comfortable, even luxurious journey—taking fifteen days, with thirty-two stops. Speed was not a priority in the 1930s.

ABOVE:
The record-setting aviator Sir Charles Kingsford-Smith (left) shown with the polar explorer Hubert Wilkins (1888–1958) in front of Wilkins' Fokker aircraft which had become famous as *Southern Cross*, first aircraft to fly the Pacific.

One last aviation achievement was claimed by Australia. In June 1939 P.G. Taylor made the first flight across the Indian Ocean, flying a Catalina flying boat from Port Hedland in Western Australia to Mombasa in Kenya to investigate possible bases for transoceanic flights for the British and Australian governments.

Rearmament

In April 1935, one month after Nazi Germany had announced the reintroduction of conscription, Australia was a member of the 14-nation Council of the League of Nations that protested at this contravention of the Treaty of Versailles. Hitler's reoccupation of the Rhineland (the buffer zone between France and Germany) in March 1936, the outbreak of the Spanish Civil War (in which Germany and Italy supported General Franco's armies against the socialist Republic), the Japanese invasion of China in 1937: all were indications that brutality reigned and that a new world war was not only possible but probable.

In 1938 Britain intensified its rearmament, especially in the production of modern fighter (or bomber interceptor) aircraft. In the same year the Lyons government, which had been returned to power in the October 1937 elections, announced that an unprecedented total of £43 million would be spent on defence over the coming year and a recruiting campaign was mounted to increase the strength of the militia. The export of iron ore to Japan was stopped (the export restrictions on minerals lasted until 1961). In radio broadcasts and speeches Billy Hughes and Monash's former chief of staff, Major-General Thomas Blamey, lent their considerable prestige to the government's efforts: by March 1939 militia strength had increased to 70,000. In 1936 three new light cruisers had been ordered from the Admiralty—*Sydney, Hobart* and *Perth*—but the destroyer force remained the five old ships dating from 1917–18, which the Admiralty wisely decided against scrapping. (Of these eight warships, five were to be lost in action in the coming war.)

HEAD O' THE RIVER

Those not so fortunate

In 1938 President Roosevelt used his considerable influence to call for the convening of a conference in Europe to discuss assistance to Germany's Jews. Australia attended the Évian conference and offered to take as refugees 15,000 homeless Jews. Jewish leaders asked whether Australia would allow refugees to create a community in the northwest. Even Hitler favoured the idea and thought it a solution to his 'Jewish problem'. But Australian politicians deemed it inadvisable to create a separate religious community and barely 7000 Jews reached Australia over the next eight years, while six million of their brethren died at Nazi hands.

The 150th anniversary of European settlement was celebrated in Sydney in January 1938 without great enthusiasm. Floats moved through the city and sailors and soldiers in costume re-enacted Governor Phillip's landing, but it was chiefly notable for a small group of Aborigines who proclaimed 26 January a Day of Mourning for their race, and demanded citizens' rights. The authorities paid them no attention.

Britain's defence priorities precluded supplying Australia with either modern aircraft or new ships. To provide the RAAF with a 'modern' fighter the Commonwealth Aircraft Corporation began manufacturing the American Harvard trainer in 1938, and ordered fifty Lockheed Hudsons from the United States. Australia had chosen the Harvard because it was considered a dual-purpose aircraft, both fighter and bomber, and because of its cheapness. The first one off the factory floor flew in March 1939. The type was dubbed the 'Wirraway'. It was slow and already obsolete before production started and the only Australian squadron to fly it in battle (defending Rabaul in 1942) was shot down in five minutes.

ABOVE:
After Lyons' sudden death two prominent conservatives fought for his place in the boat: a cartoonist depicted their battle as a Head of the River. Robert Menzies ended up captain and Richard Casey had to take second place, while Billy Hughes rocked the boat in his usual fashion.

1939: Menzies becomes Prime Minister

The Lyons government was displaying little leadership to the nation, for the Prime Minister was a dying man. When Robert Gordon Menzies announced on returning from Germany in 1938 that Australia needed 'inspiring leadership' his words were interpreted as an attack on his leader. On 15 March 1939 Menzies resigned dramatically from the government when Lyons postponed a national insurance scheme. Only three weeks later Lyons died, leaving Menzies and R.G. Casey to contest the leadership.

There was little difference between them. Both were more British than the British in their speech and demeanour. Menzies won narrowly. 'Fellow Australians,' the new Prime Minister said in a wireless broadcast on 26 April, 'I am a singularly plain man, born in the little town of Jeparit, on the fringe of the Mallee. Apart from having parents of great character, intelligence and fortitude, I was not born to the purple …' Earle Page, however, refused to serve with him and many UAP members wondered if Bob Menzies' air of self-importance would increase. 'I am a Labor woman,' Mary Gilmore wrote after hearing the new Prime Minister broadcast in May on Australia's need for 'honest pride', 'but there are things that Menzies says that make me say in my heart "Here is a man one could follow!"'

The fragile peace of Munich collapsed in March 1939 when Germany encouraged Slovak nationalists to declare their independence from Czechia and hours later (on 15 March) sent forces into Prague to 'protect' the Czechs. The Dominions had already pledged their unwavering support to Britain in the event of war. While Prime Minister Mick Savage of New Zealand warned his people to 'prepare themselves for the worst', the British government sought to deter further German aggression by pledging military aid in April 1939 to Poland, Rumania and Greece, reintroduced conscription and made the first tentative moves towards forming an alliance with Stalin's Soviet Union. But on 23 August Hitler and Stalin signed a non-aggression pact, sealing Poland's fate. War now seemed inevitable. France began to mobilise.

1939: Australia goes to war

On 1 September 1939 German forces invaded Poland. On Sunday 3 September the British ambassador in Berlin presented Hitler's government with an ultimatum demanding that German forces be withdrawn from Poland within two hours. No reply was expected from Hitler and none was received. At 11 am Prime Minister Chamberlain announced on radio from Downing Street in a sad voice that Britain had declared war on Germany. His broadcast, which reached Australians at 7.15 pm, 3 September, was immediately followed by the announcement on the radio from Prime Minister Menzies that Australia was also at war. New Zealand's Prime Minister Savage also issued an immediate declaration of war. The two nations were thus the first to join Britain in the war against Nazism. The French declaration of war on Germany followed six hours later, at 5 pm, European time, 3 September 1939.

RIGHT:
The liner *Straithaird*, converted to a troop-ship, leaving with Australian troops for the Middle East, early 1940.

Chapter 9
Fighting for a Better World

From 1939 to 1949

THE BRITISH EMPIRE WENT TO WAR IN 1939 with less unity than it had in 1914, but in other respects the similarities were striking: once more a British army crossed the Channel to France and the Belgian frontier, while the Royal Navy imposed a blockade that would hopefully cripple Germany as it had in 1918.

Once again, the Empire went to war to the command of Scots. The counterparts of Menzies and Governor-General Lord Gowrie in Canada, Prime Minister Mackenzie King and his Governor-General, Lord Tweedsmuir, issued Canada's declaration of war on 10 September. India's Viceroy, a Scot, declared war on Germany without summoning the Council of Princes. Ireland declared neutrality, and South Africa tried to, but General Smuts was appointed to lead the Union by the Governor-General, another Scot, and declared war on 4 September. The United States proclaimed its neutrality, and Italy its 'non-belligerency'.

On the fourth day of war Prime Minister Menzies introduced a National Security Bill empowering the government to rule by regulations. Several Labor firebrands—Eddie Ward, H.P. Lazzarini and Maurice Blackburn—denounced it strongly, reminding Australians that 'men who are vested with absolute power will abuse that power'. But the press accepted censorship, price controls were instituted, rationing begun. The Communist Party and fascist parties were banned in 1940. After the entry of Italy into the war in June 1940 Italians—and numerous Australians of Italian parentage—joined Germans in internment camps. But for the first two years of war there was little other regimentation of the Australian people, for the war seemed remote.

1940: The Second AIF is formed

On 16 September 1939 Prime Minister Menzies called for volunteers for a 'Special Force', but did not disclose for two months whether it would serve overseas. Once again, Australia's hand was forced by New Zealand's offer to Britain of an expeditionary force. Volunteers soon filled the ranks Australia's new expeditionary force, which was named the 6th Division (five militia infantry divisions were already in existence) and commanded by Major-General Blamey. When the government announced that a second division—the 7th—was to be formed, Blamey was made Lieutenant-General in charge of the entire Corps, and the 6th sailed for the Middle East in January 1940, accompanied by ships bearing New Zealand's first echelon. Thus was born the embryo 2nd Australian Imperial Force—the new Anzacs.

The inactivity on the Western Front—the Phoney War, as an American senator called the conflict—lulled Australians into a false sense of security. Volunteers for

OPPOSITE:
Volunteers of the Second Australian Imperial Force leave for war, 1940.

the air force were called for, to be trained in Canada under an 'Empire Air Training Scheme' for service in the European theatre. More Australians attempted to join the air force than the army in the first months of war. Almost all units of Australia's navy were by early 1940 serving under Admiralty command in the Northern Hemisphere, for the nation's shores appeared safe from any external enemy. The chiefs of staff—the professional heads—of both the Australian army and the RAAF were replaced by British officers. The navy was already under British command. Australia's subordination to Britain's war needs was quickly decided upon and implemented.

John Curtin and Labor rejected Menzies' invitation to join his government in a coalition but the Country Party accepted in March 1940. The Blitzkrieg broke in Western Europe on 10 May 1940 (the day Winston Churchill replaced Chamberlain as Britain's prime minister) and the calamitous events of June—the fall of France, the entry of Italy into the war, and Britain facing invasion—saw an immediate response to the government's plea for recruits. Yet in some ways the appeals were unnecessary, for thousands of Australians now understood that the conflict had become a war of survival. In June nearly 49,000 men enlisted in the AIF (which soon grew to four divisions—6th, 7th, 8th and 9th). Australians read of the Battle of Britain, in which an understrength RAF, including Australian fighter pilots and crew, broke the *Luftwaffe*'s bomber assaults, with great pride, and wondered when their own forces would see action and prove their worth.

ABOVE:
Cliffhanger: In the September 1940 elections both the Menzies government (UAP–Country) and the Australian Labor Party (ALP) each won 36 seats in the House, and Menzies depended for the next year on the support of two Independents to retain office. He is seen welcoming the United States envoy in 1941, with the Governor-General Lord Gowrie and (on right) the influential Country Party minister John McEwen.

THIS WEEK'S DAILY NET CIRCULATION—228,476 · FORECAST.—CHIEFLY FINE, BUT CLOUDY

The Herald
LAST EDITION

Hundred and First Year

No. 19,734 | Registered at General Post Office, Melbourne | MELBOURNE, TUESDAY EVENING, AUGUST 13, 1940 | Price 1½d. | 16 PAGES

THREE MINISTERS DIE IN CRASH

TEN VICTIMS OF R.A.A.F. DISASTER

Army Chief Included

TRAGIC SPIN NEAR CANBERRA 'DROME

From Our Special Representative

CANBERRA, Tuesday.—Ten people, including three Federal Cabinet Ministers and the Chief of the General Staff were killed when a Royal Australian Air Force bomber crashed in hilly country about eight miles from Canberra, and a mile from the Canberra Air Force aerodrome, about 10.15 a.m. today.

Those Killed Were:

MR G. A. STREET, Minister for the Army and Minister for Repatriation.
MR J. V. FAIRBAIRN, Minister for Air and Civil Aviation.
SIR HENRY GULLETT, Vice-President of the Executive Council.
GENERAL SIR BRUDENELL WHITE, Chief of the General Staff.

War Leaders In Today's Disaster

Mr Street

61 Enemy Planes Down

AIR OFFENSIVE ON BRITAIN CONTINUES

Australian Associated Press

LONDON, Monday. — The air Battle for Britain, now being waged ceaselessly day and night with thousands of planes taking part, today exacted a further enemy toll of 61 raiders, while 13 British fighters were lost.

The scope and severity of the German bombing is increasing beyond anything yet known.

Numbers of reports of raid incidents reaching the Australian Associated Press office from points over a wide area reveal the extent of the operations, but there is not one report of serious damage to shipping or defences.

The British communiques give only a conservative estimate of the German losses. Even the Berlin Official News Agency felt obliged today to amend from time to time the absurdly fractional estimates of German losses. Eventually it admitted that 19 German planes had not returned.

German Bid For Propaganda

The Daily Mail says experts believe that the air war is not a preliminary to "an immediate invasion." Germany, it says, apparently hopes to attain great propaganda value from the raids.

The German wireless is broadcasting ceaselessly graphic but fictitious versions of the operations. Today raiding planes attempted sky-writing over two English towns. It was impossible to read it except for a huge query mark.

Where Is Nazi Raid 'Damage'?

From GEOFFREY TEBBUTT, a Special Representative of The Herald

BRISTOL, Monday. — In a timely effort to counteract the possible effect of persistent German claims, having ravaged certain parts, Ministry of Information today American and Dominion journalists opportunity to see for themselves what the bombers had achieved city of their own selection.

I can testify that Bristol, far being devastated, is as normal are to be found throughout and although, according to the Controller, some 250 bombs have in that area since June 17, all the national and war enterprises continue unimpeded.

There have been some near misses of important objectives but the results of raids to 6 p.m. can be summarised thus:—

5 killed;
50 injured;
Some private property destroyed;
77 hours' work lost.
(Continued in Page 2)

Stop Press

Late Stocks

ABOVE:
A sailor of the newly
arrived light cruiser
HMAS *Perth*, pho-
tographed in Sydney
with his family, 1940.
Perth saw service in the
Mediterranean and went
down in battle against the
Japanese in the Sunda
Strait, 28 February 1942,
with the loss of nearly
300 of her officers and
men.

OPPOSITE:
The crash in August
1940 of a RAAF aircraft
at Canberra carrying
General White and three
of Menzies' most loyal
cabinet ministers
horrified the nation and
almost destroyed Menzies'
narrow hold on power.

In August 1940 the plane carrying from Melbourne the Chief of the General Staff, General White, and Menzies' political colleagues Sir Henry Gullett, Air Minister Fairbairn, and the Army Minister, Street, crashed at Canberra airport, and all aboard were killed. Their deaths were a devastating personal and political blow to the Prime Minister, for the politicians were among his strongest supporters, and his opponents were growing in number. The September 1940 election proved a cliff hanger. Both the coalition and Labor won thirty-six seats in the House and Menzies retained power only with the support of two independents, Coles and Wilson.

The Japanese threat

As early as July 1940 Japan had entered northern Indochina, securing bases there from the Vichy French authorities without a shot being fired. Within days of the September 1940 election Japan had signed in Berlin the 'Tri-partite Alliance' with Germany and Italy, in which the three militarist powers pledged their determination to create a 'New Order' in the world. Menzies was concerned about Britain's lack of awareness of Japanese intentions. He resolved to fly to London to confer with Churchill and secure reinforcements for the Far East. He left by Qantas Empire flying boat from Rose Bay on 24 January 1941 and wrote in his diary of his first view of Asia as they flew low over Java's rice paddies: 'Intense cultivation, chiefly rice … an occasional oil well, a distant volcano; but chiefly rice—curiously shaped little terraces, millions of them, the peasants working in water; every few hundred yards a village of say 50 or 100 cottages, surrounded by trees.' After addressing the Australian troops in Egypt Menzies was to reach London and confront Winston Churchill, whose own energy was volcanic.

1941: Desert victory

In January 1940 the British army in Egypt crossed the Libyan frontier to begin he conquest of Italy's ramshackle North African empire. It was an understrength force, and a polyglot one. British forces in Egypt could muster only one division of tanks (the 7th Armoured Division) but another vast Imperial army was gathering in the Nile Delta; the 6th and 7th Australian Divisions (soon joined by the 9th Australian Division), the New Zealand Division, the 4th and 5th Indian, while by mid-1941 the 1st and 2nd South African Divisions were travelling overland from the south. It was this army of Empire and Dominion infantry that would fight the major Mediterranean and African campaigns for the first two years of war.

On 3 January 1941, Major-General Mackay's 6th Australian Division and twenty-four British tanks stormed the Italian fortress of Bardia, capturing it in two days along with 40,000 prisoners, 120 tanks and 400 guns. On 21 January the 15,000 Australians attacked Tobruk with the aid of twelve British tanks, broke the defences and next day accepted its surrender. For the loss of 180 men killed and 600 wounded, the Australians in two battles had captured 65,000 Italians. It was one of the most remarkable victories in military history. 'Well done, Australia!' their Corps commander cabled Mackay. On 6 February 1941 Australian Bren-gun carriers rolled into Benghazi and prepared for an advance on Tripoli, the great prize.

At Benghazi the offensive halted. The attacking troops were exhausted and their supply lines were dangerously extended; the British tanks were breaking down and captured Italian ones useless. In February 1941, when Prime Minister Menzies was visiting the victorious Australians in Libya, Churchill ordered the Desert Army to be shipped to Greece, which since October 1940 had been standing alone against Italian attack.

1941: Greece

'This expedition to Greece doesn't stand a dog's chance,' the over-all AIF commander, General Blamey was heard to say. It seemed strategically unsound to pause just short of victory in North Africa and send an army to the Balkans. Churchill saw it otherwise: to maroon Greece, Britain's only ally, would be morally indefensible and he saw an opportunity to form the wavering states of Yugoslavia, Greece and Turkey into a new 'Balkan Front' to block Hitler's designs. The entry of German forces into Bulgaria on 1 March 1941 left Greece's north-eastern frontier dangerously exposed to German attack but the dispatch of the expeditionary force to Greece proceeded. The army for Greece would consist of the 6th and 7th Australian Divisions, the New Zealand Division and a brigade of 100 British tanks, supported by British non-combatant units.

THREE DEAD IN CAR CRASH—Page 3

WEATHER FORECAST: Cool, cloudy at times.

AUSTRALIA'S LARGEST SALE—260,302 DAILY

The Sun
NEWS—PICTORIAL
With Which Is Incorporated The Morning Post

Melbourne: Monday, April 7, 1941

NAZIS MARCH IN BALKANS

Across Greek and Jugoslav Frontiers

BOMBS ON BELGRADE AS
WAR IS DECLARED:
ADVANCING ON THRACE

ABOVE:

HMAS *Sydney*, which achieved fame in the Mediterranean during 1940. A light cruiser named in honour of her famous predecessor which sank the *Emden* in 1914, *Sydney*, commanded by Captain John Collins, RAN, boldly attacked two enemy cruisers off the coast of Crete in July 1940 and sank one of them, driving the other one off. She fought through numerous actions against the Italians without suffering a single battle fatality before returning to a hero's welcome in Australia early in 1941. She was lost in a battle to the death with the German raider *Kormoran* off the Western Australian coast in November 1941, disappearing with the loss of all her 645 men. Her loss was regarded as a national tragedy. It was not until February 2008 that the wrecks of HMAS *Sydney* and *Kormoran* were located, lying in waters more than two kilometres deep.

'The whole of the fighting troops are Australian and New Zealand,' Blamey wrote with concern to Menzies on 15 March. 'Past experience has taught me to look with misgiving on a situation where British leaders have control of considerable bodies of first-class Dominion troops while Dominion commanders are excluded from all responsibility in control, planning and policy.'

Eleven days later Yugoslavia joined the Axis; but on the following day, 26 March 1941, Serbian officers carried out a coup, replacing the pro-German government while pledging neutrality. Hitler, losing his self-control, ordered Yugoslavia crushed 'militarily and as a national unit'. His planned invasion of Russia, scheduled for 15 May, would be postponed until 22 June. It was probably Hitler's single most disastrous strategic mistake.

Once again Anzac forces were near the centre of the storm of great events. The storm fell on the Balkans on 6 April 1941; three days later Australian troops on the Greek–Yugoslav frontier opened fire on units of the Adolf Hitler Division moving south through the Monastir Gap. Marooned in the snow-covered mountains north of Thessaly the 6th Division and the New Zealanders (the 7th Division was never to join them) faced an avalanche of ten German divisions.

The fighting retreat of Anzac Corps (as it was named on 12 April) was skilfully managed. By the eve of Anzac Day the force had delayed the German columns sufficiently to enable evacuation to begin from beaches near Athens, but 14,000 British and Empire non-combat troops were left behind, with most of the forces' transport and weapons. On the day the Australians entered battle in Greece (10 April) the newly arrived 9th Division was surrounded in Tobruk, where the garrison had been marooned by the collapse of the British front.

ABOVE:

Menzies' rival Richard Casey took up a diplomatic career, opening Australia's first legation in Washington and later (1942) serving as Britain's Minister of State in the Middle East. He is shown here (left) in London with British Prime Minister Churchill.

1941: Menzies in London

In London Menzies could barely control his distress. He was heartened by the spirit of England's people under the bombing of the Blitz but appalled by Churchill's meddling in strategy. Attending a War Cabinet meeting when Churchill described the beleaguered fortress of Tobruk as an invaluable sally port from which the Australians could harry and harass the Axis forces, Menzies exploded 'With *what!*' He confessed to Major-General Kennedy in London that with one Australian division surrounded at Tobruk and another high and dry in Greece, he hardly dared return home and 'might as well go on a trip to the North Pole'.

Flying home via Canada in late May, he spoke to Mackenzie King of the dire need for the Dominions to be represented by someone in the British War Cabinet. King guessed correctly that the Australian saw himself as the man for the job. Menzies arrived back in Sydney with 'a sick feeling of repugnance and apprehension' (as he wrote in his diary) at the thought of returning to the pettiness of party politics and personal abuse. During his six months' absence he had won international stature, but had failed in the main objective of his mission: to obtain from Churchill modern aircraft for the Singapore base and Australia's defence, and British recognition of the threat Australia faced from the growing power of Japan.

The battle for Crete

On 20 May 1941 the Anzac and British forces on the island of Crete faced another deadly storm—a massive airborne invasion by German paratroopers and glider-borne troops. Ill-armed and lacking air cover, the 7000 Australians, 7000 New Zealanders and 15,000 British troops and Greek units fought a losing battle for a week under constant bombardment from a *Luftwaffe* fleet of 1000 aircraft. The evacuation of the troops from Crete's southern coast began on 28 May and continued for three nights, when the chances of air attacks were lessened. Nearly 4000 Australians and 5000 New Zealanders were among those killed, wounded or left behind on Crete, yet they had fought well and bravely, sustained by the support of the Cretans. Hundreds of Anzacs were hidden from the Germans by villagers in the mountains of mainland Greece and of Crete and aided in escaping to Turkey and freedom. British naval losses had been staggering.

It seemed that Australians and New Zealanders were destined to fight in classic surroundings as their fathers had done in the Dardanelles and the Holy Land; but Greece and Crete were calamities, and concern grew that Anzac soldiers were again being sacrificed callously by British blunders and miscalculations.

BELOW:
Australians defending Crete against a German airborne invasion, May 1941.

The defence of Tobruk, 1941

Only Tobruk remained of all the gains jeopardised by the errors of 1941. On 10 April a violent sandstorm enveloped the fortress, filling trenches as soon as they were dug, reducing visibility to a metre. As German armoured cars and infantry approached the perimeter they were met by a deluge of fire from the defenders. The action marked the beginning of an eight-month siege and a famous defence by the 9th Australian Division.

The Germans and Italians had never encountered small arms fire of such intensity, nor a defence so aggressive. Sustained and supplied by the British Fleet, including the five old Australian destroyers of the 'Scrap Iron Flotilla,' the 9th Division held Tobruk with British gunners and a handful of tanks through the long summer months of intense heat, despite shortages of water and food, until September when the first of its brigades, physically exhausted, was relieved by British infantry. Major-General Morshead, the commander of 'the Rats of Tobruk', was evacuated with the remainder of the division in late October 1941, only a month before the beginning of the British counteroffensive. The defence of Tobruk cost another 3000 Australian casualties but it denied Rommel's *Afrika Korps* the port they needed to maintain their advance. It was a remarkable victory—the first time resolute infantry had withstood tank attack, the first outright defeat suffered by the German army in the war—and brought great fame to the Australians, entering legend alongside Gallipoli.

ABOVE:
The easy victories over the Italians ended when German forces entered the Balkans and Libya in strength. Some of the Australians who defended Tobruk during 1941 clown for the camera.

In June 1941 the 7th Division fought its way into Syria in a month-long campaign that claimed 1,600 Australian casualties. Apart from the defence of Tobruk and the rapid quelling of the Iraqi revolt, it was the sole lasting victory in the Middle East in 1941.

Menzies replaced by Fadden

The Fairfax press now joined in those questioning Menzies' capacity to head a wartime government. His position crumbling, Menzies wrote on 26 August 1941 to John Curtin, asking Labor to join him in a coalition and offering to serve under him in any capacity. 'Your letter,' replied Curtin, 'indicates that you are not now able as P.M. to give Australia stable government.' Two days later Menzies' own party asked him to step down. 'Mr Menzies has been offered as Australia's scapegoat on the altar of political ambition, under the coercion of constantly applied pressure,' one witness of the meeting, A.W. Coles, told the press. 'I witnessed a lynching organised by mass hysteria. It was something so unclean that it will never be erased from my memory.' Arthur Fadden, the Country Party leader, assumed Menzies' post. A blunt farmer, he lasted barely five weeks before Coles and Wilson, angered by the lack of strong leadership, crossed the floor of the House on 7 October to sit with the Opposition, giving Labor a majority—and government.

BELOW:
Australia's new Prime Minister, Labor's John Curtin, walks to Parliament in Canberra with his friend and deputy Ben Chifley, who was destined to succeed him as Prime Minister in 1945.

1941:
Labor takes power

Australia's new Prime Minister, John Curtin, was an unknown quantity. 'We shall carry on the war effort, don't make any mistake about that,' Curtin announced. *The Age* echoed most Australians' feelings about the new government: 'They are entitled to reasonable time to get properly into the saddle …' Time was the element Australia lacked. Japan's increasing belligerence was shown in July 1941, when its forces entered Saigon and annexed French Indochina, a move that brought the Japanese dangerously close to Malaya.

Malaya and the naval base at its southern tip, Singapore, were considered effective barriers to Japanese expansion. The Malay Peninsula's mountain range and jungles were viewed as impenetrable. Churchill described the Singapore naval base as an 'impregnable fortress'. The Japanese themselves had proved incapable of subjugating China in four years of war and had intelligence enough, Churchill thought, to avoid

PIX

Vol. 8, No. 21.   NOVEMBER 22, 1941

No. 1 GLAMOR GIRL
OF 1941
(Pages 30-33)

6d

EVERY
WEEK

conflict with the American, Dutch and British empires in South-East Asia. President Roosevelt's reaction to Japan's conquest of Indochina had however been swift and sudden; a complete embargo on exports of oil and rubber to Tokyo and a freezing of Japanese assets in America. This action strengthened the hand of the war party in Tokyo and in October 1941 General Tojo, the War Minister, replaced the neutralist Prince Konoye as prime minister. Tojo retained the post of War Minister and added that of Home Minister to his portfolios. Answerable only to the Emperor, his power was complete. War plans were made for a sudden conquest of South-East Asia's rich natural resources of oil, rubber and rice by sudden, massive air, land and naval strikes; after which a peace could perhaps be negotiated with the Allies.

The weakness of British defences in Malaya was known to the Japanese, if not to the Australian people. A British Commonwealth conference of senior officers meeting in Singapore in October 1940 had recommended that, as Singapore lacked a fleet and strong land defences, priority should be giving to strengthening air defences; they recommended a minimum of 566 aircraft—twenty-two squadrons of modern aircraft (i.e. Spitfires and Hurricanes). When the Japanese struck there were only a dozen squadrons (four of them RAAF and one RNZAF) with a total of barely 166 aircraft, all of them obsolete and soon shot out of the sky by the remarkable Japanese Zero fighters. Apart from several British battalions on Singapore the only ground troops were two understrength Indian divisions and the 8th Australian Division, which, destined for the Middle East, had been directed to Malaya in February 1941. The Malaya garrison had no tanks. Churchill, in November 1941, dispatched to Singapore the battleship *Prince of Wales* and the battle cruiser *Repulse* in the hope that these fast, powerful ships would deter Japan from risking war with the British Empire. It was a romantic gesture on Churchill's part but an empty one, for the two ships had arrived without the aircraft carrier that was to have accompanied them. Lacking air cover, both great ships were to be sunk by swarms of Japanese torpedo-bombers on the third day of combat.

ABOVE:
For most Australians the war from 1939 to 1942 was remote, seldom displacing bathing beauties and Hollywood stars from the covers of popular magazines. This issue of *PIX* appeared just two weeks before Japan struck in the Pacific.

The Japanese onslaught

A violent thunderstorm broke over northern Malaya in the dark early hours of 8 December 1941; the rains turned airfields into seas of mud. The Australian Hudson squadron at Kota Bharu airfield was on alert, for two days earlier one of their aircraft had spotted a large convoy steaming south in the Gulf of Siam, but had lost contact with it in the low monsoonal cloud.

The Courier-Mail

FORECAST : Fine; cloudy. Map, Page &

GREATEST DAILY SALES IN QUEENSLAND

No. 2579 — BRISBANE, TUESDAY, DECEMBER 9, 1941. 10 PAGES 2d

JAPAN STRIKES HARD AT PACIFIC BASES

Bombs on Nauru, Singapore, Hong Kong: Fierce Hawaiian Battle

ENEMY TROOPS LAND IN NORTH MALAYA

Heavy Damage at U.S.A. Naval Key Points

JAPAN has invaded Malaya and Thailand, and has attacked Singapore and Hong Kong. She has bombed Nauru and Ocean Island, close to the Australian Mandated Territory one of New Guinea and the Solomon Islands.

This follows swiftly upon her treacherous and sudden attack on the great U.S. Naval base of Hawaii and the other American key points in the Pacific.

No official information has been received in Australia to indicate that the A.I.F. has yet been in action. Our troops are in southern Malaya.

The Prime Minister (Mr. Churchill) told the House of Commons yesterday that Cabinet had met at noon, and he had been authorised to make an immediate declaration of war against Japan. That declaration had been presented at 1 p.m.

Her bombers have done heavy damage to the U.S. sea and air bases in Hawaii and are reported virtually to have destroyed America's advanced base at Guam. Bases in the Philippines have been raided.

AUSTRALIA TO DECLARE WAR: WIDE NATIONAL DECISIONS

ABOVE:
Japan launches war in the Pacific. The attacks were sudden and devastating.

The Japanese ships began landing troops before dawn on the coast at Kota Bharu, whose beaches were flimsily defended by Indian troops, and within hours the invaders were being bombed by RAAF Hudsons. But by afternoon the airfield only two kilometres from the beaches was under sniper fire and the surviving aircraft were ordered flown south. This action was the first of the Pacific War, occurring hours before the first Japanese dive bombers appeared over the American naval base at Pearl Harbor in Hawaii (morning of 7 December, because of the time difference) where they sank four American battleships and effectively destroyed the U.S. Pacific Fleet. Further Japanese attacks fell on Hong Kong and the American bases at Wake Island, Midway Island and the Philippines. Churchill's declaration of war on Japan was followed by America's. Speaking before Congress President Roosevelt described Sunday 7 December as 'a day which will live in infamy'. Japan's attack had transformed the European War into the Second World War. 'Now, only the stars are neutral,' Curtin said.

1942: The fall of Malaya

The first week of war sealed the fate of Malaya. Their flimsy air cover destroyed, their defensive positions on the roads outflanked by Japanese trained in jungle fighting, both Indian divisions were, by the first days of January 1942, in disorganised retreat to the south. On 27 December, as Malaya's defences disintegrated, Prime Minister Curtin issued a statement that was widely reprinted in Australia and overseas: 'We refuse to accept the dictum that the Pacific struggle must be treated as a subordinate segment of the general conflict. Without any inhibitions of any kind I make it quite clear that Australia looks to America, free of any pangs as to our traditional links of kinship with the United Kingdom.'

349

4   THE AUSTRALASIAN, February 7, 1942.

THE WAR IN MALAYA :: ALLIED PACIFIC LEADERS

JAPANESE TANKS destroyed by Australian anti-tank guns when they tried to pass trees felled across the road as a defence measure.

CAMOUFLAGED A I F ANTI-TANK GUN in a forward area: Ten Japanese tanks were destroyed in one battle by units like this in fighting in the Muar area.

GNR. A. D. LANG, of Hurstville, NSW, is amused by a Japanese propaganda pamphlet, dropped from the air.

THE MONKEY MASCOT which Gnr. George Martin and Bdr. G. T. Mansfield are attaching to the army vehicle may look fearsome, but that's the taxidermist's fault!

GNR. H. M. FISHER, of Manly, NSW, who evaded Japanese captors and dived into the Muar River. He was in the water 10 hours before joining Indian troops, who nearly shot him, thinking him an enemy.
—(*Dept. of Information pictures*)

Roosevelt, far from being impressed, saw this as a sign of Australia's 'flagging morale'. But in the War Department, Washington, a recently promoted Brigadier-General named Dwight Eisenhower drafted a strategic plan for the President that recommended: 'Our base must be Australia.' An American division sailing for the Philippines was ordered to Australian ports. Curtin had already ordered Blamey, with Churchill's agreement, to ship the 6th and 7th Divisions from Egypt to the Dutch East Indies.

Major-General Bennett's 8th Australian Division first entered battle on 14 January by mounting a spectacular ambush on the Gemas road; it was the first attempt in the campaign to play the Japanese at their own game. On 20 January two Australian battalions and an Indian force holding the Japanese near Bakri were cut off by the collapse of the British-Indian line on the coast, and fought their way out in a three-day battle from which only 1000 of the 4000-strong force survived. On 31 January the defenders of Malaya crossed over to Singapore Island and detonated the causeway connecting it to the mainland. For the loss of 4500 casualties, the majority of these incurred by the Australians, a force of 35,000 Japanese had driven an army of 65,000 men from Malaya.

ABOVE:
Malaya's defences crumbled under the suddenness of the Japanese attacks, despite the optimistic reports of Allied reporters. When Singapore fell in February 1942 the entire 8th Australian Division passed into captivity.

1942: The fall of Singapore

The Japanese landed on Singapore Island on 8 February and within two days had pushed the defenders from the western end to a barely defensible line running down the centre of the island. By 14 February 1942 the enemy, well supplied with tanks, had taken the reservoirs. Singapore surrendered on the following day. In the largest mass surrender in British history an army of 130,000 men passed into Japanese captivity. Among the captured were 16,000 Australian soldiers—the entire 8th Division.

ABOVE:
Birth of the 'United Nations': In January 1942 President Roosevelt (wearing a black armband for his men killed at Pearl Harbor) and Prime Minister Churchill meet in Washington with representatives of the Allied powers and issued 'The Declaration of the "United Nations"', pledging to fight on against Germany, Italy and Japan until victory was achieved.
Australia's Owen Dixon (second from left) signed for his country.

Equally horrifying was the fate suffered by Australian Army nurses in Singapore. Australian women had staffed AIF hospitals in the Middle East—and served in Greece—without suffering casualties, but the ship carrying sixty-five Australian nurses from Singapore just before its fall was torpedoed and the survivors were massacred. Only one Australian nurse survived the horror and subsequent captivity. The Japanese refused to honour the Geneva Convention or to respect the Red Cross.

The day before Singapore's fall the first echelons of the 7th Division reached Java where, in response to the pleas of the British Supreme Commander, Wavell, a brigade was landed. It was overwhelmed in mid-March. In January and February 1942 the small isolated Australian garrisons at Rabaul (where the Wirraways were shot down in minutes), Ambon and Timor were overwhelmed and forced to surrender. Few of the men survived massacres or brutality at Japanese hands. Only a small group of commandos in Portuguese Timor eluded capture, retreating into the mountains to wage a guerrilla war. In April, Darwin picked up the faint wireless messages from those remarkable men (nearly all of them West Australian bushmen) and reinforcements, ammunition and supplies soon flowed in. Darwin itself was struck by bombs from Japanese aircraft on 19 February 1942. The attack destroyed shipping and caused 556 casualties

On the night of 28 February, as the Japanese began invading Java, the Australian cruiser *Perth* and USS *Houston*, seeking to reach Australian waters, encountered a sixty-ship Japanese fleet near the north of Sunda Strait and were sunk after a desperate battle; the little sloop HMAS *Yarra,* escorting ships fleeing from Java, was sunk in action the next day. HMAS *Sydney*, the hero of the Mediterranean battles, had been lost with all 645 of her crew off Carnarvon four months earlier, sinking her assailant the German raider *Kormoran* in the process. None of *Sydney's* men were ever found, and only 200 of *Perth's* crew survived battle and captivity.

On 21 February 1942 Churchill had diverted to Rangoon the convoy carrying elements of the 7th Division, for Burma was now collapsing under Japanese attack. In an angry cable to Churchill two days later Curtin protested to Churchill: 'All our northern defences are gone, or going. Now you contemplate using the AIF to save Burma. All this has been done, as in Greece, without adequate air support.' The convoy was rerouted to its original course and proceeded to Australian ports. The 6th Division following in its wake was similarly diverted to Colombo where, following a request from Churchill, two brigades were landed to garrison the island. Australia's own defence needs, John Curtin felt, were of minor concern to Churchill.

The Japanese advanced south and east, barely having to pause. In March 1942 they landed at Lae in New Guinea. It seemed that nothing stood between Japan and the conquest of Australia itself.

ABOVE:

General Douglas MacArthur, who was ordered to leave the besieged Philippines for Australia to command the Allied forces there, is shown with Prime Minister Curtin, with whom he forged a rare friendship.

MacArthur and the 'Yanks'

On 16 March 1942 a tall American general, Douglas MacArthur, commander of the embattled American forces in the Philippines, clambered from a B-17 bomber onto Australian soil at an airfield in the Northern Territory. Darwin itself had been under continuous Japanese air attack for the past four weeks and it was considered unsafe to land there. In the shade of a gum tree the general was handed a cable from President Roosevelt appointing him Supreme Commander, Allied Forces South West Pacific. His headquarters and base would be Australia.

MacArthur was hailed as a conquering hero instead of a defeated general when he arrived in Melbourne on 23 March. 'My faith in our ultimate victory is invincible,' he informed Australia in the language that came easily to him. 'We shall win or we shall die and to this end I pledge the full resources and all the mighty power of my country and all the blood of my countrymen.' He quickly established a warm relationship with Curtin and Blamey, but he was dismayed by the pitiful resources and power at his disposal. Only two American army divisions (the 32nd and the 41st), originally destined for the Philippines, were arriving in, or were en route to, Australia.

Australia's defence rested on an ill-equipped army of 330,000 militia, 33,000 newly arrived US personnel and a handful of aircraft. The 6th and 7th Divisions had left half their strength in Java and Ceylon; the 8th had been lost at Singapore; the 9th remained in the Middle East. The Commander-in-Chief Home Forces, General Mackay, reported that existing forces were too few in number to defend much more than the 'vital' Brisbane-to-Melbourne region, and stated: 'It may be necessary to submit to the occupation of certain areas by the enemy should resistance be overcome'; both Townsville and Tasmania would have to be considered expendable. The Labor firebrand Eddie Ward accused the government of planning to retreat to defences behind a 'Brisbane Line'.

ABOVE:
The poet, Dame Mary
Gilmore.

TOP:
Herbert Vere Evatt,
Foreign Minister under
Curtin, fought tenaciously
for Australia's interests;
many British and Ameri-
can leaders found his
mind brilliant but his
manner unbearable.

1942: Fortress Australia — 'great, tragic days'

Lacking adequate modern fighter aircraft, the RAAF ordered the construction of a local aircraft: The brilliant Lawrence Wackett designed and constructed the first Boomerang fighter (similar to the Buffalo) in fourteen weeks. In March Curtin sent Minister for External Affairs H.V. Evatt to Washington and London to convey the seriousness of Australia's plight to Roosevelt and Churchill. In England Evatt's suspicion was confirmed that the 'big two' had considered Australia expendable. 'We would have got you back after the war,' Churchill assured him. 'Oh, but they're our own kith and kin,' Clementine Churchill chided her husband. The London press reminded its readers of Australia's generosity in assigning its aircraft allocation to Britain and shipping its reserve of rifles to England in 1940. Evatt obtained enough Spitfires from Churchill to equip three squadrons. (They arrived in time to blunt the Japanese air offensive on Darwin that lasted until September 1943.)

Japanese submarines began operating in Australian waters, sinking merchantmen (a total of twenty-six ships by war's end) as far south as Bass Strait. Japanese submarines raided Sydney Harbour on the night of 31 May and a week later shelled both Sydney and Newcastle. For the first time in their history, Australians faced war—and possible defeat—on their own shores.

'The battle of Australia is about to begin,' Prime Minister Curtin warned the nation. Blackouts of cities were enforced, travel was restricted, rationing extended. 'The next few months may decide not only whether we are to survive as a nation, but whether we deserve to survive,' wrote Vance Palmer in *Meanjin.* 'We could vanish and leave singularly few signs that, for some generations, there had lived a people who had made a homeland of this Australian earth.' He called on the true resource of the nation to show itself: 'But there is an Australia of the spirit, of men who came here to form a new society, of hard conflicts in many fields, it has developed a toughness all its own. These are great, tragic days. Let us accept them stoically, and make every yard of Australian earth a battle-station.' Mary Gilmore called on the spirit of the pioneer men and women to stiffen Australians' resolve:

No foe shall gather our harvest,
Or sit on the stockyard rail

In April 1942 a Japanese strike force sailed into the Indian Ocean, sinking a British carrier and the destroyer HMAS *Vampire* off Ceylon under a deluge of bombs and torpedoes. On 7 May the last American forces holding out in the Philippines surrendered. Japan's conquest of South-East Asia was complete.

Turning the tide: The battles of Coral Sea and Midway

Six months of unremitting disaster ended on 7 May 1942 when Prime Minister Curtin was handed a message in the half-empty House of Representatives and stood up to make a brief but stirring announcement: 'I have just received a communiqué from the Commander-in-Chief of the Allied Forces in the South-West Pacific Area stating that a great naval battle is proceeding in the South-West Pacific Zone.' He had few details of the course of the battle but called on all Australians to dedicate themselves to achieving victory as loyally as were their fighting men. Only hours before, the first naval battle in history fought between fleets of aircraft carriers had begun in the blue waters of the Coral Sea between the coast of northern Queensland and the Solomons. An American fleet and an Australian cruiser task force, forewarned by code-breakers of Japanese plans to seize Port Moresby by sea, had made contact with the enemy. On the following day MacArthur's headquarters announced that American aircraft had sunk a Japanese aircraft carrier, for the loss of thirty-three US planes, forcing the enemy to turn back. (One American carrier and numerous aircraft were also lost, but the Japanese never again attempted to seize Port Moresby by sea.)

On 4 June, again forewarned of Japanese moves, the US Navy's last remaining carrier fleet in the Pacific, stationed off Midway Island, confronted a strong Japanese fleet; at the end of a desperate day-long air battle American pilots located and sank four enemy carriers in quick succession for the loss of only one of their own carriers. The 'Glorious Fourth of June' was the battle that stopped Japan's seaborne advance and rendered impossible any invasion of Australia, but Australians would mythologise the earlier action in the Coral Sea as 'The Battle that Saved Australia', making its anniversary 'Friendship Day' in tribute to America's role.

ABOVE:
Without adequate aircraft the Allies could neither strike back at the enemy nor defend their bases. As a stopgap, Australian factories produced Australia's own fighter aircraft, the Boomerang, but it was too slow to successfully tackle the Japanese Zeros. The arrival of American aircraft helped turn the tide of the war.

1942: Collapse in the desert

Hopes that the Allies had now achieved the initiative were dashed by events in the Middle East. On 20 June 1942 Rommel's Afrika Korps, having launched a sudden counteroffensive three weeks before, captured Tobruk from the 1st South African Division after a siege of two days. Six days later the last remaining Australian division in the Middle East, the 9th—the 'Rats of Tobruk' who had defended the seaport for eight months during 1941—was ordered south from Syria to rejoin the 8th Army in Egypt. Ahead of the Diggers lay fighting more bloody and intense than Tobruk: the four-month battle to hold the enemy at El Alamein, the 'last ditch' before Cairo.

OPPOSITE:
Prime Minister Curtin facing a question from the Opposition in the House of Representatives, 13 May 1942. General MacArthur was invited to sit near the Speaker and see Australian democracy at work.

New Guinea

Within days of Midway the Joint Chiefs of Staff in Washington ordered MacArthur to forestall Japanese moves in New Guinea and the Solomons. But the enemy

ABOVE:

Jungle fighting: From July to November 1942 ill-equipped Australian troops resisted and then defeated a determined Japanese attempt to take Port Moresby on the Kokoda Track. The fighting was intense and fought in nightmarish conditions of mud, disease and the threat of sudden ambush.

LEFT:

During the bitter fighting in Gona and Buna, the Australian Commander-in-Chief General Blamey (left) confers with Lieutenant-General Eichelberger, the American commander. Both men were rankled by complaints from General MacArthur that the Japanese were not being attacked with sufficient vigour.

WORK · SAVE · FIGHT

and so AVENGE THE NURSES !

ABOVE:
When a Japanese submarine sank the Australian hospital ship *Centaur* off Brisbane in 1943, nurses were among the 268 who died.

seized the initiative. In July 1942 the Japanese, while extending their hold in the Solomons, landed a force of 5000 troops at Buna and Gona on the north-eastern coast of New Guinea. They struck inland rapidly, heading for the village of Kokoda from where a rough mountain track led over the rugged Owen Stanley Range to the foothills near their goal—Port Moresby. The march over the mountains would, they planned, take seven days.

New Guinea was a nightmare battleground. The great island was mountainous for the most part, a forbidding realm of numerous and savage tribes into which few Australians apart from missionaries and miners had ventured. The island lay under a suffocating blanket of heat and humidity; disease was rampant; torrential rain was constant in the Highlands, turning tracks into rivers of mud; the humidity of the coast was enervating. The highest peaks of the Owen Stanley Range were lost in clouds of perpetual mist and its ridges and valleys were covered in almost impassable jungle. Two of MacArthur's staff officers returning from New Guinea told him they didn't know how men could live there, much less fight. New Guinea would be the major battlefield between Australian and Japanese forces for the next three years.

1942: The Kokoda Track

It is still not known why Port Moresby was defended by only an underequipped brigade of young militia troops. Japanese air raids on the forlorn port sapped their morale until two RAAF squadrons of Kittyhawk fighters arrived in March 1942 to tackle the raiders. In June 1942 the first companies of the best battalion there, the

39th Battalion, a Melbourne unit, set out from Moresby accompanied by native bearers to hike over the Owen Stanley Range to defend Kokoda, a small village with an airfield at the vital 'gap' at the northern base of the range.

On 23 July 1942 the Australians sighted Japanese advancing inland from Buna, and opened fire; it was the beginning of a week-long battle to hold the village and rubber groves of Kokoda. Outnumbered, the Militia companies fell back, fighting a rearguard action on the Kokoda Track for four weeks before digging in at Isurava, midway across the range, where they were joined by battle-hardened AIF troops of the 7th Division on 23 August. For another four weeks the Australians fought an impossible battle against the invaders. By 17 September the combined Australian force had been pushed back to Imita, the last ridge before Moresby. The seven-day hike over the mountain track planned by the Japanese had become ten weeks of some of the most bitter jungle fighting of the war.

The Japanese, depleted in numbers, were by now exhausted and starving, and began to fall back to Buna on 26 September, by which date a second attempt to seize a base on the eastern tip of New Guinea had been thwarted by Australian troops at Milne Bay, after a week-long battle fought in mangrove swamps and mud. On the Kokoda Track the Australians counterattacked and by 23 October had reached the Japanese stronghold high above a roaring torrent of Eora Creek. It was the first day of a bitter five-day combat in rain and mud to break the Japanese grip.

On that same day, 23 October, half a world away in Egypt, the 9th Australian Division went forward in the north of the line at Alamein in General Montgomery's great counteroffensive to drive the Axis armies from Egypt.

ABOVE:
While the battle of the Kokoda Track was raging the 9th Australian Division—the famed 'Rats of Tobruk'—was turning stalemate into victory in the great offensive at El Alamein in the deserts of Egypt, October–November 1942. The last Australian formation in the Middle East, the 9th Division, sailed for Australia in March 1943 to join the war against the Japanese.

ABOVE:
Australian army nurses.

ABOVE, RIGHT:
Australian factories including General Motors-Holden produced 700 Beauforts, an adaptable reconnaissance aircraft and light bomber widely flown by the RAAF in the Pacific.

1942: *Victory at Alamein*

These two battles, fought at the same time, were possibly the supreme achievements of Australian infantry in a war now entering its fourth year. The offensive at Alamein stalled on the third day. The Australians, already weary from combat since July, were ordered to absorb the bulk of the enemy's tank attacks while pushing their line forward, in an attempt to 'crumble' Rommel's armour. 'All now depended on the Australians,' Montgomery was to write. It was the last great ordeal of Australian troops in the desert war. By 2 November 1942, the day when equally exhausted Diggers reached Kokoda and raised the Australian flag, the New Zealanders, Highland Division and British tanks were able to launch the breakthrough thrust that caused Rommel to order a general retreat. 'The magnificent forward drive of the Australians, achieved by ceaseless bitter fighting, had swung the entire battle in our favour', Churchill wrote in tribute. Of the 15,000 men of the 9th Division, 6000 had been lost in four months of constant battle.

The closing months of 1942 were, on all fronts, a climax of the war. The first snows were falling on the encircled German army at Stalingrad; in North Africa, hampered by winter rains, the 8th Army was in pursuit of the Afrika Korps. In the Pacific, by February 1943 the Americans (reliant on Australian Coastwatchers on Bougainville for warning of Japanese naval and air movements) finally forced the Japanese from the southern Solomons after eight months of land, sea and air battles.

1943: The strain of war

In January 1943 Australian veterans of Kokoda, reinforced by fresh battalions and by American troops, overcame the last Japanese bunkers on the coast at Buna–Gona–Sanananda. The two-month battle amid the mangrove swamps was bloodier than Kokoda. The Papuan campaign from Kokoda to Buna cost 2165 Australian killed and 3500 wounded. Nearly 14,000 Diggers were struck by malaria and dengue fever. American casualties were lighter—2600—though MacArthur's headquarters gave the public the impression that US troops had played the major role. 'The American troops cannot be classified as attack troops,' Blamey informed Curtin. 'They are definitely not equal to the Australian militia and from the moment they met opposition, sat down and have hardly gone forward a yard.'

Whatever the frontline troops thought of the fighting capacities of the green American units they saw in New Guinea, the presence and power of a growing American army on the Australian mainland transformed Australia's role in the war, and its society. By war's end nearly one million American servicemen had passed through Australia and their impact on the nation was lasting. Australian women found the neatly uniformed, highly paid, well-mannered GIs glamorous and charming; Diggers returning from overseas derided the newcomers and picked fights with them. (Though the notorious free-for-all, the battle of Brisbane in 1942, began when two Australians tried to stop American military police from bashing up a harmlessly drunk GI, and the battle of Melbourne early in 1943 between the returning 9th Division and the battle-hardened 1st US Marine Division ended with

ABOVE:
'The Yanks are here!': American troops (top of photograph) marching through Sydney after their arrival in 1942.

Australian troops march separately. The Allies fought alongside each other in the battles ahead, but kept a certain distance.

drinks all round.) Curtin was alarmed to hear that black troops were accompanying American units to Australia and sought to have them directed elsewhere, but Australians found the Afro-American soldiers the most pleasant visitors of all.

'No more Bunas!' was MacArthur's order to his commanders: no more set-piece battles. He would instead by-pass Japanese strongholds using his growing fleet of amphibious craft and aircraft. The Pacific War, however, was low among the priorities of Allied grand strategy. At Casablanca in January 1943 Churchill and Roosevelt demanded the 'unconditional surrender' of the three Axis powers but resolved to concentrate Allied strength on the destruction of Germany and Italy. In a broadcast to the Australian people Curtin told the nation that the Pacific would be a 'holding war' that could last another three years.

Prisoners of war

For the 22,000 Australians captured by the Japanese after the collapse in Malaya, Java and the islands, those three years were to be one long hell. Nearly 35 per cent of them died in captivity—a total of 7777 soldiers, in addition to sailors and airmen. In mid-1942 the first Australian groups left Changi camp on Singapore for Burma and Thailand, where the Japanese had decided to build a railway to connect Rangoon to Bangkok using local labourers and Allied prisoners. Nearly 100,000 workers died from disease or brutality; 6800 of them were Britons and 2700 Australians. Another 1500 Australians died at sea when the transports carrying them to Japan were tragically sunk by American submarines. Nearly 2000 Australians died of starvation or disease or by execution in the death marches from Sandakan

RIGHT:

The conditions of Allied prisoners of war in the hands of the Japanese was largely unknown until 1944, when survivors of a torpedoed prison ship were picked up by American submarines and recounted their stories.

Australian artist Murray Griffin, who survived captivity, painted this picture of the Hospital on the Burma–Thailand railway; few of those stricken with dysentery, beri-beri or cholera survived.

From the painting in the Australian War Memorial, Canberra.

"10 DAYS THAT SHOOK THE WORLD"

LEFT:
In January 1943, Roosevelt and Churchill met at Casablanca and announced their determination to defeat the Axis powers.

in northern Borneo in 1945 when those who collapsed from exhaustion were shot or bayoneted by their guards. Nearly 600 Australians were executed brutally for attempting to escape, or for defying their captors. The suffering of Australians in Japanese hands deeply affected Australia's attitude to Asia for a generation.

Of the 7000 Australian soldiers who fell into German and Italian hands during the Mediterranean campaigns only 242 died in captivity. In Australian camps German and Japanese prisoners were treated and fed decently according to the Geneva Convention; the Italian prisoners were particularly fortunate, especially after 1943 when Italy joined the Allies and the POWS enjoyed much freedom as workers on country properties. Many of them were well liked and later returned as immigrants. Among Australians interned during the war was the editor and nationalist P.R. Stephensen. A former Rhodes Scholar, Stephensen had become increasingly right wing. As a leader of the tiny Australia First movement he was perceived as a fascist sympathiser. He was later to ghost-write Australian adventure books for Frank Clune.

BELOW:
In the 1943 elections Labor's Dorothy Tangney became the first woman elected to the Senate.

1943: *The home front*

In Australia 830,000 men and women were in uniform, but the shortage of manpower in secondary industry was acute. A gradual reduction in army strength was made and in March 1943 Curtin risked splitting Labor by pushing through Parliament a bill making Militia conscripts liable for active service anywhere south of the equator. The August 1943 elections saw Curtin and Labor win a healthy majority—49 seats in the 74-seat House of Representatives—an endorsement of Curtin's vigorous leadership.

In mid-1942 the federal government had taken over the collection of all income tax; they would henceforth allocate grants to the states. In the same year Curtin's government ratified the Statute of Westminster.

1943: Birth of the Liberal Party

The election marked the demise of the United Australia Party. Since the fall of the UAP–Country Party coalition in October 1941, Robert Menzies had returned to the back benches and his law practice in Melbourne. His attempts to obtain a responsible position overseas were rejected by Churchill, who possibly saw the self-assured Australian as a threat to his own position. In 1944 Menzies called a conference in Albury of the UAP and other anti-Labor parties to forge a viable opposition party. From the deliberations arose a new Liberal Party, one devoted to the 'freedom of the individual' and to 'individual enterprise'. From 1944 onwards Menzies would be an increasingly effective critic of Labor's policies.

Stirrings of modernism

By late 1944 indeed both government and people were preparing themselves for peace. The campaigns in Europe were remote, and posting of aircrew to the European theatre ceased. Prominent foreigners visiting Australia were astonished by the casual attitude of the people to the war itself. War controls and rationing were strict but a black market flourished. In the south-west Pacific a RAAF strength of nearly 150,000 ground crew and airmen were left behind in the backwater of war with no enemy left to fight. The two biggest stories of the year (apart from that of the Allied invasion of Europe in June 1944) were William Dobell's defence in court of his 1943 Archibald Prize-winning portrait—described by the conservative art world as a cruel caricature, not a portrait—and the publication of lines of apparent nonsense by a contributor named 'Ern Malley' in the literary magazine *Angry Penguins*. The magazine's editor, Max Harris, described the poet as a

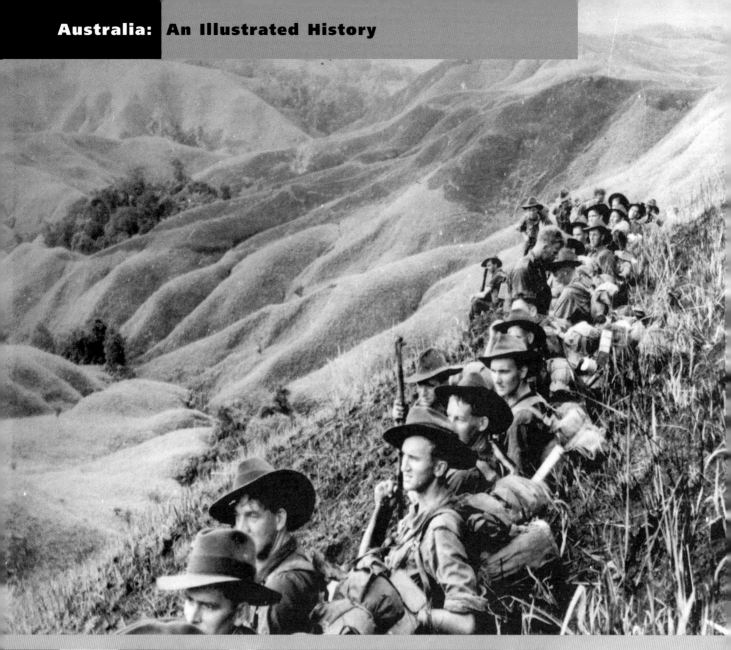

ABOVE:
Australian troops stop for a breather on the track across the Finisterre Ranges. Madang on the north-east coast of Papua New Guinea fell early in 1944.

LEFT:
A powerful British Fleet returned to the Pacific late in 1944, using Australia as its base. Here its commander, Admiral Sir Bruce Fraser, addresses officers and men of an Australian destroyer.

genius, but it soon became known that the whole thing was a hoax. The poems had been written by two writers in Army Intelligence to point out the absurdity of modernist poetry, and out of sheer boredom.

In Europe the Royal Air Force (nearly half of whose pilots by 1945 were Australians, New Zealanders and Canadians) continued to suffer staggering losses in the 'round the clock' bombing offensives of Hitler's Europe.

1943–44: South-west Pacific

In June 1943 a major Allied counteroffensive in the south-west Pacific began in New Guinea with American landings at Nassau Bay and Australian advances in the mountainous hinterland, preludes to an Allied drive on Lae. Lae fell to Australian infantry in September, a fortnight before the 9th Division landed near Finschhafen on the Huon Gulf and the 7th Division pushed to the base of the Finisterre mountains. Shaggy Ridge and Old Vickers joined Eora Creek, Kokoda and Buna as definitions of hell in the lexicon of the Australian soldier in New Guinea; the Japanese were driven from the ridges in January, opening the way to Madang.

In December 1943 General Blamey announced the end of Australian Army operations in New Guinea, in accordance with MacArthur's directive that American forces take over offensive operations. When the Australians straggled over the Finisterre mountains into Madang on Anzac Day 1944, they closed a chapter in Australian military history. Over the previous seven months alone, five divisions—the 7th and 9th AIF and the 3rd, 5th and 11th Militia—had outfought an army of 100,000 Japanese, causing the death of 35,000 enemy soldiers at the cost of 4000 Australian casualties. It was a remarkable achievement.

In April 1944 MacArthur bypassed the 100,000 Japanese at Wewak on New Guinea's north coast and landed at Aitape; in September Morotai was seized and in October 1944, two months ahead of schedule, the Americans landed in the Philippines. Covering the landings in the task force, the flagship HMAS *Australia* was struck by the first Kamikaze attacks of the war but survived. The complex series of naval battles known as Leyte Gulf saw the American Navy's greatest victory—the destruction of four Japanese carriers, three battle ships and six cruisers. The Imperial Japanese Navy had now virtually ceased to exist.

1945 The last offensives

The operations of Australian land forces in the last year of the Pacific War have been widely criticised as a waste of young lives. Japan's defeat was assured when Australians took over from American garrisons to drive the remaining Japanese forces from

BELOW:
It was left to Australian troops to clear the last Japanese from Papua New Guinea. Brigadier Windeyer, a veteran of Alamein (and later a justice of the High Court), watches as soldiers of the 9th Division embark for the landings in the Huon Gulf of Papua, September 1943.

Bougainville, New Ireland and New Guinea's northern coast in November 1944. The strength of the enemy was underestimated. The Australian and New Zealand governments issued in November what an American diplomat called 'the Anzac Monroe Doctrine'. Both countries, as founding members of the United Nations, declared their intention of retaining their mandated Pacific territories at war's end. On Curtin's direction Australian forces would remain on active operation until war's end.

In May 1945 the 9th Division landed in Borneo, an island whose strategic value was small, for the Allied navies and American air forces were now bombarding Japan itself. Tarakan and Brunei Bay, seized by the 9th Division, and Balikpapan (where the 7th Division landed under smoke from burning oil tanks in July) cost nearly 600 Australian dead and thousands of wounded. As MacArthur was preparing for a mass invasion of Japan scheduled for 1946, an American aircraft on 6 August 1945 dropped the first atomic bomb (possessing explosive power equiva-

ABOVE:
Image of the Digger: an unnamed Australian soldier in jungle green and carrying a Bren (machine-gun), New Guinea, 1943–44. The Australians facing the Japanese in the 1942 battles on the Kokoda Track were less well armed. 'We weren't heroes,' a soldier said when peace came. 'We were just ordinary men doing a horrible job.'

lent to 20,000 tonnes of TNT) on Hiroshima. Three days later a second atomic bomb fell on Nagasaki; six days later the Japanese Emperor, Hirohito, asked his people to 'accept the unacceptable' and ordered unconditional surrender.

Victory over Japan, 1945

'At this moment, let us all offer thanks to God,' Prime Minister Chifley said to Australians in a victory broadcast on 15 August 1945. 'Let us remember those whose lives were given so that we may enjoy this glorious moment and look forward to a peace which they have earned for us.' In Sydney crowds estimated at 'a million' danced in the streets, as millions were doing in nearly every town and city of the Allied nations. Most would remember the day as the happiest of their lives.

ABOVE:
When the atomic bombs fell on Japan, Australian forces were still 'cleaning up' Japanese garrisons left behind by the swift American amphibious offensives of 1944. Despite their hopeless position the Japanese resisted to the death in northern New Guinea, Borneo and Bougainville where a wounded Australian soldier is being helped by islanders.

Prime Minister Curtin, ailing for six months, had died in office, of a heart attack, on 5 July 1945, worn out by the strain and anxiety of war. A contemporary wrote: 'Delegating authority and responsibility to members like Chifley, Evatt, Beasley and Forde, he freed himself from departmental duties in order to concentrate on general matters of national importance.'

Curtin's deputy, Frank Forde, became acting Prime Minister for eleven days before the Treasurer, Ben Chifley, was chosen by Caucus to succeed their dead leader. Of Curtin, Chifley said: 'Australia has lost a great man and myself a great friend. He was a great gentleman to be associated with, and was too fine a man to be associated with the feuds and personal animosities that come with politics.' Billy Hughes added his own tribute to Curtin: 'Of no man can it be more truly said that he literally gave his life for his country. He was a great Australian.'

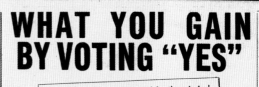

Few of the wartime leaders were left. Churchill had lost power in July in a Labour landslide that seemed to mock his great role in leading Britain's survival. President Roosevelt had died in April 1945, mourned as the greatest President since Lincoln. Hitler had shot himself in Berlin on 30 April, the day after Mussolini had been executed by Italian partisans. Tojo attempted suicide but recovered. An Australian, Sir William Webb, would be the presiding judge of an international tribunal convened in Japan that two years later sentenced to death Tojo and six other Japanese war leaders for crimes against humanity. Only Stalin remained to cast a malignant shadow over Eastern Europe.

In the south-west Pacific the Australian army of 165,000 men in the war zone accepted the surrender of 344,000 Japanese personnel. At Rabaul alone 90,000 emaciated Japanese, nineteen generals and two admirals, capitulated to the 5th Division. On Bougainville, where 18,000 Japanese had died in operations against the Australians over the past nine months, barely 23,000 were alive to surrender.

On 2 September 1945 Japan officially signed the documents of surrender on the deck of the American battleship USS *Missouri* anchored in Tokyo Bay. General MacArthur dominated the ceremony, for the victory had been American; but it was appropriate that officers from Britain, Australia and New Zealand witnessed and signed the documents: Among the fifty members of the new United Nations Organisation convening in San Francisco, they alone had lasted the entire course of six years of war, from 3 September 1939.

Australia had lost nearly 30,000 war dead, including 8000 soldiers who had died as prisoners of the Japanese. Australian forces (all of them volunteer apart from the militia divisions that saw action in 1944–45) had fought in all theatres of war, from the air war's bomber offensives of 1942 to 1945 to the naval and air battles of the Mediterranean and Pacific campaigns. Of the aircrew who saw action, barely one in four survived unscathed. Nearly 50,000 Australian women had served in uniform. Australia's contribution to victory had been great and unselfish and her society had been transformed and reshaped.

FOR QUALITY!

AKUBRA
hats

ALTHOUGH war-time require-
ments for the services have
restricted the output of these
famous Australian Pure Fur
Felt Hats for civilian needs,
you should always select an
AKUBRA. . . . Style and long-
wearing qualities, combined
with comfort, ensure sound
money and *coupon value.*

A2

LOOK YOUR BEST IN AN AKUBRA

A B O V E :
Transition to peace:
soldiers swapped their
slouch hats for Akubras.

The Chifley years: socialism for the people

'We shall build a new Jerusalem 'in Australia's pleasant land',
J.J. Dedman, Labor Minister for Post War Reconstruction had
pledged in May 1945 in presenting a Bill to provide 'full
employment'. It was a time of great idealism. With mon-
strous tyrannies crushed, the era of the common man had
dawned.

Prime Minister Ben Chifley, a former train driver, was
'another Curtin' but stronger, more robust. He continued
the Irish Catholic Labor tradition, one dedicated to removing the abuses of capitalism and replacing them, under
socialim, with opportunities for the betterment of all.

Australia's first Christmas of peace was a grey one: rolling
strikes by communist-led unions shut down electricity in capital cities and produced numerous shortages. The sufferings of the Russian people—as many as 20
million dead—and the triumph of the Red Army had seen the Communist Party
grow in prestige, but as early as 1946 the Labor Party refuted any link between
Marx and democratic (and intensely Catholic) socialism, announcing: 'We declare
the Communist Party to be a danger to Australian democracy and a permanent foe
to the Australian Labor Party.' The suspicion remained among conservatives and
many Labor voters that Labor was 'soft' on communists.

1945: *Nationalising the banks — or trying to*

Chifley moved quickly to reform the structure of Australian society. In 1945 he
made his first move to nationalise the trading banks—the merchant banks—for he
saw them not as a force for good but as institutions motivated solely by profit-making. The Prime Minister, who retained the Treasury portfolio, announced: 'Since the
influence of money is so great, the entire monetary and banking system should be
entrusted to public authorities [i.e. the Commonwealth Bank in its role as the central bank] responsible to Parliament.'

The leader of the opposition, Menzies, denounced the Bill as 'the most revolutionary, unwarranted and un-Australian measure' introduced in Parliament's history, one that would place the flow of money in the hands of a government monopoly. He reminded the House that profit-making was not improper, but indeed the
key to the growth of the British Empire and of Australia itself. The 'battle of the
banks' would dominate domestic politics for the next four years.

Keynesian economics

Even before the war had ended, Australia was one of forty-four nations that sent
representatives to a conference in 1944 at Bretton Woods in the United States to
work out a new economic plan that would, it was hoped, save the world from
more economic depressions and their disastrous consequences by freeing up
world trade. The resulting General Agreement on Tariffs and Trade (GATT, now

369

replaced by the World Trade Organisation), was an attempt to stabilise world currencies; also created were a World Bank to provide long-term loans and an International Monetary Fund to provide funds to cover trade imbalances.

This was one outcome of the endeavours of the influential British economist and government adviser John Maynard Keynes. One of his admirers, the Australian economist H.C. 'Nugget' Coombs, wrote in the opening words of his memoirs: 'The publication in 1936 of John Maynard Keynes' *General Theory of Employment, Interest and Money*, was for me and for many of my generation the most seminal intellectual event of our time … soon I had become convinced that in the Keynesian analysis lay the key to comprehension of the economic system.' Keynes' theories were to provide a basis for the rebuilding of wartime (and mostly war-shattered) economies. His policies had been adopted by the Roosevelt administration in the 1930s to haul the United States out of the Depression and later support the industries of wartime expansion: infusions of government (public) money and loans, government spending even in recession, tight control of wages and prices, regulations to curb excess profits. In the United Kingdom after the Labour Party win in 1945 there emerged a mixture of private companies and 'public' ones (notably when the coal, steel, and railway industries were nationalised). Where Britain and Western Europe followed a program of nationalisation of major industries, the United States imposed regulations while allowing private enterprise to flourish if it could. By the late 1970s governments would realise that

ABOVE:
Surprise visit. Aviator Polly Potter lands in a paddock to say hello to her grazier husband, who is driving sheep on their western New South Wales property in 1946.

OPPOSITE:
Australia's political leaders in the immediate postwar years: In 1950 Ben Chifley (far right), Labor Prime Minister 1945–49, attends a naturalisation ceremony presided over by his successor, the newly elected Liberal leader, Robert Menzies (left). Behind Menzies sits Harold Holt, who succeeded him in 1966; next to Holt is Arthur Calwell, Labor's leader between 1960 and 1967.

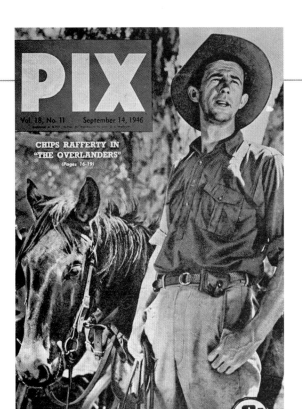

PIX
Vol. 18, No. 11   September 14, 1946

CHIPS RAFFERTY IN
"THE OVERLANDERS"
(Pages 16-19)

6^D

LEFT
The making of the 1946 film *The Overlanders* (based on a famous droving epic of the war years) was seen as the rebirth of the local film industry, but hopes were dashed, for Hollywood dominated cinema production with the escapist fare that audiences liked. Australian film would undergo a rejuvenation in the 1970s.

their economies, despite two decades of astonishing growth and spectacular progress, were stagnating amid inflation and unemployment, strikes, union demands and falling productivity. Keynes predicted that full employment was perhaps impossible to achieve, but governments would attempt to prove him wrong. For thirty-five years after the war they carefully implemented Keynesian economic theory.

For all its tragedy, the Second World War had transformed Australia economically, giving rise to a range of industries that quickly adapted to peacetime production. The war had cost Australia in money terms £2500 million, of which close to half had been paid through revenue, the balance subscribed by loans. Australia emerged from the conflict with no overseas debt; indeed, the United Kingdom owed all the Dominions significant amounts for wartime purchases. Australia, once principally an agricultural economy,

had become a small industrial power, one that looked beyond Britain to America for future guidance.

'Populate or perish!': Postwar immigration

In 1945 Arthur Calwell, Labor's Immigration Minister, signed an agreement with Britain to jointly encourage the migration to Australia of up to 70,000 Britons a year. Faced with a lowered Australian birth rate in the 1930s and 1940s, Calwell planned to increase the population of seven million by one per cent annually by immigration, and announced his campaign simply: 'Populate or perish'. (Nearly sixty years later Australia's population is still boosted by more than 100,000 migrants annually.)

The first postwar immigrants arrived in 1947. British immigrants were soon encouraged to make a new home in Australia by being asked to pay only £10 towards the cost of their passage; the balance was paid by the Australian government. Like all assisted passage 'migrants' (the word was coined by Australians), they were required to stay at least two years. Among the earliest postwar arrivals were those drawn from the 8.5 million 'displaced persons' living in squalor in camps in the Allied Occupation Zones in Germany. They were mainly refugees from an Eastern Europe now ruled by Soviet armies—people from Latvia, Lithuania, Estonia (known collectively as 'Balts') and Poland. Chifley was afraid that they would form closed communities—like Milwaukee in the United States, where the population was almost entirely Polish—but they didn't. They merged into the Australian population, as did those who followed—Czechs, Yugoslavs, Germans and Dutch.

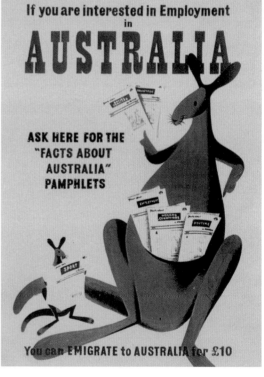

Australians received them coldly, calling them 'reffos' or 'wogs', but postwar migration boosted Australia's population to eight million by 1949 and Calwell asked Australians to welcome the newcomers and to desist from calling them insulting nicknames. He coined for the non-British migrants the name 'New Australians'. Their arrival was to transform Australia within a generation from a dull, inward-looking Anglo-Celtic backwater into a multiracial nation comprising a lively mix of cultures and languages.

In the 1950s, Italians came in their thousands. The first came from the poverty-stricken south, from where entire villages would make the journey to Australia. Italian migration fell after the mid-1960s when conditions in Italy improved. By the end of the 1970s nearly 400,000 Italians had come to Australia, and though a quarter of them returned to Italy or moved on to other countries, those who remained became Australia's largest non-British segment of the population—and its most vivacious.

ABOVE:
Poster to entice British migrants.

TOP:
Immigration Minister Arthur Calwell welcomes migrant number 100,000, a young Briton, in 1949.

ABOVE:
Federal election, 1949:
Voters picking up their
ballot papers.

Second in number were the Yugoslavs, of whom more than 160,000 arrived. Australians thought it strange that many Yugoslavs refused to mix with their brethren; they were unaware of the deep religious and racial divisions among Serbs, Croats, Slovenes and Bosnian Muslims. Next were the Greeks, of whom 150,000 had arrived by the late 1970s. Children of migrants inherited few of the animosities of their parents but much of their nature—other Australians found them outgoing, humorous, generous and ambitious. There is hardly a field of endeavour in which their descendants have not made a mark.

The English assimilated quickly and so did the Dutch; though the British were the slowest to take up 'Australian nationality' after it was introduced in 1949, and the Dutch the quickest. Others were treated without hostility, but with indifference. They in time assimilated successfully and their children showed little interest in their parents' heritage. The immigration policy was one of Labor's boldest successes, but Calwell remained opposed to Asian immigration, believing that Asians would not assimilate into a European environment. History was to prove him wrong.

A brilliant young Polish-born academic who had fought in the Resistance against the Germans arrived from London in 1956 to take up a position as a demographer at the Australian National University in Canberra. He was saddened to see how little the government did to help the newcomers overcome language problems and cultural differences and thought that brilliant talent was being wasted by Australia. Jerzy Zubrzycki would pioneer a government program to teach English-language skills to migrants and become a founder of 'multiculturalism'.

1946: *Labor returned to power*

In 1946 Chifley confirmed that the wartime measure of Commonwealth collection of income tax would remain in force; the states would be funded by the federal

LEFT:
Many critics saw
Borovansky's ballet *Terra
Australis,* first performed
in 1946, as a milestone
in Australia's postwar
cultural rebirth; to play an
Aborigine, dancer Vassilie
Trunoff donned black
leotards and greasepaint.

government after Premiers' Conferences, held annually.
Chifley asked the people by referendum to give Canberra
power to introduce a nationwide health insurance
scheme. Oddly, one-third of voters said No. The powerful
British Medical Association warned Australians of the dangers of the new British 'National Health' scheme. The Chifley government's campaign to eradicate tuberculosis—
the disease born of malnutrition that claimed 28 per cent
of deaths among 20- to 40-year-olds—began with compulsory X-rays of citizens. It was a complete success; the
campaign against the other killer of the young, polio,
would be delayed until the development of the Salk
vaccine in 1955.

Labor won the 1946 elections and in that year the
government formed a new domestic airline, TAA, as a
competitor to ANA; it proved profitable from the first year
of operation. In 1947 the government bought out the
British government's 50 per cent share of Qantas Empire
Airways. The fully nationalised Qantas became Australia's international airline—
'the flag carrier'—and to the distress of the British aircraft industry later adopted
American aircraft.

Overseas telecommunications were nationalised and the federal government
bought shares in the coalmines to partly own the nation's major power source.
The Australian National University was created as a centre for post-graduate
research in all disciplines from the humanities to the sciences, though the foundation stone for the first buildings in Canberra was not laid for another three years.
Chifley appointed an Australian (the Labor politician William McKell) to the post
of Governor-General in 1947 and put an end to the practice of appointing British

ABOVE:
Many Australian artists
continued to leave their
country for London or
New York, where their
talents were better appreciated. George Johnston,
who had won acclaim
as a war correspondent,
moved to London and
then the Greek islands
with his wife Charmian
Clift. They returned to
Australia only in the
mid-1960s.

officers to senior posts in the defence forces by naming the young Rear-Admiral John Collins, captain of the famous wartime cruiser HMAS *Sydney*, as Chief of Naval Staff in 1948. Generally, the defence forces were run down but the navy benefited from the Chifley government's decision to place an order with Britain for an aircraft carrier—HMAS *Sydney* arrived in time to serve off the coast of Korea in 1951—and was followed by a second one, HMAS *Melbourne*, in 1956.

In 1945 an attempt was made to foster a healthy Australian book publishing industry, but in 1947 British publishers regained their monopoly of the old Commonwealth markets and were to retain them until the late 1970s.

Australia offered few opportunities to artists, writers and musicians, the free spirits who create culture. 'The people are beginning to develop and take an interest in books and painting and music,' the novelist Patrick White wrote on returning from war service in 1946; he felt that 'a great deal was about to happen'. But little did happen. Until the late 1960s artists and journalists, actors and playwrights, dancers and composers would continue to leave for London or Europe where work was abundant. Two of Australia's outstanding war correspondents, Chester

Wilmot and Alan Moorehead, remained in England, where they achieved renown for their works of history. Patrick White remained in Australia, a lonely figure even in the small community of local writers. His novel *The Tree of Man* was published in New York in 1955, where it was hailed as a masterpiece, majestic and memorable. More than a dozen English publishers rejected the book, for the author's style was difficult and his view of life seemed bleak, and the English edition that reached Australian a year later was barely reviewed. In 1973 Patrick White would become the first Australian to be awarded the Nobel Prize for literature, but the bitterness of his early rejection never left him.

In 1947 the High Court found parts of Chifley's bank nationalisation legislation to be unconstitutional. Refusing to accept defeat the Prime Minister appealed for a ruling from the Privy Council in London, an odd move by a nationalist to make. The decision would take more than a year to emerge.

1947 was the year that was the high-water mark for Labor governments in Australia, with the ALP seemingly permanently established as the governing party in the states: New South Wales had Labor governments from 1941 to 1965, Queensland from 1932 to 1957, Tasmania from 1934 to 1969, Western Australia from 1933 to 1947. The introduction of a 40-hour working week appeared to set the seal on Australia's quiet emergence from wartime austerity.

BELOW:
Australia played a prominent part in the new United Nations Organisation and in mediation efforts in the Dutch East Indies, where Indonesian nationalists demanded complete independence. Among the Australians meeting Indonesian leaders in Jakarta in September 1947 was Squadron Leader Len Spence (figure shaking hands), who was later killed in action leading the RAAF Mustang squadron in Korea.

Birth of the Holden,
'Australia's national car':
Prime Minister Chifley
at the release of the first
completed vehicle, 1948.

An independent path

In international affairs, Australia's name stood high. In 1947 Britain granted India
and Pakistan independence; both republics remained within the Commonwealth
of Nations. In 1948 H.V. Evatt was elected President of the United Nations' General Assembly by thirty-one votes to twenty; against Britain's wishes, Australia voted
with the United States for the creation of the state of Israel and against continued
Dutch presence in Indonesia (the republic achieved independence in 1949).

Domestically, the production of the first Holden in 1948 gave promise of a car
within the means of all. Manufactured by General Motors, it was the first automobile specifically designed for Australia's harsh road conditions.

In October 1949 the Governor-General pushed the button that launched the
greatest federal initiative of all: the Snowy Mountains Hydro-Electric Scheme. For
a generation men had wondered how they could harness the torrents of the
Snowy River to irrigate land or power electricity. The 'Snowy Scheme' involved
building a series of twelve dams and sixteen tunnels to respectively store and
divert the Snowy's flow into the Murray and Murrumbidgee to increase water
available for irrigation. On its downward passage the water would turn turbines to
provide electricity for south-eastern Australia. Under the scheme's chief, William
'Big Bill' Hudson, a New Zealander, a workforce of 100,000 men, two-thirds of them
New Australians, completed the scheme twenty-five years later, at the cost of more
than a hundred lives. Nearly fifty years after construction began, when the once-
mighty Snowy River had been reduced to a trickle, people questioned the wisdom
of diverting its flow for irrigation.

ABOVE:
Governor-General William McKell opens the Snowy Mountains Hydro-Electric Scheme, October 1949; on the left stands Prime Minister Chifley.

LEFT:
Harnessing the waters of the Snowy River: Khancoban spillway, one of the many in the network that permits the controlled release of water.

Industrial unrest plagued Australia in the last years of Labor's rule. Demonstration outside Parliament House, Sydney, February 1949.

In 1949 the Chifley government extended the franchise to Aborigines but left registration of Aboriginal voters to the states. It was at least a step towards recognising Australia's indigenous peoples as citizens. Calwell's Nationalisation Act, effective from Australia Day 1949, clarified Australians' ambiguous national identity: they were henceforth 'Australian Citizens' while remaining British Subjects. In introducing the Bill, Calwell reaffirmed that Australia, although less British, would remain European. 'Our grandfathers and great-grandfathers laid the foundations of Australia … and made it possible for this democracy to exist as it is today. I respect Asiatic people, I do not regard them as inferior but they have different cultures and history, different living conditions and different religions.'

By the winter of 1949 the Labor government was losing much of its support. Chifley refused to abolish petrol rationing, and communist-led rolling strikes in the coalmines, with miners demanding a 35-hour week, cut power supplies. Chifley sent in the army to dig the coal but the damage done to Labor was deep. The Privy Council's decision against Chifley's bank nationalisation legislation was announced in October 1949. Chifley requested a double-dissolution from the Governor-General, prelude to a new election.

1949: Labor loses power

In December 1949 Labor was swept from power, retaining only forty-seven seats in the new 121-seat House of Representatives. It was the end of the greatest of Australia's reform governments.

'I try to think of the Labor movement as (one) bringing something better to the people, better standards of living, greater happiness for the mass of the people,' Chifley had said in a Sydney speech in June 1949. 'We have a great objective—the light on the hill—which we aim to reach by the betterment of mankind, not only here but anywhere we may give a helping hand.' He died, like Curtin, in Canberra, of a stroke, only two years later, while Australia was celebrating the 50th anniversary of Federation. When informed of Chifley's death, Menzies appeared stricken, as if he had lost a friend.

Chapter 10
The Lucky Country

From 1950 to 1983

NOTHING IN ROBERT MENZIES' LIFE rivalled his satisfaction when he became Prime Minister again in December 1949. Discarded by his party in 1941 as a failed wartime leader incapable of inspiring loyalty among his colleagues or the trust of the people, he became the consummate peacetime leader, and his rule would last sixteen years. In creating a new Liberal Party successfully allied to the Country Party, he also created a political force whose philosophy appealed to Australians tired of socialism, shortages and restrictions.

Some said he was the same old Menzies; others saw in him a more benign, avuncular quality, a maturity. During the rowdy election campaign 'Pig Iron Bob' had responded to hecklers with wit and humour instead of sarcasm and ridicule. Australians craved stability and a prosperity too long denied them. Menzies would give them change but would shape it to his own ends.

1950: The Korean War

The real and imagined threat of world communism dominated the politics of the 1950s. China had fallen to the communists in October 1949, creating fear of a southward thrust towards Australia by her militant millions and Menzies' warnings of 'red' aggression seemed justified when communist North Korea's forces invaded South Korea on 25 June 1950. Two days later the United Nations branded the action blatant aggression and called on member nations to provide forces to expel the invaders. Australia was the first of the United States' allies to respond materially. On 2 July the Australian squadron based in Japan were flying their Mustang fighters over Korea in support of General MacArthur's forces.

Menzies reintroduced national service (six months' military training for 18-year-old youths) and approved use of Australian ground forces. The thousand men of the 3rd Battalion Royal Australian Regiment (3RAR), brought up to wartime strength by volunteers, were airlifted to the front in September 1950. Forming part of the British Commonwealth Brigade, the battalion would achieve a remarkable reputation in the fighting and win a Presidential Citation for its valour in the desperate stand at Kapyong that blunted the Chinese offensive in April 1951. Australian infantry, serving with British troops in the 'Commonwealth Division', remained in action in Korea until the armistice of June 1953.

OPPOSITE, TOP:
Manly Lifesavers and a new acquaintance: an image of the 1960s.

OPPOSITE, BOTTOM:
Father figures of the 1950s: Prime Minister Menzies and Field Marshal Sir William Slim, who served as Governor-General from 1953 to 1960. This photograph was taken when Menzies farewelled Slim on the latter's departure from Canberra airport in 1960; their wives follow in their wake.

ABOVE:
Within eight months of taking office the Menzies government committed Australia to war in Korea. Australia was the only nation apart from the United States to commit all three of her armed services to the conflict. Australian troops clearing a village in Korea in the first year of fighting.

The ANZUS Treaty

Fear of a resurgent Japan was now added to
the threat posed by communist China. On
the urging of the United States both Australia
and New Zealand signed a non-punitive
peace treaty with Japan in 1951, and their
reward was the offer of a defence alliance
with the United States. The ANZUS Treaty
was signed by the three governments in September 1951 (and ratified in Federal Parliament the next year). Fifty years later the
alliance between the United States and Australia was almost unbreakable, with Australia
the site of key US communications bases
that form part of the superpower's web of
early warning systems around the globe.

In many respects Australia remained suspicious of American power and wedded to
Britain and Britishness. The Chifley government had begun the construction of a township at Woomera, 500 kilometres north-west
of Adelaide, for British missile testing and
Menzies was happy to provide more of the
deserts of South Australia and the nation's
offshore islands to the British as testing
grounds for rockets and atomic weapons
after 1952. Australia had the dubious distinction of being the only country in the
Commonwealth to serve as a testing ground
for nuclear weapons for more than a decade.
In 1954 British hydrogen-bomb tests took
place in the Montebellos, and in two months
late in 1956 four nuclear weapons were

exploded at Maralinga in the South Australian desert. 'What the bloody hell is
going on?' the deputy Prime Minister, Arthur Fadden, cabled London when an unexpected wind shift blew an atomic cloud over populated areas. Tests ended in 1957
but testing of radioactive weapons components continued until 1963. A generation later, when it was discovered that radioactivity was still present in the deserted test sites, a Australian royal commission (1984) found that the British government had failed to take adequate precautions to contain radioactivity.

Reverence for Britain and the Crown was perpetuated in the Governors-Gener-
al chosen by Menzies. All were Britons: Field Marshal Viscount Slim, the stalwart
British soldier whose term at Yarralumla lasted from 1953 to 1960; Viscount Dun-
rossil and his successor, Viscount De Lisle VC. Britain's prestige was immense and
all three were respected but only Slim was widely popular. He was a former Manchester schoolteacher who had risen from the ranks and on outback trips he often
stopped for a beer in the public bar with the regulars.

ABOVE:
Australia invented the
'ute', a cut-down sedan
with carrying space in
the rear. GMH launched
the first 'utility model' in
1951.

The communist threat

In March 1951 Menzies' Bill to 'dissolve' the Communist Party was rejected as unconstitutional by the High Court (Mr Justice Latham alone dissenting from the decision of his five colleagues). Walter Murdoch, Australia's homespun philosopher, wrote in the Melbourne *Herald:* 'The Government is asking for a sinister power—the power to punish a man for his beliefs—or for what some spy alleges him to believe. It will be a sad day for Australia if she allows this spiritual poison to get into her system'. Menzies won the elections he called in May 1951 but in the September 1951 referendum Australians voted No to the proposal to outlaw the Communist Party, but only by a slender majority: 50.4 per cent.

A boom begins

The Korean War presented Menzies with a second bonus: a panic purchase of Australia's wool clip by American textile makers providing uniforms for US forces. (American troops, without woollen battledress, were freezing in Korea's harsh winters.) In 1950 Australia's wool sold for 240 pence a pound—'a pound a pound'—a huge leap from the 18 pence a pound of the war years. The wool boom continued in 1951 when it fetched 375 pence a pound, bringing to growers the first real prosperity they had known in nearly twenty years. It came as the rabbit scourge was finally overcome by the introduction of myxomatosis, developed by the CSIRO.

Comic Court Winner Of Melbourne Cup 1950
...non. of Adelaide, returns to scale on Comic Court after winning the Melbourne Cup 1950. Comic Court, aged 5 year by Powerscourt-Witty Maid, and is owned by Messrs. R. A., J. D., and A. J. Lee of Adelaide.

But by 1952 Australia's economy was dangerously overheated. By 1951 Britain's shipping and export industries had recovered from wartime shortages, and imports from both the United Kingdom and the United States were reducing Australia's reserves of sterling and American dollars. To curb inflation Menzies, who never professed to be an expert in economics, introduced a 'horror budget' that increased income tax by 10 per cent, reduced jobs in the growing public service and restricted the outflow of money. In 1952 Menzies announced that the introduction of television would be 'indefinitely postponed'.

Australia was the only Western nation that succumbed to the same anti-communist hysteria that swept the United States between 1948 and 1954. Despite the exposure of an atomic scientist, Fuchs, as a Soviet agent and the defection of two diplomats, Burgess and Maclean, to Moscow in 1951, Britain remained blithely immune to witch hunts, though some explanation for this is found in Britain's strong libel laws and its long tolerance of homosexuals in the higher reaches of diplomacy and the civil service. In 1951 Australian church leaders issued a 'Call to the People' reminding them to fight 'the mortal enemies of mankind' by advancing their moral standards, and to 'Fear God, Honour the King'. In 1952 Liberal backbencher William Wentworth accused two respected writers, Vance Palmer and Flora Eldershaw, of having had associations with the Communist Party; an ALP member, Stan Keon, told Parliament that the Australian National University had become 'a nest of communists'. When Frank Hardy was unsuccessfully prosecuted for criminal libel after publication in 1950 of his novel *Power Without Glory* (whose central character bore an uncanny resemblance to the corrupt Melbourne figure John Wren) many suspected that the prosecution was launched because Hardy was a communist, a 'dangerous subversive'.

ABOVE:

The visit to Australia of Queen Elizabeth II and her husband the Duke of Edinburgh in 1954 was the first made by a reigning British monarch. The royal party photographed during their visit to Parliament House, Canberra.

SOVIET SPY RING DIRECTED FROM CANBERRA, SAYS MENZIES

Red envoy

The Argus

FOUNDED 1846

WEDNESDAY APRIL 14 1954
Telephone FO411 Price 4d
Registered at the G.P.O. Melb. for transmission by post as a newspaper.

WEATHER BUREAU: Today: Cooler. Cloudy. Some light rain.

Australians named by Embassy fugitive

GRANTED ASYLUM

Canberra, Tuesday

A SPY RING, involving the Russian Embassy in Canberra, secret Russian agents and Australian ... by Mr. Menzies, Prime ... tonight

City's trams stopped indefinitely

MELBOURNE will be without trams and tramway buses indefinitely. Tramway workers yesterday voted overwhelmingly in favor of a strike until their terms are met by the Tramways Board.

And Mr. Risson, Tram Board chairman, said last night: "There will be no compromise.

"To settle this dispute the men must come back and agree to abide by the award," he said.

LATE NEWS

JAP CHECK ON WATER

1954: Royal visit and Russian spies

The accession in 1952 of a new monarch, Elizabeth II, renewed Australia's fascination with the royal family. The coronation in 1953 and the visit to Australia of the Queen and her husband the Duke of Edinburgh early in 1954 were affirmation of Australia's wild affection for the monarchy. A fortnight after the Queen's departure Prime Minister Menzies announced in Parliament (on 14 April 1954) that that an official of the Soviet embassy in Canberra, Vladimir Petrov, had asked for political asylum and had produced proof of a Soviet spy ring in Australia. One week later Petrov's wife was dragged protesting onto an aircraft at Mascot by two Soviet couriers charged with escorting her to Moscow. On Menzies' order the couriers were overpowered when the aircraft landed at Darwin and Mrs Petrov joined her husband as the nation's two newest migrants.

On 30 April Menzies—who had been accused of 'manipulating' the announcement of Petrov's defection to improve the Liberals' chances in the May elections—informed the House that a royal commission had been appointed to investigate Petrov's assertions. In the elections of May 1954 the Menzies government was returned to power. The royal commission failed to find or name any traitors but discovered that classified information had been leaked to the Soviets. Labor's bitter denunciation of Menzies' tactics did it electoral harm.

ABOVE:
This dramatic photograph shows Petrov's wife being dragged by Soviet agents to a plane for Moscow.

TOP:
The Petrov Affair burst on Australia soon after the end of the royal visit.

1954: The Labor split

Labor was in the process of disintegrating, not from pressure by communist-leaning factions but from extreme anti-communist groups within the party. The Catholic Industrial Group, led by the Melbourne Catholic intellectual B.A. Santamaria and supported publicly by Archbishop Mannix, had effectively supplanted communist leaders in numerous unions, but party leader H.V. Evatt saw their influence as dangerous to Labor itself. At the ALP national conference held in Hobart in March 1955, a majority of members voted to withdraw support from the 'Groupers'—the Industrial Movement. 'An outside organisation has no right to subvert the Labor Party and use it to force its policies on the people,' Evatt announced.

The purge was swift: in one night the left-dominated Victorian branch expelled 104 members. The result was catastrophic for the Australian Labor Party. One month later the Catholic bishops collectively condemned Labor for its action; Evatt responded with name-calling. The anti-communist right-wing Labor groups gradually coalesced into a new party, the Democratic Labor Party (DLP). The 'Labor Split' effectively prevented the ALP winning office for another seventeen years, for DLP preferences automatically went to the conservatives.

1956: The coming of television

Weary of years of scare-mongering about the 'Reds' and political squabbling, Australians looked forward in 1956 to the Olympic Games, due to open in Melbourne in November, and to the coming of television. The medium arrived late in Australia. The first local broadcast was made in 1934 but the coming of war delayed all progress. The Chifley Labor government had pledged in 1949 to

ABOVE:
Menzies held in great respect Vice-Admiral Sir John Collins, who had commanded HMAS *Sydney* brilliantly in the Mediterranean battles of 1940 and survived severe wounds in the battles off the Philippines.
Here Collins, long-term Chief of Naval Staff, welcomes the visiting Fleet Admiral 'Bull' Halsey, USN, during Coral Sea week in 1954.
Australia's Navy Minster—and future Prime Minister—William McMahon stands on the left.

BELOW:
Australian family, early 1960s. Modernism adapted for Australian conditions.

ABOVE:
In the Olympic Games held in Melbourne in 1956 sprinter John Landy, who had become the second athlete to break the four-minute mile in 1954, was given the honour of reading the oath at the opening ceremony.
Landy later became Governor of his home State, Victoria.
Long-distance champion Ron Clarke is in the foreground in this picture with John Landy behind.

introduce television, but the innovation met powerful opposition from newspaper and radio proprietors, who lobbied successfully for its introduction to be postponed. In 1955, however, the Commonwealth government authorised two commercial stations to operate alongside the national broadcaster, the ABC, in major cities. TCN 9 began broadcasting in Sydney on 16 September 1956, and by 1969, 98 per cent of Australians were able to view television on a nationwide network of stations.

The Olympic Games of 1956 were a triumph for Australian athletes—the nation won thirty-five medals, thirteen of them gold—but coverage of the sports on television was interrupted by news bulletins showing grim footage of more fighting—this time in Egypt and Hungary.

Suez and Hungary, 1956

The death of Stalin in 1953 had removed a dark and menacing shadow from the world. He had grown increasingly unstable and cold-blooded and history would show him to have been even more inhuman than Hitler—his tyrannical regime killed as many as 18 million Soviet citizens. Under his successor, Khrushchev, a definite 'thaw' occurred in the Cold War, beginning with Khrushchev's public denunciation of Stalin's crimes early in 1956. In January 1956 Menzies had won his third election victory in seven years.

ABOVE:
Employment for all:
Holden assembly line,
late 1950s.

In July 1956 Egypt suddenly nationalised the Anglo-French 'Suez Canal Company', which Britain's Prime Minister Eden regarded as a flouting of international agreements. He called on the Commonwealth's elder statesman Robert Menzies to mediate with Egypt's President Nasser. Their meeting in Cairo was not a success. Nasser refused to pass on control of the canal to an international body and was understandably irritated when Menzies remonstrated with him and called him 'my boy'.

Early in 1956 riots broke out in Poland and then in Hungary, where the Stalinist government was replaced by a moderate one in October 1956 and Soviet forces began to leave Budapest. Their tanks returned a week later, brutally crushing the freedom fighters, and the world paid little attention because British and French forces had landed at the mouth of the Suez on 31 October to recover it by force and bring down Nasser if possible, while Israeli forces struck across the Sinai Desert to the east bank of the canal. Menzies approved the Anglo-French invasion as a justified reaction but his foreign minister Richard Casey was appalled, as were the United Nations and Britain's greatest ally, the United States, which had been kept in the dark. The fighting was quickly terminated and British and French forces were withdrawn in humiliating fashion. Nasser became the unofficial leader of an Arab world that became stridently nationalist, Eden was forced to resign on grounds of 'ill health' (and was replaced by Harold Macmillan), the West's influence in the Middle East was damaged beyond repair, and the canal, filled with sunken Egyptian blockships, was unusable for years. The Suez crisis was a turning point in twentieth-century history.

That year, 1956, marked the climax of the first period of the Cold War. The following ten years would be marked by easing world tensions and, in Australia, by peaceful, undisturbed growth.

1958: Economic superplan

In elections held in December 1958 the Menzies government was again returned to power. No previous prime minister had won four elections in succession. Menzies had little interest in economics, and he was happy to defer to his new deputy

RIGHT:
Country children regularly went to the coast for their annual holidays; for many, seeing the ocean for the first time was a shock.

BELOW:
The 1950s saw the end of the golden age of radio, which had provided a constant diet of children's serials, quiz shows, variety shows, dramas and comedies. Members of the popular ABC radio program *The Argonauts.*

Prime Minister, John McEwen, who had been Minister for Trade since 1956 and took over from Fadden as Country Party leader in 1958.

'Black Jack' McEwen was a formidable man. He came from Protestant Scotch-Irish stock. As a soldier settler after 1919 he had known hunger and privation during his years on the land; this experience had forced him into Country Party politics. His belief in Australia was immense. As Minister for Trade and Industry (he took on this added portfolio in 1958) until 1971, McEwen influenced Australia's rate of economic growth for a quarter of a century. He envisaged an Australia rich in untapped natural resources and completely self-sufficient. He initiated wider trade with Japan, welcoming Japan's Prime Minister to Australia on an official visit; it aroused great hostility among those unable to forget the horrors of the war.

Under McEwen, manufacturing growth would provide full employment, and high wages would be maintained by protective tariffs on imports, even if Australian-made goods were as a result more expensive than goods manufactured overseas. By 1960, nine automobile manufacturing plants were established in Australia, supplied by more than 300 thriving parts-manufacturing businesses. Many of the consumer goods people demanded were manufactured here under licence—television sets, for example. Australians bought cars readily but at a price twice that of American vehicles. The market was small, but Australians' capacity to pay was high. By the end of the 1960s Australians owned four million cars (and three million television sets)—one of the highest levels of vehicle ownership in the Western world.

Local manufacturers could apply for tariffs or duties to be imposed on imported items that threatened their market share. Few profits were ploughed back into research and development (R&D) or in modernising plant. Twenty years later, when a generally free market economy was the world norm, this protectionist policy would leave Australia unable to compete in manufacturing and reliant on

They keep Australia strong

primary produce and minerals to correct a balance of payments deficit of calamitous proportions. A committee was appointed in 1962 to look into the nation's economic affairs. The resulting Vernon Report, which recommended that politicians abdicate economic planning in favour of experts, was rejected by Menzies in 1965.

ABOVE:
Services recruiting poster, 1950s.

The 1950s

The Menzies years would be remembered as an era of material progress and political and cultural stagnation. Australians had a keen interest in the outside world—in the 1950s many young Australians sailed overseas to live for two or three years in England and Europe ('working holidays') before returning to 'settle down' permanently in suburban life. This generation of innocents is immortalised in the monologues of one of its members, the Melbourne satirist Barry Humphries, who saw comic aspects in the great ordinariness of Australians.

Few imagined a world in which jet airliners could carry them to London in little more than twenty-four hours. In 1958 Qantas initiated its round the world service and the coming of Boeing jets in 1960 brought faster journeys to Europe and low air fares within the reach of most Australians, ending the era of sea travel.

The Menzies government adopted a paternalistic foreign policy in Asia. The Colombo Plan of 1950, by which the Commonwealth's developed countries pledged to train students from the newly emergent nations and provide material aid to them as a counterweight to communism, was very much the initiative of Australia's Minister for External Affairs, Percy Spender. His successor, Richard Casey, showed an unexpected openness and interest in Australia's Asian neighbours: a wartime period as Governor of Bengal had transformed Casey's once lofty view of imperialism.

...ersonality, Graham Kennedy, excelled as host of the long-running late-night ...n variety show *In Melbourne Tonight*.

"It is indeed a lovely shirt sir!"

ABOVE:
Australia prided itself on manufacturing nearly everything its people needed. Men's shirts came in one colour: white. Few realised that the cost of goods' production made them far more expensive than items produced overseas, but in an age of high wages few questioned the wisdom of the economic planners.

...mbert's novel *The ...Thousand Thieves,* ...ed in 1951, was ...in tribute to the ...the 9th Division. ...Scottish writer ...ry Millington found ...ference in mood ...n Australia's outback ...cities, just a stultify-...eness, and summed ...mpressions in her ...*Nation of Trees*

a nation of trees | australian rites
rosemary millington
New Authors Limite[d]

Eric Lambert
THE TWENTY THOUSAND THIEVES

Australians of the 1950s lived simply and frugally. This was the golden age of radio: most families listened nightly to serials, dramas, musical shows, comedies and quizzes and radio 'stars' became household names. Every weekend the 'kids' in the street trudged off to the pictures—'the Saturday arvo flicks'—or built billy carts in their back yards, just as their parents had done. In many ways the 1950s was the last age of innocence; for the young, a drowsy decade disturbed only by the arrival of rock'n'roll in 1955 and television in 1956, harbingers of a new and noisy age of 'mass culture'. Half a century later Australians would be more critical of the decade that history forgot. It was a repressed era, and the level of education was poor. Much of schooling was brutish and in schools and homes run by both Protestants and Catholics some youngsters suffered abuse that in some cases was sexual—practices considered intolerable nowadays.

The outside world had little interest in Australia. The few celebrities who arrived in the country were usually asked bluntly by journalists at airports why had they come—and did they like Australia? Some visitors passing through airline terminals noticed that only two passenger airlines appeared to be operating—ANA and its counterpart TAA. (Qantas was restricted to overseas routes.) In 1952 the Menzies government introduced its 'two airlines policy' that lasted, with modifications, until 1990: only two carriers were given permission to service the main inter-capital routes, charging identical fares.

In 1952 also, a Scottish journalist, John Douglas Pringle, who had been trained on the great *Manchester Guardian* newspaper, arrived in Sydney to begin work with the Fairfax press. Six years later he published *Australian Accent*, one of the most perceptive portraits of the Australia of the late 1950s. He found Sydney a city of rare beauty—'it is beautiful, far more beautiful, indeed, than I had ever imagined'. On the drive to Canberra he saw the Australian bush for the first time. 'I fell in love with it,' he wrote. 'It is not easy to describe its charm though the different kinds of gum trees have an obvious beauty. I think it is partly the great swing and sweep of

ABOVE:
Sidney Nolan executed many of the striking cover illustrations for his friend Patrick White's novels. Axel Poignant took this photograph when White (right) visited Nolan in his studio in 1963. The two men later had a bitter falling out.

ABOVE:
White's novel *Voss*, which was published in 1957 to critical acclaim but public indifference.

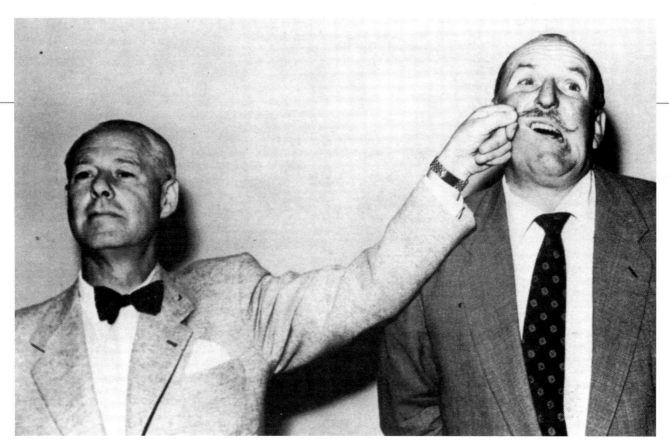

Popular comperes of radio shows Jack Davey (left) and Bob Dyer made the transition to television on its beginning in 1956 and continued their mock feud on—and off—camera.

the countryside; the wide horizons, the marching trees, the mountain ranges receding in the distance, and always the hard, clear edge to everything and the brilliant light.'

'Canberra itself seems very odd,' he wrote. 'A few public buildings with a rather startled look as though they were surprised to be there at all.' Of Menzies he wrote:

He is an impressive man, still handsome though too fat, with an obvious but easy intellectual brilliance that makes him outstanding in this country. He was very bitter—and very amusing—about the lot of a Prime Minister in Australia—badgered by the press, always expected to hob nob with every politician, and hampered by inefficient advisers and staffs … 'Here', he said, 'a Prime Minister was expected to think of the idea, draft the report, persuade the cabinet, bully his party, push it through Parliament and act as chief publicity officer in the country.'

'He told good stories about Churchill who, he said, now treats him very nearly as an equal,' Pringle wrote. 'I did not have a chance to speak to many other Ministers. MacMahon (is) bright but I think a lightweight; McEwen the strongest and most impressive.' The journalist was impressed also by the leader of the Opposition, Evatt—'slow, kindly, very intelligent' but 'cordially disliked and distrusted by everyone, including his own party'.

'A land without culture'

The visitor found Australians healthy and loud, the menfolk rough, and all Australians victims of a glorious climate. The nation seemed to lack a culture, a soul. 'If culture is judged by the general standard of education and the arts among the population, it must be said that Australia has little or none. Everything', Pringle wrote, 'seems to discourage intellectual effort.'

In 1950 the academic A.A. Phillips had used the term 'cultural cringe' in a *Meanjin* article to describe Australians' almost Pavlovian subservience to overseas models and lack of pride in its own achievements. In 1958 the Sydney publisher

Angus & Robertson published the first edition of the multi-volume *Australian Encyclopaedia* since 1926. It was a magnificent production but too few Australians bought it and the cost of its printing and many years of preparation were not recovered. In the same year, when the *Bulletin* was still being published in the layout of the 1880s, two new journals, *Nation* and *Observer* first appeared. Modelled on the bright London journals of comment, they were published and funded by journalists who wished only to enhance the quality of discussion in Australian society. They too had to struggle for a readership. Creative Australians continued to leave for the great city of London, where talent was more quickly recognised. The poet and critic Peter Porter left Queensland for England in 1951, explaining later that he wanted to escape Australia's philistinism and physicality. The writers Clive James and Phillip Knightley departed ten years later, and also achieved renown.

Most Australian households bought magazines like *Australian Women's Weekly*, which had grown from a circulation of 550 000 in 1942 to more than 800 000 in 1959—a publishing phenomenon in a country of only nine million people; and men often surreptitiously read the 'barber shop' monthlies, *Pix*, *People* and *Australasian Post* (or *Man*, the pale imitation of the American *Esquire*). On the subject of art, many Australian families bought prints of the paintings of the Aboriginal artist Albert Namatjira, of the Aranda people, who brilliantly painted landscapes of central Australia in the European style. In 1957 Namatjira became the first Aborigine to be made an 'honorary Australian citizen', but he continued to live at the Hermannsburg mission near Alice Springs. He was convicted of supplying liquor to relatives in 1957 and, as providing alcohol to Aborigines was prohibited, he was sentenced to a short period in gaol. His spirit was broken and he died of a stroke in 1959.

ABOVE:

In an incongruous meeting in 1956 Australia's best-known Aborigine, the painter Albert Namatjira, is seen (left) with Cardinal Gilroy of Sydney. Namatjira finds it hard to show much interest in his friend Frank Clune's latest book, a travelogue on New Zealand.

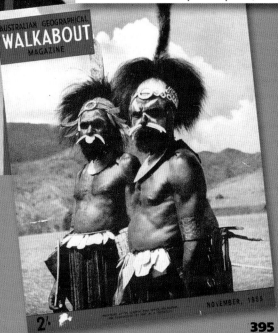

Above & Right:
Images of the 1950s from magazines of the time: Stamina 'self-supporting' trousers were high fashion for men; 'a hostie', the image of glamour was the widely reproduced advertising icon of TAA; the Australian travel magazine Walkabout tried to stimulate tourist interest in Papua New Guinea, where Australians had fought bitter battles (few found the land welcoming); boxed chocolates were promoted as the way to a girl's heart.

LEFT:
Far from the cities:
An Australian Inland Mission padre visits stockmen in the Northern Territory. Within two decades motorbikes and even helicopters would be used to help muster cattle herds in the outback.

Stagnating politics

State politics stagnated during the 1950s. In South Australia Sir Thomas Playford served as Premier of a conservative government that lasted from 1937 to 1965, a period in power far exceeding Menzies' sixteen years. On the drive to his office in Adelaide Playford often gave a lift to a near neighbour, a young Labor leader named Don Dunstan, who would later become a reformist premier of the state. In 1955 the NSW Cahill Labor government became the first after Queensland's to abolish the death penalty (Victoria followed only in 1975, eight years after the controversial hanging of Ronald Ryan in 1967) and it made a long-delayed move in 1958 to end sexual inequality by introducing equal pay. Women received only 60 per cent of the pay of a male doing the equivalent job, but pay for women would be increased 5 per cent per annum until parity was reached. 'The Bill is very simple,' the minister, Abe Landa, announced in State Parliament. 'It confers simple justice on the womenfolk of this state. Australia, a new world country bursting with the life of new ideas, began this century well by giving women political equality with men in 1902. Only now, after more than 50 years of gross social injustice, are we giving them wage justice.'

OPPOSITE, TOP:
Primary schoolchildren in Sydney, early 1960s.

OPPOSITE, BELOW:
In 1956 when this photograph was taken, Iron Monarch in South Australia was BHP's greatest source of iron ore and the true extent of the nation's mineral wealth was as yet undiscovered.

The Sydney Opera House

The new government-funded Elizabethan Theatre Trust had presented its first productions in 1956, when it staged Ray Lawler's play *Summer of the Seventeenth Doll*, and announced plans to create both an Australian ballet and an opera company. But Sydney's people were amused when Premier Cahill announced in 1955 that the tram sheds occupying the Fort Macquarie buildings on Bennelong Point would be demolished to provide the site for Australia's first Opera House (which would include concert halls for symphony performances) and the world's finest architects would be asked to submit designs. Public fascination in the grandiose project quickened in 1957 when Cahill announced that a winner had been chosen from 233 designs received. The successful design was from a 38-year-old Danish architect, Joern Utzen, and his design looked like a giant clipper with the wind

Lee Gordon presents

Bill HALEY
AND HIS COMETS
IN
The "BIG SHOW"

LA VERN BAKER

JOE TURNER

FREDDIE BELL and THE BELLBOYS

1st Australian Tour 1957

LEFT:
In the late 1950s Australia's quiet complacency was shaken by the coming of rock 'n' roll and the emergence of first generation of 'teenagers'.
One of the top performers was Johnny O'Keefe, seen in a 1970s photograph under a portrait of Elvis Presley, beside singer Jade Hurley.

filling its sails; to others it looked like a pile of lobster shells. Its cost was budgeted at £3.5 million ($7 million). The Sydney Opera House was completed only in 1973, long after the architect had walked off the site in dismay at the modifications made to his concept. It cost $100 million (the bulk of this was raised through lotteries) but has been acclaimed as one of the greatest buildings in the world—one without precedent and without imitators.

In 1958 an 'entry permit' replaced the absurd dictation test that had restricted immigration of non-British migrants and—in the words of the then Immigration Minister—'caused much resentment outside Australia, and has tarnished our good name in the eyes of the world'. The change did not open the gates to Asia; as late as 1965 there were barely 25,000 Asians in the Commonwealth, and half of them were Colombo Plan students studying on temporary residency visas.

The 1960s: bright dawn of a new Australia

The economy, again overheating, was cooled down by a sudden 'credit squeeze' and the December 1961 elections saw the Menzies government retain office with only a one-seat majority. But boom years were coming. In 1961 immense iron-ore deposits were found in the Pilbara region of Western Australia, and export restrictions on Australia's minerals were lifted in 1961. Oil was discovered at Moonie, in Queensland. Japan was becoming the major purchaser of Australia's mineral output and the balance of trade was substantially in Australia's favour.

In the early 1960s Australia was changing and it would soon achieve for the first time since the gold rush of the 1850s a kind of glamour in the eyes of the world. Small events insignificant at the time would be seen by historians as important strides towards a more modern society. In 1960 a play called *The One Day of the Year* was staged in Adelaide. It had been considered by the new Adelaide Festival of the Arts but rejected by the board, who were shocked by its theme—a young man's contempt for his father's reverence for Anzac Day, which many of the younger generation saw as a boozy celebration of mateship. The play's author, Alan Seymour, left for London in 1961 and became a successful writer there. In that year the moribund *Bulletin* was converted by its new owners, the Packers, into a weekly news magazine similar to the American *Time* and *Newsweek*. Until December 1960 the slogan 'Australia for the White Man' had been carried on its masthead and until 1961 the White Australia policy remained part of the Labor Party's platform.

In London, Australians were flattered when an exhibition of their painters at the Whitechapel Gallery in 1961 was acclaimed as the advent of an exciting and unique school of painting. England's discovery of Australian artists—Sidney Nolan and Russell Drysdale in particular—was long overdue. In the same year the Sydney publishers Ure Smith revived their famous quarterly journal devoted to Australian art, *Art and Australia*; its success was assured by the attention its contributors paid to abstract art and sculpture and by the number of galleries that advertised in its pages. Also in 1961 the ABC began broadcasting a weekly hour-long television program that explored contentious issues. *Four Corners* was modelled on the BBC Panorama program. More than forty years later it is still broadcast, the winner of more awards for excellence than any other Australian television program. In 1962 historian C.M.H. Clark published the first volume of his huge work *A History of Australia*. It would stretch to six volumes over the next twenty-five years and though few Australians read it through, many of them bought it, flattered that their country, which had such a short history, was considered worthy of such a majestic opus.

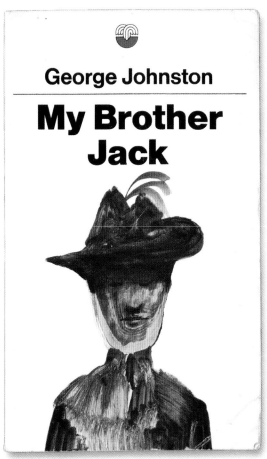

George Johnston

My Brother Jack

Things were changing, and none more dramatically than the skylines of the major cities. In 1962 Sydney's first skyscraper of shining glass—the AMP building—rose above the Victorian-era buildings at Circular Quay. Previously buildings of this height had been forbidden by local councils. Soon office towers arose, each one taller than its neighbours, and cities reverberated to the hammering of pneumatic drills.

British immigrants tended to settle principally in Western Australia and in South Australia (many of them in the new satellite city of Elizabeth), but Sydney attracted the young, the ambitious, the transient. It had always been the nation's seaport, fascinating, fast-paced, in parts sleazy, where anything could be bought. In 1962 the visiting

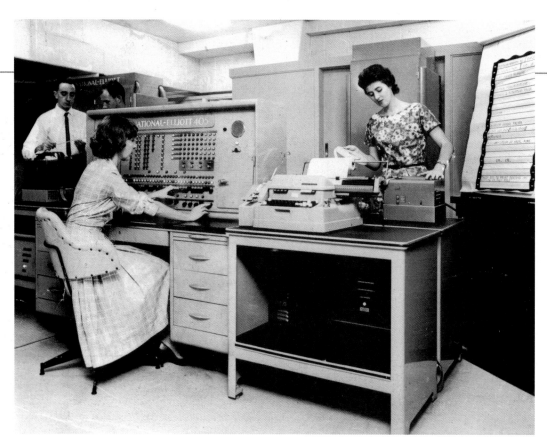

British journalist James Morris described Sydney as little more than 'a harbour sur-rounded by suburbs—its origins unsavoury, its temper coarse, its organization slip-shod'. Further visits softened his harsh early impressions and more than twenty years later, as Jan Morris, the same author wrote a rapturous book on Sydney, describing it as 'by general consent, one of the world's great cities'. Visitors to Canberra late in 1963 were astonished to see that a lake had appeared as if by magic—the waters of the Molonglo had been released and, as the development of the federal capital was one of Menzies' enthusiasms, the dull township soon took on a futuristic look, with government buildings of bold design appearing behind avenues of trees.

Lifestyles were changing. By the early 1960s cities were sprawling outward into oceans of suburbs lapping the main roads. Dry bushland was bulldozed, sub-divid-ed and landscaped to provide young couples with the Australian dream—a quar-ter-acre block with their own home and garden. Most families by the 1960s had their own car (half the cars sold were Holdens) and this new mobility saw roads clogged on weekends with vehicles heading for the beaches or the bush. The beaches became the focus of teenage life and culture, the place where the sexes discovered each other. (Teenage girls had access to the contraceptive pill by the mid-1960s.) Newcomers and old critics of a sexually repressed society saw in the young a fresh, gloriously healthy Australia emerging, a generation careless and disrespectful of their parents' values but wonderfully free of bigotry. The great change born of affluence had come to Australia.

In the elections of 30 November 1963—held just one week after the assassina-tion of the young American President John Kennedy—Menzies was again returned to power, this time with an increased majority.

The economy was thriving. In 1964 the *Financial Times* of London described Australia as having 'the healthiest economy in the world' and *Time* magazine devoted a special issue to 'The New Australia.'

ABOVE:
By the mid-1960s many city offices were installing computers. Development of the silicon chip (invent-ed in 1958 but developed to extraordinary capacity nearly two decades later) later made it possible to shrink the size of comput-ers like this to models smaller than a television set.

ABOVE:
Surf Life Savers carnival on Manly Beach, early 1960s. This photograph was taken at almost the same spot as that on page 266.

The new universities

In 1961 Menzies, using federal funds, extended state aid to private schools, including church schools, but in his retirement he would say that his proudest achievement was federal spending on universities. The Murray Report of 1957 informed the government that Australia's existing state-funded universities were insufficient. Menzies made federal funding available—Monash University, which opened in 1961, was the first of the new tertiary institutions. Increased state government funding of education was forced by the pressure of the postwar baby boom, but few children were progressing to their final year in overcrowded schools. 'We consider that a "survival rate" of 16 per cent to the final year of the secondary school, if continued, is likely to deprive the community of sufficiently educated young people,' the NSW Wyndham Committee observed in 1957. An extra year was added to schooling in 1962.

In the late 1960s an intelligent, educated body of university undergraduates would become the conscience of Australia, leading opposition to the Vietnam War.

1964: 'The Lucky Country'

So far Australia's writers had remained silent. Few made a living from their pen, and the book market was dominated by British publishers who were pleased that Australians bought so many books by British writers—and by Australian writers living overseas such as the novelists Catherine Gaskin, Jon Cleary, Charmian Clift and her husband George Johnston. Other writers living overseas and celebrated a generation later were then almost unknown except by critics: among them Christina Stead and Shirley Hazzard. As late as the 1970s, 90 per cent of the books Australians read were imported titles. But in 1964 the British company Collins published George Johnston's novel *My Brother Jack*, which drew heavily on the author's early years in prewar Melbourne, and the author returned to Australia for the

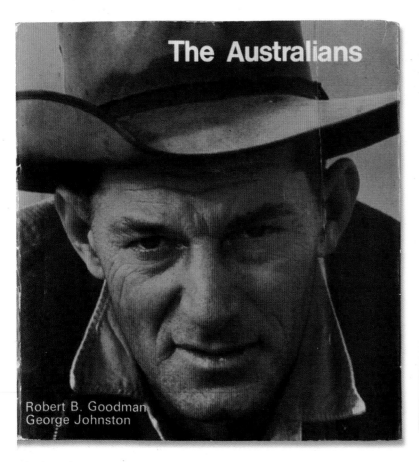

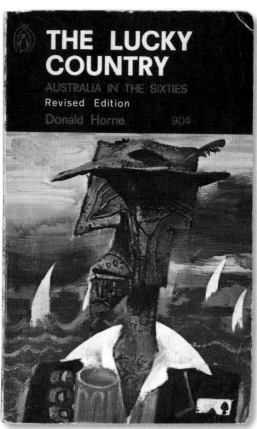

launch. The book, with its jacket showing a Sidney Nolan painting of a digger, was a success. In the same year, Penguin Books in Australia published a paperback destined to be the non-fiction bestseller since the war: *The Lucky Country* by Donald Horne, a mordant look at the newly prosperous nation. Its title was intended to be ironic, for the author saw Australia as a country enjoying a run of luck—'a first rate country run by second rate people'. Australians took the title to be complimentary and bought the book in the thousands.

Also in 1964 a television show modelled on the satirical BBC program *This Was the Week That Was* was broadcast—*The Mavis Bramston Show*, in which the stars poked sly fun at Australian personalities, events and institutions. Previous Australian television humour had come straight from the 'pie in the face' school of comedy— or in men dressing up as women, which always got a laugh—but viewers enjoyed the sharp satire. And in Brisbane a small schoolbook publisher published a book of poems by an Aboriginal woman writer. *We Are Going* seemed to be a lament for a disappearing race. Its author, Kath Walker, would later adopt her people's name, Oodgeroo Noonuccal.

In 1965 Australians bought thousands of copies of a slim book that mocked their diction—*Let Stalk Strine* ('strine' for 'Let's Talk Australian'). If the ability to laugh at oneself is the hallmark of a sense of humour, Australians were richly endowed with it.

1965: Giant strides forward

In 1965 two lively Adelaide identities, the lecturer and writer Geoffrey Dutton (a former RAAF fighter pilot) and the poet and bookseller Max Harris, founded a new publishing house in Melbourne to bring out something more serious: an all-Australian paperback series, which they named Sun Books. One of their first titles was Geoffrey Blainey's *The Tyranny of Distance*, which traced the influence of

ABOVE, LEFT:
By the mid-1960s Australia was one of the most envied countries in the world—a booming economy, widespread prosperity, and a relaxed lifestyle attracted immigrants and an increasing number of tourist. The flattering picture book *The Australians*, published in 1965, sold an unprecedented 35,000 copies in its first three days and was still selling ten years later.

ABOVE, RIGHT:
Donald Horne's lively review of Australia's society and mores, published in 1964, was critical but became a surprise bestseller and gave Australia a new name — 'The Lucky Country' (cover painting by Albert Tucker).

NOT REGISTERED FOR TRANSMISSION AT THE G.P.O.

(the Bureaucratic Alfs have been pondering our application for 18 months now)

No. 20, 1965: 2/-

OZ

CIRCULATION: 30,000.

GIVE US YOUR VIETNAM LINE AGAIN, BOB

THE BIG JOKE

ABOVE:
Prime Minister Menzies committed Australian troops to fight in Vietnam in 1965 on the request of the Americans. Criticism of his decision grew immediately, for many observers described the conflict as a civil war, not a trial between Communism and democracy.
The satirical monthly *Oz* shows Britain's Prime Minister Wilson and Canada's Prime Minster Pearson as being highly amused by Menzies' reasoning.

distance from Europe on Australia's development. They were astonished to see a work of history become a bestseller. Australians were beginning to show an interest in their own country and this interest would become a fascination and then an obsession.

In 1966 appeared Craig McGregor's *Profile of Australia* (modelled to some extent on the American John Gunther's books of reportage) and also a handsome pictorial book filled with colour plates, *The Australians*, which broke all Australian sales records. The volume (planned by the American photographer, written by the Australian George Johnston and designed by an Englishman) was immensely flattering to Australians and its success spawned dozens of highly illustrated imitations, launching a boom in books about Australia. They were printed cheaply in Asia, for Australian printing plants were as outmoded as much of its industry. In 1969 John Gunther himself visited Australia, which he now thought interesting enough to merit an *Inside Australia* book (his volume was published in 1972). And in 1966 also an ambitious work of more limited interest but enduring importance appeared—the first volume of *The Australian Dictionary of Biography*, published by Melbourne University Press. Many Australians doubted whether there were enough prominent figures to fill a second volume but a quarter of a century later the ADB had reached fifteen volumes, with more to come.

In inner suburban Sydney and Melbourne the terraces once occupied by workers and long the haunt of artists were bought up by young couples, and restored and 'gentrified' (often this process took little more than a coat of white paint). There was appearing an alternative to the double-fronted brick veneer home in remote outer suburbs where so many dreams had died and marriages failed.

Not least among visitors were a pop group called the Beatles, who spoke in the heavy accents of Midlands England but produced a music that was universal in appeal. On their arrival in Australia in 1964 the foursome were mobbed in cities by hysterical teenagers. Popular culture, riding on an ocean of sound, had arrived, and was here to stay.

The new Asia

Even turbulent South-East Asia seemed to be more stable. No sooner had the bulk of the Australian troops returned from Korea after the 1953 ceasefire than Menzies announced that Australian forces would form part of a 'British Commonwealth Strategic Reserve' based with British and New Zealand units in Malaya, where they would also help fight the last of the communist insurgents. An Australian battalion arrived in Penang in 1955, and was soon joined by three RAAF squadrons based at Butterworth. RAN ships would also serve on patrol there. Malaya achieved independence from Britain in 1957 and in 1960 the 'emergency' was declared at an end.

In 1959 the Menzies government ended national service. Since 1951 it had put more than 250,000 young Australians through six months of military service but most of the 'Nashos' would look back on their days as soldiers with great amusement. With no foreseeable threat to Australia's security the government found the cost of training them prohibitive.

SEATO

After the French admitted defeat in June 1954 following the fall of their fortress of Dien Bien Phu in northern Vietnam, a form of peace had been brokered at Geneva by which Vietnam was to be divided along the 17th parallel, with the victorious Communist regime in the North, and a 'Republic of Vietnam', backed by the West, in the south. A plebiscite was to be held in two years' time to decide whether both Vietnams would be united under a government of their own choosing. Unfortunately South Vietnam's rulers were as corrupt as the North Vietnam's were ruthless.

Alarm at the forward march of communism resulted in the creation of the South-East Asian Treaty Organisation in September 1954, when delegates from the United States, the United Kingdom, France, Australia, New Zealand, Thailand, Pakistan and the Philippines signed a mutual assistance pact in Manila. It was modelled on NATO, the West's defensive shield in Europe, but SEATO remained a paper tiger, lacking a central military command. Its first challenge came not in Vietnam but in the tiny land-locked kingdom of Laos, with its two million people, on Thailand's border, where communist Pathet Lao guerrillas in 1962 broke their truce with the royal government and seemed poised to take over the country. Britain and Australia sent air force squadrons to Thailand, and the United States dispatched naval units and troops, deterring any further move and alleviating Thailand's fears.

Vietnam's problems were not so easily resolved. South Vietnam's President Diem refused to hold elections and persecuted anyone known to harbour communist sympathies. By 1962 American intelligence officers were reporting to Washington that communist Viet Cong guerrillas, using cruel intimidation, had control of 40 per cent of South Vietnam, that roads and highways were unsafe and that Diem's

ABOVE:
Vietnam was a divisive issue in the second half of the 1960s and cast its shadow long afterwards. Australian forces, including Centurion tanks, served in South Vietnam from 1965 to 1972.

army was inept and its provincial heads mostly corrupt. By year's end 10,000 American military advisers were helping to train the South Vietnam Army in counter-insurgency, joined by a small group of Australian jungle warfare experts—the Advisory Team. But conditions in South Vietnam deteriorated during 1963 and the Viet Cong seemed about to take control. In 1954 President Eisenhower, whose knowledge of South-East Asia was limited, likened its countries to a row of dominoes: if Vietnam fell to communism, so would Cambodia, and then Thailand, the Philippines, Malaya and Indonesia. Western leaders confused nationalism with communism and saw Asia's faceless millions as a mass aspiring only to live under Western systems, little realising that the departure of the great powers had left Asia's political situation confused and unresolved, borders contested, governments corrupt.

'Confrontation' with Indonesia

Australia's eyes were fixed on Indonesia, which, under President Sukarno, had adopted an expansionist foreign policy. In 1957 he had expelled the last of the Dutch, nationalising their businesses, and vowing to lead his country, richly endowed with natural resources, into the future by 'guided democracy'. The result was economic chaos, and Sukarno sought economic and military aid from the Soviet Union. He demanded that the Dutch hand over to Indonesia the last of their East Indies possessions, western New Guinea, even though its people were Melanesians with no cultural, racial or historic links with Malay and Islamic Indonesia. The United Nations supported the demand, and awarded the region to Indonesia in 1962. In September 1963 the new state of Malaysia was born, a federation of Malaya, Singapore, and the former British colonies in Borneo of Sarawak and Sabah, but the new union pleased few of its neighbours. Singapore left the union peaceably in 1965 and even the pro-Western Philippines challenged Malaysia's claim to Sabah, while Sukarno vowed to destroy Malaysia, seeing it as a threat and possible rival. By 1964 Indonesian forces were skirmishing in Borneo with Malaysian, British and Australian units rushed to the area, and soon landed infiltrators in Malaya itself.

In South Vietnam communist insurgency was intensifying. An army coup had killed the republic's unpopular President Diem in 1963 but the generals who replaced him seemed unable to eradicate the guerillas.

Rearmament and conscription

The Menzies government was alarmed. In November 1964, as if in warning of a major new development in policy, the Australian government announced a massive increase in defence spending. Personnel of the RAN and the RAAF would be increased 25 per cent and new aircraft would be purchased—namely French-designed Mirage jet fighters and American F-111 long-range jet 'strike' aircraft,

LEFT:
Australian troops landing in Vietnam.

BELOW:
A wounded Australian soldier being helped in Vietnam.

along with another squadron of Hercules transports, and long-distance Orion maritime reconnaissance aircraft. These planes were a wise choice. The revolutionary F-111 'swing wing' bomber was delayed by design problems and the Mirage was later replaced by the more modern F-A/18 Hornet fighters, but forty years later the F-111 and the other aircraft were still doing sterling service in the Royal Australian Air Force.

Menzies announced that the army would be increased from 22,000 to 33,000 men to provide nine complete battalions (the strength of three wartime 'brigade groups'). To achieve this expansion conscription would be reintroduced: all 20-year-old males were to register for national service, and a number of them would then be chosen for service by ballot.

The 'Indonesian threat'—'confrontation' with Malaysia—was to end suddenly. In September 1965 communist officers mounted a coup in Jakarta that misfired; six senior generals were brutally killed but the strongly Muslim Indonesian army, which had long viewed Sukarno's flirtation with the communists with concern, struck back. Sukarno was deposed by his army chiefs and at least half a million 'suspected communists' were killed in retaliation in the following year by mobs or the army. General Suharto took Sukarno's place as President in 1967 and set out to normalise relations with the West. His country benefited from an inflow of American investment and Suharto, his family and his army cronies grew rich on a rake-off, establishing a corrupt but pro-Western oligarchy that would last until 1998.

RIGHT:
In 1966 Lyndon Johnson became the first US President to visit Australia.

1965: Australians in Vietnam

In Vietnam the fighting dragged on and America's commitment was deepening. In August 1964, when the destroyer USS *Maddox*, operating with South Vietnamese forces in the Gulf of Tonkin, reported an 'attack' by North Vietnamese coastal defence boats (the attack was later found to have been imaginary), American aircraft were ordered to bomb targets in North Vietnam in 'retaliation'. A few days later Congress granted the bellicose President Johnson (Kennedy's successor) authority to pursue the war in Vietnam. In March 1965, following the deaths of American personnel in random attacks in Vietnam, Johnson ordered three months of intensive bombing of North Vietnam—'Operation Rolling Thunder'—often choosing the targets himself and in April he met in Honolulu with his commander in South Vietnam, General William Westmoreland. The general asked that American ground forces be increased to more than 80,000 and that Australia be asked to contribute at least a battalion and South Korea three battalions, to give the appearance of Allied solidarity. Before the year was out there would be 125,000 American troops in Vietnam and the first units of the North Vietnamese army were infiltrating the south to reinforce the Viet Cong guerrillas. Escalation by both sides had begun.

On 29 April 1965 Menzies announced to a half-empty House that, in response to a request for military assistance from the South Vietnamese government, Australia would dispatch an infantry battalion to the war zone. No such request had been received, but it was apparent that the Australian government was treating Vietnam as another Korea, a conflict in which solidarity with the United States must be tangibly demonstrated. Menzies explained that the threat to South Vietnam 'must be seen as part of a thrust by Communist China between the Indian and Pacific Oceans'.

The opposition leader, Arthur Calwell, said of the decision to send troops: 'We do not think it will help the fight against Communism ... We do not think it will promote the welfare of the people of Vietnam.' The Vietnam War would provoke more division within Australian society than any dispute since the conscription campaigns of 1916–17.

ABOVE:
Australian soldier on the morning after the battle of Long Tan, 1966.

1966: Holt succeeds Menzies

Sir Robert Menzies retired on Australia Day (26 January) 1966 after sixteen years of unbroken rule. His successor was the Treasurer, Harold Holt, a well-liked man who had struck up an immediate rapport with the American President, Lyndon Johnson. Holt's pledge that Australia would go 'all the way with LBJ' drew from Johnson a promise to visit Australia, but the first visit by a serving American President in October 1966 was not a complete success. Anti-war demonstrators booed and jeered the visitor and some lay on the road to halt the official motorcade. 'Ride over the bastards,' NSW Premier Askin told one driver. (The phrase entered folklore alongside Colonel Tom Price's 'Fire low and lay them out.')

Battle of Long Tan — and after

By May 1966 two Australian battalions were based in Vietnam, and with the arrival of a Logistics Support Group, the sizeable '1st Australian Task Force', took over responsibility for the security of Phuoc Tuy province south-east of Saigon. A long war of patrols had begun.

On 18 August 1966 Australian troops fought their first pitched battle in Vietnam. One day earlier mortars had shelled the Australian base at Nui Dat, and several strong patrols were sent out to locate the attackers. Late in the afternoon of 18 August 'D Company' (107 officers and men) of the 6th Battalion Royal Australian Regiment were entering a rubber plantation at the hamlet of Long Tan when they were suddenly attacked by 2500 North Vietnamese troops. The Australians fought back wave after wave of attacks well into the night, lying in mud and pouring rain,

losing seventeen men killed before reinforcements clanking to the scene in armoured personnel carriers (APCs) drove off the attackers. The bodies of 245 enemy dead were counted around the Australians' perimeter.

In 1966 the first New Zealanders (gunners, later joined by infantry) and Australian SAS units arrived. The Special Air Service belied its name: the men were commandos, more highly trained than infantry, and they were given the loneliest of patrols and the toughest of assignments. In 1967 Phuoc Tuy province and its vital highway Route 15 were secured, though small bands of Viet Cong remained to mount sudden attacks. The Task Force grew in strength and was joined by 50-tonne Centurion tanks, artillery and engineers. Three RAAF squadrons served in Vietnam, including 9 Squadron, which flew Iroquois helicopters (which they later armed with machine guns—the 'Bushrangers'). The guided-missile destroyers Perth, Hobart and Brisbane each served two tours of duty in Vietnam waters and the troop carrier HMAS *Sydney* made twenty-five voyages to Vietnam and earned the nickname 'the Vung Tau Ferry'. The war would be one of long patrols and constant sweeps through jungle and villages, to the ever-present sound of the helicopters carrying them into action, lifting out the wounded, or spraying the jungle with machine-gun fire.

The Australians preferred to fight alone or with the small New Zealand units, whom they knew they could also rely on. All Australian troops had been trained in jungle warfare; the majority of Americans had not. American forces by 1967 totalled 500,000, yet victory over their elusive enemy seemed as remote as the day when they had arrived. In an effort to destroy the communists' jungle hideouts, American aircraft sprayed a new defoliant named 'Agent Orange'. It proved to be a poison and Vietnam veterans were displaying its after-effects for a generation after the war. Small compensation payments were later made to men whose health had been destroyed.

In the December 1966 election, fought largely on the Vietnam issue, the Liberal – Country Party coalition won handsomely over Labor. To Australians still concerned about the communist threat, events in China, where Mao Zedong had unleashed the Cultural Revolution, seemed to confirm that Asia was a natural enemy, capable of extremes of violence. A Morgan opinion poll on the eve of the election had shown that only 27 per cent of Australians were opposed to sending troops to Vietnam.

'Americanisation'

Australia's bonds with the United States were growing stronger as ties to Britain were weakening. Britain had brought in a Commonwealth Immigrant Act in 1962 to restrict entry of Asian and West Indian immigrants; Australians and New Zealanders no longer had an automatic right to enter the United Kingdom and live there. When Britain devalued the pound in 1967 Australia, for the first time in history, did not follow suit.

Australia by the mid-1960s was almost a different society from that of twenty years before. The population had nearly doubled—from seven million (in 1947) to more than 12 million, 2.5 million of whom were postwar immigrants. Australians were more worldly, and quite proud of their country, enjoying the new prosperity. Modern Australian culture dates from this era. The journalist J.D. Pringle, contributing to a supplement on Australia published in the *Times* early in 1968, found the country almost transformed. 'Sydney and Melbourne are now huge sophisticated cities ... There has been a tremendous improvement in superficial manners and morals.' There was less drunkenness and brutishness; restaurants and galleries abounded. 'The wild colonial boy has been tamed,' the writer decided. The rising Sydney Opera House, the Victorian Arts Centre, the new National Library in Canberra were evidence of a new Australia. Increasing numbers of women were entering the workforce—the proportion of women of 'working age' in the workforce grew from 23 per cent in 1960 to 51 per cent thirty years later.

'If anything worries one—and it certainly worries intellectuals—it is the fear that at the same time Australia is losing her old character and succumbing to the insidious pressures of Americanism,' Pringle wrote. 'Some Australian nationalists find a painful irony in the circumstance that, having fought against British influence all their lives, they have won their battle only to find that American influence has taken its place.'

ABOVE:

A triumph of the time: in 1967 Australians voted overwhelmingly to include Aborigines in the census, thus recognising them as Australian citizens.

Aboriginal rights

'The old suspicious racialism is nearly gone,' Pringle noted. In 1962 voting rights were extended to Aborigines in state and territory elections, and in 1964 the Menzies government set up the Australian Institute of Aboriginal Studies. In the following year Charles Perkins graduated in Arts from the University of Sydney—the first Aboriginal university graduate. He had been born in Alice Springs and taken at the age of ten to a home for Aboriginal children in Adelaide, and later trained as a fitter and turner. But rather than just finding a job he went to England, where he played soccer, and then took himself to university. Early in 1965 he led a group of university students on buses on a 'freedom ride' to towns in the far west of New South Wales, where racial discrimination persisted. At Moree, where Aboriginal

OCTOBER 1966   THIRTY CENTS

Walkabout
AUSTRALIA'S WAY OF LIFE MAGAZINE

FEATURING SPECIAL COLOUR OFFE

special features inside	MELBOURNE CUP IN COLOUR • DAISY BATES OF OOLDEA A PLEA FOR OUR WILDLIFE • TERMITE MYSTERIES FAREWELL, CURL CURL • LAST OF THE BULLOCKIES

ABOVE & LEFT:
The 1960s were the golden age of general interest magazines. Few titles survived into the 1990s.

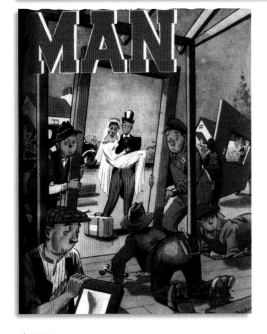

ABOVE:
Man, notable for its fine illustrations, died in 1974.

children were forbidden to use the public swimming pool, the townspeople's hostility towards the travellers was captured by television newsfilm, and the consciences of liberal Australians grew uneasy. (One of the freedom riders, Jim Spigelman, later became Chief Justice of New South Wales.)

In 1965 the Yolngu people of Yirrkala in the Northern Territory's Gove Peninsula protested to the federal government by way of a bark petition against mining on their land. In 1966 the Gurindji people working on the great Wave Hill cattle station walked off the job, weary of being paid a pittance, and demanded ownership of their traditional land. In that year Aborigines achieved equal pay.

In 1967 Prime Minister Holt asked the respected public servant H.C. 'Nugget' Coombs, a compassionate man, to be chairman of two new bodies—the Council for Aboriginal Affairs and the Council for the Arts (predecessor of today's Australia Council). A program of limited Asian immigration had begun and Australians voted overwhelmingly (93 per cent) in a referendum in May 1967 to count the indigenous peoples as part of Australia's population—that is, to give rights of citizenship to the nation's 44,000 surviving full-blood Aborigines and Torres Strait Islanders and the 200,000 of mixed blood. There have been some fine moments in Australian history and this was one of them.

A bluff New Zealander, Dr Fred Hollows, the professor of ophthalmology at the recently created University of New South Wales, first met the writer and activist

Frank Hardy in 1968. Both men were sincere communists and devoted to the righting of social inequalities. On journeying into central Australia Hollows was appalled by the high incidence of eye disease among the Aboriginal stockmen and their families at the Gurindji camp at Watti Creek. Nearly all of them were afflicted with loss of sight (caused by the blinding sun), others with cataracts and trachoma (caused by chlamydia). He had never seen anything like it—'eye diseases of the kind and degree that hadn't been seen in western society for generations!' He was later to co-found the Aboriginal Medical Service, and lead teams of volunteers and doctors into the outback with help from the federal government and equipment from the Australian army.

ABOVE:
The death by drowning of Prime Minister Harold Holt on 17 December 1967 shocked Australia.

1968: Gorton succeeds Holt

On 19 December 1967 Prime Minister Holt, a keen swimmer, disappeared in the strong surf off the beach near his holiday home at Portsea. Navy divers searched for days but the waters were turbulent, the underwater rockshelves jagged and cavernous, and most of the divers were themselves injured before the search was called off. Holt's body was never found and for three weeks the Country Party leader John McEwen, who refused to accept McMahon as Holt's successor, served as Acting-Prime Minister until the Coalition could decide on a replacement. Coombs saw Holt's death as a 'tragic personal loss'. He wrote:

There is little doubt that in the latter months of [Holt's] life the burden of the

ABOVE:
Holt's successor was
another Victorian, John
Grey Gorton.

Prime Ministership, intensified by some ill-health and personal worries, became increasingly heavy. It was perhaps because of these anxieties that he turned to initiatives in the Arts and Aborigines as relief, but also as work which better expressed his own generous and human spirit.

The new leader, John Grey Gorton, who assumed the prime ministership in January 1968, was a rough diamond of a man. A Victorian like his two Liberal predecessors, he was a former RAAF fighter pilot whose craggy face showed traces of his wartime injuries. He had been a success as Minister for the Navy, where his obvious love for the navy and his breezy informality had even won over the admirals in the nation's most tradition-encrusted service. 'Unfortunately,' Coombs wrote,

Gorton's image of Australia's society, like that of many of his compatriots, had no place for Aborigines as such. He saw no justification or need for special policies to help them and the idea that Aborigines had valid rights to land based on traditional title was to him wholly unacceptable. He went along with proposals to assist Aboriginal children to get access to secondary education and occupational training and to create a fund to assist Aboriginal entrepreneurs to establish or develop their own business. But he ignored the Gurindji and Yirrkala Aboriginal demands for land, pushed aside [the responsible minister] Wentworth's pleas to protect Aboriginal sacred sites from miners, and dismissed the Yirrkala community's objections to the opening of a hotel near their settlement with an offer to them of a share in the ownership!

Gorton shared the nation's growing feeling that the Vietnam War was stalemated if not unwinnable. The communist Tet Offensive, launched in February 1968, revealed that American boasts that 'victory is around the corner' were empty ones. The Viet Cong fought their way into the grounds of the US Embassy in Saigon and captured the northern city of Hue, but the offensive was stemmed—Australian forces were heavily engaged defending their firebases north of Saigon. The damage done to the American cause was irreparable, as were reports of several American atrocities that matched in horror the terror campaign the Viet Cong had waged against their own people. During 1968, as demands for withdrawal from Vietnam swept America, Richard Nixon was swept into the White House on a pledge to reduce the scale of the war, and in November 1969 Gorton won the elections, though the Labor vote improved substantially compared to that of 1966.

1967: American bases

In 1967, at the height of the Vietnam War, a joint US-Australian communications facility began operating at North-West Cape in Western Australia, followed by one at Pine Gap near Alice Springs in 1969, and another at Nurrungar nearly 500 kilometres north of Adelaide in 1971. These top secret, highly guarded bases are still vital links in the US Defence Department's communications and monitoring network, providing the United States with electronic eyes and ears over a vast seg-

LEFT:
Leonard French's stained glass window for the
new National Library in Canberra, 1968.
BELOW:
'Nugget' Coombs (right), champion of Aboriginal reform,
at an art exhibition in the 1970s.

ABOVE:
Australian actors Jeannie Drynan and Harold Hopkins starred in the 1960s ABC television serial *Pastures of the Blue Crane*; the story of a girl, prejudiced against Aborigines, who discovers a secret about her own past.

ment of the world's surface—the Indian Ocean and the regions to Australia's north. Australia thereafter could not remain a passive onlooker to any conflict involving the United States, for it was—and remains—a part of the American defensive shield.

The mineral boom

Despite an unpopular war the 1960s ended on a high note that set the tone for the next ten years. In September 1969 the Western Australian mining company Poseidon announced a nickel find that saw its shares soar from 50 cents to $280 in six months. Australians discovered in the share market all the excitement of gambling, for the mineral boom promised quick profits and better odds than the races, the poker machines and the lotteries combined. (In May 1969 a national strike was averted when a Sydney lottery winner paid a gaoled unionist's fines with a slice of his windfall, explaining: 'This country is not ready for martyrs.' Money was for the spending.)

Poseidon's mineral find was discovered to be overrated and when the shares' value fell to a few cents, thousands of speculators lost fortunes, for much stock had been bought for quick re-sale by individuals without money. In 1970 Minsec, another mining complex, collapsed when many of its claims were found to be spurious. Tasminex shares fell from $90 in January to just over $7 in March. The basic wage was abolished in 1967, but in the following decade salaries rose to match the rise in real estate prices, as did union demands for increased wages and benefits.

Britain says farewell

When Queen Elizabeth II visited Australia in 1970 to commemorate the 200th anniversary of the landing of Captain Cook at Botany Bay, she came as the figurehead of a British Empire than had now all but disappeared.

Australia's economic ties with Britain were lessening every year, and so was her reliance on Britain as a partner in defence In the early 1970s Britain bought only 8 per cent of Australia's exports and supplied only 18 per cent of her imports, and within twenty years both these figures had fallen to just 5 per cent. In 1968 the Wilson Labour government had announced that Britain would withdraw all her armed forces presently on duty 'east of Suez' over the next three years and concentrate them in Europe. During 1970–71 the last British troops left their bases and airfields in Malaysia and Singapore without fanfare. Even the reassuring sight of Royal Navy's dark-grey warships in South-East Asian waters became just a memory. Soon the only outpost of Empire was Hong Kong (itself fated to be handed back to China in 1997).

'It was one of the great turning points in British history,' wrote one British historian with wistfulness:

Marlborough's and Wellington's victories, the great eighteenth century sea-fights, mercantile expansion, the industrial revolution, world empire, world power—all of it was past. Britain again stood where she had stood in the reign of Elizabeth I, a second-class, perhaps a third-class power in terms of relative economic strength and warlike capacity, living precariously in the face of keen trade rivalry and sandwiched between the superpowers.

In 1973 the United Kingdom was one of three new countries admitted to the ranks of 'The Six' (France, Germany, Italy, Belgium, the Netherlands and Luxembourg) that formed the European Common Market (now the European Union), marking her final break with the past. British investment in Australia and the region, however, remained high—and would increase.

The 1970s: A more open society

The warning signs of an ailing Australian economy were there and also the first indications of the New Technology; both were largely ignored. By 1970 nearly 900 computers were in operation in Australia, most of them huge mainframe installations capable of processing figures at a phenomenal speed, and used principally in banking, accounting and invoicing. The computer business and the huge sales commissions attracted a new class of sales reps. 'The age group of these entrepreneurs is typical of the industry and their employees average around 28 years of age', ran a report in 1970. Within fifteen years the terms 'entrepreneur' and 'electronic data processing' were everyday jargon.

By the early 1970s the Liberal Party was losing cohesion and direction. Vietnam had tarnished the government's image: the mass marches of the 1970 moratoriums, led by Labor's conscience, Jim Cairns, showed that much of 'middle Australia' was as adamantly opposed to the war as the radicals. Malcolm Fraser, the Victorian groomed by Menzies for greater things, resigned in 1971 as Defence Minister on the grounds of Gorton's 'extreme disloyalty', an action indicating Cabinet's growing dissatisfaction with the Prime Minister's idiosyncratic style of leadership. Gorton did much. He pledged federal money to foster an Australian film industry, creating what would be the Australian Film Commission in 1971; and, significantly, began the withdrawal of the bulk of the Australian troops from Vietnam, where American forces (after a disastrous incursion into Cambodia) were also being reduced in number.

The Liberal Party's adoption of a policy of gradual change was being outpaced by developments overseas and by demands for accelerated reform from the Labor opposition. The liberalisation of Australian censorship began under a broad-minded minister, Don Chipp, and in 1970 even *Portnoy's Complaint*, a disturbingly frank portrait of male adolescence by the American novelist Phillip Roth, was published without its publishers being prosecuted. Scandinavian countries had, since

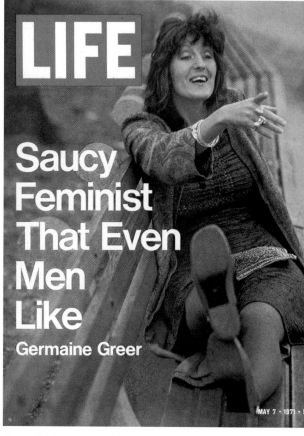

ABOVE:

Women's Liberation: Germaine Greer's *The Female Eunuch*, published in 1970, transformed the Australian author into one of the leading voices in the international feminist movement and often the most outrageous and amusing.

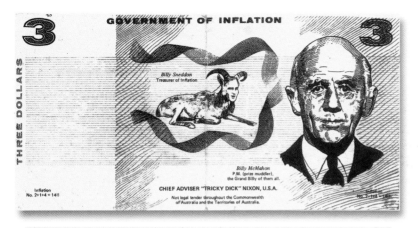

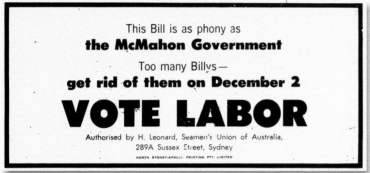

the early 1960s, begun removing restrictions on the circulation of sexually explicit works, whether magazines, books or films, and statistics showed that the new permissiveness had not resulted in any increase in sexual offences. Judges had always found it difficult to define pornography, for one person's view of obscenity differed from another's. In 1972 South Australia, under young Labor Premier Don Dunstan, was the first Australian state to decriminalise homosexual acts between consenting adults. By the end of the 1970s, rigid censorship of works freely available overseas existed only in Queensland.

ABOVE:
Lacklustre Prime Minister William McMahon, who succeeded Gorton in 1971, faced a rejuvenated Labor Party and an electorate weary of Vietnam and growing inflation. The Labor campaign of 1972 made the most of his shortcomings.

Women's liberation—and civil rights

The 1970s became a decade of innovation and experimentation, awash with American influences, and this was seen even before the arrival of the Whitlam Labor whirlwind in 1972. It was a decade of street marches and protests by minority groups bravely espousing unpopular causes—conservation, female liberation, black rights, and even homosexual liberation. In 1970 expatriate academic Germaine Greer published her feminist best-seller, *The Female Eunuch*.

In 1971 a Melbourne-based academic, Dennis Altman, published *Homosexual Liberation and Oppression*, a demand for 'gay rights' that also became, like *The Female Eunuch*, a world best-seller. In 1972, as wowserism died, the Packer-owned ACP group launched a magazine for the 'New Woman'—*Cleo*, edited by Ita Buttrose. Instead of the predictable features on cooking, TV stars and the royal family it contained articles on men, sex, careers—and a foldout, Playboy-fashion, of a nude male pin-up.

Aboriginal tent embassy

In 1970 C.K. Rowley published *The Destruction of Aboriginal Society*, an influential work that reminded white Australians that terrible wrongs had been done to their indigenous people. In the following year, when a court admitted that Aborigines had the right to apply for fifty-year leases on land (which after all was their own, having been taken from them without compensation) indigenous activism flared. Aborigines unfurled their own flag—a black sun on a red and yellow background—and flew it over their own makeshift 'embassy' in Canberra in the park opposite Parliament House. They explained that they were foreigners in their own country and had every right to their own representation. Most Australians chuckled and agreed. After police moved in and cleared it, Aboriginal leaders vowed to bring in their people by the busload and restore the tents. Nugget Coombs, trusted completely by Aboriginal leaders, intervened. No police moved in to remove the embassy; thirty years later it was still there.

THE AUSTRALIAN

NUMBER 2617   MONDAY DECEMBER 4 1972   SEVEN CENTS*   WESTERN AUSTRALIA 10 CENTS

WHITLAM TAKES OVER

THE AUSTRALIAN
More than a Labor victory

MR WHITLAM has had a massive victory in a campaign which matched an appeal for reform against a rather old-fashioned appeal to bigotry.

During the campaign the Liberal-CP coalition descended, in the footsteps of the DLP, to an attack on the Labor Party over moral issues which was as unsuccessful as it was unimaginative. The decision, in 1972, to try to fight a major national election on trumped-up fears of the permissive society displayed a bankruptcy of both policy and leadership.

It also demonstrated how totally out of touch with the needs and ambitions of the Australian people the leadership of both the Liberal Party and the DLP had become. The only consolation in this depressing spectacle was that the electorate, in rejecting the attempt to play politics with morality, also turned its back on the DLP in such numbers that the party's baneful influence on Australian politics would appear to be nearly at its end.

While Mr McMahon and his more desperate followers climbed aboard the DLP's moral bandwagon to oblivion, Mr Whitlam wisely continued to put forward positive proposals for the development of Australia. While Mr McMahon tried to make us shiver at Senator Gair's nightmare, Mr Whitlam was left looking like the only man who knew where he — and Australia — ought to be going.

The electorate took the only possible intelligent choice and opted for constructive policies rather than scare electioneering. The bulk of voters, like this newspaper, decided that it was time for a change. But Mr Chipp was probably right on Saturday night when he said, commenting on the returns, that the Opposition had not won the election so much as the Government had lost it.

We are now standing on a totally fresh stage. The electorate, quite confounding the cherished beliefs of old-time politicians, has exercised a sophisticated judgment and given Mr Whitlam the chance he asked for. The grounds on which that decision was taken, and its effects, will radically change the shape of Australian politics.

In the first place, we have to see what Mr Whitlam makes of his chance. He will not have an easy task. Committed to a huge programme of urgent reforms, he inherits at the same time a decidedly delicate economic situation.

Meeting with department heads prepares the way for Labor rule

By ALAN RAMSEY

LABOR'S Prime Minister-elect, Mr Gough Whitlam, 56, flew to Canberra yesterday to begin taking over the reins of Australia's second post-war Federal Labor Government.

He drove through cheering crowds at Canberra airport to his Parliament House office for more than three hours of talks with four of the Government's senior departmental heads.

He arranged the meeting from Sydney with the Secretary of the Prime Minister's Department, Sir John Bunting, and the head of foreign affairs, Sir Keith Waller.

Also at the meeting were the chairman of the Commonwealth Public Service Board, Mr A. S. Cooley, and the secretary of the Attorney-General's Department, Mr C. W. Harders.

The discussions centred on Labor's planned reconstruction of the ministry and various government departments.

Mr Whitlam will continue these talks today with his two senior Cabinet ministers — the proposed Defence Minister, Mr Barnard, and the likely Attorney-General, Senator Murphy, Labor's Senate leader.

SWEARING IN

A key topic in yesterday's talks was the constitutional legality of the new Labor Government pending the formal swearing in of the ministry next week.

The out-going Prime Minister, Mr McMahon, telephoned Mr Whitlam at his Sydney home early yesterday. He told him he would tender his Government's resignation to the Governor-General, Sir Paul Hasluck, tomorrow.

Sir Paul is then expected to call Mr Whitlam and swear him in as Prime Minister.

Labor's ministry will not be formed until it is elected at a caucus meeting, tentatively scheduled for next Monday.

Mr Whitlam is concerned at the constitutional legality of his Government in the in-tervening week and sought to have this

Conservation …

In 1970 Jack Mundey, the communist leader of the Builders Labourers Federation, placed the first 'green ban' on land that was threatened by developers. Green bans were later effectively used nationally to preserve parkland and historic buildings or sites from destruction or development. The Australian Conservation Foundation, founded only six years earlier, gathered thousands of new members; Green Peace was founded in Britain in 1971, and the movement soon had offices in Australia. In March 1972 a group was formed in Tasmania to attempt to save Lake Pedder from being flooded; it has been called the world's first environmental political party, sending 'Green' independent members to Tasmania's Parliament from that date. Green was the colour of the 1970s.

… and corruption

Yet the 1970s was a decade of corruption in state politics, particularly in New South Wales. The Liberals' Robert Askin had ended twenty-four years of Labor rule in the state in 1965 and he ruled until 1975. He inherited a police force proud of its uniformed men, but riddled with accusations that its detectives accepted pay-offs from organised prostitution, drugs and gambling, and he seemed unwilling to eradicate it. The profits for all participants were great: Much gambling was then illegal, and during the Vietnam War Sydney was the mecca of hundreds of thousands of American servicemen on leave ('rest and recreation'). The drug culture was established in this period. It would take more than twenty-five years to clean

ABOVE:
Edward Gough Whitlam, who led Labor back into power in December 1972. 'Gough'—as even his opponents called him—was committed to rapid and dramatic reform. He remains probably the most charismatic Australian political figure of his century.

up police corruption, and the drug culture remained.

It took even longer to clean up corruption in the Queensland Police Force. Following a penetrating *Four Corners* investigation the Fitzgerald Inquiry of 1987–89 unearthed evidence of police misconduct that led to the gaoling of a Chief Commissioner.

Eve of election

In March 1971 Gorton, whose individualistic style was angering many in his own party, was voted out of office by one vote—his own—in Cabinet. Four years he later was elected to the Senate—as an independent. The lacklustre and ageing William McMahon, who came from a wealthy Sydney background, replaced him as Prime Minister. McMahon created a new ministry, that of Environment, Aborigines and the Arts—some cynics called them the 'three lost causes'.

On the eve of the 1972 general election the Women's Electoral Lobby was formed to sponsor or endorse candidates favourable to reforming the position of women and children in society. Labor's policies won their endorsement. In 1972 the Arbitration Court awarded women equal pay with men (though this advance was easier to legislate than enforce). The Australian singer Helen Reddy living in the United States gave the women's movement worldwide its theme and marching song—'*I am Woman*'.

In late November 1972, only a week before Australia's polling day, New Zealand—like Australia, under conservative rule since 1949 (apart from a three year interregnum)—gave Norman Kirk's Labour Party a landslide victory and some Australians saw it as an omen.

1972: The Labor victory

Gough Whitlam's revitalised Labor Party ended 23 years of conservative rule in its electoral victory of 2 December 1972. Labor won 67 seats in the House (the Coalition won 57) but still lacked a majority in the Senate. Edward Gough Whitlam, who had replaced the admired but doctrinaire Caldwell as federal leader in 1967, dwarfed the diminutive Billy McMahon both physically and intellectually. Labor's progressive platform and respectable image—Whitlam was a former Queen's Counsel—and slogan 'It's Time' appealed to women, to blue-collar and white-collar workers, to New Australians and to young 'swinging voters' alike. The poor showing of the DLP candidates marked the end of the DLP and a split Labor vote, and proved that a democratic socialist government was not only acceptable to the mass of Australians but eagerly awaited.

In their first week in office, before Cabinet had been sworn in, Whitlam and his deputy announced a withdrawal of the last Australian personnel from Vietnam, the cessation of conscription, an amnesty for draft evaders and recognition of communist China. This set the pace for the changes that followed. In its first year the Whitlam Labor government introduced 253 bills, a record unmatched by any previous administration.

The new Labor government promised increased federal spending on education and welfare and relief for the disadvantaged. In December 1972 a Department of Aboriginal Affairs was created, and all states except Queensland passed to the federal government the right to legislate on behalf of indigenous peoples. In the same month the Whitlam government announced the creation of Medibank—a national health insurance scheme. After a stormy evolution it became operative in July 1975, and though many of its benefits have been eroded it remains in existence as Medicare. Pensions and unemployment benefits were increased and extended. The voting age in federal elections was lowered to eighteen years. In 1973 a Community Health Program brought funding for women's refuges, childcare centres and halfway houses; a single-mothers benefit was introduced. In 1973 tariffs on imports were cut by 25 per cent 'across the board' in an effort to make Australian industry improve its performance—a move described by one newspaper as one of the boldest strokes ever made by a government since Federation. In 1974 worker training at government expense was initiated.

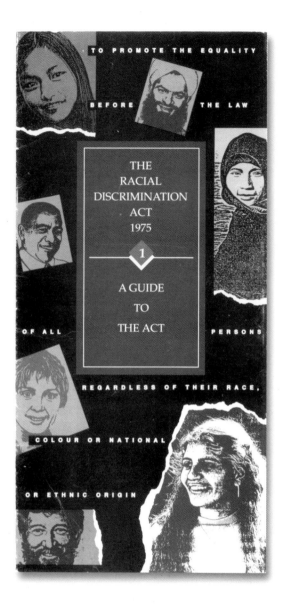

When the hostile Senate rejected or amended dozens of Bills and twice rejected the Bills establishing Medibank, Whitlam requested a double dissolution from Governor-General, Sir Paul Hasluck. In May 1974 Labor was narrowly returned to office, retaining 66 seats in the new 127-seat House of Representatives. But in the Senate, Labor and the Coalition won 29 seats each, the balance of power being held by two independents. A historic joint sitting of Parliament passed the Medibank Bills and three electoral reform Bills in August 1974.

ABOVE:

Australians were taken aback by Labor's program of social legislation. The 1975 Act ending any form of racial discrimination helped remodel Australian society and make it one of the most tolerant and open in the world.

1975: The end of 'White Australia'

The White Australia policy was effectively ended in 1974 when a 'non-discriminatory' immigration program was adopted; from the following year aspiring British and Irish migrants—to their shock—no longer enjoyed automatic right of entry. (The policy of increasing Asian immigration was extended by the Liberal government after Labor fell.) In 1975 Federal Parliament passed an Act making racial and sexual discrimination illegal, enacting a UN convention. With multiracialism came, in the late 1970s, 'multiculturalism', a federal government initiative aimed at encouraging Australia's diverse ethnic groups to celebrate and preserve their own languages, cultures, and traditions. Multiculturalism (like the model for Medibank) was a Canadian initiative dating from 1968 and devised to bond together its antag-

BELOW:
By the 1970s Australia's trade imbalance was growing.
A container ship unloads imports at Swanston Dock, Melbourne.

ABOVE:
Vast coal reserves formed an important component in Australia's economy and by 1984 the nation had taken over from the United States as the world's largest coal exporter. The high carbon content of coal makes it an ideal fuel but also one of the principal causes of atmospheric pollution.

onistic communities—the English-speaking and the French. Australia had no such divisions but the adoption of multiculturalism was, in effect, an admission that assimilation of ethnic groups in the American way was not working and that many groups in the community felt disadvantaged and outside the mainstream of Australian life.

Outraged by the Tasmanian government's flooding of Lake Pedder to create a dam for hydro-electric power, conservation groups grew in strength and in 1974 the Whitlam government ratified the World Heritage Convention that obligated signatories to protect and preserve natural heritage areas.

Labor's pains

In less than two years of dynamic change, Labor's progress was disturbing many. Its policies were generous but spendthrift. All disadvantaged sections of the community had benefited, but the cost was high. The oil shortages and the rise in prices introduced by the Organisation of Petroleum Exporting Countries (OPEC) in 1973 affected all Western economies. Inflation rose to 13 per cent by late 1973 and reached 15 per cent in 1975. Speculators moved to the safe ground of real estate, buying and selling properties at a rate that saw some Sydney home prices rise from $25,000 in 1972 to more than $90,000 in 1980; twenty years later the price would be close to $400,000. Many Australians realised that speculating in real estate was more rewarding and enriching than working for a wage or salary.

Despite an unwise 'credit squeeze' in 1973, growing inflation and an epidemic of strikes, the 1970s were the last truly carefree decade Australians were to know. In 1974 most Australian adults received in the post a gift from the banks: a plastic

Bankcard that offered them varying degrees of credit. Bankcard was accepted by most retailers and hotels and sparked a spending spree of national proportions. Nearly thirty years later, in 2003, Australians would owe $22 billion on their credit cards.

Australia was also becoming—in the phrase of one critic—'the land of the long weekend', with its workers enjoying more leisure time than those of any other country on earth.

Most Australians worked a 40-hour, five-day week and enjoyed three weeks' annual leave and nine public holidays—the equivalent of 4.5 weeks of paid leisure. (Many Americans, by contrast, had only two weeks' vacation, and two public holidays.) National productivity lagged and only mineral exports to Japan helped to redress the growing trade imbalance.

1970s: Modern culture

The Whitlam government's support for the arts was one of its enduring achievements. In 1974 it abolished university fees (the federal government would meet the cost of courses). The new-look 'Australia Council', now drawing on bountiful Federal funding, was created in 1975. Originally established by the Coalition as the Council for the Arts, it was expanded to overcome the lack of public interest in the arts, and it provided financial assistance for poets, potters, painters, writers and other creative souls. Many thought it would eventually be disbanded but it still existed in 2004, playing a powerful role in deciding what constitutes culture and what doesn't. A flood of subsidised books, plays, films and music began projecting a recognisably Australian identity. For all their lack of sophistication, they established an awareness that an Australian culture existed. With it came an unexpectedly aggressive nationalism, which intellectual maturity normally discourages. Book publishers, film-makers and television producers found rich lodes in every aspect of Australian history—the convict era, bushrangers, the Anzacs, the gold rush. Contemporary issues or themes were regarded as commonplace.

The haunting Peter Weir film *Picnic at Hanging Rock* was more mature. It appeared in 1975, the year in which colour television was first broadcast in Aus-

ABOVE:
Singer Helen Reddy achieved fame in the United States.

ABOVE, LEFT:
Australian soprano Joan Sutherland. (Australian Opera photo) Sydney-born soprano Joan Sutherland, who left for London to continue her singing studies, achieved fame there and in Europe during the 1960s. She toured Australia in 1974 to acclaim.

tralia—eight years after it had started in Britain. By the 1970s Barry Humphries, who had left Australia for London in 1959, and returned in the 1960s a celebrity, was now a national treasure. Gough Whitlam and his wife Margaret even appeared in cameo roles in Bruce Beresford's film version of his *Adventures of Barry Mackenzie*, the crudest but funniest product of the Australian Film Commission.

Humphries found Australia's cultural renaissance droll. He was to invent yet another memorable character—Les Patterson, a vulgar retired politician who had landed a soft job as a cultural liaison officer and was now promoting 'Australian culture' while trying to remain sober. Within a decade life had imitated art and armies of cultural bureaucrats were determining who received taxpayer funding for their artistic enterprises, and who didn't. Australian academics were soon to adopt 'post structuralist' approaches to their disciplines, investigating hitherto hidden aspects of Australian art, history and literature—the influences of race, gender and class, for example—but much of their reasoning in search of 'subtext' was confused and their language incomprehensible. 'Post modernism' was arriving.

Some few continued to write in the clear, pellucid lines that echo in readers' minds—A.D. Hope and Judith Wright won long-overdue praise as two of the outstanding poets in the English language. They were to die within days of each other in July 2000, as if they had decided to sign off together from a world that no longer made much sense.

Australia's best-known playwright, David Williamson, emerged during these years, and he had a sharp ear for the phoniness and pretensions of suburban middle-class life, picking ambitious young professionals and academics (and their spouses) as his targets. *Don's Party* was released as a film in 1973 (it had first been performed in 1971). Set at a suburban barbecue thrown by Laborites to celebrate Labor's anticipated win on the night of the 1969 elections, it portrayed their despair as the figures came in and they dissolved into anger, brawls, accusations of infidelity, and bad language. Within a decade both Humphries' and Williamson's satire was becoming heavier and sharper, but their victims were no longer laughing at themselves.

The 'new nationalism'

The new nationalism disturbed a basically conservative electorate. Whitlam made no moves towards republicanism but he replaced 'God Save the Queen' with 'Advance Australia Fair' as the national anthem and introduced an Australian honours system (the Order of Australia) to replace Imperial knighthoods and awards. Britain, in entering the European Common Market, had finally turned its back on the Imperial past. But the monarchy, paradoxically, remained popular in Australia, the doings of the royal family constantly paraded in print in the Sunday papers and women's magazines to an extent that astonished even English migrants.

1946-52 | 1953 | 1964 | COLOURS OF THE | 70's

ABOVE:
Airline stewardesses—
the term air hostesses or
'hosties' was discontin-
ued—model the change
in fashions over nearly
30 years, as skirts gor
shorter and shorter.

1974: Birth of the Australian Defence Force

In 1974 the three armed services became the Australian Defence Force (ADF) under a single minister for defence, though the navy, army and air force preserved their separate uniforms and entities (unlike the unpopular Canadian experiment, where all personnel wore the same green uniform; they later reverted to the their old ones). A small, professional defence force took shape. In 1985 females were admitted to the three services in all arms except the combat units; the separate women's services (the WRANS, WRAAF, WRAC) had been dissolved. In 1986 the Australian Defence Force Academy opened in Canberra, adjacent to the Royal Military College (Duntroon); it was a campus of the University of New South Wales and would soon have a student body of a thousand male and female officer cadets, studying for degree courses of three to four years.

The 'permissive generation'

In the wider world increasing numbers of teenagers, and even career-oriented couples relaxing from the stresses of city life, smoked 'pot' (marijuana), despite its illegality. (By the mid-1980s, when organised crime introduced heroin to Australia, drug addiction among the young would become a social cancer.) In 1975 a sweeping reform of divorce law came with an Act (the initiative of the reformist Attorney-General, Senator Lionel Murphy) that did away with fault clauses. Critics said that it would make marriage and divorce too easy, but the Act removed much of the pain and trauma from divorce.

As church attendances fell (the Methodists, Presbyterians and Congregationalists combined in 1977 to form the Uniting Church), many of the young sought some spirituality or guidance in life from Eastern religions such as the gentle faith of Buddhism, or the colourful one of Hinduism—or from noisier American fundamentalist sects. The educated classes remained Anglophile, their attitudes shaped by English culture; intellectuals remained anguished; but the mass of Australians read American bestsellers and magazines, watched American television shows and films and bought American music. The historian Manning Clark said that Australians

had, like all Western societies, left the kingdom of God and entered the Kingdom of Nothingness, but a new tolerance was being born, freed of religious dogma.

1975: New Guinea, Vietnam and Timor

The Whitlam government had given impetus to 'decolonising' New Guinea. By the end of 1973 the Territory of Papua-New Guinea was, in practice, already self-governing, with its own Westminster-style parliament. Full independence came on 16 September 1975. Some maintain that nationhood was conferred too quickly, for fourteen years later the people of the mineral-rich island of Bougainville, which supplied 40 per cent of the new nation's revenue, rebelled against the central government. It was the beginning of a tragic war that cost thousands of lives while in PNG's capital, Port Moresby, corruption and lawlessness went unchecked.

ABOVE:
The flag of independent
New Guinea

The Whitlam government's indifference to events to the north puzzled many. In April 1975 the Vietnam conflict came to an end with a sudden, massive communist offensive that swept into Saigon itself. The last Australian diplomats and some of their Vietnamese staff took off from Saigon airport in an RAAF Hercules transport on Anzac Day 1975. North Vietnamese tanks crashed the gates of the Presidential Palace in Saigon six days later while American helicopters ferried staff and Vietnamese refugees from the roof of the burning US embassy to aircraft carriers lying offshore—a humiliating end to a war that had been prolonged beyond endurance. As many as 50,000 Australians had served in Vietnam, and they suffered 3000 casualties including 501 fatalities; 40 per cent of casualties were young conscripts. The majority of casualties were caused by landmines.

A new bloodbath in Vietnam was expected, but the communist government instead undertook a 're-education' program of its former enemies in the south. Nevertheless, ten of thousands of Vietnamese fled the regime in small boats—the first 'boat people'. The bloodbath took place to Vietnam's west, in Cambodia where the communist Khmer Rouge forces of Pol Pot took control in 1975 and instituted a murderous regime that was to kill more than 2 million Cambodians before Vietnamese troops invaded the country in 1978, this time as liberators. Significantly, SEATO was wound up in 1977. New forces, new groupings, were emerging in South-East Asia.

In November 1975, only six months after the fall of Saigon, Indonesian forces invaded Portuguese East Timor. There was no reaction from the Australian government. Ever since a military coup in Lisbon in April 1974—carried out by officers despairing of the mounting cost in lives of maintaining the Portuguese empire in Angola and Mozambique—Timor had been in political ferment and it seemed likely that a Marxist party there would win control by elections or other means. A group of Australian television journalists reporting on the increasing Indonesian raids across East Timor's border dis-

ABOVE:
Malcolm Fraser became Liberal Party leader in March 1975. He was to lead the Liberal–National coalition government from 1975 to 1983.

appeared in October 1975. It took their next of kin a quarter of a century to establish that the Indonesian military had killed them. In early November 1975—only days before Australia's own change of government—Indonesian forces landed in Dili and began occupying East Timor. Over the next twenty years reports of Indonesian atrocities in Timor caused anguish to Australians who remembered the support the Christian Timorese had given their soldiers in 1942–43.

Australia thereafter followed a policy of military non-involvement in world affairs, its people helpless onlookers at unrestrained genocide in Timor and Cambodia and violence in Africa and the Middle East. They were the last battles of the Cold War, in which each side was supplied with arms by the communist powers or the West. Few Australians objected when their governments accepted increasing numbers of Indochinese refugees from these horrors—140,000 of them (mainly Vietnamese) have been given refuge in Australia.

1970s: Arab oil and Middle East crises

In 1973 the Arab oil-producing countries suddenly doubled oil prices, adding to the West's woes. Cheap petrol was now a thing of the past. The rise was politically motivated in that it set out to remind the West that its continuing support for Israel was dooming the expectations of millions of Palestinian refugees and hampering chances of lasting peace in the region. Palestinian terrorists of the 'Black September' group began hi-jacking airliners and in the 1972 Munich Olympics kidnapped and murdered Israeli athletes. After the 1973 Arab nations' attack on Israel, which was only narrowly defeated, violence spread to Lebanon. Peace between Jews and Muslim extremists in the Middle East seemed unattainable.

RIGHT:
Queen Elizabeth II returned to Australia to open the Sydney Opera House in November 1973. She stands between the Governor-General, Sir Paul Hasluck (on her right) and the controversial Premier Askin of New South Wales. In the row behind are (far left) Sir John Kerr, Prime Minister Whitlam and his wife Margaret; in the row below them, the Governor, Sir Roden Cutler VC.

ABOVE:
Wattie Creek in the Northern Territory: Prime Minister Whitlam hands back documents of ownership of 3238 square kilometres of Wave Hill land to the Aboriginal people, 16 August 1975.

The fall of Labor

The first rip in the fabric of unity in the Whitlam government came in December 1974 when Whitlam replaced Frank Crean as Treasurer with Jim Cairns. The Treasury was harbouring misgivings as to how continued government developments could be funded.

The Minister for Minerals and Energy, Rex Connor, had a vision for Australia, one in which growth and prosperity would be assured by harnessing the nation's immense natural resources—minerals, oil, natural gas—for the good of the people. He had commissioned a distinguished financial journalist, Tom Fitzgerald, to investigate the mining industry, where vast fortunes were being made by overseas companies. The Fitzgerald Report revealed that though the government was reaping large royalties from mining companies, profits equal to five times the amount of royalties were being repatriated from Australia. To Connor it was confirmation that the 'multinationals' were raping Australia's resources. In December 1974 the Executive Council authorised the raising of an overseas loan of $4 billion for national development. This coincided with the devastating Cyclone Tracy, which struck Darwin on Christmas Day, destroying the city and taking sixty-two lives.

On 7 January 1975 the loans decision was reversed before it became public knowledge, but three weeks later the rarely convened Executive Council approved a plan to obtain a reduced amount—$2 billion. On 20 May Whitlam ordered that all moves by his ministers to sound out foreign lenders be made through the normal channel—Treasury. In June Jim Cairns, who had written to a loans broker in March, was sacked as Treasurer and replaced by Bill Hayden. Rex Connor's efforts to obtain overseas loans were exposed in October and resulted in his forced resignation.

Two days later, on 15 October, the opposition leader, Malcolm Fraser, announced that as a result of 'extraordinary and reprehensible circumstances'—namely the 'loans scandal'—the opposition would refuse to pass the government's budget Bills unless a general election was called. It was unheard of to 'block supply' in the Senate and thus render a government penniless.

Labor's narrow hold on the Senate had been eroded since February 1975, when Senator Murphy resigned to join the High Court. Breaking constitutional precedent, the NSW Liberal government had filled the vacancy with a non-Labor person. In June the death of a Labor senator saw his seat filled by another non-Labor appointment, by Queensland's Bjelke-Petersen government. To the conservatives, the Whitlam government was hell-bent on ruining Australia; to Labor sympathisers the conservatives were conspiring to destroy all parliamentary precedents.

Mounting public outrage forced the opposition to offer a compromise on 3 November: the Supply Bill would be passed if the government promised to call an election within the next six months. This offer was rejected by Whitlam. His party had the majority in the Lower House—the 'people's house'. To Whitlam the crisis was political, not constitutional. Within a week several Coalition senators, concerned at the break with parliamentary precedent, were considering voting with Labor to pass the Bill. But events took an extraordinary turn.

ABOVE:

Remembrance Day, 11 November 1974.

Exactly one year later, Prime Minister Gough Whitlam was sacked by the man he stands beside, Governor-General Sir John Kerr. Margaret Whitlam, wearing green, stands to Gough's right.

ABOVE:
Prior to the election, Gough Whitlam addresses supporters outside Parliament House in Canberra, November 1975.

The Dismissal

On the evening of 10 November 1975, Governor-General Sir John Kerr, a Whitlam appointee, was advised by Chief Justice Barwick, a former Liberal minister (and a long-time antagonist of Whitlam), that he (Kerr) could break this extraordinary deadlock by using his 'reserve powers'. The nature of these reserve powers was revealed the next day. Just before noon on 11 November 1975—Remembrance Day—Prime Minister Whitlam drove to Government House at Yarralumla to be told by Kerr that he—the Prime Minister—had been dismissed from office. Kerr informed him that he had commissioned the opposition leader, Malcolm Fraser, as leader of a 'caretaker government' until an election could be held. Parliament was dissolved and along with it much of Australia's faith in the past and hope for the future.

On the steps of Parliament House, the Governor-General's secretary, David Smith, read out the official notice. Whitlam appeared behind him, and promised the crowd: 'Nothing will save the Governor-General!' But the 13 December election—the most bitter ever waged in Australia—was a foregone conclusion. While securing only 54 per cent of the popular vote the Liberals and National Party (as the Country Party was now known) were swept into power with ninety-one seats, with Labor retaining only thirty-six seats. Ahead lay eight years of conservative rule.

The Fraser years

From 1975 to 1983, Australia was governed by a conservative Coalition saddled with severe economic problems not traceable solely to three years of Labor. It was a new, tough economic world. In the United States the industrial boom brought about by the Vietnam War had petered out, and in 1971 the US had a trade a deficit for the first time since 1893. Twenty years of budget surpluses in Australia had also ended. In 1976/77 the government announced the third year of budget deficits and the following year severely cut government spending.

ABOVE:
The completed Sydney Opera House. Its architect, aghast at the changes made to his original concept, did not attend its official opening.

The Fraser government began restructuring Medibank in 1977 because of its excessive cost and attempted to tighten company laws to prevent fraud and misuse of shareholders' funds by crooked directors (some of whom, for example, had hidden profits in secretive 'bottom of the harbour' schemes) but this latter initiative was blocked by the High Court of Sir Garfield Barwick, which viewed increased regulations as detrimental to commercial initiative. Chief Justice Barwick retired in 1980 on the eve of a decade of corporate chaos and excess, much of which could have been averted by tighter government controls. His name does not stand high in Australia's history.

Strikes were the norm of the late 1970s. In 1976 a one-day general strike was called to protest against the Fraser government's attempts to amend Medibank; Telecom was hit by a month-long strike by unionists protesting against the rapid introduction of new technology, and soon journalist on metropolitan newspapers struck when their typewriters were replaced by computers. In 1979 Commonwealth public servants went on strike and in 1982 bank employees struck in support of reduced hours—a 72-hour fortnight—the first strike of this nature for sixty-three years.

1977: Kerr resigns

Political bitterness was intense for the remainder of the 1970s. Sir John Kerr was often abused when he appeared in public, though he seemed oblivious for he was sometimes embarrassingly drunk. He resigned as Governor-General in 1977 and chose to spend most of his remaining years out of Australia. To succeed him Fraser chose a public figure who was widely admired, the distinguished Jewish academic Sir Zelman Cowen.

In the same year, 1977 a progressive MP and former minister Don Chipp resigned from the Liberal Party and formed a new one—the Democrats, one of the numerous 'third parties' that appear and disappear in Australian political life, serving as a safety valve for mounting frustrations and attracting voters dissatisfied with both major parties. In the December 1977 elections Fraser retained power, but both major parties lost votes to the Democrats, two of whose candidates were elected to the Senate.

ABOVE:
Malcolm Fraser (second
from left) and his cabinet,
1976. Andrew Peacock sits
on the right,

In the following year Gough Whitlam resigned as leader of the ALP and retired from politics. He later became Australia's ambassador to UNESCO in Paris, and his wit and a certain gift for self-mockery soon returned to strengthen the affection in which he was held. He never grew embittered and lived long enough to see himself celebrated as a historic phenomenon, revered, indeed loved, even by those who never voted for him. Animosity toward his old foe Malcolm Fraser disappeared in later years when the two men appeared together in public forums fighting the same battle to protest foreign ownership of the Fairfax newspapers, and they enjoyed an unusual friendship. Recalling the dramas of 1975, Whitlam wrote in his 1997 book *Abiding Interests*: 'Malcolm Fraser took advantage of Kerr's and Barwick's shortcomings, but he did not set out to deceive me. Accordingly we have always had civil relations or better.'

Seventies style

The 1970s was the last splutter of individualism. Seen by many as just an extension of the swinging sixties, the decade had a spontaneity and outrageousness all its own. Probably everyone enjoyed the 1970s except those with taste. Twenty years later many fathers would deny to their children that they wore their hair to their shoulders and Mexican moustaches; favoured pastel-coloured terylene safari suits or figure-hugging body-shirts and chunky jewellery, flared trousers and high-heeled clogs, or listened to 'wall of sound' disco music so loud that conversation was impossible. Even the popular culture of the time seems gauche: predictable TV miniseries on the bushrangers and the outback, or soap operas about the new pioneers—families stranded in bleak suburbia. There was little originality.

In 1977 cricket became a glamour sport when the media magnate Kerry Packer (owner of the Nine Network) founded World Series Cricket and enticed the top cricketers away from the national cricket boards that had controlled Test matches, to play professionally in unofficial matches that were televised and highly publicised. The players also wore coloured outfits—and used a white ball instead of the traditional red. So many players were attracted by the contracts offered that

LEFT:
Nobel Prize winning
scientist Sir Macfarlane
Burnet (left) in 1979
with his successor as
Director of the Walter
& Eliza Hall Institute,
Sir Gustav Nossal, the
Austrian-born immun-
ologist who was
knighted in 1977.

in the 1978–79 England–Australia Tests, England won 5-1 over the weakened
Australian side.

Even Australia's record in the 1972 and 1976 Olympic Games was a disappoint-
ing one. Government funding was introduced to encourage sport and in 1981 the
Australian Institute of Sport opened in Canberra. Since that date Australia, whose
sportsmen and women have had the advantage of professional and constant training, has restored a reputation in competitive sports unequalled by any nation of
equivalent population, but the cost to the taxpayer has been high.

1980: Fraser's last term

The Fraser government was again returned to power in the elections of 1980, but
in that year the giant GMH (General Motors-Holden) plant at Pagewood in New
South Wales closed, an indication of the dislocation to the economy made by
imports of Japanese vehicles. In 1982 recession came. GMH, BHP and Alcoa
announced a program of 'restructuring'. With unemployment growing, Fraser's

leadership came under question from his own party: in mid-1981 Andrew Peacock became the fifteenth minister to leave Fraser's government, protesting that the Prime Minister 'was impossible to work with'.

The authoritarian Fraser was a far more liberal and human man than his critics allowed. His record in conservation was outstanding. He continued the Whitlam government's initiatives and in 1982 alone proclaimed the Upper Franklin River a World Heritage site to deter the Tasmanian government from damming its rivers, led the successful campaign to halt whaling and handed back Kakadu—established as a national park in 1979—in Arnhem Land to its traditional owners (who now lease it back to the government). He reduced the barriers against non-European immigration and encouraged the development of 'ethnic' broadcasting; SBS-TV began transmitting news bulletins and innovative programs specially for immigrants in 1982, and within twenty years most Australians were able to receive them, enjoying a stimulating bonus in the shape of European and Asian feature films that had never been previously shown in Australian cinemas. Fraser's outspoken denunciation of racism made him one of the few statesmen in the British Commonwealth, and the Howard Liberal government's attitude to refugees in the 1990s and beyond would cause him grief. Fraser can be seen as the last of the giant political figures on the Australian scene.

Concerned about the rapidly changing world economic scene, Fraser constituted in 1982 an important Inquiry into the entire Australian financial system under the chairmanship of the influential Sir Keith Campbell, with a special emphasis on banking. The Campbell Report recommended that most government controls on banking be removed to encourage more competitive trading. Indeed, many of those saving to buy a house used building societies and other cooperatives instead of the established banks, because the latters' interest rates on deposits (set by the government) were too low, their charges too high, loans too difficult to obtain. Mergers of revered institutions had formerly occasioned howls of outrage, but two major banks—the Bank of New South Wales ('the Wales') and the Commercial Bank of Australia (CBA)—merged in 1982 under the name 'Westpac' and the National Bank of Australia ('the Nat') merged with the Commercial Banking Company of Sydney (CBC) to form the National Australia Bank. The number of mergers, takeovers, and name changes would soon be dizzying.

As wool prices continued to fall in the early 1980s so did the sheep population, to 174 million (ten sheep for every Australian). The Australian Wool Corporation guaranteed to buy growers' wool at a set 'floor price' but international buyers were few and soon the unsold wool accumulated. By the early 1990s the wool stockpile reached 4.7 million bales, stored in more than 100 warehouses—there was so much unsold wool that if the bales were placed in a row they would stretch from Brisbane to Perth. (The hapless AWC was dissolved in 1991, when the nation's sheep population had been reduced to around 100 million, and the stockpile was slowly sold off at the best price offered. The last bale was proudly presented in 2002 to the National Wool Museum in Geelong where it is a prized exhibit.)

Australia could no longer ride to prosperity on the sheep's back or the seat of the tractor. By 1982 exports were falling, employment had risen to 10 per cent, and inflation was climbing. With a general election looming, the Country Party changed its name to the National Party in the hope of attracting a greater number of conservative votes.

Australians were becoming alarmed at reports that in American cities patients were suffering from a strange and deadly new disease known as AIDS for which there was no known cure.

The only bright news was that Australia's foreign debt was only $20 billion. It was to increase tenfold in the next twelve years. In that same year the Labor Party's intellectual Barry Jones published his plea for Australians to grasp the opportunities of the new technology in a rapidly changing world. It was called *Sleepers, Wake!* But Australians continued to slumber.

When Labor took office in 1983 Australia was economically ailing. Twenty years later its economy would be thriving, but the transformation was a savage one, dislocating peoples' lives and hopes. A hard new world was emerging.

The economic revolution

In the outside world—as Australians called it— enormous changes were taking place. Within less than a decade the clearly defined world order and the societies that had existed since 1945, Australia's included, were to undergo a shattering transformation.

In 1980 Ronald Reagan was elected President of the United States, one year after Margaret Thatcher had led the Conservatives to victory over Labour in Britain. It is difficult to imagine less likely leaders or allies than these two figures; yet Britain's first female prime minister and Reagan, the ageing former Hollywood cowboy star, established an extraordinary rapport and not only dominated the decade but reshaped it. They inherited troubled economies. The USA and Britain—in common with most of the nations of the developed world including Australia—were faced with runaway inflation and mounting unemployment but with no increase in productivity: a state known as 'stagflation'. In both countries government regulated the economy on Keynesian lines—imposing price controls, for example, when inflation began to climb; but this measure was proving ineffective. Britain's 'mixed economy' of government-owned and privately-owned businesses was inefficient. A generation earlier, the Labour government had nationalised major industries—aviation, railways, coalmining and steel, for example—but none was now profitable. Even in the United States, where private enterprise had always thrived, innovations in aviation and airlines (areas in which the US led the world) were cramped by numerous federal regulatory bodies, a holdover of the Roosevelt era, when big business was placed under surveillance.

The Reagan–Thatcher model

The Reagan and Thatcher governments broke with long-accepted economic approaches. Thatcher had been impressed by the theories of Friedrich von Hayek, an Austrian émigré economist whose disciples at the London School of Economics became the 'monetarist' school; their theories could be explained simply as: 'Markets work—governments don't'. In October 1979, less than six months after taking office, Thatcher abolished remaining exchange controls and then began a ruthless policy of selling off government-owned utilities and corporations such as British Steel, which had been a constant drain on British taxpayers. To the astonishment of the public—and of workers laid off in the drastic restructuring—the newly constituted businesses soon made profits. These profits were lightly taxed.

As late as 1981 France's newly elected socialist government, ending more than two decades of Gaullist rule, announced a program of nationalising industries, but it too soon came under the spell of the new economic theories.

In the United Kingdom Thatcher went further. In 1984 shares in the nation's communications network, British Telecom, were offered to the public. Social security benefits were pared, and so were company taxes. Closures of uneconomic coalmines led to a national coalminers strike during 1984 but after a year of violent confrontation the strikers accepted the government's conditions and the power of their union was broken. Thatcher applauded the way the Australian newspaper proprietor Rupert Murdoch had challenged the unions by building his own modern printing plant in London in 1985 and then running it with staff who accepted his employment conditions: 500 non-union printers replaced a work force of 5000. The plant was picketed by 12,000 unionists and in one day of savage rioting more than 150 policemen were injured by the mob: for a century Britain had never known social division or violence on this scale but Prime Minister Thatcher proceeded on the course she had set, earning the sobriquet 'The Iron Lady'.

In the United States Reagan cut government spending and abolished regulations, while lowering corporate and personal taxes. By 1983, after a painful recession, America's economy had picked up. At the same time, a technological revolution pioneered by computers was under way in North America, Great Britain and Europe, transforming business methods. But Australia seemed to lag.

435

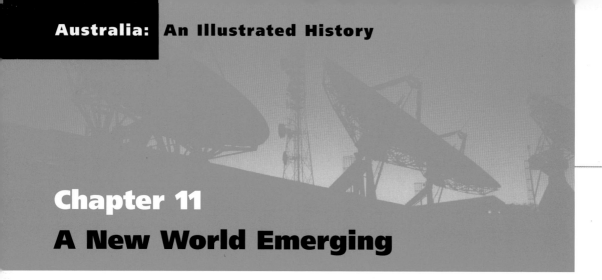

Chapter 11
A New World Emerging

From 1983 to the present

The Hawke era begins

LABOR BIDED ITS TIME. On 3 February 1983 Prime Minister Fraser, confident of victory over a Labor Party led by Whitlam's successor Bill Hayden, called on the Governor-General seeking a double dissolution. But on that very day, before Fraser could obtain a response from the Governor-General and announce the election, Hayden was encouraged to resign as leader. Fraser had his election, but found he would be combating the popular Bob Hawke, the former president of the ACTU. Labor fought the campaign with an absence of the pyrotechnics characteristic of their tactics in the past, while horrifying February ('Ash Wednesday') bushfires ravaged Victoria and South Australia, taking seventy-one lives.

The old rowdy Labor militancy had gone; Labor's program promised a 'middle way', an end to confrontation and the birth of a policy of 'consensus' by which employees and management would reach agreements on how best to solve problems that were becoming mountainous. The new conservative Labor program was about to bury much of socialism.

In the March 1983 elections Hawke and the Labor Party swept into power, winning seventy-five House seats, the Coalition retaining only fifty. In the following month union leaders and captains of industry met in Canberra in an unusual gathering in the chambers of Parliament itself. Here the Prime Minister and his Treasurer Paul Keating (aged thirty-nine, he was one of the youngest Treasurers in Australian history) explained the new policy of consensus: both sides undertook to follow restraint in dealing with wage claims and industrial action. This was an Australian 'first' and was emulated by several European governments. In September 1983 the Hawke government introduced 'Medicare' to replace the truncated Medibank—but the rest of its time in office was to see an abandonment of some of Labor's basic tenets.

1984: 'Deregulation'

In December 1983 the Treasurer took another step in the new direction Labor had marked out. Keating announced that the Australian dollar would be allowed to 'float'—that is, its value would be decided not by the government (Treasury and the Reserve Bank) but by the international money market. Its value fell immediately—a sobering shock to Australians—before stabilising.

Early in 1984 Keating announced that exchange controls would be eliminated and banking 'deregulated'—in short, the remaining controls on the inflow or outflow of money would be abolished, in keeping with the world's new 'free market' economic practice. Foreign banks would be allowed to operate in Australia to

OPPOSITE:
Labor back in power: Bob Hawke and his wife Hazel acknowledge the cheers on victory night, March 1983

RIGHT:
Prime Minister Hawke; an official photo.

stimulate competition. These decisions were, in the view of the political columnist Paul Kelly, 'the most influential decisions of the Hawke–Keating years'. He explains: 'Hawke and Keating looked out to the world and sought to internationalise the Australian economy … They grasped that the revolutionary changes in the world economy meant that a new benchmark of international competitiveness was fundamental for Australian prosperity.'

The deregulation of banking opened the gates to a greater inflow of capital than anyone had imagined. In a world economy stricken by Third World debt, the impending bankruptcy of European communist regimes and a United States emerging from recession, Australia's renowned social and political stability made it a good investment risk for dollar-rich international merchant banks. During 1985–86, sixteen foreign-owned banking groups began trading in Australia, and within ten years of deregulation there were more than seventy foreign-exchange dealers. Many building societies became fully fledged banks. Payment for goods or services by cash card or credit card (electronic funds transfer arrived in 1983) was common by the mid-1980s, as were automatic teller machines (ATMs) dispensing cash as if by magic. The monthly balance of trade figures quickly became the barometer of Australia's health, a guide to the strength or weakness of the Australian dollar.

The Bond era

The early years of the Hawke government were up-beat ones. The euphoria of the millionaire Alan Bond's victory in the September 1983 America's Cup yacht race in *Australia II* coincided with an economic recovery and carried through to the 1988 Bicentenary, the nation's birthday party.

Alan Bond would be a representative figure of the 1980s. Born in England in 1938, he had migrated with his parents to Western Australia in 1950, and began work as a sign-writer. In 1956 he was arrested on two charges of housebreaking; released (ironically) on a good behaviour bond, he formed his own sign company next year and by 1960 was involved in real estate, borrowing heavily from banks to develop his resort Yanchep Sun City. Bond mounted challenges for the America's Cup in 1977 and 1980—in the latter year he was so well known that he was named 'Australian of the Year'. On the day of Bond's 1983 America's Cup victory the Western Australian government under the entrepreneur-minded Labor Premier Burke paid Bond Corporation $42 million for shares in a diamond mine. By 1988 Bond Corporation had grown 20-fold, borrowing billions of dollars to fund acquisitions ranging from

ABOVE:
Treasurer Paul Keating.

ABOVE:
Entrepreneur Alan Bond from a Bond Corporation annual report. By the early 1990s he and most of his directors were under investigation for flouting corporate regulations, or in prison

breweries to media (purchasing Kerry Packer's TV and radio network for more than $1 billion) in addition to the Bell Group; over 1982–88 it had earned $700 million in profits but, by using ploys such as tax havens, had paid only $20 million in tax, and rumours were soon rife that losses had been hidden and profits wildly overstated.

AIDS

In this up-beat time, the only dampener was the arrival in the early 1980s of a deadly new disease known as AIDS (acquired immune deficiency syndrome). The first cases in the world had been diagnosed in New York in 1981, when homosexual men were afflicted with a wasting disease that destroyed their immune system. The first AIDS case was diagnosed in Australia in November 1982. The actual virus was discovered a year later—human immunodeficiency virus (HIV)—and more cases were reported in Sydney, again among homosexuals. The virus had quickly travelled around the world, at the speed of jet aircraft. Before mid-1985 blood from HIV-infected donors was unwittingly given in transfusions to 400 Australians. The disease can also be spread by drug users sharing infected hypodermic needles.

The onset of the disease occurred at a time when homosexuality had been accepted and no longer penalised. In 1984 New South Wales decriminalised homosexual acts between consenting adults and it was accepted by the federal government that homosexuals should be granted equality in employment and should not be discriminated against.

BELOW:
Replaced as Labor leader by Bob Hawke, Bill Hayden (seen here addressing the United Nations) served loyally as Labor's Minister for Foreign Affairs and was later appointed Governor-General.

By the mid-1990s nearly 20,000 Australians were infected with HIV and 4000 had died, but a government warning campaign on television using shock tactics had a traumatic effect on Australians—and on their love life. The development of drugs to combat the worst ravages of the disease has given many sufferers hope but in other parts of the world such as Africa and South-East Asia, where AIDS had been spread by heterosexual contact, the disease had claimed 20 million lives by 2003, with another 30 million people infected.

1986: 'Banana republic'

Warnings about the consequences of growing deficits and a national spending spree were voiced by Prime Minister Hawke in 1986, when he told Australians that their problems were in some ways 'worse than the war'. Treasurer Keating, a more picturesque speaker, warned Australia during an interview on commercial radio that the nation was approaching the state of a 'banana republic'. The Queensland Premier, the eccentric Joh Bjelke-Petersen, announced that he would run for Federal Parliament and the 'Joh for PM' movement began, much to the distress of Liberal leader John Howard. Fortunately the push ended soon afterwards, but Howard was replaced by Andrew Peacock in 1989.

It seemed that the Liberals were no longer of appeal to the electorate.

Hawke's popularity was still high. He created the Office of the Status of Women and in 1986 introduced 'self-assessment' for taxpayers while announcing plans to introduce an 'Australia Card' to force registration of all financial dealings. Hawke fought and won the July 1987 elections on the issue. Most Australians who had paid their taxes honestly regarded it as an invasion of civil liberties and the Australia Card was never introduced. It was found to be unconstitutional, and it would soon have been irrelevant, for electronic monitoring of financial transactions would soon tell governments all they needed to know about their citizens' financial affairs.

ABOVE:

When courts found in 1985 that banning women from the armed forces was discriminatory, females were allowed to enter the service of their choice (excluding combat roles). A government-sponsored exhibition toured the nation in the 1990s, demonstrating cheekily the remarkable advances women had achieved in Australia over a century

Many of the overseas loans of the 'easy money' 1980s were squandered on unproductive activities—speculation, luxuries by farmers, 'conglomerate building' by growth companies purchasing smaller firms at greatly inflated prices. These loans were taken out at deceptively low interest rates in the mid-1980s but by the 1990s interest rates had risen in some cases past 25 per cent per annum. Farmers were among the first to seek loans; the collapse of commodity prices and rural land values at the end of the decade left up to 70 per cent of farmers carrying unrepayable debts. Australia's foreign debt—which was non-existent forty years before—began to grow, and soon the ability of governments to simply pay the interest on their debts would be the indication of their own credit rating.

A restructuring of Australia's industrial base was necessary. By 1990 the nine car assembly plants in the nation had been reduced to three, and these were battling to compete against the Japanese and Korean cars entering the country under lowered tariffs. In technology, Australia had fallen behind the developing Asian nations—Singapore, Taiwan and Korea were now out-producing even Japan on a per capita basis. It was a strange new competitive world in which Australians felt uneasy. Australia was slowly evolving into a 'post-Industrial society', a service economy where products (from farms, mines or manufacturing) were employing fewer workers than the expanding 'service industries' of retail, banking, finance, transport, education and tourism. China would be the prime beneficiary of the liberalisation of world trade. Her work force was immense, labour costs low, resources great. Within a decade China was producing much of the clothing Australians bought at a fraction of the cost of locally made merchandise.

Universities galore

'Australia, in addition to being the Lucky Country, must be the Clever Country,' Prime Minister Hawke announced. Pledging to increase the number of university graduates, John Dawkins, the Minister responsible over 1987–88, set in train the merger of the nineteen existing 'old' universities with fifty of the colleges of advanced education (CAEs) to form a total of thirty-six large universities; some

ABOVE:
Age of technology: by the mid-1980s computers were in almost universal use in business

remote colleges became campuses of the main university. They were soon joined by the first of the 'private universities', Bond University in Queensland. Fees were introduced, and these were to rise alarmingly. The cost of studying at university became a major investment for students, but their degree on graduating was their entry card into highly paid employment in the burgeoning professional work force of the 1990s.

1980s: Computers and CDs

By the mid-1980s desktop electronic computers were found in most offices and an increasing number of homes. Long sceptical of computers, Australians soon embraced them with enthusiasm. In 1979 and 1980 journalists on metropolitan newspapers had struck for extra pay when typewriters were replaced with desk-top computers (visual display units) that converted their copy directly into type. With every year computers were becoming smaller, with higher storage capacity and speed of operation—and cheaper, too. In 1984 the first 'easy-to-use' compact computer, the Apple Mackintosh, was released. In addition to a keyboard it had a sort of remote control—a mouse—and soon rival manufacturers using 'IBM compatible' operating systems stole Apple's thunder, taking over the market. The modern 'personal computer' (PC) had arrived, looking reassuringly like a television set.

But three generations of computers had preceded it, and for thousands of years humans have used primitive calculating machines (the wooden abacus, for example, is still used in Arab lands). In the seventeenth century Blaise Pascal invented a gear-driven adding machine and Gottfried Leibniz one that could not only add but also subtract, multiply, divide and calculate square roots. The Englishman Charles Babbage created a mechanical calculator as early as the 1830s. In December 1943 British mathematical geniuses created the first modern computer powered by electricity—'Colossus'—to process and decipher intercepted German 'Enigma' wireless messages (a job previously carried out by hundreds of female clerks with pencil and paper). In 1944 Harvard University, in association with engineers from International Business Machines (IBM) built a gigantic computer; it also converted numbers into electronic impulses that could be added up using vacuum tubes. In 1951 the United States Census Bureau purchased UNIVAC, developed by Sperry Rand, which was shown on television predicting the results of the 1952 US

ABOVE:
Cartoonist Peter
Nicholson satirised
prominent figures of
the 1980s (all except
one of them politicians)
in his *Rubbery Figures*
series on ABC television.
Caught in the act from
left to right: Andrew
Peacock, Malcolm Fraser
(standing behind Bob
Hawke), John Howard,
Paul Keating, John Elliott
and Joh Bjelke-Petersen.

election. In Australia Dr Trevor Pearcey of the CSIRO began building the world's fourth digital computer, CSIRAC, in 1949, and in 1960 the AMP and MLC insurance companies installed the first computers in Australia to be used in business. The 360 series of computer developed by IBM was in common use during the 1960s. Developments in 'electronics'—the invention of the transistor in 1958 (replacing bulky valves) and then the integrated circuit, which could hold on a silicon chip the capacity of hundreds (and soon thousands) of miniaturised transistors—led to the table-top 'mini-computer'. By late 1983, when the revolutionary compact disc arrived on the market—enabling music and images, in addition to text, to be converted and stored digitally—there were more than 100,000 computers in Australia. Two years later the number had risen to 200,000, and since that time growth has averaged 30 per cent or more each year. By the year 2000, more than 50 per cent of Australians had computers or were familiar with their use—one of the highest rates of acceptance in the world. The sleepers had wakened—and some users stayed up all night, enthralled by computers' magic.

The end of Anzac?

In the 1980s New Zealand seemed to be drifting away. Always independent and keen to show their self-reliance, New Zealanders had pursued actively a campaign to declare the Pacific a nuclear-free zone, a policy in which all her political parties concurred. When France persisted in testing atomic bombs on her Pacific atolls, New Zealand dispatched an RNZN frigate in protest to the test zone. Quicker than most to see that the Cold War's tensions were ending, New Zealand refused to admit a visiting US warship to her harbours in 1984 in case it was nuclear-armed, and in the February 1985 ANZUS naval exercises the United States refused to allow New Zealand's forces to participate, effectively expelling her from ANZUS. Australia tried to mediate in the dispute but without success, and accused its partner of failing to share the responsibilities of defending the region. In 1985 French agents sank the Green Peace protest ship *Rainbow Warrior* in Auckland harbour, adding to New Zealanders' anger. The New Zealand government bought only two of the Australian-built Anzac frigates and cancelled orders for the rest, and in 2002 announced that the RNZAF would soon scrap its last fighter aircraft and not

RIGHT:
NZ troops marching
off a parade.

replace them. Its reduced armed forces would concentrate on peacekeeping duties when required; but ANZUS was now effectively dead and with it possibly the unique emotional link forged in war by the men of the two nations. The number of New Zealanders fleeing a depressed economy to live in Australia, where they had automatic right of entry, rose from 175,000 in 1981 to 275,000 ten years later. In the famous quip of the acerbic New Zealand politician Sir Robert Muldoon, their departure for Australia 'raised the IQ of both countries'.

With a population of only 3.5 million, it is possible that New Zealand will forge a closer union with Australia and this could be an advantage. New Zealanders have often pioneered progress while others lagged behind: in 2004 their Governor-General, Chief Justice and Prime Minister were women. The contribution of New Zealanders to Australian life has already been enormous: the founder of AMPOL, Bill Walkley; the Commissioner of the Snowy Mountains Scheme, 'Big Bill' Hudson; the bibliophile and life-long collector of Australiana Rex Nan Kivell; the artists Dorothy Wall (creator of 'Blinky Bill'), Elioth Gruner and David Low; the writers Douglas Stewart, Ruth Park, Florence James; the satirist John Clarke, the actors Rebecca Gibney, Sam Neill and Russell Crowe… all were New Zealand–born.

End of the 'classless society'?

Australians enjoyed the illusion of prosperity as the 1980s ended. Foreign debt rose but investors benefited in the short term from rising share values, record dividends, and absurdly high interest on investments in building societies, especially in Victoria. Most growth lay in the 'sunrise' industries—the new areas of high technology, tourism and leisure.

Others marvelled at the extravagant lifestyles of the entrepreneurs and millionaires—merchant bankers, property barons, corporate executives. Sydney, Melbourne, Adelaide, Brisbane and Perth became skyscraper cities, their central business districts monuments to postmodernist architecture and capitalist success. 'The rich grew richer; a 1986 estimate credited Australia with about 30,000 millionaires,' writes the historian Geoffrey Bolton. 'Ten per cent of Australia's families owned 60 per cent of its wealth.' In 1985 the giant Coles and Myer retail groups merged and soon controlled 25 per cent of Australian retailing.

Large corporations swallowed smaller ones. The Hawke–Keating government attempted to break up the media empires so that owners of newspapers could no longer also control television stations in the same market. But the result after 1987 has been described as the newspaper world's 'greatest upheaval in its history' accompanied by the closure of many dailies and the unforeseen concentration of ownership in two or three owners. Rupert Murdoch had taken out American citizenship in 1985 and his giant News Corporation earned most of its profit outside Australia; but News Corp took over the Herald & Weekly Times Group of Melbourne for $2.5 billion in 1987. After the collapse of Fairfax—publishers of the *Sydney Morning Herald*, *The Age* and the *Australian Financial Review*—in 1990 its majority shareholding passed into the hands of the Canadian Conrad Black. Thus by the end of the turbulent decade ten of the twelve capital-city dailies were under foreign control. So were most of the book publishers—and all of them repatriated their profits overseas.

World Bank statistics suggested that Australia in the late 1980s had the most unequal distribution of wealth of any Western nation. The rich in Australia had seldom flaunted their wealth; they kept their money to themselves, and the nation prided itself on its freedom from class distinctions based on affluence and a fortunate birth. But a new generation of successful businessmen splashed their money around in a vulgar display and some achieved celebrity status. Soon Australia would be divided between the successful (for professional earnings were rising) and the poor.

The poor got poorer. Almost one in four school leavers were without work during the 1980s and had little chance of obtaining jobs; a similar proportion of the population as a whole lived close to the poverty line and faced a distressing future in which medical and unemployment benefits were being reduced. It would take another decade before Australians adjusted to a world in which full-time employment for all was recognised as impossible.

1987: Stock market collapse

The bust came suddenly. On 20 October 1987 the over-heated New York stock market crashed; in one day $700 billion was wiped off the value of shares, and the shock waves struck Australian stock exchanges savagely. It was the beginning of

ABOVE:
The New York stock market crash of 1987 struck Australia savagely.

the end for the overvalued, debt-laden entrepreneurial empires and a crash more devastating than the 1890s bust. Some predicted the coming of a depression on the scale of the 1929–30 slump, but the world economy was now too resilient or perhaps too elastic, and it absorbed the shock before it became an earthquake.

On Thursday 22 October 1987 depositors made a rush on Perth's best-known merchant bank, Rothwells, withdrawing $250 million in the week before its doors closed. Of the other $750 million of depositors' funds little could be found. On the following weekend a $370 million 'rescue package' for Rothwells was put together by a host of the banker's business associates, headed by Alan Bond, who flew to Perth in his corporate jet. 'The rescuers read like a *Business Who's Who* of Australia—Kerry Packer, Robert Holmes à Court, John Elliott and Larry Adler all agreed to throw a lifeline; Brian Yuill and Alan Bond also held out a hand', wrote Paul Barry in his remarkable biography of Bond. Fifteen years later Packer would be the wealthiest man in Australia and the other names would be dead, business failures or forgotten.

When Rothwells crashed in October 1988 'it was the harbinger of doom, the first star to fall in the great Australian corporate collapse,' wrote Barry. 'By 1990, and much earlier for some, Ariadne was gone, so were Equiticorp, Spedley Securities, Tricontinental, Girvan, Hooker Corporation, Quintex, Westmex, Rothwells, Parry Corporation and a host of smaller fry besides.' By late 1988 Bond's empire in mining, property, media and brewing had debts of $10 billion. In 1989 an ABC investigative report revealed that the Bond group had evaded tax on a monumental scale. Having paid Packer more than $1 billion for the Nine Network, Bond had to sell it back for little more than $200 million. By 1991 Christopher Skase of Quintex was filing for bankruptcy and in the following year Alan Bond was declared bankrupt. Other casualties of the bust were ordinary Australians who had invested their superannuation or savings in 'financial plans' on professional advice, and found their investment portfolios almost worthless.

Alan Bond was eventually gaoled for illegally stripping $1.2 billion from Bell Resources (much of the money still remains unaccounted for). In 1995, having paid back to the liquidators just over $3 million to clear his personal debts of $625 million, he was discharged from bankruptcy. Christopher Skase, denying that he had acted illegally, fled to Majorca from where he fought extradition to Australia. He died there in 2001.

1988: The Bicentennial

The celebration of two centuries of European settlement began well before the official festivities. An avalanche of pictorial books celebrating Australia's achievements flooded the bookshops, and the boyish millionaire and record-breaking aviator Dick Smith (in 1983 he had made the first solo helicopter round-the-world flight) launched in 1986 a glossy quarterly magazine called *Australian Geographic* that within ten years had a circulation of 250,000. In the same year Paul Hogan's film *Crocodile Dundee* broke box office records around the world. A year earlier (1985) one of the nation's symbols (as much an icon as the Sydney Harbour Bridge or Paul Hogan)—the giant central Australian monolith Ayers Rock (Uluru)—had been given back to its original owners, the Mutijulu people, and Australians applauded the act. Australia's international reputation was high and tourism boomed.

The celebrations in Sydney on 26 January 1988 were the colourful climax to an overheated decade. The Queen of Australia's representatives Charles, Prince of Wales, and his wife Diana sailed in review on a harbour thick with the sails and masts of visiting warships, windjammers and liners, yachts and pleasure craft, including replica vessels of the First Fleet. The Prince was seen to wave enthusiastically to a passing yacht crowded with young bare-breasted girls who shouted 'Good on yer, Charlie!' and the two sunny faces of Australia narrowly avoided collision. Unlike the bicentennial of 1770, celebrations were carefully planned to include respectful reference to the Aboriginal people, many of whom understandably boycotted the party as a celebration of the European 'invasion'. Several Aborigines gate-crashed the launch of the official Bicentennial history of Australia on the shores of Sydney Harbour and hurled a copy of it into the water, but this was the extent of their protest, and many reflected that the nation's healthy tolerance and humour were still intact.

The Queen herself arrived in May 1988 to open Australia's new Parliament House, sited on a hill overlooking the city, and the old Houses of Parliament became a museum and art gallery. Like many buildings from the 1980s, the new Parliament House was breathtaking in design, but extravagant. With a budget in 1978 of $220 million, it was completed at a cost of $1.2 billion, and many wondered where the money was found to build it. Australia's foreign debt mounted.

1989: The end of the Cold War

Australia was so involved in its own changes that many of the dramas in the wider world passed it by. On 8 December 1987 President Reagan and the Soviet Union's Mikhail Gorbachev announced in Washington their agreement to remove nuclear missiles from Europe. It was the effective end of the Cold War. The Soviet Union announced that its five-million-strong armed forces would be reduced by 10 per cent within two years and divisions would be begin withdrawing from Eastern Europe. After more than forty years of Cold War, the Soviet Union was facing bankruptcy and unable to maintain its empire.

Ironically, the pace of disarmament had been forced by President Reagan's announcement in 1981 that the United States intended to build a missile defence shield in space capable of destroying any approaching enemy missiles. It was denounced by critics in the United States as a 'Star Wars' concept; others called it pie in the sky, for it was still on the drawing boards. But it alarmed the Soviet Union, whose space technology and economy were failing. Reagan then sent powerful Pershing nuclear-armed cruise missiles (capable of hitting Moscow three minutes after launch) to US bases in Western Europe. In Britain and Germany protesting crowds blockaded the bases but Reagan reminded his critics that the Soviet Union was still an 'evil empire'.

It seemed that a new arms race and a new era of tension were about to begin. In 1985, however, the realist Mikhail Gorbachev took over the helm in the Soviet Union. In his first meeting with Reagan he suggested that both sides dismantle all their nuclear weapons —an idea so novel that the normally loquacious Reagan was lost for words. In later meetings Gorbachev offered to withdraw nuclear missiles from Eastern Europe if the United States scrapped the missile shield and removed the Pershings. This proposal was acceptable. Sanity triumphed. The Cold War had ended.

Early in 1988 President Reagan and Gorbachev walked together amid friendly crowds in Moscow's Red Square. When a Western reporter asked Reagan whether he thought the Soviet Union was still an 'evil empire' the President replied: 'No. I was talking about another time, and another era.'

In mid-1989 East Germany remained the only part of the Soviet bloc that refused to allow its citizens to travel to the West—from which they were cut off by concrete walls, electrified fencing and minefields—and the state was bankrupt. Many East Germans began to leave via the more open frontiers of Czechoslovakia and the trickle became a river. When the East German authorities announced that travel restrictions would be lifted, a human flood of East Berliners surged through the checkpoints at the Brandenburg Gate while the security forces looked on. Soviet troops remained in their barracks. Over the following months people took to the streets in Hungary, Czechoslovakia, Rumania, Bulgaria and Albania, forcing the resignation of the communist governments. The communist empire fell without a shot fired (except in Bucharest where fighting between secret police and the army lasted for days and the hated rulers, Nicolae Ceaucescu and his malevolent wife, were executed). The reunification of Germany in 1990 (an event opposed by Britain and France, each of which had long memories of German wars) marked the burial of Communism as a credible political force. In 1991 the Soviet Union broke up into fifteen independent states, including the Russian Federation, and the accumulated detritus of seventy years of grey dictatorship, coercion and state control began to be dismantled. In the same years the Communist Party of Australia was dissolved; few Australians had taken it seriously.

1990s: The media giants—Murdoch and Packer

By 1990 even the great Fairfax newspaper group was bankrupt, victim of an attempt by a younger member of the Fairfax family to buy back total control. He was left instead with unrepayable debts and sold the company off before leaving to live permanently in the United States. Sydney's Kerry Packer was able to buy a sizeable shareholding in Fairfax, and, once more in control of the television and radio interests he had bought back cheaply from Alan Bond, emerged from the 1980s as Australia's wealthiest man. He was soon to invest in Sydney's first legal casino, which opened in 1995.

Rupert Murdoch's rise to global power was phenomenal. After inheriting a handful of small newspapers from his father Sir Keith Murdoch in 1953, Rupert moved into Sydney in 1960 by purchasing the tabloid *Daily Mirror*, initiating a circulation war with its rival the Sun (which later folded) and founding the quality newspaper the *Australian* in 1964. He took over the flagging London daily tabloid *The Sun* in 1969, making it a vulgar (and successful) copy of his *Daily Mirror*, with daily sales of 3.6 million copies (a world press record) and an annual profit of around $100 million. To the consternation of the snobby English Establishment, he then took over two revered papers, *The Times* and the *Sunday Times* in 1981 (and a significant share of the long-established book publisher, Collins). He broke the power of the printing unions by setting up his own London printing works in 1985 and then replacing unionists with contracted (non-union) staff, winning the admiration of Prime Minister Thatcher for his initiative. News Corporation narrowly avoided collapse in 1991 following the share market plunge when bank loans became due for repayment (the company's debts amounted to $9 billion) and revenue was falling. Rolling over the loans, Murdoch expanded his acquisitions wildly until by 1993 News Corporation had more than 500 subsidiary companies in Europe, America and Asia. The brash Australian-born magnate was by the year 2000 running a media empire of newspapers, magazines, book publishers (HarperCollins), film studios (including Fox) and television networks that spanned the world—and much of space, for many of his pay-TV programs were bounced from satellite.

'End of certainty'

Financial collapses continued. The Victorian government, borrowing heavily overseas to finance newly arising 'sunrise' industries revealed in 1990 that its debts were close to $30 billion. After the collapse of Geelong's main housing bank, public outrage forced the resignation of Premier John Cain, just as Western Australia's

Hong Kong here we come!

Ansett Australia.

Ansett Australia.

ABOVE:
Deregulation was the cry of the 1980s: Ansett Airlines, which had swallowed ANA, took on the challenge to fly international routes, but collapsed in 2002.

Premier Burke had been forced to resign because of dealings with discredited entrepreneurs in 'WA Inc.' South Australia's Bannon government was shaken by the collapse of the Bank of South Australia. John Cain, Brian Burke and John Bannon had been seen as Labor's brightest stars—seemingly skilled, dedicated men who had inspired trust.

The 1990s: Privatisation

The 1980s was the decade of globalisation and computers. The 1990s was that of privatisation and a new innovation in communications—the Internet. It is hard to know which of the two had a more immediate effect on Australians, for both were revolutions.

In October 1990 the federal government ended the two airlines policy in civil aviation and a new, deregulated industry took off. By December 1991 one of the new airlines, Compass, had collapsed with debts of $154 million. Only six months earlier the government had announced that Qantas and Australian Airlines (the old TAA) would be merged and privatised: three days later Qantas offered $400 million for Australian Airlines; this made it a fleet of eighty-four aircraft and one of the world's major airlines. Ansett Airlines was to survive until 2002, victim of the modern cut-throat aviation world, and leaving a new player, the Briton Richard Branson's Virgin Blue, to take its place.

In 1991 the government began privatising the Commonwealth Bank—'the peoples' bank'—by selling off shares in it to the public. By 1993 it had sold 49 per cent of it, and the balance was eagerly purchased before the decade was finished. In their rush to reduce costs and pay handsome dividends to shareholders, the banks were to alienate their customers. Within a decade the Commonwealth Bank had closed 870 branches (mainly in country towns), laid off 17,000 staff, eliminating small savers whose accounts had never been profitable and replacing them with big investors. The Hawke–Keating government's legislation in the early 1990s

forcing all employees to invest a percentage (about 10 per cent) of their wages or salaries in superannuation saw the rise of a new growth industry, 'fund management'. It produced high dividends when the market was booming, sad losses when the market fell.

Next in the federal government's sights were its properties—not only its airport terminals, office buildings and military bases, but its major utilities and public-owned companies. The most valuable of all was Telstra, which some analysts valued at close to $100 billion. A new communications company, Optus, was selected in October 1991 as the 'second carrier' (it later purchased the satellite provider AUSSAT) and in 1992 a 'third carrier' was authorised to compete with Telstra and Optus in the growing mobile telephone market.

The Australian Labor Party, the world's oldest parliamentary socialist party, marked its 100th anniversary in 1991 without fanfare, presiding over the ruin of most of its ideals. In that year Michael Pusey published *Economic Rationalism in Canberra*, suggesting that the new economic policies were driven by a localised ideology rather than global influences. In the following year (1992) the skilled political journalist Paul Kelly published *The End of Certainty*, tracing the changes over the nine Labor years that had seen the 'collapse of the ideas Australia had embraced nearly a century before' and 'a campaign to re-invent the Australian political tradition … driven by economic crises'. He felt that Australia had delayed longer than most nations in addressing the true definition of nationhood—the ability to accept responsibility for its own future—and predicted that a new economically competitive Australia was emerging from the scandalous 1980s, guided by pragmatic political leaders. Others wondered if the healthy scepticism of Australians was being eroded by the confusing language used by politicians and academics to explain the inexplicable and the intolerable—almost an Orwellian 'newspeak' based on a vocabulary of obscure new words and phrases ('downsizing', 'technical correction', etc.). Australia was now living in a new 'postmodern' world, halfway between the past and the future. The term 'politically incorrect' was used to describe those who objected to new policies or who displayed sentiments out of keeping with the new times.

ABOVE:
In 1985 the first AUSSAT communications satellite was deployed by the NASA Space Shuttle Discovery. The international satellite consortium, of which Australia was a part, was soon operating 400 transmission and control facilities (earth stations) in 150 countries. Easy-to-use table-top personal computers were common and the 'Internet' was about to be born

Broader developments

Out of the blue came another war: In 1990–91 the United Nations authorised operations to eject Iraqi forces from Kuwait and the RAN's guided-missile destroyer *Brisbane*, photographed here in Sydney Harbour, sailed for active service in the Persian Gulf.

In 2004 *Brisbane*, Australia's last destroyer, was towed to Queensland where she will be scuttled off the coast as a diving wreck.

1991: Arab extremism and the first Iraq War

Only the virulent Arab nationalisms that had disturbed Middle Eastern politics since the creation of the state of Israel in 1948 seemed insoluble. For more than a thousand years Jew and Arab lived side by side in Palestine, but since the wars of 1948, 1956, 1967 and 1973 the two sides seemed irreconcilable. In 1979, however, President Carter brought about a peace treaty between Egypt and Israel; it is a peace that has endured. But other events in 1979 were to produce further instability in the region. In that year Russian forces entered Afghanistan to replace the rabidly Marxist and anti-Islamic regime they had earlier installed, and found themselves at the start of a ten-year war with a powerful new force—the Islamic Mujahidin (holy warriors) who were supplied with arms via Pakistan by the United States. In 1979, too, the Shah of Iran was forced from power and his Westernising but corrupt regime replaced with a fundamentalist Islamic government that showed unrelenting hostility to the West and pathological hatred for America. Also in 1979, Saddam Hussein achieved total power in Iraq.

When war broke out in 1980 between Iran and its smaller neighbour Iraq, the West supplied Iraq with weapons during the bloody but unresolved conflict, which ended in stalemate in 1988. Saddam Hussein of Iraq proved as unpredictable as Iran's leaders, and then made demands on another neighbour, the small oil-rich kingdom of Kuwait. In August 1990 Iraqi forces invaded Kuwait. The United Nations demanded that Iraq withdraw its forces from Kuwait. Reagan's successor, President George Bush, undertook to contribute American forces to evict the Iraqis and amassed naval task forces, air forces and an army of 450,000 men in

Saudi Arabia. Iraq was militarily strong in conventional weapons, possessing nearly 6000 tanks alone, but the United States had confidence in its technological advantages in weaponry (including night-fighting Abrams tanks, guided missiles and 'smart bombs', and Apache attack helicopters firing laser beam-guided missiles tipped with 'uranium-depleted' warheads). In January 1991 missile and bomber strikes on Iraq began and on 24 February the Americans led the great ground offensive, supported by United Nations land, air and naval forces (including Australian warships) comprised of units from forty nations including Britain, France, Egypt, Syria and Pakistan. In just four days Kuwait was liberated, and the bulk of Iraq's army was destroyed, with few Allied casualties.

But Saddam's murderous regime itself survived this defeat, under a form of quarantine. It was ordered to disarm its 'weapons of mass destruction' (i.e. chemical, biological or nuclear). The Kurd areas in the north became an autonomous region and US and British aircraft were to be permitted to fly regularly over two-thirds of Iraq on close aerial surveillance, while the country's sea-borne trade was monitored by Allied warships. As early as the mid-1990s the Atomic Energy Agency established that Iraq was taking steps to perfect a nuclear capability and in 1999 the United States asserted that Iraq still possessed 25,000 litres of anthrax, and an even larger quantity of botulin toxin. Australian warships were still on interception duty in the Gulf when a new Iraq crisis arose twelve years later. Australia and Britain were America's only allies when President George W. Bush sent an army into Iraq to March 2003 to overthrow the regime of Saddam Hussein.

Australia after Hawke

1991: Keating takes over

Prime Minister Hawke retained a high personal popularity, for most Australians respected his pugnacity and sincerity in trying to tackle the nation's problems and Labor was again returned to power in the elections of April 1990, benefiting from the inability of the opposition to produce an attractive leader. Yet Labor lost seats in the Senate to the rising 'third party' of the 1980s—the Democrats, who were committed to popular causes ranging from conservation to a more equable distribution of the nation's resources—and the 'Greens', who fought any measure that would further deplete the nation's natural resources. It was Hawke's fourth election win and he enjoyed his job so much that he postponed plans to hand over power to his Treasurer Paul Keating. Keating's challenge in Caucus for the prime ministership in June 1991 failed but he succeeded in a second attempt in December 1991.

During Labor's long term in office in Canberra, the states, as so often in Australian history, went the other way. Their Labor governments had been mostly discredited by their financial mismanagement during the 1980s. In March 1991 the Liberals won power in New South Wales, and in October 1992 Jeff Kennett's Liberal-led Coalition won government in Victoria (the Liberals had taken office earlier in that year in Tasmania). In January 1993 the Liberals under Richard Court (son of former Premier Sir Charles Court) took power from Labor in Western Australia and by year's end Labor was to lose office in South Australia.

ABOVE:
Australia's young Prime
Minister Paul Keating
regarded his close
relationship with
Indonesia's President
Suharto as a triumph.
Here the leaders
witness the signing of
the Australia–Indonesia
Treaty in Jakarta in
1995.

In the federal elections of March 1993 few predicted that Labor would survive. It faced a new opposition leader in John Hewson, whose program—called Fightback!—promised to combat the nation's economic woes principally by rationalising the tax system and replacing the tangled web of taxes by a single goods and services tax (GST). Australians were not ready for such a threatening new levy and re-elected the Keating government. 'This is the sweetest victory of all,' Keating told his supporters on victory night, savouring every moment.

1993: Mabo and its consequences

The Hawke–Keating Labor government was outstanding in its commitment to the welfare of Australia's indigenous people. So far the history of Australia has been the story of Europeans in an alien environment and how they created a society that flourished. Now the indigenous people make their re-entry.

In 1989 the Aboriginal and Torres Strait Islander Commission (ATSIC) was established by legislation, and its council met for the first time in the following year; it consisted of twenty members, seventeen of whom were directly elected by Aborigines and Torres Strait Islanders. In December 1992 Keating, in a speech at Redfern in Sydney's inner suburbs to commemorate the international Year of Indigenous People, apologised to Australia's own Aborigines, saying; 'With some noble exceptions, we failed to make the most basic human response and enter into their hearts and minds … As a consequence we failed to see that what we were doing degraded all of us.' Some Australians took exception to these remarks, but the many who knew of the few opportunities offered to Aborigines, their appallingly high infant mortality rate and shortened life span caused by European selfishness and neglect, felt it was just one of the first steps towards righting an injustice.

And in 1993 Federal Parliament passed the native title legislation, the greatest victory yet for forces determined to do justice to Aboriginal land claims. It had begun in 1982 when three men from the Murray Islands in Torres Strait, led by Eddie Mabo, asserted their right to their land and instituted proceedings against the State of Queensland. The case ended up in the High Court in Canberra, which in June 1992 confirmed that the islanders were entitled to the possession of their lands. The Native Title Act followed the High Court decision. Ahead lay numerous attempts by Aboriginal groups to establish before the Native Title Tribunal and the courts claims to the land, not all of them successful. When the Wik people claimed a pastoral lease in Queensland, the matter went to the High Court in Canberra which decided against them in 1996. The Wik decision meant that native title could coexist with pastoral leases, but not supersede them.

An inquiry into the inordinately high number of Aborigines committing suicide in prison cells (the Royal Commission into Aboriginal Deaths in Custody) failed to confirm widespread police brutality. But in 1995 the federal government established a further inquiry, under the joint chairmanship of former High Court justice Sir Ronald Wilson and the Aboriginal leader Mick Dodson, to investigate Aboriginal claims that their children in past generations had been forcibly removed from their families. Its findings would not be released until 1997, by which time a Howard-led Coalition had won office in Canberra.

ABOVE:
Melbourne skyline, 1990s.

Decline of the unions

In the 1990s the great century of the unions and their power was ebbing. By the middle of the decade 25 per cent of Australian workers were employed part-time, and only 31 per cent were members of a union (compared with 51 per cent in the 1960s). The scores of unions themselves had been consolidated into seventeen large unions. Strikes and cases of industrial unrest were rare.

OPPOSITE:
Images of the 1990s.

The youthful Keating had great personal style, but many of his initiatives angered the electorate. In 1994 the Labor government brought in a new Industrial Relations Reform Act to facilitate 'collective bargaining' between employers and workers, while ensuring that workers still had the 'safety net' of minimum wages and working conditions. In March 1995 Labor under Bob Carr won power in New South Wales and two months later Keating outlined in Parliament plans for a republic, which would be decided by a referendum. The majority of Australians favoured Australia becoming a republic in the centenary year 2001, but the method of choosing a head of state was to prove a stumbling block.

1995: Wooing Indonesia and closer ties with Asia

In foreign affairs Hawke and Keating moved closer to South-East Asia and particularly to Indonesia, our nearest neighbour. The Labor government committed Australia to a new regional grouping in 1989 known as APEC (Asia-Pacific Economic Cooperation forum), which comprised the ASEAN nations (Indonesia, Singapore,

The Australian Women's Weekly

100 NEW BABY NAMES

JULY 1994 $3.50*

REVENGE!
Rogues pay high price for selling royal scandals

JACKIE O
Intimate memories of her last great love affair

EXCLUSIVE
Zany star's FABULOUS pet project

FREE RECIPE CARDS
NO-SUGAR DISHES

TV'S FAB FOUR
Under pressure to stay beautiful

PSYCH SECRE OF YO INITIA

SOUV
25 y
ago..
walk
the

DOLLY SPECIAL

Every totally cool thing yo ever wanted to know abo

SEX, LOVE & ROCK 'N' ROLL

Australasian POST

PUZZLES!
KIDS' PAGE!
PRIZES!

$2

YOUR ALL-AUSTRALIAN FAMILY MAGAZINE

SEPTEMBER 10, 1994 52*

My Family

HOME, A TOWNSVILLE HUT

MONTY TAKES TO THE AIR...

RUSH FOR GOLD ON AGAIN

HOPE FOR A LITTLE ANGEL

KIDS TAKEN AWAY: OUR SHAME

Reverend Doctor Doug woos a new flock

AUSTRALIA Today ABC

KITTSON AND FAHEY
The sting behind the smiles

EVERY MONTH
Jennifer Byrne
George Negus
Helen Wellings
Robyn Williams
Caroline Jones
Ian Parmenter
WRITE JUST FOR YOU

Monarchy or Republic?
PAUL LYNEHAM
LETS RIP

WE WILL SURVIVE
Aussie Ukrainians speak out
PHOTO SPECIAL

RUTH AND GARRY
WHO IS THE REA MINDER

PLUS 24-PAGE LIFT-OUT
TV AND RADIO PROGRAM GUIDE

FIRST ISSUE

Malaysia, Thailand, the Philippines and Brunei) and Canada, the USA, Japan, Korea, New Zealand and Australia. In 1991 China, Hong Kong and Taiwan joined, and other 'Pacific rim' countries did later, all of them pledged to eliminate all tariffs by 2020. The Asian economies were now thriving. In this period units of the Australian Defence Force under the aegis of the United Nations supervised the cease-fire in Cambodia (1992–93), provided

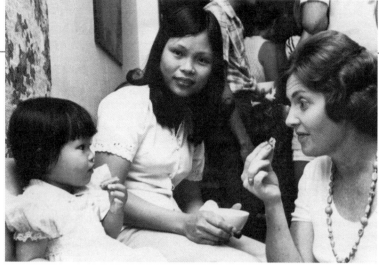

ABOVE:
An Australian carer helps make welcome an Asian refugee family in Canberra.

nearly a thousand soldiers for peacekeeping in Somalia early in 1993, a medical team for Rwanda, the small African country decimated by genocide—among other commitments of small bodies of uniformed personnel in trouble spots ranging from the Sahara to the Sinai. On these duties the Australian personnel achieved a high reputation for humanity, discipline and professionalism.

In 1995 Prime Minister Keating and his high-profile foreign minister Gareth Evans signed a 'security pact' with Indonesia, an act deeply disturbing to many Australians. It lasted only four years.

1996: Howard in power

Early in 1995 John Winston Howard had taken over the Liberal leadership from Alexander Downer. He was 56 years old and had been a fairly colourless figure in his twenty-odd years in Parliament, holding numerous portfolios with competence—including Treasury—but making little impression on Australians. He came from middle-class Sydney, son of a service station owner. A skilled debater at Canterbury High School he later practised law in Sydney before entering Parliament in 1974. In 1985 he had replaced the genial Andrew Peacock as Liberal leader, but in 1988 had angered many in his own party by his widely reported criticisms of multiculturalism. In the words of his most recent biographers, Wayne Errington and Peter van Onselen: 'Howard's lack of empathy for Aborigines, asylum seekers

BELOW
Broad smiles for Liberal Party leader John Howard after his election win in 1996.

and welfare recipients is rooted in the values he imbibed around the dinner table as a child.' Replaced as Liberal leader by Peacock in 1989, Howard regained the leadership in January 1995 after Alexander Downer fumbled the job (visiting Aboriginal communities Downer had pledged to repeal the Mabo decision and things went downhill from there). When Keating called a new election for March 1996, Coalition hopes were high.

Howard knew it would be political suicide to campaign for a Goods and Services Tax (GST) in 1996, going on Hewson's disastrous attempt three years earlier, and instead played on voters'

ABOVE:
Children who appeared in
a series of popular Qantas
commercials were a cross-
section of the multi-racial
society Australia had
achieved in the 1990s.

disillusionment with Keating, who had promised massive tax cuts in 1993 and had then reneged. Howard accused him of giving Australia a bare 'five minutes of economic sunlight' followed by financial mismanagement. 'When we hear from John Howard, the very much recycled leader of the Opposition, it is a case of back to the future,' Keating responded. Rumours of new taxes grew stronger when it was revealed that Labor had run up a 'black hole' budget deficit of close to $10 billion. In March 1996 Howard's Coalition won 94 parliamentary seats to Labor's 49. He had undisputed control of the House but not of the Senate, where a handful of 'third party' members could scuttle legislation, including his plan to sell off 30 per cent of Telstra.

Howard and his Treasurer Peter Costello began reducing federal spending immediately, with cuts in the public service (even six of the 18 department heads in Canberra lost their jobs), reductions in funding for ATSIC, the Office of the Status of Women and, to no one's surprise, the ABC, soon followed by a toughening of welfare qualifications. Annual immigration was cut from 100,000 to 76,000. Hard hit was funding for apprentice training: unwise cuts, as ten years later Australia had such a shortage of tradespeople that the government had to seek them overseas.

1997: 'One Nation'

Among the new members elected to the House in 1996 was an independent named Pauline Hanson. The shopkeeper from Ipswich, Queensland, was disendorsed as a Liberal candidate for racist remarks. 'She has to go,' Howard ordered. She won nevertheless and in her maiden speech in September 1996 said bluntly: 'I believe we are being swamped by Asians,' describing ATSIC as 'a failed, hypocritical and discriminatory organization.' Prime Minister Howard did not censure her.

Worse was to come. In 1997 Hanson became leader of a new political party named One Nation, which soon gathered momentum. In a mid-1998 Queensland election One Nation candidates won an astonishing 11 seats, attracting 'protest votes' from those opposed to the multicultural policies of both major parties. In the 2001 federal elections, however, Hanson failed to win a Senate seat and the party dissolved amid recriminations, in-fighting, scandals and court cases. She stood again for the Senate in 2007 but failed, obtaining just 4 per cent of the primary vote.

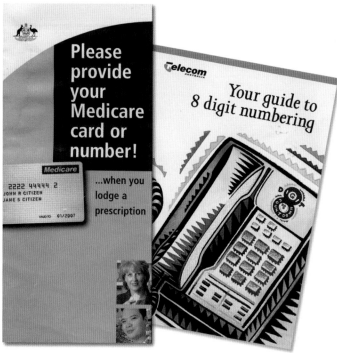

1997: Kyoto and global warming

During the 1960s the terms 'ecology' and 'environment' came into everyday use when attention was drawn to the damage being inflicted on nature by industrial nations and untrammelled growth; soon the term 'greenhouse effect' was coined to describe a progressive warming of the Earth's atmosphere: a gradual, closely monitored rise in the Earth's temperature, increasing dry periods, climatic fluctuations and a certain rise in ocean levels. The change in Earth's temperature was caused by the increase in the atmosphere of carbon dioxide, which with other greenhouse gases—such as water vapour, methane, nitrous oxide and CFCs (chlorofluorocarbons)—absorb the Sun's radiation and then re-emit it, warming the atmosphere and eroding the ozone layer that protects life on Earth. These poisons are also entering the oceans. It is a natural cycle but over the past century humankind has thrown it out of balance.

Faced by evidence that the ozone layer was disappearing over the polar regions, the 1987 United Nations–sponsored Montreal conference had achieved the banning of the manufacture of the harmful CFC gases widely used in refrigeration and spray cans (their production ceased in 1995). It was seen as an unusual example of international co-operation; the ozone hole's growth, despite fluctuations, was halted. Mounting evidence that the world was warming at a faster rate than scientists had predicted led ten years later to the 1997 Kyoto Accord.

By the 1990s the burning of fossil fuel, the polluted smoke from cities, factories and motor vehicles had added 3 billion tons of carbon dioxide (CO_2) to the atmosphere annually, and this has been accompanied by the progressive destruction of the Earth's lungs—its oxygen-producing forests. Some authorities predicted that by 2050 the polar ice caps will almost disappear, causing ocean levels to rise as much as a metre. Sydney's temperate climate may become as warm as Brisbane's, winter rain could decrease by up to 20 per cent, while summer rain may increase by up to 20 per cent as the monsoonal rains move south.

At a Climate Change conference convened by the United Nations at Kyoto in Japan in December 1997 signatories to an Accord pledged to progressively reduce their nations' greenhouse gas emissions by the year 2010. Australia, along with the United States, refused to sign the Accord (which expires in 2012), citing the calamitous effect it would have on their economies.

ABOVE:
In an age of anxiety, Australians remained a nation of optimists and continued to take advantage of low-interest credit and to spend freely, running up the highest per capita debts in the Western world. Cash dispensing machines and 'electronic funds transfer' (EFT) were introduced in the 1980s. The government pleaded with citizens to spend wisely and to provide for their retirement.

The Internet

Its origins lay in a network by which computers could contact each other over telephone lines. The Internet was developed by the US Defense Department who saw its value in communications but handed it back to the universities and commercial interests in 1988, possibly because it was so easy to penetrate ('access'). With the development of new communications links—fibre-optic cable (both underground and under-ocean) and satellites—a 'web' of networks developed: computers could contact 'web sites' across the world for the cost of a local phone call. By 1996 institutions as familiar as the International Red Cross and the *Sydney Morning Herald* had web sites; newspapers, journals, even encyclopaedias were soon available 'online', mostly free of charge. Over the next decade ease of access to the Internet increased—wireless broadband was the circuit breaker—while the speed and capacity of new personal computers doubled every year as their size and price halved, offering information, communications and entertainment to millions.

1998: Industrial Relations reforms

Early and radical Industrial Relations (IR) reforms late in 1996 introduced Australian Workplace Agreements (AWAs), but a hostile Senate emasculated most of its provisions.

Australia's inefficient wharves became the next test case for IR reforms. In 1998 a belligerent new minister, John Reith, encouraged shipping owners and wharf handlers to introduce cost-saving measures; they began by sacking the work force and hiring non-union labour to the outrage of their unions. Violent scenes followed but modern cargo-handling practices and machinery were introduced.

BELOW:
The champions: the Australian Test Team celebrating victory in 1999. Australia lost the Ashes to England in 2005 but gained them back in spectacular fashion in December 2006 when Shane Warne, master of legspin bowling (centre) took his 700th Test wicket. Australian favourite cricket larrikin, he announced his retirement shortly afterwards.

1997: Aboriginal Australia

In 1997, in a period of 'reconciliation', Prime Minister Howard publicly criticised the newly released 'Bringing Them Home' report on the removal of Aboriginal children from their families, and disassociated himself from its conclusions, accusing some historians of exaggerating accounts of European brutality and of wanting all Australians to wear a 'Black Armband' of guilt. In 1998 tens of thousands of Australians nevertheless signed 'Sorry' books and in 2000 marched en masse as an act of contrition.

Many prominent Black leaders avoided involvement with the board of the scandal-plagued Aboriginal and Torres Strait Islander Commission (ATSIC) and an exasperated Howard government abolished it in 2004. Some Outback Aboriginal communities remained backwaters of despair, lacking even a single police officer or doctor, suffering from poor diet and ill-health, and plagued by the easily accessible curses of modern civilisation—alcoholism and pornography—which in turn led to domestic physical and sexual violence. When reports of these activities were confirmed in 2007 the federal government sent in social workers, medical teams, police and Army personnel under an Army major-general to more than 70 Aboriginal communities in the Northern Territory.

1998: The GST election

Presenting his budget in May 1998, Treasurer Costello had reason to look smug: in two years he had changed a $10 billion deficit into a surplus of $2.7 billion and reduced interest rates. It was time to revive the GST issue and sell the electorate on the need for a thorough reform of taxation by replacing the web of wholesale taxes with a single consumption tax. Similar to that in operation in Britain and Western Europe, the GST would be 10 per cent of the value of all transactions. This revenue would be given entirely to the state governments who would in turn abolish numerous state taxes and relinquish about $18 billion annually in federal grants.

The electorate had panicked at the threat of a new tax in 1993, but in 1998 Howard offered them massive tax cuts and 'packages' in compensation. Costello pointed out that most households would be $50 a week better off. 'It was a genuine reform measure that went to the structural heart of the economy,' writes Tracey Aubin, Costello's biographer. Labor responded by offering tax cuts to lower-income workers. On 3 October 1998 the Coalition was returned to power, but with their 44-seat majority reduced to 12. Still lacking control of the Senate and determined to pass the legislation intact ('no exemptions'), Howard courted the Democrats, who demanded—and obtained—many exemptions (food for example, was exempted from GST, but meals, like books, were not). The GST was passed in mid-1999 and came into effect in July 2000.

The government soon benefited from an embarrassment of riches from GST—$24 billion in the first year. As the economy grew, rising company taxes added to the windfall. The Coalition was jubilant and even the state governments were happy.

Privatisation of public assets accelerated. Between 1990 and 1998 the federal government bolstered its coffers by $30 billion from privatisation and the states made an equivalent sum. Public servants who were regarded as superfluous or resistant to change were encouraged to accept 'voluntary redundancy'.

OPPOSITE RIGHT:
Prime Minister Keating's dedication to improving the conditions of the indigenous people was sincere and his speeches eloquent. A NSW Police photographer shows a rare occasion when harmony reigned in the inner-city suburb of Redfern; Keating chose the location to make his apology to Aboriginal leaders for past wrongs.

1999: The republic referendum

Early in 1998 representatives of Australia's diverse society met in the Old Parliament House in Canberra to debate the changes in the Constitution necessary before the people could vote on the issue of forming a republic in a referendum. The chief question was how to choose a Head of State (President).

Howard, a devoted monarchist, spoke out strongly against any projected change in the Constitution and asked Australians to vote No against the 'preferred model' offered to them in November 1999. His Treasurer, Costello, was an outspoken republican (a cause for growing coldness between the two men). After the electorate voted No, a future Liberal minister, the lawyer and merchant banker Malcolm Turnbull said that the Prime Minister had 'broken Australia's heart'. Most Australians still favoured a republic but wanted to elect the Head of State by direct vote. Further debate on the subject was deferred indefinitely.

BELOW:
Gabi Hollows (left), an unidentified Aboriginal man, former Prime Minister Malcolm Fraser and Dr Lowitja O'Donoghue hold hands after the *Journey of Healing* ceremony at *Corroboree 2000*.

1999: Indonesia and Timor

In 1997 the over-heated South-East Asian economies went into a spiral. The collapse began in Thailand and spread quickly. Banks crippled by over-generous and unrepayable loans closed down, the share market plummeted, factories closed. Rioters in Jakarta demanded an end to the Suharto regime. In 1998 Suharto was forced to resign, while Indonesia itself was wracked by separatist uprisings.

Since the Indonesian invasion of 1975 the East Timorese had suffered under alien rule and up to 100,000 had died. In March 1999 the UN Secretary-General announced that Indonesia had agreed that a referendum would be held in which the East Timorese could choose their future. Groups of armed 'militia' sponsored by the Indonesian Army immediately began a program of intimidation, forcibly removing 150,000 East Timorese to the Islamic west of the island, and carrying out killings of pro-independence leaders. Jakarta's leaders professed regret at the state of affairs, admitting that they had no control whatever over the military. On 30 August the East Timorese people's will for independence was shown in the results of the referendum. Indonesian-backed militias then went on a revenge rampage of burning and killing.

One week later the UN called on Indonesia to halt the violence and accept a peace-keeping force. The Howard government, having alerted the brigade at Darwin for instant deployment, offered to provide a peace-keeping force for the UN. On 9 September Indonesian President Habibie agreed to this. On 20 September 1999 the first of 4500 Australian troops landed in the ashes of Dili. Within 30 days the Diggers had occupied all of East Timor. Later joined by units from 12 nations, the UN force (Interfet) oversaw the peaceful departure of the last Indonesians and the creation of the world's newest and smallest nation, Timor-Leste, in 2002. The Howard government won popular approval for its action but drove a hard bargain for liberating the one million East Timorese: the lion's share from the new nation's oil and gas fields in the Timor Sea go to Australia.

2000: BHP moves offshore

For 80 years Australia's industrial giant BHP—the 'Big Australian'—had made the world's finest steel at their works in Newcastle and Wollongong, firing their furnaces with Hunter Valley coal. But locally produced iron and steel, like Australian shipbuilding, could no longer compete in price and speed of manufacture with Korea and Japan. In 2000 BHP closed down its works to manufacture 'offshore', and in 2001 merged with an overseas company, Billiton, moving its headquarters to London. Newcastle plunged into recession but adapted itself to the hard new age, developing tourism while remaining the world's largest coal-exporting port. In 2006 BHP Billiton made profits of $17 billion—about the same income as the federal government's.

Other old institutions were vanishing or being reconstituted. As in the public service, efficiency was obtained at the cost of dislocating people's lives. The 'job security' that had been an Australian tradition was now a valueless concept, but Howard could point to the fact that Australia was one of the few Western countries whose economy was showing steady growth. Unemployment began to fall, but most of the new jobs were temporary ones. Australia had a remarkably effective and efficient government but it seemed to lack a heart.

End of the Millennium

Not a single act of terrorism detracted from the televised celebrations across the world on the night of 31 December 1999—eve of a new millennium—nor did anything mar the success of the Sydney Olympic Games held late in 2000. Australia won a total of 58 medals including 16 gold—improving on the nation's total

OPPOSITE, BOTTOM: Triumph: Major-General Peter Cosgrove shown here with Indonesian officers, used tact backed by strong armed force and the full authority of the United Nations to negotiate the peaceful withdrawal of Indonesian forces from East Timor. He went on to be Australian of the Year in 2001, Chief of the Defence Staff, retiring in 2005 as a full General after forty years' army service.

Now the world's youngest nation, Timor-Leste is still plagued by the consequences of 25 years of Indonesian rule, its people divided between those who benefited from Indonesian rule and those who opposed it. Timor-Leste's elected leader Jose Ramos Horta was severely wounded in an attempted coup by renegades in his own army in February 2008 and peacekeeping detachments from Australia and thirty other nations are still on duty there.

of 41 medals in the previous Olympics (1996) and making her the fifth highest medal-winner in the world. It seemed that the madness of the twentieth century had died and a new age of peace was dawning. But it was not to be.

2001: New York attacked

On the morning of 11 September 2001 Islamic fanatics hijacked and then crashed two airliners into the twin towers of the World Trade Center in New York and a third into the Pentagon building in Washington; a fourth plane struck the earth in Pennsylvania after the passengers had attempted to regain control of the aircraft. Millions across the world watched in horror as television relayed the burning and collapse of the twin towers. Nearly 3000 people died in these attacks, among them 20 Australians. Prime Minister Howard was in Washington at the time, attending the 50th anniversary commemoration of the signing of the ANZUS Pact, and he announced immediately that Australia would assist the

United States under the terms of the Treaty. British Labour Prime Minister Tony Blair, who had just been re-elected to power, also pledged Britain's support.

The terrorist attacks were catastrophic. America's airlines faced bankruptcy, business confidence crumbled and recession loomed (it was avoided by the US Federal Reserve injecting billions of dollars into the financial system to kick along the American economy—the spending spree and cheap mortgages came to a shattering halt six years later). President George W. Bush (son of the former President) called the attacks acts of war against the United States and vowed to bring to justice those who had planned them. In his later State of the Union address Bush described the existence of a new 'axis of evil' based in Iraq, Iran and North Korea, where terrorism was fostered. Bush's Intelligence soon revealed that the terrorists were members of an extremist Islamic group—al-Qaeda—led by a billionaire fanatic Osama bin Laden, who had already orchestrated attacks on US embassies and targets in Africa and the Middle East from his headquarters in Afghanistan, where Taliban extremists had been in power in Kabul since 1996. Intelligence officers found evidence of something long suspected: al-Qaeda was a world-wide terrorist network with cells not only throughout the Middle East but in western Europe and the United States itself.

2001: Into Afghanistan

When the Taliban leadership refused the United States' demands that bin Laden be handed over, President Bush moved quickly. Obtaining bases around Afghanistan, American aircraft struck Taliban centres on 7 October 2001 while the Northern Alliance forces, well supplied with tanks and supported by US and British aircraft, missile-strikes and Special Forces units, moved south with ease, entering Kabul in mid-November. Australian SAS soldiers saw action in the skirmishes against Taliban pockets, and suffered one fatality. The ragtag Taliban leadership—and Osama bin Laden—had fled, mostly to the mountain fastnesses along the Pakistan border where they still remain, rearming. Seven years later Australian troops were among the international force of 40,000 troops (principally from NATO countries) attempting to rebuild Afghanistan under increasingly heavy attacks by Taliban fighters.

The asylum seekers

Australia had given refuge annually to about 12,000 refugees but the mounting numbers of illegal immigrants sailing from Indonesian ports in leaky vessels panicked the Howard government.

In September 2001 the Norwegian tanker *Tampa* picked up 483 refugees from a sinking boat near the Australian territory Christmas Island but was forbidden to land them there. To solve the problem of where to put the refugees, the Howard government hit upon the 'Pacific Solution' and arranged that they would be detained on Pacific Islands, including Manus and Nauru. Other refugees were put in detention behind barbed wire at camps at Woomera in South Australia and Port Hedland in Western Australia. Conditions there were appalling.

2001: Howard's third win

Early in October 2001, just before the federal election, the warship HMAS *Adelaide* was preparing to escort an overloaded refugee boat back to Indonesian waters when it began to founder. The warship radioed Defence Headquarters in Canberra that people were jumping into the sea, but the phrase 'children were being thrown overboard' was passed to Prime Minister Howard who mentioned this disturbing revelation in pre-election speeches, and the news was headlined in newspapers appearing on Monday 7 October, the day when US and British forces began the invasion of Afghanistan, crowding out reasoned debate. Defence personnel quickly informed the prime minister's office that the report was unconfirmed (it was later found to be untrue) but Howard, who was well behind in the polls and facing a possible challenge to his leadership from his impatient Treasurer, Costello, did not retract his assertion.

Opinion polls supported Howard in his strong stand against those they termed 'aliens'; others thought it a heartless reaction to the plight of ordinary people who wished only to live free of terror. Howard's Coalition won the election on 10 November 2001, ending with 82 seats in the 150-seat House.

Many asylum seekers spent years in Australian camps and the children in particular are reported to have suffered mental trauma. For the first time since the war in Vietnam some Australians felt deep shame at the country's policies.

The Labor Party accused Howard of politicizing the higher ranks of the Defence Forces (senior officers had appeared before Senate committees, where their competence was questioned and their dignity shaken over the conflicting reports issued over the refugee boats issue). Many Australians thought the government, in introducing tough surveillance and security laws, was over-reacting to an imagined

threat, but on 12 October 2002, 88 Australians were among the 203 killed by Islamic terrorist bombs in the peaceful holiday resort of Bali. Australian Federal Police assisted Indonesian authorities in tracking down the culprits, who proved to be products of one of the Islamic schools in Indonesia well known to the police and allied to the extremist Jemaah Islamiah network. Their curriculum had included military training and bomb-making.

2003: Invading Iraq—and aftermath

The United States had decided that the time had come to settle accounts with Iraq. Many experts maintained that Saddam Hussein's cruel regime was crumbling of its own accord and had no links whatever with al-Qaeda but to President Bush and his warlike neo-conservative advisers, Iraq was not only a threat to the stability of the Middle East (source of 60 per cent of the world's oil reserves) but also a present or future breeding ground of terrorism. Saddam was suspected, moreover, of constructing Weapons of Mass Destruction (WMDs) including primitive nuclear and biological bombs. Saddam, already a pariah in the Arab world, had done little to mollify his critics, expelling UN inspectors in 1998. Readmitted under UN pressure in 2002 they found no evidence of WMDs.

When the UN Security Council refused to authorise armed action against Iraq, the United States pledged to move of its own accord. At this stage only Britain and Australia had promised direct military assistance to the United States.

Soon 2000 Australian Defence Force personnel were on duty in the Gulf. Australia was once more in the firing line, her men and women sailing again to a war zone. The nation was not only divided but also enduring its second year of the worst drought since 1901–02. After months of intense heat without rain, bushfires in south-east Australia turned into a firestorm that reached into the suburbs of Canberra itself, consuming nearly 500 homes. The fires were doused by scattered rains a month later but expected autumn rainfall was inadequate. By winter farm land still lay dry and barren. The nation had to import wheat and more than eight million sheep had died.

On 20 March 2003 American and British ground forces invaded Iraq from Kuwait, accompanied by devastating air attacks on Iraq's forces and infrastructure. Australian SAS units and Hornet fighters were in action from the first day while Navy units helped secure the waterways leading to Basra. Within three weeks American tanks were entering Baghdad, from where Saddam and his government had fled. In the great city of 6 million people no police or authority existed; rioters and looters ran wild. In early May President Bush claimed: 'Mission Accomplished'. In the following months no WMDs or deadly missiles were found in Iraq but President Bush and Prime Ministers Blair and Howard remained unrepentant and unapologetic.

The United States had won a campaign without preparing for its aftermath. Within months the glow of victory had become the fire of arson and explosion with random attacks on American forces, a violent campaign by fanatics that grew in intensity. Al-Qaeda did not die; it grew. Even the presence of forces from 30 of America's allies and the capture of Saddam Hussein in December 2003 (he was hanged for war crimes three years later) brought no end to the violence. Newly raised Iraqi army and police units and moderate political figures were targeted, pipelines and mosques bombed as the conflict sank into a civil war between Kurd, Sunni and Shiite; it is estimated that at least 70,000 Iraqi men, women and children have died at the hands of terrorists. Six years later most utilities—including fresh water and electricity—are still in ruins.

In May and June 2003, as Australia's peace-keepers completed their task of restoring order in Bougainville, the Howard government announced that they would provide 2000 troops and a police contingent to restore order and safeguard civil authorities rebuilding government in the lawless Solomons—another 'failed state'. Australia had become the policeman of the South Pacific.

In 2006, following complaints by American and Canadian wheat growers, a Royal Commission began investigating evidence that the Australian Wheat Board (AWB) had paid $300 million in bribes after 1996 to Saddam Hussein's government (through a 'front', a trucking company registered in Jordan) in order to obtain grain sales. Prime Minister Howard and Foreign Minister Downer claimed they had never been informed of the claims. They escaped censure but several AWB executives faced criminal charges. 'If Howard didn't know something, it was because somewhere along the chain of command someone thought that telling the Prime Minister was a bad idea,' explains his most recent biographers. The ensuing controversy was reminiscent of the 'people overboard' scandal of 2001.

Islam and the West

Europe is now home to 20 million Muslims; followers of Islam in Australia number around 150,000. All but a small minority bear no animosity towards their non-Muslim neighbours. Christianity and Islam indeed rose from the same Judaic origins, sharing a common belief in a single almighty God. But international Islamic terrorism, in which a hundred Australians have died, soon spawned suspicion and hostility. In 2004 Islamic terrorist bombs caused 2000 casualties including 200 dead in Madrid, leading Spain to withdraw its forces from Iraq; in July 2005 terrorists detonated bombs (and themselves) in the London Underground rail network, killing 50 commuters; and in 2007 terrorist groups mounted an attack in Glasgow. Lebanon, homeland of many Islamic Australians, has been wracked by civil war for nearly 30 years. In December 2005 Australians witnessed on TV news vicious race riots between nationalistic 'Anglos' and youths of Lebanese backgrounds on Sydney's southern beaches. It was a violent outburst revealing an ugly underbelly to our multicultural society.

2004: Howard's fourth win

Beazley's successor, the quietly spoken Simon Crean, failed to attract public or Party attention or support. On 17 October 2003 the rising young Labor member Mark Latham flew from Canberra to Jim Cairns' funeral in Melbourne, sitting next

to the influential Labor Senator John Faulkner. Latham wrote in his diary:
'He [Faulkner] is agonizing over whether it is his responsibility to tell Simon to go.
Does he pole-axe a federal Labor Leader or watch the Party get slaughtered in the
next general election? … John wanted to know if I would contest a leadership
vacancy.' In a Caucus vote in December Latham beat Beazley for the leadership.

Latham was self made, a tough in-fighter from the western suburbs of Sydney, at
once idealistic and roughhouse; but he had made lots of enemies on his way up.
During 2004 he caused the government to back-track on its lavish new parliamentary superannuation scheme and hounded it to amend clauses unfavourable to
Australia in the new Free Trade Agreement with the USA which came into effect in
January 2005. Calling President Bush 'the most incompetent and dangerous
president in living memory' and angered by Australia's involvement in Iraq, Latham
pledged to 'bring the troops home by Christmas'. When Howard called an election
for 9 October 2004 Latham was pursued relentlessly by the Fairfax and Murdoch
press for past indiscretions. Howard was returned to power with 87 seats to
Labor's 60. Mark Latham resigned from politics in January 2005. He was one of the
brief meteors of the political scene, but Australia arguably needs more of them.

Other losers in 2004 were the Democrats, the once-admired third party. Howard
now controlled the Senate—the first time any party had control of both houses of
parliament since 1981. Nothing could now delay his legislation.

Telecommunications

Control of the Senate allowed the Howard government to sell off its last 51 per
cent shareholding of Telstra (by October 2006) after the Coalition partners, the
National Party, secured assurances that rural areas would receive priority attention
from the telecommunications giant. Telstra's shares came on the market at just
$2 but quickly rose to $3—well below the $7 value the prime minister banked on
but providing a windfall for some lucky gamblers. Still subject to a degree of
government regulation, Telstra's tough new management complained that their
hands were still tied as their smaller competitors achieved market share. Telstra's
savage staff reductions provoked anger, as did its announcement that its broadband
CDMA network would be switched off in 2008 and replaced by a 'Next
Generation' wireless broadband network which malfunctioned when first demonstrated. Australians continue to complain that their broadband service is not only
expensive but among the world's slowest, transmitting one kilobyte per second
(1 kbps) compared with Japan's 50 kbps.

But the introduction of broadband had allowed rapid access to the growing
Internet and Australians were now spending more time in front of their
computers than watching television. Many households use the Internet—'the
Web'—to 'download' music or films, or look up (or contribute articles to) the

amazing 'Wikipedia', and to pay accounts (phone banking), or book holidays and airline tickets, and purchase goods. When the government announced that analog TV transmissions would be switched off by 2012 to make way for digital broadcasts, it hardly created a ripple; Australians were slow to buy digital television sets, possibly because they were weary of the predictable fare from the networks and were obtaining livelier home entertainment.

The compact disc (CD) and its successor the DVD are now challenged by even more compact and easy-to-use electronic marvels. Computers are getting smaller—laptop models and 'notebooks' now outsell desktop models. Even schoolchildren own pocket-sized mobile phones to organise their social life; some mobiles can store and transmit film and iPods can download audio and film from the Internet and store more than 10,000 pop songs. An age of abundance has become one of excess, but also an age of wonders.

Affluence and anxieties

With unemployment low (well below five per cent) the Howard government's rigorous new 'Work Choice' laws came into force in March 2006. They granted employers the right to set wages, hours and conditions by individual contracts (Australian Workplace Agreements or AWAs), replacing their employees' collective agreements negotiated by unions; 'unfair dismissal' claims were abolished. Many employees found themselves offered work for lower pay and longer hours. Amid mounting criticism the government claimed that it provided flexibility for a changing work force (two-thirds of Australians now worked in the 'service industries'—a term that embraced everything outside manufacturing, mining and agriculture) and that average annual earnings were a healthy $50,000. But for the majority of Australians it seemed that the traditional security of a lifetime career in their chosen profession or trade—including paid holidays and sick leave—was a thing of the past. The Labor Opposition denounced Work Choices and vowed to 'roll back' its provisions if they were elected. This was done by the new Labor government in February 2008.

In the same year the Organisation for Economic Co-operation and Development (OECD) announced that Australia had the second-highest living standards in the world. Coal worth $25 billion a year was the nation's single biggest export earner and Prime Minister Howard, soon to announce a $20 billion sale of natural gas to China, had paid off all $100 billion dollars of government overseas debt, in itself a remarkable achievement. But private sector debt was climbing to around $400 billion dollars. Like the United States, Australia had for years been importing more than it exported, and was on a seemingly unstoppable consumer spending spree, borrowing continually. The Howard government had pledged to keep interest rates low but as house prices began to soar (inner city or harbourside cottages in Sydney were selling for $1 million) purchasers with large mortgages dreaded even fractional interest-rate rises. John Howard quipped that no one had complained to him that their homes had doubled in value in just a few years. The real estate industry explained that inadequate land was being zoned for new housing development; state governments complained that while GST provided more than half their revenue, their budgets were inadequate to fund the infrastructure for development and that more federal money was needed; most state services—

OPPOSITE RIGHT:
Sydney's rival: Melbourne, capital of Victoria, has a population of more than 3 million ranking as Australia's second largest city. It has been transformed by new developments along the Yarra River and some of the world's tallest buildings but preserves more of its solid Victorian-era architecture than any other Australian city.

ABOVE:
Facing the future.

notably hospitals, schools and transport—were suffering from inadequate funding. All six states and both territories were Labor-led and inherently hostile to the Coalition. The ALP's new leader, Kevin Rudd, was quick to capitalise on voters' disenchantment and promised increased federal involvement in education and medical care. A major public concern was the Howard government's seeming indifference to the problem of climate change.

Climate change

The United States and Australia alone had refused to sign the 1997 Kyoto Accords and their leaders professed scepticism of the whole notion of climate change. 'The jury's still out,' Prime Minister Howard had stated in 2006. Australia's six-year drought was ascribed to the periodic El Niño climate effect that arises in the Pacific Ocean. Others blamed the astonishing increase in the world's population from 2 billion to 6.6 billion over the previous century for the destruction of the world's natural resources. But in that year Australia's cities began running out of water: major dams were emptying and severe water restrictions were enforced. Heavy rains finally came to south-east Australia in mid-2007, replenishing dams and reservoirs but failing to fill them. The states announced plans to build desalination plants on the coasts at massive cost. In September 2006 Sir Nicholas Stern released a United Nations–sponsored report originally commissioned by the British government that described climate change as a reality and warned of the calamitous effects it would have on human society— from economic depression to political upheavals—unless governments spent part of their GDP to start mitigating its effects.

Prime Minister Howard saw nuclear power as a solution for the 'clean' generation of electricity, but announced a plan to spend $20 billion over the next 25 years to develop alternative power sources. To many it was a case of too little too late.

2007: Labor wins

Facing the need to call a general election within three years and three months of the 2004 election, John Howard delayed his decision to the last moment, hoping for a change in public opinion polls during 2007 indicating that only 45 per cent of the electorate would vote again for the Coalition. For nearly 12 years Howard had been, in the words of the columnist Paul Kelly, 'the government's greatest asset,' successful as both conservative and populist, dominating his Cabinet as few leaders had done since the days of his idol, Robert Menzies. Unprepossessing in appearance yet amazingly fit for a 68-year-old, he excelled in long pre-election campaigns that wore out his younger opponents and gave him the opportunity to offer funds, grants and largesse to the deserving, and to greet the public in quick tours of shopping malls. While admitting that he intended to retire in 18 months and hand over the reins to Treasurer Costello, he reminded Australians of their prosperity (the London *Economist* in 2006 had written of the nation's 'miracle economy'), promised an astonishing $34 billion in tax cuts over the next seven years (people remained unconvinced) and harped constantly on the inexperience of his opponent, the 50-year-old Labor leader Kevin Rudd, a youthful, softly spoken Queenslander who had begun his career in the diplomatic service and had been in parliament for only nine years. Rudd launched his quiet campaign with the words: 'If the economy is going so well, why are so many finding it so tough?' Last-minute polls predicted a close election.

Within two hours of the booths closing, early counting of votes showed a massive swing against the Howard government, and within four hours the prime minister had conceded defeat. John Howard became the first prime minister since Stanley Bruce in 1929 to lose his own seat, when his electorate of Bennelong in Sydney was won for Labor by the former ABC journalist Maxine McKew (44,685 votes to 42,251). After postal votes came in (close to one million Australians are currently overseas) it was announced that Labor had 83 seats in the House to the Coalition's 65; the Labor government was sworn in by the Governor-General on 3 December. With new Senators taking their seats in mid-2008, both the Coalition and Labor (and Greens) will be represented by 37 Senators, with two independents holding the balance of power.

Appointing Julia Gillard as the nation's first female deputy prime minister, Rudd left for overseas in December, visiting Australian forces in Iraq (where he announced plans to withdraw most troops) and Afghanistan (where he promised a continuing military presence) and, to the applause of Climate Conference delegates, signed the Kyoto Accord. Two nations alone remain non-signatories— the United States and Kazakhstan. (The world's two rising industrial giants, China and India, are signatories of Kyoto but not yet bound by emissions control provisions.) Like Scullin in 1929, a Labor prime minister was entering office as leader of a seemingly prosperous country at the very moment when the world's most powerful nation, the United States, was facing the prospect of economic recession.

On 13 February 2008, on the first day's sitting of Parliament in Canberra, Prime Minister Rudd carried out his election promise and apologised on Australia's behalf to the nation's indigenous peoples for past wrongs and indignities inflicted on them; his speech was seconded by the new Opposition leader, Dr Brendan Nelson. Most Australians agreed it was an important and overdue step towards reconciliation.

Facing the future

Australians still regard themselves as the luckiest people in the world. They enjoy life and are unashamedly materialist. Their anxieties are principally focussed on their own well-being and financial security. In their democratic society class counts for little; comfort counts for all. But many dreams have died. For the first time in Australia's history there seem to be limits to growth and deep anxieties about the future. Cities continue to grow—some suggest that 'NSW' stands for Newcastle–Sydney–Wollongong, and planners predict that the most populous state's three largest cities (Sydney alone has a population of 4 million) will soon form a single giant, congested coastal 'mega-city'. For the first time in history Australians purchased one million new vehicles in a single year (2007), in a time when vehicle pollution and fuel costs are reaching new highs. Future climatic fluctuations place water supplies in jeopardy. Over-use of irrigation has drained the waters of the Murray–Darling Basin, the nation's breadbasket and principal fruit-growing region. Some primary industries, already facing declining profits in the competitive global market, are dying, and so are the smaller country towns. 'The Bush', the heart of Australian legend and folklore, is also losing its people. As farms are consolidated into giant 'agri-businesses' and rural canneries, flour mills and factories close down, the young unemployed drift to the cities. When the populations of country towns fall, so do the services—schools, buses, service stations, banks. The sense of community dies.

In cities, many parents, appalled by the lacklustre standards and poor discipline of many public schools, are opting for private schooling for their children despite the expense. Prime Minister Howard decried the failure to teach history in any depth and the post-modernist bias of much teaching, and threatened to impose a national curriculum. Some futurists even predict that the states themselves—historical oddities—might be replaced by more logical geographically based administrative entities. The population is falling as couples are having an average of only 1.8 children and one in four people choose to remain single. As the social critic Hugh Mackay observed wryly, houses are getting bigger as families get smaller. Population growth can only be stimulated by immigration, principally from Asia. Europe, also enjoying peaceful union and prosperity, no longer supplies emigrants, for her population is also falling. Soon one in four Australians will be aged 65 or more, resulting in massive future government outlays in pensions and medical care for a greying population. The young are also prey to the diseases of affluence and self-indulgence—obesity and diabetes—and half the population is classified as overweight. Australian forces remain on duty in Afghanistan and Iraq as part of the war against Islamic extremism, garrison Timor-Leste, and help police the islands of the south Pacific—the 'failing states' that are plagued by internal anarchy and face rising sea levels, another grim consequence of global warming. Australia has already made significant advances in developing alternative power to replace the burning of fossil fuels—solar (photovoltaic) cells and windmills generating power are now common sights. Despairing about seeming government inaction over climate change, many Australians have installed solar panels, catch their own rainwater and recycle waste to prove that a form of self-sufficiency is possible, even in cities.

ABOVE:
Rare moment of amity. John Howard and the Labor leader and future Prime Minister, Kevin Rudd, at an Aboriginal reconciliation ceremony in Canberra in 2007, prior to the federal election.

Yet fewer countries are richer in natural resources than Australia. Exports of coal, minerals and natural gas have funded her prosperity for decades. In human resources she is even richer. One in four Australians is of non-European origin and sociologists point proudly to the fact that the nation is one of the Earth's most successful examples of a racially mixed society. Australia is equal in landmass to the United States (excluding Alaska)—nearly eight million square kilometres. Where America's population exceeds 300 million, providing an enormous economy—and tax base—to fund progress, Australians number only 21 million, yet they have criss-crossed their continent with highways, railways, air services, communications and communities. Australia's society is harmonious, her personality distinctive, at once unfailingly optimistic and refreshing. The question now is whether governments of the future can meet the challenges of the 21st century, and start leading instead of following.

Appendix:

Australia's Prime Ministers since 1901

Sir Edmund Barton	Protectionist1	Jan. 1901 - 24 Sept. 1903
Alfred Deakin	Protectionist	24 Sept. 1903 - 27 April 1904
J.C. Watson	Labor	7 April 1904 - 17 Aug. 1904
G.H. Reid	Free-Trade/Protectionist	18 Aug. 1904 - 5 July 1905
Alfred Deakin	Protectionist	5 July 1905 - 13 Nov. 1908
Andrew Fisher	Labor	3 Nov. 1908 - 2 June 1909
Alfred Deakin	Fusion	2 June 1909 - 28 April 1910
Andrew Fisher	Labor	29 April 1910 - 24 June 1913
Joseph Cook	Liberal	24 June 1913 - 17 Sept. 1914
Andrew Fisher	Labor	7 Sept. 1914 - 27 Oct. 1915
W.M. Hughes	Labor	27 Oct. 1915 - 14 Nov. 1916
W.M. Hughes	Nationalist - Labor	14 Nov. 1916 - 17 Feb. 1917
W.M. Hughes	Nationalist	17 Feb. 1917 - 10 Jan. 1918
W.M. Hughes	Nationalist	10 Jan. 1918 - 9 Feb. 1923
S.M. Bruce	Nationalist - Country Party	9 Feb. 1923 - 22 Oct. 1929
J.H. Scullin	Labor	22 Oct. 1929 - 6 Jan. 1932
J.A. Lyons	United Australia Party	6 Jan. 1932 - Sept 1934
J.A. Lyons	UAP - Country Party	Sept 1934 - 7 Nov 1938
J.A. Lyons	UAP - Country Party	7 Nov. 1938 - 7 April 1939
Sir Earle Page	Country - UAP	7 April 1939 - 26 April 1939
R.G. Menzies	UAP	26 April 1939 - 14 March 1940
R.G. Menzies	UAP - Country Party	14 March 1940 - 28 Oct. 1940
R.G. Menzies	UAP - Country Party	28 Oct. 1940 - 29 Aug. 1941
A.W. Fadden	Country - UAP	29 Aug. 1941 - 7 Oct. 1941
J. Curtin	Labor	7 Oct. 1941 - 21 Sept. 1943
J. Curtin	Labor	21 Sept. 1943 - 6 July 1945
F.M. Forde	Labor	6 July 1945 - 13 July 1945
J.B. Chifley	Labor	13 July 1945 - 1 Nov. 1946
J.B. Chifley	Labor	1 Nov. 1946 - 19 Dec. 1949
R.G. Menzies	Liberal - Country Party	19 Dec. 1949 - 11 May 1951
R.G. Menzies	Liberal-Country Party	11 May 1951 - 11 Jan. 1956
R.G. Menzies	Liberal-Country Party	11 Jan. 1956 - 10 Dec. 1958
R.G. Menzies	Liberal-Country Party	0 Dec. 1958 - 18 Dec. 1963
Sir Robert (R.G.) Menzies	Liberal - Country Party	18 Dec. 1963 - 26 Jan. 1966
H.E. Holt	Liberal - Country Party	26 Jan. 1966 - 14 Dec. 1966
H.E. Holt	Liberal - Country Party	14 Dec. 1966 - 19 Dec. 1967
J. McEwen	Liberal - Country Party	19 Dec. 1967 - 10 Jan. 1968
J.G. Gorton	Liberal - Country Party	10 Jan. 1968 - 28 Feb. 1968
J.G. Gorton	Liberal - Country Party	28 Feb. 1968 - 12 Nov. 1969
J.G. Gorton	Liberal - Country Party	12 Nov. 1969 - 10 Mar. 1971
W. McMahon	Liberal - Country Party	10 Mar. 1971 - 5 Dec. 1972
E.G. Whitlam	Labor	5 Dec. 1972 - 19 Dec. 1972
E.G. Whitlam	Labor	9 Dec. 1972 - 12 Jun. 1974
E.G. Whitlam	Labor	12 Jun. 1974 - 11 Nov. 1975
J.M. Fraser	Liberal - National/Country	11 Nov. 1975 - 22 Dec. 1975
J.M. Fraser	Liberal - National/Country	22 Dec. 1975 - 20 Dec. 1977
J.M. Fraser	Liberal - National	20 Dec. 1977 - 3 Nov. 1980
J.M. Fraser	Liberal - National	3 Nov 1980 - 11 Mar. 1983
R.J. Hawke	Labor	11 Mar. 1983 - 13 Dec. 1984
R.J. Hawke	Labor	13 Dec. 1984 - 24 July 1987
R.J. Hawke	Labor	24 July 1987 - 4 April 1980
R.J. Hawke	Labor	4 April 1990 - 20 Dec. 1991
P.J. Keating	Labor	20 Dec. 1991 - 24 Mar. 1993
P.J. Keating	Labor	24 Mar. 1993 - 11 Mar. 1996
J.W. Howard	Liberal - National	11 March 1996 - 3 Oct 1998
J.W. Howard	Liberal - National	3 Oct. 1998 - 10 Nov. 2001
J.W. Howard	Liberal - National	10 Nov. 2001 - 9 Oct. 2004
J.W. Howard	Liberal - National	9 Oct. 2004 - 3 Dec. 2007
K.M. Rudd	Labor	3 Dec. 2007 -

Acknowledgements

This book is the concluding volume of a trilogy I set myself to write on aspects of Australia's past. The first book, *The Great Treasury of Australian Folklore* was published in 1990, the second, *Australians at War*, in 1991. This book's publication was postponed when I was appointed Editor-in-Chief of the eight-volume *Australian Encyclopaedia* in 1993, but the text has, I hope, been improved as a result of that enriching experience: the original opening and closing chapters have been substantially revised and expanded. I am grateful to my copy editor Richard McGregor for his close reading of the text and his many helpful suggestions, to my publishers for their patience as text and images were brought together and for the book's handsome format, and to my dear wife Veronica who once again did the hard work - the typing and retyping of the manuscript.

Like *Australians at War* this is principally a pictorial history, but I hope the narrative covers the important milestones in our history. It is a re-telling, the result of a long fascination in Australian history and of wide and enjoyable reading and is not a work of original research, so it would be pretentious to list all the books I consulted or the sources of all quoted material. Authorities that I have found particularly valuable are acknowledged in the text, but my principal debts are to *The Australian Encyclopaedia*, whose six editions and current eight volumes are a mine of historical fact, to Manning Clark's six-volume *History of Australia* (published between 1961 and 1987) and to the numberless biographies of our outstanding figures which bring history so vividly to life.

Illustrations

The pictures in this book are drawn from the author's collection of historic photographs, portraits, engravings and printed ephemera gathered over forty years in book publishing. The author and publishers wish to acknowledge those who provided illustrations and especially the following archives or copyright holders for kindly granting permission to reproduce pictures from their collections:

The Trustees of the Mitchell Library and Dixon Galleries (State Library of New South Wales), Sydney, for illustrations on pages 15, 16, 68, 75, 76, 78, 82, 87 top left, 91, 94 both, 96 lower, 97 lower, 99, 104, 107, 111 both, 114, 120, 121, 122, 126, 128, 129, 131, 133, 136, 138 top, 142 top, 143, 157 lower, 160 top, 161, 169 top, 181, 204 top, 206, 207 lower, 209, 214 top, 219 top, 231 top, 232 both, 237, 242, 245, 249 top, 258 top, 261 both, 263 top, 265 top right, 284, 290 top, 303 top, 307 top, 315 lower right.

NSW Government Printer collection: photographs on pages 166, 184 lower, 212 lower, 217, 218 top, 224 top, 225, 226 top, 240 top, 241, 247 lower, 250, 255, 263 lower, 266 top.

National Library of Australia, Canberra, for illustrations on pages 1, 3, 5-6, 9, 14 (top), 17, 21, 27, 35, 38, 41, 42, 52, 54, 55, 56 (top), 57 (top), 59, 63, 65, 66 (top), 71 top, 72, 79, 81, 83, 85 lower, 86 left, 87 lower left, 88, 89, 90, 92, 97 top, 98, 105, 106 top, 109 top, 117, 119, 132, 139, 140 top, 144, 146, 148, 162, 190 top, 198, 207 top, 211, 215, 218 lower, 224 lower, 239 both, 253 top, 256, 257 top, 260, 267 lower, 268 lower right, 269 lower, 272 lower, 273 top, 286, 304 top left, 319 both, 314 top, 325 top, 327 lower, 328 lower, 329 top and lower left, 347, 351, 374 top, 376, 384, 394, 396, 414 both, 426, 427 lower, 439 lower, 459 top left, 461, 462.

National Archives of Australia (and former DEFAT collection/Australian News and Information Bureau, Canberra) for illustrations on pages 212 top, 243, 285, 303 lower, 304 lower, 334, 337, 339, 370, 371 lower, 372, 373, 375, 377, 378 top, 381 lower, 383 top, 385, 387 both, 397 top, 403 top, 407, 409, 428, 429, 431, 432, 453, 456 both, 459 top right.

Australian War Memorial, Canberra, for photographs on pages 275, 277, 279, 280, 282 both, 287, 288, 291, 292, 293 top, 294, 295, 296, 297, 298, 335, 340 top, 341, 343 lower, 345, 346, 354, 356 both, 357, 358, 359 left, 360, 361, 363, 364 both, 365, 366, 367 top two, 390, 406 top.

Australian Defence Forces Digital Media, Canberra, for images on pages 443, 463 both, 464, 468, 469 all, 471, 473.

Art Gallery of New South Wales for paintings on pages 20, 299, 325 bottom.

National Gallery of Victoria for painting on page 227.

Tasmanian Museum and Art Gallery for painting on page 95.

Latrobe Library, State Library of Victoria for images on pages 171, 184 top, 193 top, 236.

Newspix for photo on page 459 bottom.

TAA for pages 424, 425 top.

Fairfax Photos for page 427 top.

Parliament of Victoria Library for William Strutt drawings on pages 170, 175, 177 top two 183, 191 lower, 194 top.

John Oxley Memorial Library, Brisbane for photo on page 213.

BHP Archives, Melbourne for photos on pages 222, 226 lower, 316, 397 lower.

ACP Publishing for permission to reproduce *Bulletin* covers on pages 437.

Roslyn Poignant for permission to reproduce photograph by Axel Poignant (via NLA) on page 392.

Norman Lindsay drawing on page 259 reproduced by permission Norman Lindsay estate and Barbara Mobbs Agency.

Peter Nicholson for image on page 442.

Life Magazine cover reproduced with permission of Time-Life, Photo by Vernon Merritt III/Time & Life Pictures/Getty Images for page 416.

Qantas Airways for page 457, 465.

Defence Department official photograph courtesy of ADF Media page 466 bottom.

AAP Image/Vision images for image on page 466 top.

istock images for image on page 471 bottom

Kiley Blatch © Newspix for image on page 472

AAP Image/Dave Hunt for image on page 473

AAP Image/Alan Porritt for image on page 474

If the source or ownership of any illustration has not been correctly acknowledged, the author and publishers apologise and undertake to correct the omission.

Index